ANALYTIC FUNCTIONS AND DISTRIBUTIONS IN PHYSICS AND ENGINEERING

ANALYTIC FUNCTIONS AND DISTRIBUTIONS IN PHYSICS AND ENGINEERING

BERNARD W. ROOS

John Jay Hopkins Laboratory
For Pure and Applied Science
Gulf General Atomic, Inc.
San Diego, California

John Wiley & Sons, Inc., New York · London · Sydney · Toronto

Library of Congress Catalog Card Number: 69-19241
SBN 471 73334 2
Printed in the United States of America

1 2 3 4 5 6 7 8 9 10

To My Mother and Father

PREFACE

The purpose of this book is to present in an informal and easily readable style an introduction to those mathematical concepts and techniques involving analytic functions and distributions that have found wide application in theoretical physics and engineering in recent years.

Originally written with an industrial educational program in mind, it has been my intention to present the material in a form suitable for students and research workers whose interest is primarily in the *application* of mathematical theories rather than in these theories themselves. I have avoided therefore abstract and involved mathematical arguments and have not attempted to present the foundations of the concepts and techniques in their most general form. Instead I have attempted to present an easily accessible introduction on the mathematical level of most research papers concerned with the applications of analytic functions and distributions to the solution of concrete physical problems.

I have assumed that the reader has some knowledge of the elements of the theory of functions of a complex variable. However, in an effort to make the book reasonably self-contained, I included a chapter on the more important aspects of this theory, and, in a few instances, presented detailed discussions of some rather elementary mathematical concepts.

The physical problems that serve to illustrate the mathematical techniques pertain to relevant current research in theoretical physics and are far from trivial. They have been taken from research papers on hydrodynamics, electrodynamics, neutron transport theory, and plasma physics. However, to make the book accessible to readers with a varied background in physics, I assumed no specialized knowledge of physics on the part of the reader and presented discussions of the physical fundamentals and derivations of the basic equations. Furthermore, it has been my policy to treat a few subjects in detail rather than many subjects superficially. As criteria for including a particular subject I used the frequency of occurrence of relevant applications of analytic functions and distributions in the research papers on the subject, the current or future relevance of these applications to other subjects, and the degree of my familiarity with the particular subjects. I included therefore rather extensive discussions of neutron transport theory and of longitudinal plasma oscillations. In addition, I have attempted to introduce the reader to those concepts and techniques of the theory of analytic functions and distributions that are important for an understanding of the applications of dispersion relations and causality arguments in classical and modern theoretical physics.

I agree with the observation made by T. Teichmann in one of his book reviews in *Physics Today* that the majority of Western books on advanced mathematical topics, which have appeared in the last few years, are either elegant but abstract descriptions of the theory or encyclopedic descriptions of applications. This has made it rather difficult for those readers who wish to learn more about the subject with no view to conducting research in it or solving arrays of engineering or physics problems. The present book is aimed precisely at such readers in the field of analytic functions and distributions. It is not a standard textbook on the theory of functions of a complex variable and its applications. Instead it stresses the more advanced theories and techniques seldom found in the current textbook literature. It is definitely applied in nature and is directed to those physicists, engineers, and applied mathematicians who are interested in becoming acquainted with the subject rather than to specialists, although I hope, of course, that the book will also be useful to the latter.

I have drawn upon many sources for my material and I feel a depth of gratitude to the authors of the books and articles from which I learned.

I am also indebted to my friends and colleagues who made the John Jay Hopkins Laboratory a place where it is enjoyable to do research and creative work. Particularly the encouragements of Dr. Lothar W. Nordheim contributed much to the completion of this book.

It is with great pleasure that I acknowledge the support received from Gulf General Atomic, Inc., and from its President, Dr. Frederic de Hoffman and its Vice President for Research and Development, Dr. Edward C. Creutz.

Finally I wish to express my sincere gratitude to my wife Nardina for her constant encouragement and for her untiring help in editing, proofreading, and indexing the manuscript.

Rancho Santa Fe *BERNARD W. ROOS*
February 23, 1969

CONTENTS

ANALYTIC FUNCTIONS AND DISTRIBUTIONS IN PHYSICS AND ENGINEERING

CHAPTER I

ANALYTIC FUNCTIONS

1.1 INTEGRAL REPRESENTATIONS OF ANALYTIC FUNCTIONS

Analytic functions of a complex variable are of great importance in the mathematical analysis of problems in theoretical physics and engineering. The reason can be found in the high degree of smoothness exhibited by these functions. This smooth behavior is well-suited to the description of the smooth variations in space and time which are characteristic of a physical process in the physics of continua such as the mechanics of material media or classical electromagnetic theory. The smooth behavior of an analytic function plays also a role in its adaptability to the description of few particle processes in the regions of space outside the immediate vicinity of singularities in the potentials. Of similar importance for the description of physical phenomena as its smooth behavior is the behavior of an analytic function of a complex variable at the points at which it ceases to be analytic. The location of such singular points of the function coincides with boundaries, interfaces, sources, sinks, or potential singularities of the physical situation, and the behavior of the function in the neighborhood of such points may yield considerable information about the singular aspects of the physical process described by the function.

To define an analytic function of a complex variable we may make use of the differential or integral properties of the function. According to the differential definition, a single-valued function of a complex variable is analytic in a region of the complex plane if it has a uniquely defined derivative at all points of this region. It is an immediate consequence of this definition that an analytic function of a complex variable has derivatives of all orders at every point of its region of analyticity. The integral definition asserts that a continuous function of a complex variable is analytic in a region if the contour integral of the function over any closed contour in this region vanishes. Thus, according to the integral definition, the theory of analytic functions of a complex variable can be developed by a consistent employment of the concept of integration. Of course, the conditions imposed on an analytic function in the integral definition must follow as logical consequences from the impositions on such a function in the differential definition and vice versa. For instance, developing the theory of analytic functions on the basis of the differential definition, we obtain Morera's theorem which is equivalent in content to the integral definition.

On the following pages we shall often write, erroneously but conveniently, that a particular function is analytic at a given point or that such a function is analytic on a given path or contour. Statements of this type should not be taken literally, since, to be consistent with our definitions, we should really write that the function is analytic in some neighborhood of the point or that the function is analytic in some neighborhood of the path or contour in the complex plane.

The fundamental theorem of the theory of functions of a complex variable, and a theorem with far-reaching practical implications, is Cauchy's theorem. This theorem states that the contour integral of an analytic function of a complex variable over a contour in its region of analyticity vanishes,

$$\oint_C F(\zeta)\, d\zeta = 0$$

We refer the reader to one of the standard textbooks on complex variables for the lengthy proof of this theorem.

It should be noted that Cauchy's theorem also applies to functions which are analytic inside a contour and which are continuous inside and on that contour. This version of the theorem is sometimes more suitable for applications in mathematical physics than the foregoing version.

Closely related to Cauchy's theorem is the Cauchy formula for the representation of an analytic function by a contour integral. If C is a contour in the region of analyticity of an analytic function $F(\lambda)$ and $\lambda = \omega + i\gamma$ is an arbitrary point inside the contour, then the function can be represented by the contour integral,

$$F(\lambda) = \frac{1}{2\pi i} \oint_C \frac{F(\zeta)}{\zeta - \lambda}\, d\zeta$$

This integral representation of the function $F(\lambda)$ can be obtained by an application of Cauchy's theorem. The function $F(\zeta)/(\zeta - \lambda)$ is analytic at all points inside the contour with the exception of the point λ and we can contract the contour to a circle Σ about the point λ. Integrating the function $F(\zeta)/(\zeta - \lambda)$ over a contour which consists of the contour C, the circle Σ, and a barrier between the contour C and the circle, we obtain, according to Cauchy's theorem,

$$\frac{1}{2\pi i}\oint_C \frac{F(\zeta)}{\zeta - \lambda}\,d\zeta = \frac{1}{2\pi i}\oint_\Sigma \frac{F(\zeta)}{\zeta - \lambda}\,d\zeta$$

since the integrals over the barrier cancel each other. The integral on the right hand side of this equation can be written as follows,

$$\frac{1}{2\pi i}\oint_\Sigma \frac{F(\zeta)}{\zeta - \lambda}\,d\zeta = F(\lambda) + \frac{1}{2\pi i}\oint_\Sigma \frac{F(\zeta) - F(\lambda)}{\zeta - \lambda}\,d\zeta$$

where we make use of the fact that,

$$\frac{1}{2\pi i}\oint_\Sigma \frac{d\zeta}{\zeta - \lambda} = \frac{1}{2\pi}\int_0^{2\pi} d\phi = 1$$

However, since the function is continuous inside the circle, the second integral on the right hand side of the penultimate equation vanishes when the radius of the circle tends to zero. Consequently, we obtain the result,

$$\frac{1}{2\pi i}\oint_C \frac{F(\zeta)}{\zeta - \lambda}\,d\zeta = F(\lambda)$$

The Cauchy integral representation of an analytic function enables us to obtain the value of this function at any point inside a contour in its region of analyticity once the function is known on the contour.

If the point λ is located outside a contour in the region of analyticity of the function $F(\lambda)$, a straightforward application of Cauchy's theorem shows that the integral of the function $F(\zeta)/(\zeta - \lambda)$ over this contour vanishes,

$$\oint_C \frac{F(\zeta)}{\zeta - \lambda}\,d\zeta = 0$$

From the point of view of the applications of the theory to problems in mathematical physics and engineering, a highly interesting situation develops when the point $\lambda = \alpha$ is located on the contour. To obtain a mathematically more manageable problem we indent the contour by a semicircle Σ in the manner shown in Figure I-1.

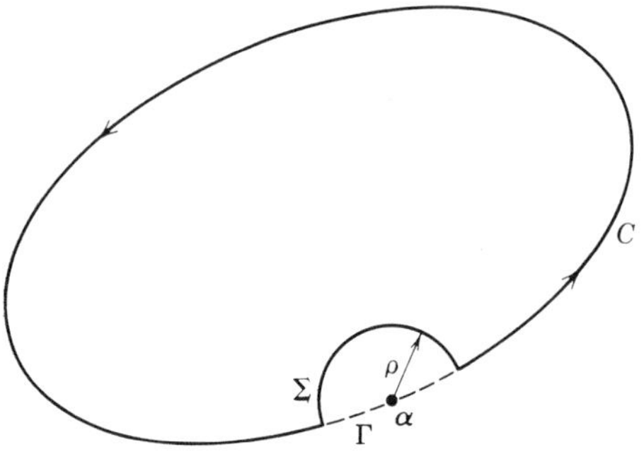

Figure I-1

For very small values of ρ the segment Γ approaches a straight line. Since the point α is located outside the indented contour we find

$$\frac{1}{2\pi i}\int_{C-\Gamma}\frac{F(\zeta)}{\zeta-\alpha}\,d\zeta+\frac{1}{2\pi i}\int_{\Sigma}\frac{F(\zeta)}{\zeta-\alpha}\,d\zeta=0$$

In the limit, as ρ tends to zero, we obtain for the first integral the value,

$$\frac{1}{2\pi i}\oint_{C}\frac{F(\zeta)}{\zeta-\alpha}\,d\zeta=\lim_{\rho\to 0}\frac{1}{2\pi i}\oint_{C-\Gamma}\frac{F(\zeta)}{\zeta-\alpha}\,d\zeta$$

The integral on the left hand side of this equation is defined by the limit relation as a Cauchy principal value integral. Such integrals will be introduced in Chapter IV, to which we refer the reader for a more detailed discussion.

The second integral over the semicircle Σ can be evaluated as follows,

$$\lim_{\rho\to 0}\frac{1}{2\pi i}\int_{\Sigma}\frac{F(\zeta)}{\zeta-\alpha}\,d\zeta=\lim_{\rho\to 0}\frac{1}{2\pi}\int_{\pi}^{0}F(\alpha+\rho e^{i\phi})\,d\phi=-\frac{1}{2}F(\alpha)$$

This implies that, whenever the point α is located on the contour, the function $F(\alpha)$ can be represented by the integral,

$$F(\alpha)=\frac{1}{\pi i}\oint_{C}\frac{F(\zeta)}{\zeta-\alpha}\,d\zeta$$

where the integral on the right hand side of this equation should be understood in the sense of a Cauchy principal value integral.

The remark we made, with respect to Cauchy's theorem, about the conditions which should be imposed on the function $F(\lambda)$ is also valid with respect to the representation integrals above, i.e., the integral formulas presented above remain valid whenever the function $F(\lambda)$ is analytic inside the contour and is continuous inside and on the contour.

In problems of mathematical physics one frequently needs to represent analytic functions which are defined in a half plane by integrals over an infinite straight line as shown in Figure I-2.

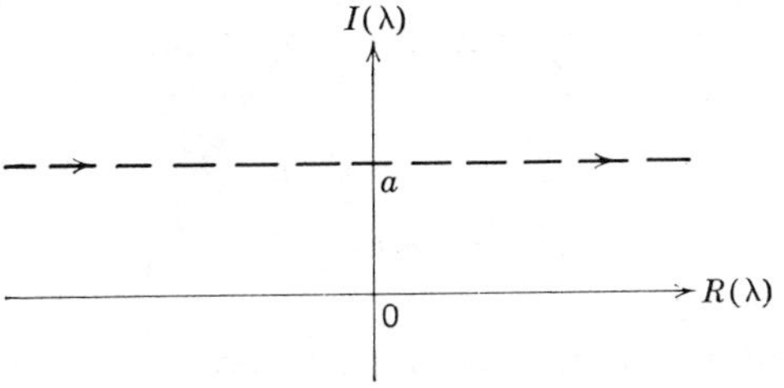

Figure I-2

If we assume that the function $F(\lambda)$ is analytic in the upper half plane $I(\lambda) > a$, is continuous in the half plane $I(\lambda) \geqq a$, and vanishes when λ tends to infinity in this half plane, the function $F(\lambda)$ can be represented by the integral,

$$F(\lambda) = \frac{1}{2\pi i} \int_{-\infty + ia}^{\infty + ia} \frac{F(\zeta)}{\zeta - \lambda} d\zeta$$

at any point λ in the half plane $I(\lambda) > a$. This integral representation for the function $F(\lambda)$ can be made plausible by considering Figure I-3.

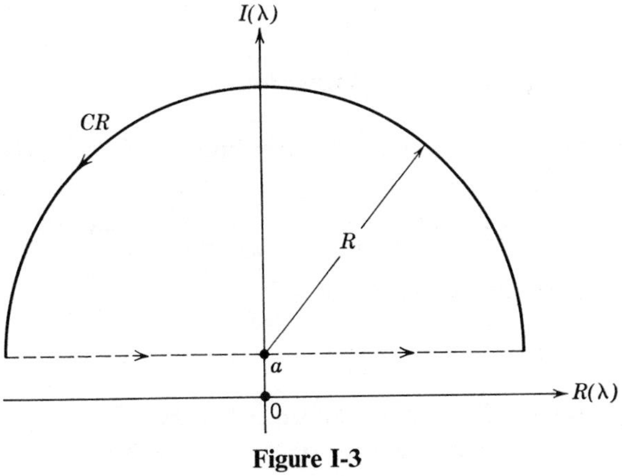

Figure I-3

The function $F(\lambda)$ is analytic inside the contour C which consists of the path $(-R + ia, R + ia)$ and the semicircle CR. Consequently, according to the Cauchy representation formula for a closed contour, we may write

$$F(\lambda) = \frac{1}{2\pi i} \oint_C \frac{F(\zeta)}{\zeta - \lambda} d\zeta = \frac{1}{2\pi i} \int_{-R+ia}^{R+ia} \frac{F(\zeta)}{\zeta - \lambda} d\zeta + \frac{1}{2\pi i} \int_{CR} \frac{F(\zeta)}{\zeta - \lambda} d\zeta$$

Since the function $F(\lambda)$ tends to zero when λ tends to infinity in the upper half plane, the second integral vanishes when R tends to infinity and we obtain the required result.

If λ is a point located in the lower half plane $I(\lambda) < a$ the point λ is located outside the contour C. In this case it is an immediate consequence of the derivation above that the integral,

$$\frac{1}{2\pi i}\int_{-\infty+ia}^{\infty+ia}\frac{F(\zeta)}{\zeta-\lambda}\,d\zeta$$

vanishes when $I(\lambda) < a$.

Now let us assume that the point $\lambda = \alpha$ is located on the path $(-\infty + ia, \infty + ia)$. To obtain the appropriate representation formula let us first take the point $\lambda = \alpha + i\varepsilon$ to be located just above the path as shown in Figure I-4.

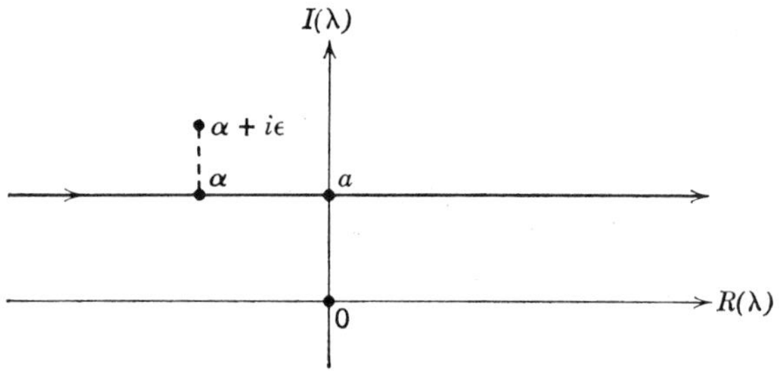

Figure I-4

Since the point $\lambda = \alpha + i\varepsilon$ is located in the upper half plane, we may write

$$F(\alpha + i\varepsilon) = \frac{1}{2\pi i}\int_{-\infty+ia}^{\infty+ia}\frac{F(\zeta)}{\zeta-\alpha-i\varepsilon}\,d\zeta$$

In order to perform the limit operation,

$$\lim_{\varepsilon\to 0} F(\alpha + i\varepsilon)$$

we indent the path in the manner shown in Figure I-5.

We shall denote the new path, $(-\infty + ia, \alpha - \rho, \Sigma, \alpha + \rho, \infty + ia)$, by Γ. The indentation of the original path is necessary, since obviously we cannot let ε tend to zero without taking certain precautions with respect to the existence of the integral and with respect to the location of the point $\lambda = \alpha + i\varepsilon$. This requires that we properly define an integral of the type,

$$\int_{-\infty+ia}^{\infty+ia}\frac{F(\zeta)}{\zeta-\alpha}\,d\zeta$$

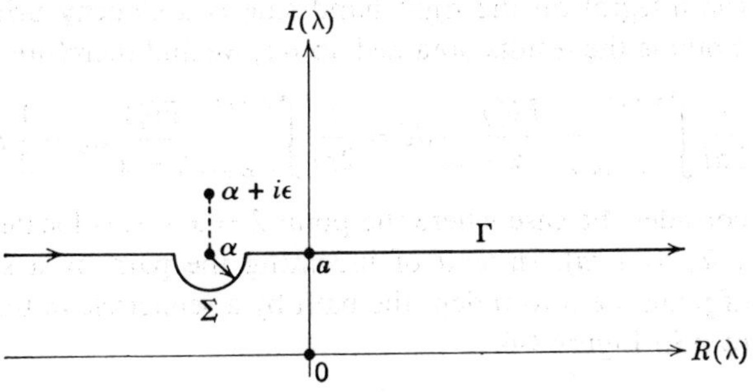

Figure I-5

Furthermore, we should take care that when ε tends to zero the point $\lambda = \alpha + i\varepsilon$ stays in the upper half plane $I(\lambda) > a$. The indentation of the path allows us to remove all ambiguities which may arise with respect to the two considerations above. For, by making use of the new path, we can evaluate the limit in the following manner,

$$\lim_{\varepsilon \to 0} \int_{-\infty + ia}^{\infty + ia} \frac{F(\zeta)}{\zeta - \alpha - i\varepsilon} \, d\zeta = \lim_{\substack{\varepsilon \to 0 \\ \rho \to 0}} \int_{\Gamma} \frac{F(\zeta)}{\zeta - \alpha - i\varepsilon} \, d\zeta$$

Letting ε tend to zero in the second integral, we are left with the evaluation of this integral when the radius ρ of the small semicircle tends to zero. We may write

$$\lim_{\rho \to 0} \int_{\Gamma} \frac{F(\zeta)}{\zeta - \alpha} \, d\zeta = \lim_{\rho \to 0} \int_{\Sigma} \frac{F(\zeta)}{\zeta - \alpha} \, d\zeta + \lim_{\rho \to 0} \left(\int_{-\infty + ia}^{\alpha - \rho} \frac{F(\zeta)}{\zeta - \alpha} \, d\zeta + \int_{\alpha + \rho}^{\infty + ia} \frac{F(\zeta)}{\zeta - \alpha} \, d\zeta \right)$$

The first limit on the right hand side of this equation yields,

$$\lim_{\rho \to 0} \int_{\Sigma} \frac{F(\zeta)}{\zeta - \alpha} \, d\zeta = \lim_{\rho \to 0} \int_{-\pi}^{0} F(\alpha + \rho e^{i\theta}) i \, d\theta = \pi i \, F(\alpha)$$

The second limit relation on the right hand side of the equation is equivalent to the definition of an integral in the sense of a Cauchy principal value. Consequently, we obtain the result,

$$\lim_{\rho \to 0} \left(\int_{-\infty + ia}^{\alpha - \rho} \frac{F(\zeta)}{\zeta - \alpha} \, d\zeta + \int_{\alpha + \rho}^{\infty + ia} \frac{F(\zeta)}{\zeta - \alpha} \, d\zeta \right) = \int_{-\infty + ia}^{\infty + ia} \frac{F(\zeta)}{\zeta - \alpha} \, d\zeta$$

where now the integral on the right hand side is a Cauchy principal value integral. Combining the results obtained above, we find therefore the relation,

$$\lim_{\varepsilon \to 0} \frac{1}{2\pi i} \int_{-\infty + ia}^{\infty + ia} \frac{F(\zeta)}{\zeta - \alpha - i\varepsilon}\, d\zeta = \frac{1}{2\pi i} \int_{-\infty + ia}^{\infty + ia} \frac{F(\zeta)}{\zeta - \alpha}\, d\zeta + \frac{1}{2} F(\alpha)$$

Let us now consider the case where the point $\lambda = \alpha - i\varepsilon$ is located below the path $(-\infty + ia, \infty + ia)$. Instead of indenting the path by a semicircle in the lower half plane we now indent the path by a semicircle in the upper half plane, as shown in Figure I-6.

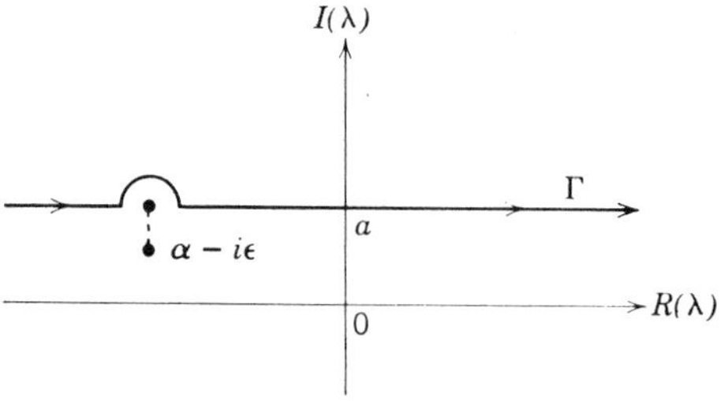

Figure I-6

In a manner similar to that explained in the preceding discussion we now obtain the result,

$$\lim_{\varepsilon \to 0} \frac{1}{2\pi i} \int_{-\infty + ia}^{\infty + ia} \frac{F(\zeta)}{\zeta - \alpha + i\varepsilon}\, d\zeta = \frac{1}{2\pi i} \int_{-\infty + ia}^{\infty + ia} \frac{F(\zeta)}{\zeta - \alpha}\, d\zeta - \frac{1}{2} F(\alpha)$$

Combining this result with the result which we obtained when we let $\lambda = \alpha + i\varepsilon$ approach the point α through values in the upper half plane, we may write

$$\begin{aligned}\lim_{\varepsilon \to 0} F(\alpha \pm i\varepsilon) &= \lim_{\varepsilon \to 0} \frac{1}{2\pi i} \int_{-\infty + ia}^{\infty + ia} \frac{F(\zeta)}{\zeta - \alpha \mp i\varepsilon}\, d\zeta \\ &= \pm \frac{1}{2} F(\alpha) + \frac{1}{2\pi i} \int_{-\infty + ia}^{\infty + ia} \frac{F(\zeta)}{\zeta - \alpha}\, d\zeta\end{aligned}$$

where the integral on the right hand side of the second equality sign must be evaluated as a Cauchy principal value integral. These two formulas are a special case of the boundary value equations of Plemelj. Subtracting and adding the two equations above, we obtain the so-called formulas of Plemelj,

$$\lim_{\varepsilon \to 0} F(\alpha + i\varepsilon) - \lim_{\varepsilon \to 0} F(\alpha - i\varepsilon) = F(\alpha)$$

and

$$\lim_{\varepsilon \to 0} F(\alpha + i\varepsilon) + \lim_{\varepsilon \to 0} F(\alpha - i\varepsilon) = \frac{1}{\pi i} \int_{-\infty + ia}^{\infty + ia} \frac{F(\zeta)}{\zeta - \alpha}\, d\zeta$$

In our case the function $F(\alpha - i\varepsilon)$ vanishes identically and we obtain therefore the representation formula,

$$F(\alpha) = \frac{1}{\pi i} \int_{-\infty + ia}^{\infty + ia} \frac{F(\zeta)}{\zeta - \alpha} \, d\zeta$$

where α is a point on the path of integration and the integral must be read as a Cauchy principal value integral. The formulas of Plemelj have been derived here for the very special case that the function $F(\lambda)$ is analytic in the upper half plane and is analytic and continuous on the line $(-\infty + ia, \infty + ia)$. In Chapter IV we shall present a more detailed discussion of these formulas for more general functions.

Some useful integral representations of some well-known functions can be obtained from the following integral representation of the function exp $(i\lambda t)$,

$$\frac{1}{2\pi i} \int_{-\infty}^{\infty} \frac{e^{i\omega t}}{\omega - \lambda} \, d\omega = e^{i\lambda t} \qquad \text{when } t \text{ is positive}$$

$$= 0 \qquad \text{when } t \text{ is negative}$$

where λ denotes a point located in the upper half of the complex plane. From the representation above we obtain immediately the following integral representation of the unit step function,

$$\frac{1}{2\pi i} \int_{-\infty}^{\infty} \frac{e^{i\omega t}}{\omega - i\varepsilon} \, d\omega = \theta(t)$$

where ε denotes a vanishingly small positive number and $\theta(t)$ is defined as the function,

$$\begin{aligned} \theta(t) &= 1 && \text{when } t \text{ is positive} \\ &= 1/2 && \text{when } t \text{ is zero} \\ &= 0 && \text{when } t \text{ is negative} \end{aligned}$$

In the limit as $I(\lambda)$ tends to zero and the point λ tends to the point ω_0 on the real axis, we indent the path in the manner shown in Figure I-7.

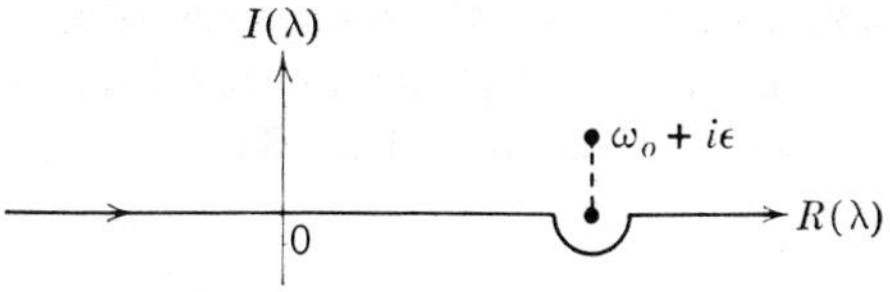

Figure I-7

Since the small semicircle is traversed in the positive direction we find in the limit as ε tends to zero that

$$\lim_{\varepsilon\to 0}\frac{1}{2\pi i}\int_{-\infty}^{\infty}\frac{e^{i\omega t}}{\omega-\omega_0-i\varepsilon}\,d\omega=\frac{1}{2}\,e^{i\omega_0 t}+\frac{1}{2\pi i}\int_{-\infty}^{\infty}\frac{e^{i\omega t}}{\omega-\omega_0}\,d\omega=e^{i\omega_0 t}$$

when the parameter t is positive, and

$$\lim_{\varepsilon\to 0}\frac{1}{2\pi i}\int_{-\infty}^{\infty}\frac{e^{i\omega t}}{\omega-\omega_0-i\varepsilon}\,d\omega=\frac{1}{2}\,e^{i\omega_0 t}+\frac{1}{2\pi i}\int_{-\infty}^{\infty}\frac{e^{i\omega t}}{\omega-\omega_0}\,d\omega=0$$

when the parameter t is negative. From these results we obtain immediately the integral representation,

$$\begin{aligned}\frac{1}{\pi i}\int_{-\infty}^{\infty}\frac{e^{i\omega t}}{\omega-\omega_0}\,d\omega &= e^{i\omega_0 t} \qquad &&\text{when } t \text{ is positive}\\ &= -e^{i\omega_0 t} &&\text{when } t \text{ is negative}\end{aligned}$$

where the integral is defined as a Cauchy principal value integral. For $\omega_0 = 0$ the representation above reduces to

$$\begin{aligned}\frac{1}{\pi i}\int_{-\infty}^{\infty}\frac{e^{i\omega t}}{\omega}\,d\omega &= 1 \qquad &&\text{when } t \text{ is positive}\\ &= 0 &&\text{when } t \text{ is zero}\\ &= -1 &&\text{when } t \text{ is negative}\end{aligned}$$

Consequently, the signum or sign function $\varepsilon(t)$, which is defined by the relation,

$$\varepsilon(t) = 2\theta(t) - 1$$

can be represented by the integral,

$$\frac{1}{\pi i}\int_{-\infty}^{\infty}\frac{e^{i\omega t}}{\omega}\,d\omega=\varepsilon(t)$$

where the integral is again defined as a Cauchy principal value integral.

The integral representations for the derivatives of an analytic function can be obtained from the integral representation of the function by straightforward differentiation. For instance, if the function $F(\lambda)$ can be represented by the contour integral,

$$F(\lambda)=\frac{1}{2\pi i}\oint_C\frac{F(\zeta)}{\zeta-\lambda}\,d\zeta$$

then the integral representation of the derivative of the function at the point λ can be obtained by differentiating the integral under the integral sign,

$$\frac{dF(\lambda)}{d\lambda} = \frac{1}{2\pi i} \oint_C \frac{F(\zeta)}{(\zeta - \lambda)^2}\, d\zeta$$

This representation is valid when λ is a point inside the contour. Similarly, we find by repeated differentiation the formula,

$$\frac{d^n F(\lambda)}{d\lambda^n} = \frac{n!}{2\pi i} \oint_C \frac{F(\zeta)}{(\zeta - \lambda)^{n+1}}\, d\zeta$$

where λ is a point inside the contour.

The integral above can be integrated by parts yielding the result,

$$\frac{d^n F(\lambda)}{d\lambda^n} = \frac{1}{2\pi i} \oint_C \frac{F^{(n)}(\zeta)}{\zeta - \lambda}\, d\zeta$$

This formula can be used to determine the integral representation of the n-th order derivative of the function $F(\lambda)$ when $\lambda = \alpha$ is a point on the contour. It can be shown, in the manner explained above, that this representation takes the form,

$$\frac{d^n F(\alpha)}{d\lambda^n} = \frac{1}{\pi i} \oint_C \frac{F^{(n)}(\zeta)}{\zeta - \alpha}\, d\zeta$$

where the integral should be interpreted as a Cauchy principal value integral. In this way we have circumvented the need to use improper integrals of the form,

$$\oint_C \frac{F(\zeta)}{(\zeta - \alpha)^{n+1}}\, d\zeta$$

In principle such an integral can be defined by the relation,

$$\oint_C \frac{F(\zeta)}{(\zeta - \alpha)^{n+1}}\, d\zeta = \frac{1}{n!} \frac{\partial^n}{\partial \alpha^n} \oint_C \frac{F(\zeta)}{\zeta - \alpha}\, d\zeta$$

Fortunately, integrals of this type do not seem to occur often in mathematical physics.

For suitable functions $F(\lambda)$ the results above can be generalized to the case in which the closed contour is replaced by an infinite straight line. We present without proof the following representation formulas for the derivatives of a function $F(\lambda)$. Assuming that $F(\lambda)$ is analytic in an upper half plane $I(\lambda) > a$ and vanishes when λ tends to infinity in this half plane, the derivatives of the function can be represented by the integrals,

$$\frac{d^nF(\lambda)}{d\lambda^n} = \frac{1}{2\pi i}\int_{-\infty+ia}^{\infty+ia} \frac{F^{(n)}(\zeta)}{\zeta-\lambda}\,d\zeta$$

when λ is a point in the upper half plane $I(\lambda) > a$, and

$$\frac{d^nF(\alpha)}{d\lambda^n} = \frac{1}{\pi i}\int_{-\infty+ia}^{\infty+ia} \frac{F^{(n)}(\zeta)}{\zeta-\alpha}\,d\zeta$$

when α is a point on the path of integration $(-\infty + ia, \infty + ia)$. These formulas can be used to obtain the integral representation of a function $F(\lambda)$ which is analytic in the upper half plane $I(\lambda) > a$ and which is of algebraic growth at infinity. For instance, let us assume that $F(\lambda) = O(\lambda^n)$ when λ tends to infinity in the upper half plane $I(\lambda) \geqq a$. Assuming that $\zeta = \alpha_0$ denotes a point on the path $(-\infty + ia, \infty + ia)$ the point $\alpha_0 - i\delta$ is located in the lower half plane $I(\lambda) < a$ when δ is an arbitrarily small positive constant. In that case, the function,

$$G(\lambda) = \frac{F(\lambda)}{(\lambda-\alpha_0+i\delta)^{n+1}}$$

is analytic in the upper half plane $I(\lambda) > a$ and vanishes as λ tends to infinity in the closed upper half plane $I(\lambda) \geqq a$. Hence, we may represent the function $G(\lambda)$ by the Cauchy integral,

$$G(\alpha + i\varepsilon) = \frac{1}{2\pi i}\int_{-\infty+ia}^{\infty+ia} \frac{G(\zeta)}{(\zeta-\alpha-i\varepsilon)}\,d\zeta$$

and letting ε tend to zero, we obtain the representation,

$$G(\alpha) = \frac{1}{\pi i}\int_{-\infty+ia}^{\infty+ia} \frac{G(\zeta)}{\zeta-\alpha}\,d\zeta$$

where the integral must be read as a Cauchy principal value integral. In terms of the function $F(\lambda)$ we may write

$$\frac{F(\alpha)}{(\alpha-\alpha_0+i\delta)^{n+1}} = \frac{1}{\pi i}\int_{-\infty+ia}^{\infty+ia} \frac{F(\zeta)}{(\zeta-\alpha_0+i\delta)^{n+1}}\frac{d\zeta}{(\zeta-\alpha)}$$

which may also be written in a more convenient form,

$$\frac{F(\alpha)}{(\alpha-\alpha_0+i\delta)^{n+1}} = \frac{1}{n!\,\pi i}\int_{-\infty+ia}^{\infty+ia} \frac{d\zeta}{(\zeta-\alpha_0+i\delta)}\frac{\partial^n}{\partial\zeta^n}\left(\frac{F(\zeta)}{\zeta-\alpha}\right)$$

From this equation we may infer, that in the limit as δ tends to zero,

$$\frac{F(\alpha)}{(\alpha-\alpha_0)^{n+1}} = -\frac{1}{n!}\frac{\partial^n}{\partial\lambda^n}\left(\frac{F(\lambda)}{\lambda-\alpha}\right)_{\lambda=\alpha_0} + \frac{1}{n!\,\pi i}\int_{-\infty+ia}^{\infty+ia} \frac{d\zeta}{\zeta-\alpha_0}\frac{\partial^n}{\partial\zeta^n}\left(\frac{F(\zeta)}{\zeta-\alpha}\right)$$

Evaluating the derivative term and multiplying through by the factor $(\alpha - \alpha_0)^{n+1}$, we obtain the representation formula,

$$F(\alpha) = F(\alpha_0) + (\alpha - \alpha_0)F'(\alpha_0) + \frac{1}{2!}(\alpha - \alpha_0)^2 F''(\alpha_0) + \cdots$$

$$+ \frac{1}{n!}(\alpha - \alpha_0)^n F^{(n)}(\alpha_0) + \frac{(\alpha - \alpha_0)^{n+1}}{\pi i} \int_{-\infty + ia}^{\infty + ia} \frac{F(\zeta)}{(\zeta - \alpha)(\zeta - \alpha_0)^{n+1}}$$

Where now the integral should be evaluated as a Cauchy principal value integral at the points α and α_0.

1.2 SERIES REPRESENTATIONS OF ANALYTIC FUNCTIONS

In the foregoing section we were concerned mainly with the representation of analytic functions and their derivatives by means of contour integrals. Other representations of analytic functions can be obtained by means of the series expansion of such functions about particular points.

Formally the analytic function $F(\lambda)$ can be represented by the infinite series,

$$F(\lambda) = u_0(\lambda) + u_1(\lambda) + \cdots + u_m(\lambda) + \cdots$$

Of course, such a representation makes sense only if the information we can obtain about the analytic properties of the series and its separate terms can be correlated with the analytic properties of the function $F(\lambda)$. The information of particular importance pertains to the ordinary and uniform convergence of the series.

The infinite series $\sum_{m=0}^{\infty} u_m(\lambda)$ is said to be convergent at a point λ in a region in the complex plane whenever the sequence of partial sums,

$$S_m(\lambda) = u_0(\lambda) + \cdots + u_m(\lambda)$$

has a finite limit. This limit is called the sum $S(\lambda)$ of the series. Hence, in order that an infinite series can be used to represent a given function it should at least be convergent. However, to represent an analytic function in its region of analyticity it is not sufficient for this series to be convergent in the ordinary sense at each particular point λ in this region. We must require that the series is uniformly convergent in this region and, moreover, that it is a uniformly convergent series of analytic functions. In other words, if the functions $u_0(\lambda), u_1(\lambda), \ldots$ are analytic in a given region of the complex plane and form a uniformly convergent series,

$$u_0(\lambda) + u_1(\lambda) + \cdots + u_m(\lambda) + \cdots$$

then the sum of this uniformly convergent series of analytic terms,

$$F(\lambda) = u_0(\lambda) + u_1(\lambda) + \cdots + u_m(\lambda) + \cdots$$

is also an analytic function in the given region. The series above is a representation of the function $F(\lambda)$ in its region of analyticity.

Let us now explain what we mean by uniform convergence. If an infinite series $\sum u_m(\lambda)$ is convergent at a point λ, the sequence of partial sums has a definite limit,

$$S(\lambda) = \lim_{m\to\infty} S_m(\lambda)$$

at this point. This implies that from some given integer M onwards the absolute value of the difference between the partial sum $S_m(\lambda)$ and the sum $S(\lambda)$ becomes arbitrarily small. In the case of ordinary convergence the magnitude of this integer M depends on the particular point λ we are considering. Hence, if each point in a given region has its own integer M assigned to it, such that $|S_m(\lambda) - S(\lambda)|$ is arbitrarily small when $m > M$, we shall say that the infinite series is convergent at each point λ of the given region. In contrast to this concept of ordinary convergence, uniform convergence requires that the integer M can be chosen uniformly for each point λ of the given region. In other words, we require that for all λ in the region considered the quantity $|S_m(\lambda) - S(\lambda)|$ is smaller than some given positive number whenever m is larger than some integer M which can be chosen independently of λ.

Because of their strong analytic properties, uniformly convergent series are of great utility. For instance, a series which is uniformly convergent can be integrated term by term, and it can be differentiated term by term whenever the series of the derivatives of the terms is uniformly convergent. Moreover, the sum of a uniformly convergent series is continuous at a point whenever the separate terms are continuous at that point. Of course, such regular analytic properties make it easy to manipulate such series and ensure the well-behaved character of the results.

A convenient test for the uniform convergence of a series $\sum u_m(\lambda)$ is Weierstrass's M-test. This is a comparison test in which we compare the separate terms of the series with the corresponding terms of a convergent series of constant terms $\sum M_m$. It can be shown that the infinite series $\sum u_m(\lambda)$ is uniformly convergent in a region D whenever the absolute value of the function $u_m(\lambda)$ is smaller than the value M_m at all points in the region.

If a function of a complex variable is analytic in some neighborhood of a point and at the point itself, then its series representation in that neighborhood can be expressed immediately in terms of its derivatives at the point. The series representation of a function $F(\lambda)$ at a point a in its region of analyticity is the Taylor series,

$$F(\lambda) = F(a) + (\lambda - a)\frac{dF(a)}{d\lambda} + \frac{1}{2!}(\lambda - a)^2\frac{d^2F(a)}{d\lambda^2} + \cdots$$

To obtain the Taylor series expansion of the function about the point a let us consider a circle C with radius R and center at the point a such that $F(\lambda)$ is analytic inside and on the circle. According to the Cauchy integral representation of the function inside the circle, we may write

$$F(\lambda) = \frac{1}{2\pi i} \oint_C \frac{F(\zeta)}{\zeta - \lambda}\, d\zeta = \frac{1}{2\pi i} \oint_C \sum_{m=0}^{\infty} \left(\frac{\lambda - a}{\zeta - a}\right)^m \frac{F(\zeta)}{\zeta - a}\, d\zeta$$

where λ is an arbitrary point inside the circle. Since the infinite series in the integrand is uniformly convergent at all points ζ on the contour, we may integrate this series term by term. Interchanging the order of integration and summation, we obtain

$$F(\lambda) = \frac{1}{2\pi i} \sum_{m=0}^{\infty} (\lambda - a)^m \oint_C \frac{F(\zeta)}{(\zeta - a)^{m+1}}\, d\zeta$$

Substitution of the Cauchy integral representations for the derivatives immediately yields the desired result,

$$F(\lambda) = \sum_{m=0}^{\infty} \frac{(\lambda - a)^m}{m!} \frac{d^m F(a)}{d\lambda^m}$$

The radius of convergence of the power series is equal to the distance between the point a and the nearest point at which the function ceases to be analytic.

A Taylor expansion of the function $F(\lambda)$ with a remainder can be obtained by terminating the expansion of the function $1/(\zeta - \lambda)$ at the n-th term,

$$\frac{1}{\zeta - \lambda} = \frac{1}{\zeta - a}\left[1 + \frac{\lambda - a}{\zeta - a} + \left(\frac{\lambda - a}{\zeta - a}\right)^2 + \cdots + \frac{(\lambda - a)^{n+1}}{(\zeta - a)^n(\zeta - \lambda)}\right]$$

Term by term integration of this expansion yields the following representation of the function $F(\lambda)$,

$$F(\lambda) = F(a) + (\lambda - a)F'(a) + \frac{1}{2!}(\lambda - a)^2 F''(a)$$

$$+ \cdots + \frac{1}{n!}(\lambda - a)^n F^{(n)}(a) + \frac{(\lambda - a)^{n+1}}{2\pi i} \oint_C \frac{F(\zeta)}{(\zeta - a)^{n+1}(\zeta - \lambda)}\, d\zeta$$

which closely resembles the representation formula for the function $F(\lambda)$ at the end of Section 1.1.

The Taylor series is a series representation of a function of a complex variable in the neighborhood of a point at which the function is analytic. We can also obtain a series representation of a function in an annular neighborhood of a point a at which it is not analytic. The only requirement is that we be able to isolate this point from all other points at which the function is not analytic by an annulus of arbitrarily small inner radius and an outer radius which extends to the nearest point of nonanalyticity of the function. If we can find such an annular neighborhood about the point a, then the function can be represented in this region by a Laurent series which is an infinite series of positive and negative powers of the quantity $(\lambda - a)$. To construct such a series, let us assume that C denotes the inner circle and that Σ denotes the outer circle of the annulus. Since $F(\lambda)$ is not analytic at the point a, we cannot expand the function in a Taylor series about the point a. However, let λ be a point in the annulus. The doubly connected region which is bounded by the circles C and Σ can be rendered simply connected by the insertion of a barrier between C and Σ. The function $F(\lambda)$ is analytic in this simply connected region and we may write, according to the Cauchy integral representation formula,

$$F(\lambda) = \frac{1}{2\pi i}\oint_{\Sigma} \frac{F(\zeta)}{\zeta - \lambda}\, d\zeta - \frac{1}{2\pi i}\oint_{C} \frac{F(\zeta)}{\zeta - \lambda}\, d\zeta$$

since the integrals over the barrier cancel each other. Expanding the integrands of the integrals above in powers of $(\lambda - a)/(\zeta - a)$ and $(\zeta - a)/(\lambda - \text{a})$ respectively, we obtain the result,

$$F(\lambda) = \frac{1}{2\pi i}\oint_{\Sigma} \frac{F(\zeta)}{\zeta - a} \sum_{m=0}^{\infty} \left(\frac{\lambda - a}{\zeta - a}\right)^m d\zeta + \frac{1}{2\pi i}\oint_{C} \frac{F(\zeta)}{\lambda - a} \sum_{m=0}^{\infty} \left(\frac{\zeta - a}{\lambda - a}\right)^m d\zeta$$

The infinite series in the integrand of the first integral is uniformly convergent on the circle Σ and the series in the integrand of the second integral is uniformly convergent on the circle C. Consequently, we may integrate both series term by term and we obtain the result,

$$F(\lambda) = \sum_{m=0}^{\infty} A_m(\lambda - a)^m + \sum_{m=1}^{\infty} B_m/(\lambda - a)^m$$

where the coefficients A_m and B_m are determined by the contour integrals,

$$A_m = \frac{1}{2\pi i}\oint_{\Sigma} \frac{F(\zeta)}{(\zeta - a)^{m+1}}\, d\zeta$$

and

$$B_m = \frac{1}{2\pi i}\oint_{C} F(\zeta)(\zeta - a)^{m-1}\, d\zeta$$

The infinite series above is called the Laurent series representation of the function $F(\lambda)$ in the region enclosed by the two circles. The Laurent series is uniformly convergent in the annulus including the two boundaries. The circle C can be expanded and the circle Σ can be contracted into a single contour C

which is located inside the annulus. Defining new coefficients a_m by the relations,

$$a_m = A_m = \frac{1}{2\pi i}\oint_C \frac{F(\zeta)}{(\zeta - a)^{m+1}}\, d\zeta$$

$$a_{-m} = B_m = \frac{1}{2\pi i}\oint_C F(\zeta)(\zeta - a)^{m-1}\, d\zeta$$

we obtain the more compact-looking Laurent representation,

$$F(\lambda) = \sum_{m=-\infty}^{\infty} a_m(\lambda - a)^m$$

where the coefficients a_m are now defined by the contour integrals,

$$a_m = \frac{1}{2\pi i}\oint_C \frac{F(\zeta)}{(\zeta - a)^{m+1}}\, d\zeta$$

1.3 SINGULARITIES AT ISOLATED POINTS

We remarked in Section 1.1 that the smooth variations of a physical process are amenable to description by analytic functions of a complex variable. In other words, such functions can be used to describe the physical process in regions which are devoid of sources and sinks and which are removed from sharp discontinuities in the physical properties of the medium. For it is obvious that the physical process cannot be represented accurately by well-behaved analytical expressions in the neighborhood of such singular variations. On the contrary in such situations we expect to see functions appear in the analysis whose singular behavior represents in a more or less exaggerated manner the singular behavior of the physical process. In other words, in order to describe such situations we shall have to use functions which are analytic at all points of a region with the exception of certain isolated points or curves. Conversely, functions with singular behavior can sometimes be used advantageously to describe smoothly varying physical situations. For example, let us consider the velocity field of the plane motion of an incompressible and irrotational fluid. Such a field can be described by the mathematical device of a complex velocity potential,

$$F(z) = \phi(x, y) + i\psi(x, y)$$

where $\phi(x, y)$ is the real velocity potential and $\psi(x, y)$ is the stream function. The conjugate functions ϕ and ψ present together a complete description of the velocity field. In the regions of the plane in which the field is smooth and finite the complex velocity potential should, in general, be analytic and well-behaved. However, to describe certain smooth streamline patterns it is sometimes advantageous to use complex velocity potentials which have some singularity, such as a logarithmic or power law infinity, at an isolated point. A simple illustration is, for instance, the logarithmic potential,

$$F(z) = q \log (z - a) = q [\log |z - a| + i \arg (z - a)] = q[\log R + i\Theta]$$

In this case the streamlines are lines of constant Θ,

$$\psi(R, \Theta) = q\Theta$$

extending radially outward from the origin, while the lines of constant potential,

$$\phi(R, \Theta) = q \log R$$

are concentric circles with center at the point a as shown in Figure I-8.

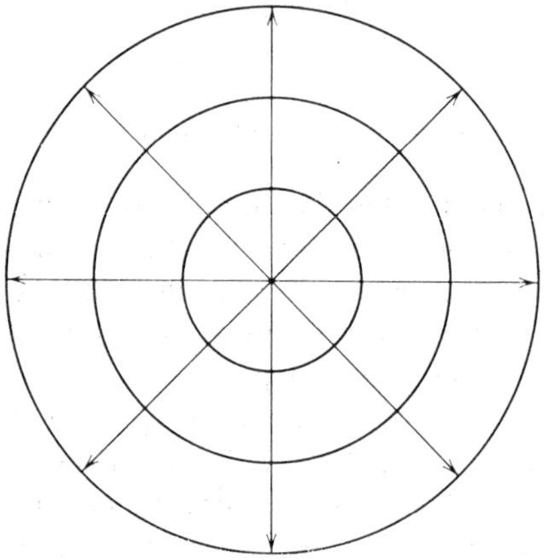

Figure I-8

In the hydrodynamical interpretation of such a streamline pattern we assume that a source or a sink of strength q is located at the point a and induces a fluid flow from or to this point. Actually a real physical counterpart of such a mathematical singularity does not exist. The concept of a point source or a point sink is a convenient mathematical abstraction. It can be used however, with great success, to construct streamline patterns which, for example, realistically depict the flow of an ideal fluid around bodies of revolution.

A. Isolated Singular Points in the Finite Plane

In the foregoing section we found that a function of a complex variable can be expanded in a Taylor series about a point, provided the function is analytic at that point. The Taylor series may be used to represent the function at all points of a circular region which is centered at the point in question and extends up to the nearest singular point of the function. We also observed that a function of a complex variable can be expanded in a Laurent series about a point at which it is not analytic, provided this point can be isolated from the other singular points of the function by an annular region which is centered at the point. The Laurent series is a convergent series representation of the function at all points of the annular region. A singular point which can be isolated from all other singularities of the function is an isolated singularity of the function.

The behavior of a function in the neighborhood of an isolated singular point can be determined completely from the Laurent series expansion of the function about this point. For let us assume that the function $F(\lambda)$ has an isolated singularity at the point a. The Laurent representation of the function about the point a may be written as the sum of two series,

$$F(\lambda) = \sum_{m=0}^{\infty} A_m(\lambda - a)^m + \sum_{m=1}^{\infty} \frac{B_m}{(\lambda - a)^m}$$

The second series in the representation of the function is called the principal part $P[F(\lambda), a]$ of the function at the point a. The nature of a singularity of a function at an isolated singular point is related to the behavior of the principal part of the function at that point.

First let us assume that the principal part of the function $F(\lambda)$ at the point a vanishes. In this case, the function is analytic at the point and can be expanded in a Taylor series about the point. The point a is called a removable singular point. If, moreover, the coefficients $A_0, A_1 \cdots, A_{n-1}$ are zero but the coefficient A_n has some finite value, then the function,

$$F(\lambda) = \sum_{m=n}^{\infty} A_m(\lambda - a)^m$$

is said to have a zero of order n at the isolated point a.

Now let us assume that the principal part of the function $F(\lambda)$ at the isolated singular point a is a finite sum,

$$P[F(\lambda), a] = \sum_{m=1}^{n} B_m/(\lambda - a)^m$$

where n is some positive integer. In this case, $F(\lambda) = O(1/(\lambda - a)^n)$ when λ tends to the point a, and we shall say that the function has a pole of order n at this point. The function can be represented in a neighborhood of this point by the expansion,

$$F(\lambda) = \sum_{m=0}^{\infty} A_m(\lambda - a)^m + \sum_{m=1}^{n} B_m/(\lambda - a)^m$$

The coefficient B_1 in this expansion can be used to evaluate the contour integral of the function $F(\lambda)$ along a contour C which encloses the singular point a but no other singularities of the function. For, integrating the series expansion of $F(\lambda)$ over the contour, we obtain, according to Cauchy's formula and theorem,

$$\frac{1}{2\pi i}\oint_C F(\zeta)\, d\zeta = B_1$$

The integral on the left hand side of this equation is called the residue of the function $F(\lambda)$ at the point a,

$$\text{Res}\,[F(\lambda), a] = \frac{1}{2\pi i}\oint_C F(\zeta)\, d\zeta$$

Consequently, the coefficient B_1 of the term $B_1/(\lambda - a)$ in the Laurent series representation of a function is equal to the residue of that function at the point a. If the function $F(\lambda)$ has a simple pole at the point a, the residue can immediately be evaluated by the limit relation,

$$\text{Res}\,[F(\lambda), a] = \lim_{\lambda\to a}\,(\lambda - a)F(\lambda)$$

If the function $F(\lambda)$ has a pole of order $(n + 1)$ at the point a, the residue can be obtained from the formula,

$$\text{Res}\,[F(\lambda), a] = \frac{1}{n!}\left(\frac{d^n}{d\lambda^n}[(\lambda - a)^{n+1}F(\lambda)]\right)_{\lambda=a}$$

Now let us assume that the function $F(\lambda)$ has p isolated singularities which are located at the points $a_1, a_2, \ldots, a_p$ and that all singularities are poles. Assuming that the contour C_m encloses the pole at the point a_m and no other singularities of the function, we may write

$$\text{Res}\,[F(\lambda), a_m] = \frac{1}{2\pi i}\oint_{C_m} F(\zeta)\, d\zeta$$

for the residue of the function $F(\lambda)$ at the pole at the point a_m. Summing over all poles, we obtain therefore

$$\sum_{m=0}^{p}\frac{1}{2\pi i}\oint_{C_m} F(\zeta)\, d\zeta = \sum_{m=0}^{p}\text{Res}\,[F(\lambda), a_m]$$

The multiple connected region, bounded by the contours C_m and the contour C, can be rendered simply connected by the barriers b_m as depicted in Figure I-9. This implies, according to Cauchy's theorem, that

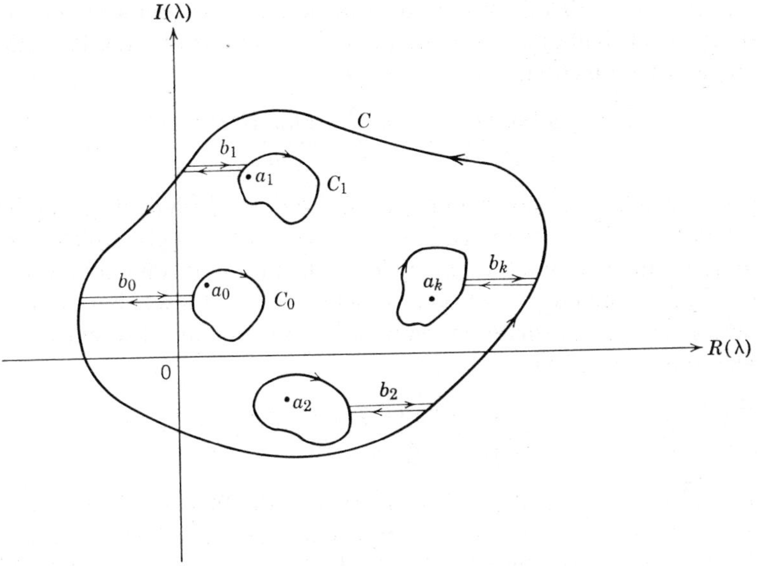

Figure I-9

$$\frac{1}{2\pi i}\oint_C F(\zeta)\,d\zeta - \sum_{m=0}^{p}\frac{1}{2\pi i}\oint_{C_m} F(\zeta)\,d\zeta = 0$$

since the barrier integrals cancel each other. Consequently, we obtain

$$\oint_C F(\zeta)\,d\zeta = \sum_{m=0}^{p}\oint_{C_m} F(\zeta)\,d\zeta = 2\pi i \sum_{m=0}^{p} \text{Res}\,[F(\lambda), a_m]$$

This is the so-called residue theorem which states that the contour integral of the function is equal to $2\pi i$ times the sum of the residues of that function at the poles which are located inside the contour.

As an application of the residue theorem we shall now derive the principle of the argument. If the function $F(\lambda)$ has a pole of order m at the point a we may write $F(\lambda) = G(\lambda)/(\lambda - a)^m$ where the function $G(\lambda)$ is analytic and nonvanishing in some neighborhood of the point a. Consequently, we find the following expression for the logarithmic derivative of the function,

$$\frac{d \log F(\lambda)}{d\lambda} = -\frac{m}{\lambda - a} + \frac{d \log G(\lambda)}{d\lambda}$$

This implies that the logarithmic derivative of a function has a simple pole with residue $-m$ at the point at which the function has a pole of order m. Similarly, if the function $F(\lambda)$ has a zero of order n at the point b we may write $F(\lambda) = (\lambda - b)^n H(\lambda)$, where the function $H(\lambda)$ is analytic and nonvanishing in a neighborhood of the point b. Consequently, the logarithmic derivative of the function,

$$\frac{d \log F(\lambda)}{d\lambda} = \frac{n}{\lambda - b} + \frac{d \log H(\lambda)}{d\lambda}$$

will have a simple pole with residue n at the point at which the function has a zero of order n. Now let us assume that the function $F(\lambda)$, which is nonvanishing on the contour C, is analytic inside and on this contour with the exception of a finite number of poles which are located inside but not on the contour. It is an immediate consequence of the residue theorem and the considerations above that

$$\frac{1}{2\pi i} \oint_C \frac{d \log F(\zeta)}{d\zeta} \, d\zeta = N - P$$

where N denotes the total number of zeros of the function $F(\lambda)$ inside the contour, each zero of order n being counted n times, and P denotes the total number of poles of the function inside the contour, each pole of order m being counted m times. Denoting the increment in the function $F(\lambda)$, as a result of a complete circuit of the contour C, by $\Delta_C F(\lambda)$, we find

$$\oint_C \frac{d \log F(\zeta)}{d\zeta} \, d\zeta = \Delta_C \log F(\zeta) = i \, \Delta_C \arg F(\zeta)$$

For, $\log F(\zeta) = \log |F(\zeta)| + i \arg F(\zeta)$ and $\log |F(\zeta)|$ returns to its starting value after one complete circuit of the contour. Consequently, substitution of this expression for the integral yields the result,

$$\Delta_C \arg F(\zeta) = 2\pi(N - P)$$

In words, the variation in the argument of the function $F(\zeta)$ over the contour C is equal to 2π times the difference in the total number of zeros and the total number of poles of the function inside the contour, where the zeros and poles are counted in the manner described above. This is the so-called principle of the argument.

An interesting application of the principle of the argument concerns the so-called simple functions. A function $F(\lambda)$ is said to be simple in a region D if it is analytic in this region and takes no value more than once in the region. We shall now show, with the help of the principle of the argument, that a function $F(\lambda)$ which is analytic inside and on a contour C and takes no value more than once on this contour is a simple function in the region bounded by the contour. The easiest way is to map the contour C by means of the transformation $w = F(\lambda)$ into the complex w-plane. Since $F(\zeta)$ is analytic and takes no value more than once on C, the transformation $w = F(\zeta)$ traces a continuous curve in the complex w-plane which does not intersect itself. Moreover, since $F(\zeta)$ is single-valued on C, the terminal value of the path in the w-plane coincides with the point at which the path is started. Thus the curve in the w-plane is a closed contour which we shall denote by Σ. Now let a be a point inside the contour C. Then, according to the principle of the argument,

$$N = \frac{1}{2\pi i} \oint_C \frac{d \log [F(\zeta) - F(a)]}{d\zeta} d\zeta$$

denotes the number of zeros of the function $F(\lambda) - F(a)$ inside the contour C. Since a is a point inside the contour, the function $F(\lambda) - F(a)$ has at least one zero inside C, namely, the point $\lambda = a$. The integer N therefore must be larger than or equal to unity. However, the mapping $w = F(\lambda)$ transforms the integral into a contour integral in the w-plane,

$$\frac{1}{2\pi i} \oint_C \frac{d \log [F(\zeta) - F(a)]}{d\zeta} d\zeta = \frac{1}{2\pi i} \oint_\Sigma \frac{du}{u - b} = N$$

where $b = F(a)$ is a point in the w-plane. According to Cauchy's theorem and Cauchy's formula, the second integral must be equal to plus or minus unity, to plus or minus one half, or to zero depending on whether the point b is located inside, on, or outside the contour. Consequently, $N = 1$ is the only admissible value of N which causes no contradiction. Hence, we may draw the conclusion that the function $F(\lambda)$ takes the value $F(a)$ no more than once. We have shown, moreover, that a point inside the contour C is mapped by the transformation $w = F(\lambda)$ into a point inside the contour Σ. Furthermore, since

$$\frac{1}{2\pi i} \oint_\Sigma \frac{du}{u - b} = 1,$$

the mapping traverses the contour Σ in the positive direction.

The function $F(\lambda)$ can have a third type of singularity at the isolated point a, namely, the principal part of the function can be an infinite series. In this case the function $F(\lambda)$ is said to have an essential singularity at the point a. An essential singularity is a very peculiar type of isolated singularity, as can be seen from the following example. The exponential function $\exp(1/\lambda)$ can be represented at the origin by the series expansion,

$$\exp(1/\lambda) = 1 + \frac{1}{\lambda} + \frac{1}{2!\,\lambda^2} + \cdots$$

It follows immediately from the definition of an essential singularity, that the function $\exp(1/\lambda)$ has such a singularity at the origin. Because of this essential singularity, the function is undefined at the origin. For let us write $\lambda = r \exp(i\theta)$. Then

$$\exp(1/\lambda) = [\cos(\sin\theta/r) - i\sin(\sin\theta/r)]\exp(\cos\theta/r)$$

On the real axis this function takes the form $\exp(1/\lambda) = \exp(1/r)$ which tends to infinity as r tends to zero. However, on the positive imaginary axis we find, $\exp(1/\lambda) = \cos(1/r) - i\sin(1/r)$ and this expression does not have a well-defined limit when r tends to zero. Similarly, on the negative real axis we obtain the function $\exp(1/\lambda) = \exp(-1/r)$ and this function tends to zero as r tends to zero. We could go on in this manner obtaining any conceivable value for the function $\exp(1/\lambda)$ at the origin.

Other examples of functions with essential singularities at the origin are the functions, $\exp(-1/\lambda)$, $\exp(1/\lambda)$, $\sin(1/\lambda)$, $\cos(1/\lambda)$, etc.

To summarize, an isolated singular point can be distinguished from a non-isolated singularity of the function by the fact that it can be isolated from any other singular point by an annular region of arbitrarily small inner radius in which the function can be expanded in a Laurent series. Furthermore, we can distinguish between the following three types of isolated singularities of a function of a complex variable: removable singularities, poles, and essential singularities. At a removable singular point or at a pole, the function $F(\lambda)$ is of algebraic growth in the immediate neighborhood of the singular point. For instance, at a removable singular point a the function $F(\lambda)$ satisfies the order relation $F(\lambda) = O(1)$ when λ tends to the point a, and at a pole of order n we may write $F(\lambda) = O(1/(\lambda - a)^n)$ when λ tends to the point a. In the neighborhood of an essential singular point the function ceases to behave algebraically and becomes undefinable.

B. Isolated Singularities at Infinity

In the foregoing section we dealt with the singularities of a function of a complex variable which are isolated and which are located in a finite region of the complex plane. In this section we shall be concerned with the singularities of functions of a complex variable at the point at infinity.

To investigate the properties of a function $F(\lambda)$ at the point at infinity, one makes use of the transformation $w = 1/\lambda$, which maps the complex λ-plane onto the complex w-plane so that the point at infinity in the complex λ-plane is mapped into the origin in the complex w-plane. The analytical properties of the function $F(\lambda)$ can now be derived from the properties of the function $G(w) = F(1/w)$ at the origin. If the function $G(w)$ has a zero, pole, or essential singularity at the origin, then the function $F(\lambda)$ will have a zero, pole, or essential singularity at the point at infinity. For let us assume that the function $G(w)$ is analytic in the region $0 < |w| < 1/r$ and can be expanded in a Laurent series,

$$G(w) = \sum_{m=-\infty}^{\infty} b_m w^m$$

about the origin. This implies that the transformed function $F(\lambda)$ is analytic in the neighborhood $r \leqq |\lambda| < \infty$ of the point at infinity and can be expanded in a Laurent series,

$$F(\lambda) = \sum_{m=-\infty}^{\infty} a_m \lambda^m$$

about the point at infinity, where $a_m = b_{-m}$. The principal part of the function $F(\lambda)$ at the point at infinity now takes the form,

$$P[F(\lambda), \infty] = \sum_{m=0}^{\infty} B_m \lambda^m$$

and we can again distinguish between three distinct types of singularities. First let us assume that the principal part of the function $F(\lambda)$ at the point at infinity is zero. In this case the function $F(\lambda)$ is analytic at the point at infinity and can be represented in the neighborhood of this point by an infinite series of inverse powers of λ,

$$F(\lambda) = \sum_{m=1}^{\infty} A_m/\lambda^m$$

We find that $F(\lambda)$ tends to zero when λ tends to infinity. Moreover, the function will have a zero of order n at infinity whenever the coefficients A_1, ..., A_{n-1} are equal to zero but the coefficient A_n has some finite value. In this case, we may also write $F(\lambda) = G(\lambda)/\lambda^n$, where the function,

$$G(\lambda) = A_n + A_{n+1}/\lambda + A_{n+2}/\lambda^2 + \cdots$$

is analytic and finite at infinity. In other words, the function $F(\lambda)$ is at most of the order of $1/\lambda^n$ when λ tends to infinity.

Now let us assume that the principal part of the function is a polynomial of degree n in λ. In this case the function $F(\lambda)$ takes the form,

$$F(\lambda) = \sum_{m=1}^{\infty} A_m/\lambda^m + \sum_{m=0}^{n} B_m \lambda^m$$

Consequently, the function will have a pole of order n at infinity. We may write $F(\lambda) = \lambda^n G(\lambda)$, where now the function,

$$G(\lambda) = B_n + B_{n-1}/\lambda + B_{n-2}/\lambda^2 + \cdots$$

is analytic and finite at infinity. In other words, the function $F(\lambda)$ is at most of the order of λ^n when λ tends to infinity.

Finally, let us assume that the principal part of the function $F(\lambda)$ at the point at infinity is an infinite series. In this case the function,

$$F(\lambda) = \sum_{m=1}^{\infty} A_m/\lambda^m + \sum_{m=0}^{\infty} B_m \lambda^m$$

will have an essential singularity at infinity. The following functions are examples of functions which have an essential singularity at infinity: $\exp \lambda$, $\exp i\lambda$, $\exp(-\lambda)$, $\sinh \lambda$, $\cosh \lambda$, etc.

To summarize, let us consider a function of a complex variable which is analytic in a neighborhood of the point at infinity and which can be represented in the neighborhood of this point by a Laurent series of the form,

$$\lambda^m(A_0 + A_1/\lambda + A_2/\lambda^2 + \cdots)$$

If m is a finite positive or negative integer or is equal to zero, we shall say that the function is of finite order m at infinity and we may distinguish between the following cases:

a. If m is negative, the function is analytic at the point at infinity and has a zero of order m at this point.
b. If m is zero, the function is analytic and finite at the point at infinity.
c. If m is positive, the function has a pole of order m at the point at infinity.

The concept of the residue of a function at a point which is located in a finite region in the complex plane can be extended to include the point at infinity. The residue of a function $F(\lambda)$ at the point at infinity is defined as the contour integral,

$$\text{Res}\,[F(\lambda), \infty] = \frac{1}{2\pi i} \oint_C F(\zeta)\, d\zeta$$

where the contour C encloses the origin and is located inside the region $r \leqq |\lambda| < \infty$. In the definition above it is assumed that the contour is traversed in the positive direction with respect to the point at infinity. Since the positive direction with respect to the point at infinity is equivalent to the negative direction with respect to the origin, we may also write

$$\text{Res}\,[F(\lambda), \infty] = -\frac{1}{2\pi i} \oint_C F(\zeta)\, d\zeta$$

where now the contour C is assumed to be traversed in the positive direction with respect to the origin. It may be noted that the expansion of the function $F(\lambda)$ in a Laurent series about the point at infinity yields the result that the residue of the function $F(\lambda)$ at infinity is equal to minus the coefficient of $1/\lambda$. Hence, this particular residue is nonzero even when the function is analytic at the point at infinity. The contour C above encloses all singularities of the function $F(\lambda)$ which are located in the finite regions of the complex plane. The point at infinity is the only possible singular point of the function which is outside the contour. Consequently, if the only singularities of the function $F(\lambda)$ in the finite regions of the complex plane are poles, which are located at the points $a_0, a_1, \ldots, a_p$, then

$$\text{Res}\,[F(\lambda), \infty] + \sum_{m=1}^{p} \text{Res}\,[F(\lambda), a_m] = 0$$

The concept of a residue of a function at the point at infinity can considerably simplify the evaluation of contour integrals by means of the residue theorem. In the foregoing section, we found that the contour integral of a function $F(\lambda)$ is equal to $2\pi i$ times the residues of the function at the poles of the function inside the contour,

$$\oint_C F(\zeta)\, d\zeta = 2\pi i \sum_m \text{Res}\,[F(\lambda), a_m]$$

provided that the contour does not enclose singularities of $F(\lambda)$ other than poles. However, we may also write

$$\sum_{m=0}^{s} \text{Res}\,[F(\lambda), a_m] + \sum_{m=s+1}^{p} \text{Res}\,[F(\lambda), a_m] + \text{Res}\,[F(\lambda), \infty] = 0$$

where $a_{s+1}, \ldots, a_p$ are the poles of $F(\lambda)$ outside the contour. This implies that the contour integral above may be evaluated as the sum,

$$\oint_C F(\zeta)\, d\zeta = -2\pi i \sum_{m=s+1}^{p} \text{Res}\,[F(\lambda), a_m] - \text{Res}\,[F(\lambda), \infty]$$

where we have assumed that $F(\lambda)$ is analytic outside and on the contour except for a finite number of poles at the points $a_{s+1}, \ldots, a_p$.

1.4 ENTIRE AND MEROMORPHIC FUNCTIONS; THEOREM OF LIOUVILLE

The character of a function of a complex variable is determined by the nature and location of its singular points. In this section we shall present a short outline of the classification of such functions by means of their singular points.

First let us consider a function which is analytic in the whole complex plane with the exception of the point at infinity at which the function may have some isolated singularity. Such functions are called entire or integral functions. The singularity at infinity can be a pole or an essential singularity, or the function may tend to zero when λ tends to infinity. Let us assume that the function is of order m at infinity where m is either a positive integer or is equal to zero. In this case the entire function $F(\lambda)$ must be a polynomial of degree m. This statement can be made plausible as follows. Since the function is of finite order m at infinity and is analytic in the whole complex plane it can be represented by the series,

$$\lambda^m(A_0 + A_1/\lambda + A_2/\lambda^2 + \cdots)$$

However, since the function must also be analytic at the origin, the expansion above cannot contain terms with negative powers of λ. This implies that the coefficients $A_{m+1}, A_{m+2}, \cdots$ must vanish, and the expansion, therefore, reduces to a polynomial of degree m.

If the entire function tends to a finite constant at infinity, in other words, if the function is of zeroth order at infinity, the considerations above imply that the function must be equal to a constant in the whole complex plane. This is an expression of Liouville's theorem, which is often quoted as follows: A function which is analytic and bounded in the whole complex plane is a constant. This theorem can also be made plausible by the following argument. Let a denote an arbitrary point in the complex plane and let C denote a circle with center at this point. The derivative of the analytic function $F(\lambda)$ at the point a can be represented by the integral,

$$\frac{dF(a)}{d\lambda} = \frac{1}{2\pi i} \oint_C \frac{F(\zeta)}{(\zeta - a)^2} \, d\zeta$$

However, since the function $F(\lambda)$ is bounded at all points of the complex plane, the integral on the right hand side of this equation must vanish when the radius of the circle tends to infinity. This implies, since the radius of the circle is independent of the location of the point a, that the derivative of the function vanishes at all points in the complex plane. In other words, the function must be a constant.

If the entire function is of a negative order m at infinity, the function vanishes at infinity. This implies, as an immediate consequence of the considerations above, that the function must vanish in the whole complex plane. In other words, if we can show that a particular entire function vanishes at infinity, we may draw the conclusion that the function vanishes in the whole complex plane.

Now let us consider a function which is analytic in all points of a region with the exception of a finite number of points at which the isolated singularities of the function are poles. Such a function is called a meromorphic function. The number of singular points of such a function in a particular region should be finite, since an infinity of poles in a finite region would result in a limit point of poles. Rational functions are examples of meromorphic functions which are meromorphic in the whole complex plane including the point at infinity.

1.5 THE LEMMA OF JORDAN

In applications of function-theoretic techniques to problems in mathematical physics, we often need to show that the contour integral of a given function over a semicircular contour, which is located either in the upper or lower half plane, vanishes as the radius of the semicircle tends to infinity. Jordan's lemma is a convenient analytical device which can assist us in some of these situations.

Let Γ denote the semicircle depicted in Figure I-10.

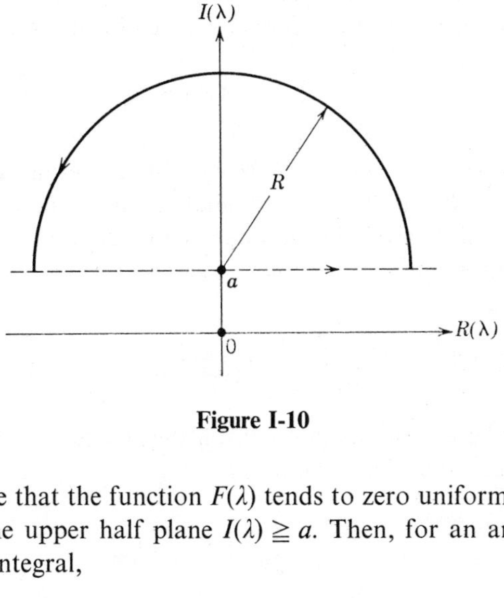

Figure I-10

Let us assume that the function $F(\lambda)$ tends to zero uniformly when λ tends to infinity in the upper half plane $I(\lambda) \geqq a$. Then, for an arbitrary positive value of t, the integral,

$$\int_\Gamma e^{i\zeta t} F(\zeta)\, d\zeta$$

vanishes when the radius R of the semicircle tends to infinity. This assertion, which is called the lemma of Jordan, can be proven as follows. Since $F(\lambda)$ tends to zero when λ tends to infinity in the upper half plane, we may write

$$\int_\Gamma e^{i\zeta t} F(\zeta)\, d\zeta = 2o(1)R \exp(-at) \int_0^{\pi/2} \exp(-Rt \sin\theta)\, d\theta$$

when R tends to infinity. Moreover, for small positive values of ϕ we find,

$$R\int_0^{\pi/2}\exp(-Rt\sin\theta)\,d\theta$$

$$<\left[R\int_0^{\phi}\exp(-Rt\sin\theta)\cos\theta\,d\theta/\cos\phi+R\int_{\phi}^{\pi/2}\exp(-Rt\sin\phi)\,d\theta\right]$$

$$=\frac{1}{t\cos\phi}+\left(\frac{\pi}{2}-\phi-\frac{1}{Rt\cos\phi}\right)R\exp(-Rt\sin\phi)$$

and for positive values of t the second term on the right hand side of this equation vanishes when R tends to infinity. Substitution of this result into the penultimate equation yields the desired result.

The following proposition is an immediate consequence of the lemma of Jordan. Let us assume that the function $F(\lambda)$ is analytic in the upper half plane $I(\lambda) \geqq a$ and tends to zero uniformly when λ tends to infinity in this half plane. Then, for an arbitrary positive value of t, the integral,

$$\frac{1}{\sqrt{(2\pi)}}\int_{-\infty+ia}^{\infty+ia}F(\zeta)e^{i\zeta t}\,d\zeta$$

is identically equal to zero. For, let C be the closed contour which consists of the line $(-R+ia, R+ia)$ and the semicircle Γ shown in Figure I-10. Since the function $F(\lambda)$ is analytic inside and on this contour and the function $\exp(i\lambda t)$ is an entire function, we obtain, according to Cauchy's theorem, the result,

$$\frac{1}{\sqrt{(2\pi)}}\oint_C F(\zeta)e^{i\zeta t}\,d\zeta=\frac{1}{\sqrt{(2\pi)}}\int_{-R+ia}^{R+ia}F(\zeta)e^{i\zeta t}\,d\zeta+\frac{1}{\sqrt{(2\pi)}}\int_{\Gamma}F(\zeta)e^{i\zeta t}\,d\zeta=0$$

However, from the conditions imposed on the function $F(\lambda)$ we may infer, by Jordan's lemma, that the integral,

$$\frac{1}{\sqrt{(2\pi)}}\int_{\Gamma}F(\zeta)e^{i\zeta t}\,d\zeta$$

vanishes when R tends to infinity. Substituting this result into the equation above yields the verification of our statement.

1.6 ANALYTIC CONTINUATION

In the foregoing sections of this chapter we have been concerned with the analytical properties of single-valued and analytic functions of a complex variable. Given such a function and its region of analyticity we have abstained from inquiring into the feasibility of extending this function by distinct but equivalent representations into the other parts of the complex plane. Inquiries of this kind are of great practical importance and we shall pursue some of their implications in this section. We shall find that in its region of analyticity an analytic function can be the single-valued representation of a larger analytical structure. Naming such a structure a complete function, we find that it is not necessarily single-valued but may have more than one value at a particular point of the complex plane. However, it can be defined as a single-valued function of position in a region, not necessarily plane, which is composed of the regions of analyticity of its analytic representations. Investigations into the continuation of analytic functions and the properties of the more general complete functions are part of the subject of analytic continuation.

Apart from its utility in the mathematical fields, the theory of analytic continuation has provided us with powerful tools which find their application in classical as well as modern mathematical physics. This assertion may be substantiated by the following historical examples.

a. At the turn of the century, Sommerfeld published his classic papers in which he presented the first exact solutions of the two-dimensional problem of the diffraction of a plane wave by a wedge or half plane. His method of solution is interwoven with the multivalued solutions of the wave equation and depends for its success, in a crucial manner, on the choice of an appropriate sheet of the Riemann surface on which these functions are defined.
b. Sommerfeld's investigations into the effect of a conducting half plane on the radiation of an oscillating dipole, which had important ramifications in the study of the propagation of radio waves, are also expositions of function-theoretic techniques in which the analytic continuation of multivalued functions plays an important role.
c. The technique of Wiener and Hopf, which has been most fruitfully applied in the fields of hydrodynamics, electrodynamics, neutron transport theory, nuclear reaction theory, plasma physics, etc., was designed to solve certain functional equations involving two unknown functions of a complex variable. These functions, which are the Fourier transforms of the solution of a partial differential equation or an integral equation, are analytic in two overlapping half planes. This provides sufficient information to conclude, by means of the theory of analytic continuation, that the two functions are the representations in their half planes of analyticity of a function which is analytic in the whole complex plane. In other words, these two functions represent an entire function. From the asymptotic behavior of this entire function enough information can be obtained to determine the Fourier transforms and from these, by inverse transformation, the solutions of the original equation.

d. In more recent years, the concept of analytic continuation of functions of a complex variable has been used to obtain a better understanding of the properties of elementary particles and their interactions.

A. Definition and Uniqueness of an Analytic Continuation

The analytic functions we have been concerned with were assumed to be given on some well-defined region by an analytic expression such as a polynomial, an exponential function, etc. Now let us consider the infinite series,

$$F(\lambda) = 1 + \lambda + \lambda^2 + \lambda^3 + \cdots$$

This series, which is uniformly convergent in the region $|\lambda| < 1$, represents in this region an analytic function of the complex variable λ, namely its sum $1/(1 - \lambda)$. Similarly, the infinite integral,

$$G(\lambda) = \int_0^\infty \exp\left[(\lambda - 1)\xi\right] d\xi$$

which is uniformly convergent in the half plane $R(\lambda) < 1$ represents in this half plane the same function, $1/(1 - \lambda)$. Consequently, the function $F(\lambda)$ which is defined by the infinite series and the function $G(\lambda)$ which is defined by the infinite integral are identically equal to each other in the region $|\lambda| < 1$ as shown in Figure I-11. It now makes sense to consider the function

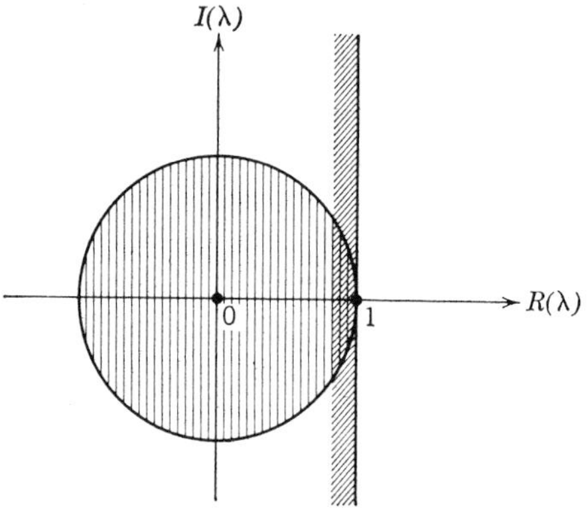

Figure I-11

$G(\lambda)$ to be the extension or continuation of the function $F(\lambda)$ into the half plane $R(\lambda) < 1$. The function $H(\lambda) = 1/(1 - \lambda)$, of which the functions $F(\lambda)$ and $G(\lambda)$ are the analytical representations in their respective regions of analyticity, is analytic in the whole complex plane with the exception of the point $\lambda = 1$ at which the function has a simple pole. This function is identically equal to the function $F(\lambda)$ in the region $|\lambda| < 1$ and to the function $G(\lambda)$ in the half plane $R(\lambda) < 1$. Hence, the function $H(\lambda)$ is the continuation of the function $F(\lambda)$ into the region $|\lambda| \geqq 1$ and of the function $G(\lambda)$ into the half plane $R(\lambda) \geqq 1$, with the provision that the point $\lambda = 1$ is excluded from both regions.

In more general terms, let us consider a function $F(\lambda)$ which is defined and analytic in some region $D(F)$ of the complex plane. We now formulate the following problem. To find a function $G(\lambda)$ which is analytic in a region $D(G)$ and which is identically equal to the function $F(\lambda)$ for all values of λ in the intersection of the regions $D(F)$ and $D(G)$.

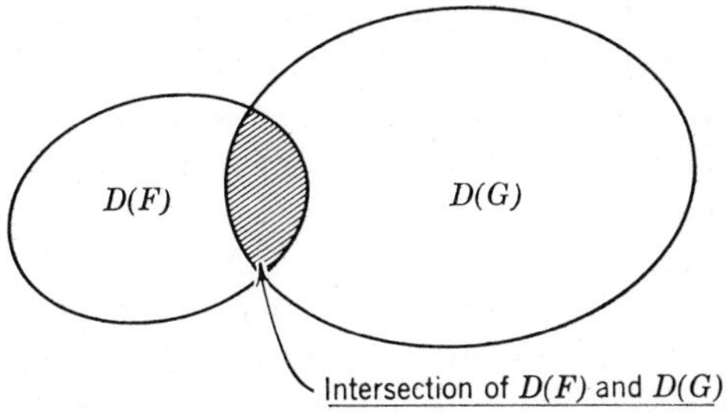

Figure I-12

If this problem has a unique solution, i.e., if we can find a uniquely determined function $G(\lambda)$ which satisfies the conditions specified above, then $G(\lambda)$ is the analytic continuation of the function $F(\lambda)$ into the region $D(G)$. The analytic continuation $G(\lambda)$ of the function $F(\lambda)$ into the region $D(G)$ is unique. This statement is an immediate consequence of the following assertion. Two functions of a complex variable which have a region of analyticity in common and which are identically equal in a subregion of this region are identically equal in the whole region. For let us assume that the two functions $F(\lambda)$ and $G(\lambda)$ have the region of analyticity D in Figure I-13 in common and that they

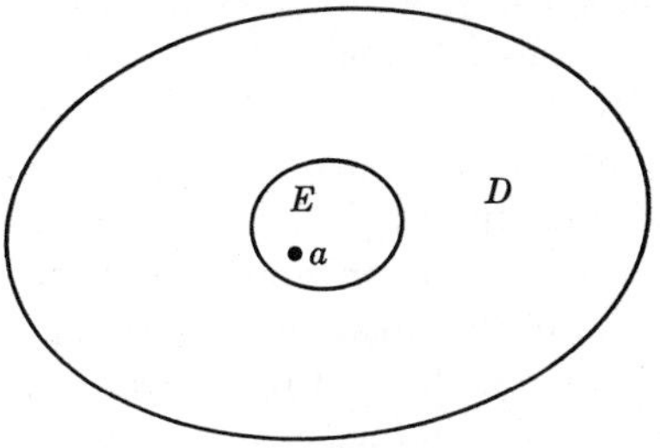

Figure I-13

are identically equal in a subregion E of this region. If a is a point in the region E, then $F(\lambda)$ and $G(\lambda)$ can be expanded in a Taylor series about the point a,

$$F(\lambda) = \sum_{m=0}^{\infty} A_m(\lambda - a)^m$$

and

$$G(\lambda) = \sum_{m=0}^{\infty} B_m(\lambda - a)^m$$

These two series have the same radius of convergence R, where R is the radius of the largest circle, centered at the point a, which lies wholly in the region D. At any point in the subregion E, the power series expansions of the two functions $F(\lambda)$ and $G(\lambda)$ are identically equal. In other words, the coefficients A_m and B_m must be equal to each other for all values of m. This implies that the two power series represent the same function at all points inside the circle and we may conclude, therefore, that $F(\lambda) = G(\lambda)$ at all points inside the circle. In general, the region which is bounded by the circle extends into that part of the region D which is outside the region E. We have extended, therefore, the region in which the two functions are identically equal. The construction above can now be repeated until all points of D have been covered.

In view of the considerations above we may make the following statement. A function which vanishes on a subregion of its region of analyticity is identically equal to zero at all other points of this region.

We now return to our assertion that the analytic continuation $G(\lambda)$ of a function $F(\lambda)$ into a region $D(G)$ is unique. The verification of this assertion can be obtained immediately with the help of the foregoing considerations. For let us assume that the function $H(\lambda)$ is a distinct continuation of the function $F(\lambda)$ into the region $D(G)$. It follows, by the definition of an analytic continuation, that $F(\lambda) = G(\lambda) = H(\lambda)$ on the intersection of the regions $D(F)$ and $D(G)$. Consequently, we may infer, since $G(\lambda)$ and $H(\lambda)$ are equal to each other on a subregion of the region $D(G)$, that $G(\lambda)$ and $H(\lambda)$ are equal to each other at all points of the region $D(G)$. This contradicts our assumption that $G(\lambda)$ and $H(\lambda)$ are distinct functions and we may conclude, therefore, that the analytic continuation of a function is unique.

Of course, the process of analytic continuation of the function $F(\lambda)$ does not have to terminate with the function $G(\lambda)$. It is possible that we can also find the analytic continuation $H(\lambda)$ of the function $G(\lambda)$ into a region $D(H)$ and so on. In this manner we obtain a chain of regions $D(F)$, $D(G)$, $D(H)$, ... as shown in Figure I-14.

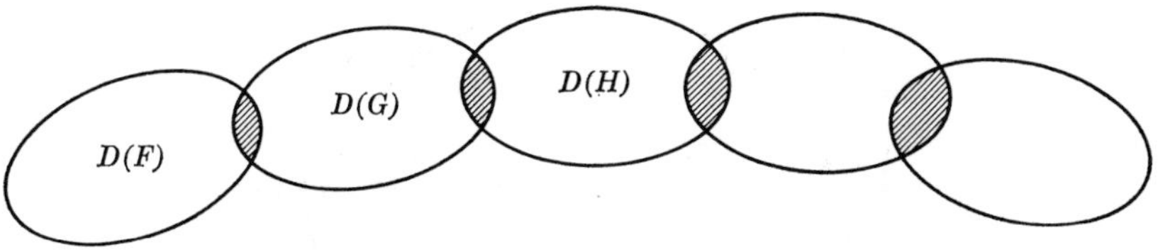

Figure I-14

The manifold of all functions $G(\lambda)$, $H(\lambda)$ ... is called the analytic continuation of the function $F(\lambda)$ into the union of the regions $D(G)$, $D(H)$, ... If no other functions can be found which fit into this scheme of analytic continuation, the manifold of all the functions $F(\lambda)$, $G(\lambda)$, $H(\lambda)$, ... is called a complete analytic function. The union of the regions, $D(F)$, $D(G)$, $D(H)$, ... is called the region of existence of the complete analytic function and the boundary of this region is called the natural boundary of this function. It is not possible to continue a representation of the complete analytic function across the natural boundary.

B. Techniques of Analytic Continuation

In this section we shall present a short outline of some of the techniques that can be used to obtain the analytic continuation of a given function.

First we shall consider a very general technique by which the continuations are obtained by means of power series expansions. Let a be a point in the region of analyticity of the function $F(\lambda)$. Then $F(\lambda)$ can be represented by its Taylor series expansion about the point a,

$$F(\lambda) = \sum_{m=0}^{\infty} A_m(\lambda - a)^m$$

If $r(a)$ is the radius of convergence of this power series, then the function $F(\lambda)$ is analytic in a circle $C(a)$ which is centered at the point a. The radius $r(a)$ of this circle is the distance between a and the nearest singularity of the function. Now let us consider a point b which is located in the circle $C(a)$ but does not coincide with the point a. Since b is a point in a region of analyticity of the function $F(\lambda)$, this function can also be expanded in a power series about the point b,

$$F(\lambda) = \sum_{m=0}^{\infty} B_m(\lambda - b)^m$$

This series is convergent in a circle $C(b)$ with center at the point b and with a radius $r(b)$ which is equal to the distance between the point b and the singularity of the function which is nearest to the point b. If this singularity $\lambda(b)$ is located as depicted in Figure I-15, then part of the area enclosed by the

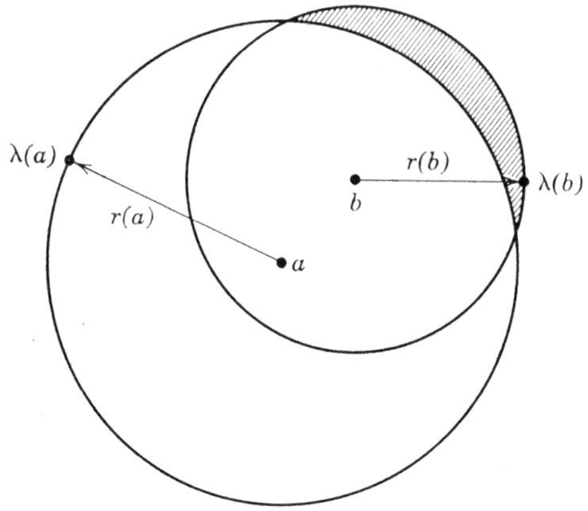

Figure I-15

circle $C(b)$ lies outside the circle $C(a)$. In this case, the Taylor series expansion of the function about the point b defines an analytic function which is the analytic continuation of the function $F(\lambda)$ into the shaded region of Figure I-15. The construction above can be repeated for a point c which is located in the shaded area. In this manner a chain of overlapping disks can be constructed in which each disk is bounded by the circle of convergence of a particular representation of the complete analytic function. The process is terminated when the natural boundary of the complete analytic function has been reached. This particular technique has important theoretical implications. It actually demonstrates, by construction, the existence of analytic continuations of an analytic function. It can be shown that a continuation which has been found by any other method can also be constructed by the series expansion method. By this method we can show, moreover, that a function which is analytic at a point in a region, and which can be analytically continued along every conceivable path in this region, represents a function which is analytic in that region. More directly applicable techniques of analytic continuation can be derived from the following principle of Riemann.

Let us consider the two adjacent regions $D(F)$ and $D(G)$ which are separated by the path Ω as shown in Figure I-16. Let us assume that the function $F(\lambda)$ is analytic in the region $D(F)$ and is continuous on the path Ω. Similarly the function $G(\lambda)$ is analytic in the region $D(G)$ and is continuous on the path Ω. Furthermore, let us assume that $F(\lambda)$ and $G(\lambda)$ are identically equal to each other for all points λ on the path Ω. Then the function $H(\lambda)$, which is equal to $F(\lambda)$ in the region $D(F)$ and to $G(\lambda)$ in the region $D(G)$, is analytic in the union of the regions $D(F)$ and $D(G)$ and on the path Ω. For let λ be a

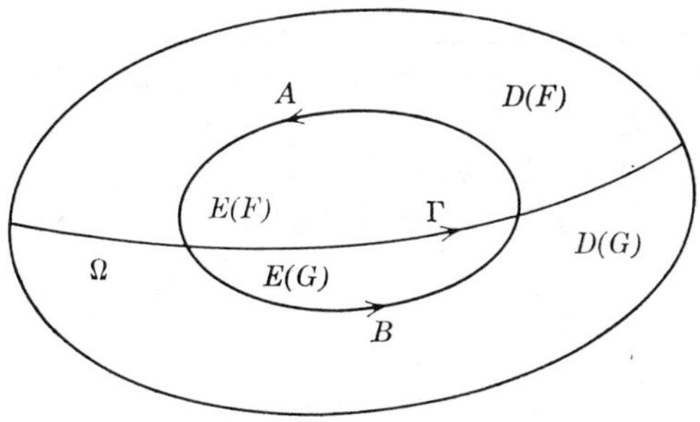

Figure I-16

point in the region $E(F)$. Then, according to Cauchy's representation formula, we may write

$$F(\lambda) = \frac{1}{2\pi i}\int_A \frac{F(\zeta)}{\zeta - \lambda}\,d\zeta + \frac{1}{2\pi i}\int_\Gamma \frac{F(\zeta)}{\zeta - \lambda}\,d\zeta$$

Furthermore, since λ is a point in the region $E(F)$,

$$0 = \frac{1}{2\pi i}\int_B \frac{G(\zeta)}{\zeta - \lambda}\,d\zeta - \frac{1}{2\pi i}\int_\Gamma \frac{G(\zeta)}{\zeta - \lambda}\,d\zeta$$

However, since $F(\lambda) = G(\lambda)$ on the path Γ, we obtain by addition the result,

$$H(\lambda) = F(\lambda) = \frac{1}{2\pi i}\int_A \frac{F(\zeta)}{\zeta - \lambda}\,d\zeta + \frac{1}{2\pi i}\int_B \frac{G(\zeta)}{\zeta - \lambda}\,d\zeta$$

where λ is a point in the region $E(F)$. In a similar manner we obtain the result,

$$H(\lambda) = G(\lambda) = \frac{1}{2\pi i}\int_A \frac{F(\zeta)}{\zeta - \lambda}\,d\zeta + \frac{1}{2\pi i}\int_B \frac{G(\zeta)}{\zeta - \lambda}\,d\zeta$$

where now λ is a point in the region $E(G)$. However, the integral representations, on the right hand side of the last and the penultimate equations, define functions which are analytic in the regions $E(F)$ and $E(G)$ and on the path Γ. This implies, in view of the arbitrariness of our choice of the regions $E(F)$ and $E(G)$ and the path Γ, that the function $H(\lambda)$ is analytic in the union of the regions $D(F)$ and $D(G)$ and on the path Ω. Furthermore, since $F(\lambda)$ and $G(\lambda)$ are the analytic representations, in the regions $D(F)$ and $D(G)$ respectively, of a function which is analytic in the union of the regions $D(F)$ and $D(G)$ and on the path Ω, we may conclude that $F(\lambda)$ is the analytic continuation of $G(\lambda)$ into the region $D(F)$ and that $G(\lambda)$ is the analytic continuation of $F(\lambda)$ into the region $D(G)$. This is the principle of Riemann.

The reflection principle of Schwarz, which is stated below, is closely related to the principle of Riemann. Let us consider the region D in Figure I-17. This region is bounded in part by a path Γ which is located on the real axis. Furthermore, let D^* denote the region which is the reflection of the region D with respect to the real axis. Now let us assume that the function $F(\lambda)$ is analytic in the region D and is real and continuous on the real axis.

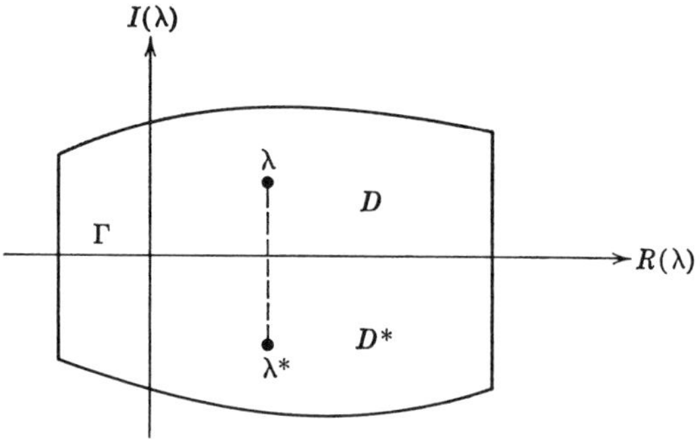

Figure I-17

Then, according to the reflection principle of Schwarz, the function $F^*(\lambda^*)$ is the analytic continuation of the function $F(\lambda)$ into the region D^*, where $F^*(\lambda)$ denotes the complex conjugate of the function $F(\lambda)$. For, assuming that the function $F(\lambda)$ is real on the path Γ which separates the regions D and D^*, we find that $F^*(\lambda^*) = F(\lambda)$ on this path. Moreover, if $F(\lambda)$ is an analytic function of the complex variable λ in the region D, then $F^*(\lambda^*)$ is an analytic function of the complex variable λ^* in the region D^*. From these two properties of the function $F^*(\lambda^*)$ we may infer, by the principle of Riemann, that this function is the analytic continuation of the function $F(\lambda)$ into the region D^*.

The principle of Riemann also leads to a simple proof of the following assertion. If an analytic function vanishes on a path which is part of the boundary of its region of analyticity, then the function vanishes at all other points of this region. For, let us assume that the function $F(\lambda)$ is analytic in the region $D(F)$ and vanishes on the path Γ which is part of the boundary of this region. Extending the region $D(F)$ by an arbitrary region $D(G)$ which is separated from the region $D(F)$ by the common boundary Γ, we assume that $D(G)$ is the region of analyticity of the trivially analytic function $G(\lambda) = 0$. Consequently, $F(\lambda) = G(\lambda) = 0$ on the path Γ and this implies, according to the principle of Riemann, that $F(\lambda)$ is the analytic continuation of $G(\lambda)$ into the region $D(F)$. Furthermore, the function $H(\lambda)$, which is represented by the function $F(\lambda)$ in $D(F)$ and by the function $G(\lambda)$ in $D(G)$, is analytic in the union of the regions $D(F)$ and $D(G)$ and on the path Γ. However, since $G(\lambda) = 0$ in $D(G)$, the function $H(\lambda)$ is identically equal to zero at all other points of its region of analyticity. This conclusion follows immediately from Section I.6A, where we found that a function which vanishes in a subregion of its region of analyticity must be zero at all other points of this region.

C. Illustrative Examples

We shall now present two examples to illustrate the applicability of the concepts which we have discussed in the foregoing two subsections. The first example offers a line of reasoning which is based on the concept of analytic continuation and is well known from its use in the Wiener-Hopf technique. The second example offers us some information about the continuation of analytic functions which are defined in parallel strips and are related to each other by an integral expression. This information is useful in the solution of integral equations by Fourier transforms.

EXAMPLE 1 Let us assume that the functions $F(\lambda)$ and $G(\lambda)$ are analytic in the half plane $I(\lambda) > a$ and the half plane $I(\lambda) < b$ respectively, and that $F(\lambda) = G(\lambda)$ in the strip $a < I(\lambda) < b$ in Figure I-18. This implies, by the

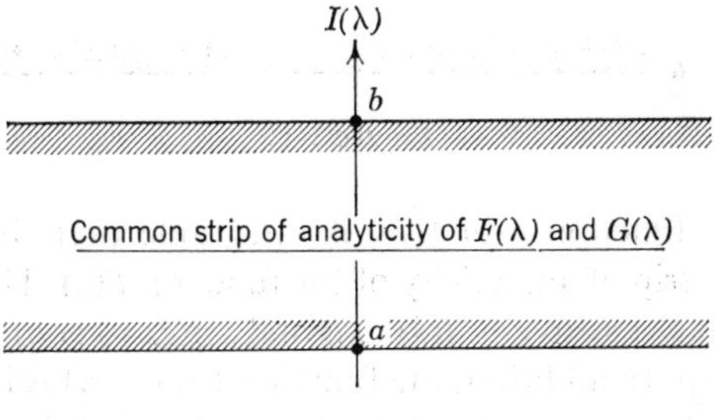

Figure I-18

definition of analytic continuation, that the function $F(\lambda)$ is the analytic continuation of the function $G(\lambda)$ into the upper half plane $I(\lambda) > a$ and that the function $G(\lambda)$ is the continuation of the function $F(\lambda)$ into the lower half plane $I(\lambda) < b$. Consequently, the functions $F(\lambda)$ and $G(\lambda)$ are analytic representations of a function $H(\lambda)$ which must be analytic in the whole complex plane. In other words, $H(\lambda)$ is an entire function. In cases of practical importance the character of this entire function can be determined more accurately from information about the behavior of the functions $F(\lambda)$ and $G(\lambda)$ at infinity. For instance, let it be known that $F(\lambda)$ and $G(\lambda)$ are of algebraic growth at infinity. In other words, $F(\lambda) = O(\lambda^{\alpha})$ when λ tends to infinity in the half plane $I(\lambda) > a$ and $G(\lambda) = O(\lambda^{\beta})$ when λ tends to infinity in the lower half plane $I(\lambda) < b$. Then $H(\lambda)$ is also of algebraic growth at infinity and we find that $H(\lambda) = O(\lambda^{\gamma})$ when λ tends to infinity, where γ is the largest of the two constants α and β. This implies, according to Liouville's theorem, that the function $H(\lambda)$ must be a polynomial of degree m, where m denotes the largest integer which is smaller than γ.

EXAMPLE 2 In this example we consider the analytical continuation of two functions of a complex variable, which are related to each other by a given integral relation and are defined in two nonoverlapping parallel strips, to an extended strip, which consists of the original strips and the region between those strips. The first function $F(\lambda)$ is analytic in the strip $a \leqq I(\lambda) \leqq b$ in Figure I-19 and tends to zero when $|\omega|$ tends to infinity inside this strip.

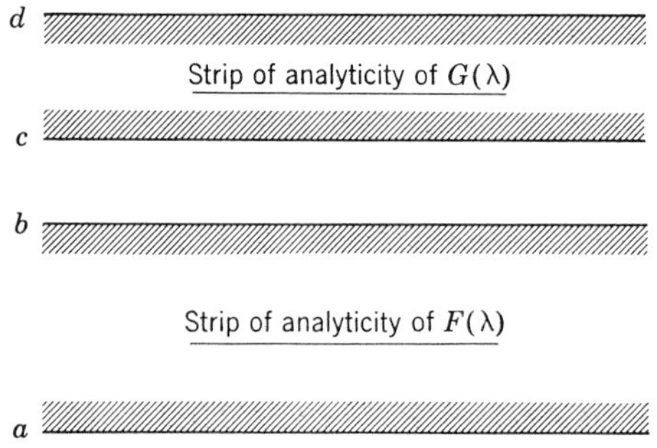

Figure I-19

Furthermore, the function $F(\omega + i\gamma)$ is integrable over the real axis for all values of γ in the strip of analyticity of the function $F(\lambda)$. The second function $G(\lambda)$ is analytic in the strip $c \leqq I(\lambda) \leqq d$ and tends to zero when $|\omega|$ tends to infinity in this strip. In addition, the function $G(\omega + i\gamma)$ is integrable over the real axis for all values of γ in the strip of analyticity of the function $G(\lambda)$.

The functions $F(\lambda)$ and $G(\lambda)$, moreover, are related to each other by the following integral relation,

$$(1.1) \qquad \frac{1}{2\pi i}\int_{-\infty+i\alpha}^{\infty+i\alpha} F(\zeta)e^{-i\zeta t}\,d\zeta + \frac{1}{2\pi i}\int_{-\infty+i\beta}^{\infty+i\beta} G(\zeta)e^{-i\zeta t}\,d\zeta = 0$$

which is valid for all real values of t and for values of α and β such that $a < \alpha < b$ and $c < \beta < d$. We now assert that these properties of the functions $F(\lambda)$ and $G(\lambda)$ imply that the following propositions are true.

a. The functions $F(\lambda)$ and $G(\lambda)$ are analytic in the extended strip, $a < I(\lambda) < d$.
b. The functions $F(\lambda)$ and $G(\lambda)$ tend to zero when $|\omega|$ tends to infinity in the extended strip, $a < I(\lambda) < d$.

c. The functions $F(\lambda)$ and $G(\lambda)$ are related to each other by the following simple algebraic relation,

$$F(\lambda) + G(\lambda) = 0$$

which is valid for all values of λ in the extended strip, $a < I(\lambda) < d$.

The assertions above can be proven as follows. Let λ be a point inside the contour $C = (-\omega + ia, \omega + ia, \omega + i\alpha, -\omega + i\alpha)$. Since the function $F(\lambda)$ is analytic inside and on the contour C it can be represented, according to Cauchy's formula, by the contour integral,

$$F(\lambda) = \frac{1}{2\pi i} \oint_C \frac{F(\zeta)}{\zeta - \lambda} d\zeta$$

However, the contribution of the vertical sides of the contour to the integral vanishes when ω tends to infinity and we obtain, therefore, the representation,

$$F(\lambda) = \frac{1}{2\pi i} \int_{-\infty + ia}^{\infty + ia} \frac{F(\zeta)}{\zeta - \lambda} d\zeta - \frac{1}{2\pi i} \int_{-\infty + i\alpha}^{\infty + i\alpha} \frac{F(\zeta)}{\zeta - \lambda} d\zeta \tag{1.2}$$

Furthermore, according to the integral relation (1.1), the following relation holds between the functions $F(\zeta)$ and $G(\zeta)$,

$$\frac{1}{2\pi i} \int_{-\infty + i\alpha}^{\infty + i\alpha} F(\zeta) e^{-i\zeta t} \, d\zeta + \frac{1}{2\pi i} \int_{-\infty + i\beta}^{\infty + i\beta} G(\zeta) e^{-i\zeta t} \, d\zeta = 0$$

Multiplying this equation by $e^{i\lambda t}$ and integrating the result over the interval $(0, \infty)$, we find

$$\frac{1}{2\pi i} \int_{-\infty + i\alpha}^{\infty + i\alpha} \frac{F(\zeta)}{\zeta - \lambda} d\zeta + \frac{1}{2\pi i} \int_{-\infty + i\beta}^{\infty + i\beta} \frac{G(\zeta)}{\zeta - \lambda} d\zeta = 0 \tag{1.3}$$

where we have justified the interchange of the order of integration by the absolute convergence of the integrals involved. Substitution of the result (1.3) into equation (1.2) yields the relation,

$$\frac{1}{2\pi i} \int_{-\infty + ia}^{\infty + ia} \frac{F(\zeta)}{\zeta - \lambda} d\zeta + \frac{1}{2\pi i} \int_{-\infty + i\beta}^{\infty + i\beta} \frac{G(\zeta)}{\zeta - \lambda} d\zeta = F(\lambda) \tag{1.4}$$

The integral expression on the left hand side of this equation represents a function which is analytic in the strip $a < I(\lambda) < \beta$ and is the analytic continuation of the function $F(\lambda)$ into this strip. Since β can be chosen arbitrarily close to the value d, proposition (a) follows immediately. In like fashion we can show that

$$\frac{1}{2\pi i} \int_{-\infty + i\alpha}^{\infty + i\alpha} \frac{F(\zeta)}{\zeta - \lambda} d\zeta + \frac{1}{2\pi i} \int_{-\infty + id}^{\infty + id} \frac{G(\zeta)}{\zeta - \lambda} d\zeta = -G(\lambda) \tag{1.5}$$

from which we may infer that the function $G(\lambda)$ is analytic in the strip $a < I(\lambda) < d$.

To prove proposition (b) let us investigate the behavior of the integral representation,

$$F(\lambda) = \frac{1}{2\pi i}\int_{-\infty+ia}^{\infty+ia} \frac{F(\zeta)}{\zeta-\lambda}\,d\zeta + \frac{1}{2\pi i}\int_{-\infty+i\beta}^{\infty+i\beta} \frac{G(\zeta)}{\zeta-\lambda}\,d\zeta \tag{1.4}$$

for large values of $|\omega|$. Considering the first integral, we may write

$$\left|\int_{-\infty+ia}^{\infty+ia} \frac{F(\zeta)}{\zeta-\lambda}\,d\zeta\right| \leqq \int_{-s}^{s}\left|\frac{F(\xi+ia)}{\xi-\omega}\right| d\xi$$
$$+\frac{1}{|a-\gamma|}\left(\int_{-\infty}^{-s}|F(\xi+ia)|\,d\xi + \int_{s}^{\infty}|F(\xi+ia)|d\xi\right)$$

Since $F(\omega + ia)$ is integrable over the real axis, the second and third integral on the right hand side of this inequality vanish when s tends to infinity. Similarly, for large fixed s and any ω which is larger than s we find,

$$\int_{-s}^{s}\left|\frac{F(\xi+ia)}{\xi-\omega}\right| d\xi \leqq \frac{1}{|s-\omega|}\int_{-s}^{s}|F(\xi+ia)|\,d\xi$$

which tends to zero when $|\omega|$ tends to infinity. We may conclude, therefore, that the integral,

$$\frac{1}{2\pi i}\int_{-\infty+ia}^{\infty+ia} \frac{F(\zeta)}{\zeta-\lambda}\,d\zeta$$

vanishes when $|\omega|$ tends to infinity. In like fashion we can show that the integral,

$$\frac{1}{2\pi i}\int_{-\infty+i\beta}^{\infty+i\beta} \frac{G(\zeta)}{\zeta-\lambda}\,d\zeta$$

vanishes when $|\omega|$ tends to infinity. Consequently, from the integral representation (1.4) of the function $F(\lambda)$, we may infer that the function $F(\lambda)$ tends to zero when $|\omega|$ tends to infinity in the extended strip. Obviously, the integral representation (1.5) for the function $G(\lambda)$ yields the verification of the statement that the function $G(\lambda)$ vanishes when $|\omega|$ tends to infinity in the extended strip. We now turn our attention to proposition (c) for which we have to prove that

$$F(\lambda) + G(\lambda) = 0$$

for all values of λ in the extended strip $a < I(\lambda) < d$. Let λ be a point in the strip $\alpha < I(\lambda) < \beta$. Since the function $F(\zeta)/(\zeta - \lambda)$ is analytic in the strip

$a \leqq I(\lambda) \leqq \alpha$ we may write, in accordance with Cauchy's theorem,

$$\frac{1}{2\pi i}\int_{-\infty+ia}^{\infty+ia}\frac{F(\zeta)}{\zeta-\lambda}\,d\zeta = \frac{1}{2\pi i}\int_{-\infty+i\alpha}^{\infty+i\alpha}\frac{F(\zeta)}{\zeta-\lambda}\,d\zeta$$

Similarly, if λ is a point in the strip $\alpha < I(\lambda) < \beta$, we find that

$$\frac{1}{2\pi i}\int_{-\infty+id}^{\infty+id}\frac{G(\zeta)}{\zeta-\lambda}\,d\zeta = \frac{1}{2\pi i}\int_{-\infty+i\beta}^{\infty+i\beta}\frac{G(\zeta)}{\zeta-\lambda}\,d\zeta$$

Substituting these two expressions into equations (1.4) and (1.5) respectively, we obtain the result,

$$F(\lambda) = \frac{1}{2\pi i}\int_{-\infty+i\alpha}^{\infty+i\alpha}\frac{F(\zeta)}{\zeta-\lambda}\,d\zeta + \frac{1}{2\pi i}\int_{-\infty+i\beta}^{\infty+i\beta}\frac{G(\zeta)}{\zeta-\lambda}\,d\zeta = -G(\lambda)$$

which verifies proposition (c) above.

1.7 MULTIVALUED FUNCTIONS

Heretofore in considering the analytic continuation of an analytic function of a complex variable, we have taken it for granted that the continuations of such a function represent in their regions of analyticity an analytic and therefore single-valued complete function. Such single-valued functions can be defined, of course, on regions in the complex plane. However, as we remarked in the introduction to the preceding section, the functions obtained by the analytic continuation of a single-valued function do not necessarily have to represent a single-valued function but may be the analytic representations of a multivalued complete function. A multivalued function has more than one value at a particular point in the complex plane and cannot be defined as a single-valued function on a plane region. However, let us assume that we encounter a multivalued function in the mathematical analysis of a physical problem. Then the single-valuedness of the physical parameters described by the function requires that we be able to assign, in an unambiguous manner, a physically meaningful value to the function. To keep track of the physically admissible values of the function, a geometrically more complicated surface than a plane must be constructed on which the function can be defined as a single-valued function of position. In other words, instead of restricting our choice to regions located in the complex plane, we must also consider regions which are located on a surface. Such Riemann surfaces are used to assign a unique value to a function at each point of its domain of definition. A Riemann surface is usually composed of several sheets, each of which is the plane region of analyticity of a particular single-valued representation of the multivalued function. Such a single-valued representation, defined on a particular sheet of the Riemann surface, is said to be a branch of the multivalued function. In general a sheet of a Riemann surface is a copy of an appropriately cut complex plane, and a specific branch of the multivalued function can be singled out by determining the location of the branch cuts in the complex plane. Such branch lines or branch cuts connect the so-called branch points of the function. Branch point singularities of a function of a complex variable have not been encountered previously in this chapter. A branch point may be defined in terms of the behavior of the function in the vicinity of the point, namely, if a function does not return to its starting value upon analytic continuation along an arbitrarily small circle around the point, then that point is a branch point of the function. For branch points are connected by branch cuts and branch cuts denote the boundaries between the separate sheets of a Riemann surface. Hence, when we circle about a branch point we are bound to cross a branch cut and to move from one sheet of the Riemann surface to the next. On the next sheet, however, the function is represented by a different branch, which explains the fact that the function changes its value on analytic continuation along a contour enclosing the branch point. This also clarifies the role of a branch cut, namely, to serve as a reminder that by crossing it we have moved into another sheet of the Riemann surface and are working with a different branch of the multivalued function. We note from the definition of a branch point that we can draw no conclusions about the behavior of the function at the point itself. Indeed the behavior of a function at a branch point can be quite regular. The function can be single-valued and even differentiable at such a point. By consistent use of a particular branch of a single-valued function, a problem in physics or engineering can be solved in terms of single-valued functions only. The branch of a function and the corresponding sheet of the Riemann surface which lead to physically meaningful values are usually called the physical branch and the physical sheet of the function. This is in contrast to other branches and sheets which are referred to as being nonphysical.

We shall now turn to the discussion of some simple examples which will serve to explain more clearly the concepts which have been discussed above in rather vague and general terms.

A. The Multivalued Function $\sqrt{\lambda}$

First we shall show, by analytic continuation, that the function $\sqrt{\lambda}$ has a branch point at the origin. Setting $\lambda = r \exp(i\theta)$ we find, $\sqrt{\lambda} = \sqrt{(r)} \exp(i\theta/2)$, where we adhere to the convention that $\sqrt{r}$ denotes the positive square root of the quantity r. We now determine the value of the function $\sqrt{\lambda}$ at the point $-r$ by continuation of the function $\sqrt{\lambda}$ from its value $\sqrt{r}$ at the point r along the semicircle $|\lambda| = r$ in the upper half plane. On this path the phase angle θ increases from 0 to π and we obtain the value $\sqrt{(-r)} = \sqrt{(r)} \exp(i\pi/2) = i\sqrt{r}$.

In like fashion, by continuing the function from its value $\sqrt{r}$ at the point r along the semicircle in the lower half plane, we find,

$$\sqrt{(-r)} = \sqrt{(r)} \exp(-i\pi/2) = -i\sqrt{r}.$$

For the phase angle decreases from 0 to $-\pi$ along this path. Hence, we obtain two distinct values for the function $\sqrt{\lambda}$ at the point $-r$ according to whether we choose a semicircle in the upper or lower half plane as our path of continuation. Since this difference in the results is not influenced by the magnitude of the radius of the circle, the origin must be a branch point of our function. The transformation $\zeta = 1/\lambda$ enables us to show that the point at infinity is also a branch point of the function.

A branch or single-valued representation of the function $\sqrt{\lambda}$ can be obtained by cutting the complex plane along a branch cut that connects the branch point at the origin with the branch point at infinity. Such a branch line or branch cut can be any line or curve connecting the two branch points. It is a reminder that we are not allowed to continue the function $\sqrt{\lambda}$ along a closed contour which encircles the origin or the point at infinity.

In the cut plane, the function $F(\lambda) = \sqrt{\lambda}$ denotes a single-valued representation of the multivalued function $\sqrt{\lambda}$, and the branch cut serves the purpose of preventing us from moving into the region of analyticity of another representation of the same function. We shall decide arbitrarily that the complex plane has been cut along the negative real axis. This amounts to the decision to choose the single-valued representation $F(\lambda) = \sqrt{\lambda}$ of the multivalued function $\sqrt{\lambda}$ which has zero phase or argument on the real axis. In the cut plane, the argument of λ lies between the limits $-\pi < \arg \lambda \leqq \pi$, and when λ moves over the cut plane the branch $F(\lambda)$ takes on the values $F(\lambda) = \sqrt{(r)} \exp(i\theta/2)$, where the phase angle θ lies between the limits $-\pi/2 < \theta \leqq \pi/2$ as shown in Figure I-20.

The representation $F(\lambda) = \sqrt{\lambda}$ of the multivalued function $\sqrt{\lambda}$ defined above is single-valued and analytic in the whole cut plane. It is obtained by

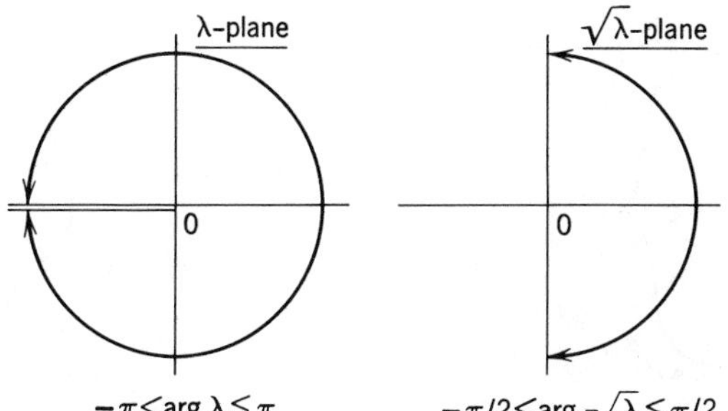

Figure I-20. Region and range of the branch $F(\lambda) = \sqrt{\lambda}$ of the multivalued function $\sqrt{\lambda}$

the analytic continuation of the function $\sqrt{\lambda}$ into the cut plane, starting with the value $\sqrt{(r)}\exp(i0/2)$ at the point r. In other words, it is that branch of the multivalued function which has zero phase angle or argument on the positive real axis. The second branch $G(\lambda) = \sqrt{\lambda}$ of the multivalued function $\sqrt{\lambda}$ is obtained by taking the argument of λ between the limits $\pi < \arg\lambda \leqq 3\pi$ as shown in Figure I-21. In this case, we obtain the single-valued and analytic representation $G(\lambda) = \sqrt{(r)}\exp(i\theta/2)$, where $\pi/2 < \theta \leqq 3\pi/2$.

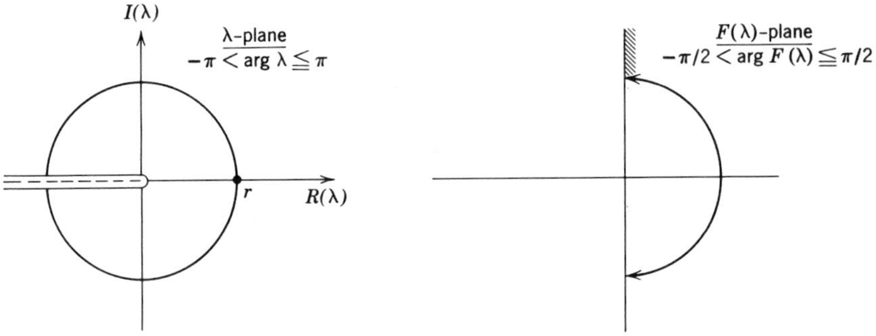

Figure I-21a. Region and range of $F(\lambda)$.

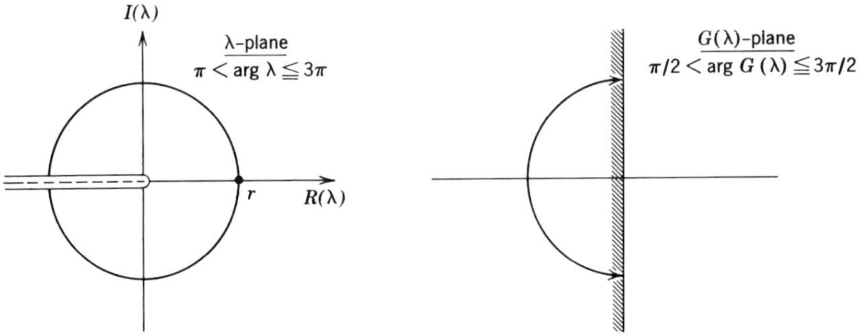

Figure I-21b. Region and range of $G(\lambda)$.

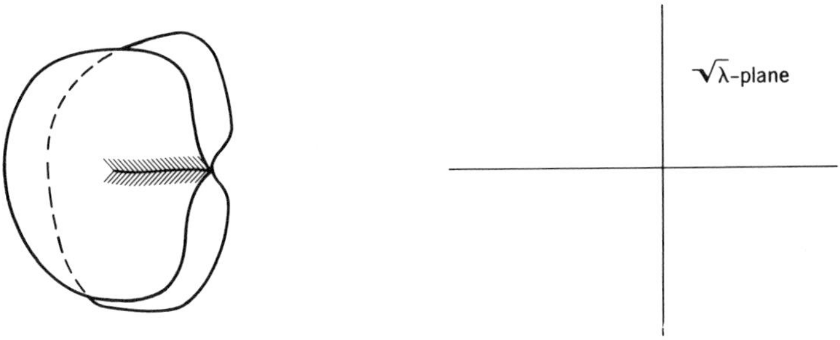

Figure I-21c. Region and range of $\sqrt{\lambda}$.

The multivalued function $\sqrt{\lambda}$ has only two distinct branches. Hence, the Riemann surface of the function $\sqrt{\lambda}$ consists of two sheets. The surface can be constructed by superimposing the regions of analyticity of the two branches $F(\lambda)$ and $G(\lambda)$ in the following manner. We take two copies of the complex plane, which is cut along the negative real axis, and place the $(\pi < \arg \lambda \leqq 3\pi)$-plane, which is used to represent $G(\lambda)$, on top of the $(-\pi < \arg \lambda \leqq \pi)$-plane, which is used to represent $F(\lambda)$. We now connect the upper bank of the branch cut in the upper plane with the lower bank of the branch cut in the lower plane and the lower bank of the cut in the upper plane with the upper bank of the cut in the lower plane.

B. Multivalued Functions in Electrostatics

To illustrate the use of multivalued functions in the mathematical description of physical phenomena we shall now consider the following simple boundary value problem in electrostatics.

Let it be required to find the potential due to a point charge of strength q, which is placed at a point a in the complex plane, when a grounded line conductor is placed along the negative real axis in Figure I-22. To solve this

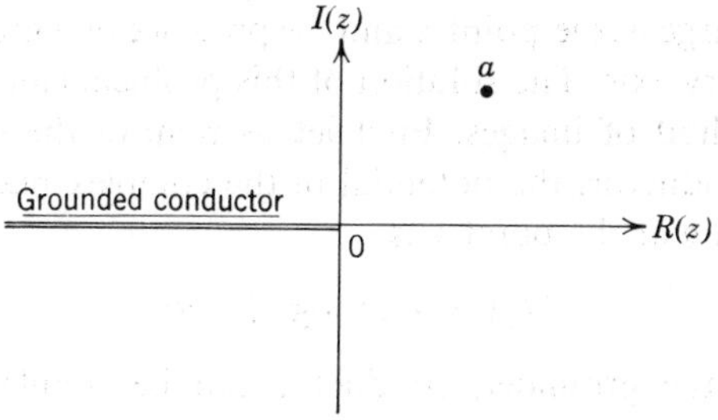

Figure I-22

problem, we introduce the complex potential, $F(z) = \phi(x, y) + i\psi(x, y)$, where $\phi(x, y)$ denotes the electrostatic potential and $\psi(x, y)$ the electrostatic force function. The functions $\phi(x, y)$ and $\psi(x, y)$ are solutions of the two-dimensional equation of Laplace, and the function $F(z)$ is an analytic function with a singularity at the location of the point charge. To obtain a more convenient geometrical configuration of charge and conductor, we map the complex z-plane into the complex ζ-plane by means of the conformal mapping $\zeta = \sqrt{z}$. As is well known, a transformation of this type maps the equipotential lines and the force lines in the z-plane into similar lines in the complex ζ-plane. Furthermore, the grounded conductor in the z-plane is mapped into a grounded conductor in the complex ζ-plane. Let us choose the branch $\zeta = \sqrt{z}$ of the multivalued function $\sqrt{z}$ which is real and positive on the real axis. Hence, we may write $z = r \exp(i\theta)$, where $-\pi < \arg z \leqq \pi$. Thus $\zeta = \sqrt{r} \exp(i\theta/2)$, where $-\pi/2 < \arg \zeta \leqq \pi/2$. Consequently, the whole complex z-plane is mapped into the right half of the complex ζ-plane. The grounded line conductor, which was represented by the negative real axis in the z-plane, now stretches along the whole imaginary axis in the ζ-plane, as shown in Figure I-23.

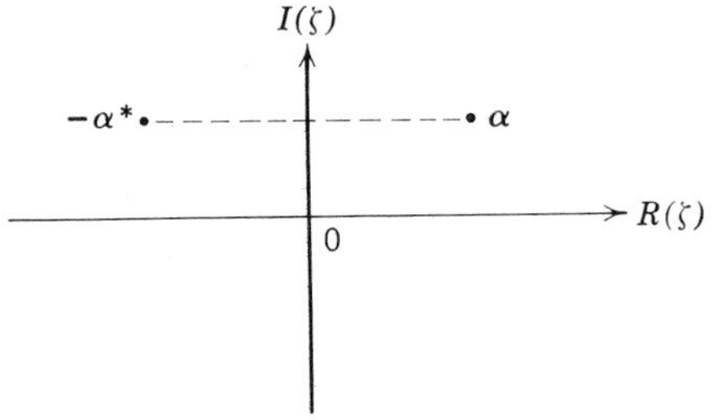

Figure I-23

This implies, that we now have to find the potential in the complex ζ-plane, due to a point charge at the point α and the presence of a grounded conductor along the imaginary axis. The solution of this problem can be obtained most easily by the method of images. First let us remove the conductor. In the absence of the conductor, the potential in the complex plane due to a point charge of strength q at the point α is

$$F(\zeta) = -2q \log(\zeta - \alpha)$$

The presence of the grounded conductor can be simulated by placing a point charge of strength $-q$, the charge induced on the conductor, at the point $-\alpha^*$ which is the reflection of the point α with respect to the imaginary axis. The complex potential, due to the two point charges, can be written down immediately,

$$F(\zeta) = -2q \log(\zeta - \alpha) + 2q \log(\zeta + \alpha^*)$$

The real part of this function is a solution of Laplace's equation and satisfies, moreover, the boundary condition that the potential vanishes on the surface of a grounded conductor. Hence, the real part of the complex potential $F(\zeta)$ must be the solution of our boundary value problem in the ζ-plane.

To obtain the solution of the boundary value problem in the z-plane, we merely have to make the substitution $\zeta = \sqrt{z}$ in the equation above and we find

$$F(z) = -2q \log(\sqrt{z} - \sqrt{a}) + 2q \log(\sqrt{z} + \sqrt{a^*})$$

This solution was obtained assuming that $\sqrt{z}$ represents the branch of the multivalued function $\sqrt{z}$ which is real and positive on the real axis. In other words, we have placed our branch line along the negative real axis, the location of the grounded line conductor, and chosen the sheet of the Riemann surface on which $-\pi < \arg z \leqq \pi$. According to the foregoing section, this is the lower sheet of the Riemann surface and we shall call this sheet the physical sheet. The upper sheet, on which $\pi < \arg z \leqq 3\pi$, is, therefore, the nonphysical sheet. The singularities of the function $F(z)$ on the Riemann surface are located at the points $|a| \exp(i \arg a)$ and $|a| \exp[i(2\pi - \arg a)]$. Only the first singularity is located on the physical sheet and represents in this sheet the location of the point charge q. The image charge $-q$, which is not a singularity of the function $F(z)$, is located at the point $|a| \exp[i(2\pi - \arg a)]$ on the nonphysical sheet.

C. Multivalued Functions in the Propagation of Harmonic Plane Waves

The physical phenomena of the two-dimensional propagation of harmonic plane waves in dissipative media can be described mathematically by the solutions of the wave equation,

$$\nabla^2\Phi(x, y, t) = c^2 \frac{\partial^2\Phi}{\partial t^2} + \frac{1}{a^2}\frac{\partial\Phi}{\partial t}$$

Let it be required to find the solutions of the two-dimensional wave equation in the half plane, $-\infty < x < \infty$, $y > 0$, which take prescribed values on the line $y = 0$ and which vanish when y tends to infinity. The harmonic wave motion which satisfies these conditions can be constructed by the superposition of elementary waves.

Since the wave motion is supposed to be harmonic we can separate off the time dependence by writing $\Phi(x, y, t) = \phi(x, y) \exp(-i\omega t)$, where the positive number ω denotes the angular frequency. The negative sign of the exponent has been chosen to ensure an outgoing wave motion at infinity. Substitution of this expression for the function $\Phi(x, y, t)$ into the wave equation above yields the Helmholtz equation,

$$\nabla^2\phi(x, y) + k^2\phi(x, y) = 0$$

where the coefficient $k^2 = \omega^2c^2 + i\omega/a^2$ has a positive imaginary part. In the following we shall assume that we have chosen the sign of the square root such that the wave number $k = \alpha + i\beta$ has also a positive imaginary part. To obtain the elementary solutions of the Helmholtz equation, we write $\phi(x, y) = \psi(y) \exp(i\lambda x)$, where λ can be a real or complex number. Substituting this expression for the function $\phi(x, y)$ into the Helmholtz equation, we obtain the following simple second order ordinary differential equation for the function $\psi(y)$,

$$\frac{d^2\psi}{dy^2} - (\lambda^2 - k^2)\psi(y) = 0$$

The general solution of this equation can be written down immediately,

$$\psi(y) = A(\lambda)e^{y\sqrt{(\lambda^2-k^2)}} + B(\lambda)e^{-y\sqrt{(\lambda^2-k^2)}}$$

Let us assume, for the moment, that it is possible to obtain a representation or branch of the multivalued function $\sqrt{(\lambda^2 - k^2)}$ such that the real part of this branch is of one sign in the whole cut plane and let us assume, to be definite, that the real part is positive. Hence, since the solution of the wave equation vanishes when y tends to infinity, the coefficient $A(\lambda)$ must vanish for all values of λ, and the elementary waves take the form,

$$B(\lambda)e^{i(\lambda x - \omega t) - y\sqrt{(\lambda^2-k^2)}}$$

The function $B(\lambda)$ can now be found from the boundary condition which is imposed on the wave function on the line $y = 0$.

We need not stress the fact that the assumptions which were made with respect to the particular branch of the function $\sqrt{(\lambda^2 - k^2)}$ are of decisive importance in the determination of the proper elementary waves. These assumptions enable us to eliminate the coefficient $A(\lambda)$ in the general solution $\psi(y)$, thus clearly demonstrating the importance of accumulating sufficient information about the branch of the function $\sqrt{(\lambda^2 - k^2)}$ which is physically admissible in the context of our problem statement above.

The multivalued functions $\sqrt{(\lambda^2 - k^2)}$ and $\sqrt{(k^2 - \lambda^2)}$ are of frequent occurrence in mathematical physics. For this reason we shall present in the remaining part of this section a discussion of their properties and of the properties of their components. Throughout this discussion we shall assume that the real and imaginary parts of the number k are positive. First let us consider the multivalued function $\sqrt{(\lambda - k)}$. The branch points of this function are the points $\lambda = k$ and the point at infinity. We choose a branch cut which extends from the point k to the point at infinity in the upper half plane, as shown in Figure I-24. Furthermore we choose the branch of the multivalued function $\sqrt{(\lambda - k)}$ such that $\arg(\lambda - k)$ tends to zero when λ tends to infinity on the positive real axis. First let us investigate the behavior of this branch when $\lambda = a$ moves on the real axis. We may write

$$\sqrt{(a - k)} = \exp\left(\frac{1}{2}\log|a - k| + \frac{1}{2}i\arg(a - k)\right)$$

Since $\arg(a - k)$ tends to zero and $\log|a - k|$ tends to $\log|a|$ when a tends to infinity on the positive real axis, we obtain the result that $\sqrt{(a - k)}$ tends

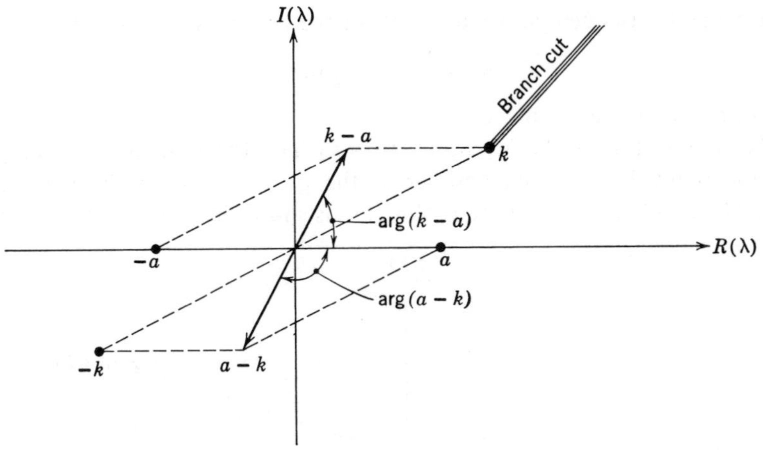

Figure I-24

to $\sqrt{a}$ when a is positive and large. Similarly, when a is large and negative, we find that $\arg(a-k)$ tends to $-\pi$, $\log|a-k|$ tends to $\log|a|$, and thus that $\sqrt{(a-k)}$ tends to $\exp(\frac{1}{2}\log|a| - \pi i/2) = -i\sqrt{(-a)}$. Furthermore, at the origin, we obtain the value,

$$\sqrt{(-k)} = \exp\left(\frac{1}{2}\log|k| + \frac{1}{2}i\arg(-k)\right)$$

$$= \exp\left(\frac{1}{2}\log|k| + \frac{1}{2}i(\arg k - \pi)\right) = -i\sqrt{k}.$$

Now let us consider the multivalued function $\sqrt{(k-\lambda)}$. The branch points of this function are the points $\lambda = k$ and the point at infinity. Assuming that the complex plane has been cut along the line depicted above and choosing the branch such that $\arg(k-\lambda)$ tends to zero when λ tends to infinity on the negative real axis, we find that $\sqrt{(k-a)} = \exp(\frac{1}{2}\log|k-a| + \frac{1}{2}\arg(k-a))$ tends to $\sqrt{(-a)}$ when a tends to infinity on the negative real axis. Furthermore, for large positive values of a we find that $\log|k-a|$ tends to $\log|a|$ and $\arg(k-a)$ tends to π. Hence, in this case the function $\sqrt{(k-a)}$ tends to the value $\exp(\frac{1}{2}\log|a| + \frac{1}{2}i\pi) = i\sqrt{a}$. At the origin we obtain the value $\sqrt{(k-a)} = \exp(\frac{1}{2}\log|k|) = \sqrt{k}$.

Comparing the behavior of this branch of the function $\sqrt{(k-a)}$ with the behavior of the branch of the function $\sqrt{(a-k)}$, which we have chosen above, we find that $i\sqrt{(a-k)} = \sqrt{(k-a)}$ when a is a point on the real axis. This relationship between the two branches, which holds true on a line in the complex plane, can be extended by analytic continuation into the whole cut plane. Consequently, we find that for the branches considered,

$$i\sqrt{(\lambda - k)} = \sqrt{(k - \lambda)}$$

at all points in the cut plane.

Now let us turn to the function $\sqrt{(\lambda + k)}$. This function has a branch point at the point $\lambda = -k$ and another at the point at infinity. The particular branch cut which we shall use in this case is shown in Figure I-25. The multi-

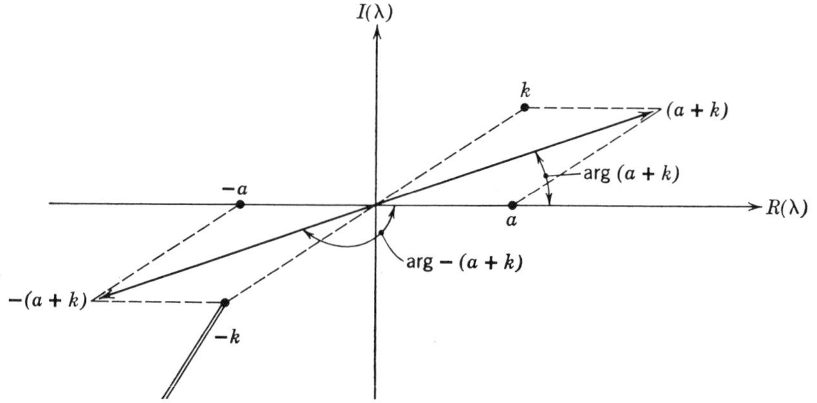

Figure I-25

valued function $\sqrt{(\lambda + k)}$ is made definite by choosing the branch such that arg $(\lambda + k)$ tends to zero when λ tends to infinity on the positive real axis.

We shall again consider the behavior of this branch when $\lambda = a$ moves on the real axis. First, since arg $(a + k)$ tends to zero and $\log |a + k|$ tends to $\log |a|$, we find for large positive values of a that $\sqrt{(a + k)}$ tends to

$$\exp\left(\frac{1}{2}\log |a|\right) = \sqrt{(a)}.$$

Similarly, when a tends to infinity on the negative real axis we find that arg $(a + k)$ tends to π and $\log |a + k|$ tends to $\log |a|$. Hence, in this case, the function $\sqrt{(a + k)} = \exp\,[\frac{1}{2}\log |a + k| + \frac{1}{2}\,i \arg (a + k)]$ tends to the value $\exp\,(\frac{1}{2}\log |a| + i\pi/2) = i\sqrt{(-a)}$. At the origin the function takes the value $\sqrt{(k)}$.

The function $\sqrt{(-\lambda - k)}$ has branch points at the same locations as the branch points of the function $\sqrt{(\lambda + k)}$, and we can cut the complex plane in the manner depicted above. Choosing a branch such that arg $(-\lambda - k)$ tends to zero when λ tends to infinity on the negative real axis we obtain the following results. The function $\sqrt{(-a - k)}$ tends to $\sqrt{(-a)}$ when a tends to infinity on the negative real axis. For in this case arg $(-a - k)$ tends to zero and

$\log|-a-k|$ tends to $\log|a|$. Furthermore, when a tends to infinity on the positive real axis the argument of this branch tends to $-\pi$ and thus the function $\sqrt{(-a-k)}$ tends to $\exp(\frac{1}{2}\log|a| - \pi i/2) = -i\sqrt{(a)}$. At the origin we find that this branch takes the value

$$\sqrt{(-k)} = \exp\left(\frac{1}{2}\log|k| + \frac{1}{2}i\arg(-k)\right)$$

$$= \exp\left(\frac{1}{2}\log|k| - \frac{1}{2}i(\pi - \arg k)\right) = -i\sqrt{k}.$$

The results obtained above, for the particular branches of the functions $\sqrt{(a+k)}$ and $\sqrt{(-a-k)}$, imply that $i\sqrt{(-a-k)} = \sqrt{(a+k)}$ when a is a point on the real axis. This relationship can again be extended, by analytic continuation, into the cut plane and we find that for the particular branches chosen,

$$\sqrt{(\lambda+k)} = i\sqrt{(-\lambda-k)},$$

at all points in the cut plane.

Finally, let us consider the functions

$$\sqrt{(\lambda^2 - k^2)} = \sqrt{[(\lambda-k)(\lambda+k)]} = \sqrt{[(-\lambda-k)(-\lambda+k)]}$$

and

$$\sqrt{(k^2 - \lambda^2)} = \sqrt{[(k-\lambda)(k+\lambda)]} = \sqrt{[(-k-\lambda)(-k+\lambda)]}.$$

The first function has branch points at the point k and $-k$. We choose a branch cut which connects these points via the point at infinity in the manner shown in Figure I-26. We should note that the point at infinity is not a branch

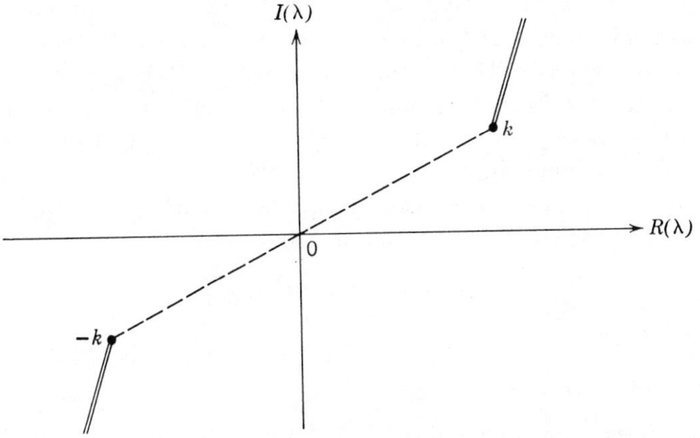

Figure I-26

point of the function $\sqrt{(\lambda^2 - k^2)}$ but that this function has a pole of first order at this point. This can be verified by the substitution $\lambda = 1/\zeta$. We find, $\sqrt{[(\lambda - k)(\lambda + k)]} = \sqrt{[(1 - \zeta k)(1 + \zeta k)]}/\zeta$ which tends to $1/\zeta$ when ζ tends to zero. The function $\sqrt{(\lambda^2 - k^2)}$ is made definite by choosing the branch such that arg $\sqrt{(\lambda^2 - k^2)}$ tends to zero when λ tends to infinity on the positive real axis. This implies that

$$\sqrt{(a^2 - k^2)} = \exp\left(\frac{1}{2}\log|a - k| + \frac{1}{2}\log|a + k| + \frac{1}{2}i\arg(a - k) + \frac{1}{2}i\arg(a + k)\right)$$

tends to $\exp(\log|a|) = a$ when a tends to infinity on the positive real axis. Similarly, $\sqrt{(a^2 - k^2)}$ tends to $\exp(\log|a|) = |a|$ when a tends to infinity on the negative real axis. For, in this case, $\arg(a + k)$ approaches the value π while $\arg(a - k)$ takes the value $-\pi$. Finally at the origin we obtain the result,

$$\sqrt{(-k^2)} = \exp\left(\log|k| + \frac{1}{2}i\arg(-k) + \frac{1}{2}i\arg k\right)$$

$$= \exp(\log|k| + i\arg k - i\pi/2) = -ik.$$

We note, that the branch of the function $\sqrt{(\lambda^2 - k^2)}$ chosen above has the property that, for positive values of y, the function $\exp[-y\sqrt{(\lambda^2 - k^2)}]$ tends to zero when $\lambda = a$ tends to plus or minus infinity. The function $\sqrt{(k^2 - \lambda^2)}$ has similar properties in the same cut plane. This function can be made definite by choosing the branch such that $\arg(k^2 - \lambda^2) = \arg k$ at the origin. This branch tends to ia when a tends to infinity on the positive real axis. For in this case $\arg(k - a)$ tends to π and $\arg(k + a)$ tends to zero. Hence $\sqrt{(k^2 - a^2)}$ tends to $\exp(\log|a| + \pi i/2) = ia$. Similarly, we find that $\arg(k - a)$ tends to zero and $\arg(k + a)$ tends to π when a tends to infinity on the negative real axis. This implies that $\sqrt{(k^2 - a^2)}$ tends to $i|a|$ for large negative values of a. From the results obtained above we may conclude that for positive values of y the function $\exp[(iy\sqrt{(k^2 - a^2)})]$ tends to zero when a tends to plus or minus infinity on the real axis.

By analytic continuation we can extend the relationship $i\sqrt{(a^2 - k^2)} = \sqrt{(k^2 - a^2)}$ into the cut plane and we find that

$$i\sqrt{(\lambda^2 - k^2)} = \sqrt{(k^2 - \lambda^2)}$$

at all points in the cut plane.

D. The Multivalued Function $\log \lambda$

Another important multivalued function is the logarithmic function $L(\lambda) = \log \lambda$. To show that the origin is a branch point of this function we analytically continue the integral,

$$L(\omega) = \log \omega = \int_1^{\omega} ds/s$$

into the complex plane. First let us obtain the value of the integral,

$$L(\lambda) = \log \lambda = \int_1^{\lambda} d\zeta/\zeta$$

at the point $\lambda = -r$ by continuation of the function $L(\lambda)$ from its value at the point $\lambda = 1$ along the path Γ as shown in Figure I-27. The path Γ consists of

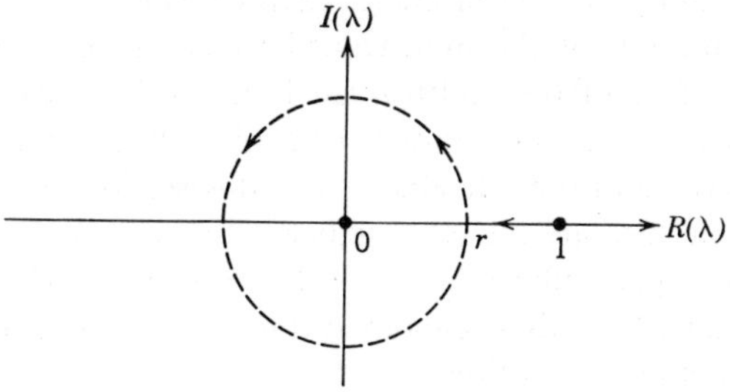

Figure I-27

the path between the point $\lambda = 1$ and $\lambda = r$ and the semicircle with radius r in the upper half plane. In this manner we obtain the following value for the integral at $\lambda = -r$,

$$L(-r) = \int_{\Gamma} d\zeta/\zeta = \int_1^r ds/s + \int_0^{\pi} i\, d\theta = \log r + i\pi$$

Similarly, if we continue the function $L(\lambda)$ along the path Ω, which consists of the line between the points $\lambda = 1$ and $\lambda = r$ and the semicircle with radius r in the lower half plane, we find the value,

$$L(-r) = \int_{\Omega} d\zeta/\zeta = \int_1^r ds/s + \int_0^{-\pi} i\, d\theta = \log r - i\pi$$

Hence, we obtain two distinct values of the function $L(\lambda)$ at the point $\lambda = -r$, depending on whether we continue the function along the semicircle in the upper or lower half plane. The difference between the two values obtained is not influenced by the magnitude of the radius of the circle. This implies that the origin must be a branch point of the multivalued function $L(\lambda) = \log \lambda$. We can easily show that the point at infinity is also a branch point of this function by means of the transformation $\zeta = 1/\lambda$. We can distinguish between the different branches or single-valued representations of the function by choosing a branch cut along the negative real axis. Each branch of the function $\log \lambda$ is single-valued and analytic in the cut plane. The so-called principal branch of the function is defined as the function $F(\lambda) = \log \lambda$ where $-\pi < \arg \lambda \leqq \pi$. The principal branch of the function $\log \lambda$ is obtained by continuation of the function $\log r$ into the cut plane. Hence, the phase angle or argument of the principal branch vanishes on the positive real axis. In other words, the principal branch of the function $\log \lambda$ is the representation of this function which has the value $\log 1 = 0$ at the point $\lambda = 1$. Other branches of the function take the form $\log \lambda = \log |\lambda| + i \arg \lambda$ where $(2n - 1)\pi < \arg \lambda \leqq (2n + 1)\pi$ and n is a positive or negative integer. There is a countable infinity of such branches each of which is a single-valued and analytic representation of the multivalued function $\log \lambda$ in the cut plane. The Riemann surface of the multivalued function $\log \lambda$ can be constructed by superimposing a countable number of copies of the cut complex plane in the manner described in the introduction to this section. The separate sheets of the Riemann surface are joined together by connecting the upper bank of the branch cut in a particular plane with the lower bank of the branch cut in the subjacent plane. On this Riemann surface the function $L(\lambda) = \log \lambda$ is a single-valued function of position.

E. Evaluation of an Integral in Neutron Transport Theory

As an example of the manipulation of multivalued functions of a complex variable let us evaluate the following integral,

$$I(a) = \lim_{R \to \infty} \frac{1}{2\pi i} \int_{-iR}^{iR} e^{-a\gamma} \frac{\operatorname{arctanh} \gamma}{1 - c(\operatorname{arctanh} \gamma)/\gamma} \, d\gamma$$

by contour integration. This integral, which arises in the computation of the neutron density due to an isotropic point source in an infinite isotropic medium, exists in the Cesaro sense. In other words, the integral oscillates about some average value when R tends to infinity and this average value is by definition the value of the integral.

Supposing that a is a positive parameter, we close the path of integration by a properly indented semicircle in the right half plane. To choose the appropriate semicircle we first need to obtain information about the location and nature of the singular points of the integrand,

$$G(a, \lambda, c) = \frac{e^{-a\lambda} \operatorname{arctanh} \lambda}{1 - c(\operatorname{arctanh} \lambda)/\lambda}$$

The singularities of this function are simple poles which are located at the zeros of the denominator,

$$H(\lambda, c) = 1 - c(\operatorname{arctanh} \lambda)/\lambda$$

and branch points which are due to the presence of the function,

$$2 \operatorname{arctanh} \lambda = \log(1 + \lambda) - \log(1 - \lambda)$$

The branch points of this function are located on the real axis at the points $\lambda = -1$ and $\lambda = 1$, as shown in Figure I-28. We connect these branch points

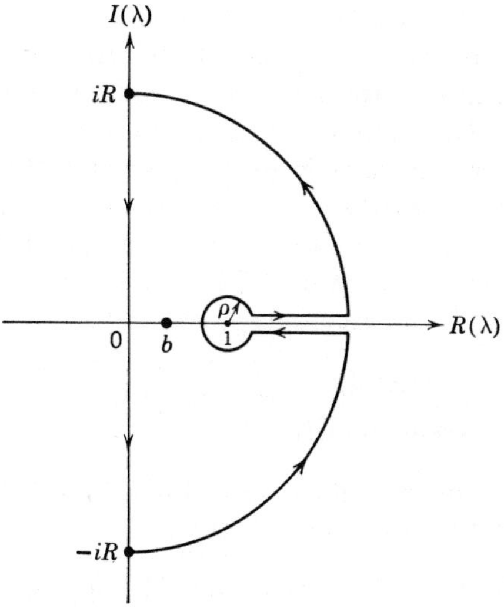

Figure I-28

via the point at infinity by branch cuts which run along the real axis from minus infinity to minus one and from plus one to plus infinity. The function arctanh λ is single-valued and analytic in the whole cut plane. We choose the branch of this multivalued function so that $\log(1 + \lambda) - \log(1 - \lambda)$ is equal to zero at the origin. This implies that the argument of $\log(1 - \lambda)$ vanishes at a point which is located between the origin and the point $\lambda = 1$. Going from such a point A to a point B, which is located on the upper bank of the branch cut, we rotate in the clockwise direction about the point $\lambda = 1$ over an angle of 180 degrees. Consequently, when λ is a point on the upper bank of the branch cut we may write $(1 - \lambda) = |\omega - 1| \exp(-i\pi)$ and thus $\log(1 - \lambda) = \log(\omega - 1) - i\pi$ at a point on the upper bank. Similarly, for a point λ on the lower bank we find the expression $\log(1 - \lambda) = \log(\omega - 1) + i\pi$.

The semicircle in the right half plane is now indented by paths which run along the upper and lower banks of the branch cut and by a circle of small radius ρ about the point $\lambda = 1$. Apart from poles, the integrand $G(a, \lambda, c)$ is single-valued and analytic inside the closed contour depicted above. The poles of the function $G(a, \lambda, c)$ can be found as the zeros of the function, $H(\lambda, c) = 1 - c(\operatorname{arctanh} \lambda)/\lambda$. The location of a root of the transcendental equation,

$$\operatorname{arctanh} \lambda = \lambda/c$$

depends, of course, on the magnitude of the parameter c. In this section we shall assume that this parameter is smaller than one. When λ is real, we find, by investigating the intersections of the curve $\gamma = \operatorname{arctanh} \omega$ with the line $\gamma = \omega/c$, that the transcendental equation above has a real root which is located on the real axis between the origin and the point $\lambda = 1$. We shall denote this point by $b(c)$, since the location of this root is clearly a function of the parameter c. We shall assume for the moment that the point $b(c)$ is the only pole of the function $G(a, \lambda, c)$ which is located inside the contour, delaying the verification of this supposition, by means of the principle of the argument, to the end of this section. Since the point $\lambda = b$ is a simple pole of the integrand, we obtain, according to the residue theorem,

$$\frac{1}{2\pi i} \oint_C \frac{e^{-a\zeta} \operatorname{arctanh} \zeta}{1 - c(\operatorname{arctanh} \zeta)/\zeta} \, d\zeta = \operatorname{Res}\,[G(a, \lambda, c), \lambda = b(c)]$$

The residue of the function $G(a, \lambda, c)$ at the simple pole $\lambda = b(c)$ can be computed by evaluation of the limit relation,

$$\operatorname{Res}\,[G(a, \lambda, c), \lambda = b(c)] = \lim_{\lambda \to b(c)} [\lambda - b(c)] G(a, \lambda, c)$$

Expanding the function $H(\lambda, c) = 1 - c(\operatorname{arctanh} \lambda)/\lambda$ in a Taylor series about the point $\lambda = b(c)$, we obtain

$$H(\lambda, c) = H[b(c), c] + [\lambda - b(c)] \, \partial H[b(c), c]/\partial\lambda + \cdots$$

However, $H[b(c), c] = 0$ and we find, therefore, by substitution of the Taylor series in to the limit relation,

$$\lim_{\lambda \to b(c)} [\lambda - b(c)] G(a, \lambda, c) = \frac{e^{-ab(c)} \operatorname{arctanh} b(c)}{\partial H[b(c), c]/\partial\lambda}$$

The derivative of the function $H(\lambda, c)$ at the point $\lambda = b(c)$ can be evaluated as follows,

$$\frac{\partial H[b(c), c]}{\partial \lambda} = -c \frac{\partial}{\partial b} \left(\frac{\operatorname{arctanh} b(c)}{b(c)} \right)$$

Moreover, since $H[b(c), c] = 1 - c[\text{arctanh } b(c)]/b(c) = 0$ we find, by differentiating this function with respect to c,

$$\frac{\partial H(b, c)}{\partial c} = -\frac{\text{arctanh } b(c)}{b(c)} - c\left[\frac{\partial}{\partial b}\left(\frac{\text{arctanh } b(c)}{b(c)}\right)\right]\frac{\partial b}{\partial c} = 0$$

Hence, the expression on the right hand side of the penultimate equation can be replaced by the quantity $[\text{arctanh } b(c)]/[b(c)(\partial b/\partial c)]$. Substitution of the relations derived above yields the following expression for the residue of the function $G(a, \lambda, c)$ at the point $\lambda = b(c)$,

$$\text{Res}\,[G(a, \lambda, c), \lambda = b(c)] = e^{-ab(c)}b(c)\,\partial b(c)/\partial c$$

Consequently, the contour integral takes the form,

$$\frac{1}{2\pi i}\oint_C \frac{e^{-a\zeta}\,\text{arctanh } \zeta}{1 - c(\text{arctanh } \zeta)/\zeta}\,d\zeta = e^{-ab(c)}b(c)\,\partial b(c)/\partial c$$

Investigating the asymptotic behavior of the integrand when the radius of the semicircle tends to infinity, we find that, in the Cesaro sense, only the paths along the upper and lower banks of the branch cuts and the path along the imaginary axis contribute to the integral. For the contribution of the path along the upper bank of the branch cut we find

$$\frac{1}{2\pi i}\int_1^\infty G(a, \zeta, c)\,d\zeta = \frac{1}{2\pi i}\int_1^\infty \frac{e^{-a\omega}(\text{arctanh } 1/\omega + i\pi/2)}{1 - c(\text{arctanh } 1/\omega + i\pi/2)/\omega}\,d\omega$$

where we make use of the fact that along this bank $\log(1 - \lambda) = \log(\omega - 1) - i\pi$. Similarly, for the contribution to the integral of the path along the lower bank of the branch cut we obtain

$$\frac{1}{2\pi i}\int_\infty^1 G(a, \zeta, c)\,d\zeta = \frac{1}{2\pi i}\int_\infty^1 \frac{e^{-a\omega}(\text{arctanh } 1/\omega - i\pi/2)}{1 - c(\text{arctanh } 1/\omega - i\pi/2)/\omega}\,d\omega$$

The integrals over the banks of the branch cut can be combined and the result substituted in the expression for the contour integral. The final result takes the form,

$$\frac{1}{2\pi i}\int_{-i\infty}^{i\infty} \frac{e^{-a\gamma}\,\text{arctanh } \gamma}{1 - c(\text{arctanh } \gamma)/\gamma}\,d\gamma = -e^{-ab(c)}b(c)\frac{\partial b(c)}{\partial c} + 2\int_0^1 \frac{e^{-a/s}\,ds}{s^2[4(1 - cs\,\text{arctanh } s)^2 + c^2\pi^2 s^2]}$$

where we made use of the substitution $s = 1/\omega$. The functions and the integral on the right hand side of this equation have been tabulated extensively.

Now we must substantiate our supposition that the simple pole, which is located on the real axis, is the only singularity of the function $G(a, \lambda, c)$ which is located inside the contour C. Verification of this supposition can be obtained by a straightforward application of the principle of the argument of Section 1.3. This principle states that the variation in the argument of a function of a complex variable, which is analytic inside and on a contour, upon a complete circuit of the contour, is equal to 2π times the excess of the number of zeros over the number of poles of the function which are located inside the contour. We shall apply this principle to show that the function $H(\lambda, c) = 1 - c(\operatorname{arctanh} \lambda)/\lambda$ has only one zero which is located inside the contour. Since the function $H(\lambda, c)$ is analytic inside the contour, this means that we have to prove that $\Delta_C \arg H(\lambda, c) = 2\pi$. First let us compute the contributions to the quantity $\Delta_C \arg H(\lambda, c)$ of the paths which run along the upper and lower banks of the branch cut. On the lower bank we may write $\log(1 - \lambda) = \log(\omega - 1) + i\pi$. Consequently, when λ is a point on the lower bank of the branch cut, the function $H(\lambda, c)$ takes the form,

$$H(\omega, c) = 1 - c[\log(1 + \omega) - \log(\omega - 1) - i\pi]/2\omega$$

The real part of this function tends to 1 through positive values and the imaginary part tends to 0 through positive values when ω tends to infinity. Similarly, the real part of the function $H(\lambda, c)$ tends to minus infinity and the imaginary part tends to $c\pi/2\omega$ when ω tends to one on the lower bank of the branch cut. Consequently, the variation in the argument of the function $H(\lambda, c)$ when λ moves along the lower bank from infinity to one is equal to π. In like fashion we find that $\Delta \arg H(\lambda, c) = \pi$ when λ runs along the upper bank of the branch cut from one to infinity. The function $H(\lambda, c) = 1 - c(\operatorname{arctanh} \lambda)/\lambda$ tends to one as λ tends to minus or plus infinity on the imaginary axis. Hence, the variation $\Delta \arg H(\lambda, c)$ vanishes on this path. Similarly, the quantity $\Delta \arg H(\lambda, c)$ vanishes on the semicircular arcs when R tends to infinity and on the circle about the point $\lambda = 1$ when ρ tends to zero. In summation we may conclude that $\Delta_C \arg H(\lambda, c) = 2\pi$. This implies, according to the principle of the argument, that the function $H(\lambda, c)$ has only one zero inside the contour.

F. Evaluation of the Inversion Integral of a Unilateral Fourier Transform

As a final example of the evaluation of an integral by means of contour integration we consider the path integral,

$$\frac{1}{2\pi i} \int_{-\infty + ia}^{\infty + ia} \zeta^{\alpha - 1} e^{-i\zeta t} \, d\zeta$$

Integrals of this type will be encountered as the inversion integrals of unilateral Fourier transforms in Chapter II. We shall assume that a is a positive constant and the path $(-\infty + ia, \infty + ia)$, therefore, runs parallel to the real axis in the upper half of the complex plane. We shall assume, moreover, that t is a positive or negative real parameter.

The integral above exists on the path of integration $(-\infty + ia, \infty + ia)$ only if $R(\alpha)$ is smaller than unity, since for all other values of α the function $\exp[(\alpha - 1)\log \zeta]$ will be a rapidly oscillating function when ζ tends to infinity on this path. If $R(\alpha)$ is smaller than one, the function $\lambda^{\alpha-1}$ vanishes when λ tends to infinity in the upper half plane $I(\lambda) > a$. Consequently, according to the corollary to Jordan's lemma obtained in Section 1.5, we may conclude that the integral above is equal to zero for all negative values of t. For positive values of t the contour must be closed in the lower half plane in such a manner that a possible branch point at the origin, which ensues for fractional values of α, is excluded from the region inside the contour. Cutting the plane by a branch cut along the imaginary axis, from 0 to $-i\infty$, we choose the contour of Figure I-29. The integrand $\lambda^{\alpha-1}\exp(-i\lambda t)$ is analytic inside

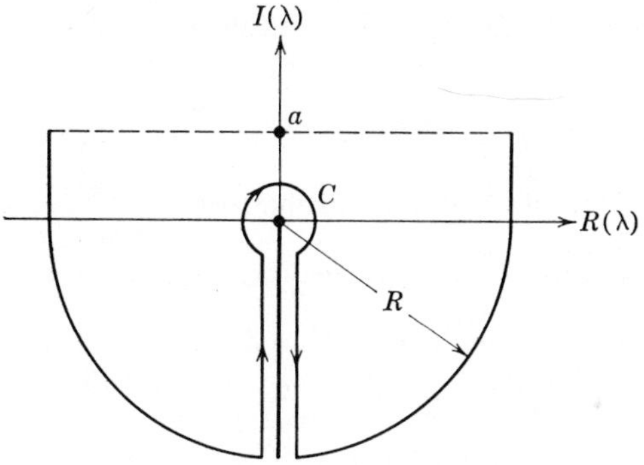

Figure I-29

the contour and, according to Cauchy's theorem, the contour integral of this function over the closed contour,

$$\oint \zeta^{\alpha-1} \exp(-i\zeta t)\, d\zeta$$

vanishes. Furthermore, by Jordan's lemma, the contributions of the circular paths to the integral vanish when the radius of the circle tends to infinity. Similarly, the contributions of the vertical paths located between the original path and the real axis, vanish when the radius R tends to infinity. In the limit as R tends to infinity, therefore, the integral over the path $(-\infty + ia, \infty + ia)$ can be reduced to the integral,

$$\frac{1}{2\pi i}\int_{\Omega} \zeta^{\alpha-1} e^{-i\zeta t}\, d\zeta$$

over the path Ω, which consists of the path from $-i\infty$ to 0 along the left bank of the branch cut, the circle C, and a path from 0 to $-i\infty$ along the right bank of the branch cut. However, although the integral over the original path $(-\infty + ia, \infty + ia)$ is only defined for values of α such that $R(\alpha)$ is smaller than unity, the integral over the path Ω is defined for all real and complex values of α. To evaluate the integral let us first consider the case in which α is positive. For these values of α the contour integral,

$$\oint_C \zeta^{\alpha-1} e^{-i\zeta t}\, d\zeta$$

vanishes when the radius of the circle C tends to zero. Consequently, in this limit the integral over the path Ω is reduced to an integral over the paths running along the banks of the branch cut. For positive fractional values of α we choose the branch of the multivalued function $\exp[(\alpha - 1)\log\lambda]$ which has zero phase on the positive imaginary axis. This implies, since $\lambda = |\lambda| \exp(i\pi)$ on the left bank and $\lambda = |\lambda| \exp(-i\pi)$ on the right bank, that the integrand takes the form,

$$\exp[(\alpha - 1)\log\lambda - i\lambda t] = \exp[(\alpha - 1)(\log u + i\pi) + iut]$$

on the left bank of the branch cut, and the form,

$$\exp[(\alpha - 1)\log\lambda - i\lambda t] = \exp[(\alpha - 1)(\log u - i\pi) + iut]$$

on the right bank of the branch cut, where u denotes the absolute value of λ. Consequently, for vanishingly small values of C, we obtain the result,

$$\frac{1}{2\pi i}\int_\Omega \zeta^{\alpha-1} e^{-i\zeta t}\, d\zeta = \frac{\sin(\alpha - 1)\pi}{\pi}\int_0^{i\infty} u^{\alpha-1} e^{iut}\, du = \frac{\sin(\alpha-1)\pi}{\pi}\left(\frac{i}{t}\right)^\alpha \Gamma(\alpha)$$

where $\Gamma(\alpha)$ denotes the gamma function. We have verified this result so far for positive values of the parameter α only. However, considered as functions of α, the function represented by the integral and the function on the right hand side of the equation are analytic functions of α in the whole complex α plane. Hence, by analytic continuation, we find that our result is true for all values of α. To summarize, for values of α, such that $R(\alpha) < 1$, we obtain the integral representation,

$$\frac{1}{2\pi i}\int_{-\infty+ia}^{\infty+ia} \zeta^{\alpha-1} e^{-i\zeta t}\, d\zeta = \frac{\sin(\alpha-1)\pi}{\pi}\Gamma(\alpha)\left(\frac{i}{t}\right)^\alpha \theta(t)$$

which, upon the substitution,

$$\frac{\sin(\alpha-1)\pi}{\pi}\Gamma(-\alpha) = \frac{1}{\Gamma(1+\alpha)}$$

is transformed into the representation,

$$\frac{1}{2\pi i}\int_{-\infty+ia}^{\infty+ia}\frac{e^{-i\zeta t}}{\zeta^{\alpha+1}}\,d\zeta = -\frac{1}{\Gamma(1+\alpha)}\left(\frac{t}{i}\right)^{\alpha}\theta(t)$$

For positive values of t we find, moreover, that these integral representations are valid for all values of α, provided that the path $(-\infty + ia, \infty + ia)$ is replaced by the path Ω delineated above.

CHAPTER II

FOURIER TRANSFORMS, CAUSALITY, AND DISPERSION RELATIONS

2.0 INTRODUCTION

In Chapter I we were concerned with functions of a complex variable and in particular with the representation of such functions by Cauchy integrals and by infinite series. In this chapter we shall consider the representation of functions of a real or complex variable by Fourier integrals. Such representations are of great utility in classical as well as modern theoretical physics.

More generally, let us consider the path or contour integral,

$$\int_{\Gamma} f(\zeta)K(\zeta, \lambda)\, d\zeta$$

where $f(\zeta)$ and $K(\zeta, \lambda)$ are functions of the variable ζ on the path Γ and $K(\zeta, \lambda)$ is also a function of the complex variable $\lambda = \omega + i\gamma$. The integral above defines a function $F(\lambda)$ of the complex variable λ which takes its values on some path, contour, or region in the complex λ-plane. In other words, the integral,

$$F(\lambda) = \int_{\Gamma} f(\zeta)K(\zeta, \lambda)\, d\zeta \tag{2.1}$$

is the integral representation of the function $F(\lambda)$ in some given region in the complex plane. From another point of view we may also consider the function

$F(\lambda)$ to be the integral transform of the function $f(\zeta)$ with kernel $K(\zeta, \lambda)$ and path Γ. For known kernel $K(\zeta, \lambda)$ and source function $F(\lambda)$, equation (2.1) is an integral equation for the function $f(\zeta)$. In certain situations the solution of this equation can be represented by an integral of the form,

$$f(z) = \int_{\Omega} F(\zeta) G(\zeta, z)\, d\zeta \tag{2.2}$$

where Ω is a path or contour in the complex z-plane and $G(\zeta, z)$ is a function of ζ and of the complex variable z. From the transform point of view, equation (2.2) is an expression for the inverse transform $f(z)$ of the transform $F(\lambda)$, and the function $G(\zeta, z)$ is the kernel of the inverse transform. If the paths Γ and Ω are the same and the kernel $K(\zeta, \lambda)$ is the complex conjugate of the kernel $G(\zeta, z)$, then the functions $f(z)$ and $F(\lambda)$ are conjugate functions and the transforms are reciprocal transformations. On the other hand, if the paths Γ and Ω are the same but the function $K(\zeta, \lambda)$ is equal to the negative of the function $G^*(\zeta, z)$, then the functions $f(z)$ and $F(\lambda)$ are skew-conjugate and the transforms are skew-reciprocal transformations.

In this chapter we shall be concerned with the reciprocal Fourier transform,

$$F(\omega) = \frac{1}{\sqrt{(2\pi)}} \int_{-\infty}^{\infty} f(t) e^{i\omega t}\, dt$$

and its inverse,

$$f(t) = \frac{1}{\sqrt{(2\pi)}} \int_{-\infty}^{\infty} F(\omega) e^{-i\omega t}\, d\omega$$

and with the analytic continuations of the function $F(\omega)$ into the complex plane. The function $F(\omega)$ can be decomposed into a positive and a negative frequency part,

$$F_+(\omega) = \frac{1}{\sqrt{(2\pi)}} \int_{0}^{\infty} f(t) e^{i\omega t}\, dt$$

and

$$F_-(\omega) = \frac{1}{\sqrt{(2\pi)}} \int_{-\infty}^{0} f(t) e^{i\omega t}\, dt$$

where both $F_+(\omega)$ and $F_-(\omega)$ are defined on the real ω-axis. This leads to the so-called unilateral Fourier transforms. Assuming that the function $f(t)$ is absolutely integrable over the real axis the functions $F_+(\omega)$ and $F_-(\omega)$ can be continued into the upper half and the lower half of the complex λ-plane respectively. For, since $f(t) \exp(-\gamma t)$ is absolutely integrable over the positive real axis for any positive value of γ, the function,

$$F_+(\lambda) = F_+(\omega + i\gamma) = \frac{1}{\sqrt{(2\pi)}} \int_{0}^{\infty} f(t) e^{i\lambda t}\, dt$$

is analytic in the upper half of the complex plane. Similarly, since $f(t)\exp(-\gamma t)$ is absolutely integrable over the negative real axis for all negative values of γ, the function,

$$F_-(\lambda) = F_-(\omega + i\gamma) = \frac{1}{\sqrt{(2\pi)}}\int_{-\infty}^{0} f(t)e^{i\lambda t}\,dt$$

is analytic in the lower half of the complex plane. Furthermore, $F_+(\lambda)$ and $F_-(\lambda)$ are continuous and bounded in the half plane $I(\lambda) \geqq 0$ and $I(\lambda) \leqq 0$ respectively. $F_+(\lambda)$ vanishes when λ tends to infinity in the upper half plane $I(\lambda) \geqq 0$, whereas $F_-(\lambda)$ vanishes when λ tends to infinity in the lower half plane $I(\lambda) \leqq 0$. Hence, according to Section 1.1, we may write

$$F_+(\lambda) = \frac{1}{2\pi i}\int_{-\infty}^{\infty} \frac{F(\zeta)}{\zeta - \lambda}\,d\zeta$$

and

$$F_-(\lambda) = -\frac{1}{2\pi i}\int_{-\infty}^{\infty} \frac{F(\zeta)}{\zeta - \lambda}\,d\zeta$$

In the limit as λ tends to ω from the upper and lower half plane respectively we obtain, according to that same section,

$$F_+(\omega) = \frac{1}{2}F(\omega) + \frac{1}{2\pi i}\int_{-\infty}^{\infty} \frac{F(\zeta)}{\zeta - \omega}\,d\zeta$$

and

$$F_-(\omega) = \frac{1}{2}F(\omega) - \frac{1}{2\pi i}\int_{-\infty}^{\infty} \frac{F(\zeta)}{\zeta - \omega}\,d\zeta$$

where the integrals now need to be interpreted as principal value integrals. Adding and subtracting the two expressions for $F_+(\omega)$ and $F_-(\omega)$ we obtain the formulas,

$$F_+(\omega) + F_-(\omega) = F(\omega)$$

and

$$F_+(\omega) - F_-(\omega) = \frac{1}{\pi i}\int_{-\infty}^{\infty} \frac{F(\zeta)}{\zeta - \omega}\,d\zeta$$

These are the Plemelj formulas for the positive and negative frequency parts of a function $F(\omega)$ which is the Fourier transform of an absolutely integrable function $f(t)$. The functions $F_+(\omega)$ and $F_-(\omega)$ are the boundary values on the real axis,

$$F_\pm(\omega) = \lim_{\gamma \to 0} F(\omega \pm i\gamma) \qquad \gamma > 0$$

of a function $F(\lambda)$ which is analytic in the whole complex plane with the exception of the real axis.

Now let us consider the case in which $f(t)$ is a causal function,

$$f(t) = f(t)\,\theta(t)$$

where $\theta(t)$ is the unit step function introduced in Section 1.1. Assuming that $f(t)$ is absolutely integrable over the positive real axis, we find

$$F(\omega) = F_+(\omega) = \frac{1}{\sqrt{(2\pi)}}\int_0^\infty f(t)e^{i\omega t}\,dt$$

The function $F(\omega) = F_+(\omega)$ is the restriction on the real axis of a function $F(\lambda)$ which is analytic in the whole upper half plane. Since $F_-(\omega) = 0$ we obtain by means of the second Plemelj formula the following integral representation for the function $F(\omega)$,

$$F(\omega) = \frac{1}{\pi i}\int_{-\infty}^\infty \frac{F(\zeta)}{\zeta - \omega}\,d\zeta$$

Taking real and imaginary parts of both sides of this representation of $F(\omega) = D(\omega) + iA(\omega)$ we find

$$D(\omega) = \frac{1}{\pi}\int_{-\infty}^\infty \frac{A(\zeta)}{\zeta - \omega}\,d\zeta \tag{2.3}$$

and

$$A(\omega) = -\frac{1}{\pi}\int_{-\infty}^\infty \frac{D(\zeta)}{\zeta - \omega}\,d\zeta \tag{2.4}$$

where the integrals are again principal value integrals. The function $D(\omega)$ is the Hilbert transform of the function $A(\omega)$ and the second formula expresses $A(\omega)$ as the inverse transform of the function $D(\omega)$. Hence, the real and imaginary parts of the Fourier transform of the causal function $f(t)\,\theta(t)$ form a pair of Hilbert transforms. Since

$$D(\omega) = \frac{1}{\sqrt{(2\pi)}}\int_0^\infty f(t)\cos\omega t\,dt$$

and

$$A(\omega) = \frac{1}{\sqrt{(2\pi)}}\int_0^\infty f(t)\sin\omega t\,dt$$

$D(\omega)$ is an even function of ω,

$$D(\omega) = D(-\omega)$$

and $A(\omega)$ is an odd function of ω,

$$A(\omega) = -A(-\omega)$$

In this case we may also write

$$D(\omega) = \frac{2}{\pi} \int_0^\infty \frac{\zeta A(\zeta)}{\zeta^2 - \omega^2} \, d\zeta$$

and

$$A(\omega) = -\frac{2\omega}{\pi} \int_0^\infty \frac{D(\zeta)}{\zeta^2 - \omega^2} \, d\zeta$$

Relations of this kind or of the type (2.3), (2.4), connecting the real and imaginary parts of a physical parameter which depends on the frequency or the energy, are called dispersion relations. Appearing in many fields of theoretical physics, they are the mathematical consequences in frequency or energy space of the causal behavior of a physical system in space-time. For instance, in scattering theory the real and imaginary parts of the scattering amplitude form a pair of dispersion relations, reflecting in energy space the fact that no outgoing wave will be observed before the incoming uncollided flux has reached the scattering center. Similarly we can obtain dispersion relations for the real and imaginary parts of the dielectric constant, the index of refraction, and several other parameters used in the description of electromagnetic phenomena. Now the dispersion relations are expressions in frequency space of the finite velocity of propagation of the electromagnetic field.

The Fourier transform technique, both in its real and complex form, is widely used in the solution of boundary value and initial value problems of mathematical physics and engineering. Fourier transformation of the underlying integral or partial differential equation and of the subsidiary conditions usually results in a less complicated problem in the space of the transform variable. If the solution of this secondary problem can easily be obtained and inverted, the transform technique is straightforward and efficient. The transform approach to the solution of a boundary value or initial value problem is in essence a formal approach. We formally solve the integral or differential equations involved by assuming that the relevant Fourier transforms and their inverses exist. The solution obtained is subsequently verified by substitution into the integral or differential equation and the auxiliary conditions. If it satisfies the equations and conditions, we may infer, by existing uniqueness theorems, that we have obtained the correct solution to our initial or boundary value problem.

2.1 SOME REMARKS ON INTEGRATION AND CAUCHY PRINCIPAL VALUE INTEGRALS

In this book we shall often encounter integrals which cannot be defined as ordinary or Riemann integrals but which must be defined as improper Riemann integrals or as Cauchy principal value integrals. At this point, therefore, a short digression into the subject of integration, mainly to explain the terminology, seems to be in order.

We know from elementary calculus that the Riemann integral of a function of a real variable over an interval of the real axis exists, provided that the function has at most a finite number of bounded discontinuities and that the interval is finite. However, in certain cases, the integral of a function which has a finite number of infinite discontinuities on a finite interval can be defined as an improper Riemann integral or as a Cauchy principal value integral. Similarly, the integral of a function over an infinite interval can sometimes be defined as an infinite Riemann integral or as an infinite principal value integral. Let us first turn our attention to the case in which the function $f(t)$ is unbounded at the point c of the finite interval (a, b). We presuppose moreover the existence of the integral of the function $f(t)$ over any subinterval of the interval (a, b) which does not contain the point c. In that case the integral of the function $f(t)$ over the interval (a, b) can be defined as the improper Riemann integral,

$$\int_a^b f(t)\,dt = \lim_{\varepsilon\to 0}\int_a^{c-\varepsilon} f(t)\,dt + \lim_{\delta\to 0}\int_{c+\delta}^b f(t)\,dt$$

provided the limits exist when the small positive quantities ε and δ tend to zero independently of each other. If the integral of a function exists either as a proper or as an improper Riemann integral we shall say that the function is Riemann integrable. In other words, a Riemann integrable function has at most a finite number of bounded or unbounded discontinuities on a finite interval. The function is absolutely integrable over an interval (a, b) if the integral of its absolute value exists either as a proper Riemann integral or as an improper Riemann integral. If a function is absolutely integrable, then it is also integrable. However, the converse of this statement is not necessarily true. Frequently we find that the limits,

$$\lim_{\varepsilon\to 0}\int_a^{c-\varepsilon} f(t)\,dt + \lim_{\delta\to 0}\int_{c+\delta}^b f(t)\,dt$$

do not exist when ε is different from δ, but that the limit,

$$\lim_{\varepsilon\to 0}\left[\int_a^{c-\varepsilon} f(t)\,dt + \int_{c+\varepsilon}^b f(t)\,dt\right]$$

does exist. In that case the integral of the function $f(t)$ over the interval (a, b) can be defined as a Cauchy principal value integral by the limit relation,

$$\int_a^b f(t)\,dt = \lim_{\varepsilon \to 0} \left[\int_a^{c-\varepsilon} f(t)\,dt + \int_{c+\varepsilon}^b f(t)\,dt \right]$$

For example, let us evaluate the integral,

$$\int_a^b \frac{dt}{t-c}$$

where c is a point on the interval (a, b). Assuming that the integral exists as an improper Riemann integral, we find

$$\int_a^b \frac{dt}{t-c} = \lim_{\varepsilon \to 0} \int_a^{c-\varepsilon} \frac{dt}{t-c} + \lim_{\delta \to 0} \int_{c+\delta}^b \frac{dt}{t-c} = \log \frac{b-c}{c-a} + \lim_{\varepsilon, \delta \to 0} \log (\varepsilon/\delta)$$

The limit on the right hand side of this equation can be any value between minus and plus infinity depending on the manner in which the quantities ε and δ tend to zero. For instance, if $\varepsilon = p\delta$ we obtain

$$\int_a^b \frac{dt}{t-c} = \log \frac{b-c}{c-a} + \log p$$

and the value of the integral, therefore, depends on p. However, the integral can be defined in an unique fashion as a Cauchy principal value integral by letting p be equal to unity and thus ε be equal to δ. We now obtain the value,

$$\int_a^b \frac{dt}{t-c} = \log [(b-c)/(c-a)]$$

which is the principal value of this integral defined in the Cauchy sense.

The following integral can also be defined as a principal value integral,

$$\int_a^b \frac{f(t)}{t-c}\,dt$$

where c is again a point located on the interval (a, b). It can be shown that this integral exists as a principal value integral at all points c of the interval (a, b) provided that the function $f(t)$ is Hölder continuous on the interval (a, b). In Chapter IV we shall present a short discussion on Hölder continuity. Here it suffices to say that a function $f(t)$ is Hölder continuous on the interval (a, b) if, at any point c on the interval (a, b), there exists a positive number α which is smaller than or equal to unity such that

$$f(t) - f(c) = O[(t-c)^\alpha]$$

when t tends to c. We now subtract the singularity in the integral above and we find

$$\int_a^b \frac{f(t)}{t-c}\,dt = \int_a^b \frac{f(t)-f(c)}{t-c}\,dt + f(c)\int_a^b \frac{dt}{t-c}$$

As we have shown, the second integral on the right hand side of this equation can be evaluated immediately as a Cauchy principal value integral. Furthermore, since $f(t)$ is Hölder continuous on the interval (a, b), we may write

$$f(t) - f(c) = (t-c)O[(t-c)^{\alpha-1}]$$

where $0 < \alpha \leqq 1$, and c is an arbitrary point on the interval (a, b). Consequently, if α is smaller than unity, the first integral on the right hand side of the penultimate equation exists as an improper Riemann integral and, if α is equal to one, this integral exists as an ordinary Riemann integral.

If the integral of a function exists as a proper Riemann integral then its value is the same as its principal value. The converse of this statement is, of course, not true.

We now turn our attention to the case of an infinite interval. Assuming that the function $f(t)$ is integrable over any finite subinterval of the semi-infinite interval (a, ∞), the infinite integral of this function can be defined as the limit,

$$\int_a^\infty f(t)\,dt = \lim_{b\to\infty}\int_a^b f(t)\,dt$$

provided this limit exists and is finite. This definition can be generalized immediately to the case in which the function is integrable over any finite subinterval of the infinite interval $(-\infty, \infty)$. The infinite integral of this function can be defined as the limit,

$$\int_{-\infty}^\infty f(t)\,dt = \lim_{a,b\to\infty}\int_{-a}^b f(t)\,dt$$

provided this limit exists and is finite when the positive quantities a and b tend to infinity independently of each other. If a function is integrable over any finite subinterval of a semi-infinite or an infinite interval and its infinite integral converges in the sense defined above, then the function is Riemann integrable over the particular infinite interval. A function is absolutely integrable over an infinite interval if the absolute value of the function is integrable over that interval. If a function is absolutely integrable over an infinite interval, then it is also integrable over this interval. However, the converse of this statement is not necessarily true.

If the limit,

$$\lim_{a,b\to\infty}\int_{-a}^b f(t)\,dt$$

exists only if a is equal to b, then the infinite integral of $f(t)$ exists as a Cauchy principal value integral and we may write

$$\int_{-\infty}^{\infty} f(t)\,dt = \lim_{a\to\infty}\int_{-a}^{a} f(t)\,dt$$

A very simple example of an integral which exists as a principal value integral but not as an infinite Riemann integral is the integral of the sign function $\varepsilon(t)$ over the infinite interval,

$$\int_{-\infty}^{\infty} \varepsilon(t)\,dt$$

The Cauchy principal value of this integral is defined as the limit,

$$\int_{-\infty}^{\infty} \varepsilon(t)\,dt = \lim_{a\to\infty}\int_{-a}^{a} \varepsilon(t)\,dt = 0$$

and vanishes therefore. However, if the upper and lower limit of the integral on the right hand side of this equation are not equal, we obtain, for instance,

$$\lim_{a\to\infty}\int_{-a}^{a+1} \varepsilon(t)\,dt = 1.$$

The value obtained for the integral depends, therefore, on the manner in which the upper and lower limits are chosen and the integral does not exist as an infinite Riemann integral. In the literature the principal value of an integral is commonly denoted by placing the letter P in front of the integral sign. Thus,

$$\int_{-\infty}^{\infty} \varepsilon(t)\,dt = P\int_{-\infty}^{\infty} \varepsilon(t)\,dt$$

We shall avoid this notation by assuming that the integrals of the functions considered exist either as proper Riemann integrals or as principal value integrals. In this book we shall depend in general on these two concepts of integration and we shall make little use of the concept of Lebesgue integration found in the mathematically more sophisticated works. In doing so we shall suffer some penalties, not only with regard to mathematical elegance, but also with regard to mathematical flexibility. For a Lebesgue integral exists for a larger class of functions than a Riemann integral. To prove that the Lebesgue integral of a function exists it is sufficient to show that the function is bounded over the interval of integration, whereas to prove that the Riemann integral exists we have to show that the function is piecewise continuous on the interval. Thus, it is in general easier to prove that a function is Lebesgue integrable than it is to prove that a function is Riemann integrable. This is also true for unbounded functions over an infinite interval. This, of course, is of great convenience in more theoretical work. However, the concept of Riemann integration, together with that of a principal value integral, is sufficient for nearly all applied work.

2.2 INFINITE INTEGRALS DEPENDING ON A PARAMETER

As defined in the introduction of this chapter, an integral transform of a function $f(z)$ of the real or complex variable z is a function $F(\lambda)$ of the real or complex variable λ which can be represented by an integral of the form,

$$F(\lambda) = \int_\Gamma f(\zeta)K(\zeta, \lambda)\, d\zeta = \int_\Gamma G(\zeta, \lambda)\, d\zeta$$

Obviously, it is important that we be able to determine the convergence properties of such integrals and the analytic properties of the functions which can be represented by them. In this section we shall present a short discussion pertaining to the convergence properties of integrals of this type, while in the next section we shall consider the analyticity of the function $F(\lambda)$.

As we mentioned at the outset of this chapter, we are mainly interested in integrals along infinite or semi-infinite straight lines which run parallel to the real axis or which coincide with the real axis. First let us consider an infinite integral of the type,

$$\int_a^\infty G(t)\, dt$$

where a denotes some arbitrary finite real number. In the foregoing section we stated that an infinite integral of this type can be defined as the limit,

$$\int_a^\infty G(t)\, dt = \lim_{b\to\infty} \int_a^b G(t)\, dt$$

provided that the function $G(t)$ is Riemann integrable over any finite subinterval (a, b) of the infinite interval (a, ∞) and that the limit exists and is finite. This definition implies that, corresponding to any arbitrarily small positive number ε, we can find a point $T(\varepsilon)$ on the interval (a, ∞) such that the absolute value of the integral,

$$\int_t^\infty G(t)\, dt$$

is smaller than ε for any value of t which is larger than $T(\varepsilon)$. In other words, the contribution of the interval (t, ∞) to the infinite integral becomes arbitrarily small when t is larger than $T(\varepsilon)$. This definition of convergence is not adequate when we are dealing with integrals of functions $G(t, \lambda)$ which depend not only on the variable t but also on a real or complex valued parameter λ. The infinite integral,

$$\int_a^\infty G(t, \lambda)\, dt$$

now represents a function of the parameter λ which is defined on a path, contour, or region D in the complex plane, and in addition to the existence of this function at each separate point of the region D we are also interested in the analytic properties of this function. Such properties depend on the uniformity of the convergence of the integral. The integral,

$$\int_a^\infty G(t, \lambda)\, dt$$

is uniformly convergent for all values of λ in a region D if, corresponding to an arbitrarily small positive number ε, we can find a point $T(\varepsilon)$ on the interval (a, ∞) such that the absolute value of the integral,

$$\int_t^\infty G(t, \lambda)\, dt$$

is smaller than ε for all values of t which are larger than $T(\varepsilon)$ and for all values of λ in the region D. We note that the value of $T(\varepsilon)$ may depend on ε but not on λ. It is a uniform value for all values of λ in the region D.

A convenient test for the uniform convergence of infinite integrals is a generalization of Weierstrass's test for the uniform convergence of infinite series. If we can find a non-negative function $F(t)$ such that $|G(t, \lambda)| \leqq F(t)$ for all values of t in the interval (a, ∞) and all values of λ in the region D, and if, moreover, the integral,

$$\int_a^\infty F(t)\, dt$$

converges, then the integral,

$$\int_a^\infty G(t, \lambda)\, dt$$

is absolutely and uniformly convergent for all values of λ in the region D. For, since the integral of the non-negative function $F(t)$ over the interval (a, ∞) is convergent, we can find, corresponding to any arbitrarily small positive number ε, a point $T(\varepsilon)$ on the interval (a, ∞) such that the integral,

$$\int_t^\infty F(t)\, dt$$

is smaller than ε when t is larger than $T(\varepsilon)$. However,

$$\left|\int_t^\infty G(t, \lambda)\, dt\right| \leqq \int_t^\infty |G(t, \lambda)|\, dt \leqq \int_t^\infty F(t)\, dt < \varepsilon$$

and, since the bound ε has been chosen independently of λ, we may infer that the integral of the function $G(t, \lambda)$ over the interval (a, ∞) is absolutely and also uniformly convergent for all λ in the region D.

The analytic properties of a function $F(\lambda)$ defined by an integral of the form,

$$F(\lambda) = \int_a^\infty G(t, \lambda)\, dt$$

can most easily be investigated at the hand of an infinite series representation of the integral. Let $a = t_0 < t_1 < t_2 < \cdots < t_m < \cdots < \infty$ be an arbitrary partition of the interval (a, ∞). Then we may write

$$F(\lambda) = \int_a^\infty G(t, \lambda)\, dt = \int_a^{t_1} G(t, \lambda)\, dt + \int_{t_1}^{t_2} G(t, \lambda)\, dt + \cdots + \int_{t_m}^{t_{m+1}} G(t, \lambda)\, dt + \cdots$$

$$= F_0(\lambda) + F_1(\lambda) + \cdots + F_m(\lambda) + \cdots$$

Referring to the short discussion on infinite series in Section 1.2 it can be shown that the infinite integral is uniformly convergent for all values of λ in the region D, provided the infinite series is uniformly convergent for all values of λ in the region D and for all possible partitions of the interval (a, ∞).

The series representation can be used to verify the following assertions. Let $G(t, \lambda)$ be a continuous function of the variable λ in the region D for all values of t on the interval (a, ∞) and let $G(t, \lambda)$ be a piecewise continuous function of the variable t on the interval (a, ∞) for all values of λ in the region D. Furthermore, let $G(t, \lambda)$ be uniformly integrable over the interval (a, ∞) for all values of λ in the region D. Then the function,

$$F(\lambda) = \int_a^\infty G(t, \lambda)\, dt$$

is a continuous function of the variable λ in the region D. Moreover, the integral of the function $F(\lambda)$ over a path or contour Γ in the region D can be evaluated by interchanging the order of integration of the corresponding integrals of the function $G(t, \lambda)$,

$$\int_\Gamma F(\lambda)\, d\lambda = \int_\Gamma d\lambda \int_a^\infty G(t, \lambda)\, dt = \int_a^\infty dt \int_\Gamma G(t, \lambda)\, d\lambda$$

Similarly, the derivative of the function $F(\lambda)$ can be evaluated by differentiating the function $G(t, \lambda)$ under the integral sign,

$$\frac{dF(\lambda)}{d\lambda} = \frac{d}{d\lambda}\int_a^\infty G(t, \lambda)\, dt = \int_a^\infty \frac{\partial G(t, \lambda)}{\partial \lambda}\, dt$$

provided that the partial derivative of the function $G(t, \lambda)$ with respect to λ is uniformly integrable over the interval (a, ∞) for all values of λ in the region D.

The considerations above pertain to infinite integrals of functions of a real variable. However, the results obtained can be extended immediately to integrals of functions of a complex variable. Let Γ be a path which connects the point a in a finite region of the complex plane with the point at infinity and let λ be a complex valued parameter which takes its values in a region D of the complex plane. Then the infinite integral,

$$\int_\Gamma G(\zeta, \lambda)\, d\zeta \tag{2.5}$$

is uniformly convergent if, corresponding to any arbitrarily small positive number ε, we can find a point $Z(\varepsilon)$ on the path Γ such that the absolute value of the integral,

$$\int_Z^\infty G(\zeta, \lambda)\, d\zeta$$

is smaller than ε for all values of z which lie between the point $Z(\varepsilon)$ and the point at infinity and for all values of λ in the region D. To test for the uniform convergence of such an integral we may use the following generalization of Weierstrass's test for the uniform convergence of infinite series. Let s denote the arc length on the path Γ. If we can find a non-negative function $F(s)$ which is integrable over the interval $(0, \infty)$ and which satisfies the condition that

$$|G(\zeta, \lambda)\, d\zeta(s)/ds| \leqq F(s)$$

for all values of λ in a region D, then the integral (2.5) is absolutely and uniformly convergent for all values of λ in the region D. For, since the function $F(s)$ is non-negative and integrable over the interval $(0, \infty)$, we can find, for any arbitrarily small positive value of ε, a point $S(\varepsilon)$ on the interval $(0, \infty)$ such that the integral,

$$\int_S^\infty F(s)\, ds$$

is smaller than ε for any value of s which is larger than $S(\varepsilon)$. This implies that

$$\left|\int_Z^\infty G(\zeta, \lambda)\, d\zeta\right| = \left|\int_{S(Z)}^\infty G(\zeta, \lambda) \frac{d\zeta(s)}{ds}\, ds\right|$$

$$\leqq \int_{S(Z)}^\infty \left|G(\zeta, \lambda) \frac{d\zeta(s)}{ds}\right| ds \leqq \int_S^\infty F(s)\, ds < \varepsilon$$

and, since the bound ε has been chosen independently of λ, it follows immediately that the function $G(\zeta, \lambda)$ is absolutely and uniformly integrable for all values of λ in the region D.

The analytic properties of the function $F(\lambda)$ which is represented by the path integral,

$$F(\lambda) = \int_\Gamma G(\zeta, \lambda)\, d\zeta$$

can be obtained by a straightforward generalization of the analogous properties of the function $F(\lambda)$ which is defined by the infinite integral of a function of a real variable.

EXAMPLE 1 The unilateral Fourier integral,

$$F_+(\lambda) = \frac{1}{\sqrt{(2\pi)}} \int_0^\infty f(t) e^{i\lambda t}\, dt$$

appears frequently in the application of function-theoretic techniques to problems in mathematical physics and engineering. If the function $g(t) = f(t) \exp(-at)$ is absolutely integrable over the positive real axis, then it can easily be shown that the infinite Fourier integral is absolutely and uniformly convergent for all values of λ in the half plane $I(\lambda) \geqq a$. For we may write

$$|F_+(\lambda)| \leqq \frac{1}{\sqrt{(2\pi)}} \int_0^\infty |f(t)| e^{-\gamma t}\, dt = \frac{1}{\sqrt{(2\pi)}} \int_0^\infty |g(t)| e^{(a-\gamma)t}\, dt$$

and the second integral is convergent for all values of γ which are larger than or equal to a. Similar conclusions can be drawn if we assume that the function $f(t)$ is absolutely integrable over any finite subinterval of the positive real axis and is of exponential growth at infinity,

$$f(t) = O(\exp at)$$

when t tends to infinity. In this case it can be shown that the unilateral Fourier integral is absolutely and uniformly convergent for all values of λ in the upper half plane $I(\lambda) > a$.

EXAMPLE 2 In the same manner we can show that the unilateral Fourier integral,

$$F_-(\lambda) = \frac{1}{\sqrt{(2\pi)}} \int_{-\infty}^{0} f(t) e^{i\lambda t} \, dt$$

is absolutely and uniformly convergent for all values of λ in the lower half plane $I(\lambda) \leqq b$, provided that the function $f(t) \exp(-bt)$ is absolutely integrable over the negative real axis. Similarly, the supposition that the function $f(t)$ is absolutely integrable over any finite subinterval of the negative real axis and is of exponential growth on the negative real axis,

$$f(t) = O(\exp bt)$$

when t tends to minus infinity, is sufficient to ensure the absolute and uniform integrability of the function $f(t) \exp(i\lambda t)$ over the negative real axis for all values of λ in the lower half plane $I(\lambda) < b$.

EXAMPLE 3 Assuming that the function $f(t) \exp(-at)$ is absolutely integrable over the positive real axis and that the function $f(t) \exp(-bt)$ is absolutely integrable over the negative real axis, we can show, at the hand of Examples 1 and 2, that the Fourier integral,

$$F(\lambda) = F_+(\lambda) + F_-(\lambda) = \frac{1}{\sqrt{(2\pi)}} \int_{-\infty}^{\infty} f(t) e^{i\lambda t} \, dt$$

is absolutely and uniformly convergent for all λ in the strip $a \leqq I(\lambda) \leqq b$. Again, it is sufficient to impose the conditions that $f(t)$ is absolutely integrable over any finite subinterval of the real axis and satisfies the order relation $O(\exp at)$ when t tends to plus infinity and the order relation $O(\exp bt)$ when t tends to minus infinity. In this case the Fourier integral $F(\lambda)$ is absolutely and uniformly convergent in the strip $a < I(\lambda) < b$. This is an immediate consequence of the conclusions reached in Examples 1 and 2, since the half planes of uniform convergence mentioned in these examples overlap in the strip $a < I(\lambda) < b$.

EXAMPLE 4 In Section 1.7 we considered the wave equation,

$$\nabla^2 \Phi(\mathbf{r}, t) = \frac{1}{c^2} \frac{\partial^2 \Phi(\mathbf{r}, t)}{\partial t^2} + a^2 \frac{\partial \Phi(\mathbf{r}, t)}{\partial t}$$

which arises in the mathematical description of the propagation of waves in a dissipative medium. Assuming that we are interested in the solutions of this equation which have a simple harmonic time dependence, we separate off the time dependence by the substitution $\Phi(\mathbf{r}, t) = \phi(\mathbf{r}) \exp(-i\omega t)$, and find

$$\nabla^2 \phi(\mathbf{r}) + k^2 \phi(\mathbf{r}) = 0$$

The wave number $k = \alpha + i\beta$ depends on the angular frequency ω, on the velocity of propagation c, and on the dissipative constant a. We shall assume that k has a positive imaginary part. In the two-dimensional problems of the wave propagation in an infinite medium it frequently occurs that we need to find the solutions of the Helmholtz equation which are symmetric about the origin and which have a logarithmic singularity at this point. If, in addition, we need to impose the condition that such solutions can be used to describe outgoing or incoming wave motion at infinity, then our choice of solutions has been limited to the zeroth order Hankel functions of the first and second kind, $H_0^{(1)}(kr)$ and $H_0^{(2)}(kr)$, respectively. For it is well known that these functions satisfy the zeroth order Bessel equation,

$$\frac{1}{r}\frac{\partial}{\partial r}\left(r\frac{\partial \phi}{\partial r}\right) + k^2\phi(r) = 0$$

and behave like $-(2 \log kr)/\pi i$ at the origin. Furthermore, the function $H_0^{(1)}(kr)$ tends to $\exp[i(kr - \pi/4)]\sqrt{(2/\pi kr)}$ for large values of the argument, whereas the function $H_0^{(2)}(kr)$ behaves like $\exp[-i(kr - \pi/4)]\sqrt{(2/\pi kr)}$ when kr becomes large. Because of this behavior and the choice of sign of the exponent in the time factor $\exp(-i\omega t)$, the Hankel function of the first kind can be used to represent an outgoing wave at infinity, whereas the Hankel function of the second kind can be used in the description of an incoming wave.

Now let us consider the functions $H_0^{(1)}(k|x|)$ and $H_0^{(2)}(k|x|)$. The Fourier transform of the Hankel function of the first kind can be defined as follows,

$$H(\lambda) = \frac{1}{\sqrt{(2\pi)}}\int_{-\infty}^{\infty} H_0^{(1)}(k|x|)e^{i\lambda x}\, dx$$

The integral converges at the origin, because the integrand has a logarithmic singularity at this point and the integral of $\log|x|$ exists at the origin. With respect to this point the convergence is uniform in any finite region of the λ-plane. For large values of the argument of the Hankel function, the integrand satisfies the order relation, $e^{i\lambda x}H_0^{(1)}(k|x|) = O[\exp(-\beta|x| - I(\lambda)x)]$. Consequently, according to the foregoing examples, the integral above converges absolutely and uniformly for all λ in the strip $-\beta < I(\lambda) < \beta$. Similar conclusions can be drawn with respect to the Fourier integral of the function $H_0^{(2)}(k|x|)$.

2.3 REPRESENTATION OF AN ANALYTIC FUNCTION BY AN INFINITE INTEGRAL

In the foregoing section we investigated the relations that exist between some of the analytic properties of the function $F(\lambda)$ and the properties of the integrand $G(\zeta, \lambda)$ of the infinite integral,

$$F(\lambda) = \int_\Gamma G(\zeta, \lambda)\, d\zeta \tag{2.6}$$

which is the integral representation of the function $F(\lambda)$. In the application of integral transforms to problems in mathematical physics we frequently need to determine the region of analyticity of the function $F(\lambda)$ by means of the analytic properties of the integrand $G(\zeta, \lambda)$. In this section we shall consider briefly how the analyticity of the function $F(\lambda)$ is related to the properties of the function $G(\zeta, \lambda)$.

First we shall consider the case of a finite contour or path Γ. In this case, the integral (2.6) is a representation of an analytic function of the complex variable λ in a region D, provided that the integrand $G(\zeta, \lambda)$ is a continuous function of the variable ζ on the path Γ and is a continuous and analytic function of the variable λ in the region D. For, since the function $G(\zeta, \lambda)$ is analytic in the region D we can represent this function by the contour integral,

$$G(\zeta, \lambda) = \frac{1}{2\pi i} \oint_C \frac{G(\zeta, \alpha)}{\alpha - \lambda}\, d\alpha$$

where C denotes an arbitrary contour in the region D which encloses the point λ. Substitution of this expression for $G(\zeta, \lambda)$ into the integral representation for $F(\lambda)$ yields the relation,

$$F(\lambda) = \frac{1}{2\pi i} \int_\Gamma d\zeta \oint_C \frac{G(\zeta, \alpha)}{\alpha - \lambda}\, d\alpha$$

Interchanging the order of integration of the integrals of the continuous function $G(\zeta, \alpha)$, we obtain

$$F(\lambda) = \frac{1}{2\pi i} \oint_C \frac{d\alpha}{\alpha - \lambda} \int_\Gamma G(\zeta, \alpha)\, d\zeta = \frac{1}{2\pi i} \oint_C \frac{F(\alpha)}{\alpha - \lambda}\, d\alpha$$

Since C denotes an arbitrary contour in the region D and encloses the point λ, we may infer that the function $F(\lambda)$ is an analytic function of the complex variable λ in the region D.

Now let us turn our attention to the case of the infinite path Γ which was defined in the previous section. The conditions which are imposed on the function $G(\zeta, \lambda)$ in the case of the finite path are not sufficient for the analyticity of the function $F(\lambda)$ in the case of the infinite path. In addition to the conditions which are imposed on the function $G(\zeta, \lambda)$ for the finite contour we must require that the integral,

$$F(\lambda) = \int_\Gamma G(\zeta, \lambda)\, d\zeta \tag{2.7}$$

is uniformly convergent for all values of λ in the region D. Hence, we can make the following statement. If $G(\zeta, \lambda)$ is a continuous and analytic function of the complex variable λ in the region D for any value ζ on the path Γ, and if $G(\zeta, \lambda)$ is a continuous function of the variable ζ on the path Γ for any value of λ in the region D and is, moreover, uniformly integrable along the path Γ for all values of λ in D, then the integral (2.7) represents an analytic function in the region D. This assertion can be made plausible as follows. Partitioning the path Γ by a sequence of points $\{a_m\}$ which are ordered from $a_0 = a$ to $\zeta = \infty$, we obtain integrals of the form,

$$F_m(\lambda) = \int_a^{a_m} G(\zeta, \lambda)\, d\zeta$$

This is a finite integral which depends on the parameter λ and we have shown above that the conditions imposed on the integrand are sufficient to assure the analyticity of the function $F_m(\lambda)$ in the region D. The sequence of integrals, $F_1(\lambda), F_2(\lambda), \ldots, F_m(\lambda), \ldots$ tends to a limit $F(\lambda)$ uniformly when m tends to infinity, and the limit of a uniformly convergent sequence of analytic functions is also an analytic function which has the same region of analyticity as the functions $F_1(\lambda), F_2(\lambda), \ldots$

EXAMPLE 1 The well-known integral representation of the gamma function,

$$\Gamma(\lambda) = \int_0^\infty e^{-t} t^{\lambda-1}\, dt$$

can be used to illustrate the discussion above. The integrand $G(t, \lambda) = t^{\lambda-1} \exp(-t)$ is continuous and analytic in the whole finite λ-plane and is continuous on any finite part of the positive real axis. Moreover, writing the integral above as the sum of two integrals,

$$\int_0^\infty e^{-t} t^{\lambda-1}\, dt = \int_0^1 e^{-t} t^{\lambda-1}\, dt + \int_1^\infty e^{-t} t^{\lambda-1}\, dt$$

we find, according to Weierstrass's test, that the first integral is uniformly convergent in any region in which the real part of λ is bounded away from zero, whereas the second integral is uniformly convergent in the whole finite λ-plane. This implies that the integral is uniformly convergent in the half plane $R(\lambda) > 0$ and is a representation of an analytic function in this half plane.

EXAMPLE 2 In the preceding section we showed that the unilateral Fourier integral,

$$F_+(\lambda) = \frac{1}{\sqrt{(2\pi)}} \int_0^\infty f(t) e^{i\lambda t}\, dt$$

is absolutely and uniformly convergent in the upper half plane $I(\lambda) \geqq a$ whenever the function $f(t) \exp(-at)$ is absolutely integrable over the positive real axis. Hence, provided that this condition is satisfied, the integral above represents a function $F_+(\lambda)$ which is analytic in the half plane $I(\lambda) > a$. Similarly we may assert that the function,

$$F_-(\lambda) = \frac{1}{\sqrt{(2\pi)}} \int_{-\infty}^{0} f(t)e^{i\lambda t}\, dt$$

is analytic in the lower half plane $I(\lambda) < b$ whenever the function $f(t) \exp(-bt)$ is absolutely integrable over the negative real axis. We may also conclude that the Fourier integral,

$$F(\lambda) = F_+(\lambda) + F_-(\lambda) = \frac{1}{\sqrt{(2\pi)}} \int_{-\infty}^{\infty} f(t)e^{i\lambda t}\, dt$$

represents an analytic function of the complex variable λ in the strip $a < I(\lambda) < b$, provided that the function $f(t) \exp(-at)$ is absolutely integrable over the positive real axis and the function $f(t) \exp(-bt)$ is absolutely integrable over the negative real axis.

EXAMPLE 3 The Fourier integral of the zeroth order Hankel function of the first kind $H_0^{(1)}(k|x|)$,

$$H(\lambda) = \frac{1}{\sqrt{(2\pi)}} \int_{-\infty}^{\infty} H_0^{(1)}(k|x|)e^{i\lambda x}\, dx$$

converges absolutely and uniformly for all λ in the strip $-\beta < I(\lambda) < \beta$, where β is defined in Example 5 of the preceding section. This implies, since the function $H_0^{(1)}(k|x|) \exp(i\lambda x)$ is continuous and analytic in the whole complex λ-plane, that the Fourier integral above represents a function $H(\lambda)$ which is analytic in the same strip. The function $H(\lambda)$, which is the Fourier transform of the function $H_0^{(1)}(k|x|)$, takes the form,

$$H(\lambda) = \sqrt{\left(\frac{2}{\pi}\right)} \frac{1}{\sqrt{(k^2 - \lambda^2)}}$$

The branch points of this multivalued function are located at the points $\lambda = \pm k$. According to Section 1.7, we can cut the complex plane and choose a branch such that $\sqrt{(k^2 - \lambda^2)} = \arg k$ at the origin. The analytic continuation of the function $H(\lambda)$ is analytic in the whole cut plane. Analogous observations can be made with respect to the Fourier transform of the zeroth order Hankel function of the second kind.

2.4 BILATERAL FOURIER TRANSFORMS

In this section we shall be concerned with the integral representation of a real or complex valued function $F(\omega)$ of the real variable ω by a Fourier integral,

$$F(\omega) = \frac{1}{\sqrt{(2\pi)}} \int_{-\infty}^{\infty} f(t) e^{i\omega t} \, dt \tag{2.8}$$

of an appropriately defined but largely arbitrary function $f(t)$ of the real variable t. In the terminology of the introduction to this chapter, the function $F(\omega)$ is the Fourier transform of the function $f(t)$ and, for given $F(\omega)$, the inverse transform $f(t)$ can be determined as the solution of the integral equation (2.8) for the function $f(t)$. The solution of this integral equation can be found formally by multiplying both sides of the equation by the factor $\exp(-i\omega t_0)/\sqrt{(2\pi)}$ and by integrating the results over the real axis. Interchanging the order of integration, we find

$$\frac{1}{\sqrt{(2\pi)}} \int_{-\infty}^{\infty} F(\omega) e^{-i\omega t_0} \, d\omega = \int_{-\infty}^{\infty} f(t) \, dt \, \frac{1}{2\pi} \int_{-\infty}^{\infty} e^{i\omega(t-t_0)} \, d\omega$$

The second integral on the right hand side of this equation is the well-known Fourier integral representation of the Dirac delta function,

$$\delta(t - t_0) = \frac{1}{2\pi} \int_{-\infty}^{\infty} e^{i\omega(t-t_0)} \, d\omega$$

Replacing the integral on the right hand side of the penultimate equation by the delta function, we obtain the following solution of the integral equation (2.8),

$$f(t_0) = \frac{1}{\sqrt{(2\pi)}} \int_{-\infty}^{\infty} F(\omega) e^{-i\omega t_0} \, d\omega$$

where we have used the sifting property of the delta function,

$$\int_{-\infty}^{\infty} \delta(t - t_0) f(t_0) \, dt_0 = f(t)$$

We have obtained therefore, in an admittedly formal manner, the inverse transform,

$$f(t) = \frac{1}{\sqrt{(2\pi)}} \int_{-\infty}^{\infty} F(\omega) e^{-i\omega t} \, d\omega$$

of the Fourier transform of the function $f(t)$,

$$F(\omega) = \frac{1}{\sqrt{(2\pi)}} \int_{-\infty}^{\infty} f(t) e^{i\omega t} \, dt$$

The formal derivation above can be justified by rigorous assertions stating the necessary and sufficient conditions which must be imposed on the function $f(t)$ to guarantee that its Fourier transform $F(\omega)$ exists and can be inverted. This is not the place, however, to make a penetrating analysis of the weakest possible conditions which must be imposed to obtain the largest possible class of functions with these properties. In this book we are mainly interested in the application of the transform technique to problems in mathematical physics and engineering and for these purposes a satisfactory procedure is to impose certain rather weak sufficient conditions on the functions we want to consider. Conditions of this kind usually involve one or more statements about the integrability and about the smoothness of the function $f(t)$. The integrability conditions are imposed on the function $f(t)$ to assure the existence of the Fourier integral,

$$\frac{1}{\sqrt{(2\pi)}}\int_{-\infty}^{\infty} f(t)e^{i\omega t}\,dt,$$

and of the function $F(\omega)$ defined by this integral. The smoothness conditions are imposed on the function $f(t)$ to assure that the function is well defined at a particular point on the real axis and can be represented at this point by the inverse transform integral,

$$\frac{1}{\sqrt{(2\pi)}}\int_{-\infty}^{\infty} F(\omega)e^{-i\omega t}\,d\omega$$

For instance, if the function $f(t)$ is absolutely integrable over the real axis, then its Fourier transform integral exists for all real values of ω and its Fourier transform $F(\omega)$ is bounded and continuous for all real values of ω. In addition, let us impose the conditions that the function $f(t)$ is piecewise smooth and is normalized on all finite subintervals of the real axis. This means that the function is piecewise continuous and has a piecewise continuous derivative. In other words, the function is continuous on all finite subintervals of the real axis with the exception of a finite number of bounded discontinuities. Moreover, at a point of discontinuity $t = a$ the function can be represented by its mean value,

$$f(a) = \tfrac{1}{2}[f(a + 0) + f(a - 0)]$$

where $f(a + 0)$ denotes the limit of the function when t tends to a through values larger than a and $f(a - 0)$ is the limit of the function when t tends to a through values smaller than a. Now we can show that the function $f(t)$ has the representation,

$$f(t) = \frac{1}{2}[f(t + 0) + f(t - 0)] = \frac{1}{\sqrt{(2\pi)}}\int_{-\infty}^{\infty} F(\omega)e^{-i\omega t}\,d\omega$$

at all points t on the real axis, provided the integral is a principal value integral.

Less stringent conditions than the Dirichlet conditions considered above require the concept of bounded variation. Let

$$a = a_0 < a_1 < a_2 < \cdots < a_M = b$$

denote an arbitrary partition of the interval (a, b). Then the function $f(t)$ is of bounded variation on the interval (a, b), provided the sum,

$$\sum_{m=1}^{M} |f(a_m) - f(a_{m-1})|$$

has a finite bound which does not depend on the integer M. In more geometrical terms we may also say that the graph of a function of bounded variation has a finite length. A function of bounded variation has only a finite number of maxima and minima on a finite interval and can be written as the difference of two monotonically increasing functions. It has, therefore, a finite number of jump discontinuities on a finite interval. At these jumps the limits $f(a + 0)$ and $f(a - 0)$ exist and the function can be normalized. If a function $f(t)$ is of bounded variation on any finite subinterval of the real axis and is absolutely integrable over the real axis, then the Fourier transform $F(\omega)$ of this function exists and the function $f(t)$ has the representation,

$$f(t) = \frac{1}{2}[f(t+0) + f(t-0)] = \frac{1}{\sqrt{(2\pi)}} \int_{-\infty}^{\infty} F(\omega) e^{-i\omega t}\, d\omega$$

at all points of the real axis, provided the integral is a principal value integral.

In some situations of practical interest these conditions are too stringent. For instance, we may want to consider functions which are truncated and vanish outside some finite subinterval of the real axis. Functions of this type, of course, do not have to be absolutely integrable over the whole real axis. Applications of a more theoretical nature may require that the functions considered are integrable square in the sense of Riemann or Lebesgue. In other words, we now must impose the condition that the Riemann or Lebesgue integral of the square of the magnitude of the function,

$$\int_{-\infty}^{\infty} |f(t)|^2\, dt$$

exists.

A mathematically symmetric theory of Fourier transforms can be built for the class of functions which are square integrable in the sense of Lebesgue. This theory is based on the concept of mean square convergence. A sequence of functions $\{f_m(t)\}$, which are defined and square integrable on the interval (a, b), converges in the mean square to a function $f(t)$ which is also square integrable on the interval (a, b), if the integral,

$$\int_a^b |f(t) - f_m(t)|^2 \, dt$$

vanishes almost everywhere when m tends to infinity. In more physical terms we may also say that the error $|f(t) - f_m(t)|$ is minimized in the sense of a least square approximation. According to a theorem of Plancherel, we can show that if the function $f(t)$ is square integrable over the real axis, then there exists a square integrable function $F(\omega)$ which is the limit in the mean of the sequence of functions,

$$F(\omega, a) = \frac{1}{\sqrt{(2\pi)}} \int_{-a}^{a} f(t) e^{i\omega t} \, dt$$

when a tends to infinity, that is,

$$\lim_{a \to \infty} \int_{-\infty}^{\infty} |F(\omega) - F(\omega, a)|^2 \, d\omega = 0$$

This function $F(\omega)$ is the Fourier transform of the function $f(t)$,

$$F(\omega) = \frac{1}{\sqrt{(2\pi)}} \int_{-\infty}^{\infty} f(t) e^{i\omega t} \, dt$$

Conversely, it car be shown that the sequence of functions,

$$f(t, a) = \frac{1}{\sqrt{(2\pi)}} \int_{-a}^{a} F(\omega) e^{-i\omega t} \, d\omega$$

converges in the mean square,

$$\lim_{a \to \infty} \int_{-\infty}^{\infty} |f(t) - f(t, a)|^2 \, dt = 0$$

to the square integrable function,

$$f(t) = \frac{1}{\sqrt{(2\pi)}} \int_{-\infty}^{\infty} F(\omega) e^{-i\omega t} \, d\omega$$

which is the inverse transform of the square integrable function $F(\omega)$.

As may be noted from this short discussion, a rigorous justification of the transform technique can be a lengthy and complicated affair. To go deeply into such rigorous investigations, however, is completely outside the scope of this book and the subsequent discussions on the special properties of Fourier transforms and on the application of the Fourier transform technique to problems in mathematical physics and engineering will be on a formal level. In other words, we shall in general take it for granted that the functions considered have Fourier transforms and that these Fourier transforms can be inverted. We shall also feel free to interchange the order of integration in the manipulation of such integral transforms without going through lengthy justifications. As we noted in the introduction to this chapter, such a procedure is perfectly satisfactory provided that the results obtained are subjected *a posteriori* to a conscientious verification by other means.

2.5 SOME ELEMENTARY PROPERTIES OF BILATERAL FOURIER TRANSFORMS

To evaluate and invert Fourier transforms efficiently it is convenient to have the following simple rules at our disposal. Assuming that $F(\omega)$ denotes the Fourier transform of the function $f(t)$ and that a and b are arbitrary real constants, we find:

1. The function $F(\omega/a)/|a|$ is the Fourier transform of the function $f(at)$. This assertion can be verified by making the substitution $t_0 = at$ in the integral,

$$\frac{1}{\sqrt{(2\pi)}}\int_{-\infty}^{\infty} f(at)e^{i\omega t}\,dt$$

and by observing that for negative values of a the limits of the integral are interchanged.

2. The function $F(\omega)\exp(ia\omega)$ is the Fourier transform of the function $f(t-a)$. Substituting $t_0 = t - a$ into the Fourier integral,

$$\frac{1}{\sqrt{(2\pi)}}\int_{-\infty}^{\infty} f(t-a)e^{i\omega t}\,dt$$

immediately yields the required result.

3. The function $F(\omega + a)$ is the Fourier transform of the function $f(t)\exp(iat)$.

4. The function $F\left(\frac{\omega + a}{b}\right)\Big/\left|b\right|$ is the Fourier transform of the function $f(bt)\exp(iat)$.

5. The function $(-i\omega)^m F(\omega)$ is the Fourier transform of the m-th derivative of the function $f(t)$, provided that the first $(m-1)$ derivatives of this function vanish when t tends to plus or minus infinity. This rule can be verified through integration by parts.

6. The function $(it)^m f(t)$ is the inverse transform of the m-th derivative of the Fourier transform $F(\omega)$ of the function $f(t)$.

We shall frequently encounter the convolution or convolution integral,

$$\int_{-\infty}^{\infty} g(t-t_0)f(t_0)\,dt_0$$

of two functions $g(t)$ and $f(t)$. Assuming that the Fourier transforms $G(\omega)$ and $F(\omega)$ of these two functions exist the Fourier transform of the convolution takes the form,

$$\frac{1}{\sqrt{(2\pi)}}\int_{-\infty}^{\infty} e^{i\omega t}\,dt \int_{-\infty}^{\infty} g(t-t_0)f(t_0)\,dt_0 = \sqrt{(2\pi)}G(\omega)F(\omega)$$

To justify the manipulations which are necessary to derive this relation, it is sufficient to require that the functions $f(t)$ and $g(t)$ are absolutely integrable or that one of these functions is absolutely integrable and the other function is the inverse transform of an absolutely integrable Fourier transform. In the latter case the function $\sqrt{(2\pi)}G(\omega)F(\omega)$ is also absolutely integrable and has an inverse,

$$\int_{-\infty}^{\infty} g(t-t_0)f(t_0)\,dt_0$$

If we assume that the inverse transforms $f(t)$ and $g(t)$ of the Fourier transforms $F(\omega)$ and $G(\omega)$ exist, we obtain, by substituting the inverse integral transforms into the convolution integral and using the Fourier representation of the delta function, the relation

$$\int_{-\infty}^{\infty} g(t-t_0)f(t_0)\,dt_0 = \int_{-\infty}^{\infty} G(\omega)F(\omega)e^{-i\omega t}\,d\omega$$

We now set $t = 0$ and we replace $g(-t)$ by $g(t)$ in the integral on the left hand side of this equation. This requires that we also replace $G(\omega)$ by $G(-\omega)$ in the integral on the right hand side of the equation, and we find

$$\int_{-\infty}^{\infty} g(t)f(t)\,dt = \int_{-\infty}^{\infty} G(-\omega)F(\omega)\,d\omega$$

Replacing, moreover, the function $g(t)$ by its complex conjugate $g^*(t)$ we simultaneously need to replace the function $G(-\omega)$ by the complex conjugate $G^*(\omega)$ of the function $G(\omega)$. This yields the Parseval relation between two functions $f(t)$ and $g(t)$ and their Fourier transforms $F(\omega)$ and $G(\omega)$,

$$\int_{-\infty}^{\infty} g^*(t)f(t)\,dt = \int_{-\infty}^{\infty} G^*(\omega)F(\omega)\,d\omega$$

If $g(t)$ is set equal to $f(t)$ this relation takes the well-known form,

$$\int_{-\infty}^{\infty} |f(t)|^2\,dt = \int_{-\infty}^{\infty} |F(\omega)|^2\,d\omega$$

The following assertion is known as the Riemann-Lebesgue lemma. The Fourier transform,

$$F(\omega) = \frac{1}{\sqrt{(2\pi)}} \int_{-\infty}^{\infty} f(t) e^{i\omega t} \, dt$$

vanishes when ω tends to plus or minus infinity. For, assuming that the function $f(t)$ is absolutely integrable over the real axis, we find

$$\frac{1}{\sqrt{(2\pi)}} \int_{-\infty}^{-a} f(t) e^{i\omega t} \, dt + \frac{1}{\sqrt{(2\pi)}} \int_{a}^{\infty} f(t) e^{i\omega t} \, dt = o(1)$$

when a tends to infinity, and we may write, therefore,

$$F(\omega, a) = \frac{1}{\sqrt{(2\pi)}} \int_{-a}^{a} f(t) e^{i\omega t} \, dt + o(1)$$

where $F(\omega, a)$ tends to the Fourier transform $F(\omega)$ of the function $f(t)$ when a tends to infinity. Integration by parts yields the relation,

$$F(\omega, a) = \frac{1}{i\omega} [e^{i\omega a} f(a) - e^{-i\omega a} f(-a)] + \frac{1}{i\omega} \int_{-a}^{a} \frac{df}{dt} e^{i\omega t} \, dt + o(1)$$

Keeping a fixed and assuming that the function $f(t)$ is boundedly differentiable on any finite subinterval of the real axis, the first two terms of this expression vanish when ω tends to plus or minus infinity. If we subsequently let a tend to infinity we obtain the desired result.

To conclude this section we shall present the Fourier transforms of some elementary functions which are of frequent occurrence in the mathematical analysis of problems in theoretical physics.

1. The Fourier transform of the Dirac delta function $\delta(t)$ can be found immediately from the definition of this function,

$$\frac{1}{\sqrt{(2\pi)}} \int_{-\infty}^{\infty} \delta(t) e^{i\omega t} \, dt = \frac{1}{\sqrt{(2\pi)}}$$

Inverting the transform, we obtain the Fourier integral representation of the delta function,

$$\delta(t) = \frac{1}{2\pi} \int_{-\infty}^{\infty} e^{-i\omega t} \, d\omega$$

The Fourier integral on the right hand side of the equation represents the spectral resolution of the delta function. The amplitude per unit frequency interval is $1/2\pi$.

2. The Fourier transform of the signum or sign function $\varepsilon(t)$, which was introduced in Section 1.1, takes the form,

$$\frac{1}{\sqrt{(2\pi)}}\int_{-\infty}^{\infty}\varepsilon(t)e^{i\omega t}\,dt = \frac{1}{\sqrt{(2\pi)}}\frac{2i}{\omega}$$

This result can be verified immediately by evaluating the inverse transform integral,

$$\frac{i}{\pi}\int_{-\infty}^{\infty}\frac{e^{-i\omega t}}{\omega}\,d\omega = \frac{2}{\pi}\int_{0}^{\infty}\frac{\sin\omega t}{\omega}\,d\omega = \varepsilon(t)$$

since the second integral is the Dirichlet integral which is a well-known representation of the sign function. The spectral resolution of the sign function is given by the integral,

$$\varepsilon(t) = \frac{i}{\pi}\int_{-\infty}^{\infty}\frac{e^{-i\omega t}}{\omega}\,d\omega$$

and has the complex amplitude $i/\pi\omega$ per unit frequency interval.

3. The Fourier transform of the unit step function $\theta(t) = [1 + \varepsilon(t)]/2$ can be obtained by using the results for the delta and sign function. We find

$$\frac{1}{\sqrt{(2\pi)}}\int_{-\infty}^{\infty}\theta(t)e^{i\omega t}\,dt = \frac{1}{\sqrt{(2\pi)}}\left[\pi\,\delta(\omega) - \frac{1}{i\omega}\right]$$

or, in terms of the Heisenberg delta function,

$$\delta_+(\omega) = \frac{1}{2}\,\delta(\omega) - \frac{1}{2\pi i\omega}$$

we may also write

$$\frac{1}{\sqrt{(2\pi)}}\int_{-\infty}^{\infty}\theta(t)e^{i\omega t}\,dt = \sqrt{(2\pi)}\delta_+(\omega)$$

The inverse Fourier transform of the $\theta(\omega)$ function takes the form,

$$\frac{1}{\sqrt{(2\pi)}}\int_{-\infty}^{\infty}\theta(\omega)e^{-i\omega t}\,d\omega = \sqrt{(2\pi)}\delta_+^*(\omega)$$

where $\delta_+^*(\omega)$ is the complex conjugate of Heisenberg's delta function,

$$\delta_+^*(\omega) = \frac{1}{2}\,\delta(\omega) + \frac{1}{2\pi i\omega} = \delta_-(\omega)$$

4. The Fourier transform of the Gaussian $\phi(t) = \exp(-t^2/2\sigma^2)$ is the Gaussian $\Phi(\omega) = \sigma\exp(-\sigma^2\omega^2/2)$ where σ denotes a positive real number.

This statement can be verified as follows,

$$\Phi(\omega) = \frac{1}{\sqrt{(2\pi)}} \int_{-\infty}^{\infty} \exp{(i\omega t - t^2/2\sigma^2)}\, dt$$

$$= \frac{\exp{(-\omega^2\sigma^2/2)}}{\sqrt{(2\pi)}} \int_{-\infty}^{\infty} \exp\left[-\left(\frac{t}{\sigma} - i\omega\sigma\right)^2 /2\right] dt$$

We now make the substitution $\sigma\zeta = t - i\omega\sigma^2$ in the integral above and obtain

$$\Phi(\omega) = \frac{\sigma \exp{(-\omega^2\sigma^2/2)}}{\sqrt{(2\pi)}} \int_{-\infty - i\omega\sigma}^{\infty - i\omega\sigma} \exp{(-\zeta^2/2)}\, d\zeta$$

For a fixed value of ω the path $(-\infty - i\omega\sigma,\ \infty - i\omega\sigma)$ can be replaced by the path $(-\infty, \infty)$. For let us consider the contour integral,

$$\oint_C \exp{(-\zeta^2/2)}\, d\zeta$$

where C is the contour shown in Figure II-1.

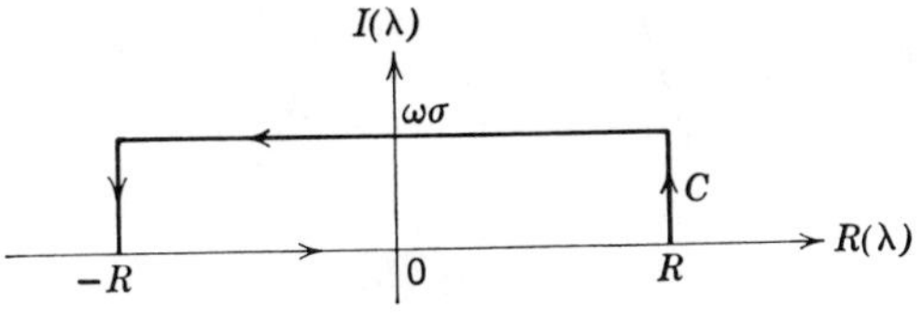

Figure II-1

Since the function $\exp{(-\lambda^2/2)}$ is analytic inside the contour, the contour integral vanishes according to Cauchy's theorem. Furthermore, the contribution of the vertical sides of the contour to the contour integral vanishes as R tends to infinity and we obtain therefore

$$\Phi(\omega) = \frac{\sigma \exp{(-\omega^2\sigma^2/2)}}{\sqrt{(2\pi)}} \int_{-\infty}^{\infty} \exp{(-\zeta^2/2)}\, d\zeta = \sigma \exp{(-\sigma^2\omega^2/2)}$$

5. The Fourier transform,

$$R(\omega) = \frac{1}{\sqrt{(2\pi)}} \frac{2 \sin \omega T}{\omega}$$

of the rectangular wave train of finite duration,

$$r(t) = \theta(t + T) - \theta(t - T)$$

shown in Figure II-2, can be found by simple integration. Inverting the Fourier

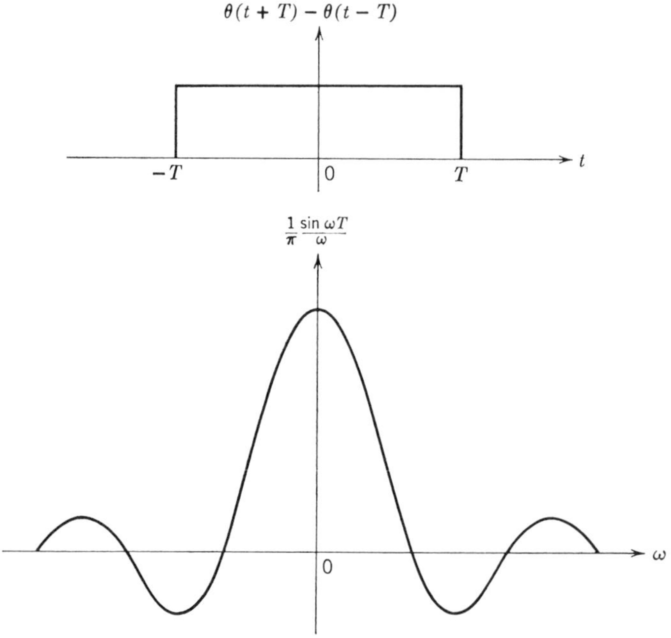

Figure II-2

transform, we obtain the spectral resolution of a rectangular wave train of finite duration,

$$r(t) = \frac{1}{\pi} \int_{-\infty}^{\infty} \frac{\sin \omega T}{\omega} e^{-i\omega t} \, d\omega$$

In frequency space, the disturbance in the neighborhood of the frequency ω has the amplitude,

$$A(\omega) = \frac{1}{\pi} \frac{\sin \omega T}{\omega}$$

per unit frequency interval.

6. The Fourier transform of the triangular wave train of finite duration,

$$\Delta(t) = \left[1 - \frac{t\varepsilon(t)}{T}\right][\theta(t + T) - \theta(t - T)]$$

can also be obtained by simple integration and we find

$$\Delta(\omega) = \frac{1}{\sqrt{(2\pi)}} \frac{4 \sin^2 \omega T/2}{\omega^2 T}$$

The spectral resolution of this wave train shown in Figure II-3 can be obtained

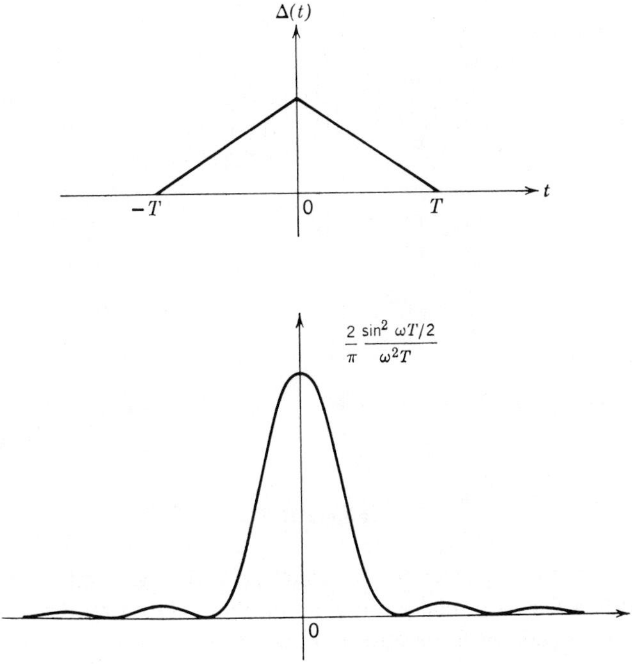

Figure II-3

by inverting the Fourier transform,

$$\Delta(t) = \frac{2}{\pi} \int_{-\infty}^{\infty} \frac{\sin^2 \omega T/2}{\omega^2 T} e^{-i\omega t} \, d\omega$$

In this case, the disturbance in the neighborhood of the frequency ω has the amplitude,

$$A(\omega) = \frac{2}{\pi} \frac{\sin^2 \omega T/2}{\omega^2 T}$$

per unit frequency interval.

7. The Fourier transform of the harmonic wave train of finite duration,

$$h(t) = \cos \omega_0 t[\theta(t + T) - \theta(t - T)]$$

shown in Figure II-4, takes the form,

$$H(\omega) = \frac{1}{\sqrt{(2\pi)}}\left[\frac{\sin(\omega_0 + \omega)T}{\omega_0 + \omega} + \frac{\sin(\omega - \omega_0)T}{\omega - \omega_0}\right]$$

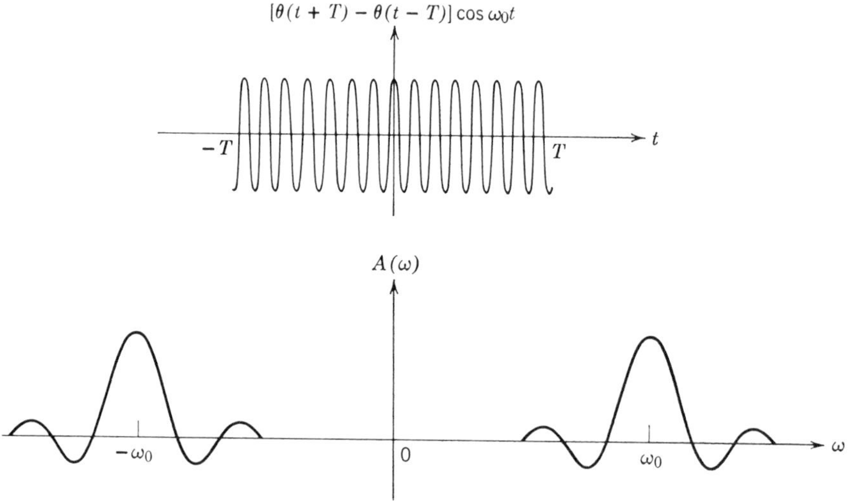

Figure II-4

A wave train of this type can be used to describe the light emitted by an atom in its transition from one energy state to another. The spectral resolution of a harmonic wave train of finite duration may be written

$$h(t) = \frac{1}{2\pi}\int_{-\infty}^{\infty}\left[\frac{\sin(\omega_0 + \omega)T}{\omega_0 + \omega} + \frac{\sin(\omega - \omega_0)T}{\omega - \omega_0}\right]e^{-i\omega t}\, d\omega$$

and the amplitude of the disturbance in frequency space is given by

$$A(\omega) = \frac{1}{2\pi}\left[\frac{\sin(\omega_0 + \omega)T}{\omega_0 + \omega} + \frac{\sin(\omega - \omega_0)T}{\omega - \omega_0}\right]$$

2.6 BILATERAL FOURIER TRANSFORMS, LINEAR PHYSICAL SYSTEMS, AND GREEN'S FUNCTIONS

The Fourier integral,

$$f(t) = \frac{1}{\sqrt{(2\pi)}}\int_{-\infty}^{\infty} F(\omega)e^{-i\omega t}\, d\omega$$

represents the Fourier resolution or frequency decomposition of an arbitrary time-dependent physical quantity described by the function $f(t)$ in its harmonic components. From this point of view, the integral is the limit of an infinite sum of simple harmonic components of angular frequency ω and amplitude $F(\omega)\,d\omega$. The function $F(\omega)$ is the spectral density or amplitude per unit frequency interval of the function $f(t)$. It is in general a complex valued function of the real variable ω. The square of the absolute value of the amplitude is the energy density or the energy per unit frequency interval. This name is derived from the use of the Fourier resolution method in the analysis of radiative processes. In such an analysis it is shown that the radiated power as a function of time is related to the square of the absolute value of the amplitude of the field intensity. For in a radiation field the radiated power is proportional to the square of the absolute value of the field intensity, $P(t) = A|f(t)|^2$, where A is some proportionality constant. Consequently, the total radiated energy is equal to the integral of the quantity $A|f(t)|^2$ over all time. Resolving the field intensity in Fourier components, we find by Parseval's theorem that the total radiated energy is also proportional to the integral of the quantity $|F(\omega)|^2$ over all frequencies,

$$A\int_{-\infty}^{\infty} |f(t)|^2\,dt = A\int_{-\infty}^{\infty} |F(\omega)|^2\,d\omega$$

In other words, the total energy is proportional to the integral of the energy in each harmonic component. The quantity $|F(\omega)|^2$ is a measure therefore of the energy radiated per unit frequency interval.

The spectral analysis or frequency decomposition technique is a valuable tool in the study of wave and oscillatory motions. In the implementation of this technique we first decompose a complex time-dependent system into its harmonic components. The simpler systems obtained in this manner can usually be analyzed more easily and the results of such an analysis can then be synthesized into corresponding results for the more complex system. Such a procedure is feasible if the physical system is linear.

For a linear physical system the validity of the spectral analysis or frequency decomposition technique is guaranteed by the principle of superposition. According to this principle, the effect on the system due to two or more superposed causes is the sum of the effects on the system due to the individual causes. For instance, in the language of the displacement-driving force relationship of a harmonic oscillator, the displacement due to two or more superposed driving forces is the sum of the displacements due to the individual driving forces. In the electrostatic analogy, the potential due to two or more superposed charges is the sum of the potentials due to the individual charges. Finally, in terms of the well-known input-output relationship of linear electrical networks, the output of the system due to two or more superposed inputs is equal to the sum of the outputs due to the individual inputs.

Linear physical systems can be described mathematically by linear differential or integral equations. Such equations can be written symbolically in the operator notation,

$$Hx(\mathbf{r}, t) = f(\mathbf{r}, t)$$

where H is a linear differential or integral operator, $f(\mathbf{r}, t)$ is a known function, and $x(\mathbf{r}, t)$ is the solution of the equation. Linear differential or integral equations are characterized by the fact that the solution of the equation with two or more inhomogeneous terms is equal to the sum of the solutions of the equations with the separate inhomogeneous terms. Symbolically, we can express this by writing

$$H[ax(\mathbf{r}, t) + by(\mathbf{r}, t)] = aHx(\mathbf{r}, t) + bHy(\mathbf{r}, t) = f(\mathbf{r}, t) + g(\mathbf{r}, t)$$

where a and b are two arbitrary real or complex constants. The rules of operation of such linear operators conform, therefore, to the requirements of the principle of superposition.

In this chapter we shall be concerned with systems in which time is the only independent variable,

$$Hx(t) = f(t)$$

In addition we shall require that the system is invariant under translations of the time axis. This implies that the differential or integral equations, which are used to describe such a system, do not contain time in an explicit fashion. For instance, if H denotes a differential operator, then the coefficients of the solution and its derivatives must be constants. In this case we may also write

$$Hx(t - t_0) = f(t - t_0)$$

The cause and effect relationship of a time-dependent linear physical system can most easily be described by means of the influence or Green's function. In this context, the Green's function $G(t \mid t_0)$ can be interpreted as the effect at time t due to an impulse cause of unit magnitude at time t_0. The linearity of the physical system and the principle of superposition then yield the relationship,

$$x(t) = \int_{-\infty}^{\infty} G(t \mid t_0) f(t_0)\, dt_0 \tag{2.9}$$

between the effect $x(t)$ at time t and a cause $f(t_0)$ at time t_0.

Let H denote the operator which maps the function $x(t)$ into the function $f(t)$,

$$Hx(t) = f(t) \tag{2.10}$$

Then, operating with H on both sides of equation (2.9), we formally obtain the relation,

$$Hx(t) = \int_{-\infty}^{\infty} HG(t \mid t_0) f(t_0)\, dt_0$$

This relationship can only be true if

$$HG(t \mid t_0) = \delta(t - t_0)$$

where $\delta(t)$ denotes Dirac's delta function. This equation confirms our interpretation of the Green's function $G(t \mid t_0)$ as the effect at time t due to an impulse cause of unit magnitude at time t_0.

We note that equation (2.10) is the inverse of the equation,

$$x(t) = \int_{-\infty}^{\infty} G(t \mid t_0) f(t_0)\, dt_0$$

This enables us to define an inverse operator H^{-1} such that,

$$x(t) = H^{-1} f(t) = \int_{-\infty}^{\infty} G(t \mid t_0) f(t_0)\, dt_0$$

If the physical system considered is invariant under a transformation involving a translation of the time axis, then

$$G(t \mid t_0) = G(t - t_0)$$

In this case we obtain the equation,

$$x(t) = \int_{-\infty}^{\infty} G(t - t_0) f(t_0)\, dt_0 = \int_{-\infty}^{\infty} G(t_0) f(t - t_0)\, dt_0$$

and the system is completely determined by its Green's function $G(t)$. The shape of this equation is familiar from the convolution theorem of the previous section. Assuming that the functions $x(t)$, $f(t)$, and $G(t)$ satisfy some weak sufficient conditions, we obtain, by means of the convolution theorem, the relationship,

$$X(\omega) = G(\omega) F(\omega)$$

between the Fourier transforms of these functions. The factor $\sqrt{(2\pi)}$ is absorbed in the Fourier transform of the Green's function. In frequency space therefore the relationship between the Fourier transforms of the effect, cause, and Green's function of a translational invariant linear physical system turns out to be particularly simple. It states that the Fourier transform of the effect function can be obtained from the Fourier transforms of the influence and cause functions by simple multiplication. The effect itself can then be obtained immediately by inverse Fourier transformation. To illustrate this procedure, we shall discuss in the next sections some simple examples taken from the fields of mechanics and electromagnetic theory. We shall analyze these problems using a more elaborate mathematical formalism than is strictly necessary. However, we feel that this approach is justified because it enables us to illustrate some useful mathematical techniques at the hand of some perspicuous physical situations.

2.7 SMALL OSCILLATIONS OF A PHYSICAL SYSTEM ABOUT A POSITION OF STABLE EQUILIBRIUM

The model of a physical system performing small oscillations about a position of stable equilibrium and the interaction of such a system with an external field has been a valuable heuristic aid in many diverse branches of theoretical physics. Let us mention, for instance, the classical investigations on the interaction between harmonically bound electrons and an electromagnetic radiation field or the interaction between such electrons and other charged particles. Studies of this kind, based on the model of a harmonically bound electron, have yielded reliable quantitative results on the scattering, absorption, and dispersion of light in material media and on the passage of charged particles through matter.

Assuming that the potential energy of a system is a function of position $U(\mathbf{x})$, a small displacement of the system from its position of stable equilibrium at the point $\mathbf{x}_0$ induces a force,

$$\mathbf{F}(\mathbf{x}) = -\nabla U(\mathbf{x})$$

which acts to restore the system to its equilibrium position. To evaluate this force, we assume that the displacement of the system from its equilibrium position is small and we expand the potential function at the position $\mathbf{x}$ in a Taylor series about the equilibrium position at $\mathbf{x}_0$,

$$U(\mathbf{x}) = U(\mathbf{x}_0) + (\mathbf{x} - \mathbf{x}_0) \cdot \nabla U(\mathbf{x}_0) + \tfrac{1}{2}((\mathbf{x} - \mathbf{x}_0) \cdot \nabla)^2 U(\mathbf{x}_0) + \cdots$$

Retaining only terms of second order in the displacement $(\mathbf{x} - \mathbf{x}_0)$ and imposing the equilibrium condition,

$$\nabla U(\mathbf{x}_0) = 0$$

we obtain the following expression for the potential energy of the system at the point $\mathbf{x}$,

$$U(\mathbf{x}) = U(\mathbf{x}_0) + \tfrac{1}{2}[(\mathbf{x} - \mathbf{x}_0) \cdot \nabla]^2 U(\mathbf{x}_0)$$

Without loss of generality we may require that the potential energy of the system vanishes at the point $\mathbf{x}_0$ and we may choose the equilibrium position to be located at the origin of the coordinate system. This yields the simple expression,

$$U(\mathbf{x}) = \tfrac{1}{2}(\mathbf{x} \cdot \nabla)^2 U(0)$$

for the potential energy of the system at the point $\mathbf{x}$. The restoring force can now be written as follows,

$$\mathbf{F}(\mathbf{x}) = -\nabla[\tfrac{1}{2}(\mathbf{x} \cdot \nabla)^2 U(0)]$$

These vector relations for the potential energy and the restoring force of the system simplify considerably in the one-dimensional case. For one-dimensional configurations the potential energy of the system takes the form,

$$U(x) = \tfrac{1}{2}kx^2$$

where k denotes the second derivative of the potential energy at the origin. This is the well-known expression for the potential energy of a harmonic oscillator. For the restoring force we obtain in the one-dimensional case the expression,

$$F(x) = -dU/dx = -kx$$

Thus, the equation of motion of a one-dimensional system which oscillates about a position of stable equilibrium is, according to Newton's second law, the simple harmonic oscillator equation,

$$\ddot{x}(t) + \omega_0{}^2 x(t) = 0$$

where $\omega_0{}^2 = k/m$ denotes the square of the natural or resonance frequency and m denotes the mass of the system. Consequently, as a result of a small displacement from its position of stable equilibrium, the system will perform harmonic oscillations under the influence of a linear elastic restoring force. The natural or resonance frequency of the oscillations $\omega_0 = \sqrt{(k/m)}$ is a function of the physical properties of the system. The total energy of such a system is a constant of the motion and, being the sum of the kinetic and potential energy, it takes the form,

$$E = (m\dot{x}^2 + kx^2)/2$$

Now let us place the system in an external, time-dependent, force field of strength $f(t)$. Since the oscillations are assumed to be small the external field must be weak. The equation of motion which describes the motion of the system in the external field now has an inhomogeneous term. It is the forced harmonic oscillator equation,

$$\ddot{x}(t) + \omega_0{}^2 x(t) = f(t)/m$$

where $\omega_0 = \sqrt{(k/m)}$ again denotes the natural frequency of the system.

The solution of this equation can be obtained by means of a Green's function technique. In this context the Green's function $G(t \mid t_0)$ is the solution of the equation,

$$\ddot{G}(t \mid t_0) + \omega_0{}^2 G(t \mid t_0) = \delta(t - t_0)/m$$

and can be interpreted as the displacement of the system at time t due to an impulse of unit magnitude at time t_0. Consequently, the Green's function vanishes at all times earlier than t_0. This causality condition actually enables us to determine the appropriate solution of the Green's function equation. We note, moreover, that the Green's function equation is invariant with respect to transformations involving a translation of the time axis. This implies that the Green's function depends on the time difference $t - t_0$ only. We now introduce the following integral representation of the Green's function,

$$G(t - t_0) = \frac{1}{2\pi} \int_{-\infty}^{\infty} G(\omega) e^{-i\omega(t - t_0)} \, d\omega$$

This amounts to the resolution of the Green's function in its harmonic components. Introducing this representation and the well-known representation for the delta function,

$$\delta(t - t_0) = \frac{1}{2\pi} \int_{-\infty}^{\infty} e^{-i\omega(t - t_0)} \, d\omega$$

into the forced harmonic oscillator equation, we obtain the following expression for the amplitude of the Green's function,

$$G(\omega) = \frac{1}{m(\omega_0{}^2 - \omega^2)}$$

Substitution of this expression into the Fourier integral representation of the Green's function yields the integral representation,

$$G(t - t_0) = \frac{1}{2\pi m} \int_{-\infty}^{\infty} \frac{e^{-i\omega(t - t_0)}}{\omega_0{}^2 - \omega^2} \, d\omega$$

This integral can easily be evaluated by means of contour integration in the complex $\lambda = \omega + i\gamma$ plane. To accomplish this, we write

$$G(t - t_0) = \lim_{R \to \infty} \frac{1}{2\pi m} \int_{-R}^{R} \frac{e^{-i\omega(t - t_0)}}{\omega_0{}^2 - \omega^2} \, d\omega$$

and close the contour by a semicircle in the upper or lower half plane. The choice of the contour depends on the sign of the time increment $t - t_0$. If we want to evaluate the Green's function at a time later than t_0 we must close the contour in the lower half plane. In this case, the convergence factor exp $\gamma(t - t_0)$ in the integrand will have a negative exponent. Similarly, the contour must be closed in the upper half plane if we want to obtain the Green's function at a time earlier than t_0. Furthermore, the contribution of the semi-circle to the contour integral vanishes when the radius R of the semicircle tends to infinity. The Green's function can be represented therefore by the contour integral,

$$G(t - t_0) = \lim_{R\to\infty} \frac{1}{2\pi m} \oint_C \frac{e^{-i(t-t_0)\zeta}}{{\omega_0}^2 - \zeta^2}\, d\zeta$$

This integral can be evaluated by means of Cauchy's theorem and the residue theorem. The integrand has simple poles at the points ω_0 and $-\omega_0$ on the real axis. This places us in a dilemma. For we must decide whether the contour for $t < t_0$ or the contour for $t > t_0$ encloses the poles of the integrand. However, the decision is made easy by the causality condition which is imposed on the Green's function. According to this condition, the Green's function vanishes at all times t which are earlier than time t_0. For these values of t the contour must be closed in the upper half plane, as shown in Figure II-5.

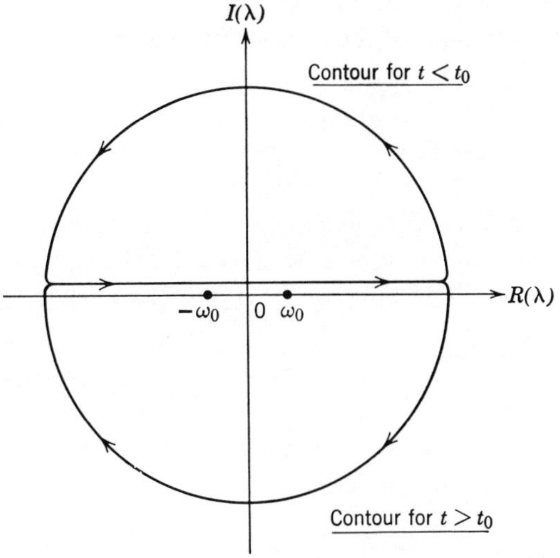

Figure II-5

Hence, letting the horizontal part of the contour run just above the real axis we find, according to Cauchy's theorem,

$$G(t - t_0) = 0$$

at times t earlier than t_0, since the integrand is analytic inside the contour.

Thus, the poles of the integrand are located inside the contour which is closed in the lower half plane and we obtain, by the residue theorem,

$$G(t - t_0) = 2\pi i \sum \text{Res}\left[\frac{e^{-i(t-t_0)\zeta}}{2\pi m(\zeta^2 - \omega_0{}^2)}, \pm\omega_0\right] = \frac{1}{m}\frac{\sin\omega_0(t - t_0)}{\omega_0}$$

at all times t later than t_0. Thus we have found the Green's function $G(t \mid t_0)$ for the forced harmonic oscillator,

$$G(t - t_0) = \frac{1}{m}\frac{\sin\omega_0(t - t_0)}{\omega_0}\,\theta(t - t_0)$$

where $\theta(t)$ denotes the unit step function.

The causal solution of the harmonic oscillator equation with an impulse-driving force of unit magnitude is also called the retarded Green's function $G_R(t \mid t_0)$. This is in contrast to the advanced Green's function $G_A(t \mid t_0)$ which satisfies the condition,

$$G_A(t \mid t_0) = 0$$

at all times later than t_0. The advanced Green's function can be obtained by letting the horizontal part of the contour run just below the real axis. In this case we find

$$G_A(t \mid t_0) = \frac{1}{m}\frac{\sin\omega_0(t - t_0)}{\omega_0}\,[1 - \theta(t - t_0)]$$

In terms of the retarded Green's function (or the response at time t due to a delta pulse of unit magnitude at time t_0) the actual response or displacement $x(t)$ of our system at time t due to the force $f(t_0)$ at time t_0 is

$$x(t) = \int_{-\infty}^{\infty} G(t - t_0)f(t_0)\,dt_0 = \frac{1}{m\omega_0}\int_{-\infty}^{t} \sin\omega_0(t - t_0)f(t_0)\,dt_0$$

A quantity of special interest is the total energy ΔE transferred to the oscillating system by the external field,

$$\begin{aligned}\Delta E &= \frac{1}{2}m[\dot{x}^2(\infty) + \omega_0{}^2x^2(\infty)]\\ &= \frac{1}{2}m[\dot{x}(\infty) + i\omega_0 x(\infty)][\dot{x}(\infty) - i\omega_0 x(\infty)]\\ &= \frac{1}{2m}\left|\int_{-\infty}^{\infty} f(t_0)e^{i\omega_0(t-t_0)}\,dt_0\right|^2\end{aligned}$$

The Fourier amplitude of the force $f(t)$ at the natural frequency ω_0 is

$$F(\omega_0) = \frac{1}{\sqrt{(2\pi)}} \int_{-\infty}^{\infty} f(t_0) e^{i\omega_0 t_0} \, dt_0$$

We find therefore the relation,

$$\Delta E = \frac{\pi}{m} |F(\omega_0)|^2$$

between the total energy transferred to the system and the Fourier amplitude of the driving force $F(\omega_0)$ at the resonance frequency.

The solution of the forced harmonic oscillator equation breaks down in the resonance region because we have neglected the effect of energy dissipation in the ambient medium. For, in a physically realistic situation the surroundings of the oscillating system are always resistive to the motion. For instance, if we depict a molecule as a harmonic oscillator, then the intermolecular collisions will absorb part of the energy which is stored in the motion of the oscillator. To account for the effects of energy dissipation in the ambient medium we have to add to the right hand side of the equation of motion a resistive force term $-m\Gamma\dot{x}(t)$, where Γ denotes a positive decay or damping constant which has the dimensions of frequency. This results in the following more realistic forced harmonic oscillator equation with a damping term,

$$\ddot{x}(t) + \Gamma\dot{x}(t) + \omega_0^2 x(t) = f(t)/m$$

The Green's function of this physical system is the solution of the same equation but now with a delta function force of unit magnitude,

$$\ddot{G}(t \mid t_0) + \Gamma\dot{G}(t \mid t_0) + \omega_0^2 G(t \mid t_0) = \delta(t - t_0)/m$$

The Fourier amplitude of this Green's function can easily be found to take the form,

$$G(\omega) = \frac{1}{m(\omega_0^2 - \omega^2 - i\Gamma\omega)}$$

It is interesting to note that, considered as a function of the complex variable $\lambda = \omega + i\gamma$, the function $G(\lambda)$ has two poles which are both located in the lower half plane. Consequently, the ambiguity, which arose with respect to the location of the poles of the Green's function of the undamped harmonic oscillator, does not exist for the harmonic oscillator in a dissipative environment. This fact can be used to evaluate the contour integral for the Green's function of the undamped harmonic oscillator. Thus, to find the solution of the Green's function equation for the undamped harmonic oscillator, we first assume that there is a slight energy dissipation in the ambient medium. This introduces a small positive decay constant, ε say, which causes the poles of the amplitude of the Green's function to move from the real axis into the lower half plane. Now there is no ambiguity with respect to the location of these poles and we can immediately perform the contour integration by means of the residue theorem. Having found the Green's function $G(t \mid t_0 \mid \varepsilon)$ for the harmonic oscillator moving in the rarefied medium, we obtain the vacuum solution by letting ε tend to zero,

$$G(t \mid t_0) = \lim_{\varepsilon \to 0} G(t \mid t_0 \mid \varepsilon)$$

The device of the temporary introduction of a dissipative term can also be used, with great benefit, in the formulation of well-posed boundary value problems involving partial differential equations. For instance, in some situations it can be used to replace the radiation condition of Sommerfeld.

Mathematically we can also consider the operator $(d/dt + \varepsilon)^2$ instead of d^2/dt^2. For instance, we can define the Green's function $G(t \mid t_0)$ as the limit as ε tends to zero of the Green's function $G(t \mid t_0 \mid \varepsilon)$ which is the solution of the equation,

$$\left(\frac{d}{dt} + \varepsilon\right)^2 G(t|t_0|\varepsilon) + \omega_0{}^2 G(t|t_0|\varepsilon) = \delta(t - t_0)/m$$

The solution of this equation in frequency space,

$$G(\omega \mid \varepsilon) = \frac{1}{m} \frac{1}{\omega_0{}^2 - (\omega + i\varepsilon)^2}$$

has poles at the point $\omega = \pm\omega_0 - i\varepsilon$ in the lower half of the complex plane. Hence,

$$G(t|t_0|\varepsilon) = \frac{1}{2\pi m} \int_{-\infty}^{\infty} \frac{e^{-i\omega(t-t_0)}}{\omega_0{}^2 - (\omega + i\varepsilon)^2} \, d\omega$$

and by contour integration we find

$$G(t|t_0|\varepsilon) = \frac{1}{m} \frac{\sin \omega_0(t - t_0)}{\omega_0} e^{-\varepsilon(t-t_0)} \theta(t - t_0)$$

Letting ε tend to zero, we obtain the retarded Green's function,

$$G(t \mid t_0) = \lim_{\varepsilon \to 0} G(t|t_0|\varepsilon) = \frac{1}{m} \frac{\sin \omega_0(t - t_0)}{\omega_0} \theta(t - t_0)$$

Similarly, we can obtain the advanced Green's function as the limit, as ε tends to zero, of the function $G(t \mid t_0 \mid \varepsilon)$ which is a solution of the equation,

$$\left(\frac{d}{dt} - \varepsilon\right)^2 G(t|t_0|\varepsilon) + \omega_0{}^2 G(t|t_0|\varepsilon) = \delta(t - t_0)/m$$

Returning to the solution of the damped harmonic oscillator equation, we pause for a moment to study the equation of motion in the space of the transform variable. Fourier transformation of the forced harmonic oscillator equation yields the following simple equation of motion in frequency space,

$$X(\omega) = G(\omega)F(\omega)$$

where $X(\omega)$ and $F(\omega)$ are the Fourier amplitude of the displacement and force, respectively, and $G(\omega)$ denotes the Fourier amplitude of the Green's function,

$$G(\omega) = \frac{1}{m} \frac{1}{\omega_0{}^2 - \omega^2 - i\Gamma\omega}$$

For more general linear physical systems, the Fourier amplitude $G(\omega)$ of the Green's function is also called the susceptibility of the system. Hence, in our case the equation of motion in frequency space simply states that the Fourier transform of the displacement is equal to the susceptibility times the amplitude of the force. The susceptibility, considered as a function of the complex variable $\lambda = \omega + i\gamma$,

$$G(\lambda) = \frac{1}{m} \frac{1}{\omega_0{}^2 - \lambda^2 - i\Gamma\lambda}$$

is analytic in the upper half of the complex plane and vanishes when λ tends to infinity in the upper half plane and on the real axis. We may infer therefore that this function can be represented by the Cauchy integral,

$$G(\lambda) = \frac{1}{2\pi i} \int_{-\infty}^{\infty} \frac{G(\zeta)}{\zeta - \lambda} \, d\zeta$$

If we subsequently let the imaginary part of λ tend to zero so that λ tends to the point ω on the real axis, we obtain, by the method outlined in Section 1.1, the integral representation,

$$G(\omega) = \frac{1}{\pi i} \int_{-\infty}^{\infty} \frac{G(\zeta)}{\zeta - \omega} \, d\zeta$$

This is a so-called dispersion relation for the susceptibility or for the Fourier amplitude of the Green's function of the harmonic oscillator. Taking real and imaginary parts of both sides of the dispersion relation, we obtain the following dispersion relations for the real and imaginary parts of the susceptibility $G(\omega) = D(\omega) + iA(\omega)$,

$$D(\omega) = \frac{1}{\pi} \int_{-\infty}^{\infty} \frac{A(\zeta)}{\zeta - \omega} \, d\zeta$$

and

$$A(\omega) = -\frac{1}{\pi} \int_{-\infty}^{\infty} \frac{D(\zeta)}{\zeta - \omega} \, d\zeta$$

The real part of the susceptibility of a linear physical system is called the dispersive part, whereas the imaginary part is known as the absorptive part. To explain the reason for this last name, let us consider a damped harmonic oscillator in the field of a simple harmonic driving force $f(t) = a \exp(-i\omega t)$. The equation of motion takes the form,

$$\ddot{x}(t) + \Gamma \dot{x}(t) + \omega_0{}^2 x(t) = \frac{a}{m} \exp(-i\omega t)$$

and the steady state solution of this equation may be written as follows,

$$x(t) = R[G(\omega) a e^{-i\omega t}] = \tfrac{1}{2}[G^*(\omega) a^* e^{i\omega t} + G(\omega) a e^{-i\omega t}]$$

The steady state motion of the system is maintained by the action of the external driving force. This force produces the necessary work to overcome the negative action of the dissipative force. The power or rate of work done by the external force field on the harmonic oscillator is

$$\frac{\Delta W}{\Delta t} = f(t)\dot{x}(t) = \frac{i\omega}{4}(a^* e^{i\omega t} + a e^{-i\omega t})[G^*(\omega) a^* e^{i\omega t} - G(\omega) a e^{-i\omega t}]$$

This implies that the energy transfer from the field to the oscillator averaged over one cycle is

$$\langle \Delta E \rangle = \frac{\omega}{2\pi}\int_0^{2\pi/\omega} \dot{x}(t) f(t)\, dt = \frac{i\omega}{4}[G^*(\omega) - G(\omega)]|a|^2 = \frac{\omega}{2}|a|^2 A(\omega)$$

where $A(\omega)$ is the imaginary part of the susceptibility $G(\omega)$. Hence, the average energy dissipated into the ambient medium or the average energy absorbed by the ambient medium is

$$\langle \Delta E \rangle = \frac{\omega}{2}|a|^2 A(\omega)$$

The imaginary part of the susceptibility $G(\omega)$ is therefore proportional to the average energy absorption in the ambient medium.

In the case of the damped harmonic oscillator the dispersive part of the susceptibility $G(\omega)$ takes the form,

$$D(\omega) = \frac{1}{m}\frac{\omega_0{}^2 - \omega^2}{(\omega_0{}^2 - \omega^2)^2 + \Gamma^2\omega^2}$$

whereas the absorptive part of the susceptibility may be written

$$A(\omega) = \frac{1}{m}\frac{\Gamma\omega}{(\omega_0{}^2 - \omega^2)^2 + \Gamma^2\omega^2}$$

In the range of frequencies ω which are small with respect to the resonance frequencies we obtain the simple relations,

$$D(\omega) = \frac{1}{m\omega_0^{\,2}}$$

and

$$A(\omega) = \frac{\Gamma\omega}{m\omega_0^{\,4}}$$

In the neighborhood of the resonance frequency ω_0, however, the absorptive part of the susceptibility is sharply peaked about the point ω_0 and has the shape of the Lorentzian of half width Γ shown in Figure II-6. This clearly

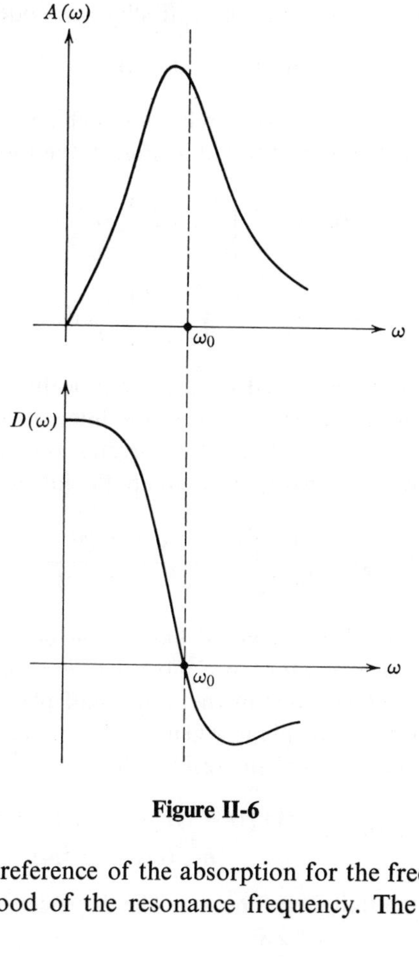

Figure II-6

demonstrates the preference of the absorption for the frequencies in the immediate neighborhood of the resonance frequency. The dispersive part of the susceptibility reverses its shape while going from a positive maximum,

$$\frac{1}{m\omega_0^2}\frac{1}{2(\Gamma/\omega_0) - (\Gamma/\omega_0)^2}$$

at the point $\omega_0\sqrt{(1 - \Gamma/\omega_0)}$ to a negative minimum,

$$-\frac{1}{m\omega_0^2}\frac{1}{2(\Gamma/\omega_0) + (\Gamma/\omega_0)^2}$$

at the point $\omega_0\sqrt{(1 + \Gamma/\omega_0)}$.

The dispersive part of the susceptibility is an even function of ω,

$$D(\omega) = D(-\omega)$$

whereas the absorptive part of the susceptibility is an odd function of ω,

$$A(\omega) = -A(-\omega)$$

These so-called symmetry or crossing relations enable us to bring the dispersion relations for the functions $D(\omega)$ and $A(\omega)$ in the form,

$$D(\omega) = \frac{2}{\pi}\int_0^\infty \frac{\zeta A(\zeta)}{\zeta^2 - \omega^2}\,d\zeta$$

$$A(\omega) = -\frac{2\omega}{\pi}\int_0^\infty \frac{D(\zeta)}{\zeta^2 - \omega^2}\,d\zeta$$

The integration is now performed over the physically meaningful positive frequency range, that is, we have reduced the integration to the physically admissible region $\omega > 0$. To obtain the Green's function $G(t\,|\,t_0)$ of the damped harmonic oscillator we again evaluate the integral,

$$G(t\,|\,t_0) = \frac{1}{2\pi m}\int_{-\infty}^{\infty} \frac{e^{-i\omega(t-t_0)}}{\omega_0^2 - \omega^2 - i\Gamma\omega}\,d\omega$$

by contour integration. The integrand has simple poles in the lower half plane at the points $\omega = \pm\sqrt{(\omega_0^2 - \Gamma^2/4)} - i\Gamma/2 = \pm\,\hat{\omega}_0 - i\Gamma/2$, shown in Figure II-7. Closing the contour in the upper half plane when t is smaller than t_0 and in the lower half plane when t is larger than t_0, we obtain by means of Cauchy's theorem and the residue theorem,

$$G(t\,|\,t_0) = e^{-\Gamma(t-t_0)/2}\,\frac{\sin[(t - t_0)\sqrt{(\omega_0^2 - \Gamma^2/4)}]}{m\sqrt{(\omega_0^2 - \Gamma^2/4)}}\,\theta(t - t_0)$$

where $\theta(t)$ denotes the unit step function. The displacement $x(t)$ can now be

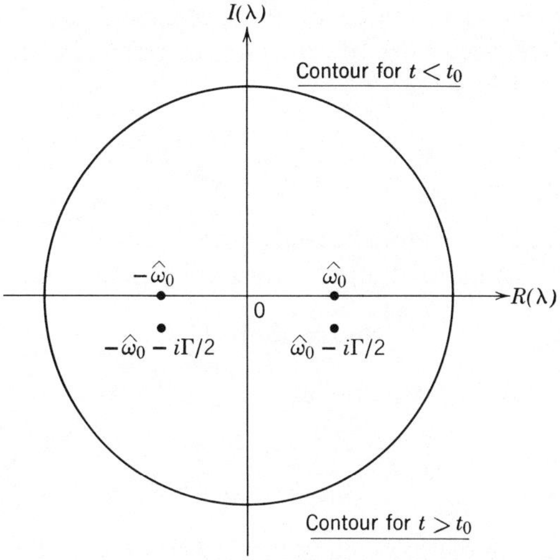

Figure II-7

obtained by evaluating the integral,

$$x(t) = \int_{-\infty}^{\infty} G(t \mid t_0) f(t_0)\, dt_0$$

2.8 ELECTRIC POLARIZATION AND DISPERSION RELATIONS

As an example we shall now apply the ideas of the previous section to the classical computation of the electric dipole moment which is induced in an atom or molecule by a rapidly varying electric field. If an atom or molecule is placed in an electric field, the field displaces the negatively charged electrons with respect to the positively charged nuclei. This transforms an atom or a molecule into a neutral charge configuration with a dipole moment, $\mathbf{p} = e\mathbf{x}$. Here we shall only consider the electronic polarization and we shall neglect the effects of the displacement and orientation polarization of the heavy molecules. The following discussion applies therefore to atoms only. To obtain an analytic expression for the polarization, we picture an atom as an assembly of harmonic oscillators, i.e., we assume that each electron is bounded to an equilibrium position by a spherically symmetric harmonic restoring force of strength $m\omega_0^2\mathbf{x}(t)$. Assuming, moreover, that the dissipative effects of interatomic collisions can be accounted for by a damping term $-m\Gamma\dot{\mathbf{x}}(t)$, the equation of motion of such an electron in a local electric field $\mathbf{E}(t)$ takes the form,

$$\ddot{\mathbf{x}}(t) + \Gamma\dot{\mathbf{x}}(t) + \omega_0^2\mathbf{x}(t) = \frac{e}{m}\,\mathbf{E}(t)$$

where ω_0 is the resonance frequency of the oscillator. The Fourier amplitude of the displacement vector can be expressed, therefore, in terms of the Fourier amplitude of the field vector,

$$\mathbf{X}(\omega) = \frac{e}{m} \frac{\mathbf{E}(\omega)}{\omega_0^2 - \omega^2 - i\Gamma\omega}$$

If we now assume that an atom has only one vibrating electron, then the Fourier amplitude of the induced dipole moment takes the form,

$$\mathbf{p}(\omega) = \alpha(\omega)\varepsilon_0 \mathbf{E}(\omega)$$

where $\alpha(\omega)$ denotes the polarizability,

$$\alpha(\omega) = \frac{e^2}{m\varepsilon_0} \frac{1}{\omega_0^2 - \omega^2 - i\Gamma\omega}$$

and ε_0 is the vacuum dielectric constant. Let us now suppose that our atom is but one of the many atoms of a dilute monatomic gas. If N is the number of atoms per unit volume of the gas, then the polarization $\mathbf{P}$ per unit volume can be defined as,

$$\mathbf{P} = N\mathbf{p} = N\alpha(\omega)\varepsilon_0 \mathbf{E}$$

However, in terms of the electric susceptibility $\chi(\omega)$ and the dielectric constant $\kappa(\omega)$ of the gas we may also write

$$\mathbf{p} = \chi(\omega)\varepsilon_0 \mathbf{E} = [\kappa(\omega) - 1]\varepsilon_0 \mathbf{E}$$

which is the well-known formula for the polarization per unit volume of a substance. Comparing this expression for $\mathbf{P}$ with the penultimate equation, we obtain the following relationship between the susceptibility, the dielectric constant, and the polarizability of a dilute gas,

$$\chi(\omega) = \kappa(\omega) - 1 = N\alpha(\omega)$$

Furthermore, in a medium in which the magnetization can be neglected, the index of refraction, which is the ratio of the velocity of light to the phase velocity in a dielectric, is equal to the square root of the dielectric constant,

$$n(\omega) = \sqrt{\kappa(\omega)}$$

Consequently, the index of refraction can also be related to the polarizability,

$$n(\omega) = \sqrt{[1 + N\alpha(\omega)]}$$

or, in the case of a dilute gas,

$$n(\omega) = 1 + \tfrac{1}{2}N\alpha(\omega)$$

We have obtained, therefore, the following four basic complex quantities which describe the dielectric behavior of a dilute gas,

The polarizability: $$\alpha(\omega) = \frac{e^2}{m\varepsilon_0} \frac{1}{\omega_0^{\ 2} - \omega^2 - i\Gamma\omega}$$

The susceptibility: $$\chi(\omega) = \frac{Ne^2}{m\varepsilon_0} \frac{1}{\omega_0^{\ 2} - \omega^2 - i\Gamma\omega}$$

The dielectric constant $$\kappa(\omega) = 1 + \frac{Ne^2}{m\varepsilon_0} \frac{1}{\omega_0^{\ 2} - \omega^2 - i\Gamma\omega}$$

The refractive index: $$n(\omega) = 1 + \frac{Ne^2}{2m\varepsilon_0} \frac{1}{\omega_0^{\ 2} - \omega^2 - i\Gamma\omega}$$

Considered as a function of the complex variable $\lambda = \omega + i\gamma$, each of these quantities is analytic in the upper half of the complex plane. The polarizability and the susceptibility vanish as λ tends to infinity in the upper half plane and on the real axis while the dielectric constant and the index of refraction tend to unity. Consequently, the real and imaginary parts of these functions obey dispersion relations which, due to the even-odd symmetry of these quantities, involve integrals over positive frequencies only. For instance, for the real and imaginary parts of the refractive index we obtain in this manner the famous Kramers-Kronig relations,

$$R[n(\omega_0) - 1] = \frac{2}{\pi} \int_0^\infty \frac{\omega I[n(\omega)]}{\omega^2 - \omega_0^{\ 2}}\, d\omega$$

and

$$I[n(\omega_0)] = -\frac{2\omega_0}{\pi} \int_0^\infty \frac{R[n(\omega) - 1]}{\omega^2 - \omega_0^{\ 2}}\, d\omega$$

2.9 CLASSICAL MOTION OF A BOUND ELECTRON IN AN ELECTRIC FIELD

As a second example of the application of the Fourier resolution method to problems in theoretical physics, we shall consider the steady state motion of a harmonically bound electron in an electromagnetic field and we shall determine the total energy imparted to the electron by the field. The classical equation of motion of a harmonically bound electron in an electromagnetic field is the Abraham-Lorentz equation,

$$\ddot{\mathbf{x}}(t) + \omega_0^2\,\mathbf{x}(t) = \frac{e}{m}\,[\mathbf{E}(t) + \dot{\mathbf{x}} \times \mathbf{B}(t)] + \frac{\Gamma}{\omega_0^{\ 2}}\,\dddot{\mathbf{x}}(t)$$

where $\mathbf{x}(t)$ denotes the displacement of the electron from its equilibrium position. The first term on the right hand side of this equation represents the total electromagnetic force on an electron moving with a velocity $\dot{\mathbf{x}}(t)$ in an electromagnetic field of electric intensity $\mathbf{E}(t)$ and magnetic intensity $\mathbf{B}(t)$. This is the so-called Lorentz force. Assuming that the electron speed is small with respect to the speed of light, the magnetic force term in the expression for the Lorentz force may be neglected. The second term on the right hand side of the equation of motion represents the radiative reaction force where

$$\Gamma = \frac{e^2 {\omega_0}^2}{6\pi m \varepsilon_0 c^3}$$

is the radiative damping constant. This force accounts for the variation in the motion due to the radiative energy loss experienced by a moving electron. All other possible dissipative influences on the motion of the electron have been neglected.

In the manner described in the foregoing sections we obtain by Fourier resolution of the displacement and field vectors the following simple equation of motion in frequency space,

$$\mathbf{X}(\omega) = G(\omega)\mathbf{E}(\omega)$$

where $G(\omega)$ denotes the Fourier amplitude of the Green's function of the simplified Abraham-Lorentz equation,

$$G(\omega) = \frac{e}{m} \frac{1}{{\omega_0}^2 - \omega^2 - i\Gamma(\omega)\omega}$$

and $\Gamma(\omega) = \Gamma\omega^2/{\omega_0}^2$ is a function of the frequency. It should be noted that in this case the denominator of the susceptibility $G(\lambda)$ is a third degree polynomial of the complex variable λ. This polynomial has three complex roots, one of which is located in the upper half plane $I(\lambda) > 0$. In the evaluation of the Green's function by contour integration, therefore, the contour closed in the upper half plane encloses a pole of the function $G(\lambda)$. This implies that the Green's function $G(t \mid t_0)$ of the Abraham-Lorentz equation is non-vanishing for values of t which are smaller than t_0 and does not satisfy the causality condition. This reflects the fact that the motion of a bound electron in an electromagnetic field as described by the Abraham-Lorentz equation is an acausal physical process.

The total work done by the electric field on the moving electron is given by the integral,

$$W = e\int_{-\infty}^{\infty} \mathbf{E}(t)\dot{\mathbf{x}}(t)\, dt$$

This integral can be evaluated by means of Parseval's relation. Since the Fourier transform of the velocity is equal to $-i\omega$ times the Fourier transform of the displacement, we obtain

$$W = -ie \int_{-\infty}^{\infty} \mathbf{E}^*(\omega)\mathbf{X}(\omega)\omega \, d\omega$$

However, the displacement and the field are real functions of t and the symmetry relations,

$$\mathbf{E}(-\omega) = \mathbf{E}^*(\omega) \quad \text{and} \quad \mathbf{X}(-\omega) = \mathbf{X}^*(\omega)$$

enable us to reduce the integral on the right hand side to an integral over positive frequencies only,

$$W = ei \int_{0}^{\infty} [\mathbf{X}^*(\omega)\mathbf{E}(\omega) - \mathbf{X}(\omega)\mathbf{E}^*(\omega)]\omega \, d\omega$$

To further reduce the integral we make use of the equation of motion in frequency space,

$$\mathbf{X}(\omega) = G(\omega)\mathbf{E}(\omega)$$

to obtain the following expression for the total energy transfer from the field to the electron,

$$\Delta E = 2e \int_{0}^{\infty} A(\omega)|E(\omega)^2|\omega \, d\omega$$

where $A(\omega)$ denotes the absorptive part of the susceptibility $G(\omega)$. Since

$$A(\omega) = \frac{e}{m} \frac{\omega\Gamma(\omega)}{(\omega_0^{\,2} - \omega^2)^2 + \omega^2\Gamma^2(\omega)}$$

the total energy transfer may also be written

$$\Delta E = \frac{2e^2}{m} \int_{0}^{\infty} \frac{|E(\omega)|^2\omega^2\Gamma(\omega)}{(\omega_0^{\,2} - \omega^2)^2 + \omega^2\Gamma^2(\omega)} \, d\omega$$

Thus, if the Fourier amplitude of the field is given, the transferred energy can be computed by the analytical or numerical evaluation of the integral above.

To obtain an approximate expression for ΔE let us assume that the function $\Gamma(\omega)$ is constant. This situation prevails whenever the effect of the radiative reaction can be simulated by a dissipative force term which is proportional to $-\omega_0^{\,2}\dot{\mathbf{x}}(t)$ instead of being proportional to $\dddot{\mathbf{x}}(t)$. For small Γ, the integrand is concentrated about $\omega = \omega_0$. Hence, replacing $\omega + \omega_0$ by 2ω, we find

$$\Delta E = \frac{e^2}{m} \int_{0}^{\infty} \frac{|E(\omega)|^2\Gamma/2}{(\omega_0 - \omega)^2 + (\Gamma/2)^2} \, d\omega$$

Making use of the following well-known representation for the delta function,

$$\lim_{\Gamma \to 0} \frac{\Gamma}{(\omega_0 - \omega)^2 + \Gamma^2} = \pi\delta(\omega - \omega_0)$$

we obtain, in the limit for small values of Γ,

$$\Delta E = \frac{\pi e^2}{m} \int_0^\infty |E(\omega)|^2 \, \delta(\omega - \omega_0) \, d\omega = \frac{\pi e^2}{m} \, |E(\omega_0)|^2$$

Thus the total energy transferred by the electric field to the moving electron is directly proportional to the square of the absolute value of the amplitude of the field at the resonance frequency and is, for vanishingly small dissipation, independent of the damping constant.

2.10 UNILATERAL FOURIER TRANSFORMS

For appropriately defined functions $f(t)$, the unilateral Fourier integral,

$$\frac{1}{\sqrt{(2\pi)}} \int_0^\infty f(t) e^{i\lambda t} \, dt$$

is the integral representation of an analytic function of the complex variable λ. For instance, in Section 2.3 we found that the integral represents an analytic function in the upper half of the complex plane, provided that the function $f(t)$ is absolutely integrable over the positive real axis. Introducing a convergence factor $\exp(-at)$ and assuming that the function $f(t)\exp(-at)$ is absolutely integrable, we find that the unilateral Fourier integral is absolutely and uniformly convergent in the upper half plane $I(\lambda) \geqq a$ and represents a function which is analytic in the upper half plane $I(\lambda) > a$. This function, moreover, is continuous and bounded for all finite values of λ in the half plane $I(\lambda) \geqq a$ and vanishes when λ tends to infinity in this half plane. We can arrive at the same conclusions by assuming that the function $f(t)$ is absolutely integrable over any finite subinterval of the positive real axis and is of exponential growth, $f(t) = O[\exp(at)]$, when t tends to infinity on this axis. The function of the complex variable,

$$F_+(\lambda) = \frac{1}{\sqrt{(2\pi)}} \int_0^\infty f(t) e^{i\lambda t} \, dt$$

delineated above, is the unilateral or generalized Fourier transform of the function $f(t)$. Similarly, the function $F_-(\lambda)$,

$$F_-(\lambda) = \frac{1}{\sqrt{(2\pi)}} \int_{-\infty}^0 f(t) e^{i\lambda t} \, dt$$

denotes the unilateral Fourier transform of a function $f(t)$ which is defined on the negative axis. Assuming that the function $f(t)\exp(-bt)$ is absolutely integrable over the negative real axis, the Fourier integral,

$$\frac{1}{\sqrt{(2\pi)}}\int_{-\infty}^{0} f(t)e^{i\lambda t}\,dt$$

is absolutely and uniformly convergent for all values of λ in the lower half plane $I(\lambda) \leqq b$, and represents an analytic function $F_-(\lambda)$ in the half plane $I(\lambda) < b$. This function is continuous and bounded at all points in the half plane $I(\lambda) \leqq b$, and vanishes when λ tends to infinity in this half plane. The function $F_-(\lambda)$ has the same properties if we assume that $f(t)$ is absolutely integrable over any finite part of the negative real axis and is of exponential growth, $f(t) = O[\exp(bt)]$, when t tends to infinity along this axis.

The analytic properties of the function $F_+(\lambda)$ enable us to represent this function by a Cauchy integral,

$$F_+(\lambda) = \frac{1}{2\pi i}\int_{-\infty+i\alpha}^{\infty+i\alpha} \frac{F_+(\zeta)}{\zeta-\lambda}\,d\zeta$$

where α is a real number which is larger than or equal to a and λ is a point in the upper half plane $I(\lambda) > \alpha$. Such integral representations have been discussed in Chapter I. The denominator of the Cauchy integral can be written

$$\frac{1}{i(\zeta-\lambda)} = \int_0^\infty e^{-i(\zeta-\lambda)t}\,dt$$

where λ denotes a point in the half plane $I(\lambda) > \alpha$. Substituting this expression in the Cauchy representation for the function $F_+(\lambda)$ and assuming that we may interchange the order of integration, we find

$$F_+(\lambda) = \frac{1}{\sqrt{(2\pi)}}\int_0^\infty e^{i\lambda t}\,dt\left\{\frac{1}{\sqrt{(2\pi)}}\int_{-\infty+i\alpha}^{\infty+i\alpha} F_+(\zeta)e^{-i\zeta t}\,d\zeta\right\}$$

Comparing the integral on the right hand side of this equation with the unilateral Fourier transform integral, we obtain the result,

$$f(t) = \frac{1}{\sqrt{(2\pi)}}\int_{-\infty+i\alpha}^{\infty+i\alpha} F_+(\zeta)e^{-i\zeta t}\,d\zeta$$

This integral can be interpreted as a representation of the solution of the integral equation,

$$F_+(\lambda) = \frac{1}{\sqrt{(2\pi)}}\int_0^\infty f(t)e^{i\lambda t}\,dt$$

or as the inversion integral of the unilateral Fourier transform $F_+(\lambda)$.

A more direct derivation of the inversion integrals for the unilateral Fourier transforms makes use of the inversion formulas for the bilateral Fourier transforms. Proceeding via this route, we introduce a function $g(t)$,

$$g(t) = e^{-\alpha t} f(t)\theta(t)$$

where $\theta(t)$ denotes the unit step function. The function $g(t)$ is absolutely integrable over the whole real axis and vanishes for all negative values of t. The bilateral Fourier transform of this function takes the form,

$$G(\omega) = \frac{1}{\sqrt{(2\pi)}} \int_{-\infty}^{\infty} g(t)e^{i\omega t}\, dt = F_+(\omega + i\alpha)$$

and, assuming that the inverse transform exists, we may write

$$g(t) = e^{-\alpha t} f(t)\theta(t) = \frac{1}{\sqrt{(2\pi)}} \int_{-\infty}^{\infty} G(\omega)e^{-i\omega t}\, d\omega$$

$$= \frac{1}{\sqrt{(2\pi)}} \int_{-\infty}^{\infty} F_+(\omega + i\alpha)e^{-i\omega t}\, d\omega$$

Hence, multiplying both sides of this equation by the factor $\exp{(\alpha t)}$, we obtain the result,

$$f(t)\theta(t) = \frac{1}{\sqrt{(2\pi)}} \int_{-\infty + i\alpha}^{\infty + i\alpha} F_+(\zeta)e^{-i\zeta t}\, d\zeta$$

We note that the inversion integral vanishes for negative values of t. A confirmation of this result has been obtained in Section 1.5 by means of the lemma of Jordan.

Assuming that the function $f(t) \exp{(-bt)}$ is absolutely integrable over the negative real axis, we obtain in a similar fashion the inversion integral,

$$f(t)[1 - \theta(t)] = \frac{1}{\sqrt{(2\pi)}} \int_{-\infty + i\beta}^{\infty + i\beta} F_-(\zeta)e^{-i\zeta t}\, d\zeta$$

for the unilateral Fourier transform,

$$F_-(\lambda) = \frac{1}{\sqrt{(2\pi)}} \int_{-\infty}^{0} f(t)e^{i\lambda t}\, dt$$

where the real number β, in the limits of the inversion integral, is smaller than b.

Summarizing the results obtained so far, we may assert: If $f(t)$ is a function of a real variable and $f(t) \exp{(-at)}$ is absolutely integrable over the positive real axis, then the unilateral Fourier transform of the function $f(t)$,

$$F_+(\lambda) = \frac{1}{\sqrt{(2\pi)}} \int_{0}^{\infty} f(t)e^{i\lambda t}\, dt$$

is analytic in the half plane $I(\lambda) > a$, is continuous and bounded in the half plane $I(\lambda) \geqq a$, and vanishes when λ tends to infinity in this half plane. If, moreover, the function $f(t) \exp(-bt)$ is absolutely integrable over the negative real axis, then the unilateral transform,

$$F_-(\lambda) = \frac{1}{\sqrt{(2\pi)}} \int_{-\infty}^{0} f(t) e^{i\lambda t}\, dt$$

is analytic in the half plane $I(\lambda) < b$, is continuous and bounded in the half plane $I(\lambda) \leqq b$, and vanishes when λ tends to infinity in this half plane. Assuming that the real number b is smaller than the real number a, we obtain the following representation for the function $f(t)$,

$$f(t) = \frac{1}{\sqrt{(2\pi)}} \int_{-\infty + i\alpha}^{\infty + i\alpha} F_+(\zeta) e^{-i\zeta t}\, d\zeta + \frac{1}{\sqrt{(2\pi)}} \int_{-\infty + i\beta}^{\infty + i\beta} F_-(\zeta) e^{-i\zeta t}\, d\zeta$$

where the paths of integration are shown in Figure II-8.

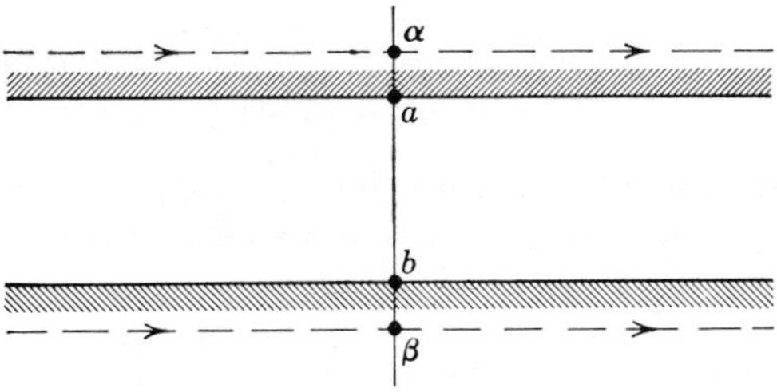

Figure II-8

We note that for positive values of t the function is represented by the first integral on the right hand side of the equation. For in that case the second integral vanishes. Conversely, the second integral represents the function when t is negative because now the first integral vanishes. If a is smaller than b, then the half planes of analyticity of the functions $F_+(\lambda)$ and $F_-(\lambda)$ overlap in the strip $a < I(\lambda) < b$, shown in Figure II-9, and the function,

$$F(\lambda) = F_+(\lambda) + F_-(\lambda) = \frac{1}{\sqrt{(2\pi)}} \int_{-\infty}^{\infty} f(t) e^{i\lambda t}\, dt$$

is an analytic function of the complex variable λ in this strip. Furthermore, the function is continuous and bounded in this strip and vanishes as λ tends to infinity in the strip. If this situation prevails, we can find a real number v

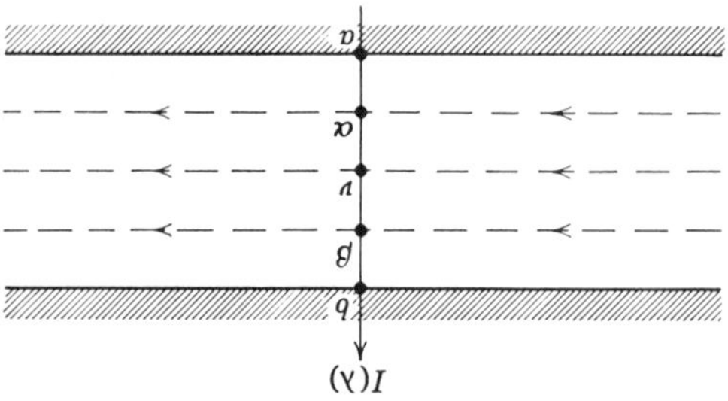

Figure II-9

which is smaller than β but larger than α so that the function $f(t)$ can be represented by the integral,

$$f(t) = \frac{1}{\sqrt{(2\pi)}} \int_{-\infty + i\nu}^{\infty + i\nu} F(\zeta) e^{-i\zeta t} \, d\zeta$$

In other words, this integral is the inversion integral for the bilateral Fourier transform,

$$F(\lambda) = F_{+}(\lambda) + F_{-}(\lambda) = \frac{1}{\sqrt{(2\pi)}} \int_{-\infty}^{\infty} f(t) e^{i\lambda t} \, dt$$

If the real axis lies inside the strip $a < I(\lambda) < b$, we may set ν equal to zero in the limits of the penultimate integral and we obtain the inversion integral,

$$f(t) = \frac{1}{\sqrt{(2\pi)}} \int_{-\infty}^{\infty} F(\omega) e^{-i\omega t} \, d\omega$$

In this case the bilateral Fourier transform,

$$F(\omega) = \frac{1}{\sqrt{(2\pi)}} \int_{-\infty}^{\infty} f(t) e^{i\omega t} \, dt$$

is the restriction to the real axis of a function $F(\lambda)$ which is analytic in the strip $a < I(\lambda) < b$. In other words, the function $F(\omega)$ can be analytically continued from the real axis into this strip in the complex plane.

2.11 CAUSAL FOURIER TRANSFORMS, DISPERSION RELATIONS, AND TITCHMARSH'S THEOREM

Because of their importance in theoretical physics, the unilateral Fourier transforms of causal functions,

$$\theta(t) f(t)$$

merit special attention. In particular we shall be concerned with a theorem of Titchmarsh which provides a link between the principle of causality and the dispersion relations of certain physical quantities. As we have already remarked in Section 2.7, the dispersive and absorptive parts of the amplitude of the Fourier resolution of certain physical quantities are related to each other by so-called dispersion relations. In more mathematical terms, the real and imaginary parts of the Fourier transform of the function describing this physical quantity form a pair of Hilbert transforms. Now it has been shown by Titchmarsh that if the real and imaginary parts of the Fourier transform of a square integrable function form a pair of Hilbert transforms, then this function must be a causal function. From this result we may infer, loosely speaking, that if the dispersive and absorptive parts of the Fourier amplitude of a function obey a dispersion relationship, then this function must describe a causal process. Titchmarsh has shown moreover that the converse of this assertion is also true. That is, he has shown that the real and imaginary parts of the Fourier transform of a causal function form a pair of Hilbert transforms. Translated into physical terms this means that the dispersive and absorptive parts of the Fourier amplitude of a causal physical quantity obey dispersion relations. Titchmarsh's theorem, in its most general form, is stated in terms of Lebesgue square integrable functions. This ensures the existence of necessary transforms and their inverses. We shall first discuss the essentials of the theorem in a less general form avoiding the use of Lebesgue integrals. At the end of this section however we shall deal briefly with the exact form of the theorem and present a short outline of its rigorous proof.

In the less general form of the theorem we shall make use of the following definition of a causal transform which will be superseded, however, by the definition used in the more general form of the theorem. A causal transform is the boundary value of a function of a complex variable which is analytic in the upper half of the complex plane $I(\lambda) > 0$, is continuous and bounded in the half plane $I(\lambda) \geqq 0$, and vanishes when λ tends to infinity in this half plane.

We are now ready to discuss the formal proof of the following assertions. The Fourier transform of a causal function which is absolutely integrable over the positive real axis must be a causal transform. Conversely, a causal transform which has an inverse must be the Fourier transform of a causal function.

For, let $f(t)$ be a causal function which is absolutely integrable over the positive real axis. Then, according to Section 2.3, the Fourier integral,

$$F(\omega) = \frac{1}{\sqrt{(2\pi)}} \int_0^\infty f(t) e^{i\omega t}\, dt$$

can be analytically continued from the real axis into the upper half plane.

The function,

$$F(\lambda) = \frac{1}{\sqrt{(2\pi)}} \int_0^\infty f(t)e^{i\lambda t}\, dt$$

so obtained, is analytic in the upper half plane $I(\lambda) > 0$, is continuous and bounded in the half plane $I(\lambda) \geqq 0$, and vanishes when λ tends to infinity in this half plane. Thus, the boundary value,

$$F(\omega) = \lim_{\gamma \to 0} F(\lambda) = \lim_{\gamma \to 0} F(\omega + i\gamma)$$

is a causal transform. Conversely, let us assume that $F(\omega)$ is a causal transform and has an inverse,

$$f(t) = \frac{1}{\sqrt{(2\pi)}} \int_{-\infty}^\infty F(\omega)e^{-i\omega t}\, d\omega$$

Then the properties of a causal transform are sufficient to ensure that the integral representation of the function $f(t)$ above vanishes for all negative values of the parameter t. This has been shown by means of Jordan's lemma in Section 1.5.

The assertions proven above are equivalent to what is generally known as the first part of Titchmarsh's theorem. The statements which are equivalent to the second part of this theorem read as follows. The real and imaginary parts of the Fourier transform of a causal function, which is integrable over the positive real axis, form a pair of Hilbert transforms. Conversely, if the real and imaginary parts of the Fourier transform of a function form a pair of Hilbert transforms and this transform has an inverse, then the inverse must be a causal function.

Let us consider the first assertion. Assuming that $f(t)$ is a causal function which is absolutely integrable over the positive real axis, we have shown above that the Fourier transform of this function is a causal transform. In other words, the Fourier transform $F(\omega)$ of this function is the restriction to the real axis of a function $F(\lambda)$, which is analytic in the upper half plane $I(\lambda) > 0$, is continuous and bounded in the half plane $I(\lambda) \geqq 0$, and vanishes as λ tends to infinity in this half plane. According to Section 1.1, these properties of the function $F(\lambda)$ are sufficient to ensure that its restriction to the real axis can be represented by the Cauchy integral,

$$F(\omega) = \frac{1}{\pi i} \int_{-\infty}^\infty \frac{F(\zeta)}{\zeta - \omega}\, d\zeta$$

Now let us assume that $D(\omega)$ and $A(\omega)$ denote the real and imaginary parts of the function $F(\omega)$ respectively. Taking real and imaginary parts of the integral representation above we find

$$D(\omega) = \frac{1}{\pi} \int_{-\infty}^\infty \frac{A(\zeta)}{\zeta - \omega}\, d\zeta$$

and

$$A(\omega) = -\frac{1}{\pi}\int_{-\infty}^{\infty} \frac{D(\zeta)}{\zeta - \omega}\, d\zeta$$

which confirms the first assertion of the second part of the theorem.

Now let us consider the second assertion. Assuming that the real and imaginary parts of the Fourier transform $F(\omega)$ of a function form a pair of Hilbert transforms we may write formally

$$F(\omega) = \lim_{\varepsilon\to 0} F(\omega + i\varepsilon) = \lim_{\varepsilon\to 0} \frac{1}{2\pi i}\int_{-\infty}^{\infty} \frac{F(\zeta)}{\zeta - \omega - i\varepsilon}\, d\zeta$$

Multiplying both sides of this equation by $e^{-i\omega t}/\sqrt{(2\pi)}$ and integrating the results over the real axis we obtain

$$\int_{-\infty}^{\infty} f(s)\, ds \frac{1}{2\pi}\int_{-\infty}^{\infty} e^{-i\omega(t-s)}\, d\omega$$

$$= \frac{1}{\sqrt{(2\pi)}}\int_{-\infty}^{\infty} F(\zeta)\, d\zeta \left\{ -\lim_{\varepsilon\to 0} \frac{1}{2\pi i}\int_{-\infty}^{\infty} \frac{e^{-i\omega t}}{\omega - \zeta + i\varepsilon}\, d\omega \right\}$$

where we have interchanged the order of integration on both sides of the equation. Such formal manipulations should, of course, be justified by subsequent more exact derivations. Substitution of the integral representations,

$$\lim_{\varepsilon\to 0} \frac{1}{2\pi i}\int_{-\infty}^{\infty} \frac{e^{-i\omega t}}{\omega - \zeta + i\varepsilon}\, d\omega = -e^{-i\zeta t}\theta(t)$$

and

$$\frac{1}{2\pi}\int_{-\infty}^{\infty} e^{-i\omega(t-s)}\, d\omega = \delta(t - s)$$

into the equation above, yields the result,

$$f(t) = \frac{\theta(t)}{\sqrt{(2\pi)}}\int_{-\infty}^{\infty} F(\omega) e^{-i\omega t}\, d\omega$$

This formally confirms the second assertion of the second part of the theorem.

A different formal proof of the second part of Titchmarsh's theorem makes use of the decomposition of $f(t)$ into even and odd functions. This proof reads as follows. *Let* $f(t)$ be a causal function. Then

$$F(\omega) = D(\omega) + iA(\omega) = \frac{1}{\sqrt{(2\pi)}}\int_{0}^{\infty} f(t) e^{i\omega t}\, dt$$

and thus

$$D(\omega) = \frac{1}{\sqrt{(2\pi)}} \int_0^\infty f(t) \cos \omega t \, dt$$

and

$$A(\omega) = \frac{1}{\sqrt{(2\pi)}} \int_0^\infty f(t) \sin \omega t \, dt$$

where ω is a point on the real axis. Since $f(t)$ is a causal function, we may write

$$f(t) + f(-t) = [f(t) - f(-t)]\varepsilon(t)$$

where $\varepsilon(t)$ denotes the sign function. This expression is valid for all values of t. Taking the Fourier transform of both sides of the equation and noting that $f(t) + f(-t)$ is an even function, we find that the transform of the left hand side of this expression is equal to $2D(\omega)$. Similarly, we find that the Fourier transform of the odd function $f(t) - f(-t)$ is equal to $2iA(\omega)$. By the convolution theorem therefore

$$\frac{1}{\sqrt{(2\pi)}} \int_{-\infty}^\infty [f(t) - f(-t)]\varepsilon(t)e^{i\omega t} \, dt = \frac{2}{\pi} \int_{-\infty}^\infty \frac{A(\zeta)}{\zeta - \omega} \, d\zeta$$

where we made use of the Fourier transform of the sign function $\varepsilon(t)$ which is equal to $2i/\omega\sqrt{(2\pi)}$. Straightforward substitution now yields the desired result,

$$D(\omega) = \frac{1}{\pi} \int_{-\infty}^\infty \frac{A(\zeta)}{\zeta - \omega} \, d\zeta$$

The inverse Hilbert transform can be obtained in a similar manner.

Now let us consider the converse assertion. Assuming that the inverse transform exists, we may write

$$f(t) = \frac{1}{\sqrt{(2\pi)}} \int_{-\infty}^\infty F(\omega)e^{-i\omega t} \, d\omega$$

From this we may infer that

$$f(t) + f(-t) = \frac{1}{\sqrt{(2\pi)}} \int_{-\infty}^\infty 2D(\omega)e^{-i\omega t} \, d\omega$$

and

$$f(t) - f(-t) = \frac{1}{\sqrt{(2\pi)}} \int_{-\infty}^\infty 2iA(\omega)e^{-i\omega t} \, d\omega$$

However, taking the Fourier transform of both sides of the relation,

$$D(\omega) = \frac{1}{\pi} \int_{-\infty}^{\infty} \frac{A(\zeta)}{\zeta - \omega} \, d\zeta$$

which is known to exist between the real and imaginary parts of $F(\omega)$, we obtain the result,

$$\begin{aligned} f(t) + f(-t) &= \frac{1}{\sqrt{(2\pi)}} \int_{-\infty}^{\infty} 2D(\omega) e^{-i\omega t} \, d\omega \\ &= \frac{1}{\sqrt{(2\pi)}} \int_{-\infty}^{\infty} 2iA(\zeta) \, d\zeta \, \frac{1}{\pi i} \int_{-\infty}^{\infty} \frac{e^{-i\omega t}}{\zeta - \omega} \, d\omega \end{aligned}$$

Making use of the representation

$$\frac{1}{\pi i} \int_{-\infty}^{\infty} \frac{e^{-i\omega t}}{\zeta - \omega} \, d\omega = e^{-i\zeta t} \varepsilon(t)$$

we find

$$f(t) + f(-t) = \frac{\varepsilon(t)}{\sqrt{(2\pi)}} \int_{-\infty}^{\infty} 2iA(\zeta) e^{-i\zeta t} \, d\zeta = \varepsilon(t)[f(t) - f(-t)]$$

Since this relation holds for all values of t we may infer that the function $f(t)$ is a causal function.

Now let us turn our attention to the exact formulation of Titchmarsh's theorem. In this formulation we shall make use of functions of a complex variable which are analytic in the upper half of the complex plane with the exclusion of the real axis. These functions moreover satisfy the condition that the Lebesgue integral of the square of their absolute value,

$$\int_{-\infty}^{\infty} |F(\omega + i\gamma)|^2 \, d\omega$$

is uniformly bounded for all values of γ in the upper half of the complex plane. This simple condition is sufficient to endow these functions with strong structural properties that are of the utmost importance in the following investigations.

For instance, if $F(\lambda)$ is such a function, it can be shown that it converges in the mean square sense to a boundary value,

$$F(\omega) = \lim_{\gamma \to 0} F(\omega + i\gamma)$$

which is square integrable and exists for almost all values of ω on the real axis. For the lengthy proof of this assertion we must refer the reader to the literature.

It can also be shown that the function $F(\lambda)$ vanishes as ω tends to infinity in the positive or negative direction on a line which runs parallel to the real axis in the upper half of the complex plane. For let a be an arbitrary positive constant and let λ denote a point in the upper half of the complex plane so that the imaginary part of λ is larger than or equal to a, as shown in Figure II-10. Constructing a circle C about the point λ of radius ρ which is smaller than a

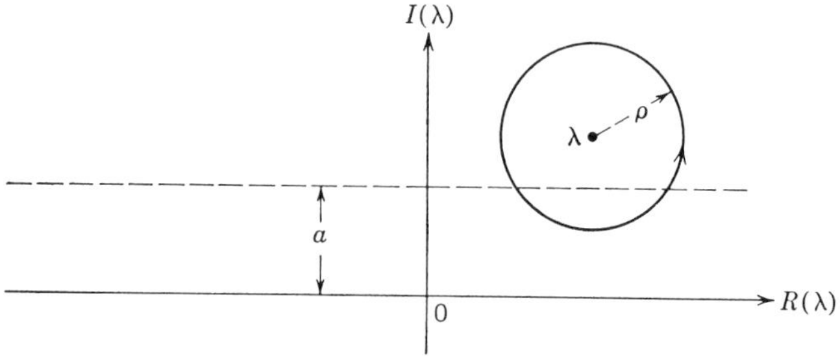

Figure II-10

we are assured that this circle lies completely inside the region of analyticity of the function $F(\lambda)$. Thus, according to Cauchy's formula, we can represent the function $F(\lambda)$ by the contour integral,

$$F(\lambda) = \frac{1}{2\pi i} \oint_C \frac{F(\zeta)}{\zeta - \lambda}\, d\zeta = \frac{1}{2\pi} \int_0^{2\pi} F(\lambda + \rho e^{i\phi})\, d\phi$$

Multiplying this equation by ρ and integrating over ρ from 0 to a, we obtain

$$\pi a^2 F(\lambda) = \int_0^a \int_0^{2\pi} F(\lambda + \rho e^{i\phi}) \rho\, d\rho\, d\phi$$

The integral on the right hand side of this equation is the integral of the function $F(\lambda + \rho e^{i\phi})$ over the region bounded by the circle C. We now make use of a well-known inequality of Schwarz. This inequality provides us with a bound on the absolute value of an integral of a product of two functions in terms of the product of the integrals of the square of the absolute values of these functions. The particular version of this inequality which is most useful for our purpose may be formulated as follows.

Let $G(\rho, \phi)$ and $H(\rho, \phi)$ denote two functions of the polar coordinates ρ and ϕ which are square integrable over the finite region $0 \leqq \rho \leqq a$, $0 \leqq \phi \leqq 2\pi$. Then the product of these functions is integrable over the same region and

$$\left| \int_0^a \int_0^{2\pi} G(\rho, \phi) H(\rho, \phi) \rho\, d\rho\, d\phi \right|^2$$
$$\leqq \int_0^a \int_0^{2\pi} |G(\rho, \phi)|^2 \rho\, d\rho\, d\phi \int_0^a \int_0^{2\pi} |H(\rho, \phi)|^2 \rho\, d\rho\, d\phi$$

A proof of Schwarz's inequality can be found in most textbooks on real analysis.

In our case, making the substitutions $G(\rho, \phi) = 1$ and $H(\rho, \phi) = F(\lambda + \rho e^{i\phi})$, we obtain the result,

$$\pi a^2 |F(\lambda)|^2 \leqq \int_0^a \int_0^{2\pi} |F(\lambda + \rho e^{i\phi})|^2 \rho \, d\rho \, d\phi$$

Referring to Figure II-11 it is obvious that the double integral of the positive

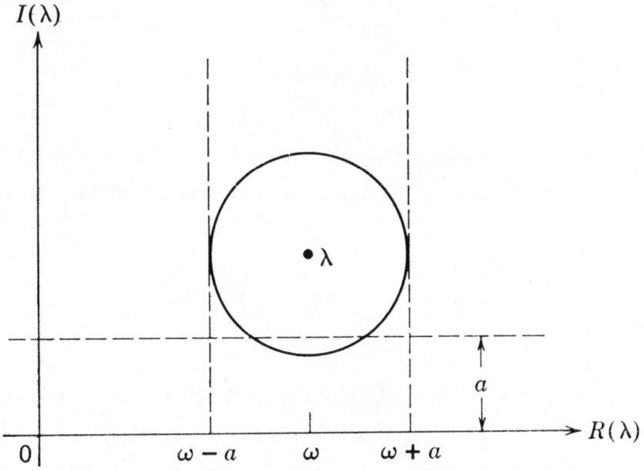

Figure II-11

quantity $|F(\lambda + \rho e^{i\phi})|^2$ over the region bounded by the circle C is smaller than the integral of the same quantity over the strip $\omega - a < \omega < \omega + a$, $0 < \gamma < \gamma + a$. Consequently, we obtain the bound,

$$\pi a^2 |F(\lambda)|^2 \leqq \int_0^{\gamma+a} \int_{\omega-a}^{\omega+a} |F(\omega + i\gamma)|^2 \, d\omega \, d\gamma$$

The inner integral on the right hand side of this inequality is bounded and vanishes as ω tends to plus or minus infinity. From this we may infer that $F(\lambda) = F(\omega + i\gamma)$ vanishes as $|\omega|$ tends to infinity on a line which runs parallel to the real axis and is located in the upper half of the complex plane.

Actually it can be shown that the function $F(\lambda)$ vanishes as λ tends to infinity in the upper half plane independently of the mode in which λ approaches infinity.

We shall now show that the function $F(\lambda)$ delineated above can be represented by a Cauchy integral,

$$F(\lambda) = \frac{1}{2\pi i} \int_{-\infty}^{\infty} \frac{F(\zeta)}{\zeta - \lambda} \, d\zeta$$

Let C denote the rectangular contour shown in Figure II-12.

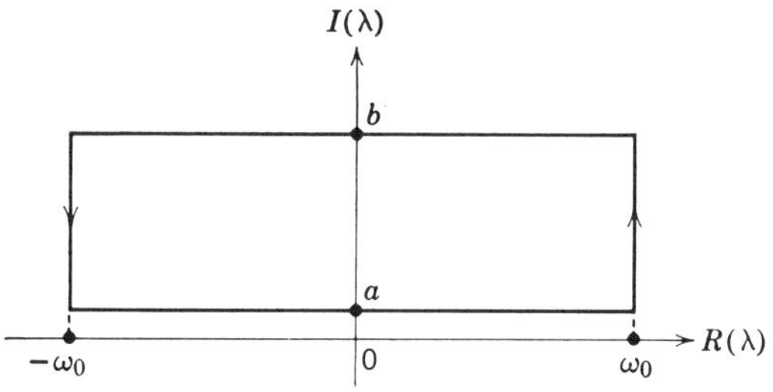

Figure II-12

Again the contour C lies wholly inside the region of analyticity of the function $F(\lambda)$ and, according to Cauchy's formula, the function can be represented by the integral,

$$F(\lambda) = \frac{1}{2\pi i} \oint_C \frac{F(\zeta)}{\zeta - \lambda}\, d\zeta$$

at any point λ inside the contour. For a fixed distance $(b - a)$, the contribution to this integral of the vertical sides of the contour vanishes when $|\omega_0|$ tends to infinity. This is a consequence of the fact, shown above, that $F(\lambda)$ vanishes when ω tends to infinity. Considering the contribution of the path $(-\infty + ib, \infty + ib)$ to the contour integral, we may write, by Schwarz's inequality,

$$\left| \int_{-\infty + ib}^{\infty + ib} \frac{F(\zeta)}{\zeta - \lambda}\, d\zeta \right|^2 \leqq \int_{-\infty}^{\infty} |F(\omega_0 + ib)|^2 \, d\omega_0 \int_{-\infty}^{\infty} \frac{d\omega}{(\omega_0 - \omega)^2 + (\gamma_0 - b)^2}$$

and the second integral on the right hand side of this inequality vanishes as b tends to infinity. Thus we obtain the result,

$$F(\lambda) = \frac{1}{2\pi i} \int_{-\infty + ia}^{\infty + ia} \frac{F(\zeta)}{\zeta - \lambda}\, d\zeta$$

and letting a tend to zero, we find the Cauchy representation formula,

$$F(\lambda) = \frac{1}{2\pi i} \int_{-\infty}^{\infty} \frac{F(\zeta)}{\zeta - \lambda}\, d\zeta$$

Moreover, in the limit as λ tends to a point ω on the real axis we obtain, in the manner of Section 1.1, the integral representation,

$$F(\omega) = \frac{1}{\pi i} \int_{-\infty}^{\infty} \frac{F(\zeta)}{\zeta - \omega}\, d\zeta$$

The integral representations above have been obtained solely on the assumption that $F(\lambda)$ is an analytic function of λ in the upper half plane $I(\lambda) > 0$, and satisfies the condition that the integral,

$$\int_{-\infty}^{\infty} |F(\omega + i\gamma)|^2 \, d\omega \tag{2.11}$$

is uniformly bounded for all positive values of γ.

In summary, a function $F(\lambda)$, which is analytic in the upper half of the complex plane with the exception of the real axis and satisfies the condition that the integral (2.11) is uniformly bounded for all positive values of γ, converges in the mean square sense, and also in the pointwise sense almost everywhere, to a boundary value,

$$F(\omega) = \lim_{\gamma \to 0} F(\omega + i\gamma)$$

which is square integrable over the real axis. The boundary value $F(\omega)$ will be called a causal transform. Thus a causal transform is the boundary value on the real axis of a function which is analytic in the upper half plane and satisfies the conditions delineated above. A causal transform can be represented by the Cauchy integral,

$$F(\omega) = \frac{1}{\pi i} \int_{-\infty}^{\infty} \frac{F(\zeta)}{\zeta - \omega} \, d\zeta$$

We are now ready to state Titchmarsh's theorem and to present an outline of Titchmarsh's rigorous proof of this theorem. Let $f(t)$ be square integrable over the real axis. Then the following two conditions are equivalent necessary and sufficient conditions for $f(t)$ to be a causal function.

(a) The Fourier transform of $f(t)$ is a causal transform.

(b) The real and imaginary parts of the Fourier transform of $f(t)$ form a pair of Hilbert transforms.

First let us consider part **(a)** of the theorem. If $f(t)$ is a causal function which is square integrable over the real axis, then for any positive value of γ the function $f(t) \exp(-\gamma t)$ is also square integrable over the real axis. According to Schwarz's inequality, we may write moreover

$$\left(\int_0^{\infty} e^{-\gamma t} |f(t)| \, dt \right)^2 \leq \int_0^{\infty} e^{-2\gamma t} \, dt \int_0^{\infty} |f(t)|^2 \, dt$$

Consequently, the function $f(t) \exp(-\gamma t)$ is absolutely integrable over the positive real axis for any positive value of γ. From this result we may infer that the Fourier transform of $f(t)$

$$F(\lambda) = \frac{1}{\sqrt{(2\pi)}} \int_0^{\infty} f(t) e^{i\lambda t} \, dt$$

is analytic in the upper half of the complex plane with the exception of the real axis. By Parseval's theorem, moreover,

$$\int_{-\infty}^{\infty} |F(\omega + i\gamma)|^2 \, d\omega = \int_0^{\infty} |f(t)|^2 e^{-2\gamma t} \, dt \leqq \int_0^{\infty} |f(t)|^2 \, dt$$

and, since the function $f(t)$ is square integrable, the integral of the square of the absolute value of the function $F(\omega + i\gamma)$ is uniformly bounded for positive values of γ. We may infer therefore that the Fourier transform of a square integrable causal function is a causal transform. Conversely, let us assume that $F(\omega)$ is a causal transform. Thus $F(\omega)$ is the boundary value on the real axis of a function $F(\lambda)$ which is analytic in the upper half of the complex plane and which satisfies the condition that the integral (2.11) is uniformly bounded for all positive values of γ. We now consider the contour integral,

$$\frac{1}{\sqrt{(2\pi)}} \oint_C F(\zeta) e^{-i\zeta t} \, d\zeta$$

where C denotes the rectangular contour depicted in Figure II-13. The con-

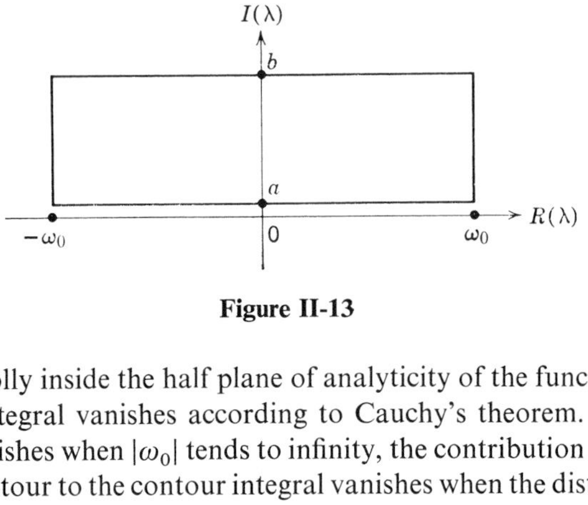

Figure II-13

tour C lies wholly inside the half plane of analyticity of the function $F(\lambda)$, and the contour integral vanishes according to Cauchy's theorem. Since $F(\lambda) = F(\omega_0 + i\gamma)$ vanishes when $|\omega_0|$ tends to infinity, the contribution of the vertical sides of the contour to the contour integral vanishes when the distance between the horizontal lines is kept constant. Consequently, we obtain the result,

$$\text{(2.12)} \quad \frac{1}{\sqrt{(2\pi)}} \int_{-\infty}^{\infty} F(\omega + ia) e^{-i(\omega + ia)t} \, d\omega = \frac{1}{\sqrt{(2\pi)}} \int_{-\infty}^{\infty} F(\omega + ib) e^{-i(\omega + ib)t} \, d\omega$$

For positive values of γ the function $F(\omega + i\gamma)$ is square integrable over the real axis. Assuming therefore that γ is a positive constant, the Fourier transform,

$$F(\omega + i\gamma) = \frac{1}{\sqrt{(2\pi)}} \int_{-\infty}^{\infty} f(t, \gamma) e^{i\omega t} \, dt$$

has a square integrable inverse which takes the form,

$$f(t, \gamma) = \frac{1}{\sqrt{(2\pi)}} \int_{-\infty}^{\infty} F(\omega + i\gamma) e^{-i\omega t} \, d\omega$$

In terms of the inverse of the Fourier transform $F(\omega + i\gamma)$, equation (2.12) may also be written

$$e^{at} f(t, a) = e^{bt} f(t, b)$$

Setting b equal to unity, we find

$$f(t, a) = e^{-at}[e^{t} f(t, 1)] = e^{-at} f(t)$$

where the function $f(t)$ is independent of a. In general,

$$f(t, \gamma) = f(t) \exp(-\gamma t)$$

The function $f(t, \gamma)$ can be written therefore as the product of an exponential factor $\exp(-\gamma t)$ and a square integrable function $f(t)$ which is independent of γ. This enables us to show that the function $f(t, \gamma)$ must vanish for all negative values of t. For, according to Parseval's equality,

$$\int_{-\infty}^{\infty} |f(t, \gamma)|^2 \, dt = \int_{-\infty}^{\infty} e^{-2\gamma t} |f(t)|^2 \, dt = \int_{-\infty}^{\infty} |F(\omega + i\gamma)|^2 \, d\omega$$

By assumption, moreover, the third integral is uniformly bounded for all positive values of γ. For positive values of γ, however, the second integral diverges at the lower limit and, to avoid inconsistencies, we must require that the contributions of the negative real axis to the first and second integral vanish. Since the integral of a positive function can be zero only if its integrand vanishes almost everywhere on the interval of integration, this implies that the function $f(t, \gamma)$ vanishes for all negative values of t. In the limit as γ tends to zero we obtain the expression,

$$f(t) = \frac{\theta(t)}{\sqrt{(2\pi)}} \int_{-\infty}^{\infty} F(\omega) e^{-i\omega t} \, dt$$

This confirms the assertion that a function is a causal function if its Fourier transform is a causal transform.

Now let us consider part **(b)** of Titchmarsh's theorem. Assuming that $F(\omega)$ is the Fourier transform of a square integrable causal function $f(t)$, we have shown above that $F(\omega)$ is a causal transform. This implies that the function $F(\omega)$ can be represented by the Cauchy integral,

$$F(\omega) = \frac{1}{\pi i} \int_{-\infty}^{\infty} \frac{F(\zeta)}{\zeta - \omega} \, d\zeta \tag{2.13}$$

Consequently, taking real and imaginary parts of both sides of this representation we find

$$D(\omega) = \frac{1}{\pi} \int_{-\infty}^{\infty} \frac{A(\zeta)}{\zeta - \omega}\, d\zeta$$

and

$$A(\omega) = -\frac{1}{\pi} \int_{-\infty}^{\infty} \frac{D(\zeta)}{\zeta - \omega}\, d\zeta$$

where $D(\omega)$ and $A(\omega)$ denote the real and the imaginary parts of the function $F(\omega)$, respectively. Thus, the real and imaginary parts of the Fourier transform of a square integrable causal function form a pair of Hilbert transforms. Conversely, if the real and imaginary parts of a function $F(\omega)$ which is square integrable over the real axis form a pair of Hilbert transforms, then this function is a causal transform and the Fourier transform therefore of a square integrable causal function. This part of the theorem can be made plausible as follows. Since $D(\omega)$ and $A(\omega)$ form a pair of Hilbert transforms, the function $F(\omega)$ has a Cauchy representation (2.13) and is the boundary value on the real axis of an analytic function $F(\lambda)$ which can be represented by the integral,

$$F(\lambda) = \frac{1}{2\pi i} \int_{-\infty}^{\infty} \frac{F(\zeta)}{\zeta - \lambda}\, d\zeta$$

This function satisfies the condition that the integral,

$$\int_{-\infty}^{\infty} |F(\omega + i\gamma)|^2\, d\omega$$

is uniformly bounded for all positive values of γ. Consequently, the function $F(\omega)$ is a causal transform and the Fourier transform therefore of a square integrable causal function.

The condition of square integrability which has been imposed on the functions in Titchmarsh's theorem places a severe limitation on its applicability to the problems of theoretical physics. Most functions encountered in the mathematical description of physical processes do not satisfy this condition. However, in some of these situations we can easily salvage the essentials of the theorem. Let us assume, for example, that the function $F(\lambda)$ does not vanish at infinity but tends to some constant value $F(\infty)$. In the terminology of Chapter I the function $F(\lambda)$ has a pole of zeroth order at infinity. We now consider the function $F(\lambda) - F(\infty)$ and apply the theorem to this function. For instance, since the function $F(\lambda) - F(\infty)$ is analytic in the upper half of the complex plane and tends to zero at infinity, it can be represented by the Cauchy integral,

$$F(\lambda) - F(\infty) = \frac{1}{2\pi i} \int_{-\infty}^{\infty} \frac{F(\zeta) - F(\infty)}{\zeta - \lambda} \, d\zeta$$

The boundary value $F(\omega) - F(\infty)$ of this function takes the form,

$$F(\omega) - F(\infty) = \frac{1}{\pi i} \int_{-\infty}^{\infty} \frac{F(\zeta) - F(\infty)}{\zeta - \omega} \, d\zeta$$

This is a useful dispersion relation for the function $F(\omega)$, provided that the value of the function at the point at infinity is known. Let us assume however that the value $F(\infty)$ cannot be obtained but that we know instead the value of the function at a point ω_0 on the real axis. In that case we may write

$$F(\omega_0) - F(\infty) = \frac{1}{\pi i} \int_{-\infty}^{\infty} \frac{F(\zeta) - F(\infty)}{\zeta - \omega_0} \, d\zeta$$

Substracting this expression from the dispersion relation above we find

$$F(\omega) - F(\omega_0) = \frac{\omega - \omega_0}{\pi i} \int_{-\infty}^{\infty} \frac{F(\zeta)}{(\zeta - \omega)(\zeta - \omega_0)} \, d\zeta - \frac{F(\infty)}{\pi i} \int_{-\infty}^{\infty} \frac{d\zeta}{\zeta - \omega} + \frac{F(\infty)}{\pi i} \int_{-\infty}^{\infty} \frac{d\zeta}{\zeta - \omega_0}$$

Since the second and the third integrals on the right hand side of this equation cancel each other we obtain the relationship,

$$F(\omega) = F(\omega_0) + \frac{\omega - \omega_0}{\pi i} \int_{-\infty}^{\infty} \frac{F(\zeta)}{(\zeta - \omega)(\zeta - \omega_0)} \, d\zeta$$

where the integral is a Cauchy principal value integral at the points ω and ω_0. This is a so-called subtracted dispersion relation.

It should be noted that although the function $F(\lambda)$ is not square integrable and does not satisfy the condition that the integral,

$$\int_{-\infty}^{\infty} |F(\omega + i\gamma)|^2 \, d\omega$$

is bounded, the function,

$$\frac{F(\lambda) - F(\omega_0)}{\lambda - \omega_0}$$

is square integrable and satisfies all the conditions of Titchmarsh's theorem.

Now let us consider the more general case in which the function $F(\lambda)$ is analytic in the upper half of the complex plane and is of algebraic growth at infinity. More specifically, let us assume that the function has a pole of order m at infinity and, thus, $F(\lambda) = O(\lambda^m)$ when λ tends to infinity. Let $\omega_0 - i\delta$ denote a point located below the real axis. Then, excluding the real axis, the function,

$$G(\lambda) = \frac{F(\lambda)}{(\lambda - \omega_0 + i\delta)^{m+1}}$$

is analytic in the upper half of the complex plane and vanishes when λ tends to infinity in this half plane including the real axis. In Section 1.1 we have shown that the function $G(\lambda)$ can be represented by the Cauchy integral,

$$G(\lambda) = \frac{1}{2\pi i} \int_{-\infty}^{\infty} \frac{G(\zeta)}{\zeta - \lambda} \, d\zeta$$

and we obtained the following representation for the function $F(\omega)$,

$$F(\omega) = F(\omega_0) + (\omega - \omega_0)F'(\omega_0) + \frac{1}{2!}(\omega - \omega_0)^2 F''(\omega_0)$$

$$+ \cdots + \frac{1}{m!}(\omega - \omega_0)^m F^{(m)}(\omega_0) + \frac{(\omega - \omega_0)^{m+1}}{\pi i} \int_{-\infty}^{\infty} \frac{F(\zeta)}{(\zeta - \omega)(\zeta - \omega_0)^{m+1}} \, d\zeta$$

This is again a subtracted dispersion relation, this time for the boundary value of a function $F(\lambda)$ which is analytic in the upper half of the complex plane and has a pole of order m at the point at infinity. By taking real and imaginary parts of both sides of the relation above, we obtain similar dispersion relations for the dispersive and absorptive parts of the function $F(\omega)$.

An interesting development of the analysis above concerns the decomposition of a square integrable function $F(\omega)$ into a positive and a negative frequency part,

$$F(\omega) = F_+(\omega) - F_-(\omega)$$

Here $F_+(\omega)$ denotes the boundary value of a function $F_+(\lambda)$ which is analytic in the upper half of the complex plane $I(\lambda) > 0$ and satisfies the condition that the integral,

$$\int_{-\infty}^{\infty} |F_+(\omega + i\gamma)|^2 \, d\omega \tag{2.14}$$

is uniformly bounded for all positive values of γ. Similarly, the function $F_-(\omega)$ is the boundary value of a function $F_-(\lambda)$ which is analytic in the lower half plane $I(\lambda) < 0$ and satisfies the condition that the integral,

$$\int_{-\infty}^{\infty} |F_-(\omega + i\gamma)|^2 \, d\omega \tag{2.15}$$

is uniformly bounded for all negative values of γ. To verify these assertions, let us assume that $F(\omega)$ is the Fourier transform of the square integrable function $f(t)$,

$$F(\omega) = \frac{1}{\sqrt{(2\pi)}} \int_{-\infty}^{\infty} f(t) e^{i\omega t}\, dt$$

If $\theta(t)$ is the unit step function, then the function $f(t)$ can be written as the difference,

$$f(t) = f_+(t) - f_-(t)$$

of the functions $f_+(t) = \theta(t) f(t)$ and $f_-(t) = [\theta(t) - 1] f(t)$ which are square integrable over the real axis. As we have shown in this section, the Fourier transform,

$$F_+(\omega) = \frac{1}{\sqrt{(2\pi)}} \int_{-\infty}^{\infty} f_+(t) e^{i\omega t}\, dt = \frac{1}{\sqrt{(2\pi)}} \int_{0}^{\infty} f(t) e^{i\omega t}\, dt$$

of the square integrable causal function $f_+(t) = \theta(t) f(t)$ is a causal transform. Consequently, $F_+(\omega)$ is the boundary value of a function $F_+(\lambda)$ which is analytic in the upper half plane $I(\lambda) > 0$ and satisfies the condition that the integral (2.14) is uniformly bounded for all positive values of γ. In a similar manner it can be shown that the Fourier transform,

$$F_-(\omega) = \frac{1}{\sqrt{(2\pi)}} \int_{-\infty}^{\infty} f_-(t) e^{i\omega t}\, dt = -\frac{1}{\sqrt{(2\pi)}} \int_{-\infty}^{0} f(t) e^{i\omega t}\, dt$$

is the boundary value of a function $F_-(\lambda)$ which is analytic in the lower half plane $I(\lambda) < 0$ and satisfies the condition that the integral (2.15) is uniformly bounded for all negative values of γ. We observe moreover that

$$F_+(\omega) - F_-(\omega) = \frac{1}{\sqrt{(2\pi)}} \int_{-\infty}^{\infty} f(t) e^{i\omega t}\, dt = F(\omega)$$

and our statements have been confirmed therefore.

With regard to the causal transform $F_+(\omega)$, we have shown that it can be represented by the Cauchy integral,

$$F_+(\omega) = \frac{1}{\pi i} \int_{-\infty}^{\infty} \frac{F_+(\zeta)}{\zeta - \omega}\, d\zeta$$

Similarly it can be shown that the function $F_-(\omega)$ can be represented by the integral,

$$F_-(\omega) = -\frac{1}{\pi i} \int_{-\infty}^{\infty} \frac{F_-(\zeta)}{\zeta - \omega}\, d\zeta$$

Combining these two representation formulas we obtain the result,

$$F_+(\omega) - F_-(\omega) = F(\omega)$$

and

$$F_+(\omega) + F_-(\omega) = \frac{1}{\pi i} \int_{-\infty}^{\infty} \frac{F(\zeta)}{\zeta - \omega} \, d\zeta$$

These are the well-known Plemelj formulas for the boundary values of a sectionally analytic function $F(\lambda)$ which is analytic in the whole complex plane with the exception of the real axis. A sectionally analytic function can be defined in terms of the functions $F_+(\lambda)$ and $F_-(\lambda)$, namely, $F(\lambda) = F_+(\lambda)$ when λ is a point in the upper half of the complex plane and $F(\lambda) = F_-(\lambda)$ when λ is a point in the lower half plane. The functions $F_+(\omega)$ and $F_-(\omega)$ are the boundary values of $F(\lambda)$ on the real axis. $F_+(\lambda)$ is defined as the value of the function $F(\lambda)$ when λ tends to the point ω through positive values of γ and $F_-(\omega)$ denotes the boundary value of $F(\lambda)$ when λ tends to the point ω through negative values of γ. We shall present a more detailed discussion of sectionally analytic functions in Chapter IV.

2.12 APPLICATIONS TO LINEAR PHYSICAL SYSTEMS

The analytical results obtained in the preceding section have been applied with considerable success to the investigation of linear physical systems. Linear physical systems were introduced in Section 2.6. The response $x(t)$ of a linear system to a driving force $f(t)$ can be found from the linear relationship,

(2.16)
$$x(t) = \int_{-\infty}^{\infty} G(t - t_0) f(t_0) \, dt_0$$

provided the system is invariant to translations of the time axis. The response of a linear physical system to a driving force is completely determined by its Green's function. The Green's function $G(t)$ of the system is defined as the response to an impulse force of unit magnitude at time $t = 0$. If the system is causal and obeys therefore the dictum that no effect shall precede its cause, then the Green's function of this system vanishes for all negative values of t, i.e.,

$$G(t) = 0 \qquad \text{when } t \text{ is negative.}$$

If we assume moreover that the Green's function is square integrable over the real axis, then according to Titchmarsh's theorem the Fourier transform of the Green's function,

$$G(\omega) = \frac{1}{\sqrt{(2\pi)}} \int_0^{\infty} G(t) e^{i\omega t} \, dt$$

must be a causal transform. We may infer therefore that the function $G(\omega)$ can be analytically continued into the upper half plane $I(\lambda) > 0$. The continuation $G(\lambda)$ satisfies the condition that the integral,

$$\int_{-\infty}^{\infty} |G(\omega + i\gamma)|^2 \, d\omega$$

is uniformly bounded for all positive values of γ. The singularities of the function $G(\lambda)$, if any, must all lie below the real axis. From the second part of Titchmarsh's theorem we may infer moreover that the real and imaginary parts of the Fourier transform $G(\omega) = D(\omega) + iA(\omega)$ of the Green's function form a pair of Hilbert transforms,

$$D(\omega) = \frac{1}{\pi} \int_{-\infty}^{\infty} \frac{A(\zeta)}{\zeta - \omega} \, d\zeta$$

and

$$A(\omega) = -\frac{1}{\pi} \int_{-\infty}^{\infty} \frac{D(\zeta)}{\zeta - \omega} \, d\zeta$$

In more physical terms we may also say that the expressions above are dispersion relations for the dispersive and absorptive parts of the susceptibility.

These conclusions are all based on the physical assumption that the Green's function of the system vanishes for negative values of t and the condition that the Green's function is square integrable over the real axis. If we assume moreover that the force function $f(t)$ is square integrable over the real axis, we find that the response function $x(t)$ is also square integrable over the real axis.

As we have shown before, the Fourier transformation of equation (2.16) yields the simple relationship,

$$X(\omega) = G(\omega)F(\omega) \tag{2.17}$$

between the square integrable Fourier transforms of the functions $x(t)$, $G(t)$, and $f(t)$. Furthermore, if we assume that the force $f(t)$ is impressed on the system at time $t = 0$ and vanishes at all earlier times, then the Fourier transform of the force is a causal transform. The response of the system to such a driving force is, of course, also a causal function and the Fourier transform of the response is a causal transform. Consequently, according to equation (2.17), the Fourier transform $G(\omega)$ of the Green's function maps the causal transform $F(\omega)$ into another causal transform $X(\omega)$. If the product of a function and a causal transform is again a causal transform, then this function is called a causal factor. The Fourier transform of the square integrable causal Green's function of the linear system delineated above is both a causal transform and a causal factor. In physical applications, however, the Green's function and its

Fourier transform are not always square integrable. However, in many of these situations we find that the force and the response functions are square integrable over the real axis and have therefore square integrable Fourier transforms. For frequently, the integrals of the square of the absolute value of these functions can be related to the total energy of the system or they may have some other physical interpretation which ensures their existence. If we assume moreover that the function $f(t)$ is a causal function, then by implication the response $x(t)$ is also a causal function. According to Titchmarsh's theorem therefore the Fourier transforms $F(\omega)$ and $X(\omega)$ are causal transforms. In this case the Fourier transform of the Green's function is a causal factor but is not a causal transform.

2.13 ANALYTIC CONTINUATION OF A FUNCTION DEFINED BY A HILBERT TRANSFORM OR CAUCHY INTEGRAL

In the preceding sections of this chapter we have been concerned mainly with functions which are defined and analytic in the upper half of the complex plane. Assuming that such a function $F(\lambda)$ vanishes when λ tends to infinity in the upper half plane, or satisfies the condition that the integral,

$$\int_{-\infty}^{\infty} |F(\omega + i\gamma)|^2 \, d\omega$$

is uniformly bounded for all positive values of γ, we can show that it has the integral representation,

$$F(\lambda) = \frac{1}{2\pi i} \int_{-\infty}^{\infty} \frac{F(\zeta)}{\zeta - \lambda} \, d\zeta$$

at all points in the upper half plane $I(\lambda) > 0$. In many problems of theoretical physics however we need to consider the more general integral,

$$\frac{1}{\pi} \int_{-\infty}^{\infty} \frac{g(\zeta)}{\zeta - \lambda} \, d\zeta$$

where now $g(\omega)$ is a real valued function of the real variable ω and is not necessarily the restriction to the real axis of a function which is analytic in the upper half plane. The theory and application of such integrals will be presented in Chapter IV. There it will be shown that the integral represents a sectionally analytic function $G(\lambda)$, provided the function $g(\omega)$ is either Hölder continuous on the real axis and at the point at infinity or absolutely integrable over the real axis. In the notation of Chapter IV we may write,

$$G(\lambda) = G^L(\lambda) = \frac{1}{\pi} \int_{-\infty}^{\infty} \frac{g(\zeta)}{\zeta - \lambda} \, d\zeta$$

when λ is a point in the upper half plane $I(\lambda) > 0$, where $G^L(\lambda)$ denotes a function which is analytic in this half plane. Similarly, if λ is a point in the lower half plane $I(\lambda) < 0$, then we shall use the notation,

$$G(\lambda) = G^R(\lambda) = \frac{1}{\pi}\int_{-\infty}^{\infty} \frac{g(\zeta)}{\zeta - \lambda}\, d\zeta$$

where $G^R(\lambda)$ denotes a function which is analytic in the lower half plane.

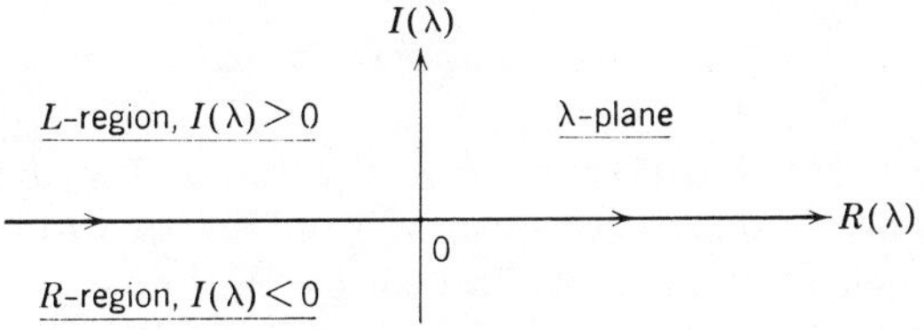

Figure II-14

It should be noted at this point that the function $G^R(\lambda)$ is not necessarily the analytic continuation of the function $G^L(\lambda)$ into the lower half plane. The functions $G^L(\lambda)$ and $G^R(\lambda)$ are analytic in the upper and lower half planes respectively but not necessarily on the real axis. This line acts as a boundary between the regions of analyticity of the functions $G^L(\lambda)$ and $G^R(\lambda)$ and it is questionable if these functions can be continued across this boundary. However, in many applications it is important to know if such an analytic continuation is possible. For instance, this question plays an important role in the investigation of the generation and damping of electron oscillations in a uniform infinite plasma in the absence of an external field. It also arises in the operator approach to quantum mechanical scattering theory. The answer to this question depends, of course, on the character of the function $g(\omega)$.

For example, if $g(\omega)$ is a so-called cut-off function,

$$g(\omega) = g(\omega)[\theta(\omega + \omega_0) - \theta(\omega - \omega_0)]$$

where $\theta(\omega)$ denotes the unit step function, then we can imagine the complex plane to be cut along the real axis from the point $-\omega_0$ to the point ω_0. By means of the reflection principle of Schwarz, the function,

$$G^L(\lambda) = \frac{1}{\pi}\int_{-\infty}^{\infty} \frac{g(\zeta)}{\zeta - \lambda}\, d\zeta$$

can be continued into the lower half plane across those parts of the real axis which are outside the cut. For, according to Schwarz's principle, the function,

$$G^R(\lambda) = (G^L(\lambda^*))^*$$

is the analytic continuation of the function $G^L(\lambda)$ across the real axis into the lower half plane, provided that the boundary value,

$$G^L(\omega) = \lim_{\gamma \to 0} G^L(\omega + i\gamma)$$

of the function $G^L(\lambda)$ is real and analytic.

In our example, the boundary values of the function $G^L(\lambda)$ on the real axis vanish outside the cut and obviously satisfy the conditions of Schwarz's principle. In general, if the boundary values $G^L(\omega)$ and

$$G^R(\omega) = \lim_{\gamma \to 0} G^R(\omega + i\gamma)$$

of the sectionally analytic function $G(\lambda)$ are real and analytic on the real axis, then they are equal to each other and the function $G(\lambda)$ is actually an entire function. In most cases of practical interest, however, the boundary values $G^L(\omega)$ and $G^R(\omega)$ of the sectionally analytic function $G(\lambda)$ are not equal to each other on the real axis. As we shall show in Chapter IV, the boundary values can be represented by the Plemelj boundary value equations,

$$G^L(\omega) = \lim_{\varepsilon \to 0} G^L(\omega + i\varepsilon) = ig(\omega) + \frac{1}{\pi} \int_{-\infty}^{\infty} \frac{g(\zeta)}{\zeta - \omega} \, d\zeta$$

and

$$G^R(\omega) = \lim_{\varepsilon \to 0} G^R(\omega - i\varepsilon) = -ig(\omega) + \frac{1}{\pi} \int_{-\infty}^{\infty} \frac{g(\zeta)}{\zeta - \omega} \, d\zeta$$

where ω denotes a point on the real axis, ε is a small positive number, and the integrals are principal value integrals. In this case the boundary values $G^L(\omega)$ and $G^R(\omega)$ are not equal to each other. Crossing the real axis, the sectionally analytic function $G(\lambda)$ suffers a jump discontinuity and the magnitude of the jump is given by the Plemelj formula,

$$G^L(\omega) - G^R(\omega) = 2ig(\omega)$$

The reflection principle of Schwarz, therefore, does not apply to this situation and we shall have to make use of so-called nonreflective techniques.

First let us consider a function $g(\omega)$ which is the real valued restriction to the real axis of an entire function $g(\lambda)$. In this case we can obtain the analytic continuation of the function,

$$G^L(\lambda) = \frac{1}{\pi} \int_{-\infty}^{\infty} \frac{g(\zeta)}{\zeta - \lambda} \, d\zeta$$

into the lower half plane by means of a technique which makes use of the Plemelj formulas. Assuming that $f(\omega)$ is the real valued restriction to the real axis of an entire function $f(\lambda)$, we define a sectionally analytic function $F(\lambda)$ by the relations,

$$F(\lambda) = F^L(\lambda) = \frac{1}{\pi}\int_{-\infty}^{\infty} \frac{f(\zeta)}{\zeta - \lambda}\, d\zeta - if(\lambda)$$

when λ is a point in the upper half plane $I(\lambda) > 0$, and by the relations,

$$F(\lambda) = F^R(\lambda) = \frac{1}{\pi}\int_{-\infty}^{\infty} \frac{f(\zeta)}{\zeta - \lambda}\, d\zeta + if(\lambda)$$

when λ is a point in the lower half plane $I(\lambda) < 0$. If ω denotes a point on the real axis then, according to the formulas of Plemelj,

$$\lim_{\varepsilon \to 0} \frac{1}{\pi}\int_{-\infty}^{\infty} \frac{f(\zeta)}{\zeta - \omega \mp i\varepsilon}\, d\zeta = \pm if(\omega) + \frac{1}{\pi}\int_{-\infty}^{\infty} \frac{f(\zeta)}{\zeta - \omega}\, d\zeta$$

where the integral on the right hand side of the equation is a principal value integral. Hence, letting λ approach the point ω through values in the upper half plane, we obtain the boundary value,

$$F^L(\omega) = \frac{1}{\pi}\int_{-\infty}^{\infty} \frac{f(\zeta)}{\zeta - \omega}\, d\zeta$$

Similarly, if we let λ approach the point ω through values in the lower half plane, we find

$$F^R(\omega) = \frac{1}{\pi}\int_{-\infty}^{\infty} \frac{f(\zeta)}{\zeta - \omega}\, d\zeta$$

Consequently, the boundary values of the analytic functions $F^L(\lambda)$ and $F^R(\lambda)$ on the real axis are equal to each other. This implies, according to the principle of Schwarz, that the function $F^R(\lambda)$ is the analytic continuation of the function $F^L(\lambda)$ into the lower half plane. Conversely, of course, the function $F^L(\lambda)$ is the analytic continuation of the function $F^R(\lambda)$ into the upper half plane. From these conclusions we may infer that the sectionally analytic function $F(\lambda)$ is analytic in the whole complex plane, including the real axis, and is therefore an entire function.

It is now easy to verify that the analytic continuation of the function,

$$G^L(\lambda) = \frac{1}{\pi}\int_{-\infty}^{\infty} \frac{g(\zeta)}{\zeta - \lambda}\, d\zeta$$

which is defined and analytic in the upper half plane, is represented by the function,

$$G^R(\lambda) = \frac{1}{\pi}\int_{-\infty}^{\infty} \frac{g(\zeta)}{\zeta - \lambda}\, d\zeta + 2ig(\lambda)$$

which is defined and analytic in the lower half plane, provided the function $g(\omega)$ is the real valued restriction on the real axis of an entire function $g(\lambda)$. The analytic continuation across the real axis into the lower half plane of the function $G^L(\lambda)$ may also be written

$$G^R(\lambda) = (G^L(\lambda^*))^* + 2ig(\lambda)$$

A useful integral representation of the function $G^L(\lambda)$ can be obtained by deforming the path along the real axis in the manner shown in Figure II-15.

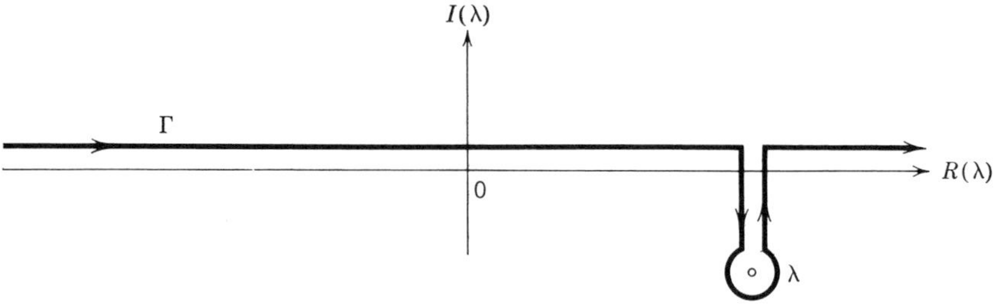

Figure II-15

The function $G^L(\lambda)$ can now be represented by the integral,

$$G^L(\lambda) = \frac{1}{\pi} \int_\Gamma \frac{g(\zeta)}{\zeta - \lambda}\, d\zeta$$

where Γ is the path shown above. For, if the imaginary part of λ is positive, the path Γ coincides with the real axis and we obtain the normal integral representation of $G^L(\lambda)$. If the imaginary part of λ is zero, the path Γ runs along the real axis and is indented by a small semicircle about the point ω. Finally, if the imaginary part of λ is negative, we obtain the path shown above. In plasma physics such a path is called a Landau path.

More generally it can be shown that if the function $g(\omega)$ is real valued and analytic on the interval (a, b) of the real axis, then the function,

$$G^L(\lambda) = \frac{1}{\pi} \int_{-\infty}^{\infty} \frac{g(\zeta)}{\zeta - \lambda}\, d\zeta$$

can be analytically continued across the interval (a, b) into the lower half plane. The analytic continuation of the function $G^L(\lambda)$ into the lower half plane takes again the form,

$$G^R(\lambda) = (G^L(\lambda^*))^* + 2ig(\lambda)$$

It can be shown, moreover, that the condition imposed on the function $g(\omega)$ is not only sufficient but also necessary. We must refer the reader to the literature for the rigorous proof of this important assertion.

In favorable circumstances the analytic continuation across the real axis into the lower half plane of the function,

$$G^L(\lambda) = \frac{1}{\pi}\int_{-\infty}^{\infty} \frac{g(\zeta)}{\zeta - \lambda}\, d\zeta$$

which is defined and analytic in the upper half plane $I(\lambda) > 0$, can also be obtained by a Fourier transform technique. Let us assume that the Fourier transform,

$$F(\alpha) = \frac{1}{\sqrt{(2\pi)}}\int_{-\infty}^{\infty} g(\zeta)e^{i\alpha\zeta}\, d\zeta$$

of the function $g(\zeta)$ exists. We shall now show that the function $G^L(\lambda)$ is the unilateral Fourier transform of the function $2iF^*(\alpha)$,

$$G^L(\lambda) = \frac{1}{\sqrt{(2\pi)}}\int_{0}^{\infty} 2iF^*(\alpha)e^{i\lambda\alpha}\, d\alpha$$

where $F^*(\alpha)$ is the complex conjugate of the Fourier transform of the function $g(\zeta)$. For let $h(\zeta) = 1/(\zeta - \lambda)$. Then, by Parseval's relation, we obtain the following expression,

$$G^L(\lambda) = \frac{1}{\pi}\int_{-\infty}^{\infty} h(\zeta)g(\zeta)\, d\zeta = \frac{1}{\pi}\int_{-\infty}^{\infty} H(\alpha)F^*(\alpha)\, d\alpha$$

where $H(\alpha)$ denotes the Fourier transform of the function $h(\zeta)$,

$$H(\alpha) = \frac{1}{\sqrt{(2\pi)}}\int_{-\infty}^{\infty} \frac{e^{i\alpha\zeta}}{\zeta - \lambda}\, d\zeta$$

In Section 1.1 we found that the Fourier transform above is the integral representation of the function,

$$\sqrt{(2\pi)}ie^{i\alpha\lambda}\theta(\alpha)$$

where $\theta(\alpha)$ denotes the unit step function. Substitution of this expression for $H(\alpha)$ into the Parseval relation yields the desired result,

$$G^L(\lambda) = \frac{1}{\sqrt{(2\pi)}}\int_{0}^{\infty} 2iF^*(\alpha)e^{i\lambda\alpha}\, d\alpha$$

However, as we have noticed before, for an appropriately defined function $F^*(\alpha)$, this integral is the representation of an analytic function of the complex variable. For instance, if $F^*(\alpha)e^{-a\alpha}$ is absolutely integrable over the positive α-axis, then the function represented by this integral is analytic in the upper half plane $I(\lambda) > \alpha$. If we can find, therefore, a negative value of a, such that the integrability condition imposed on the function $F^*(\alpha)\exp(-a\alpha)$ is satisfied, then the function $G^L(\lambda)$ can be analytically continued across the real axis into the lower half plane by means of the Fourier integral representation above.

As an example of the techniques introduced above let us consider the Hilbert transform of the Gaussian,

$$G^L(\lambda) = \frac{1}{\pi}\int_{-\infty}^{\infty} \frac{e^{-\zeta^2}}{\zeta - \lambda}\, d\zeta$$

which is defined and analytic in the upper half of the complex plane. This function is of considerable importance in the fields of plasma physics and neutron cross-section analysis. Since $\exp(-\lambda^2)$ is an entire function, we obtain by the Plemelj formula technique the following expression for the analytic continuation of the function $G(\lambda)$ across the real axis into the lower half of the complex plane,

$$G^R(\lambda) = \frac{1}{\pi}\int_{-\infty}^{\infty} \frac{e^{-\zeta^2}}{\zeta - \lambda}\, d\zeta + 2ie^{-\lambda^2} = [(G^L(\lambda^*)]^* + 2ie^{-\lambda^2}$$

This expression can also be verified by means of the Fourier transform representation of the function $G^L(\lambda)$. The Fourier transform of the function $\exp(-\zeta^2)$ is the real valued function $F(\alpha) = \exp(-\alpha^2/4)/\sqrt{2}$ and the unilateral Fourier transform of the function $2iF^*(\alpha) = 2iF(\alpha)$ is, as we have shown, equal to the function $G^L(\lambda)$. Consequently,

$$G^L(\lambda) = \frac{1}{\sqrt{(2\pi)}}\int_0^{\infty} 2iF^*(\alpha)e^{i\lambda\alpha}\, d\alpha = \frac{2ie^{-\lambda^2}}{\sqrt{(\pi)}}\int_{-\infty}^{i\lambda} e^{-\beta^2}\, d\beta$$

From this representation for the function $G^L(\lambda)$ we can immediately verify the expression,

$$G^R(\lambda) = (G^L(\lambda^*))^* + 2ie^{-\lambda^2}$$

for the analytic continuation of the function $G^L(\lambda)$ across the real axis into the lower half plane. If Γ denotes the Landau path, then

$$G(\lambda) = \frac{1}{\pi}\int_{\Gamma} \frac{e^{-\zeta^2}}{\zeta - \lambda}\, d\zeta$$

is a more compact representation of the Hilbert transform of the Gaussian and its analytic continuation into the lower half plane.

2.14 ASYMPTOTIC REPRESENTATIONS OF UNILATERAL FOURIER TRANSFORMS

It is an interesting and highly useful fact that the asymptotic behavior of the unilateral Fourier transform,

$$F_+(\lambda) = \frac{1}{\sqrt{(2\pi)}}\int_0^{\infty} f(t)e^{i\lambda t}\, dt$$

for large and small values of λ is to a great extent determined by the behavior of the function $f(t)$ for small and large values of t, respectively. Similarly, the behavior of the inversion integral,

$$f(t) = \frac{1}{\sqrt{(2\pi)}} \int_{-\infty + ia}^{\infty + ia} F_+(\zeta) e^{-i\zeta t}\, d\zeta$$

can sometimes be determined from the behavior of the function $F_+(\lambda)$ in the neighborhood of a single point. This last situation is, of course, of great importance in the application of the transform method to the solution of boundary valve problems because, in general, we can easily determine the transform $F_+(\lambda)$ but it is often difficult to evaluate the inverse transform integral. In such cases one is satisfied with the information that can be obtained about the behavior of the integral at some special value of t. Many theorems on the asymptotic behavior of the unilateral transforms and their inversion integrals are known. In this section we shall present a short discussion of some of the more important of these theorems.

A. Asymptotic Representations of Functions of a Real or Complex variable

An infinite series $\sum_{m=0}^{\infty} A_m u_m(x)$ can sometimes be used to approximate a function $F(x)$ at a constant value of x in the sense that the quantity,

$$\left| F(x) - \sum_{n=0}^{m} A_n u_n(x) \right|$$

can be made arbitrarily small when m tends to infinity. In other words, the partial sums $S_m(x) = \sum_{n=0}^{m} A_n u_n(x)$ of the infinite series are approximate representations of the function $F(x)$ at the point x. The partial sums are evaluated at a constant value of x and yield for increasing values of m successively better approximations to the function $F(x)$. This implies that the infinite series should be convergent.

In some situations, however, the function $F(x)$ can also be approximated in the neighborhood of some finite or infinite point a by the partial sums of a divergent series. To define such an approximation, we consider the behavior of the difference $F(x) - S_m(x)$ when x tends to a and m is held constant. (Note the switch in role between m and x). If this difference is of a lower order of magnitude than the last term of the sum $S_m(x)$,

$$F(x) - S_m(x) = o[u_m(x)]$$

when x tends to a, then the expansion,

$$\sum_{m=0}^{\infty} A_m u_m(x)$$

is an asymptotic representation of the function $F(x)$ in the neighborhood of the point a. In other words, the series $\sum_{m=0}^{\infty} A_m u_m(x)$ is an asymptotic expansion of the function $F(x)$ in the neighborhood of the point a, provided that the quantity,

$$\frac{F(x) - S_m(x)}{u_m(x)}$$

vanishes when x tends to a and m is held constant. This is Poincaré's definition of an asymptotic expansion. The notation used most frequently is

$$F(x) \approx \sum_{m=0}^{\infty} A_m u_m(x) \qquad (x \to a)$$

which may be read as, "$F(x)$ can be asymptotically represented by the series $\sum_{m=0}^{\infty} A_m u_m(x)$ in the neighborhood of the point a," or also as, "The series $\sum_{m=0}^{\infty} A_m u_m(x)$ is an asymptotic expansion of the function $F(x)$ in the neighborhood of the point a."

The error made in approximating the function $F(x)$ by the sum $S_m(x)$ is of the order of the first term neglected. Computing the error for a fixed value of m we find that it decreases when x tends to a. However, the following behavior of the error can be observed when x is held constant and m tends to infinity. In this case, for increasing values of m, the error first decreases, attains a minimum, and then starts to increase without bound. The value of m for which the minimum is attained is called the optimum value of m. The optimum value increases for values of x which are closer to a. In other words, if x is closer to a than some other point, then the optimum number of terms in the asymptotic expansion for the function at the point x is larger than the optimum number of terms in the asymptotic expansion of the function at this other point. For all values of m which are smaller than the optimum value, adding a term to the expansion will improve the approximation. However, for values of m which are larger than the optimum value, the approximation deteriorates when more terms are added.

For values of x which are sufficiently close to a, the error incurred in replacing the function by its asymptotic expansion with the optimum number of terms is very small and this expansion represents the function at that particular value of x with high accuracy. Since the optimum number of terms is usually small, asymptotic expansions are a very efficient approximation device. Being assured that we obtain a sufficiently accurate approximation if we do not exceed the optimum number of terms, the eventual divergence of the infinite series is of no concern to us.

In applications, asymptotic representations involving integer or fractional powers of $(x - a)$ or $1/x$ occur most frequently. For instance, let α_m denote a member of a monotonically increasing sequence of positive real numbers. Then from the notation,

$$F(x) \approx \sum_{m=0}^{\infty} A_m/x^{\alpha_m} \qquad (x \to \infty)$$

we may infer that the function $F(x)$ can be represented asymptotically by the expansion $\sum_{m=0}^{\infty} A_m/x^{\alpha_m}$ for large values of x. In other words, holding m constant, the quantity,

$$x^{\alpha_m}\left[F(x) - \sum_{n=0}^{m} A_n/x^{\alpha_n}\right]$$

vanishes when x tends to infinity. In this case we may also write

$$F(x) - \sum_{n=0}^{m} A_n/x^{\alpha_n} = o(1/x^{\alpha_m})$$

when x tends to infinity and m is held constant.

Instead of the point at infinity the limit point can also be some point on a finite part of the real axis. In this case we shall write

$$F(x) \approx \sum_{m=0}^{\infty} A_m(x-a)^{\alpha_m} \qquad (x \to a)$$

implying that the infinite sum on the right hand side is an asymptotic representation of the function $F(x)$ at the point a. In the o-notation this may be written

$$F(x) - \sum_{n=0}^{m} A_n(x-a)^n = o[(x-a)^{\alpha_m}]$$

when x tends to a.

The following properties of asymptotic expansions should be noted.

a. An asymptotic expansion of the form,

$$F(x) \approx \sum_{m=0}^{\infty} A_m u_m(x) \qquad (x \to a)$$

is a unique representation of the function $F(x)$ in terms of the reference functions $u_m(x)$ at the point a. In other words, if $\sum_{m=0}^{\infty} A_m u_m(x)$ and $\sum_{m=0}^{\infty} B_m u_m(x)$ are two asymptotic representations of the function $F(x)$ at the point a, then the coefficients A_m and B_m must be equal to each other for all values of m. For we may write

$$F(x) - \sum_{n=0}^{m} A_n u_n(x) = o[(u_m(x)] \qquad (x \to a)$$

and

$$F(x) - \sum_{n=0}^{m} B_n u_n(x) = o[(u_m(x)] \qquad (x \to a)$$

This implies however that

$$\sum_{n=0}^{m} (A_n - B_n)u_n(x) = o[(u_m x)] \qquad (x \to a)$$

which can be true only if A_n is equal to B_n for all values of n.

b. In some situations a particular function can be represented asymptotically at a given point in terms of more than one set of reference functions. For instance, we may find that

$$F(x) \approx \sum_{m=0}^{\infty} A_m u_m(x) \qquad (x \to a)$$

but also that

$$F(x) \approx \sum_{m=0}^{\infty} B_m v_m(x) \qquad (x \to a)$$

In this case, of course, the coefficients A_m and B_m are not necessarily equal to each other.

c. A function cannot be determined uniquely from its asymptotic expansion at a given point. In other words, two distinct functions $F(x)$ and $G(x)$ can have the same asymptotic representation at a given point. For instance, since

$$e^{-x} \approx 0 + 0/x + 0/x^2 + \cdots \qquad (x \to \infty)$$

the functions $F(x)$, $G(x) = F(x) + e^{-px}$, $H(x) = G(x) + e^{-qx}$, etc., have the same asymptotic representation for large values of x, provided p and q are positive constants.

The following rules pertain to the more common algebraic and analytic operations with asymptotic expansions.

(**a**) Asymptotic expansions can be added or subtracted term by term.

(**b**) Asymptotic expansions can be multiplied according to the following rule. If

$$F(x) \approx \sum_{m=0}^{\infty} A_m u_m(x)$$

and

$$G(x) \approx \sum_{m=0}^{\infty} B_m u_m(x)$$

then

$$F(x)G(x) \approx \sum_{m=0}^{\infty} C_m u_m(x)$$

where the coefficients C_m are related to the coefficients A_m and B_m by the convolution product,

$$C_m = A_0 B_m + A_1 B_{m-1} + \cdots + A_m B_0$$

(c) Asymptotic expansions can be divided if the divisor has at least one nonvanishing coefficient.

(d) Asymptotic expansions can be integrated term by term.

(e) An asymptotic expansion of a function can be differentiated term by term to obtain the asymptotic expansion of its derivative, provided such an expansion for the derivative exists.

We shall now present some elementary examples of the asymptotic expansion of some well-known functions. In the first example we consider the asymptotic expansion of the exponential integral,

$$E_n(x) = \int_1^{\infty} \frac{e^{-xt}}{t^n}\, dt = x^{n-1} \int_x^{\infty} \frac{e^{-u}}{u^n}\, du$$

Integration by parts yields the following asymptotic expansion of this function for large values of x,

$$E_n(x) \approx \frac{e^{-x}}{x}\left[1 + \sum_{m=0}^{\infty} \frac{(-1)^{m+1} n(n+1)\cdots(n+m)}{x^{m+1}}\right]$$

The infinite series on the right hand side is divergent. For, by applying the ratio test, we find that the absolute value of the ratio of the $(m+1)$-th term and the m-th term is equal to $(n+m+1)/x$. This tends to infinity when x is kept fixed and m increases without bound.

The true asymptotic character of the expansion can be verified by keeping m fixed and considering the behavior of the quantity,

$$x^m[E_n(x) - S_m(x)] = (-1)^{m+1} n(n+1)\cdots(n+m) x^{n+m-1} \int_x^{\infty} \frac{e^{-u}}{u^{n+m+1}}\, du$$

as x tends to infinity. We find

$$x^m |E_n(x) - S_m(x)| \leqq \frac{(n+m-1)!\, e^{-x}}{(n-1)!\, x}$$

and the right hand side of this inequality tends to zero when x tends to infinity. In a similar manner we can obtain the asymptotic representation for large values of x of the complementary error function,

$$\operatorname{erfc}(x) = \frac{2}{\sqrt{(\pi)}} \int_x^{\infty} e^{-t^2}\, dt \approx \frac{e^{-x^2}}{x\sqrt{\pi}}\left[1 + \sum_{m=1}^{\infty} \frac{(-1)^m 1 \,.\, 3 \,.\, 5 \ldots (2m-1)}{(2x^2)^m}\right]$$

This expansion can also be obtained by the series expansion solution of the ordinary differential equation,

$$\frac{dF}{dx} = 2xF(x) - 2/\sqrt{\pi}$$

This equation is satisfied by the function $F(x) = \operatorname{erfc}(x) \exp x^2$. The asymptotic expansion of this function for large values of x is obtained by making the substitution $z = 1/t$ in the differential equation and obtaining the series expansion solution of the equation for small values of t.

So far in this section we have been concerned with the asymptotic expansion of a function of a real variable. Without substantial changes the concepts discussed in this section can be generalized to functions of a complex variable. We should note, however, that in a limit relation concerning a function of a real variable the variable x always tends to the limit along a straight line. Hence, only one degree of freedom is involved in the approach of x to a particular limit point. In the case of functions of a complex variable, however, we have to specify the two-dimensional sector in the complex plane in which the variable z is allowed to approach the limit point. In this case the uniformity of the approach of z to the limit may be important. For instance, uniform asymptotic expansions are of particular importance in the approximation of the solutions of boundary value problems. Since the character of the asymptotic expansion may change drastically when we move from one sector of the plane into another, we must be careful that the asymptotic expansion of the solution in a particular sector is commensurate with the boundary condition in that sector.

The same rules apply for the addition, subtraction, multiplication, etc., of asymptotic expansions of a function of a complex variable as for the analogous operations for the asymptotic expansions of functions of a real variable. In combining two or more asymptotic expansions of a function of a complex variable, we should be careful, however, that the sectors of uniformity of these expansions have a region in common.

B. Asymptotic Representation of Unilateral Fourier Transforms

We now return to our point of departure in the introduction to this section, and we shall discuss briefly the asymptotic behavior of unilateral Fourier integrals and the corresponding inversion integrals.

Assuming that the function $f(t)e^{-at}$ is absolutely integrable over the positive real axis, we find that the unilateral Fourier transform,

$$F_+(\lambda) = \frac{1}{\sqrt{(2\pi)}} \int_0^\infty f(t) e^{i\lambda t}\, dt$$

is analytic in the upper half plane $I(\lambda) > a$. Now let us assume that the function $f(t)$ can be represented at the origin by the following asymptotic expansion,

$$f(t) \approx \sum_{m=0}^{\infty} A_m t^m$$

Hence, by definition of an asymptotic expansion, we may write

$$f(t) - \sum_{n=0}^{m} A_n t^n = o(t^m)$$

when t tends to zero. In this case, we can easily show that the function $F_+(\lambda)$ can be represented by the asymptotic expansion,

$$\sqrt{(2\pi)}F_+(\lambda) \approx \sum_{m=0}^{\infty} \frac{i^{m+1} A_m \Gamma(m+1)}{\lambda^{m+1}}$$

when λ tends to infinity in the upper half plane $I(\lambda) > a$. For let us assume that λ is purely imaginary so that $i\lambda = -\gamma$ is real. Multiplying the order relation,

$$f(t) - \sum_{n=0}^{m} A_n t^n = o(t^m)$$

by the function $\exp(-\gamma t)$ and integrating the result over the positive real axis, we find

$$\int_0^{\infty} e^{-\gamma t} f(t)\, dt - \sum_{n=0}^{m} A_n \int_0^{\infty} e^{-\gamma t} t^n \, dt = o\left[\int_0^{\infty} t^m e^{-\gamma t}\, dt\right]$$

The integrals can be evaluated as follows,

$$\int_0^{\infty} e^{-\gamma t} t^m \, dt = \frac{1}{\gamma^{m+1}} \int_0^{\infty} e^{-t} t^m \, dt = \frac{\Gamma(m+1)}{\gamma^{m+1}}$$

Substitution of this result in the penultimate equation yields the proof of our assertion for purely imaginary values of λ,

$$\sqrt{(2\pi)}F_+(i\gamma) - \sum_{n=0}^{m} \frac{A_n \Gamma(n+1)}{\gamma^{n+1}} = o\left(\frac{\Gamma(m+1)}{\gamma^{m+1}}\right)$$

However, since $F_+(\lambda)$ is an analytic function of λ for all values of λ in the upper half plane $I(\lambda) > a$, we may infer, by analytic continuation into the upper half plane, that the assertion is true for all values of λ in $I(\lambda) > a$.

We have shown, therefore, that if the integral,

$$\frac{1}{\sqrt{(2\pi)}} \int_0^{\infty} f(t) e^{i\lambda t}\, dt$$

represents an analytic function, $F_+(\lambda)$, of the complex variable $\lambda = \omega + i\gamma$ in the upper half plane $I(\lambda) > a$ and if the function $f(t)$ can be asymptotically represented by the expansion,

$$f(t) \approx \sum_{m=0}^{\infty} A_m t^m$$

for small values of t, then the function $F_+(\lambda)$ can be asymptotically represented by the expansion,

$$\sqrt{(2\pi)}F_+(\lambda) \approx \sum_{m=0}^{\infty} \frac{A_m i^{m+1}\Gamma(m+1)}{\lambda^{m+1}}$$

for large values of λ in the upper half plane $I(\lambda) > a$.

A special case occurs when $f(t)$ is regular at the origin and can be expanded in a Taylor series about this point,

$$f(t) = \sum_{m=0}^{\infty} \frac{f^{(m)}(0)}{m!} t^m$$

In this case, term by term integration of the Taylor series yields the following asymptotic representation of the function $F_+(\lambda)$,

$$\sqrt{(2\pi)}F_+(\lambda) = \sum_{m=0}^{\infty} \frac{i^{m+1} f^{(m)}(0)}{\lambda^{m+1}}$$

for large values of λ in the upper half plane $I(\lambda) > a$.

Another special case occurs when $f(t)$ has a branch point of order p at the origin. In this case the following lemma of Watson is applicable.

Let $F_+(\lambda)$ be an analytic function defined, in the upper half plane $I(\lambda) > a$, by the integral,

$$\frac{1}{\sqrt{(2\pi)}} \int_0^\infty f(t)e^{i\lambda t}\, dt$$

Let us assume, moreover, that the function $f(t)$ can be asymptotically represented by the convergent series,

$$f(t) = \sum_{m=1}^{\infty} A_m x^{m/p-1}$$

for small values of t. Then the function $F_+(\lambda)$ can be asymptotically represented by the expansion,

$$\sqrt{(2\pi)}F_+(\lambda) \approx \sum_{m=1}^{\infty} \frac{i^m A_m \Gamma(m/p)}{\lambda^{m/p}}$$

for large values of λ in the upper half plane $I(\lambda) > a$.

In the discussion above, we have considered the asymptotic representations of the unilateral Fourier transform $F_+(\lambda)$ for large values of λ. These representations could be derived from the behavior of the function $f(t)$ for small values of t. Similarly, the behavior of the function $F_+(\lambda)$ in the neighborhood of a singular point can be related to the behavior of the function $f(t)$ for large values of t. We state without proof.

Let $f(t)$ be absolutely integrable over the positive real axis and be asymptotically approximated by the finite sum,

$$f(t) = \sum_{m=0}^{M} A_m t^m e^{-i\lambda_0 t}$$

when t tends to infinity. Then the unilateral Fourier transform $F_+(\lambda)$ of the function $f(t)$ is analytic in the upper half plane $I(\lambda) > b$ and has a singularity at the point $\lambda_0 = \omega_0 + ib$. Furthermore, the function $F_+(\lambda)$ can be represented by the expansion,

$$\sqrt{(2\pi)}F_+(\lambda) \approx \sum_{m=0}^{M} \frac{A_m i^{m+1}\Gamma(m+1)}{(\lambda - \lambda_0)^{m+1}}$$

in the neighborhood of this singular point.

C. Asymptotic Behavior of an Inversion Integral for Large Values of t

In the foregoing section we have obtained some asymptotic representations of the unilateral Fourier transform. These representations were derived from the behavior of the function $f(t)$ for large or small values of its argument. In many problems of mathematical physics, however, the solution of a particular differential or integral equation in the space of the transform variable can easily be found. Actually the whole merit of the transform method rests on the fact that the solutions of the transformed equations can easily be obtained. Hence, in solving a particular problem by the transform method, we usually end up with an exact analytical expression for the function $F_+(\lambda)$ from which we have to determine the function $f(t)$ by evaluation of the inversion integral,

$$f(t) = \frac{1}{\sqrt{(2\pi)}} \int_{-\infty+ia}^{\infty+ia} F_+(\zeta)e^{-i\zeta t}\, d\zeta$$

It is obvious, however, that this is not always an easy task. The function $F_+(\lambda)$ can be quite complicated and an evaluation of the contour integral by analytical or numerical means may be difficult or impossible. In such a case we are usually satisfied with the behavior of the function $f(t)$ when the physically meaningful parameter t tends to some interesting limit value. For instance, the behavior of the function $f(t)$ for large values of t can be related to the behavior of the function $F_+(\lambda)$ in the neighborhood of a singular point. This can be shown in the following manner.

Let us assume that the function $F_+(\lambda)$ is analytic in the upper plane $I(\lambda) > a$ and in the region D enclosed by the contour C, as shown in Figure II-16.

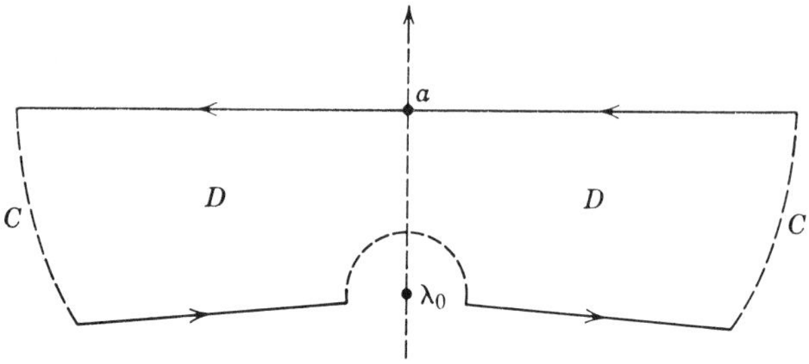

Figure II-16

Let us furthermore assume that $F_+(\lambda)$ tends to zero uniformly when λ tends to infinity in the region D. Then, if $F_+(\lambda)$ can be represented asymptotically by the expansion,

$$F_+(\lambda) \approx \sum_{m=0}^{\infty} A_m(\lambda - \lambda_0)^{\alpha_m}$$

in the neighborhood of the point λ_0, $f(t)$ can be represented asymptotically by the expansion,

$$f(t) = \sqrt{(2\pi)} \sum_{m=0}^{\infty} \frac{A_m\, i^{\alpha_m}}{t^{\alpha_m+1}\Gamma(-\alpha_m)}\, e^{-i\lambda_0 t}$$

for large values of t. Again, the α_m's are members of a sequence of positive or negative real constants which is bounded below by some positive or negative number. It should be noted that for $\alpha_m = 0, 1, 2, \ldots$ the quantity $[1/\Gamma(-\alpha_m)]$ vanishes.

Since the function $F_+(\zeta)e^{-i\zeta t}$ is analytic inside the contour C, the contour integral,

$$\oint_C F_+(\zeta)e^{-i\zeta t}\, d\zeta$$

vanishes. Furthermore, the contributions of the large circle segments to the contour integral vanish when λ tends to infinity. Thus, we obtain the result,

$$\frac{1}{\sqrt{(2\pi)}} \int_{-\infty+ia}^{\infty+ia} F_+(\zeta)e^{-i\zeta t}\, d\zeta = \frac{1}{\sqrt{(2\pi)}} \int_{\Gamma} F_+(\zeta)e^{-i\zeta t}\, d\zeta$$

where Γ is the path which consists of the two slanted straight lines and the circular path around the point λ_0. Moreover, by a slight modification of the formulas in Section 1.7, we find

$$\int_\Gamma (\zeta - \lambda_0)^\alpha e^{-i\zeta t}\, d\zeta = \frac{2\pi i^\alpha e^{-i\lambda_0 t}}{t^{\alpha+1}\Gamma(-\alpha)}\, \theta(t)$$

where $\theta(t)$ denotes the unit step function. This implies that the result can be obtained by a term by term integration of the expansion of the function $F_+(\lambda)$ about the point $\lambda = \lambda_0$.

2.15 APPLICATIONS TO INTEGRAL EQUATIONS WITH A DISPLACEMENT KERNEL

Integral equations with infinite limits such as the inhomogeneous Fredholm equation,

$$f(t) = g(t) + \int_{-\infty}^{\infty} k(t \mid t_0) f(t_0)\, dt_0$$

or with semi-infinite limits such as the inhomogeneous Wiener-Hopf equation,

$$f(t) = g(t) + \int_0^{\infty} k(t \mid t_0) f(t_0)\, dt_0$$

are amenable to solution by function-theoretic techniques. These techniques are a blend of the complex transform techniques and the techniques of analytic continuation discussed in this and the previous chapter, the important provision being that the kernel of the equations is of the convolution or displacement type. In other words, the kernel must be a function of the difference $t - t_0$ only. Such kernels arise, for instance, when the underlying physical process which is described by the solution of the integral equation is invariant to translation in the time coordinate or has translational invariance with respect to a spatial coordinate. The class of equations described above include the so-called Volterra equation,

$$f(t) = g(t) + \int_{-\infty}^{t} k(t - t_0) f(t_0)\, dt_0$$

For this equation may be written as an equation with infinite limits,

$$f(t) = g(t) + \int_{-\infty}^{\infty} k(t - t_0)\theta(t - t_0) f(t_0)\, dt_0$$

where $\theta(t)$ denotes the unit step function. Similarly, by means of this function, the Volterra equation,

$$f(t) = g(t) + \int_0^{t} k(t - t_0) f(t_0)\, dt_0$$

can always be written as a Wiener-Hopf equation,

$$f(t) = g(t) + \int_0^\infty k(t - t_0)\theta(t - t_0)f(t_0)\,dt_0$$

The integral part of an integral equation with a displacement kernel is a convolution of the kernel and the solution of the equation. This is the reason why an equation of the displacement type is amenable to solution by Fourier transform techniques. For the Fourier transformation of such an equation usually results in a particularly simple equation in the space of the real or complex transform variable. For instance, by formally Fourier transforming the integral equation,

$$f(t) = g(t) + \int_{-\infty}^\infty k(t - t_0)f(t_0)\,dt_0$$

we obtain a simple functional relationship between the Fourier transform of the solution, the kernel, and the source term,

$$F(\omega)[1 - \sqrt{(2\pi)}K(\omega)] - G(\omega) = 0$$

Solving this equation for the transform of the solution and inverting the result, we find the integral representation,

$$f(t) = \frac{1}{\sqrt{(2\pi)}}\int_{-\infty}^\infty \frac{G(\omega)e^{-i\omega t}}{1 - \sqrt{(2\pi)}K(\omega)}\,d\omega$$

for the solution of the integral equation.

By a mixture of unilateral and bilateral Fourier transforms, the Wiener-Hopf integral equations can also be reduced to simple functional equations in the space of a complex transform variable. The functional equations obtained in this manner can be solved by means of the analytic continuation technique referred to in Section 1.6. The so-called Wiener-Hopf technique for the solution of such equations is the subject of discussion of the next chapter.

As an interesting aside, we mention the fact that the homogeneous Wiener-Hopf equation,

$$f(t) = \int_0^\infty k(t - t_0)f(t_0)\,dt_0$$

can be written as a Fredholm equation over the real axis,

$$f(t) = \int_{-\infty}^\infty k(t - t_0)\theta(t_0)f(t_0)\,dt_0$$

Fourier transforming this equation, we obtain a singular integral equation of the Cauchy type,

$$F(\omega) = \frac{K(\omega)}{2\pi i} \int_{-\infty}^{\infty} \frac{F(\omega_0)}{\omega_0 - \omega}\, d\omega_0 + \frac{1}{2} K(\omega)F(\omega)$$

where $F(\omega)$ and $K(\omega)$ denote the Fourier transforms of the functions $f(t)$ and $K(t)$ and where we have absorbed a factor $\sqrt{(2\pi)}$ in the function $K(\omega)$. In the derivation of this equation we made use of the convolution theorem and of the Fourier transform of the unit step function,

$$\sqrt{(2\pi)}\Theta(\omega) = \pi\delta(\omega) - \frac{1}{i\omega}$$

This transform was obtained in Section 2.5.
Integral equations with Cauchy kernels are discussed briefly in Chapter IV.

A. Homogeneous Integral Equations

To substantiate our assertions, we shall now discuss a solution technique for the homogeneous integral equation,

$$f(t) = \int_{-\infty}^{\infty} k(t - t_0) f(t_0)\, dt_0$$

Assuming that the function $k(t) \exp [b|t|]$ is absolutely integrable over the real axis, we search for solutions $f(t)$ such that the function $f(t) \exp [-a|t|]$ is absolutely integrable over the real axis. From the integrability condition imposed on the kernel we may infer that the Fourier transform,

$$K(\lambda) = \frac{1}{\sqrt{(2\pi)}} \int_{-\infty}^{\infty} k(t) e^{i\lambda t}\, dt$$

is an analytic function of the complex variable λ in the strip $-b < I(\lambda) < b$. Similarly, from the integrability condition imposed on the solution of the equation, we may conclude that the unilateral transform,

$$F_+(\lambda) = \frac{1}{\sqrt{(2\pi)}} \int_0^{\infty} f(t) e^{i\lambda t}\, dt$$

represents an analytic function in the upper half plane $I(\lambda) > a$, whereas the transform,

$$F_-(\lambda) = \frac{1}{\sqrt{(2\pi)}} \int_{-\infty}^{0} f(t) e^{i\lambda t}\, dt$$

is an analytic function of λ in the lower half plane $I(\lambda) < -a$. Thus, supposing the positive number a is smaller than b, the transforms $K(\lambda)$ and $F_+(\lambda)$ are analytic in the strip $a < I(\lambda) < b$ shown in Figure II-17. Similarly, the transforms $K(\lambda)$ and $F_-(\lambda)$ share a strip of analyticity $-b < I(\lambda) < -a$. Now let α be a positive number which is larger than a but smaller than b. Then, according to Section 2.10, the function $f(t)$ can be represented as follows,

$$f(t) = \frac{1}{\sqrt{(2\pi)}} \int_{-\infty + i\alpha}^{\infty + i\alpha} F_+(\zeta) e^{-i\zeta t}\, d\zeta + \frac{1}{\sqrt{(2\pi)}} \int_{-\infty - i\alpha}^{\infty - i\alpha} F_-(\zeta) e^{-i\zeta t}\, d\zeta$$

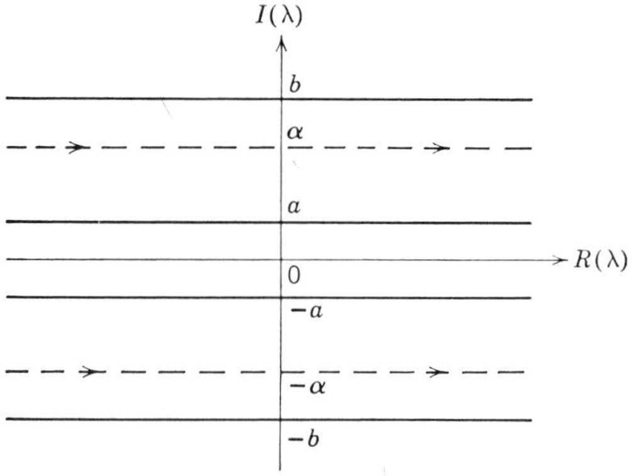

Figure II-17

Substituting the representation of the solution into the integral equation and interchanging the order of integration, we obtain the result,

$$\int_{-\infty + i\alpha}^{\infty + i\alpha} F_+(\zeta)[1 - \sqrt{(2\pi)} K(\zeta)] e^{-i\zeta t}\, d\zeta$$
$$+ \int_{-\infty - i\alpha}^{\infty - i\alpha} F_-(\zeta)[1 - \sqrt{(2\pi)} K(\zeta)] e^{-i\zeta t}\, d\zeta = 0$$

This result can be interpreted in the light of the second example on analytic continuation in Section 1.6 from which we may draw the following conclusions. The functions $F_+(\lambda)[1 - \sqrt{(2\pi)}K(\lambda)]$ and $F_-(\lambda)[1 - \sqrt{(2\pi)}K(\lambda)]$ are analytic in the strip $-b < I(\lambda) < b$ and vanish when $R(\lambda)$ tends to plus or minus infinity in this strip. Furthermore, the sum of these functions vanishes for all values of λ in the strip. Hence, we can define a function $G(\lambda)$,

$$G(\lambda) = F_+(\lambda)[1 - \sqrt{(2\pi)}K(\lambda)] = -F_-(\lambda)[1 - \sqrt{(2\pi)}K(\lambda)]$$

which is analytic in the strip $-b < I(\lambda) < b$ and vanishes when $R(\lambda)$ tends to plus or minus infinity in this strip. By means of the function $G(\lambda)$ the integral representation of the solution can be brought into the form,

$$f(t) = \frac{1}{\sqrt{(2\pi)}} \int_{-\infty + i\alpha}^{\infty + i\alpha} \frac{G(\zeta) e^{-i\zeta t}}{1 - \sqrt{(2\pi)} K(\zeta)}\, d\zeta - \frac{1}{\sqrt{(2\pi)}} \int_{-\infty - i\alpha}^{\infty - i\alpha} \frac{G(\zeta) e^{-i\zeta t}}{1 - \sqrt{(2\pi)} K(\zeta)}\, d\zeta$$

The integrands of these integrals have simple or multiple poles at the points in the strip at which the denominator $1 - \sqrt{(2\pi)}K(\lambda)$ vanishes. This enables us to evaluate the integral representation of the function $f(t)$ by means of contour integration and the residue theorem. For let us assume that all the zeros of the function $1 - \sqrt{(2\pi)}K(\lambda)$ are of first order and are located in the strip $-a \leqq I(\lambda) \leqq a$. Then, according to the residue theorem, the contour integral,

$$\frac{1}{2\pi i}\oint_C \frac{G(\zeta)e^{-i\zeta t}}{1 - \sqrt{(2\pi)}K(\zeta)}\, d\zeta$$

is equal to the sum of the residues of the integrand at the poles enclosed by the rectangular contour C of Figure II-18.

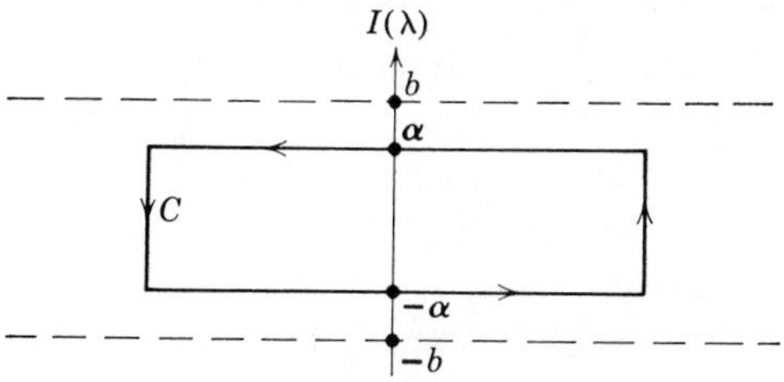

Figure II-18

However, in the limit as $R(\lambda)$ tends to plus or minus infinity, the contribution of the vertical sides of the contour to the integral vanishes. Thus we obtain

$$\frac{1}{\sqrt{(2\pi)}}\int_{-\infty+i\alpha}^{\infty+i\alpha} \frac{G(\zeta)e^{-i\zeta t}}{1 - \sqrt{(2\pi)}K(\zeta)}\, d\zeta$$

$$-\frac{1}{\sqrt{(2\pi)}}\int_{-\infty-i\alpha}^{\infty-i\alpha} \frac{G(\zeta)e^{-i\zeta t}}{1 - \sqrt{(2\pi)}K(\zeta)}\, d\zeta = \sum_m \frac{iG(a_m)e^{-ia_m t}}{dK(a_m)/d\lambda}$$

where a_m denotes the location of the zeros of the function $1 - \sqrt{(2\pi)}K(\lambda)$. The left hand side of this equation is just the integral representation of the solution of the integral equation. Thus we may write

$$f(t) = \sum_m \frac{iG(a_m)e^{-ia_m t}}{dK(a_m)/d\lambda}$$

A similar result can be obtained when the function $1 - \sqrt{(2\pi)}K(\lambda)$ has zeros of higher order than the first at the points a_m. To conclude this section we briefly consider the following two examples.

EXAMPLE 1 The Fourier transform of the kernel of the integral equation,

$$f(t) = \int_{-\infty}^{\infty} e^{-|t-t_0|} f(t_0)\, dt_0$$

takes the form,

$$K(\lambda) = \frac{1}{\sqrt{(2\pi)}} \int_{-\infty}^{\infty} e^{-|t|+i\lambda t}\, dt = \sqrt{\left(\frac{2}{\pi}\right)} \frac{1}{1+\lambda^2}$$

Hence, $K(\lambda)$ is an analytic function of λ in the strip $-1 < I(\lambda) < 1$. The integrand of the contour integral,

$$\oint_c \frac{G(\zeta)e^{-i\zeta t}}{1 - \sqrt{(2\pi)}K(\zeta)}\, d\zeta$$

has simple poles which are located at the positions of the zeros of the function,

$$1 - \sqrt{(2\pi)}K(\lambda) = \frac{\lambda^2 - 1}{\lambda^2 + 1}$$

That is, they are located at the points ± 1 on the real axis. We find, therefore, the following expression for the sum of the residues of the integrand at the simple poles enclosed by the contour,

$$\sum_m \text{Res}\left[\frac{G(\lambda)e^{-i\lambda t}}{\sqrt{(2\pi)}[1 - \sqrt{(2\pi)}K(\lambda)]}, \pm 1\right] = a \exp(it) + b \exp(-it)$$

Thus the solution of the integral equation may be written

$$f(t) = a \exp(it) + b \exp(-it)$$

where a and b are arbitrary constants which can be determined from the auxiliary conditions.

EXAMPLE 2 As a second example we consider an integral equation which arises in the study of the diffusion of mono-energetic neutrons in a uniform infinite medium with isotropic scattering but without sources,

$$f(x) = \int_{-\infty}^{\infty} k(x - \xi) f(\xi)\, d\xi$$

where $f(x)$ denotes the neutron density. The kernel of this equation is a so-called Milne kernel,

$$k(|x|) = \frac{c}{2} \int_{|x|}^{\infty} \frac{e^{-u}}{u}\, du$$

From the asymptotic expansion of the exponential integral in Section 2.11, we obtain the order relation,

$$k(|x|) = O(e^{-|x|}/|x|)$$

when $|x|$ tends to infinity. The Fourier transform of the kernel takes the form,

$$K(\lambda) = \frac{1}{\sqrt{(2\pi)}} \int_{-\infty}^{\infty} k(|x|)e^{-i\lambda x}\, dx = \frac{c}{\sqrt{(2\pi)}} \frac{\arctan \lambda}{\lambda} = \frac{c}{2i\lambda\sqrt{(2\pi)}} \log \frac{i - \lambda}{i + \lambda}$$

This function has two logarithmic branch points, which are located at the points $\pm i$, and is analytic in the strip $-1 < I(\lambda) < 1$. The location of the zeros of the function,

$$1 - \sqrt{(2\pi)}K(\lambda) = 1 - c\frac{\arctan \lambda}{\lambda}$$

depends on the magnitude of the positive constant c. If c lies between zero and one, then this function has two roots of the first order at the point $\pm i\gamma_0$ on the imaginary axis. Since $|\gamma_0|$ is smaller than one, these points are located inside the strip $-1 < I(\lambda) < 1$. The function has a double root at the origin when c is equal to one, and has two real roots at the points $\pm \omega_0$ on the real axis when c is larger than one. Hence, excluding the case in which c is equal to one, the function $1 - \sqrt{(2\pi)}K(\lambda)$ has two zeros of the first order inside the strip. Proceeding in the manner outlined in the first example, we find that the solution of the integral equation may again be written as the sum of two exponentials,

$$f(x) = a \exp(i\lambda_0 x) + b \exp(-i\lambda_0 x)$$

where λ_0 denotes the location of a root of the function $1 - \sqrt{(2\pi)}K(\lambda)$ inside the strip.

B. Inhomogeneous Integral Equations

The solution of the inhomogeneous integral equation with a displacement kernel,

$$f(t) = g(t) + \int_{-\infty}^{\infty} k(t - t_0)f(t_0)\, dt_0$$

can be obtained by a straightforward extension of the solution method for the homogeneous equation. We shall assume that the kernel and the solution of the inhomogeneous equation satisfy the conditions imposed on the kernel and the solution of the homogeneous equation in the foregoing section. In addition we shall assume that the function $g(t) \exp(-d|t|)$ is absolutely integrable over the real axis. Let d be a positive number which is smaller than b. Then the unilateral transform $G_+(\lambda)$ of the function $g(t)$ is analytic in the upper half plane $I(\lambda) > d$ and the transform $G_-(\lambda)$ is analytic in the lower half plane $I(\lambda) < -d$. Moreover, since a and d are smaller than b, the functions $F_+(\lambda)$, $G_+(\lambda)$, and $K(\lambda)$ are analytic in the strip $\max(a, d) < I(\lambda) < b$, shown in Figure II-19. Similarly, the functions $F_-(\lambda)$, $G(\lambda)$, and $K(\lambda)$ are analytic in the strip

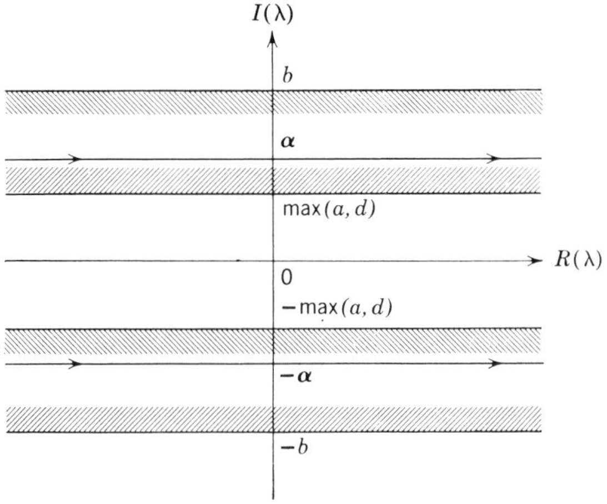

Figure II-19

$-b < I(\lambda) < -\max(a, d)$. We now choose a constant α which is smaller than b but larger than $\max(a, d)$. Then, substituting the integral representaions of the functions $f(t)$, $g(t)$, and $K(t)$ into the integral equation, we obtain

$$\frac{1}{\sqrt{(2\pi)}}\int_{-\infty+i\alpha}^{\infty+i\alpha}[F_+(\zeta)\{1-\sqrt{(2\pi)}K(\zeta)\}-G_+(\zeta)]e^{-i\zeta t}\,d\zeta$$
$$+\frac{1}{\sqrt{(2\pi)}}\int_{-\infty-i\alpha}^{\infty-i\alpha}[F_-(\zeta)\{1-\sqrt{(2\pi)}K(\zeta)\}-G_-(\zeta)]e^{-i\zeta t}\,d\zeta=0$$

Referring again to the analytic continuation argument of Section 1.6, we may conclude that the functions

$$H_+(\lambda) = F_+(\lambda)[1-\sqrt{(2\pi)}K(\lambda)] - G_+(\lambda)$$

and

$$H_-(\lambda) = F_-(\lambda)[1-\sqrt{(2\pi)}K(\lambda)] - G_-(\lambda)$$

are analytic in the strip $-b < I(\lambda) < b$ and vanish when $R(\lambda)$ tends to infinity in this strip. Furthermore, the sum of these functions vanishes identically at all points in the strip. From these conclusions we may infer that the solution of the inhomogeneous equation has the integral representation,

$$f(t) = \frac{1}{\sqrt{(2\pi)}} \int_{-\infty + i\alpha}^{\infty + i\alpha} \frac{H_+(\zeta) + G_+(\zeta)}{1 - \sqrt{(2\pi)}K(\zeta)} e^{-i\zeta t}\, d\zeta + \frac{1}{\sqrt{(2\pi)}} \int_{-\infty - i\alpha}^{\infty - i\alpha} \frac{H_-(\zeta) + G_-(\zeta)}{1 - \sqrt{(2\pi)}K(\zeta)} e^{-i\zeta t}\, d\zeta$$

where $H_+(\lambda) = -H_-(\lambda)$. The integrands of these integrals are analytic functions of λ in the strip $-b < I(\lambda) < b$ with the exception of possible poles which arise from the zeros in the denominator $1 - \sqrt{(2\pi)}K(\lambda)$. Proceeding in the manner as explained for the homogeneous equation, the solution $f(t)$ of the inhomogeneous equation can again be evaluated by contour integration. Since $H_+(\lambda) = -H_-(\lambda) = -H(\lambda)$, the solution of the integral equation can be represented by the sum,

$$f(t) = \frac{1}{\sqrt{(2\pi)}} \int_{-\infty + i\alpha}^{\infty + i\alpha} \frac{G_+(\zeta)e^{-i\zeta t}}{1 - \sqrt{(2\pi)}K(\zeta)}\, d\zeta + \frac{1}{\sqrt{(2\pi)}} \int_{-\infty - i\alpha}^{\infty - i\alpha} \frac{G_-(\zeta)e^{-i\zeta t}}{1 - \sqrt{(2\pi)}K(\zeta)}\, d\zeta + \frac{1}{\sqrt{(2\pi)}} \oint_C \frac{H(\zeta)e^{-i\zeta t}}{1 - \sqrt{(2\pi)}K(\zeta)}\, d\zeta$$

where C denotes an arbitrary contour which is located between the parallel lines $(-\infty + i\alpha, \infty + i\alpha)$ and $(-\infty - i\alpha, \infty - i\alpha)$ and encloses the zeros of the denominator $1 - \sqrt{(2\pi)}K(\lambda)$. According to this representation, the solution of the integral equation can be written as the sum of the solution of the homogeneous equation,

$$\frac{1}{\sqrt{(2\pi)}} \oint_C \frac{H(\zeta)e^{-i\zeta t}}{1 - \sqrt{(2\pi)}K(\zeta)}\, d\zeta$$

and a particular solution of the inhomogeneous equation reflecting the effect of the source term.

CHAPTER III

THE WIENER-HOPF TECHNIQUE

3.0 INTRODUCTION

In this chapter we shall be concerned with the Wiener-Hopf technique for the solution of functional equations of the form,

$$A(\lambda)F_+(\lambda) + B(\lambda)F_-(\lambda) = 0 \tag{3.1}$$

and

$$A(\lambda)F_+(\lambda) + B(\lambda)F_-(\lambda) = C(\lambda) \tag{3.2}$$

which are defined in a strip of the complex plane. Functional equations of this type are obtained by the Fourier transformation of certain integral equations and partial differential equations, and the ability to solve such functional equations is of great value in the solution of some boundary value and initial value problems of mathematical physics.

The homogeneous equation (3.1) defines a relationship between two known functions $A(\lambda)$ and $B(\lambda)$ of the complex variable λ and two functions $F_+(\lambda)$ and $F_-(\lambda)$ which we seek to obtain. Similarly, given the functions $A(\lambda)$, $B(\lambda)$, and $C(\lambda)$, we are required to solve the inhomogeneous equation (3.2) for the functions $F_+(\lambda)$ and $F_-(\lambda)$.

Let us consider the solution of the homogeneous equation,

$$A(\lambda)F_+(\lambda) + B(\lambda)F_-(\lambda) = 0 \tag{3.1}$$

Assuming that the function $F_+(\lambda)$ is analytic in the upper half plane $I(\lambda) > a$ and that the function $F_-(\lambda)$ is analytic in the lower half plane $I(\lambda) < b$, where $a < b$, the functions $F_+(\lambda)$ and $F_-(\lambda)$ have the common strip of analyticity $a < I(\lambda) < b$, as shown in Figure III-1.

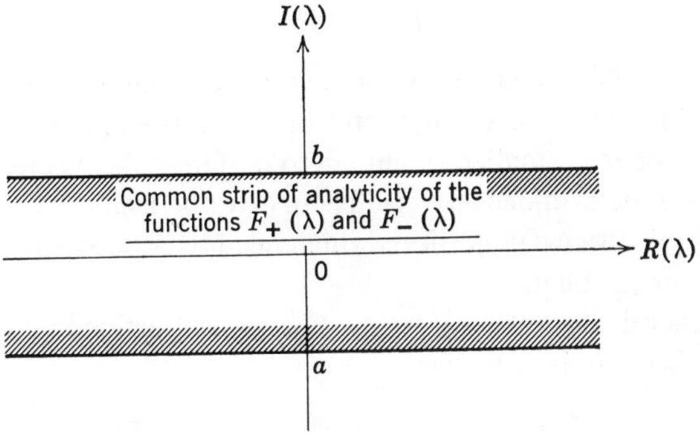

Figure III-1

If it is known moreover that the functions $A(\lambda)$ and $B(\lambda)$ are analytic in strips which contain or coincide with the strip $a < I(\lambda) < b$, then equation (3.1) is well defined in this strip since it pertains to a relation between functions which have this strip as a common region of analyticity.

We now consider the special case that the function $A(\lambda)$ is analytic and nonvanishing in the upper half plane $I(\lambda) > a$ and that the function $B(\lambda)$ is analytic and nonvanishing in the lower half plane $I(\lambda) < b$. The function $A(\lambda)F_+(\lambda)$ is analytic therefore in the upper half plane $I(\lambda) > a$ and the function $B(\lambda)F_-(\lambda)$ is analytic in the lower half plane $I(\lambda) < b$. Both functions have the strip of analyticity $a < I(\lambda) < b$ in common. This implies, according to the analytic continuation argument of Section 1.6, that the function $A(\lambda)F_+(\lambda)$ is the analytic continuation of the function $-B(\lambda)F_-(\lambda)$ into the upper half plane $I(\lambda) > b$, whereas the function $-B(\lambda)F_-(\lambda)$ is the analytic continuation of the function $A(\lambda)F_+(\lambda)$ into the lower half plane $I(\lambda) < a$. Consequently, in their respective regions of analyticity, the functions $A(\lambda)F_+(\lambda)$ and $-B(\lambda)F_-(\lambda)$ are the representations of a single function which is analytic in the whole complex plane. In other words, they are the representations of an entire function, $E(\lambda)$. The nature of this entire function can be determined from the order properties of the functions $A(\lambda)F_+(\lambda)$ and $B(\lambda)F_-(\lambda)$ for large values of λ.

For example, let us assume that the functions $A(\lambda)F_+(\lambda)$ and $B(\lambda)F_-(\lambda)$ are of algebraic growth at infinity, more specifically

$$A(\lambda)F_+(\lambda) = O(\lambda^\alpha)$$

when λ tends to infinity in the upper half plane $I(\lambda) > a$, and

$$B(\lambda)F_-(\lambda) = O(\lambda^\beta)$$

when λ tends to infinity in the lower half plane $I(\lambda) < b$. In this case, the entire function $E(\lambda)$ is also of algebraic growth at infinity, and

$$E(\lambda) = O(\lambda^\nu)$$

when λ tends to infinity in the whole complex plane, where $\nu = \max(\alpha, \beta)$. According to Liouville's theorem, therefore, the entire function $E(\lambda)$ must be a polynomial of degree smaller or equal to ν. Once the degree of the polynomial has been determined, its coefficients can be found by means of other mathematical or physical conditions which need to be satisfied by the solution of the particular problem.

Thus, in general, the entire function $E(\lambda)$ is well defined and the functions $F_+(\lambda)$ and $F_-(\lambda)$ may be written

$$F_+(\lambda) = \frac{E(\lambda)}{A(\lambda)} \quad \text{and} \quad F_-(\lambda) = -\frac{E(\lambda)}{B(\lambda)}$$

The solution of the problem above has been relatively straightforward because we have assumed that the functions $A(\lambda)$ and $F_+(\lambda)$ share an upper half plane of analyticity whereas the functions $B(\lambda)$ and $F_-(\lambda)$ have a lower half plane in common.

A slightly more complicated problem arises when the functions $A(\lambda)$ and $B(\lambda)$ are analytic and nonvanishing in the strip $a < I(\lambda) < b$. We now construct two functions $H_+(\lambda)$ and $H_-(\lambda)$, which are analytic and nonvanishing in the upper half plane $I(\lambda) > a$ and the lower half plane $I(\lambda) < b$ respectively, and satisfy the equation,

$$\frac{A(\lambda)}{B(\lambda)} = \frac{H_+(\lambda)}{H_-(\lambda)}$$

in the strip $a < I(\lambda) < b$. Substitution of this relation into equation (3.1) yields the homogeneous functional equation,

$$H_+(\lambda)F_+(\lambda) + H_-(\lambda)F_-(\lambda) = 0$$

and this equation can be solved in the manner described above.

The inhomogeneous equation,

$$A(\lambda)F_+(\lambda) + B(\lambda)F_-(\lambda) = C(\lambda) \tag{3.2}$$

can be subjected to a similar analysis. Assuming that the functions $F_+(\lambda)$ and $F_-(\lambda)$ are analytic in the upper half plane $I(\lambda) > a$ and the lower half plane $I(\lambda) < b$ respectively, and that the functions $A(\lambda)$, $B(\lambda)$, and $C(\lambda)$ are analytic and nonvanishing in the strip $a < I(\lambda) < b$, we again construct two functions, $H_+(\lambda)$ and $H_-(\lambda)$, such that

$$\frac{A(\lambda)}{B(\lambda)} = \frac{H_+(\lambda)}{H_-(\lambda)} \tag{3.3}$$

and $H_+(\lambda)$ and $H_-(\lambda)$ are analytic and nonvanishing in the upper half plane $I(\lambda) > a$ and the lower half plane $I(\lambda) < b$, respectively. Substitution of equation (3.3) into equation (3.2) yields the functional equation,

$$H_+(\lambda)F_+(\lambda) + H_-(\lambda)F_-(\lambda) = \frac{C(\lambda)}{B(\lambda)} H_-(\lambda) \tag{3.4}$$

Subsequently we construct two functions, $G_+(\lambda)$ and $G_-(\lambda)$, which are analytic in the upper half plane $I(\lambda) > a$ and the lower half plane $I(\lambda) < b$ respectively, and satisfy the relation,

$$G_+(\lambda) - G_-(\lambda) = \frac{C(\lambda)}{B(\lambda)} H_-(\lambda)$$

Substituting this expression into equation (3.4), we find

$$H_+(\lambda)F_+(\lambda) + H_-(\lambda)F_-(\lambda) = G_+(\lambda) - G_-(\lambda)$$

and rearranging terms, we obtain a homogeneous functional equation,

$$H_+(\lambda)F_+(\lambda) - G_+(\lambda) + H_-(\lambda)F_-(\lambda) + G_-(\lambda) = 0$$

which can be subjected to the same analysis as before.

We note that a successful execution of the Wiener-Hopf technique for the solution of homogeneous and inhomogeneous functional equations depends in large measure on our ability to factor a function of a complex variable $H(\lambda)$, which is analytic in a strip $a < I(\lambda) < b$, into a product,

$$H(\lambda) = H_+(\lambda) \frac{1}{H_-(\lambda)}$$

where the functions $H_+(\lambda)$ and $H_-(\lambda)$ are analytic and nonvanishing in the upper half plane $I(\lambda) > a$ and the lower half plane $I(\lambda) < b$ respectively.

In addition we have to be able to decompose a function $G(\lambda)$, which is analytic in a strip $a < I(\lambda) < b$, into two functions $G_+(\lambda)$ and $G_-(\lambda)$ which are analytic in the upper half plane $I(\lambda) > a$ and the lower half plane $I(\lambda) < b$, respectively, and satisfy the equation,

$$G(\lambda) = G_+(\lambda) - G_-(\lambda)$$

In some elementary problems the factorization and decomposition can be accomplished by inspection. In more complicated problems recourse must be sought in known product and sum rules. The derivation of such rules will be the subject of discussion of the next few sections. However, to conclude this section, we shall first present a simple example.

EXAMPLE. Let it be required to solve the functional equation,

$$A(\lambda)F_+(\lambda) + F_-(\lambda) = C(\lambda) \tag{3.5}$$

where the functions $A(\lambda)$, $C(\lambda)$, $F_+(\lambda)$, and $F_-(\lambda)$ are defined as follows

a. The function,

$$A(\lambda) = \frac{B}{\sqrt{(k^2 - \lambda^2)}}$$

where $k = \alpha + i\beta$, β is a positive number, and B is an arbitrary constant, is analytic in the strip $-\beta < I(\lambda) < \beta$.

b. The function,

$$C(\lambda) = \frac{D}{\lambda - \mu}$$

where $\mu = a + ib$, $0 < b < \beta$, and D is an arbitrary constant, is analytic in the upper half plane $I(\lambda) > b$.

c. The function $F_+(\lambda)$ is analytic in the upper half plane $I(\lambda) > b$, and $F_+(\lambda)$ vanishes as $(1/\lambda)^{1/2}$ when λ tends to infinity in this half plane.

d. The function $F_-(\lambda)$ is analytic in the lower half plane $I(\lambda) < \beta$ and vanishes as $1/\lambda$ when λ tends to infinity in this half plane.

To obtain the solution of this equation, we factor the function $A(\lambda)$ in the following manner,

$$A(\lambda) = \frac{B}{\sqrt{(k^2 - \lambda^2)}} = \frac{H_+(\lambda)}{H_-(\lambda)}$$

where the function $H_+(\lambda) = B/\sqrt{(k + \lambda)}$ is analytic and nonvanishing in the upper half plane $I(\lambda) > -\beta$, and $H_-(\lambda) = \sqrt{(k - \lambda)}$ is analytic and nonvanishing in the lower half plane $I(\lambda) < \beta$. Equation (3.5) can be written therefore

$$H_+(\lambda)F_+(\lambda) + H_-(\lambda)F_-(\lambda) = H_-(\lambda)C(\lambda)$$

It can be shown, by the method of Section 3.2, that the decomposition,

$$H_-(\lambda)C(\lambda) = D\,\frac{\sqrt{(k - \lambda)}}{\lambda - \mu} = G_+(\lambda) - G_-(\lambda)$$

where the function,

$$G_+(\lambda) = D\,\frac{\sqrt{(k - \mu)}}{\lambda - \mu}$$

is analytic in the upper half plane $I(\lambda) > b$ and the function,

$$G_{-}(\lambda) = D\,\frac{\sqrt{(k-\mu)} - \sqrt{(k-\lambda)}}{\lambda - \mu}$$

is analytic in the lower half plane $I(\lambda) < \beta$, is appropriate for our purpose. This decomposition reduces our functional equation to the form,

$$H_{+}(\lambda)F_{+}(\lambda) - G_{+}(\lambda) = -[H_{-}(\lambda)F_{-}(\lambda) + G_{-}(\lambda)]$$

The function represented by the left hand side of this equation is analytic in the upper half plane $I(\lambda) > b$, whereas the function represented by the right hand side of this equation is analytic in the lower half plane $I(\lambda) < \beta$. These functions moreover have the strip of analyticity $b < I(\lambda) < \beta$ in common and are representations therefore of the same function $E(\lambda)$ which is analytic in the whole complex plane. In other words, $E(\lambda)$ is an entire function. Consequently,

$$H_{+}(\lambda)F_{+}(\lambda) - G_{+}(\lambda) = -[H_{-}(\lambda)F_{-}(\lambda) + G_{-}(\lambda)] = E(\lambda)$$

To define the entire function $E(\lambda)$ more closely, we note that the functions $H_{+}(\lambda)F_{+}(\lambda)$ and $G_{+}(\lambda)$ vanish as $1/\lambda$ when λ tends to infinity in the upper half plane $I(\lambda) > b$. Similarly, the functions $H_{-}(\lambda)F_{-}(\lambda)$ and $G_{-}(\lambda)$ vanish as $(1/\lambda)^{1/2}$ when λ tends to infinity in the lower half plane $I(\lambda) < \beta$. $E(\lambda)$ vanishes therefore when λ tends to infinity and, according to Liouville's theorem, this function must vanish identically in the whole complex plane. Hence we may conclude that

$$F_{+}(\lambda) = \frac{G_{+}(\lambda)}{H_{+}(\lambda)} = \frac{D}{B}\,\frac{\sqrt{(k-\mu)}\sqrt{(k+\lambda)}}{\lambda - \mu}$$

and

$$F_{-}(\lambda) = -\frac{G_{-}(\lambda)}{H_{-}(\lambda)} = D\,\frac{\sqrt{(k-\lambda)} - \sqrt{(k-\mu)}}{(\lambda-\mu)\sqrt{(k-\lambda)}}$$

3.1 THE MITTAG-LEFFLER EXPANSION

As a first example of a decomposition or summation formula, we shall consider the well-known Mittag-Leffler representation of a meromorphic function by a sum of partial fractions.

Let $G(\lambda)$ be a meromorphic function and let us assume that all its poles, $a_0, a_1, a_2, \ldots$, are simple. We may write formally

$$E(\lambda) = G(\lambda) - \sum_{m=0}^{\infty} \frac{b_m}{\lambda - a_m}$$

where b_m is the residue of the function $G(\lambda)$ at the pole a_m, and $E(\lambda)$ is an entire function. If we assume that $G(\lambda)$ is bounded at infinity, then $E(\lambda)$ is also bounded at infinity and this implies, according to Liouville's theorem, that $E(\lambda)$ is a constant. Consequently, if $G(\lambda)$ is analytic at the origin, then

$$E(\lambda) = E(0) = G(0) + \sum_{m=0}^{\infty} \frac{b_m}{a_m}$$

Furthermore,

$$G(\lambda) = E(0) + \sum_{m=0}^{\infty} \frac{b_m}{\lambda - a_m}$$

and we obtain therefore the summation formula,

$$G(\lambda) = G(0) + \sum_{m=0}^{\infty} \left(\frac{b_m}{\lambda - a_m} + \frac{b_m}{a_m} \right) \tag{3.6}$$

Thus we have shown, in a rather formal manner, that a meromorphic function, which is analytic at the origin and has simple poles only, can be represented by a sum of partial fractions. The summation formula derived above is a special case of the Mittag-Leffler expansion of a meromorphic function in a sum of partial fractions.

A more rigorous derivation of the representation (3.6) follows. Let $G(\lambda)$ be a meromorphic function which has simple poles only. Let these poles be located at the points $a_0, a_1, \ldots,$ which are indexed in order of increasing magnitude, and let $C_0, C_1, \ldots,$ denote the concentric circles with center at the origin and radii $R_0, R_1, \ldots,$ such that R_n tends to infinity and such that no pole is located on a circle. We shall assume moreover that $G(\lambda)$ is analytic at the origin and is bounded on the circles with a bound that is independent of the particular circle considered. If $b_0, b_1, \ldots, b_M$ are the residues of the function $G(\lambda)$ at the poles $a_0, a_1, \ldots, a_M$ and λ is a point inside the circle C_M, which encloses the poles $a_0, a_1, \ldots, a_M$, then, according to the residue theorem of Section 1.3,

$$\frac{1}{2\pi i} \oint_{C_M} \frac{G(\zeta)}{\zeta - \lambda}\, d\zeta = G(\lambda) + \sum_{m=0}^{M} \frac{b_m}{a_m - \lambda}$$

The integral may also be written

$$\begin{aligned} \frac{1}{2\pi i} \oint_{C_M} \frac{G(\zeta)}{\zeta - \lambda}\, d\zeta &= \frac{1}{2\pi i} \oint_{C_M} \frac{G(\zeta)}{\zeta}\, d\zeta + \frac{\lambda}{2\pi i} \oint_{C_M} \frac{G(\zeta)}{\zeta(\zeta - \lambda)}\, d\zeta \\ &= G(0) + \sum_{m=0}^{M} \frac{b_m}{a_m} + \frac{\lambda}{2\pi i} \oint_{C_M} \frac{G(\zeta)}{\zeta(\zeta - \lambda)}\, d\zeta \end{aligned}$$

and we find, therefore,

$$G(\lambda) + \sum_{m=0}^{M} \frac{b_m}{a_m - \lambda} = G(0) + \sum_{m=0}^{M} \frac{b_m}{a_m} + \frac{\lambda}{2\pi i} \oint_{C_M} \frac{G(\zeta)}{\zeta(\zeta - \lambda)} d\zeta$$

However, since the function $G(\lambda)$ is bounded on the circle C_M and the bound is independent of M, the integral on the right hand side of this equation vanishes when M tends to infinity and we may conclude that

$$G(\lambda) = G(0) + \sum_{m=0}^{\infty} \left(\frac{b_m}{\lambda - a_m} + \frac{b_m}{a_m} \right)$$

3.2 THE DECOMPOSITION OF A FUNCTION THAT IS ANALYTIC IN A STRIP

If the function $G(\lambda)$ is analytic in a strip $\alpha < I(\lambda) < \beta$, then, depending on the behavior of the function $G(\lambda)$ when λ tends to infinity in this strip, a straightforward application of Cauchy's formula may lead to the decomposition,

$$G(\lambda) = G_+(\lambda) - G_-(\lambda)$$

where the functions $G_+(\lambda)$ and $G_-(\lambda)$ are analytic in the upper half plane $I(\lambda) > \alpha$ and the lower half plane $I(\lambda) < \beta$ respectively.

For, if C denotes the contour shown in Figure III-2, then according to

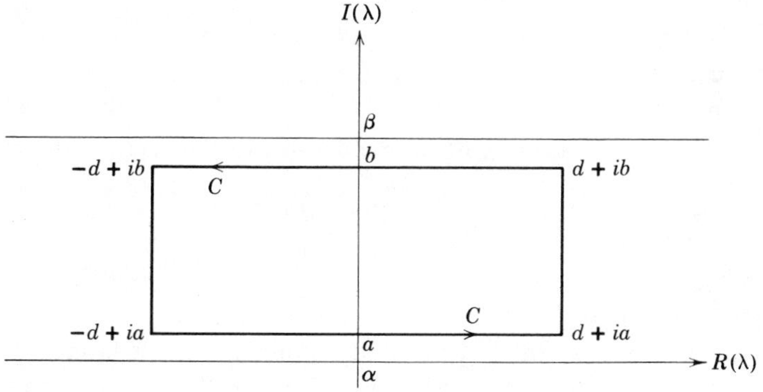

Figure III-2

Cauchy's formula,

$$G(\lambda) = \frac{1}{2\pi i} \oint_C \frac{G(\zeta)}{\zeta - \lambda} d\zeta$$

when λ is a point inside C.

Assuming that the function $G(\lambda)/\lambda$ tends to zero as λ tends to infinity uniformly in this strip, the contribution of the vertical sides of the contour to the integral vanishes when d tends to infinity, and we find

$$G(\lambda) = \frac{1}{2\pi i}\int_{-\infty+ia}^{\infty+ia} \frac{G(\zeta)}{\zeta-\lambda}\,d\zeta - \frac{1}{2\pi i}\int_{-\infty+ib}^{\infty+ib} \frac{G(\zeta)}{\zeta-\lambda}\,d\zeta = G_+(\lambda) - G_-(\lambda)$$

where the functions $G_+(\lambda)$ and $G_-(\lambda)$ have the following integral representations,

$$G_+(\lambda) = \frac{1}{2\pi i}\int_{-\infty+ia}^{\infty+ia} \frac{G(\zeta)}{\zeta-\lambda}\,d\zeta$$

and

$$G_-(\lambda) = \frac{1}{2\pi i}\int_{-\infty+ib}^{\infty+ib} \frac{G(\zeta)}{\zeta-\lambda}\,d\zeta$$

Since λ is not a point on the path $(-\infty + ia, \infty + ia)$, the first integral represents a function $G_+(\lambda)$ which is analytic for all values of λ in the upper half plane $I(\lambda) > a$. Similarly, the second integral represents a function $G_-(\lambda)$ which is analytic in the lower half plane $I(\lambda) < b$. Moreover, since the points a and b can be chosen arbitrarily close to the points α and β respectively, the functions $G_+(\lambda)$ and $G_-(\lambda)$ have a strip of analyticity $\alpha < I(\lambda) < \beta$ in common.

To illustrate the discussion above we shall now present some simple examples.

EXAMPLE 1 To decompose, in the manner of this section, the function

$$G(\lambda) = \frac{\sqrt{(\lambda + k)}}{\lambda - i\mu}$$

where $k = \alpha + i\beta$ and β and μ are positive numbers.

This function has a simple pole at the point $\lambda = i\mu$, a branch point at $\lambda = -k$, and is analytic in the strip $-\beta < I(\lambda) < \mu$. We choose a branch cut in the lower half plane and consider the integral,

$$\oint_C \frac{\sqrt{(\zeta + k)}}{\zeta - i\mu}\,\frac{d\zeta}{\zeta - \lambda}$$

where C is the contour shown in Figure III-3 and λ is a point inside this

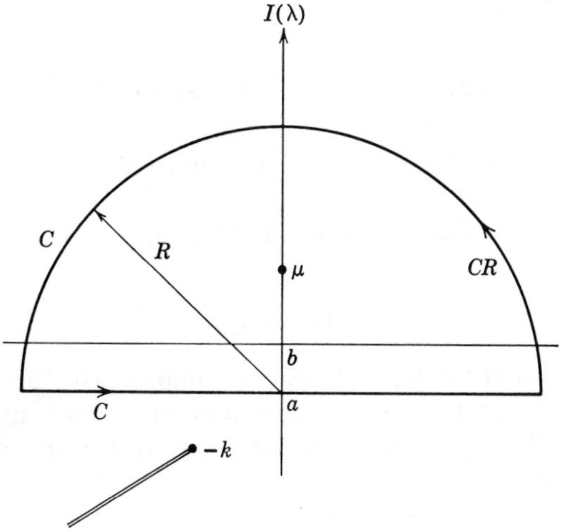

Figure III-3

contour. By the residue theorem of Section 1.3 we find

$$\oint_C \frac{\sqrt{(\zeta+k)}}{\zeta-i\mu}\frac{d\zeta}{\zeta-\lambda} = \int_{-R+ia}^{R+ia} \frac{\sqrt{(\zeta+k)}}{\zeta-i\mu}\frac{d\zeta}{\zeta-\lambda} + \int_{CR} \frac{\sqrt{(\zeta+k)}}{\zeta-i\mu}\frac{d\zeta}{\zeta-\lambda}$$

$$= 2\pi i \sum \text{Res}\left[\frac{\sqrt{(\zeta+k)}}{\zeta-i\mu}\frac{1}{\zeta-\lambda}, \zeta = i\mu \quad \text{and} \quad \zeta=\lambda\right]$$

$$= 2\pi i \frac{\sqrt{(\lambda+k)}-\sqrt{(k+i\mu)}}{\lambda-i\mu}$$

The contribution of the semicircle CR to the contour integral vanishes in the limit as R tends to infinity and we obtain, therefore,

$$G_+(\lambda) = \frac{1}{2\pi i}\int_{-\infty+ia}^{\infty+ia} \frac{\sqrt{(\zeta+k)}}{\zeta-i\mu}\frac{d\zeta}{\zeta-\lambda} = \frac{\sqrt{(\lambda+k)}-\sqrt{(k+i\mu)}}{\lambda-i\mu}$$

This function is analytic in the upper half plane $I(\lambda) > -\beta$. In a similar manner we obtain the function,

$$G_-(\lambda) = \frac{1}{2\pi i}\int_{-\infty+ib}^{\infty+ib} \frac{\sqrt{(\zeta+k)}}{\zeta-i\mu}\frac{d\zeta}{\zeta-\lambda} = -\frac{\sqrt{(k+i\mu)}}{\lambda-i\mu}$$

which is analytic in the lower half plane $I(\lambda) < \mu$. Thus we have found the following decomposition,

$$G(\lambda) = \frac{\sqrt{(\lambda + k)}}{\lambda - i\mu} = G_+(\lambda) - G_-(\lambda)$$

where the functions $G_+(\lambda)$ and $G_-(\lambda)$ are defined above.

EXAMPLE 2 To decompose the function,

$$G(\lambda) = \frac{1}{(\lambda + ic)\sqrt{(\lambda - k)}}$$

where $k = \alpha + i\beta$ and c and β are positive numbers. The function $G(\lambda)$ has a simple pole at the point $\lambda = -ic$, a branch point at $\lambda = k$, and is analytic in the strip $-c < I(\lambda) < \beta$. Hecne, the functions $G_+(\lambda)$ and $G_-(\lambda)$ have the integral representations,

$$G_+(\lambda) = \frac{1}{2\pi i}\int_{-\infty+ia}^{\infty+ia} \frac{1}{(\zeta + ic)\sqrt{(\zeta - k)}}\frac{d\zeta}{\zeta - \lambda}$$

and

$$G_-(\lambda) = \frac{1}{2\pi i}\int_{-\infty+ib}^{\infty+ib} \frac{1}{(\zeta + ic)\sqrt{(\zeta - k)}}\frac{d\zeta}{\zeta - \lambda}$$

where $-c < a < b < \beta$. Cutting the plane by a branch cut in the upper half plane, we close the paths in the lower half plane and, noting that the closed contours are traversed in the negative direction, we obtain the results,

$$G_+(\lambda) = \frac{1}{(\lambda + ic)\sqrt{(-ic - k)}}$$

and

$$G_-(\lambda) = \frac{1}{\lambda + ic}\left[\frac{1}{\sqrt{(-ic - k)}} - \frac{1}{\sqrt{(\lambda - k)}}\right]$$

where $G_+(\lambda)$ is analytic in the upper half plane $I(\lambda) > -c$ and $G_-(\lambda)$ is analytic in the lower half plane $I(\lambda) < \beta$.

EXAMPLE 3 The results obtained in the previous examples immediately lead to the decomposition,

$$G(\lambda) = D\left[\frac{\sqrt{(\lambda + k)}}{\lambda - i\mu} + \frac{1}{(\lambda + ic)\sqrt{(\lambda - k)}}\right] = G_+(\lambda) - G_-(\lambda)$$

where the function,

$$G_+(\lambda) = D\left[\frac{1}{(\lambda + ic)\sqrt{(-ic - k)}} - \frac{1}{\lambda - i\mu}\{\sqrt{(i\mu + k)} - \sqrt{(\lambda + k)}\}\right]$$

is analytic in the upper half plane $I(\lambda) > -c$, and the function,

$$G_-(\lambda) = D\left[\frac{1}{\lambda + ic}\left\{\frac{1}{\sqrt{(-ic-k)}} - \frac{1}{\sqrt{(\lambda - k)}}\right\} - \frac{\sqrt{(i\mu + k)}}{\lambda - i\mu}\right]$$

is analytic in the lower half plane $I(\lambda) < \beta$.

3.3 WEIERSTRASS'S FACTORIZATION FORMULA

As we remarked in the introduction to this chapter, the factorization of an analytic function into the product of functions which are analytic in appropriate regions of the complex plane is a crucial step in the execution of the Wiener-Hopf technique.

In this section we shall derive a special case of the well-known formula of Weierstrass for the factorization of an entire function, while in the next section we shall discuss some Wiener-Hopf formulas for the factorization of a function that is analytic in a strip into the product of two functions that are analytic in overlapping half planes.

Weierstrass's formula can be derived, in a straightforward manner, from the Mittag-Leffler formula for the expansion of a meromorphic function into a sum of partial fractions which was derived in Section 3.1.

Let us assume that the function $H(\lambda)$ is analytic in the whole complex plane with the possible exception of the point at infinity. Assuming, in addition, that the zeros $a_0, a_1, a_2, \ldots,$ of this entire function are all of the first order and that no zero is located at the origin, the logarithmic derivative,

$$\frac{d \log H(\lambda)}{d\lambda} = \frac{1}{H(\lambda)}\frac{dH(\lambda)}{d\lambda}$$

is a meromorphic function with simple poles at the points $a_0, a_1, a_2, \ldots$ If this function satisfies the conditions imposed on the function $G(\lambda)$ in Section 3.1, then, since the residue of the logarithmic derivative of the function $H(\lambda)$ at one of its poles is equal to $+1$, the Mittag-Leffler representation of the logarithmic derivative of $H(\lambda)$ takes the form,

$$\frac{d \log H(\lambda)}{d\lambda} = \frac{d \log H(0)}{d\lambda} + \sum_{m=0}^{\infty}\left[\frac{1}{\lambda - a_m} + \frac{1}{a_m}\right]$$

Integrating this expression between the limits 0 and λ, we find

$$\log H(\lambda) = \log H(0) + \lambda\frac{d \log H(0)}{d\lambda} + \sum_{m=0}^{\infty}\left[\log\left(1 - \frac{\lambda}{a_m}\right) + \frac{\lambda}{a_m}\right]$$

Consequently, the entire function $H(\lambda)$ can be represented by an infinite product,

$$H(\lambda) = H(0) \exp\left[\lambda \frac{d \log H(\lambda)}{d\lambda}\right] \prod_{m=1}^{\infty} \left(1 - \frac{\lambda}{a_m}\right) e^{\lambda/a_m}$$

This formula is a special case of Weierstrass's factor formula. It can be used to factor an entire function which has zeros of the first order and no zeros of higher order.

If $H(\lambda)$ is an even function, then $dH(0)/d\lambda$ vanishes and $a_m = -a_{-m}$. In this case we obtain the formula,

$$H(\lambda) = H(0) \prod_{\substack{m=-\infty \\ m \neq 0}}^{\infty} \left(1 - \frac{\lambda}{a_m}\right) e^{\lambda/a_m} = H(0) \prod_{m=1}^{\infty} \left(1 - \frac{\lambda^2}{a_m{}^2}\right)$$

To conclude this section we shall present a few examples to illustrate the preceding discussion.

EXAMPLE 1

$$H(\lambda) = \frac{\sin \lambda}{\lambda}$$

$H(\lambda)$ is an even function with roots at the points $a_m = -a_{-m} = m\pi$. $H(0) = 1$ and hence

$$\sin \lambda = \lambda \prod_{m=1}^{\infty} \left[1 - \frac{\lambda^2}{m^2\pi^2}\right]$$

EXAMPLE 2

$$H(\lambda) = \sqrt{(\lambda^2 + k^2)} \sinh d\sqrt{(\lambda^2 + k^2)}$$

where d and k are positive numbers. Substitution of $\lambda = i\zeta$ in the factor formula of Example 1 yields

$$\sinh \zeta = \zeta \prod_{m=1}^{\infty} \left[1 + \frac{\zeta^2}{m^2\pi^2}\right]$$

and for $\zeta = d\sqrt{(\lambda^2 + k^2)}$ we obtain

$$\sqrt{(\lambda^2 + k^2)} \sinh d\sqrt{(\lambda^2 + k^2)} = d(\lambda^2 + k^2) \prod_{m=1}^{\infty} \left[1 + \frac{d^2(\lambda^2 + k^2)}{m^2\pi^2}\right]$$

This may also be written

$$\sqrt{(\lambda^2 + k^2)} \sinh d\sqrt{(\lambda^2 + k^2)}$$
$$= d(k + i\lambda)(k - i\lambda) \prod_{m=1}^{\infty} \left[\left(1 + \frac{d^2k^2}{m^2\pi^2}\right)^{1/2} \pm \frac{i\, d\lambda}{m\pi}\right] e^{\pm i\, d\lambda/m\pi}$$

The zeros of this function are at $\lambda = \pm ik$ and at $\lambda = \pm i\sqrt{(k^2 + m^2\pi^2/d^2)}$. Consequently, we may define two functions, $H_+(\lambda)$ and $H_-(\lambda)$, such that

$$H(\lambda) = \frac{H_+(\lambda)}{H_-(\lambda)}$$

where the function,

$$H_+(\lambda) = d(k - i\lambda)\prod_{m=1}^{\infty}\left[\sqrt{\left(1 + \frac{d^2k^2}{m^2\pi^2}\right)} - \frac{i\,d\lambda}{m\pi}\right]e^{i\,d\lambda/m\pi}$$

is analytic and nonvanishing in the upper half plane $I(\lambda) > -k$ and the function,

$$\frac{1}{H_-(\lambda)} = (k + i\lambda)\prod_{m=1}^{\infty}\left[\sqrt{\left(1 + \frac{d^2k^2}{m^2\pi^2}\right)} + \frac{i\,d\lambda}{m\pi}\right]e^{-i\,d\lambda/m\pi}$$

is analytic and nonvanishing in the lower half plane $I(\lambda) < k$.

EXAMPLE 3

$$H(\lambda) = \sqrt{(\lambda^2 + k^2)}\sinh d\sqrt{(\lambda^2 + k^2)} - m\cosh d\sqrt{(\lambda^2 + k^2)}$$

Consider the function,

$$H(\zeta) = \frac{1}{d}\zeta\sinh\zeta - m\cosh\zeta$$

This function is an even function of ζ and has a vanishing derivative at the origin. The roots of the equation $H(\zeta) = 0$ occur in pairs $\zeta_n = -\zeta_{-n}$ and there are two real roots $\zeta = \pm a_0$ and a sequence of imaginary roots $\zeta = \pm ia_n$ where $n = 1,2, \ldots$ Hence

$$H(\zeta) = H(0)\left(1 - \frac{\zeta^2}{a_0^2}\right)\prod_{n=1}^{\infty}\left[1 + \frac{\zeta^2}{a_n^2}\right]$$

where $H(0) = -m$. Consequently, if we make the substitution $\zeta = d\sqrt{(\lambda^2 + k^2)}$ we obtain

$$H(\lambda) = m\left[\frac{d^2(\lambda^2 + k^2)}{a_0^2} - 1\right]\prod_{n=1}^{\infty}\left[1 + \frac{d^2(\lambda^2 + k^2)}{a_n^2}\right]$$

We may write, therefore

$$H(\lambda) = \frac{H_+(\lambda)}{H_-(\lambda)}$$

where, assuming that $k^2 < a_0{}^2/d^2$, the function,

$$H_+(\lambda) = \left[\frac{d^2(\lambda^2 + k^2)}{a_0{}^2} - 1\right] \prod_{n=1}^{\infty} \left[\sqrt{\left(1 + \frac{d^2k^2}{a_n{}^2}\right)} - \frac{i\,d\lambda}{a_n}\right] e^{i\,d\lambda/n\pi}$$

is analytic and nonvanishing in the upper half plane $I(\lambda) > 0$ and the function

$$\frac{1}{H_-(\lambda)} = m \prod_{n=1}^{\infty} \left[\sqrt{\left(1 + \frac{d^2k^2}{a_n{}^2}\right)} + \frac{i\,d\lambda}{a_n}\right] e^{-i\,d\lambda/n\pi}$$

is analytic and nonvanishing in the lower half plane $I(\lambda) < \sqrt{(k^2 + a_1{}^2/d^2)}$

3.4 WIENER-HOPF FACTORIZATION FORMULAS

Rules on the factorization of a function $H(\lambda)$ that is analytic in a strip in the complex plane into the product of two functions $H_+(\lambda)$ and $1/H_-(\lambda)$ that are analytic and nonvanishing in an upper and lower half plane respectively are of special importance in applications of the Wiener-Hopf technique. The two half planes are required to overlap in the strip of analyticity of the function $H(\lambda)$, and this strip is therefore a common strip of analyticity of the functions $H_+(\lambda)$ and $1/H_-(\lambda)$.

To derive the first formula of this type, let us consider a function $H(\lambda)$ which is analytic and nonvanishing in the strip $\alpha < I(\lambda) < \beta$. Taking logarithms of both sides of the equation,

$$H(\lambda) = \frac{H_+(\lambda)}{H_-(\lambda)}$$

we obtain the expression,

$$\log H(\lambda) = \log H_+(\lambda) - \log H_-(\lambda)$$

where we have chosen the branch of the logarithm such that $\log 1 = 0$. If we now assume that $[\log H(\lambda)]/\lambda$ vanishes when λ tends to infinity uniformly in the strip $\alpha < I(\lambda) < \beta$, then, according to the decomposition formula of Section 3.2, the functions $\log H_+(\lambda)$ and $\log H_-(\lambda)$ will have the integral representations,

$$\log H_+(\lambda) = \frac{1}{2\pi i} \int_{-\infty + ia}^{\infty + ia} \frac{\log H(\zeta)}{\zeta - \lambda}\, d\zeta$$

and

$$\log H_-(\lambda) = \frac{1}{2\pi i} \int_{-\infty + ib}^{\infty + ib} \frac{\log H(\zeta)}{\zeta - \lambda}\, d\zeta$$

where $\alpha < a \leqq I(\lambda) \leqq b < \beta$. Hence, the functions $H_+(\lambda)$ and $H_-(\lambda)$ take the form,

$$H_+(\lambda) = \exp\left[\frac{1}{2\pi i}\int_{-\infty+ia}^{\infty+ia} \frac{\log H(\zeta)}{\zeta - \lambda}\, d\zeta\right]$$

and

$$H_-(\lambda) = \exp\left[\frac{1}{2\pi i}\int_{-\infty+ib}^{\infty+ib} \frac{\log H(\zeta)}{\zeta - \lambda}\, d\zeta\right]$$

where the first function is analytic and nonvanishing in the upper half plane $I(\lambda) \geqq a > \alpha$ and the second function is analytic and nonvanishing in the lower half plane $I(\lambda) \leqq b < \beta$.

The factorization formula just derived is based on the assumption that the function $H(\lambda)$ is analytic and nonvanishing in a strip $\alpha < I(\lambda) < \beta$. However, many problems in mathematical physics to which the Wiener-Hopf technique is applied involve functions which have a finite number of zeros in the strip of analyticity. In view of what we have just learned it is possible to construct factorization formulas for such more general functions.

Suppose, for example, that the function $L(\lambda)$ is analytic in the strip $a < I(\lambda) < d$ and tends to 1 when $R(\lambda)$ tends to infinity in this strip. Assuming, moreover, that $L(\lambda)$ has a finite number of zeros $a_1, a_2, \ldots, a_m$ in a strip $\alpha \leqq I(\lambda) \leqq \beta$, which is located inside the strip $a < I(\lambda) < d$, and that all the zeros are of first order, we are able to construct the factor formula,

$$L(\lambda) = (\lambda - a_1)(\lambda - a_2)\cdots(\lambda - a_m)\frac{L_+(\lambda)}{L_-(\lambda)}$$

where the functions $L_+(\lambda)$ and $L_-(\lambda)$ are analytic and nonvanishing in the upper half plane $I(\lambda) > \alpha$ and the lower half plane $I(\lambda) < \beta$ respectively.

The formula can be obtained by first constructing a function $H(\lambda)$ to which the factorization of the first part of this section can be applied.

To be definite, we want to construct a function $H(\lambda)$ which is analytic in a strip $a < b \leqq I(\lambda) \leqq c < d$ such that $\log H(\lambda)$ vanishes when $R(\lambda)$ tends to plus or minus infinity in this strip. Assuming that the zeros $a_1, \ldots, a_m$ are the only zeros in the strip $b \leqq \alpha \leqq I(\lambda) \leqq \beta \leqq c$, we consider, as a first step in the construction of $H(\lambda)$, the function,

$$\log \frac{L(\lambda)}{(\lambda - a_1)\cdots(\lambda - a_m)} \tag{3.7}$$

This function is analytic and nonvanishing in the strip $b \leqq I(\lambda) \leqq c$, but does not vanish when $R(\lambda)$ tends to plus or minus infinity in this strip.

To let the real part of the function (3.7) vanish when $R(\lambda)$ tends to plus or minus infinity in the strip $b \leqslant I(\lambda) \leqslant c$, we add a term,

$$\log [(\lambda - ia)^{m/2}(\lambda - id)^{m/2}]$$

to the function above, choosing the branch cuts from id to $i\infty$ and from ia to $-i\infty$ and branches such that $\log(\lambda - ia)$ and $\log(\lambda - id)$ tend to $\log \lambda$ when $R(\lambda)$ tends to plus infinity in the strip $b \leqq I(\lambda) \leqq c$.

To let the imaginary part of the function (3.7) vanish as $R(\lambda)$ tends to plus or minus infinity in the strip $b \leqslant I(\lambda) \leqslant c$ we add a term,

$$\log [(\lambda - ia)^{p}(\lambda - id)^{-p}]$$

where p is a real number determined such that $\log H(\lambda)$ vanishes as $R(\lambda)$ tends to plus or minus infinity in the strip.

These additions result in the function,

$$\log H(\lambda) = \log \frac{L(\lambda)(\lambda - ia)^{m/2+p}(\lambda - id)^{m/2-p}}{(\lambda - a_1)\cdots(\lambda - a_m)}$$

which satisfies all the conditions imposed on it. Hence, by means of the first factor formula of this section, we may write

$$\log H(\lambda) = \log H_{+}(\lambda) - \log H_{-}(\lambda)$$

where the function,

$$H_{+}(\lambda) = \exp\left[\frac{1}{2\pi i}\int_{-\infty+ib}^{\infty+ib} \frac{\log H(\zeta)}{\zeta - \lambda}\, d\zeta\right]$$

is analytic and nonvanishing in the upper half plane $I(\lambda) > \alpha$ and the function

$$H_{-}(\lambda) = \exp\left[\frac{1}{2\pi i}\int_{-\infty+ic}^{\infty+ic} \frac{\log H(\zeta)}{\zeta - \lambda}\, d\zeta\right]$$

is analytic and nonvanishing in the lower half plane $I(\lambda) < \beta$.

Defining the functions $L_{+}(\lambda)$ and $L_{-}(\lambda)$ by the relations,

$$L_{+}(\lambda) = H_{+}(\lambda)(\lambda - ia)^{-p-m/2}$$

and

$$L_{-}(\lambda) = H_{-}(\lambda)(\lambda - id)^{-p+m/2}$$

we finally obtain the factor formula,

$$L(\lambda) = (\lambda - a_1)\cdots(\lambda - a_m)\frac{L_{+}(\lambda)}{L_{-}(\lambda)}$$

we set out to construct.

To illustrate the theory of this section we shall discuss the following rather lengthy example which is of great practical utility in the study of the radiation of acoustic and electromagnetic waves from the open ends of parallel plane wave guides.

Let us consider the function,

$$H(\lambda) = 1 + \exp\,[id\sqrt{(k^2 - \lambda^2)}]$$

where $k = \alpha + i\beta$ and β and d are positive numbers. The function $H(\lambda)$ has branch points at $\lambda = \pm k$ and choosing the branch of $\sqrt{(k^2 - \lambda^2)}$ such that $\arg\sqrt{(k^2 - \lambda^2)} = \arg k$ when $\lambda = 0$, we find that $I[\sqrt{(k^2 - \lambda^2)}]$ is always positive and that $\sqrt{(k^2 - \lambda^2)}$ tends to $i|R(\lambda)|$ when $R(\lambda)$ tends to plus or minus infinity in the strip $-\beta < I(\lambda) < \beta$. For the branch cuts we choose the parts of the hyperbola $\omega\gamma = \alpha\beta$ that lie above the point $\lambda = k$ and below the point $\lambda = -k$ as shown in Figure III-4. On these parts of the hyperbola

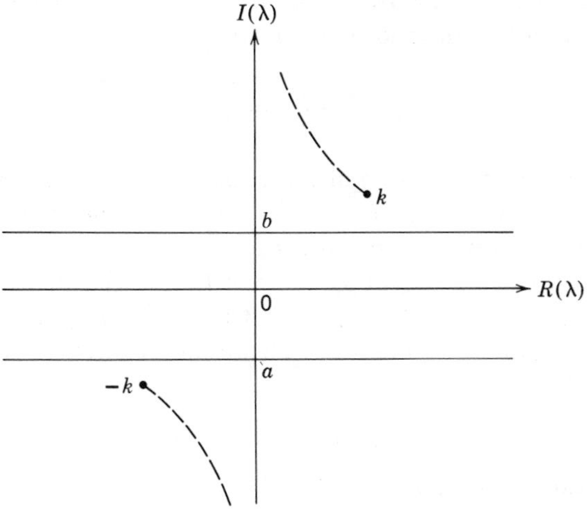

Figure III-4

the imaginary part of $\sqrt{(k^2 - \lambda^2)}$ vanishes. The function $H(\lambda)$ is analytic and nonvanishing in the strip $-\beta < I(\lambda) < \beta$, and, on the particular branch chosen, the functions $\exp\,[id\sqrt{(k^2 - \lambda^2)}]$ and $\log H(\lambda)$ vanish when $R(\lambda)$ tends to plus or minus infinity in this strip. Consequently, since $H(\lambda)$ satisfies the appropriate conditions, we may write, according to the first factorization rule of this section,

$$H(\lambda) = H_+(\lambda)/H_-(\lambda)$$

or

$$\log H(\lambda) = \log H_+(\lambda) - \log H_-(\lambda)$$

where $H_+(\lambda)$ and $H_-(\lambda)$ are analytic and nonvanishing in the upper half plane $I(\lambda) > -\beta$ and the lower half plane $I(\lambda) < \beta$ respectively. To obtain explicit expressions for the functions $H_+(\lambda)$ and $H_-(\lambda)$, it is more convenient to consider the logarithmic derivative of the function $H(\lambda)$,

$$G(\lambda) = \frac{1}{H(\lambda)} \frac{dH(\lambda)}{d\lambda} = -id \frac{\lambda \exp [id\sqrt{(k^2 - \lambda^2)}]}{[1 + \exp id\sqrt{(k^2 - \lambda^2)}]\sqrt{(k^2 - \lambda^2)}}$$

The function $G(\lambda)$ has branch points at $\lambda = \pm k$ and, in addition, simple poles at the zeros of the function $1 + \exp [id\sqrt{(k^2 - \lambda^2)}]$, namely, at the points,

$$\lambda = \pm a_m = \pm \left[k^2 - \frac{\pi^2}{d^2}(2m - 1)^2 \right]^{1/2}$$

where $m = 1,2, \ldots$.

All the poles, and of course the branch points, lie on the branch cuts defined above. For a pole is defined by the relation,

$$\sqrt{(k^2 - \lambda^2)} = \frac{\pi}{d}(2m + 1)$$

and, since the right hand side of this equation is real, the left hand side must be real also. However, $I[\sqrt{(k^2 - \lambda^2)}] = 0$ is just that part of the hyperbola $\omega\gamma = \alpha\beta$ which forms the branch cuts.

Since all the singularities of the function $G(\lambda)$ are located on the branch cuts, the function $G(\lambda)$ is analytic in the strip, $-\beta < I(\lambda) < \beta$, and vanishes as $R(\lambda)$ tends to infinity in this strip. Hence, according to Section 3.2, we may write

$$G(\lambda) = G_+(\lambda) - G_-(\lambda)$$

where the functions,

$$G_+(\lambda) = \frac{1}{H_+(\lambda)} \frac{dH_+(\lambda)}{d\lambda} = \frac{1}{2\pi i} \int_{-\infty + ia}^{\infty + ia} \frac{G(\zeta)}{\zeta - \lambda} d\zeta$$

and

$$G_-(\lambda) = \frac{1}{H_-(\lambda)} \frac{dH_-(\lambda)}{d\lambda} = \frac{1}{2\pi i} \int_{-\infty + ib}^{\infty + ib} \frac{G(\zeta)}{\zeta - \lambda} d\zeta$$

are analytic in the upper half plane $I(\lambda) > -\beta$ and the lower half plane $I(\lambda) < \beta$ respectively.

Let us consider the first integral. Since all the singularities of the integrand are on the branch cuts, we may deform the path of integration into a path Γ

which runs along the banks of the branch cut in the lower half plane as shown in Figure III-5,

$$G_+(\lambda) = -\frac{d}{2\pi}\int_\Gamma \frac{\exp\,[id\sqrt{(k^2-\zeta^2)}]}{1+\exp\,[id\sqrt{(k^2-\zeta^2)}]}\frac{\zeta\,d\zeta}{(\zeta-\lambda)\sqrt{(k^2-\zeta^2)}}$$

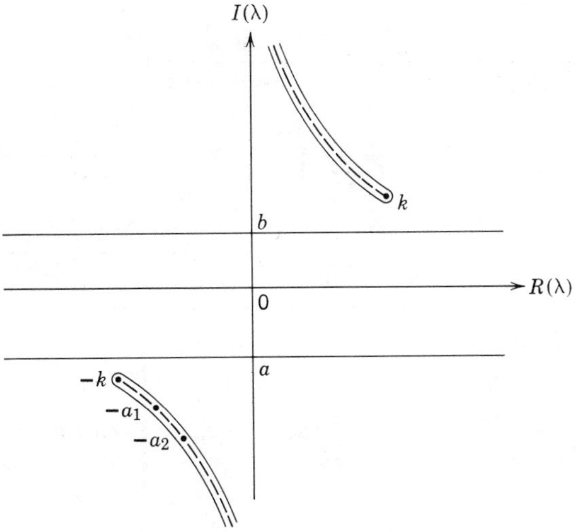

Figure III-5

The integral along the path Γ is equal to $-2\pi i$ times the sum of the residues of the integrand at the poles plus the sum of the principal value integrals over the paths connecting the poles. Taking note of the fact that the function $\sqrt{(k^2-\lambda^2)}$ changes its phase when we turn around the branch point, we find

$$G_+(\lambda) = \sum_{m=1}^{\infty}\frac{1}{\lambda+a_m} + \frac{d}{2\pi}\int_{-i\infty}^{-k}\frac{\exp\,[-id\sqrt{(k^2-\zeta^2)}]}{1+\exp\,[-id\sqrt{(k^2-\zeta^2)}]}\frac{\zeta\,d\zeta}{(\zeta-\lambda)\sqrt{(k^2-\zeta^2)}}$$

$$-\frac{d}{2\pi}\int_{-k}^{-i\infty}\frac{\exp\,[id\sqrt{(k^2-\zeta^2)}]}{1+\exp\,[id\sqrt{(k^2-\zeta^2)}]}\frac{\zeta\,d\zeta}{(\zeta-\lambda)\sqrt{(k^2-\zeta^2)}}$$

$$= \sum_{m=1}^{\infty}\frac{1}{\lambda+a_m} + \frac{d}{2\pi}\int_{k}^{i\infty}\frac{\zeta\,d\zeta}{(\zeta+\lambda)\sqrt{(k^2-\zeta^2)}}$$

To compute the integral it is convenient to make the substitutions,

$$\zeta = k\sin s, \qquad \sqrt{(k^2-\zeta^2)} = k\cos s, \qquad \lambda = k\sin z$$

This substitution transforms the path $(k, i\infty)$ in the λ-plane into the path $(\pi/2, i\infty)$ in the z-plane. Hence, defining the points,

$$z_m = \arcsin\left(\frac{a_m}{k}\right) \quad \text{and} \quad z_0 = \pi/2$$

we find

$$\begin{aligned}
\int_k^{i\infty} \frac{\zeta}{(\zeta+\lambda)\sqrt{(k^2-\zeta^2)}}\, d\zeta &= \int_{\pi/2}^{i\infty} \frac{\sin s}{\sin s + \sin z}\, ds \\
&= \sum_{m=0}^{\infty} \int_{z_m}^{z_{m+1}} \left(1 - \frac{\sin z}{\sin s + \sin z}\right) ds \\
&= \sum_{m=0}^{\infty} (z_{m+1} - z_m) - \frac{\sin z}{2} \int_{\pi/2}^{i\infty} \frac{ds}{\sin \dfrac{s+z}{2} \cos \dfrac{s-z}{2}} \\
&= \sum_{m=0}^{\infty} (z_{m+1} - z_m) - \left[\tan z \log \frac{\sin \dfrac{s+z}{2}}{\cos \dfrac{s-z}{2}} \right]_{\pi/2}^{1\infty} \\
&= \sum_{m=0}^{\infty} (z_{m+1} - z_m) - \tan z[\log(ie^{-iz}) - \log 1]
\end{aligned}$$

To determine the branch of the logarithm, we consider the case $z = 0$. The path may now be deformed into the path from $\pi/2$ to ρ, the circular path from ρ to $i\rho$, and the path from $i\rho$ to $i\infty$, as shown in Figure III-6. For

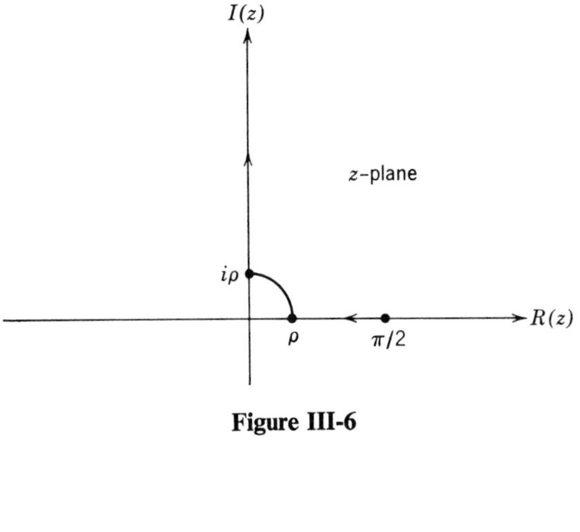

Figure III-6

vanishing ρ the contribution of the straight line segments to the integral is

$$\lim_{\rho\to 0}\left\{\left[\log\tan\frac{1}{2}s\right]_{\pi/2}^{\rho}+\left[\log\tan\frac{1}{2}s\right]_{i\rho}^{i\infty}\right\}=0$$

The contribution of the circular path is $\pi i/2$ times the residue of $(\sin s)^{-1}$ at $s = 0$. Hence, the value of the integral is $\pi i/2$ for $z = 0$. Consequently,

$$\int_k^{i\infty}\frac{\zeta}{(\zeta+\lambda)\sqrt{(k^2-\zeta^2)}}\,d\zeta=\sum_{m=0}^{\infty}(z_{m+1}-z_m)-i\left(\frac{\pi}{2}-z\right)\tan z$$

and substitution yields the expression,

$$\frac{1}{H_+(\lambda)}\frac{dH_+(\lambda)}{d\lambda}=G_+(\lambda)=\sum_{m=0}^{\infty}\left[\frac{1}{\lambda+a_{m+1}}+\frac{d}{2\pi}(z_{m+1}-z_m)\right]$$
$$-\frac{id}{2\pi}\left(\frac{\pi}{2}-z\right)\tan z.$$

Integration between the limits 0 and λ yields

$$\log H_+(\lambda)=\int_0^{\lambda}G_+(\zeta)\,d\zeta$$
$$=\sum_{m=0}^{\infty}\left[\log\left(1+\frac{\lambda}{a_{m+1}}\right)+\frac{d}{2\pi}(z_{m+1}-z_m)\lambda\right]+G_1(z)+\text{constant}$$

where

$$G_1(z)=id\frac{k}{2\pi}\left[\left(\frac{\pi}{2}-z\right)\cos z+\sin z\right]$$

Hence

$$H_+(\lambda)=Ae^{G_1(z)}\prod_{m=0}^{\infty}\left(1+\frac{\lambda}{a_{m+1}}\right)\exp\left[\frac{d}{2\pi}(z_{m+1}-z_m)\lambda\right]$$

In a similar manner we obtain

$$\frac{1}{H_-(\lambda)}=Be^{G_2(z)}\prod_{m=0}^{\infty}\left(1-\frac{\lambda}{a_{m+1}}\right)\exp\left[-\frac{d}{2\pi}(z_{m+1}-z_m)\lambda\right]$$

where

$$G_2(z)=id\frac{k}{2\pi}\left[\left(\frac{\pi}{2}+z\right)\cos z-\sin z\right]$$

The constants A and B may be determined as follows. Since

$$H(\lambda)=\frac{H_+(\lambda)}{H_-(\lambda)}=1+\exp\left[id\sqrt{(k^2-\lambda^2)}\right]$$

we find

$$ABe^{id(k/2)\cos z}\prod_{m=0}^{\infty}\left(1-\frac{\lambda^2}{a_{m+1}^2}\right)=1+\exp\left[id\sqrt{(k^2-\lambda^2)}\right]$$

However,

$$\cos\frac{1}{2}kd\prod_{m=0}^{\infty}\left(1-\frac{\lambda^2}{a_{m+1}^2}\right)=\cos\frac{d}{2}\sqrt{(k^2-\lambda^2)}=\cos\left(\frac{dk}{2}\cos z\right)$$

and we must choose therefore the constants A and B such that

$$AB=2\cos\tfrac{1}{2}kd.$$

The following choice is satisfactory,

$$A=B=\sqrt{(2\cos\tfrac{1}{2}kd)}$$

and we obtain, finally,

$$H_+(\lambda)=\sqrt{\left(2\cos\frac{1}{2}kd\right)}e^{G_1(z)}\prod_{m=0}^{\infty}\left(1+\frac{\lambda}{a_{m+1}}\right)\exp\left[\frac{d}{2\pi}(z_{m+1}-z_m)\lambda\right]$$

$$\frac{1}{H_-(\lambda)}=\sqrt{\left(2\cos\frac{1}{2}kd\right)}e^{G_2(z)}\prod_{m=0}^{\infty}\left(1-\frac{\lambda}{a_{m+1}}\right)\exp\left[-\frac{d}{2\pi}(z_{m+1}-z_m)\lambda\right]$$

3.5 WIENER-HOPF INTEGRAL EQUATIONS OF THE SECOND KIND

In 1931, Wiener and Hopf published their now famous solution of the integral equation,

$$f(t)=\int_0^{\infty}k(t-t_0)f(t_0)\,dt_0 \qquad -\infty<t<\infty \tag{3.8}$$

Their paper also contains the first formulation of the Wiener-Hopf technique, by means of which the solution of the integral equation was obtained, and the very important factorization formula of Section 3.4. The homogeneous integral equation (3.8) and its inhomogeneous counterpart,

$$f(t)=g(t)+\int_0^{\infty}k(t-t_0)f(t_0)\,dt_0 \qquad -\infty<t<\infty \tag{3.9}$$

are so-called Wiener-Hopf integral equations. They are characterized by a semi-infinite interval of integration and by a displacement kernel $k(t-t_0)$ which is a function of the difference $t-t_0$ only. We note that, although the integration interval extends over the positive real axis only, the solutions of these equations are defined over the whole real axis.

Equations (3.8) and (3.9) are integral equations of the second kind. A Wiener-Hopf integral equation of the first kind is

$$g(t) = \int_0^\infty k(t - t_0) f(t_0)\, dt_0 \tag{3.10}$$

where $g(t)$ and $k(t)$ are known functions and the equation needs to be solved for the function $f(t)$.

By means of the unilateral Fourier transforms of Section 2.10, we can Fourier transform the integral equations (3.8), (3.9), and (3.10) into functional equations of the type presented in Section 3.0 which can be solved by the Wiener-Hopf technique. Inverting the Fourier transforms of the appropriate functions, we subsequently obtain the solutions of the integral equations. To ensure the existence of the unilateral Fourier transforms we must limit the growth of the kernel $k(t)$ and the inhomogeneous term $g(t)$ of the integral equations. In other words, the Wiener-Hopf technique can only be applied to integral equations of the type (3.8), (3.9), or (3.10) if the behavior of the functions $g(t)$ and $k(t)$ at infinity is appropriate. This is usually the case for the Wiener-Hopf equations arising in the mathematical description of physical phenomena. An interesting feature of these equations is that the growth properties of the solution and the inhomogeneous term are governed by the growth properties of the kernel.

The analysis in this and the next few sections is of a formal nature. As is usual in solution methods that involve transform techniques, the transforms of the appropriate functions are assumed to exist and the results are verified *a posteriori* by substitution or by other techniques. Existing uniqueness theorems then assure us that the solution obtained in this manner is correct.

We shall now consider the solution by means of the Wiener-Hopf technique of the homogeneous integral equation of the second kind,

$$f(t) = \int_0^\infty k(t - t_0) f(t_0)\, dt_0 \qquad -\infty < t < \infty \tag{3.8}$$

Assuming that the kernel is of exponential growth at infinity, namely, that

$$k(t) = O(e^{-b|t|})$$

when t tends to plus or minus infinity, we want to obtain the solution which satisfies the condition,

$$f(t) = O(e^{at})$$

when t tends to plus infinity, where $0 < a < b$.

According to Section 2.3, the order properties imposed on the kernel and the solution imply that the Fourier transform of the kernel,

$$K(\lambda) = \frac{1}{\sqrt{(2\pi)}} \int_{-\infty}^{\infty} k(t) e^{i\lambda t} \, dt$$

is analytic in the strip $-b < I(\lambda) < b$, whereas the unilateral Fourier transform of the solution,

$$F_+(\lambda) = \frac{1}{\sqrt{(2\pi)}} \int_0^{\infty} f(t) e^{i\lambda t} \, dt$$

is analytic in the upper half plane $I(\lambda) > a$. Since $0 < a < b$, the functions $K(\lambda)$ and $F_+(\lambda)$ have a common strip of analyticity $a < I(\lambda) < b$. We now define the following functions,

$$\begin{aligned} f_+(t) &= f(t) && \text{when } t > 0 \\ &= 0 && \text{when } t < 0 \\ f_-(t) &= 0 && \text{when } t > 0 \\ &= f(t) && \text{when } t < 0 \end{aligned}$$

In terms of these functions, the integral equation takes the form

$$f(t) = f_+(t) + f_-(t) = \int_{-\infty}^{\infty} k(t - t_0) f_+(t_0) \, dt_0$$

The function $f_-(t)$ satisfies the equation,

$$f_-(t) = \int_0^{\infty} k(t - t_0) f_+(t_0) \, dt_0$$

and from the growth property of the kernel at minus infinity we may infer that

$$f_-(t) = O\left(e^{bt} \int_0^{\infty} e^{-bt_0} f_+(t_0) \, dt_0 \right)$$

when t tends to minus infinity. Furthermore, since $f_+(t) = O\,(\exp at)$ when t tends to plus infinity and $a < b$, the integral,

$$\int_0^{\infty} e^{-bt_0} f_+(t_0) \, dt_0$$

is bounded and we may conclude that $f_-(t) = O(\exp bt)$ when t tends to minus infinity. This implies that the unilateral Fourier transform,

$$F_-(\lambda) = \frac{1}{\sqrt{(2\pi)}} \int_{-\infty}^{0} f_-(t) e^{i\lambda t} \, dt$$

is analytic in the lower half plane $I(\lambda) < b$.

Consequently, the functions $F_+(\lambda)$, $F_-(\lambda)$, and $K(\lambda)$ have the common strip of analyticity $a < I(\lambda) < b$ as shown in Figure III-7.

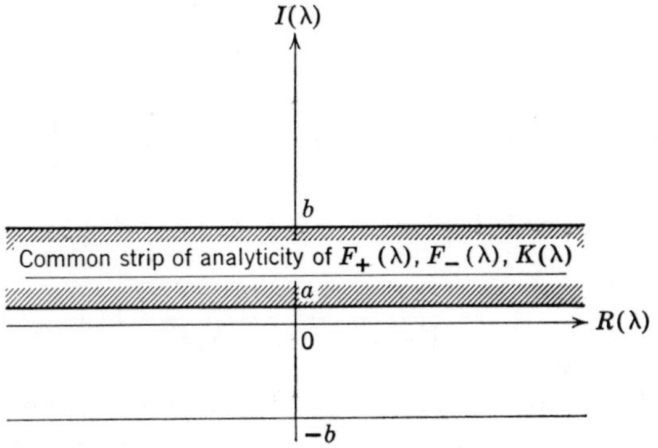

Figure III-7

Fourier transformation of the integral equation (3.8) yields the functional equation,

$$F_+(\lambda) + F_-(\lambda) = \sqrt{(2\pi)}K(\lambda)F_+(\lambda)$$

which may also be written

$$[1 - \sqrt{(2\pi)}K(\lambda)]F_+(\lambda) + F_-(\lambda) = 0$$

This functional equation of the Wiener-Hopf type, defining a relation between the unilateral Fourier transforms of the functions $f_+(t)$ and $f_-(t)$ and the Fourier transform of the kernel, is well defined in the strip $a < I(\lambda) < b$. For it only involves functions that share this strip of analyticity.

To obtain the solution of the functional equation by means of the Wiener-Hopf technique, let us assume that the function $1 - \sqrt{(2\pi)}K(\lambda)$ has simple zeros $a_1, a_2, \ldots, a_m$ in the strip $a < I(\lambda) < b$ and no other zeros in this strip. According to Section 3.4, we may write

$$1 - \sqrt{(2\pi)}K(\lambda) = \frac{K_+(\lambda)}{K_-(\lambda)}(\lambda - a_1)\cdots(\lambda - a_m)$$

where the functions $K_+(\lambda)$ and $K_-(\lambda)$ are analytic and nonvanishing in the upper half plane $I(\lambda) > a$ and the lower half plane $I(\lambda) < b$, respectively, In that same section we found the following expressions for these functions.

$$K_+(\lambda) = H_+(\lambda)(\lambda - ia)^{-p-m/2}$$

and

$$K_-(\lambda) = H_-(\lambda)(\lambda - ib)^{-p+m/2}$$

where the function,

$$H_+(\lambda) = \exp\left[\frac{1}{2\pi i}\int_{-\infty+ic}^{\infty+ic} \frac{\log H(\zeta)}{\zeta - \lambda}\, d\zeta\right]$$

is analytic in the upper half plane $I(\lambda) > a$, the function,

$$H_-(\lambda) = \exp\left[\frac{1}{2\pi i}\int_{-\infty+id}^{\infty+id} \frac{\log H(\zeta)}{\zeta - \lambda}\, d\zeta\right]$$

is analytic in the lower half plane $I(\lambda) < b$, $a < c < d < b$, and

$$H(\lambda) = \frac{H^+(\lambda)}{H^-(\lambda)} = \frac{(\lambda - ia)^{p+m/2}(\lambda - ib)^{-p+m/2}}{(\lambda - a_1)\cdots(\lambda - a_m)}[1 - \sqrt{(2\pi)}K(\lambda)]$$

Substitution of this expression for $1 - \sqrt{(2\pi)}K(\lambda)$ into the functional equation,

$$[1 - \sqrt{(2\pi)}K(\lambda)]F_+(\lambda) + F_-(\lambda) = 0$$

yields the equation,

$$(3.11) \qquad (\lambda - a_1)\cdots(\lambda - a_m)K_+(\lambda)F_+(\lambda) = -K_-(\lambda)F_-(\lambda)$$

The left hand side of this equation is analytic in the upper half plane $I(\lambda) > a$ and the right hand side is analytic in the lower half plane $I(\lambda) < b$. These half planes of analyticity overlap in the strip $a < I(\lambda) < b$ and we may conclude, by the analytic continuation argument of Section 3.0, that the left and right hand sides of equation (3.11) are the representations of the same function $E(\lambda)$ which is analytic in the whole complex plane. Hence

$$E(\lambda) = \frac{(\lambda - a_1)\cdots(\lambda - a_m)}{(\lambda - ia)^{p+m/2}} H_+(\lambda)F_+(\lambda) = -(\lambda - ib)^{-p+m/2}H_-(\lambda)F_-(\lambda)$$

Furthermore, since the functions, $F_+(\lambda)$, $F_-(\lambda)$, $K_+(\lambda)$, and $K_-(\lambda)$ are bounded in their half planes of analyticity, we observe that the function $E(\lambda)$ satisfies the order property,

$$E(\lambda) = O(\lambda^{-p+m/2})$$

when λ tends to infinity. This implies, according to Liouville's theorem, that the entire function $E(\lambda)$ must be a polynomial of a degree less than or equal to $-p + m/2$. Thus we may write

$$F_+(\lambda) = \frac{(\lambda - ia)^{p+m/2}}{(\lambda - a_1)\cdots(\lambda - a_m)} \frac{E(\lambda)}{H_+(\lambda)}$$

and

$$F_-(\lambda) = -\frac{(\lambda - ib)^{p-m/2}}{H_-(\lambda)} E(\lambda)$$

and substitution of these expressions for the unilateral Fourier transforms $F_+(\lambda)$ and $F_-(\lambda)$ into the inversion integrals,

$$f_+(t) = \frac{1}{\sqrt{(2\pi)}} \int_{-\infty+ic}^{\infty+ic} F_+(\zeta)e^{-i\zeta t}\, d\zeta$$

and

$$f_-(t) = \frac{1}{\sqrt{(2\pi)}} \int_{-\infty+id}^{\infty+id} F_-(\zeta)e^{-i\zeta t}\, d\zeta$$

enables us to obtain the functions $f_+(t)$ and $f_-(t)$ by contour integration.

The ideas above can be extended, and a procedure to solve the inhomogeneous integral equation,

$$f(t) = g(t) + \int_0^\infty k(t - t_0)f(t_0)dt_0$$

can be obtained. By Fourier transformation we obtain the functional equation,

$$F_+(\lambda)[1 - \sqrt{(2\pi)}K(\lambda)] + F_-(\lambda) = G_+(\lambda) + G_-(\lambda)$$

where the notation should be clear. This equation can be solved in the manner outlined for equation (3.2) of Section 3.0.

EXAMPLE Let us consider the integral equation,

$$f(t) = \int_0^\infty e^{-|t-t_0|} f(t_0)\, dt_0$$

The transform $K(\lambda)$ of the kernel $k(t) = e^{-|t|}$,

$$K(\lambda) = \sqrt{\left(\frac{2}{\pi}\right)} \frac{1}{\lambda^2 + 1}$$

has simple poles at the points $\lambda = \pm i$. The function,

$$1 - \sqrt{(2\pi)}K(\lambda) = \frac{\lambda^2 - 1}{\lambda^2 + 1}$$

has simple zeros at $\lambda = \pm 1$, and we write

$$1 - \sqrt{(2\pi)}K(\lambda) = \frac{K_+(\lambda)}{K_-(\lambda)}(\lambda + 1)(\lambda - 1)$$

where the function $K_+(\lambda) = 1/(\lambda + i)$ is analytic and nonvanishing in the upper half plane $I(\lambda) > -1$ and the function $K_-(\lambda) = (\lambda - i)$ is analytic and nonvanishing in the lower half plane $I(\lambda) < 1$. Hence we obtain

$$E(\lambda) = F_+(\lambda)\frac{1}{\lambda + i}(\lambda + 1)(\lambda - 1) = -F_-(\lambda)(\lambda - i)$$

which implies that the function $E(\lambda)$ is a polynomial of a degree smaller than one. Hence $E(\lambda)$ must be a constant A, and we find therefore

$$F_+(\lambda) = \frac{A(\lambda + i)}{(\lambda + 1)(\lambda - 1)}$$

$$F_-(\lambda) = -\frac{A}{\lambda - i}$$

The inverse Fourier transforms,

$$f_+(t) = \frac{A}{\sqrt{(2\pi)}} \int_{-\infty + ia}^{\infty + ia} \frac{\zeta + i}{(\zeta + 1)(\zeta - 1)} e^{-i\zeta t} \, d\zeta$$

and

$$f_-(t) = -\frac{A}{\sqrt{(2\pi)}} \int_{-\infty + ib}^{\infty + ib} \frac{e^{-i\zeta t}}{\zeta - i} \, d\zeta$$

where $0 < a \leqq b < 1$, are obtained by contour integration. To evaluate the first integral we note that $t > 0$ and close the contour in the lower half plane. The integrand has two simple poles at $\lambda = \pm 1$ and we find, by means of the residue theorem,

$$f_+(t) = B[\sin t + \cos t]$$

where $t > 0$. The second integral is evaluated by closing the contour in the upper half plane. The simple pole at $\lambda = i$ yields the result,

$$f_-(t) = C\, e^t$$

where $t < 0$. Hence, the solution of the integral equation may be written

$$f(t) = f_+(t) + f_-(t) = B[\sin t + \cos t]\, \theta(t) + C\, e^t[1 - \theta(t)]$$

where $\theta(t)$ denotes the unit step function.

3.6 WIENER-HOPF INTEGRAL EQUATIONS OF THE FIRST KIND

We now turn our attention to the Wiener-Hopf integral equations of the first kind,

$$\int_0^\infty k(t - t_0) f(t_0) \, dt_0 = g(t)$$

Let us assume that the functions $f(t)$, $g(t)$, and $k(t)$ have exponential growth at infinity, in particular, $f(t) = O(\exp at)$ when t tends to plus infinity, $g(t) = O(\exp ct)$ when t tends to plus infinity, and $k(t) = O[\exp(-b|t|)]$ when t tends to plus or minus infinity, where $0 < a < b$ and $0 < c < b$. Assuming moreover that the function $g(t)$ has been given for all positive values of t and that the function $f(t)$ vanishes for all negative t values, we want to find the functions $f(t)$ and $g(t)$ for positive and negative values of t respectively.

We again define the functions,

$$
\begin{aligned}
f_+(t) &= f(t) && \text{when } t \text{ is positive} \\
&= 0 && \text{when } t \text{ is negative} \\
g_+(t) &= g(t) && \text{when } t \text{ is positive} \\
&= 0 && \text{when } t \text{ is negative} \\
g_-(t) &= 0 && \text{when } t \text{ is positive} \\
&= g(t) && \text{when } t \text{ is negative}
\end{aligned}
$$

where the function $f_+(t)$ and $g_-(t)$ are to be determined.

The order properties imposed on the functions $f_+(t)$, $g_+(t)$, and $k(t)$ imply that the unilateral Fourier transforms $F_+(\lambda)$ and $G_+(\lambda)$ are analytic in the upper half planes $I(\lambda) > a$ and $I(\lambda) > c$ respectively and that the Fourier transform $K(\lambda)$ is analytic in the strip $-b < I(\lambda) < b$. In addition, since

$$g_-(t) = \int_0^\infty k(t - t_0) f_+(t_0)\, dt_0$$

when t is negative, the order properties imposed on the functions $k(t)$ and $f_+(t)$ imply that the function $g_-(t)$ is of exponential growth when t tends to minus infinity, or more precisely, $g_-(t) = O(\exp bt)$ when t tends to minus infinity. Consequently, the unilateral Fourier transform $G_-(\lambda)$ is analytic in the lower half plane $I(\lambda) < b$.

We now define a positive number $d = \max(a, c)$ and because $0 < d = \max(a, c) < b$, the functions $F_+(\lambda)$, $G_+(\lambda)$, $G_-(\lambda)$, and $K(\lambda)$ have a common strip of analyticity $d < I(\lambda) < b$.

The functional equation,

$$G_+(\lambda) + G_-(\lambda) = \sqrt{(2\pi)} K(\lambda) F_+(\lambda)$$

which is obtained by Fourier transformation of the integral equation, is well defined in this strip therefore. The unknown functions in this equation are $F_+(\lambda)$ and $G_-(\lambda)$ and we rearrange terms such that

$$\sqrt{(2\pi)} K(\lambda) F_+(\lambda) - G_-(\lambda) = G_+(\lambda)$$

If $M(\lambda) = K(\lambda)/N(\lambda)$ is analytic and nonzero in the strip, except for simple zeros at $a_1, a_2, \ldots, a_m$, and $M(\lambda) \to 1$ as $R(\lambda) \to \pm\infty$ in this strip, we may write

$$\sqrt{(2\pi)} M(\lambda) = \frac{M_+(\lambda)}{M_-(\lambda)} (\lambda - a_1) \cdots (\lambda - a_m)$$

Supposing, moreover, that $N(\lambda)$ can be factored by inspection and that $N_+(\lambda)$ and $N_-(\lambda)$ are of algebraic growth, the functions

$$M_+(\lambda) = K_+(\lambda)/N_+(\lambda) = H_+(\lambda)(\lambda - id)^{-p-m/2}$$

and

$$M_-(\lambda) = K_-(\lambda)/N_-(\lambda) = H_-(\lambda)(\lambda - ib)^{-p+m/2}$$

are analytic and nonvanishing in the upper half plane $I(\lambda) > d$ and the lower half plane $I(\lambda) < b$ respectively. The function $H_+(\lambda)$ has the integral representation,

$$H_+(\lambda) = \exp\left[\frac{1}{2\pi i}\int_{-\infty+i\alpha}^{\infty+i\alpha} \frac{\log H(\zeta)}{\zeta - \lambda}\, d\zeta\right]$$

and is analytic and nonvanishing in the upper half plane $I(\lambda) > d$, whereas the function $H_-(\lambda)$ is defined by the relation,

$$H_-(\lambda) = \exp\left[\frac{1}{2\pi i}\int_{-\infty+i\beta}^{\infty+i\beta} \frac{\log H(\zeta)}{\zeta - \lambda}\, d\zeta\right]$$

and is analytic and nonvanishing in the lower half plane $I(\lambda) < b$, where $d < \alpha < \beta < b$. The function $H(\lambda)$ takes the form,

$$H(\lambda) = \sqrt{(2\pi)}M(\lambda)\,\frac{(\lambda - id)^{p+m/2}(\lambda - ib)^{-p+m/2}}{(\lambda - a_1)\cdots(\lambda - a_m)}$$

and substitution yields the expression,

$$K_+(\lambda)F_+(\lambda)(\lambda - a_1)\cdots(\lambda - a_m) - K_-(\lambda)G_-(\lambda) = K_-(\lambda)G_+(\lambda)$$

This is an inhomogeneous equation of the type discussed in Section 3.0. The inhomogeneous term is analytic in the strip $d < I(\lambda) < b$ and must be decomposed in the manner described in Section 3.2. According to the decomposition formula derived in that section, we may write

$$K_-(\lambda)G_+(\lambda) = L_+(\lambda) - L_-(\lambda)$$

where the function $L_+(\lambda)$ is analytic in the upper half plane $I(\lambda) > d$ and can be represented by the integral,

$$L_+(\lambda) = \frac{1}{2\pi i}\int_{-\infty+i\alpha}^{\infty+i\alpha} \frac{K_-(\zeta)G_+(\zeta)}{\zeta - \lambda}\, d\zeta$$

whereas the function $L_-(\lambda)$ is analytic in the lower half plane $I(\lambda) < b$ and has the integral representation,

$$L_-(\lambda) = \frac{1}{2\pi i}\int_{-\infty+i\beta}^{\infty+i\beta} \frac{K_-(\zeta)G_+(\zeta)}{\zeta - \lambda}\, d\zeta$$

Substitution yields the functional equation,

$$K_+(\lambda)F_+(\lambda)(\lambda - a_1)\cdots(\lambda - a_m) - L_+(\lambda) = K_-(\lambda)G_-(\lambda) - L_-(\lambda)$$

and we find, by the now familiar analytic continuation argument, that both sides of this equation are equal to the same entire function $E(\lambda)$. This entire function is a polynomial and the degree of the polynomial is determined by the order properties of the functions of which it is composed. Solving for the functions $F_+(\lambda)$ and $G_-(\lambda)$, we find

$$F_+(\lambda) = \frac{E(\lambda) + L_+(\lambda)}{(\lambda - a_1)\cdots(\lambda - a_m)K_+(\lambda)}$$

and

$$G_-(\lambda) = \frac{E(\lambda) + L_-(\lambda)}{K_-(\lambda)}$$

The functions $f_+(t)$ and $g_-(t)$ can now be found by evaluating the inverse Fourier transform integrals,

$$f_+(t) = \frac{1}{\sqrt{(2\pi)}}\int_{-\infty+i\gamma}^{\infty+i\gamma} \frac{E(\zeta) + L_+(\zeta)}{(\zeta - a_1)\cdots(\zeta - a_m)K_+(\zeta)} e^{-i\zeta t}\, d\zeta$$

and

$$g_-(t) = \frac{1}{\sqrt{(2\pi)}}\int_{-\infty+i\gamma}^{\infty+i\gamma} \frac{E(\zeta) + L_-(\zeta)}{K_-(\zeta)} e^{-i\zeta t}\, d\zeta$$

where $d < \gamma < b$.

EXAMPLE The following integral equation of the first kind appears in the theory of diffraction of plane sound waves incident on a rigid screen,

$$\int_0^\infty H_0^{(1)}(k|x - \xi|)f(\xi)\, d\xi = e^{-i\mu x} \qquad x > 0$$

where $k = \alpha + i\beta$ and $\mu = a + ib$ are complex parameters with positive imaginary parts $b < \beta$.

The physically admissible solutions $f(x)$ are zero for negative x, become infinite like $x^{-1/2}$ when x tends to zero, and are of exponential growth, $f(x) = O(\exp bx)$, when x tends to plus infinity. We discussed some of the properties of $H_0^{(1)}(k|x|)$, which is a Hankel function of the first kind, in Sections 2.2 and 2.3. This function decreases exponentially for large values of $|x|$

$$H_0^{(1)}(k|x|) = O(x^{-1/2}e^{-\beta|x|})$$

Its Fourier transform,

$$K(\lambda) = \sqrt{\left(\frac{2}{\pi}\right)} \frac{1}{\sqrt{(k^2 - \lambda^2)}}$$

is analytic in the strip $-\beta < I(\lambda) < \beta$. We now define the functions,

$$g_+(x) = e^{-i\mu x} = \int_0^\infty H_0^{(1)}(k|x - \xi|)f(\xi)\, d\xi \qquad \text{for positive } x$$

$$= 0 \qquad \text{for negative } x$$

$$g_-(x) = \qquad = \int_0^\infty H_0^{(1)}(k|x - \xi|)f(\xi)\, d\xi \qquad \text{for negative } x$$

$$= 0 \qquad \text{for positive } x$$

where $g_+(x)$ is of exponential growth, $g_+(x) = O(e^{bx})$, when x tends to plus infinity. Its Fourier transform,

$$G_+(\lambda) = \frac{1}{\sqrt{(2\pi)}} \int_0^\infty e^{-i\mu x} e^{i\lambda x}\, dx = \frac{i}{\sqrt{(2\pi)}} \frac{1}{\lambda - \mu}$$

is analytic in the upper half plane $I(\lambda) > b$. The function $g_-(x)$ satisfies the order property,

$$g_-(x) = O\left\{x^{-1/2} e^{\beta x} \int_0^\infty e^{-\beta\xi} f(\xi)\, d\xi\right\}$$

for large negative values of x and is bounded for small values of x. Consequently, its Fourier transform, $G_-(\lambda)$, is analytic and vanishes as $1/\lambda$ in the lower half plane $I(\lambda) < \beta$. Furthermore, since $f(x) = O(e^{bx})$ when x tends to plus infinity and $f(x) = O(x^{-1/2})$ when x tends to zero, the unilateral transform $F_+(\lambda)$ is analytic and vanishes as $(1/\lambda)^{1/2}$ in the upper half plane $I(\lambda) > b$. Hence, the functional equation,

$$\sqrt{(2\pi)} K(\lambda) F_+(\lambda) = G_+(\lambda) + G_-(\lambda)$$

which is obtained as the Fourier transform of the integral equation, is defined in the strip $b < I(\lambda) < \beta$. We have therefore to find the solution of the functional equation,

$$\sqrt{(2\pi)} K(\lambda) F_+(\lambda) = G_+(\lambda) + G_-(\lambda)$$

where

a. $K(\lambda) = \sqrt{\left(\frac{2}{\pi}\right)} \frac{1}{\sqrt{(k^2 - \lambda^2)}}$

b. $G_+(\lambda) = \frac{i}{\sqrt{(2\pi)}} \frac{1}{\lambda - \mu}$

c. $F_+(\lambda)$ is analytic and vanishes as $(1/\lambda)^{1/2}$ in the upper half plane $I(\lambda) > b$
d. $G_-(\lambda)$ is analytic and vanishes as $1/\lambda$ in the lower half plane $I(\lambda) < \beta$

This functional equation has been solved in Section 3.0. There we found

$$F_+(\lambda) = \frac{i}{2\sqrt{(2\pi)}} \frac{\sqrt{(k-\mu)}\sqrt{(k+\lambda)}}{\lambda - \mu}$$

$$G_-(\lambda) = \frac{i}{\sqrt{(2\pi)}} \frac{\sqrt{(k-\mu)} - \sqrt{(k-\lambda)}}{(\lambda-\mu)\sqrt{(k-\lambda)}}$$

The solution of the integral equation has therefore the integral representation

$$f(x) = \frac{1}{\sqrt{(2\pi)}} \int_{-\infty+ic}^{\infty+ic} F_+(\zeta) e^{-i\zeta x}\, d\zeta = \frac{i}{4\pi} \int_{-\infty+ic}^{\infty+ic} \frac{\sqrt{(k-\mu)}\sqrt{(k+\lambda)}}{\zeta - \mu} e^{-i\zeta x}\, d\zeta$$

where $b < c < \beta$. This integral can be evaluated by contour integration.

An elegant solution method for a homogeneous Wiener-Hopf equation of the first kind,

$$\int_0^\infty k(x-\xi) f(\xi)\, d\xi = 0 \qquad x > 0$$

has been presented by Vainstein who studied equations of this type in relation to the problems of the radiation of acoustic and electromagnetic waves from the open ends of parallel-plane and cylindrical wave guides. In his method the integral equation above is first replaced by the dual integral equations,

$$\int_\Gamma F(\zeta) e^{-i\zeta x}\, d\zeta = 0$$

for negative values of x, and

$$\int_\Gamma F(\zeta) K(\zeta) e^{-i\zeta x}\, d\zeta = 0$$

for positive values of x, where $F(\lambda)$ and $K(\lambda)$ are the Fourier transforms of the solution and the kernel respectively. These equations are fully equivalent to the original integral equation and are solved by a combination of Jordan's lemma and the Wiener-Hopf technique. The procedure is best illustrated at the hand of an example.

EXAMPLE The integral equation,

$$\int_0^\infty k(x-\xi) f(\xi)\, d\xi = 0 \qquad x > 0$$

with the kernel,

$$k(x) = H_0^{(1)}(k|x|) + H_0^{(1)}[k\sqrt{(d^2 + x^2)}]$$

arises in the investigation of the phenomenon of radiation of electromagnetic waves from the open end of a parallel-plane wave guide. The functions $H_0^{(1)}(k\,|x|)$ and $H_0^{(1)}[k\sqrt{(d^2 + x^2)}]$ are Hankel functions of the first kind and the wave number $k = \alpha + i\beta$ has a positive imaginary part. The quantity d represents a length and hence is positive also. The physically admissible solutions $f(x)$ vanish for negative values of x and may be written as follows,

$$f(x) = f_0(x) + ae^{-ibx}$$

where b is a complex number with a positive imaginary part. The function $f_0(x)$ vanishes at infinity and may be represented by the Fourier integral,

$$f_0(x) = \frac{1}{\sqrt{(2\pi)}} \int_{-\infty}^{\infty} e^{-i\zeta x} F(\zeta)\, d\zeta$$

The idea now is to represent the solution $f(x)$ by a Fourier integral in the complex λ-plane,

$$f(x) = \frac{1}{\sqrt{(2\pi)}} \int_{\Gamma} e^{-i\zeta x} F(\zeta)\, d\zeta$$

and to construct a function $F(\lambda)$ which has a pole with residue $-a/[i\sqrt{(2\pi)}]$ at the point $\lambda = b$. Contour integration over the path Γ, shown in Figure III-8, then yields the required representation of $f(x)$,

$$f(x) = f_0(x) + ae^{-ibx}$$

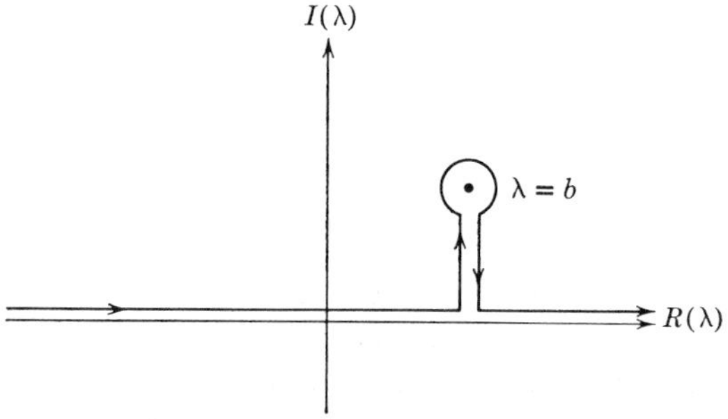

Figure III-8

Since $f(x)$ is zero for all negative values of x, $F(\lambda)$ must satisfy the equation,

$$\int_{\Gamma} e^{-i\zeta x} F(\zeta)\, d\zeta = 0 \tag{3.12}$$

for negative values of x.

Substitution of the Fourier integral for $f(x)$ in the integral equation yields moreover the equation,

$$\int_\Gamma e^{-i\zeta x} F(\zeta) K(\zeta)\, d\zeta = 0 \tag{3.13}$$

which must be satisfied for all positive values of x. According to the conclusions derived from Jordan's lemma in Section 1.5, equation (3.12) is satisfied if $F(\lambda)$ is analytic in the upper half plane, including Γ, and tends to zero uniformly when $|\lambda|$ tends to infinity in this half plane. Similarly equation (3.13) is satisfied if $F(\lambda)K(\lambda)$ is analytic in the lower half plane, including Γ, and vanishes when $|\lambda|$ tends to infinity in this half plane. To construct the functions $F(\lambda)$ and $F(\lambda)K(\lambda)$, the function $K(\lambda)$ is factored as follows,

$$K(\lambda) = \frac{K_+(\lambda)}{K_-(\lambda)} (\lambda^2 - b^2)$$

where $K_+(\lambda)$ and $K_-(\lambda)$ are analytic in the upper and lower half planes separated by and including the path Γ, respectively. We now choose

$$F(\lambda) = \frac{C}{\lambda^2 - b^2} \frac{1}{K_+(\lambda)}$$

and

$$F(\lambda)K(\lambda) = \frac{C}{K_-(\lambda)}$$

and it may be shown that the functions $F(\lambda)$ and $F(\lambda)K(\lambda)$ defined in this manner satisfy the conditions specified above. For example, in the case of the kernel,

$$k(x) = H_0^{(1)}(k\,|x|) + H_0^{(1)}[k\sqrt{(d^2 + x^2)}]$$

the Fourier transform is

$$K(\lambda) = \sqrt{\left(\frac{2}{\pi}\right)} \frac{1 + \exp\,[id\sqrt{(k^2 - \lambda^2)}]}{\sqrt{(k^2 - \lambda^2)}}$$

The function $1 + \exp\,[id\sqrt{(k^2 - \lambda^2)}]$ was factored in Section 3.4, and we found

$$1 + \exp\,[id\sqrt{(k^2 - \lambda^2)}] = \frac{H_+(\lambda)}{H_-(\lambda)}$$

Consequently, we obtain

$$K_+(\lambda) = \sqrt{\left(\frac{2}{\pi}\right)} \frac{H_+(\lambda)}{(\lambda + b)\sqrt{(k + \lambda)}}$$

and

$$K_-(\lambda) = (\lambda - b)\sqrt{(k - \lambda)}H_-(\lambda)$$

This implies that

$$F(\lambda) = \frac{C}{(\lambda^2 - b^2)}\frac{1}{K_+(\lambda)} = C\sqrt{\left(\frac{\pi}{2}\right)}\frac{\sqrt{(k + \lambda)}}{(\lambda - b)H_+(\lambda)}$$

and that

$$F(\lambda)K(\lambda) = \frac{C}{(\lambda - b)\sqrt{(k - \lambda)}H_-(\lambda)}$$

The solution of the integral equation can be represented therefore by the integral,

$$f(x) = \frac{1}{\sqrt{(2\pi)}}\int_\Gamma F(\zeta)e^{-i\zeta x}\,d\zeta = \frac{C}{2}\int_\Gamma \frac{\sqrt{(k + \zeta)}}{(\zeta - b)H_+(\zeta)}\,e^{-i\zeta x}\,d\zeta$$

The integral is evaluated by closing the path Γ in the lower half plane. If we cut the plane along the branch line from $-k$ to $-\alpha - i\infty$ the integral may be written as a sum of residues at the simple poles of the integrand plus an integral over a path C which runs along the banks of the branch cut. The poles of the integrand are located at the points which are the simple zeros of the function $H_+(\lambda)$, namely, at the points $\lambda = -a_m$ of Section 3.4 and at $\lambda = b$.

3.7 REMARKS ON SOME PARTIAL DIFFERENTIAL EQUATIONS OF MATHEMATICAL PHYSICS

The partial differential equation,

$$\nabla^2\Phi - \frac{1}{c^2}\frac{\partial^2\Phi}{\partial t^2} - a^2\frac{\partial\Phi}{\partial t} = 0$$

provides the mathematical formulation of many diverse physical phenomena which involve wave propagation, with wave velocity c, in dissipative media which may be characterized by a measure of dissipation a.

For example, in electromagnetic theory the equation takes the form,

$$\nabla^2\Phi - \mu\varepsilon\frac{\partial^2\Phi}{\partial t^2} - \mu\sigma\frac{\partial\Phi}{\partial t} = 0$$

This equation describes the propagation of electromagnetic waves in a conducting medium with conductivity σ, magnetic permeability μ, and dielectric constant ε. In rectangular coordinates the function Φ represents the components of the intensities of the electric or magnetic field. The wave motion is propagated with a velocity $c = (\mu\varepsilon)^{-1/2}$ which is independent of the conductivity of the medium and is attenuated exponentially in the direction of propagation with an attenuation factor which is proportional to the conductivity.

In neutron transport theory it has been recognized that the wave equation above, including a term in Φ and a source term S, forms the true P_1 approximation to the neutron transport equation. In this approximation the equation describes the propagation or diffusion of neutrons in an absorbing medium with a velocity c. An infinite neutron velocity reduces the equation to the ordinary diffusion equation. In most applications this turns out to be an excellent approximation, but it is not always possible to ignore the finite neutron velocity.

In the theory of mechanical vibrations the wave equation with dissipation is encountered as the equation of motion of a flexible string or membrane vibrating in a medium that exerts a frictional force. Now the coefficient of the first-time derivative is proportional to the frictional resistance of the medium while c represents the velocity of the wave motion.

The well-known wave equation,

$$\nabla^2\Phi = \frac{1}{c^2}\frac{\partial^2\Phi}{\partial t^2}$$

and the diffusion equation,

$$\nabla^2\Phi = a^2\frac{\partial\Phi}{\partial t}$$

are special cases of the more general wave equation with dissipation. They may be obtained from this equation in the limit of zero dissipation or infinite velocity of propagation, respectively. For example, in the case of the propagation of electromagnetic waves the wave equation depicts the propagation of waves in a conductionless medium whereas the diffusion equation describes the propagation of long waves in an ideal conductor.

It is interesting to note the conceptual differences between the three equations above. The ordinary wave and diffusion equations mark two extremes in the description of the modes of propagation of a physical disturbance. The solutions of the wave equation depict the propagation of a disturbance which is characterized by a clean-cut wave front which marks the boundary between the part of the region which has just been disturbed and the part of the region which has not yet been reached by the disturbance. The mathematical vehicle of the wave equation does not allow for the description of permanent residual disturbances. In the case of the diffusion equation there is no demarcation line between the disturbed and undisturbed parts of the medium. This equation calls for instantaneous propagation. For, due to the infinite velocity of propagation, the influence of a source, introduced at a certain point in the undisturbed medium, is felt instantaneously in all other points of the medium. The wave equation with the dissipation term offers a description of both the diffusion and the wave type of propagation. In the solutions of this equation one easily discerns the difference between the instantaneous mode of propagation which is characteristic of the diffusion equation and the retardation mode of propagation which is inherent in the wave equation.

From a mathematical standpoint there are sometimes distinct advantages to be gained by considering the wave equation with a dissipative term even if the physics of the problem prescribes the wave equation. We shall see below that the wave equation with a dissipative term allows us to go into the complex plane and to obtain solutions by means of the techniques outlined in the previous sections. In the limit of zero dissipation the solutions of this equation immediately yield the solutions of the ordinary wave equation.

To be specific, we shall limit ourselves in the following to two-dimensional steady state problems. In rectangular coordinates the general wave equation may be written as follows,

$$\frac{\partial^2 \Phi}{\partial x^2} + \frac{\partial^2 \Phi}{\partial y^2} - \frac{1}{c^2}\frac{\partial^2 \Phi}{\partial t^2} - a^2 \frac{\partial \Phi}{\partial t} = 0$$

We assume that the elementary harmonic solutions are of the form,

$$\Phi(x, y, t) = \phi(x, y)e^{-i\omega t}$$

Substitution yields the two-dimensional Helmholtz equation in rectangular coordinates,

$$\frac{\partial^2 \phi}{\partial x^2} + \frac{\partial^2 \phi}{\partial y^2} + \frac{1}{c^2}(\omega^2 + ia^2c^2\omega)\phi = 0$$

We now introduce the propagation constant,

$$k = \frac{1}{c}\sqrt{(\omega^2 + ia^2c^2\omega)}$$

and obtain

$$\frac{\partial^2 \phi}{\partial x^2} + \frac{\partial^2 \phi}{\partial y^2} + k^2\phi = 0$$

In this equation ω is positive and, since a is assumed to be nonzero, k is a complex quantity. We choose the sign of the square root in the definition of k such that the imaginary part of $k = \alpha + i\beta$ is positive.

The boundary value problems which involve the Helmholtz equation above and which are susceptible to analysis by the Wiener-Hopf technique can be classified according to the geometry underlying the physical phenomena. The following three types of problems are encountered most frequently.

a. In the so-called half plane problems we are required to obtain the solution of the Helmholtz equation, representing outgoing waves at infinity, in the upper half plane $y \geq 0$, $-\infty < x < \infty$, in the special case that the boundary value condition for $y = 0$ and $x < 0$ is different from the condition for $y = 0$ and $x > 0$. Boundary value problems of this type are encountered in the investigation of the diffraction of electromagnetic and sound waves, in the propagation of radio waves, in the theory of gravity waves on a sea, and in many other fields of mathematical physics.

b. In the semi-infinite parallel-plane problems of wave guide theory, the guide extends over the region $-\infty < x < 0$, $-d < y < d$, $-\infty < z < \infty$. On the surfaces of the guide the boundary conditions are in general of the form $\phi = 0$ or $\partial\phi/\partial y = 0$. The other boundary conditions are specified by one of the following two physical requirements.

1. Radiation in the form of an electromagnetic or an acoustic wave is incident on the mouth of the wave guide and excites other waves inside the guide.
2. Electromagnetic or sound waves which travel inside the guide to the mouth generate radiation outside the guide.

The problem of a dock over a sea of finite depth can also be classified among the boundary value problems with this type of geometry.

c. If the basic geometry is a semi-infinite cylinder, it is natural to make the transformation to cylindrical coordinates,

$$x = r\cos\theta,\ y = r\sin\theta,\ z = z$$

In this manner, we obtain the Helmholtz equation in cylindrical coordinates,

$$\frac{1}{r}\frac{\partial}{\partial r}\left(r\frac{\partial\phi}{\partial r}\right) + \frac{1}{r^2}\frac{\partial^2\phi}{\partial\theta^2} + \frac{\partial^2\phi}{\partial z^2} + k^2\phi = 0$$

and if we assume axial symmetry we find

$$\frac{1}{r}\frac{\partial}{\partial r}\left(r\frac{\partial\phi}{\partial r}\right) + \frac{\partial^2\phi}{\partial z^2} + k^2\phi = 0$$

The boundary conditions are of the form $\phi = 0$ or $\partial\phi/\partial r = 0$ on the surface $r = a$ and ϕ is finite at $r = 0$. Again this type of geometry is encountered in problems that deal with the radiation from the open end of a cylindrical wave guide or the excitation of electromagnetic or sound waves inside the tube by waves which are incident on the mouth of the tube.

Of course the above three geometries serve only as illustrations and many more complex geometrical configurations can be dealt with.

3.8 BOUNDARY VALUE PROBLEMS INVOLVING THE HELMHOLTZ EQUATION

In this chapter we have shown that the Wiener-Hopf technique can be applied with great success to solve integral equations of the Wiener-Hopf type. We shall now turn our attention to some applications of this technique to the solution of boundary value problems involving the Helmholtz equation.

As in the case of integral equations, the Helmholtz equation is first reduced, by means of Fourier transformation, to a functional equation defined in a strip in the complex plane of the transform variable. This equation is solved subsequently by an application of the Wiener-Hopf technique. The method can be explained most clearly at the hand of the following boundary value problem.

To find the solution, representing outgoing waves at infinity, of the Helmholtz equation,

$$\frac{\partial^2 \phi}{\partial x^2} + \frac{\partial^2 \phi}{\partial y^2} + k^2 \phi = 0$$

where $k = \alpha + i\beta$, when the solution ϕ is defined in the half plane, $y > 0$ and $-\infty < x < \infty$, and is subject to the boundary conditions,

$$\phi(x, 0) = f(x) \qquad \text{when } x \text{ is negative}$$

$$\frac{\partial \phi(x, 0)}{\partial y} = g(x) \qquad \text{when } x \text{ is positive}$$

We shall assume moreover that $f(x) = O(\exp bx)$ when x tends to minus infinity and $g(x) = O(\exp ax)$ when x tends to plus infinity, where $-\beta < a < b < \beta$.

Our strategy will be to search for the continuations of the functions $f(x)$ and $g(x)$ on the half axes $0 < x < \infty$ and $-\infty < x < 0$, respectively. We define therefore the functions,

$$\begin{aligned} f(x) &= f_+(x) \qquad \text{for positive values of } x \\ &= f_-(x) \qquad \text{for negative values of } x \end{aligned}$$

and

$$\begin{aligned} g(x) &= g_+(x) \qquad \text{for positive values of } x \\ &= g_-(x) \qquad \text{for negative values of } x \end{aligned}$$

The functions $f_-(x)$ and $g_+(x)$ are given and we want to find the functions

$f_+(x)$ and $g_-(x)$. We now introduce the unilateral Fourier transforms,

$$\Phi_+(\lambda, y) = \frac{1}{\sqrt{(2\pi)}} \int_0^\infty \phi(x, y) e^{i\lambda x}\, dx$$

and

$$\Phi_-(\lambda, y) = \frac{1}{\sqrt{(2\pi)}} \int_{-\infty}^0 \phi(x, y) e^{i\lambda x}\, dx$$

We require the solution to represent an outgoing wave at infinity, in particular $\phi(x, y) = O[\exp(-\beta x)]$ when x tends to plus infinity for a fixed value of y and $\phi(x, y) = O(\exp \beta x)$ when x tends to minus infinity for a fixed y value. This implies that the functions $\Phi_+(\lambda, y)$ and $\Phi_-(\lambda, y)$ are analytic in the upper half plane $I(\lambda) > -\beta$ and the lower half plane $I(\lambda) < \beta$ respectively, whereas the function $\Phi(\lambda, y) = \Phi_+(\lambda, y) + \Phi_-(\lambda, y)$ is analytic in the strip $-\beta < I(\lambda) < \beta$. At $y = 0$, we find

$$\Phi_+(\lambda, 0) = F_+(\lambda) = \frac{1}{\sqrt{(2\pi)}} \int_0^\infty f_+(x) e^{i\lambda x}\, dx$$

$$\Phi_-(\lambda, 0) = F_-(\lambda) = \frac{1}{\sqrt{(2\pi)}} \int_{-\infty}^0 f_-(x) e^{i\lambda x}\, dx$$

and

$$\frac{\partial \Phi_+(\lambda, 0)}{\partial y} = G_+(\lambda) = \frac{1}{\sqrt{(2\pi)}} \int_0^\infty g_+(x) e^{i\lambda x}\, dx$$

$$\frac{\partial \Phi_-(\lambda, 0)}{\partial y} = G_-(\lambda) = \frac{1}{\sqrt{(2\pi)}} \int_{-\infty}^0 g_-(x) e^{i\lambda x}\, dx$$

The Fourier transform of the Helmholtz equation can easily be obtained. Noting that the solution $\phi(x, y)$ has the integral representation,

$$\phi(x, y) = \frac{1}{\sqrt{(2\pi)}} \int_{-\infty + ic}^{\infty + ic} \Phi(\zeta, y) e^{-i\zeta x}\, d\zeta$$

where $-\beta < c < \beta$, we obtain, upon substitution, the homogeneous ordinary differential equation of the second order,

$$\frac{d^2 \Phi(\lambda, y)}{dy^2} - \mu^2(\lambda) \Phi(\lambda, y) = 0 \tag{3.14}$$

where

$$\mu(\lambda) = \sqrt{(\lambda^2 - k^2)}$$

The general solution of this equation is of the form,

$$\Phi(\lambda, y) = A(\lambda)e^{-\mu(\lambda)y} + B(\lambda)e^{\mu(\lambda)y}$$

where $A(\lambda)$ and $B(\lambda)$ are functions of λ which can be determined from the boundary conditions.

The function $\Phi(\lambda, y)$ has branch points at $\lambda = \pm k$. Choosing the branch cuts and the branches of the functions $\sqrt{(\lambda - k)}$ and $\sqrt{(\lambda + k)}$ in the same manner as in Section 1.7, we find that the real part of the function $\sqrt{(\lambda^2 - k^2)}$ is positive when λ tends to plus or minus infinity along the real axis. Hence, in order that the function $\Phi(\lambda, y)$ stays bounded for all values of λ in the cut plane when y tends to plus infinity, the coefficient $B(\lambda)$ must vanish identically. The solution of equation (3.14) may be written therefore

$$\Phi(\lambda, y) = A(\lambda)e^{-\mu(\lambda)y}$$

and its derivative with respect to y takes the form,

$$\frac{\partial\Phi(\lambda, y)}{\partial y} = -\mu(\lambda)A(\lambda)e^{-\mu(\lambda)y}$$

Consequently, for $y = 0$, we obtain the functional equations,

$$F_+(\lambda) + F_-(\lambda) = A(\lambda)$$

and

$$G_+(\lambda) + G_-(\lambda) = -\mu(\lambda)A(\lambda)$$

Eliminating the coefficient $A(\lambda)$ from these equations, we find

$$G_+(\lambda) + G_-(\lambda) = -\mu(\lambda)[F_+(\lambda) + F_-(\lambda)]$$

or, by substitution of $\mu(\lambda) = \sqrt{(\lambda^2 - k^2)}$,

$$\sqrt{(\lambda + k)}F_+(\lambda) + G_-(\lambda)/\sqrt{(\lambda - k)} = -\sqrt{(\lambda + k)}F_-(\lambda) - G_+(\lambda)/\sqrt{(\lambda - k)}$$

This is an inhomogeneous functional equation of the type (3.2) discussed in Section 3.0, which needs to be solved for the functions $F_+(\lambda)$ and $G_-(\lambda)$.

Decomposing the right hand side of this equation in the manner of Section 3.2, we find

$$L(\lambda) = -\sqrt{(\lambda + k)}F_-(\lambda) - G_+(\lambda)/\sqrt{(\lambda - k)} = L_+(\lambda) - L_-(\lambda)$$

where the function,

$$L_+(\lambda) = \frac{1}{2\pi i}\int_{-\infty + ia}^{\infty + ia} \frac{L(\zeta)}{\zeta - \lambda}\, d\zeta$$

is analytic in the upper half plane $I(\lambda) > -\beta$, and the function,

$$L_-(\lambda) = \frac{1}{2\pi i}\int_{-\infty+ib}^{\infty+ib} \frac{L(\zeta)}{\zeta - \lambda}\,d\zeta$$

is analytic in the lower half plane $I(\lambda) < \beta$, and $-\beta < a < b < \beta$.

Substitution and the usual analytic continuation argument now lead to the conclusion that

$$\sqrt{(\lambda + k)}F_+(\lambda) - L_+(\lambda) = -G_-(\lambda)/\sqrt{(\lambda - k)} - L_-(\lambda) = E(\lambda)$$

where $E(\lambda)$ is an entire function. Hence

$$F_+(\lambda) = \frac{E(\lambda) + L_+(\lambda)}{\sqrt{(\lambda + k)}}$$

and

$$G_-(\lambda) = -[E(\lambda) + L_-(\lambda)]\sqrt{(\lambda - k)}$$

Furthermore, since $A(\lambda) = F_+(\lambda) + F_-(\lambda)$, we obtain the following expression for the coefficient $A(\lambda)$,

$$A(\lambda) = \frac{E(\lambda) + L_+(\lambda)}{\sqrt{(\lambda + k)}} + F_-(\lambda)$$

This implies that the Fourier transform of the solution of the Helmholtz equation takes the form,

$$\Phi(\lambda, y) = A(\lambda)e^{-\mu(\lambda)y} = \left[\frac{E(\lambda) + L_+(\lambda)}{\sqrt{(\lambda + k)}} + F_-(\lambda)\right]e^{-\mu(\lambda)y}$$

and that the solution itself has the integral representation,

$$\phi(x, y) = \frac{1}{\sqrt{(2\pi)}}\int_{-\infty+ic}^{\infty+ic}\left[\frac{E(\zeta) + L_+(\zeta)}{\sqrt{(\zeta + k)}} + F_-(\zeta)\right]e^{-\mu(\zeta)y - i\zeta x}\,d\zeta$$

where $-\beta < a < c < b < \beta$.

To illustrate the technique introduced above we shall now discuss a more concrete boundary value problem.

To find the solution, representing outgoing waves at infinity, of the Helmholtz equation,

$$\frac{\partial^2\phi}{\partial x^2} + \frac{\partial^2\phi}{\partial y^2} + k^2\phi = 0$$

in the half plane $y > 0$ and $-\infty < x < \infty$, subject to the boundary conditions,

$$\phi(x, 0) = f(x) = e^{bx} \qquad \text{for negative values of } x$$

$$\frac{\partial\phi(x, 0)}{\partial y} = g(x) = e^{-ax} \qquad \text{for positive values of } x$$

where $k = \alpha + i\beta$ and $-\beta < a < b < \beta$.

For this problem the unilateral Fourier transforms $F_-(\lambda)$ and $G_+(\lambda)$ take the form,

$$F_-(\lambda) = \frac{1}{\sqrt{(2\pi)}} \int_{-\infty}^{0} e^{bx+i\lambda x}\, dx = \frac{1}{i\sqrt{(2\pi)}} \frac{1}{\lambda - ib}$$

and

$$G_+(\lambda) = \frac{1}{\sqrt{(2\pi)}} \int_{0}^{\infty} e^{-ax+i\lambda x}\, dx = \frac{i}{\sqrt{(2\pi)}} \frac{1}{\lambda + ia}$$

Hence, the functions $F_-(\lambda)$ and $G_+(\lambda)$ are analytic in the lower half plane $I(\lambda) < b$ and the upper half plane $I(\lambda) > -a$ respectively. The decomposition of the function,

$$L(\lambda) = L_+(\lambda) - L_-(\lambda) = -\frac{1}{i\sqrt{(2\pi)}} \left[\frac{\sqrt{(\lambda + k)}}{\lambda - ib} - \frac{1}{(\lambda + ia)\sqrt{(\lambda - k)}} \right]$$

was obtained in Section 3.2. There we found

$$L_+(\lambda) = \frac{1}{i\sqrt{(2\pi)}} \left[\frac{\sqrt{(ib + k)} - \sqrt{(\lambda + k)}}{\lambda - ib} + \frac{1}{(\lambda + ia)\sqrt{(-ia - k)}} \right]$$

and

$$L_-(\lambda) = \frac{1}{i\sqrt{(2\pi)}} \left[\frac{\sqrt{(ib + k)}}{\lambda - ib} - \frac{\sqrt{(-ia - k)} - \sqrt{(\lambda - k)}}{(\lambda + ia)\sqrt{(-ia - k)}\sqrt{(\lambda - k)}} \right]$$

These functions satisfy therefore the order properties $L_+(\lambda) = O(\lambda^{-1/2})$ and $L_-(\lambda) = O(\lambda^{-1})$ when λ tends to infinity.

Assuming that $F_+(\lambda) = O(\lambda^{-1})$ and $G_-(\lambda) = O(\lambda^{-1/2})$ when λ tends to infinity, we may infer from Liouville's theorem that the entire function $E(\lambda)$ vanishes. Hence

$$F_+(\lambda) = \frac{L_+(\lambda)}{\sqrt{(\lambda + k)}}$$

and

$$G_-(\lambda) = -L_-(\lambda)\sqrt{(\lambda - k)}$$

The solution of the boundary value problem is found therefore by inverting the Fourier transform,

$$\Phi(\lambda, y) = A(\lambda)e^{-\mu(\lambda)y}$$

where

$$A(\lambda) = F_+(\lambda) + F_-(\lambda)$$

Consequently, the solution has the integral representation,

$$\phi(x, y) = \frac{1}{\sqrt{(2\pi)}} \int_{-\infty+ic}^{\infty+ic} [F_+(\zeta) + F_-(\zeta)]e^{-\mu(\zeta)y - i\zeta x}\, d\zeta$$

$$= \frac{1}{2\pi i} \int_{-\infty+ic}^{\infty+ic} \left[\frac{\sqrt{(ib + k)}}{(\zeta - ib)\sqrt{(\zeta + k)}} + \frac{1}{(\zeta + ia)\sqrt{(-ia - k)}\sqrt{(\zeta + k)}}\right] e^{-\mu(\zeta)y - i\zeta x}\, d\zeta$$

The evaluation by contour integration of this integral is left to the reader.

3.9 SMALL AMPLITUDE THEORY OF WATER WAVES

The Wiener-Hopf technique has been applied with great success to the solution of some boundary value problems arising in the small amplitude theory of water waves. To provide a basis for the discussion of an example, we shall first present a brief outline of this theory.

We shall be concerned with certain aspects of the motion of waves on a sea, in particular with the motion of the surface of a sea under influence of a gravitational force. Because of the gravitational force the elevation of the waves above sea level varies in space and time. Representing the undisturbed free surface of the sea by the horizontal xz-plane, y is the vertical coordinate axis and the disturbed sea surface can be described by an equation of the form,

$$y = f(x, z, t)$$

We shall assume that we are dealing with the irrotational motion of an incompressible, nonviscous fluid.

Since the motion of the fluid is irrotational, the curl of the velocity field $\mathbf{v}(\mathbf{r}, t)$ vanishes,

$$\nabla \times \mathbf{v}(\mathbf{r}, t) = 0$$

where $\mathbf{r} = (x, y, z)$ denotes the position vector. This implies that the velocity vector is equal to the gradient of a scalar function $\Phi(\mathbf{r}, t)$, the so-called velocity potential,

$$\mathbf{v}(\mathbf{r}, t) = \nabla\Phi(\mathbf{r}, t)$$

The motion of the fluid can be described completely in terms of this function.

Since the fluid is assumed to be incompressible and nonviscous, the continuity equation,

$$\frac{\partial \rho(\mathbf{r}, t)}{\partial t} + \nabla \cdot (\rho \mathbf{v}) = 0$$

which states that the time rate of change of the fluid mass at a particular point in space is equal to the divergence of the quantity $\rho \mathbf{v}$, takes the simple form,

$$\nabla \cdot \mathbf{v}(\mathbf{r}, t) = 0$$

The velocity field $\mathbf{v}(\mathbf{r}, t)$ is therefore both irrotational and solenoidal. From these conclusions we may infer that the velocity potential $\Phi(\mathbf{r}, t)$ is a solution of Laplace's equation,

$$\nabla \cdot \nabla \Phi(\mathbf{r}, t) = \nabla^2 \Phi(\mathbf{r}, t) = 0$$

For a particular fluid configuration this equation is solved subject to certain boundary conditions imposed on the boundary surfaces of the region under consideration.

The types of surfaces most commonly encountered are the so-called fixed surfaces, such as the shore and the bottom of the sea, and the free surfaces such as the sea-air interface.

On a fixed impenetrable surface we must impose the physically obvious condition that the component of the fluid velocity normal to the surface must vanish. Thus, on a fixed surface, we must require that

$$\mathbf{n} \cdot \mathbf{v}(\mathbf{r}, t) = \mathbf{n} \cdot \nabla \Phi(\mathbf{r}, t) = \frac{\partial \Phi(\mathbf{r}, t)}{\partial n} = 0$$

where $\mathbf{n}$ denotes the unit vector normal to the surface.

On a free surface we assume that a fluid particle moving on the sea-air interface stays on this surface and cannot escape. Consequently, defining the surface by the implicit equation,

$$s(x, y, z, t) = y - f(x, z, t) = 0$$

we find

$$\frac{ds}{dt} = \frac{\partial s}{\partial t} + \mathbf{v} \cdot \nabla s = 0$$

However, $\partial s/\partial y = 1$, and we obtain therefore the relation,

$$v_y = \frac{\partial y}{\partial t} + v_x \frac{\partial y}{\partial x} + v_z \frac{\partial y}{\partial z} \qquad \text{on a free surface}$$

In terms of the velocity potential, this equation may also be written

$$\frac{\partial \Phi}{\partial y} = \frac{\partial y}{\partial t} + \frac{\partial y}{\partial x}\frac{\partial \Phi}{\partial x} + \frac{\partial y}{\partial z}\frac{\partial \Phi}{\partial z} \qquad \text{on a free surface}$$

This is the so-called kinematic boundary condition. Another free surface boundary condition follows from Bernoulli's law. Assuming that the pressure on such a surface is constant, we must require that

$$gf(x, z, t) + \frac{\partial \Phi}{\partial t} + \frac{1}{2}\nabla\Phi \cdot \nabla\Phi = \text{constant} \qquad \text{on a free surface}$$

where g denotes the acceleration of gravity.

The kinematic and the Bernoulli boundary conditions are nonlinear and an attempt to find the solution of Laplace's equation subject to such boundary conditions by means of existing analytical techniques is doomed to failure. Recourse must be sought in an approximate theory, namely, the small amplitude theory of water waves. This theory is based on the assumption that the fluid particle velocity, the elevation of the waves above sea level, and all appropriate derivatives are small quantities. These assumptions lead to the following linearized free surface boundary conditions,

$$gf(x, z, t) + \frac{\partial \Phi}{\partial t} = 0 \qquad \text{on a free surface}$$

and

$$\frac{\partial \Phi}{\partial y} - \frac{\partial f}{\partial t} = 0 \qquad \text{on a free surface}$$

Eliminating f from these two equations, we obtain the linear boundary condition,

$$\frac{\partial^2 \Phi}{\partial t^2} + g\frac{\partial \Phi}{\partial y} = 0$$

which is to be imposed on the undisturbed sea level position of a free surface.

To summarize, in the small amplitude theory of water waves we seek solutions of the potential equation,

$$\nabla^2\Phi(\mathbf{r}, t) = 0$$

for the velocity potential $\Phi(\mathbf{r}, t)$, subject to the boundary conditions,

$$\frac{\partial \Phi}{\partial n} = 0 \qquad \text{on a fixed surface}$$

$$\frac{\partial^2 \Phi}{\partial t^2} + g\frac{\partial \Phi}{\partial y} = 0 \qquad \text{on a free surface}$$

3.10 SEMI-INFINITE DOCK ON A SEA OF FINITE DEPTH

In this section, we shall formulate a boundary value problem of the small amplitude theory of water waves and solve it by means of the Wiener-Hopf technique.

We shall investigate the problem of progressive waves on an infinite sea of finite depth which is covered by a semi-infinite dock. We assume that the z-axis is taken along the dock side which is the separation line between the dock and the undisturbed free surface. The dock covers the left half of the xz-plane

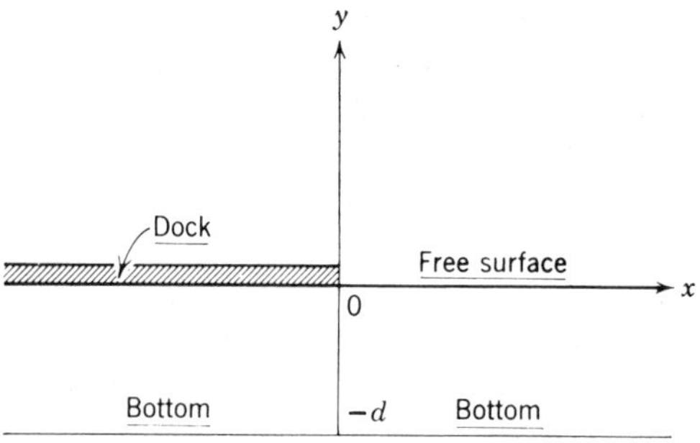

Figure III-9

whereas the undisturbed free sea surface coincides with the right half of this plane. Assuming that the surface waves are incident on the dock from the right, we are interested in the steady state behavior of these waves.

Let us suppose that the wave motion is harmonic in time and that the normal to the direction of propagation of the waves is oblique to the dock. Introducing the mode,

$$\Phi(\mathbf{r}, t) = \phi(x, y) \exp\left[i(kz - \omega t)\right]$$

we obtain, by substitution in the Laplace equation for the velocity potential the following Helmholtz equation for the steady state functions $\phi(x, y)$,

$$\frac{\partial^2 \phi}{\partial x^2} + \frac{\partial^2 \phi}{\partial y^2} - k^2 \phi = 0$$

As we have found in the preceding section, the boundary condition imposed on a free surface in the small amplitude theory of water waves takes the form,

$$\frac{\partial^2 \Phi}{\partial t^2} + g \frac{\partial \Phi}{\partial y} = 0$$

This implies that we must impose the following boundary condition on the function $\phi(x, y)$ on the right half of the xz-plane.

$$\frac{\partial \phi}{\partial y} = m\phi \qquad 0 < x < \infty$$

where $m = \omega^2/g$. At a fixed surface we must impose the condition,

$$\frac{\partial \phi}{\partial n} = 0$$

and for our problem this implies that

(a) on the bottom of the sea, $y = -d$,

$$\frac{\partial \phi(x, -d)}{\partial y} = 0 \qquad -\infty < x < \infty$$

(b) on the dock-sea interface,

$$\frac{\partial \phi(x, 0)}{\partial y} = 0 \qquad -\infty < x < 0$$

These boundary conditions specify the behavior of the function $\phi(x, y)$ on the free surface, on the bottom of the sea, and on the interface between dock and sea. We must also specify the behavior of this function for large positive and negative values of x and at the origin.

For large positive values of x we expect plane waves and the behavior of ϕ for these values of x can be derived therefore by solving the auxiliary boundary value problem,

$$\frac{\partial^2 \phi}{\partial x^2} + \frac{\partial^2 \phi}{\partial y^2} - k^2\phi = 0, \qquad x > 0$$

subject to the boundary conditions,

1. $\dfrac{\partial \phi}{\partial y} = m\phi \qquad y = 0, \quad x > 0$

2. $\dfrac{\partial \phi}{\partial y} = 0 \qquad y = -d, \quad x > 0$

3. wave motion exists for large positive values of x.

The solution of this boundary value problem can easily be obtained by separation of variables. The normal modes satisfying this problem are of the form,

$$\phi_0(x, y) = A_0 \exp(\pm ih_0 x) \cosh v_0(y + d)$$

where $h_0 = \sqrt{(v_0^2 - k^2)}$, $v_0^2 > k^2$, and $v_0 = \pm a_0/d$ are the real roots of the dispersion equation,

$$v \tanh dv = m$$

There are also modes of the form,

$$\phi_n(x, y) = A_n \exp(-h_n x) \cosh v_n(y + d)$$

which correspond to the purely imaginary roots $v_n = \pm i a_n/d$ of the same dispersion equation, where $a_n = -a_{-n}$ is a real parameter. These modes represent the exponentially damped motion.

For large negative values of x we expect the wave motion to be damped by the dock. To obtain the behavior of the function $\phi(x, y)$ for such values of x, we consider the auxiliary boundary value problem,

$$\frac{\partial^2 \phi}{\partial x^2} + \frac{\partial^2 \phi}{\partial y^2} - k^2 \phi = 0, \qquad x < 0$$

subject to the boundary conditions,

1. $\dfrac{\partial \phi}{\partial y} = 0 \qquad y = -d, \quad x < 0$

2. $\dfrac{\partial \phi}{\partial y} = 0 \qquad y = 0, \qquad x < 0$

3. ϕ vanishes for large negative values of x.

The normal modes satisfying this problem are of the form,

$$\phi_n(x, y) = B_n \exp(p_n x) \cos n\pi y/d$$

where $p_n = \sqrt{(k^2 + n^2\pi^2/d^2)}$. Hence, for large negative values of x, the function $\phi(x, y)$ satisfies the order property $\phi(x, y) = O(\exp kx)$.

Finally, we come to the condition we have to impose on the function $\phi(x, y)$ at the edge of the dock $x = 0$, $y = 0$. It can be shown, that conservation of energy leads to a velocity potential that has a logarithmic singularity at the origin. Hence we shall assume that

$$\phi(x, y) = f(r) \log r + g(r)$$

for sufficiently small values of $r = \sqrt{(x^2 + y^2)}$, where $f(r)$ and $g(r)$ are bounded at the origin and have bounded first and second derivatives at this point.

The conditions, derived above, completely specify the boundary value problem and, to summarize, we want to find a function $\phi(x, y)$ which is a solution of the Helmholtz equation,

$$\frac{\partial^2 \phi}{\partial x^2} + \frac{\partial^2 \phi}{\partial y^2} - k^2 \phi = 0$$

subject to the boundary conditions,

1. $\dfrac{\partial \phi}{\partial y} = m\phi \qquad y = 0, \qquad 0 < x < \infty$

2. $\dfrac{\partial \phi}{\partial y} = 0 \qquad y = 0, \qquad -\infty < x < 0$

3. $\dfrac{\partial \phi}{\partial y} = 0 \qquad y = -d, \quad -\infty < x < \infty$

4. $\phi(x, y)$ is bounded for large positive values of x
5. $\phi(x, y) = O(\exp kx)$ when x tends to minus infinity
6. $\phi(x, y) = f(r) \log r + g(r)$ when r tends to zero.

To solve this boundary value problem we make use of the Wiener-Hopf technique. We introduce the unilateral transforms,

$$\Phi_+(\lambda, y) = \frac{1}{\sqrt{(2\pi)}} \int_0^\infty \phi(x, y) e^{i\lambda x}\, dx$$

and

$$\Phi_-(\lambda, y) = \frac{1}{\sqrt{(2\pi)}} \int_{-\infty}^0 \phi(x, y) e^{i\lambda x}\, dx$$

where, according to the boundary conditions 4 and 5, the function $\Phi_+(\lambda, y)$ is analytic in the upper half plane $I(\lambda) > 0$ and the function $\Phi_-(\lambda, y)$ is analytic in the lower half plane $I(\lambda) < k$. Consequently, the function $\Phi(\lambda, y) = \Phi_+(\lambda, y) + \Phi_-(\lambda, y)$ is analytic in the strip $0 < I(\lambda) < k$. The Fourier transform $\Phi(\lambda, y)$ is the solution of the boundary value problem,

$$\frac{d^2\Phi}{dy^2} - \mu^2(\lambda)\Phi(\lambda, y) = 0, \qquad \mu(\lambda) = \sqrt{(\lambda^2 + k^2)}$$

subject to the boundary conditions,

1. $\dfrac{d\Phi_+(\lambda, 0)}{dy} = m\Phi_+(\lambda, 0)$

2. $\dfrac{d\Phi_-(\lambda, 0)}{dy} = 0$

3. $\dfrac{d\Phi(\lambda, -d)}{dy} = 0$

The general solution of this second order ordinary differential equation,

$$\Phi(\lambda, y) = A(\lambda)e^{-\mu(\lambda)y} + B(\lambda)e^{\mu(\lambda)y}$$

has branch points at $\lambda = \pm ik$ and, cutting the plane along the lines $(-ik, -i\infty)$ and $(ik, i\infty)$, we choose branches of the functions $\sqrt{(\lambda + ik)}$ and $\sqrt{(\lambda - ik)}$ such that $R(\lambda)$ is positive when λ tends to plus or minus infinity along the real axis.

The coefficients $A(\lambda)$ and $B(\lambda)$ can be found by means of the boundary conditions. The boundary condition on the bottom, $y = -d$, yields

$$B(\lambda) = A(\lambda) \exp(2\mu d)$$

and we may write

$$\Phi(\lambda, y) = \Phi_+(\lambda, y) + \Phi_-(\lambda, y) = A(\lambda)[e^{-\mu y} + e^{\mu(2d+y)}] \tag{3.15}$$

and

$$\frac{\partial\Phi(\lambda, y)}{\partial y} = \frac{\partial\Phi_+(\lambda, y)}{\partial y} + \frac{\partial\Phi_-(\lambda, y)}{\partial y} = \mu A(\lambda)[e^{\mu(2d+y)} - e^{-\mu y}] \tag{3.16}$$

However, on the surface, $y = 0$, we have

$$\frac{\partial\Phi_+(\lambda, 0)}{\partial y} = m\Phi_+(\lambda, 0)$$

and

$$\frac{\partial\Phi_-(\lambda, 0)}{\partial y} = 0$$

Hence, substitution into equation (3.16) yields

$$\frac{\partial\Phi_+(\lambda, 0)}{\partial y} = m\Phi_+(\lambda, 0) = \mu A(\lambda)[e^{2\mu d} - 1]$$

Eliminating the coefficient $A(\lambda)$ from this equation, by means of equation (3.15) evaluated at $y = 0$, we find

$$\Phi_+(\lambda, 0) + \Phi_-(\lambda, 0) = \frac{m}{\mu} \coth \mu d \Phi_+(\lambda, 0)$$

or

$$\left(1 - \frac{m}{\mu} \coth \mu d\right)\Phi_+(\lambda, 0) + \Phi_-(\lambda, 0) = 0$$

To solve this functional equation by the Wiener-Hopf technique, we must now factor the function,

$$H(\lambda) = \frac{\mu \sinh \mu d - m \cosh \mu d}{\mu \sinh \mu d} = \frac{H_+(\lambda)}{H_-(\lambda)}$$

where $\mu = \sqrt{(\lambda^2 + k^2)}$, so that $H_+(\lambda)$ and $H_-(\lambda)$ are analytic and non-vanishing in the upper half plane $I(\lambda) > 0$ and $I(\lambda) < k$ respectively. The factorization of this function was obtained in Section 3.3. There we found

$$H_+(\lambda) = \frac{[1 - d^2(k^2 + \lambda^2)/a_0{}^2] \prod_{n=1}^{\infty} [\sqrt{(1 + d^2k^2/a_n{}^2)} - id\lambda/a_n] e^{id\lambda/n\pi}}{d(k - i\lambda) \prod_{n=1}^{\infty} [\sqrt{(1 + d^2k^2/n^2\pi^2)} - id\lambda/n\pi] e^{id\lambda/n\pi}}$$

and

$$H_-(\lambda) = -\frac{(k + i\lambda) \prod_{n=1}^{\infty} [\sqrt{(1 + d^2k^2/n^2\pi^2)} + id\lambda/n\pi] e^{-id\lambda/n\pi}}{m \prod_{n=1}^{\infty} [\sqrt{(1 + d^2k^2/a_n{}^2)} + id\lambda/a_n] e^{-id\lambda/n\pi}}$$

Hence, both functions are at most of the order of λ when λ tends to infinity in their half planes of analyticity. By means of this factorization, the functional equation for the functions $\Phi_+(\lambda)$ and $\Phi_-(\lambda)$ may be written

$$\Phi_+(\lambda)H_+(\lambda) = -\Phi_-(\lambda)H_-(\lambda)$$

and the familiar analytic continuation argument leads to the conclusion,

$$\Phi_+(\lambda)H_+(\lambda) = -\Phi_-(\lambda)H_-(\lambda) = E(\lambda)$$

where $E(\lambda)$ is an entire function. Since the unilateral Fourier transforms $\Phi_+(\lambda)$ and $\Phi_-(\lambda)$ vanish when λ tends to infinity in the strip $0 < I(\lambda) < k$, we obtain, in view of the order properties of $H_+(\lambda)$ and $H_-(\lambda)$,

$$E(\lambda) = \Phi_+(\lambda)H_+(\lambda) = O(\lambda^\alpha)$$

when λ tends to infinity in the upper half plane $I(\lambda) > 0$, and

$$E(\lambda) = -\Phi_-(\lambda)H_-(\lambda) = O(\lambda^\beta)$$

when λ tends to infinity in the lower half plane $I(\lambda) < k$, where α and β are positive numbers smaller than one. This implies, according to Liouville's theorem, that the function $E(\lambda)$ must be a constant, $E(\lambda) = D$ say. Consequently,

$$\Phi_+(\lambda, 0) = D/H_+(\lambda), \qquad \Phi_-(\lambda, 0) = -D/H_-(\lambda)$$

and

$$\Phi(\lambda, 0) = D\left[\frac{1}{H_+(\lambda)} - \frac{1}{H_-(\lambda)}\right] = \frac{D}{H_+(\lambda)} \frac{m}{\mu} \coth \mu d$$

However, we found above that

$$\Phi(\lambda, y) = A(\lambda)[e^{-\mu y} + e^{\mu(2d+y)}]$$

and we obtain therefore the following expression for the coefficient $A(\lambda)$,

$$A(\lambda) = \frac{\Phi(\lambda, 0)}{2e^{\mu d} \cosh \mu d}$$

Substitution now yields the Fourier transform,

$$\Phi(\lambda, y) = \frac{mD}{\mu H_+(\lambda)} \frac{\cosh \mu(d + y)}{\sinh \mu d}$$

and inverting this transform, we obtain the following integral representations for the solution of our boundary value problem,

$$\phi(x, y) = \frac{mD}{\sqrt{(2\pi)}} \int_{-\infty+ic}^{\infty+ic} \frac{\cosh \mu(d + y)}{\mu \sinh \mu d} \frac{e^{-i\zeta x}}{H_+(\zeta)} d\zeta$$

$$= \frac{mD}{\sqrt{(2\pi)}} \int_{-\infty+ic}^{\infty+ic} \frac{\cosh \mu(d + y)}{\mu \sinh \mu d - m \cosh \mu d} \frac{e^{-i\zeta x}}{H_-(\zeta)} d\zeta$$

where $0 < c < k$ and $\mu = \sqrt{(\zeta^2 + k^2)}$.

To evaluate these integrals, we close the contour C by a semicircle CR of radius R and center at the point $(0, c)$ The contour is closed in the lower half plane when x is positive and in the upper half plane when x is negative. Since $H_+(\lambda)$ is analytic and nonvanishing in the upper half plane we choose the first integral representation when x is negative, and consider the contour integral,

$$\oint_C \frac{\cosh \mu(d + y)}{\mu \sinh \mu d} \frac{e^{-i\zeta x}}{H_+(\zeta)} d\zeta$$

The contribution of the semicircle to the integral vanishes when R tends to infinity and we obtain, by means of the residue theorem,

$$\phi(x, y) = mD\sqrt{(2\pi)}\left[\sum_{n=1}^{\infty} \frac{(-1)^n \exp\{x\sqrt{(k^2 + n^2\pi^2/d^2)}\} \cos n\pi(y + d)/d}{\sqrt{(n^2\pi^2 + d^2k^2)}H_+[i\sqrt{(k^2 + n^2\pi^2/d^2)}]} + \frac{e^{kx}}{2kH_+(i\ldots}\right.$$

when x is negative. In a similar manner we find

$$\phi(x, y) = mD\sqrt{(2\pi)}\left[\sum_{n=1}^{\infty} \frac{a_n^2 \exp\{-x\sqrt{(k^2 + a_n^2/d^2)}\} \cos a_n(y + d)/d}{\sqrt{(a_n^2 + d^2k^2)}H_-[-i\sqrt{(k^2 + a_n^2/d^2)}] \cos a_n\sqrt{(a_n^2 - d + \ldots}}\right.$$

$$\left. + \frac{a_0^2 \sinh(hx + \theta) \cosh a_0 y/d}{hd \cosh a_0\sqrt{(a_0^2 - d + d^2)}}\right]$$

when x is positive, where

$$\theta = -\sum_{n=1}^{\infty} [\arcsin dh\sqrt{(a_n^2 + a_0^2)} - dh/n\pi]$$

$$+ \sum_{n=1}^{\infty} [\arcsin dh\sqrt{(n^2\pi^2 + a_0^2)} - dh/n\pi] + \arcsin dh/a_0$$

and h denotes the positive square root $\sqrt{(-k^2 + a_0^2/d^2)}$.

The function $\phi(x, y)$ satisfies all the conditions imposed on the solution of the boundary value problem. However, we shall not here verify this fact but rather refer the reader to the literature for a more complete discussion.

CHAPTER IV

BOUNDARY VALUE PROBLEMS FOR SECTIONALLY ANALYTIC FUNCTIONS

4.0 INTRODUCTION

The foregoing chapter has been devoted to the Wiener-Hopf technique and its application to the solution of integral equations and partial differential equations of mathematical physics. As we have shown such an equation can sometimes be solved by first reducing it to a functional equation in the space of a Fourier transform variable. This functional equation is of the form,

$$A(\lambda)F_+(\lambda) + B(\lambda)F_-(\lambda) + C(\lambda) = 0$$

To obtain the solution of such an equation by means of the Wiener-Hopf technique it is necessary that the functions $F_+(\lambda)$, $F_-(\lambda)$, $A(\lambda)$, $B(\lambda)$, and $C(\lambda)$ have a strip of analyticity in common. However, this can be a rather severe restriction on the solutions and kernels of the original differential or integral equation. For some of the differential and integral equations of mathematical physics there exists only a line of convergence on which all necessary transforms are well defined. In such cases it has been noted that the partial differential or integral equation can be reduced to a Hilbert problem in the space of the transform variable.

For example, let us consider the homogeneous Wiener-Hopf equation of the second kind,

$$f(t) = \int_0^\infty k(t - t_0)f(t_0)\,dt_0$$

Proceeding in the usual manner, we Fourier transform this integral equation into a functional equation,

$$F_+(\lambda)[1 - \sqrt{(2\pi)}K(\lambda)] + F_-(\lambda) = 0 \tag{4.1}$$

Now let us assume that the function $k(t)\exp(-at)$ is absolutely integrable over the whole real axis. This implies that the Fourier integral,

$$K(\lambda) = \frac{1}{\sqrt{(2\pi)}}\int_{-\infty}^{\infty} k(t)e^{i\lambda t}\,dt$$

is absolutely convergent on the path $(-\infty + ia, \infty + ia)$. Similarly, assuming that the function $f(t)\exp(-at)$ is absolutely integrable over the real axis, we find that the unilateral transform,

$$F_+(\lambda) = \frac{1}{\sqrt{(2\pi)}}\int_0^\infty f(t)e^{i\lambda t}\,dt$$

is absolutely and uniformly convergent in the upper half plane $I(\lambda) \geqq a$, and that the transform,

$$F_-(\lambda) = \frac{1}{\sqrt{(2\pi)}}\int_{-\infty}^{0} f(t)e^{i\lambda t}\,dt$$

is absolutely and uniformly convergent in the lower half plane, $I(\lambda) \leqq a$. Furthermore, the function $F_+(\lambda)$ is analytic in the upper half plane $I(\lambda) > a$ and the function $F_-(\lambda)$ is analytic in the lower half plane $I(\lambda) < a$. Consequently, the line $\zeta = -\infty + ia$ to $\zeta = \infty + ia$ is a line of convergence for the three transforms $F_+(\zeta)$, $F_-(\zeta)$, and $K(\zeta)$.

The functional equation (4.1) can now be interpreted as a boundary value condition satisfied by the boundary values $F^L(\zeta) = F_+(\zeta)$ and $F^R(\zeta) = F_-(\zeta)$ of a sectionally analytic function $F(\lambda)$, namely, a function which is analytic in the whole complex plane with the exception of the path $(-\infty + ia, \infty + ia)$. In other words, the function $F(\lambda)$ is analytic in the plane cut along the path $(-\infty + ia, \infty + ia)$. This path is called the boundary of the sectionally analytic function.

A boundary value problem in which we are required to find a function $F(\lambda)$ that is sectionally analytic in the plane cut along a given contour or path on which its left and right boundary values $F^L(\zeta)$ and $F^R(\zeta)$ satisfy the condition,

$$F^L(\zeta) = A(\zeta)F^R(\zeta)$$

is called a homogeneous Hilbert problem.

Problems of this type can be solved by a technique which we shall present in Section 4.10. The conditions which must be imposed on the transforms of the solution and kernel of the integral equation to solve the Hilbert problem by this technique are rather mild. They are much less restrictive, in fact, than the conditions which must be imposed on these functions in the Wiener-Hopf technique. For instance, in the Hilbert problem technique the boundary condition does not have to be analytically continued into a strip in the complex plane as is necessary for the Wiener-Hopf technique. In other words, it is no longer necessary for the functions $F^L(\zeta)$, $F^R(\zeta)$, and $A(\zeta)$ to be the restrictions on the path $(-\infty + ia, \infty + ia)$ of analytic functions which share a strip of analyticity. Furthermore, it is not necessary for the boundary to be an infinite path which is parallel to the real axis. Hilbert problems can be formulated and solved for functions which are sectionally analytic in a plane cut along arbitrary contours and/or paths. In this chapter, however, we shall restrict ourselves to the case in which the boundary of the sectionally analytic function is either a single closed contour, a finite path, or an infinite straight line parallel to the real axis.

In the solution of a Hilbert problem extensive use is made of sectionally continuous and analytic functions and of the representation of such functions by Cauchy integrals. Although of considerable theoretical and practical interest, such functions and their representations are often neglected in the standard textbooks on functions of a complex variable. In the next few sections we shall present a short outline of those aspects of the theory of these functions and their representations of immediate importance to the topics of discussion in the rest of this book.

4.1 HÖLDER CONTINUOUS FUNCTIONS

A function $f(\lambda)$ of a complex variable is continuous in a given region of the complex plane if it approaches the value $f(a)$ when λ tends to the point a in this region. Symbolically,

$$f(\lambda) - f(a) = o(1)$$

when λ tends to a. A stronger mode of approach of the function $f(\lambda)$ to the value $f(a)$ is expressed by the condition of Hölder continuity. A function $f(\lambda)$ is Hölder continuous in a region of the complex plane if it satisfies the inequality,

$$|f(a) - f(a_0)| \leqq K|a - a_0|^\beta$$

for every pair of points a and a_0 in that region, where $0 < \beta \leqq 1$. The constants K and β are called the Hölder constants. The actual value of K is usually immaterial, but the value of β is of course important. One emphasizes the importance of β by saying that the function $f(\lambda)$ is Hölder continuous with exponent β in a given region.

If the function $f(\lambda)$ satisfies the order relation,

$$f(\lambda) - f(a) = O[(\lambda - a)^\beta]$$

for all values of λ in a given neighborhood of the point a, where $0 < \beta \leqq 1$, then $f(\lambda)$ is said to be Hölder continuous in the point a. Since

$$f(\lambda) - f(a) = O[(\lambda - a)^\beta] = o(1)$$

a function which is Hölder continuous at a given point is also continuous at that point. In other words, Hölder continuity implies ordinary continuity, or Hölder continuity is a stronger property than ordinary continuity.

Similarly, if the function $f(\lambda)$ has a bounded derivative at the point a, then

$$f(\lambda) - f(a) = O(\lambda - a)$$

when λ tends to a. Consequently, a function which is boundedly differentiable at a given point is also Hölder continuous with exponent $\beta = 1$ at this point. In other words, Hölder continuity is a weaker condition than differentiability.

A function can also be Hölder continuous at the point at infinity. If the function $f(\lambda)$ satisfies the order relation,

$$f(\lambda) - f(\infty) = O(\lambda^{-\beta})$$

when λ tends to infinity, then $f(\lambda)$ is said to be Hölder continuous with exponent β at infinity, where β is assumed to be a positive number.

In the subsequent sections of this chapter we shall be concerned with functions $f(\zeta)$ which are defined on paths and contours instead of in regions of the complex plane. In this case, the function $f(\zeta)$ is assumed to be a real or complex valued point function of the variable ζ on the path or contour. This means that $f(\zeta)$ is in general defined on a path or contour only and is not the boundary value on that path or contour of a function which is analytic in the neighborhood of that path or contour. However, $f(\zeta)$ can still be a complex valued function in the sense that $f(\zeta) = g(\zeta) + ih(\zeta)$ where $g(\zeta)$ and $h(\zeta)$ are real valued functions of ζ.

The following definitions of Hölder continuity for a function defined on a path or contour are straightforward extensions of the definitions of Hölder continuity for a function defined in a region.

The function $f(\zeta)$ is Hölder continuous on a path or contour C if $f(\zeta)$ satisfies the inequality,

$$|f(\alpha) - f(\alpha_0)| \leqq K|\alpha - \alpha_0|^\beta$$

where α and α_0 are two arbitrary points on C and $0 < \beta \leqq 1$. Similarly, the function $f(\zeta)$ is Hölder continuous at a given point α on C if it satisfies the order relation,

$$f(\zeta) - f(\alpha) = O[(\zeta - \alpha)^\beta]$$

when ζ is a point in a given neighborhood of the point α, where $0 < \beta \leqq 1$. Finally, the function $f(\zeta)$ is said to be Hölder continuous at infinity if it satisfies the order relation,

$$f(\zeta) - f(\infty) = O(\zeta^{-\beta})$$

when ζ tends to the point at infinity on the path C, where β is a positive constant.

An example of a function which is Hölder continuous but not differentiable at a given point is the function of the real variable $f(x) = |x|$. This function is Hölder continuous with exponent $\beta = 1$ at $x = 0$ but it is not differentiable at this point. It should furthermore be noted that specifying a Hölder condition on a function $f(\zeta)$ with exponent $\beta > 1$ has no special significance. For, if $f(\zeta)$ is Hölder continuous at a point α with exponent $\beta > 1$, then the derivative of this function is zero at the point α. If, moreover, the function is Hölder continuous with exponent $\beta > 1$ at every point of a given path, then the function is a constant on the path. Hence, we shall only consider functions which are Hölder continuous with exponent $0 < \beta \leqq 1$.

4.2 SECTIONALLY CONTINUOUS FUNCTIONS

In this section we shall define still another kind of continuity, namely sectional continuity.

Let C be a contour in the complex plane and let $F(\lambda)$ be a function which is continuous in a neighborhood of this contour and is defined in this neighborhood by the relations,

$$F(\lambda) = F^L(\lambda) \qquad \text{when } \lambda \text{ is a point inside } C$$
$$F(\lambda) = F^R(\lambda) \qquad \text{when } \lambda \text{ is a point outside } C$$

where the superscript L denotes the fact that the particular function considered is defined inside the contour and the superscript R indicates that the function is defined outside the contour C. Let us assume moreover that λ is a point in the region L and α is a point on the contour. If the function $F^L(\lambda)$ approaches a finite limit value $F^L(\alpha)$ when λ tends to the point α from inside the contour, as shown in Figure IV-1, then the function $F(\lambda)$ is continuous from the left at the point α on this contour. It is assumed that the point λ never leaves the region L in its approach to the point α.

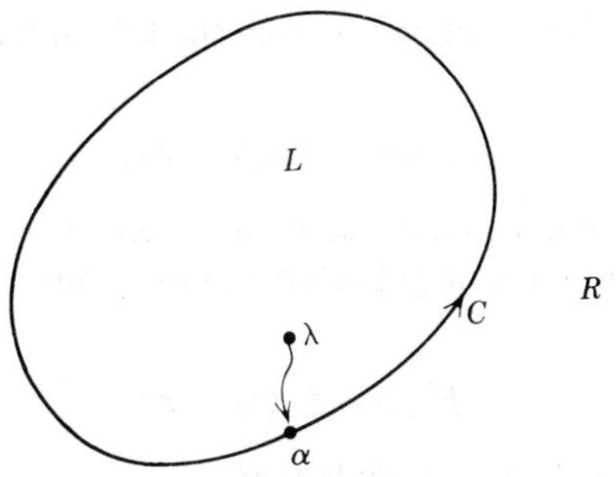

Figure IV-1

The limit value of the function $F^L(\lambda)$ at α,

$$F^L(\alpha) = \lim_{\lambda \to \alpha} F^L(\lambda) = \lim_{\lambda \to \alpha} F(\lambda)$$

as λ approaches the point α from inside the contour C is called the left boundary value of the function $F(\lambda)$ on C.

In a similar manner we may define the right boundary value of $F(\lambda)$ at a point α as the limit,

$$F^R(\alpha) = \lim_{\lambda \to \alpha} F^R(\lambda) = \lim_{\lambda \to \alpha} F(\lambda)$$

when λ approaches the point α from outside the contour C, as shown in Figure IV-2. The function $F(\lambda)$ is said to be continuous from the right at the

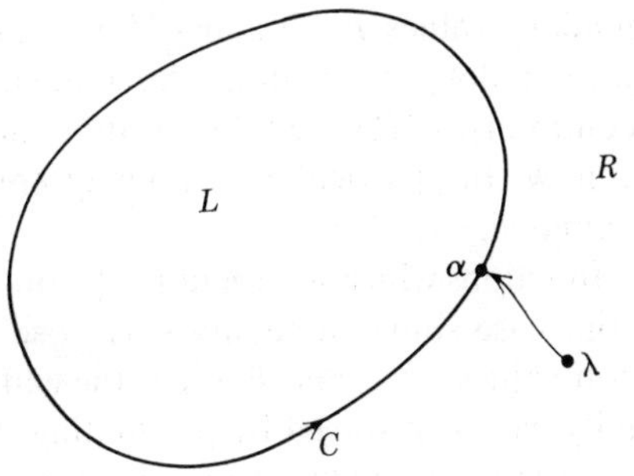

Figure IV-2

point α on C if $F^R(\alpha)$ exists.

If $F(\lambda)$ has a left boundary value $F^L(\zeta)$ at all points ζ on C, then $F(\lambda)$ is said to be continuous from the left on C. Similarly, $F(\lambda)$ is said to be continuous from the right on C if $F(\lambda)$ has a right boundary value $F^R(\zeta)$ at all points ζ on C.

If the function $F(\lambda)$ is continuous from the left on the contour C, we may write

$$F^L(\lambda) - F^L(\zeta) = o(1)$$

when λ tends to the point ζ on the contour C. Let α be a point on the contour C which is located in some neighborhood of the point ζ. In that case it is also true that

$$F^L(\lambda) - F^L(\alpha) = o(1)$$

The two order relations above imply that

$$F^L(\zeta) - F^L(\alpha) = o(1)$$

when ζ tends to α. In other words, the boundary value $F^L(\zeta)$ of the function $F(\lambda)$, which is continuous from the left on C, is a continuous function of ζ on the contour C. Similarly, the right boundary value $F^R(\zeta)$ of a function $F(\lambda)$, which is continuous from the right on a contour C, is a continuous function of ζ on C.

In conclusion, a function $F(\lambda)$ which is continuous inside a contour C and has a boundary value $F^L(\zeta)$ on C is continuous inside and on the contour C. Similarly, a function $F(\lambda)$ which is continuous outside a contour C and has the boundary value $F^R(\zeta)$ on C is continuous outside and on the contour C.

Consider a function $F(\alpha)$ which is continuous inside L and R and has the boundary values $F^L(\zeta)$ and $F^R(\zeta)$. Since the boundary values are in general not equal to each other, $F(\lambda)$ is not continuous in the whole complex plane. A function $F(\lambda)$ which is continuous in the neighborhood of a contour and possesses distinct boundary values $F^L(\zeta)$ and $F^R(\zeta)$ is said to be sectionally continuous in the plane cut along the contour. A sectionally continuous function has a jump discontinuity, $F^L(\zeta) - F^R(\zeta)$, on its boundary and we shall show in this chapter how, for particular sectionally continuous functions, such jumps can be evaluated.

We may also define functions which are sectionally continuous in the plane cut along a path. In this case some ambiguity may arise with respect to the meaning of the function values $F^L(\zeta)$ and $F^R(\zeta)$ at the end points of the path. However, this ambiguity can be resolved by postulating that the left and the right boundary values of the sectionally continuous function $F(\lambda)$ at the end points of a path are equal to each other. For example, if a is such an end point, then

$$F^L(a) = F^R(a) = F(a)$$

Hence, no distinction is made between the left and the right boundary values of a sectionally continuous function at the end point of a path.

4.3 SECTIONALLY ANALYTIC FUNCTIONS

A function $F(\lambda)$ is said to be sectionally analytic in the plane cut along the contour C if it is analytic in all finite regions of the complex plane with the exception of the contour C on which it is sectionally continuous and has the boundary values $F^L(\zeta)$ and $F^R(\zeta)$. It is important to note that a sectionally analytic function which is defined by the relations,

$$F(\lambda) = F^L(\lambda) \qquad \text{when } \lambda \text{ is a point in } L$$

$$F(\lambda) = F^R(\lambda) \qquad \text{when } \lambda \text{ is a point in } R$$

is not a complete analytic function in the sense of Section 1.6. In other words, the function $F^R(\lambda)$ is not obtained by analytic continuation of the function $F^L(\lambda)$ over the contour C or vice versa. The boundary value on the left,

$$F^L(\zeta) = \lim_{\lambda \to \zeta} F^L(\lambda)$$

when λ approaches the point ζ from inside L is, in general, not equal to the boundary value on the right,

$$F^R(\zeta) = \lim_{\lambda \to \zeta} F^R(\lambda)$$

when λ approaches the point ζ from inside R. This implies that the Riemann principle of Section 1.6 is not applicable and that in general $F^R(\lambda)$ and $F^L(\lambda)$ cannot be analytically continued over the boundary. For example, let us consider the function $f(\lambda)$ which is analytic inside the contour C and is continuous inside and on C. According to the Cauchy formulas, this implies that there exists a function $F(\lambda)$ which can be represented by the following integrals,

$$F(\lambda) = f(\lambda) \quad = \frac{1}{2\pi i}\oint_C \frac{f(\zeta)}{\zeta - \lambda}\, d\zeta \qquad \text{when } \lambda \text{ is inside } C$$

$$F(\alpha) = \frac{1}{2} f(\alpha) = \frac{1}{2\pi i}\oint_C \frac{f(\zeta)}{\zeta - \alpha}\, d\zeta \qquad \text{when } \alpha \text{ is on } C$$

$$F(\lambda) = 0 \quad = \frac{1}{2\pi i}\oint_C \frac{f(\zeta)}{\zeta - \lambda}\, d\zeta \qquad \text{when } \lambda \text{ is outside } C$$

The function $F(\lambda)$ which is represented by these integral relations is analytic inside and outside the contour C but not on the contour C. This can be seen as follows. Approaching the point α on the contour C from inside the contour, we obtain the boundary value,

$$F^L(\alpha) = \tfrac{1}{2} f(\alpha)$$

However, we find the boundary value,

$$F^R(\alpha) = 0$$

when we approach the point α from outside the contour. Consequently, the function $F(\lambda)$ is sectionally analytic in the plane cut along the contour C. Furthermore, we may conclude that this function is analytic in the whole complex plane, including the contour C, only if $F^L(\zeta) = F^R(\zeta) = 0$ on this contour. This implies that the function $f(\zeta)$ has to vanish in the whole complex plane.

We shall also consider functions which are sectionally analytic in a plane cut along a path instead of a contour. Such a function $F(\lambda)$ is analytic in all finite parts of the complex plane with the exception of a path on which it is sectionally continuous with boundary values $F^L(\zeta)$ and $F^R(\zeta)$. We require moreover that $F(\lambda)$ satisfies the order relation,

$$F(\lambda) = O[(\lambda - a)^\beta]$$

at an end point a of the path, where $\beta + 1$ is a positive quantity.

4.4 CAUCHY INTEGRAL REPRESENTATIONS OF SECTIONALLY ANALYTIC FUNCTIONS

Cauchy integral representations of sectionally analytic functions are important tools for the mathematical investigation of physical phenomena. The theory of these representations was established at the turn of the century but it has been only recently that its powers have been brought to the attention of mathematical physicists and engineers. In this section we shall discuss the properties of Cauchy representations for a limited class of density functions, and for contours and paths only. For a more detailed and rigorous treatment we refer the reader to the literature.

Let us consider the integral,

$$\frac{1}{2\pi i} \oint_C \frac{f(\zeta)}{\zeta - \lambda}\, d\zeta$$

over the closed contour C. According to Cauchy's formula, the integral above represents the function,

$$f(\lambda) = \frac{1}{2\pi i} \oint_C \frac{f(\zeta)}{\zeta - \lambda}\, d\zeta$$

for all λ inside C, provided that the function $f(\lambda)$ is analytic inside C and is continuous inside and on C. In other words, the value of $f(\lambda)$ at each point of the region enclosed by C is completely defined by the integral of $f(\zeta)/(\zeta - \lambda)$ over the contour C. Thus, the integral provides us with the means to analytically continue the function $f(\zeta)$, defined on C, to all points inside C. However, the function $f(\zeta)$ is a very special function, being the boundary value of a function $f(\lambda)$ which is analytic inside C and is continuous inside and on C. It satisfies moreover the condition,

$$\frac{1}{2\pi i}\oint_C \frac{f(\zeta)}{\zeta-\lambda}\,d\zeta = 0 \tag{4.2}$$

when λ is a point outside the contour.

Now let us consider a complex valued function $f(\zeta)$, which is defined on the contour C only, instead of the function with the special properties above. In other words, $f(\zeta)$ is a point function, which is defined on the contour C only, and is not the boundary value of a function which is analytic inside the contour. Assuming that the function $f(\zeta)$ is integrable on the contour, the contour integral,

$$\frac{1}{2\pi i}\oint_C \frac{f(\zeta)}{\zeta-\lambda}\,d\zeta$$

represents an analytic function, $F(\lambda)$ say. This function is defined and analytic for all values of λ which are not located on the contour. For, since $f(\zeta)$ is integrable on the contour, the function $F(\lambda)$ possesses a derivative with respect to λ. The analyticity of the function $F(\lambda)$ is determined by the function $1/(\zeta - \lambda)$ only. However, the condition (4.2) is in general not satisfied and the integral is not the representation of a function which is analytic inside C, continuous inside and on C, and vanishes outside the contour. It defines instead the more general function,

$$F(\lambda) = \frac{1}{2\pi i}\oint_C \frac{f(\zeta)}{\zeta-\lambda}\,d\zeta$$

which is sectionally analytic in the plane cut along the contour C. Integrals of this type are called Cauchy integrals. The function $1/(\zeta - \lambda)$ is called a Cauchy kernel and the function $f(\zeta)$ is called the density of the Cauchy integral.

The point λ can be located either inside, outside, or on the contour. In this section we shall consider only the first two possibilities and we shall postpone the discussion of the third instance, which requires the concept of a Cauchy principal value, to the next section.

The sectionally analytic function $F(\lambda)$, which is defined by the Cauchy integral above, can be decomposed into the functions $F^L(\lambda)$ and $F^R(\lambda)$ which are defined in the regions L and R by the integrals,

$$F^L(\lambda) = \frac{1}{2\pi i}\oint_C \frac{f(\zeta)}{\zeta-\lambda}\,d\zeta$$

when λ is a point in L, and

$$F^R(\lambda) = \frac{1}{2\pi i} \oint_C \frac{f(\zeta)}{\zeta - \lambda} \, d\zeta$$

when λ is a point in R. The function $F^R(\lambda)$ satisfies the order property,

$$F^R(\lambda) = O(1/\lambda)$$

when λ tends to infinity. This property is an immediate consequence of the integral representation above. Although the function $F^L(\lambda)$ is analytic inside the contour and the function $F^R(\lambda)$ is analytic outside the contour, it should be noted that the function $F^R(\lambda)$ is in general not the analytic continuation of the function $F^L(\lambda)$ into the region R. We shall show in the subsequent sections of this chapter that the boundary values of the sectionally analytic function $F(\lambda)$ suffer a jump discontinuity upon crossing the boundary. This implies, according to the principle of Riemann, that the functions $F^L(\lambda)$ and $F^R(\lambda)$ are not the analytic continuations of each other.

We shall also consider Cauchy integral representations of functions which are sectionally analytic in a plane cut along a path instead of a contour. Now the density function $f(\zeta)$ is defined and integrable on a path Γ and to reduce this situation to the one discussed above we close this path by means of another path Ω to form a contour. Subsequently, we define the extension of the function $f(\zeta)$ on this new path Ω to be identically equal to zero and we obtain in this manner the representations,

$$F^L(\lambda) = \frac{1}{2\pi i} \int_\Gamma \frac{f(\zeta)}{\zeta - \lambda} \, d\zeta$$

when λ is a point inside the region L, and

$$F^R(\lambda) = \frac{1}{2\pi i} \int_\Gamma \frac{f(\zeta)}{\zeta - \lambda} \, d\zeta$$

when λ is a point inside the region R.

4.5 THE PRINCIPAL VALUE OF A CAUCHY INTEGRAL

If the point $\lambda = \alpha$ is located on the path Γ, the Cauchy integral,

$$\frac{1}{2\pi i} \int_\Gamma \frac{f(\zeta)}{\zeta - \alpha} \, d\zeta$$

does not exist as an ordinary Cauchy integral but must be defined as a Cauchy principal value integral. In this section we shall be concerned with Cauchy integrals which are defined in the sense of a principal value integral and we shall show that such a definition is possible, provided that the function $f(\zeta)$ satisfies a Hölder condition at the point α.

Let α be a point located on the simple arc AB of the path Γ shown in Figure IV-3. We draw a circle with radius ρ and center at the point α and we

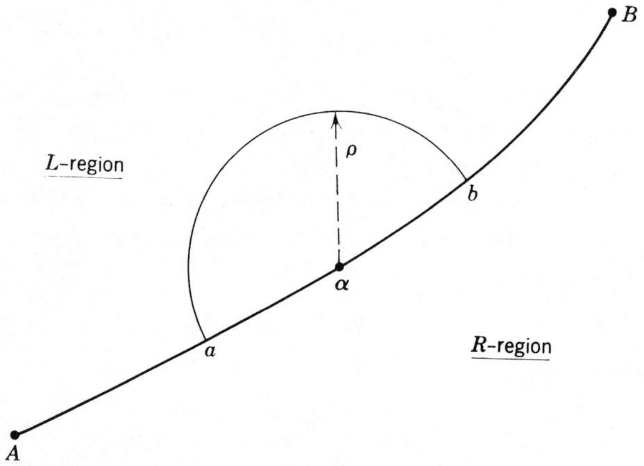

Figure IV-3

assume that this circle intersects the path AB in the points a and b such that

$$a = \alpha + \rho \exp(i\theta_a) \qquad \text{and} \qquad b = \alpha + \rho \exp(i\theta_b)$$

The angles θ_a and θ_b are measured from the line which is tangent to the curve at the point α.

The principal value of the Cauchy integral at the point $\lambda = \alpha$ on the path AB is defined as the limit,

$$\frac{1}{2\pi i}\int_{AB} \frac{f(\zeta)}{\zeta - \alpha}\, d\zeta = \lim_{\rho \to 0} \frac{1}{2\pi i}\int_{AB-ab} \frac{f(\zeta)}{\zeta - \alpha}\, d\zeta$$

This limit, and thus the Cauchy principal value, exists if $f(\zeta)$ is Hölder continuous at the point $\zeta = \alpha$. For we may write

$$\lim_{\rho \to 0}\int_{AB-ab} \frac{f(\zeta)}{\zeta - \alpha}\, d\zeta = \lim_{\rho \to 0} \frac{1}{2\pi i}\int_{AB-ab} \frac{f(\zeta) - f(\alpha)}{\zeta - \alpha}\, d\zeta + \lim_{\rho \to 0} \frac{f(\alpha)}{2\pi i}\int_{AB-ab} \frac{d\zeta}{\zeta - \alpha}$$

Furthermore, since $f(\zeta)$ satisfies a Hölder condition at the point $\zeta = \alpha$, there exists a positive constant β, smaller than or equal to one, such that

$$\frac{f(\zeta) - f(\alpha)}{\zeta - \alpha} = O[(\zeta - \alpha)^{\beta - 1}]$$

when ζ tends to α. This implies that the first integral above exists as an ordinary Riemann integral. The second integral takes the form,

$$\lim_{\rho\to 0}\frac{f(\alpha)}{2\pi i}\int_{AB-ab}\frac{d\zeta}{\zeta-\alpha}=\lim_{\rho\to 0}\frac{f(\alpha)}{2\pi i}\left(\int_A^a\frac{d\zeta}{\zeta-\alpha}+\int_b^B\frac{d\zeta}{\zeta-\alpha}\right)$$

$$=\lim_{\rho\to 0}\frac{f(\alpha)}{2\pi i}\{[\log(\zeta-\alpha)]_A^a+[\log(\zeta-\alpha)]_b^B\}$$

The multivalued function $\log(\zeta-\alpha)$, which has a branch point at the point $\zeta=\alpha$, can be made definite by choosing the branch such that $\log(\zeta-\alpha)$ changes continuously from $\log(a-\alpha)$ to $\log(b-\alpha)$ when ζ traverses the semicircle which is located wholly in the region L to the left of the contour. This can be accomplished by a branch cut along the path ab. We find, in that case,

$$\lim_{\rho\to 0}\frac{f(\alpha)}{2\pi i}\int_{AB-ab}\frac{d\zeta}{\zeta-\alpha}=\frac{f(\alpha)}{2\pi i}\left(\log\frac{B-\alpha}{A-\alpha}+\lim_{\rho\to 0}\log\frac{a-\alpha}{b-\alpha}\right)$$

$$=\frac{f(\alpha)}{2\pi i}\left[\lim_{\rho\to 0}i(\theta_a-\theta_b)+\log\frac{B-\alpha}{A-\alpha}\right]$$

In the limit as ρ tends to zero, the phase angle θ_a approaches the value π and the angle θ_b tends to zero. The net result is that

$$\lim_{\rho\to 0}\frac{f(\alpha)}{2\pi i}\int_{AB-ab}\frac{d\zeta}{\zeta-\alpha}=\frac{f(\alpha)}{2\pi i}\left(\pi i+\log\frac{B-\alpha}{A-\alpha}\right)$$

In view of the results above, we obtain by substitution

$$\frac{1}{2\pi i}\int_{AB}\frac{f(\zeta)}{\zeta-\alpha}\,d\zeta=\frac{1}{2\pi i}\int_{AB}\frac{f(\zeta)-f(\alpha)}{\zeta-\alpha}\,d\zeta+\frac{f(\alpha)}{2\pi i}\log\frac{B-\alpha}{A-\alpha}+\frac{1}{2}f(\alpha)$$

This formula can be simplified considerably when the path AB is a contour C. In that case, the point A coincides with the point B and we find

$$\frac{1}{2\pi i}\oint_C\frac{f(\zeta)}{\zeta-\alpha}\,d\zeta=\frac{1}{2\pi i}\oint_C\frac{f(\zeta)-f(\alpha)}{\zeta-\alpha}\,d\zeta+\frac{1}{2}f(\alpha)$$

In some applications of Cauchy integrals to problems in mathematical physics it is important to know the behavior of the function,

$$F(\lambda)=\frac{1}{2\pi i}\int_\Gamma\frac{f(\zeta)}{\zeta-\lambda}\,d\zeta$$

when λ approaches an end point A or B of the path Γ. At the end point A of the path Γ the integral may also be written

$$F(\lambda) = \frac{1}{2\pi i}\int_\Gamma \frac{f(\zeta) - f(A)}{\zeta - \lambda}\, d\zeta + \frac{f(A)}{2\pi i}\int_\Gamma \frac{d\zeta}{\zeta - \lambda}$$

$$= \frac{1}{2\pi i}\int_\Gamma \frac{f(\zeta) - f(A)}{\zeta - \lambda}\, d\zeta + \frac{f(A)}{2\pi i}\log\frac{B - \lambda}{A - \lambda}$$

Assuming that $f(\zeta)$ is Hölder continuous on the path Γ, the first integral stays well defined when the point λ tends to the end point A of Γ. Consequently, the function $F(\lambda)$ can be brought into the form,

$$F(\lambda) = F_A(\lambda) - \frac{f(A)}{2\pi i}\log(A - \lambda)$$

where we have introduced the quantity,

$$F_A(\lambda) = \frac{f(A)}{2\pi i}\log(B - \lambda) + \frac{1}{2\pi i}\int_\Gamma \frac{f(\zeta) - f(A)}{\zeta - \lambda}\, d\zeta$$

This implies that the function $F(\lambda)$ has a logarithmic singularity at the end point A.

In a similar manner we may show that the behavior of $F(\lambda)$ near the end point B is given by

$$F(\lambda) = F_B(\lambda) + \frac{f(B)}{2\pi i}\log(B - \lambda)$$

where

$$F_B(\lambda) = -\frac{f(B)}{2\pi i}\log(A - \lambda) + \frac{1}{2\pi i}\int_\Gamma \frac{f(\zeta) - f(B)}{\zeta - \lambda}\, d\zeta$$

4.6 THE FORMULAS OF PLEMELJ

From the point of view of the application of function-theoretic techniques to the solution of the boundary value problems of mathematical physics and engineering, great interest lies in the boundary values $F^L(\zeta)$ and $F^R(\zeta)$ of a sectionally analytic function $F(\lambda)$, which can be represented by a Cauchy integral,

$$F(\lambda) = \frac{1}{2\pi i}\int_C \frac{f(\zeta)}{\zeta - \lambda}\, d\zeta \qquad (4.3)$$

where C denotes a given path or contour. The boundary values of such a sectionally analytic function can be evaluated by means of the Plemelj formulas which are the topic of discussion of this section.

We shall first consider the case in which the function $F(\lambda)$ is sectionally analytic in the plane cut along a contour and can be represented by a Cauchy integral (4.3) where the density function $f(\zeta)$ is Hölder continuous on the contour. Formally, we may write

$$F(\lambda) = \frac{1}{2\pi i} \oint_C \frac{f(\zeta) - f(\lambda)}{\zeta - \lambda}\, d\zeta + \frac{f(\lambda)}{2\pi i} \oint_C \frac{d\zeta}{\zeta - \lambda}$$

where, according to Cauchy's formula, the second term on the right contributes a value $f(\lambda)$ when λ is a point inside the contour and vanishes when λ is a point outside the contour. Consequently,

$$F^L(\lambda) = \frac{1}{2\pi i} \oint_C \frac{f(\zeta) - f(\lambda)}{\zeta - \lambda}\, d\zeta + f(\lambda)$$

when λ is a point inside the contour, and

$$F^R(\lambda) = \frac{1}{2\pi i} \oint_C \frac{f(\zeta) - f(\lambda)}{\zeta - \lambda}\, d\zeta$$

when λ is a point outside the contour. Hence, assuming that α denotes a point on the contour, we obtain the relation,

$$F^L(\alpha) = \lim_{\lambda \to \alpha} F^L(\lambda) = \frac{1}{2\pi i} \oint_C \frac{f(\zeta) - f(\alpha)}{\zeta - \alpha}\, d\zeta + f(\alpha)$$

when λ approaches the point α from inside the contour, and

$$F^R(\alpha) = \lim_{\lambda \to \alpha} F^R(\lambda) = \frac{1}{2\pi i} \oint_C \frac{f(\zeta) - f(\alpha)}{\zeta - \alpha}\, d\zeta$$

when λ approaches the point α from outside the contour.

The existence of the integrals as either proper or improper Riemann integrals is assured by the assumption that $f(\zeta)$ is Hölder continuous on the contour. Writing the formulas in a more symmetric form, we find

$$F^L(\alpha) = \frac{1}{2} f(\alpha) + \frac{1}{2\pi i} \oint_C \frac{f(\zeta)}{\zeta - \alpha}\, d\zeta \tag{4.4}$$

and

$$F^R(\alpha) = -\frac{1}{2} f(\alpha) + \frac{1}{2\pi i} \oint_C \frac{f(\zeta)}{\zeta - \alpha}\, d\zeta \tag{4.5}$$

These formulas enable us to evaluate the boundary values of the sectionally analytic function $F(\lambda)$ defined above.

Subtracting and adding the equations (4.4) and (4.5), we may infer that the left and right boundary values of a sectionally analytic function,

$$F(\lambda) = \frac{1}{2\pi i} \oint_C \frac{f(\zeta)}{\zeta - \lambda}\, d\zeta \tag{4.3}$$

are related to each other by the formulas,

$$F^L(\alpha) - F^R(\alpha) = f(\alpha)$$

and

$$F^L(\alpha) + F^R(\alpha) = \frac{1}{\pi i} \oint_C \frac{f(\zeta)}{\zeta - \alpha}\, d\zeta$$

These formulas are known as the formulas of Plemelj.

We shall now present a less formal derivation of these formulas and, at the same time, obtain some conditions which are sufficient for their existence.

Let us consider the Cauchy integral (4.3), where $f(\zeta)$ is a continuous function on the boundary C, shown in Figure IV-4. Let α be a point on the contour

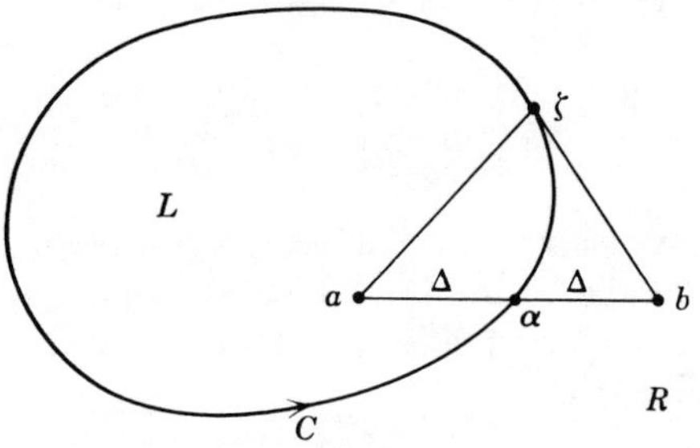

Figure IV-4

and let a in L and b in R be two points on a line through α which is not tangent to C. The points a and b are at equal distances Δ from α measured on the line through α. This implies that

$$\Delta = |a - \alpha| = |b - \alpha|$$

To be definite let $a = \alpha - \Delta$ and $b = \alpha + \Delta$. The function $F^L(\lambda)$ at the point $\lambda = a$ takes the form,

$$F^L(a) = F^L(\alpha - \Delta) = \frac{1}{2\pi i} \oint_C \frac{f(\zeta)\, d\zeta}{(\zeta - \alpha) + \Delta} = \frac{1}{2\pi i} \oint_C \frac{f(\zeta) - f(\alpha)}{(\zeta - \alpha) + \Delta}\, d\zeta + f(\alpha)$$

Similarly, at the point $\lambda = b$ we may write

$$F^L(b) = F^R(\alpha + \Delta) = \frac{1}{2\pi i} \oint_C \frac{f(\zeta)\, d\zeta}{(\zeta - \alpha) - \Delta} = \frac{1}{2\pi i} \oint_C \frac{f(\zeta) - f(\alpha)}{(\zeta - \alpha) - \Delta}\, d\zeta$$

Subtracting the second equation from the first, we obtain

$$F^L(\alpha) - F^R(\alpha) = \lim_{\Delta \to 0} [F^L(\alpha - \Delta) - F^R(\alpha + \Delta)]$$

$$= f(\alpha) - \lim_{\Delta \to 0} \frac{\Delta}{\pi i} \oint_C \frac{f(\zeta) - f(\alpha)}{(\zeta - \alpha)^2 - \Delta^2} \, d\zeta$$

Since $f(\zeta)$ is continuous at $\zeta = \alpha$, the integral expression is uniformly continuous with respect to Δ and vanishes in the limit as Δ tends to zero.

We obtain therefore the first formula of Plemelj,

$$F^L(\alpha) - F^R(\alpha) = f(\alpha).$$

It is interesting to note that in the derivation above it was sufficient to impose the condition that the density function $f(\zeta)$ be continuous. This implies that the first formula of Plemelj exists even for densities which satisfy the condition of continuity instead of the stronger condition of Hölder continuity.

To obtain the second formula of Plemelj, let us write

$$F^L(\alpha) + F^R(\alpha) = \lim_{\Delta \to 0} [F^L(\alpha - \Delta) + F^R(\alpha + \Delta)]$$

$$= \lim_{\Delta \to 0} \frac{1}{\pi i} \oint_C \frac{(\zeta - \alpha) f(\zeta)}{(\zeta - \alpha)^2 - \Delta^2} \, d\zeta = \frac{1}{\pi i} \oint_C \frac{f(\zeta)}{\zeta - \alpha} \, d\zeta$$

In Section 4.5 we have shown that the last integral exists as a principal value integral, provided that the function $f(\zeta)$ is Hölder continuous on the boundary. Hence, assuming that $f(\zeta)$ is Hölder continuous on the contour C, we obtain the second formula of Plemelj,

$$F^L(\alpha) + F^R(\alpha) = \frac{1}{\pi i} \oint_C \frac{f(\zeta)}{\zeta - \alpha} \, d\zeta$$

The formulas of Plemelj have been derived so far only for functions which are sectionally analytic in a plane cut along a contour. These formulas remain true, however, for functions which are sectionally analytic in a plane cut along a path Γ instead of a contour. This we can verify by closing the path Γ by another path Ω to form a closed contour C and subsequently postulating that the density function $f(\zeta)$ vanishes on the path Ω.

The Plemelj formulas can be used to verify the following statements. If a density function $f(\zeta)$ is Hölder continuous with exponent $\beta < 1$ on the boundary of the sectionally analytic function $F(\lambda)$, then the boundary values $F^L(\zeta)$ and $F^R(\zeta)$ are also Hölder continuous with exponent $\beta < 1$ on this boundary. However, if the density function is Hölder continuous with exponent $\beta = 1$, then the boundary values are Hölder continuous with exponent $\beta = 1 - \varepsilon$ where ε is an arbitrarily small positive constant.

4.7 BOUNDARY VALUE PROBLEMS OF PLEMELJ

In the preceding section we found that the boundary values $F^L(\zeta)$ and $F^R(\zeta)$ of a function $F(\lambda)$, which is sectionally analytic in the plane cut along a path or contour Γ and can be represented by a Cauchy integral,

$$F(\lambda) = \frac{1}{2\pi i} \int_{\Gamma} \frac{f(\zeta)}{\zeta - \lambda} \, d\zeta$$

satisfy the following boundary value or jump condition,

$$F^L(\zeta) - F^R(\zeta) = f(\zeta) \tag{4.6}$$

on the path or contour Γ. For this first Plemelj formula to be valid it is sufficient for the density function $f(\zeta)$ to be continuous on the boundary.

Now let us consider the following boundary value problem of Plemelj: Construct a function $F(\lambda)$ which is sectionally analytic in the plane cut along the path or contour Γ, vanishes at infinity, and has boundary values $F^L(\zeta)$ and $F^R(\zeta)$ that satisfy the condition,

$$F^L(\zeta) - F^R(\zeta) = f(\zeta) \tag{4.7}$$

on the boundary Γ. In addition we shall assume that the function $f(\zeta)$ is continuous on the boundary.

Interpreting the boundary value condition (4.7) in terms of the first Plemelj formula (4.6), we can immediately draw the conclusion that the solution of our boundary value problem can be represented by the Cauchy integral,

$$F(\lambda) = \frac{1}{2\pi i} \int_{\Gamma} \frac{f(\zeta)}{\zeta - \lambda} \, d\zeta$$

where the path Γ denotes the boundary of the sectionally analytic function $F(\lambda)$.

It can easily be shown that this solution is unique. For let $F(\lambda)$ and $G(\lambda)$ denote two distinct solutions of the boundary value problem of Plemelj. Defining the function,

$$H^L(\lambda) = F^L(\lambda) - G^L(\lambda)$$

when λ is a point in the region L, and

$$H^R(\lambda) = F^R(\lambda) - G^R(\lambda)$$

when λ is a point in the region R, we note that $H^L(\lambda)$ and $H^R(\lambda)$ are the analytic representations of a function $H(\lambda)$ which vanishes at infinity. Furthermore,

$$H^L(\zeta) - H^R(\zeta) = [F^L(\zeta) - G^L(\zeta)] - [F^R(\zeta) - G^R(\zeta)] = f(\zeta) - f(\zeta) = 0$$

and, consequently, $H^L(\zeta) = H^R(\zeta)$ when ζ is a point on the boundary. Hence, the function $H(\lambda)$ is analytic in the plane cut along the boundary and is continuous on the boundary. This implies, according to the principle of Riemann of Section 1.6, that the function $H(\lambda)$ is analytic in the whole complex plane. In other words, $H(\lambda)$ is an entire function. Furthermore, since $H(\lambda)$ vanishes at infinity, we may conclude by Liouville's theorem that it vanishes in the whole complex plane. This means that the functions $F(\lambda)$ and $G(\lambda)$ are identically equal and that the solution of the boundary value problem of Plemelj is unique.

A slightly different version of this boundary value problem may be stated as follows: Construct a function $F(\lambda)$ which is sectionally analytic in the plane cut along the path or contour Γ, is of algebraic growth at infinity, and has boundary values $F^L(\zeta)$ and $F^R(\zeta)$ which satisfy the condition,

$$F^L(\zeta) - F^R(\zeta) = f(\zeta)$$

on the boundary Γ.

Assuming that the function $f(\zeta)$ is continuous on the boundary and that $F(\lambda) = 0(\lambda^m)$ when λ tends to infinity, the solution $F(\lambda)$ of this boundary value problem has the integral representation,

$$F(\lambda) = \frac{1}{2\pi i} \int_\Gamma \frac{f(\zeta)}{\zeta - \lambda} d\zeta + P_m(\lambda)$$

where Γ denotes the boundary of $F(\lambda)$ and $P_m(\lambda)$ is an arbitrary polynomial of degree m. The real or complex coefficients of this polynomial can be determined from other conditions imposed on the function $F(\lambda)$.

4.8 REPRESENTATION OF SECTIONALLY ANALYTIC FUNCTIONS BY CAUCHY INTEGRALS OVER AN INFINITE LINE

In the preceding sections of this chapter we have been concerned with the representation of sectionally analytic functions by Cauchy integrals over a finite path or contour. In this section we shall consider the representation of such functions by so-called infinite Cauchy integrals, more specifically, representations of the form,

$$F(\lambda) = \frac{1}{2\pi i} \int_{-\infty + ib}^{\infty + ib} \frac{f(\zeta)}{\zeta - \lambda} d\zeta$$

where we have assumed, to be definite, that the integration path is a line parallel to the real axis.

Let us assume that the function $f(\zeta)$ is integrable and finite on any finite part of the path $(-\infty + ib, \infty + ib)$. Let it furthermore be assumed that

$f(\zeta)$ satisfies a Hölder condition at infinity,

$$f(\zeta) = f(\infty) + O(\zeta^{\beta})$$

where β is a negative constant and $f(\infty)$ denotes the value of $f(\zeta)$ when ζ tends to plus or minus infinity on the path $(-\infty + ib, \infty + ib)$. For any finite value of a the integral,

$$F(a, \lambda) = \frac{1}{2\pi i} \int_{-a+ib}^{a+ib} \frac{f(\zeta)}{\zeta - \lambda}\, d\zeta \tag{4.8}$$

exists in the sense of a finite Cauchy integral and, provided that certain regularity conditions are satisfied, this integral defines a function which is sectionally analytic in the plane cut along the path $(-\infty + ib, \infty + ib)$. For let us consider the limit,

$$\lim_{a\to\infty} F(a, \lambda) = \lim_{a\to\infty} \frac{1}{2\pi i} \int_{-a+ib}^{a+ib} \frac{f(\zeta)}{\zeta - \lambda}\, d\zeta$$

Introducing the value $f(\infty)$, the integral on the right hand side may be written as the sum of an integral which is defined as an infinite Riemann integral and an integral which can be defined as a Cauchy principal value at infinity,

$$\lim_{a\to\infty} \frac{1}{2\pi i} \int_{-a+ib}^{a+ib} \frac{f(\zeta)}{\zeta - \lambda}\, d\zeta$$

$$= \lim_{a\to\infty} \frac{1}{2\pi i} \int_{-a+ib}^{a+ib} \frac{f(\zeta) - f(\infty)}{\zeta - \lambda}\, d\zeta + \lim_{a\to\infty} \frac{f(\infty)}{2\pi i} \int_{-a+ib}^{a+ib} \frac{d\zeta}{\zeta - \lambda}$$

Since $f(\zeta)$ satisfies a Hölder condition at infinity, the first limit on the right hand side defines the infinite Riemann integral,

$$\lim_{a\to\infty} \int_{-a+ib}^{a+ib} \frac{f(\zeta) - f(\infty)}{\zeta - \lambda}\, d\zeta = \frac{1}{2\pi i} \int_{-\infty+ib}^{\infty+ib} \frac{f(\zeta) - f(\infty)}{\zeta - \lambda}\, d\zeta$$

The second integral on the right hand side of the penultimate equation can be evaluated as a Cauchy principal value. We assume that the point λ is located in the upper half plane $I(\lambda) > b$. Then, as can easily be seen from Figure IV-5,

$$\lim_{a\to\infty} \int_{-a+ib}^{a+ib} \frac{d\zeta}{\zeta - \lambda} = \lim_{a\to\infty} \log\left(\frac{\lambda - a - ib}{\lambda + a - ib}\right)$$

$$= \lim_{a\to\infty} \left[\log\left|\frac{\lambda - a - ib}{\lambda + a - ib}\right| + i \arg(\lambda - a - ib) - i \arg(\lambda + a - ib) \right] = i\pi$$

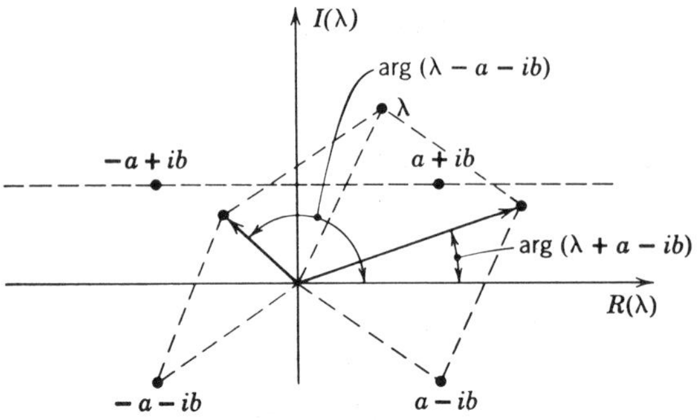

Figure IV-5

These relations imply that we may write

$$F^L(\lambda) = \frac{1}{2\pi i}\int_{-\infty+ib}^{\infty+ib} \frac{f(\zeta)}{\zeta-\lambda}\,d\zeta = \frac{1}{2}f(\infty) + \frac{1}{2\pi i}\int_{-\infty+ib}^{\infty+ib} \frac{f(\zeta)-f(\infty)}{\zeta-\lambda}\,d\zeta$$

when λ is a point in the upper half plane, $I(\lambda) > b$. The integral on the left hand side of this equation is defined as a Cauchy principal value integral at the point at infinity. The integral on the right hand side of the equation is defined as an infinite Riemann integral.

In a similar manner we obtain the expression,

$$F^R(\lambda) = \frac{1}{2\pi i}\int_{-\infty+ib}^{\infty+ib} \frac{f(\zeta)}{\zeta-\lambda}\,d\zeta = -\frac{1}{2}f(\infty) + \frac{1}{2\pi i}\int_{-\infty+ib}^{\infty+ib} \frac{f(\zeta)-f(\infty)}{\zeta-\lambda}\,d\zeta$$

where λ is a point in the lower half plane, $I(\lambda) < b$. The integral on the left hand side is again a Cauchy principal value integral and the integral on the right hand side is an infinite Riemann integral.

Now let us return to the integral,

$$F(a, \lambda) = \frac{1}{2\pi i}\int_{-a+ib}^{a+ib} \frac{f(\zeta)}{\zeta-\lambda}\,d\zeta \tag{4.8}$$

In Section 4.5 we found that this integral can be defined in the sense of a Cauchy principal value integral whenever the point $\lambda = \alpha$ is located on the path $(-a + ib, a + ib)$ and the function $f(\zeta)$ satisfies a Hölder condition at the point α. In our particular case this integral can be defined as a Cauchy principal value by the limit process,

$$F(a, \alpha) = \frac{1}{2\pi i}\int_{-a+ib}^{a+ib} \frac{f(\zeta)}{\zeta-\alpha}\,d\zeta = \lim_{\rho\to 0}\frac{1}{2\pi i}\left[\int_{-a+ib}^{\alpha-\rho} \frac{f(\zeta)}{\zeta-\alpha}\,d\zeta + \int_{\alpha+\rho}^{a+ib} \frac{f(\zeta)}{\zeta-\alpha}\,d\zeta\right]$$

This implies that to define the infinite Cauchy integral,

$$F(\alpha) = \frac{1}{2\pi i} \int_{-\infty+ib}^{\infty+ib} \frac{f(\zeta)}{\zeta - \alpha} \, d\zeta$$

as a Cauchy principal value at the point α and at the point at infinity, a double limit process is necessary,

$$F(\alpha) = \frac{1}{2\pi i} \int_{-\infty+ib}^{\infty+ib} \frac{f(\zeta)}{\zeta - \alpha} \, d\zeta$$

$$= \lim_{a\to\infty} \lim_{\rho\to 0} \frac{1}{2\pi i} \left[\int_{-a+ib}^{\alpha-\rho} \frac{f(\zeta)}{\zeta - \alpha} \, d\zeta + \int_{\alpha+\rho}^{a+ib} \frac{f(\zeta)}{\zeta - \alpha} \, d\zeta \right]$$

A sufficient condition for the existence of these limits is that $f(\zeta)$ is Hölder continuous at the point α and satisfies a Hölder condition at infinity.

Again returning to the integral (4.8) we can obtain, by the methods of Section 1.1, an expression for the left boundary value of $F(\lambda)$. Let us consider the limit,

$$F^L(a, \alpha) = \lim_{\varepsilon\to 0} \frac{1}{2\pi i} \int_{-a+ib}^{a+ib} \frac{f(\zeta)}{\zeta - \alpha - i\varepsilon} \, d\zeta$$

Deforming the path $(-a + ib, a + ib)$ by a semicircle about the point α, in the lower half plane as shown in Figure IV-6, we find

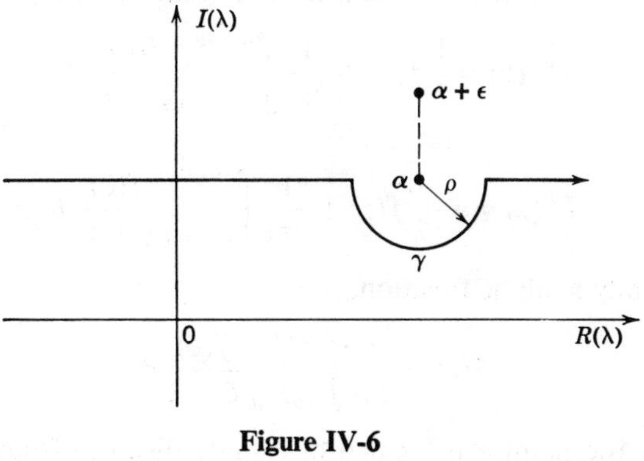

Figure IV-6

$F^L(a, \alpha) =$

$$\lim_{\varepsilon\to 0} \lim_{\rho\to 0} \frac{1}{2\pi i} \left[\int_{-a+ib}^{\alpha-\rho} \frac{f(\zeta)}{\zeta - \alpha - i\varepsilon} \, d\zeta + \int_{\alpha+\rho}^{a+ib} \frac{f(\zeta)}{\zeta - \alpha - i\varepsilon} \, d\zeta + \int_{\gamma} \frac{f(\zeta)}{\zeta - \alpha - i\varepsilon} \, d\zeta \right]$$

In the double limit as first ε and then ρ tends to zero, we find

$$\lim_{\rho\to 0} \lim_{\varepsilon\to 0} \frac{1}{2\pi i} \int_{\gamma} \frac{f(\zeta)}{\zeta - \alpha - i\varepsilon} \, d\zeta = \lim_{\rho\to 0} \frac{1}{2\pi} \int_{-\pi}^{0} f(\alpha + \rho e^{i\theta}) \, d\theta = \frac{1}{2} f(\alpha)$$

Substituting into the equation for $F^L(a, \alpha)$, we obtain the following expression for the left boundary value of $F(a, \lambda)$,

$$F^L(a, \alpha) = \frac{1}{2} f(\alpha) + \frac{1}{2\pi i} \int_{-a+ib}^{a+ib} \frac{f(\zeta)}{\zeta - \alpha} d\zeta$$

In a similar manner, by deforming the path $(-a + ib, a + ib)$ by a semicircle in the upper half plane, it can be shown that the right boundary value of $F(a, \lambda)$ takes the form,

$$F^R(a, \alpha) = -\frac{1}{2} f(\alpha) + \frac{1}{2\pi i} \int_{-a+ib}^{a+ib} \frac{f(\zeta)}{\zeta - \alpha} d\zeta$$

The Plemelj relations between the left and right boundary values of the sectionally analytic function $F(a, \lambda)$,

$$F^L(a, \alpha) - F^R(a, \alpha) = f(\alpha)$$

and

$$F^L(a, \alpha) + F^R(a, \alpha) = \frac{1}{\pi i} \int_{-a+ib}^{a+ib} \frac{f(\zeta)}{\zeta - \alpha} d\zeta$$

are immediate consequences of the expressions for the boundary values derived above.

With the assistance of the results obtained for the finite integral $F(a, \lambda)$ we immediately obtain, in the limit as a tends to infinity, the boundary values,

$$F^L(\alpha) = \frac{1}{2} f(\alpha) + \frac{1}{2\pi i} \int_{-\infty+ib}^{\infty+ib} \frac{f(\zeta)}{\zeta - \alpha} d\zeta$$

and

$$F^R(\alpha) = -\frac{1}{2} f(\alpha) + \frac{1}{2\pi i} \int_{-\infty+ib}^{\infty+ib} \frac{f(\zeta)}{\zeta - \alpha} d\zeta$$

of the sectionally analytic function,

$$F(\lambda) = \frac{1}{2\pi i} \int_{-\infty+ib}^{\infty+ib} \frac{f(\zeta)}{\zeta - \lambda} d\zeta \tag{4.9}$$

provided that the point α is located at a finite distance from the imaginary axis. We also obtain, in the limit as a tends to infinity, the Plemelj relations,

$$F^L(\alpha) - F^R(\alpha) = f(\alpha)$$

and

$$F^L(\alpha) + F^R(\alpha) = \frac{1}{\pi i} \int_{-\infty+ib}^{\infty+ib} \frac{f(\zeta)}{\zeta - \alpha} d\zeta$$

between the left and right boundary values of $F(\lambda)$.

Now let us consider the case in which α tends to infinity on the path $(-\infty + ib, \infty + ib)$. The transformation $\lambda - ib = -1/w$ maps the function $f(\zeta)$, which is assumed to be Hölder continuous on any finite part of the path $(-\infty + ib, \infty + ib)$, into the function $g(u)$ which is Hölder continuous on any finite part of the real axis in the w-plane. Furthermore, the integral (4.9) is transformed into the integral,

$$G(w) = F(ib - 1/w) = \frac{w}{2\pi i}\int_{-\infty}^{\infty} \frac{g(u)}{u(u-w)}\,du$$

This integral may also be written

$$G(w) = \frac{1}{2\pi i}\int_{-\infty}^{\infty} \frac{g(u)}{u-w}\,du - \frac{1}{2\pi i}\int_{-\infty}^{\infty} \frac{g(u)}{u}\,du$$

Let us assume that w is located in the upper half plane. According to the Plemelj formulas for the infinite Cauchy integral, we may write

$$\lim_{\varepsilon\to 0} \frac{1}{2\pi i}\int_{-\infty}^{\infty} \frac{g(u)}{u-i\varepsilon}\,du = \frac{1}{2}\,g(0) + \frac{1}{2\pi i}\int_{-\infty}^{\infty} \frac{g(u)}{u}\,du$$

This implies, as can be verified by substitution, that $G^L(0) = \frac{1}{2}g(0)$ is the left boundary value of the function $G(w)$ at the origin. Similarly we find the value $G^R(0) = -\frac{1}{2}g(0)$ for the right boundary value of $G(w)$ at the origin. In terms of the variable λ these results take the form,

$$F^L(\infty) = G^L(0) = \tfrac{1}{2}g(0) = \tfrac{1}{2}f(\infty)$$

and

$$F^R(\infty) = G^R(0) = -\tfrac{1}{2}g(0) = -\tfrac{1}{2}f(\infty)$$

Consequently, since

$$F^L(\lambda) = \frac{1}{2}\,f(\infty) + \frac{1}{2\pi i}\int_{-\infty+ib}^{\infty+ib} \frac{f(\zeta) - f(\infty)}{\zeta - \lambda}\,d\zeta$$

and

$$F^R(\lambda) = -\frac{1}{2}\,f(\infty) + \frac{1}{2\pi i}\int_{-\infty+ib}^{\infty+ib} \frac{f(\zeta) - f(\infty)}{\zeta - \lambda}\,d\zeta$$

we obtain the result,

$$\lim_{\lambda\to\infty} \frac{1}{2\pi i}\int_{-\infty}^{\infty} \frac{f(\zeta) - f(\infty)}{\zeta - \lambda}\,d\zeta = 0$$

Thus, assuming that α is a point on the line $(-\infty + ib, \infty + ib)$, we find

$$\frac{1}{2\pi i}\int_{-\infty}^{\infty} \frac{f(\zeta)}{\zeta - \alpha}\, d\zeta = 0$$

when α tends to infinity.

4.9 THE POINCARÉ-BERTRAND TRANSFORMATION FORMULA

In some applications the need arises to interchange the order of integration of two Cauchy integrals. The Poincaré-Bertrand transformation formula, which regulates such an interchange, may be written as follows,

$$\frac{1}{2\pi i}\oint_C \frac{d\zeta}{\zeta - \alpha}\left(\frac{1}{2\pi i}\oint_C \frac{f(\zeta, \beta)}{\beta - \zeta}\, d\beta\right)$$
$$= \frac{1}{4} f(\alpha, \alpha) + \frac{1}{2\pi i}\oint_C d\beta\left(\frac{1}{2\pi i}\oint_C \frac{f(\zeta, \beta)\, d\zeta}{(\zeta - \alpha)(\beta - \zeta)}\right)$$

We refer the reader to the literature for the somewhat lengthy proof of this formula. However, in order to gain some insight into the operations involved, we shall attempt to make the formula plausible. Introducing the function,

$$g(\beta, \lambda) = \frac{\beta - \lambda}{2\pi i}\oint_C \frac{f(\zeta, \beta)}{(\zeta - \lambda)(\beta - \zeta)}\, d\zeta$$

and integrating the function $g(\beta, \lambda)$ over the contour C, we obtain the function,

$$G(\lambda) = \frac{1}{2\pi i}\oint_C \frac{g(\beta, \lambda)}{\beta - \lambda}\, d\beta = \frac{1}{2\pi i}\oint_C d\beta\left(\frac{1}{2\pi i}\oint_C \frac{f(\zeta, \beta)}{(\zeta - \lambda)(\beta - \zeta)}\, d\zeta\right) \tag{4.10}$$

Assuming that we may interchange the order of integration of the ordinary integral and the Cauchy integral, we may write

$$G(\lambda) = \frac{1}{2\pi i}\oint_C \frac{d\zeta}{\zeta - \lambda}\left(\frac{1}{2\pi i}\oint_C \frac{f(\zeta,\beta)}{\beta - \zeta}\, d\beta\right) \tag{4.11}$$

We now make use of the Plemelj formulas and find

$$G^L(\alpha) = \frac{1}{4\pi i}\oint_C \frac{f(\alpha, \beta)}{\beta - \alpha}\, d\beta + \frac{1}{2\pi i}\oint_C \frac{d\zeta}{\zeta - \alpha}\left(\frac{1}{2\pi i}\oint_C \frac{f(\zeta, \beta)}{\beta - \zeta}\, d\beta\right) \tag{4.12}$$

Similarly, writing the Plemelj formulas for the function $G(\lambda)$ defined by the equation,

$$G(\lambda) = \frac{1}{2\pi i}\oint_C \frac{g(\beta, \lambda)}{\beta - \lambda}\, d\beta$$

we obtain

$$G^L(\alpha) = \frac{1}{2}\, g^L(\alpha, \alpha) + \frac{1}{2\pi i} \oint_C \frac{g^L(\beta, \alpha)}{\beta - \alpha}\, d\beta \tag{4.13}$$

Furthermore, since

$$g(\beta, \lambda) = \frac{\beta - \lambda}{2\pi i} \oint_C \frac{f(\zeta, \beta)}{(\zeta - \lambda)(\beta - \zeta)}\, d\zeta$$

the Plemelj formulas allow us to write

$$g^L(\beta, \alpha) = \frac{1}{2}\, f(\alpha, \beta) + \frac{\beta - \alpha}{2\pi i} \oint_C \frac{f(\zeta, \beta)}{(\zeta - \alpha)(\beta - \zeta)}\, d\zeta$$

This implies that

$$g^L(\alpha, \alpha) = \tfrac{1}{2} f(\alpha, \alpha)$$

Substitution of these expressions for $g^L(\beta, \alpha)$ and $g^L(\alpha, \alpha)$ into equation (4.13) yields

$$\begin{aligned} G^L(\alpha) &= \frac{1}{4}\, f(\alpha, \alpha) + \frac{1}{2\pi i} \oint_C \frac{d\beta}{\beta - \alpha} \left[\frac{1}{2}\, f(\alpha, \beta) + \frac{\beta - \alpha}{2\pi i} \oint_C \frac{f(\zeta, \beta)}{(\zeta - \alpha)(\beta - \zeta)}\, d\zeta \right] \\ &= \frac{1}{4}\, f(\alpha, \alpha) + \frac{1}{4\pi i} \oint_C \frac{f(\alpha, \beta)}{\beta - \alpha}\, d\beta + \frac{1}{2\pi i} \oint_C d\beta \frac{1}{2\pi i} \oint_C \frac{f(\zeta, \beta)}{(\zeta - \alpha)(\beta - \zeta)}\, d\zeta \end{aligned}$$

Comparison of this expression for $G^L(\alpha)$ with that of equation (4.12) immediately yields the Poincaré-Bertrand transformation formula,

$$\begin{aligned} &\frac{1}{2\pi i} \oint_C \frac{d\zeta}{\zeta - \alpha} \left(\frac{1}{2\pi i} \oint_C \frac{f(\zeta, \beta)}{\beta - \zeta}\, d\beta \right) \\ &\qquad = \frac{1}{4}\, f(\alpha, \alpha) + \frac{1}{2\pi i} \oint_C d\beta \left(\frac{1}{2\pi i} \oint_C \frac{f(\zeta, \beta)}{(\zeta - \alpha)(\beta - \zeta)}\, d\zeta \right) \end{aligned}$$

4.10 BOUNDARY VALUE PROBLEMS FOR SECTIONALLY ANALYTIC FUNCTIONS IN A PLANE CUT ALONG A CONTOUR

We are now prepared to tackle the boundary value problems we referred to in the introduction to this chapter, namely, the homogeneous Hilbert problems. These problems belong to the class of two-dimensional boundary value problems involving analytic or sectionally analytic functions of a complex variable. A well-known example of such a problem is Dirichlet's problem in which we are required to construct a function $F(\lambda)$ which is analytic inside a region D of the complex plane, is continuous inside and on the boundary of D, and is equal to some given continuous function on that boundary. It is well known that the real and imaginary parts of this function $F(\lambda)$ are solutions of Laplace's equation. Problems of this type are treated extensively in the standard textbooks on partial differential equations.

In this chapter we shall be concerned with boundary value problems for sectionally analytic functions. In such problems we are required to construct a function which is sectionally analytic in the plane cut along a path or contour and has boundary values satisfying a given boundary condition on this path or contour.

To be more specific, let us assume that $A(\zeta)$ and $B(\zeta)$ are Hölder continuous functions on a contour C which encloses the origin and that $A(\zeta)$ is non-vanishing on this contour. In the next two sections of this chapter we shall be concerned with the following boundary value problem: Construct a function $F(\lambda)$ which is sectionally analytic in the plane cut along the contour C, is of algebraic growth at infinity, and has boundary values $F^L(\zeta)$ and $F^R(\zeta)$ satisfying the boundary condition,

$$F^L(\zeta) = A(\zeta)F^R(\zeta) + B(\zeta) \tag{4.14}$$

on the contour C.

This boundary value problem is called the inhomogeneous Hilbert problem. The homogeneous Hilbert problem is obtained by setting $B(\zeta) = 0$ in the boundary condition (4.14). As we shall see, the inhomogeneous problem can easily be solved once the solution of the homogeneous problem is known. We shall therefore first direct our attention to the solution of the homogeneous Hilbert problem.

A. The Homogeneous Hilbert Problem for a Contour

Assuming that the contour C encloses the origin and that the function $A(\zeta)$ is Hölder continuous and nonvanishing on this contour, the homogeneous Hilbert problem may be stated as follows: Construct a function $F(\lambda)$ which is sectionally analytic in the plane cut along the contour C, is of algebraic growth at infinity, and has boundary values $F^L(\zeta)$ and $F^R(\zeta)$ which satisfy the boundary condition,

$$F^L(\zeta) = A(\zeta)F^R(\zeta) \tag{4.15}$$

on the boundary C.

The easiest way to obtain the solution of this problem is by reducing it to a boundary value problem of Plemelj. To illustrate this procedure let us make the simplifying assumption that $\log A(\zeta)$ is single-valued on the contour C. Taking the logarithm of both sides of equation (4.15), we obtain the boundary condition,

$$\log F^L(\zeta) - \log F^R(\zeta) = \log A(\zeta) \tag{4.16}$$

However, $A(\zeta)$ is Hölder continuous on the contour and we have thus reduced the original Hilbert problem to a boundary value problem of Plemelj with boundary condition (4.16). The solution of the Plemelj problem has been found in Section 4.7. According to the discussion in that section, the solution of the Plemelj problem may be written

$$\log F(\lambda) = \frac{1}{2\pi i} \oint_C \frac{\log A(\zeta)}{\zeta - \lambda} d\zeta$$

Consequently, under the simplifying assumption that $\log A(\zeta)$ is a single-valued function on the contour C, we find the solution,

$$F(\lambda) = \exp\left(\frac{1}{2\pi i} \oint_C \frac{\log A(\zeta)}{\zeta - \lambda} d\zeta\right)$$

of the homogeneous Hilbert problem. The Cauchy integral on the right hand side of the equation vanishes for large values of λ and this implies that the solution $F(\lambda)$ tends to one when λ tends to infinity.

The reduction of the Hilbert problem to the Plemelj problem was made easy by the assumption that $\log A(\zeta)$ is single-valued on C. This is not always true and, in general, when ζ traverses the contour we return to the starting point with a value of $\arg A(\zeta)$ which is different from the value of $\arg A(\zeta)$ with which we started. In this case $\log A(\zeta)$ is a multivalued function of ζ on the contour. The ambiguities which arise in the solution of problems with such coefficients may be circumvented in the following manner. We first consider a slightly different homogeneous Hilbert problem with a coefficient $A_0(\zeta)$ which is related to the coefficient $A(\zeta)$ but is so constructed that the function $\log A_0(\zeta)$ is a single-valued function of ζ on the contour. Such a function can be constructed as follows.

Let $2\pi p$ be the change in the argument of $A(\zeta)$ when ζ traverses the contour C. The integer p is called the index of the homogeneous Hilbert problem and can be found by evaluating the integral,

$$p = \frac{1}{2\pi i} \oint_C \frac{d \log A(\zeta)}{d\zeta} d\zeta$$

Since the contour C encloses the origin, the argument of the function ζ^p increases by $2\pi p$ when ζ traverses the contour C. The function,

$$\log A_0(\zeta) = \log [A(\zeta)/\zeta^p]$$

is single-valued therefore on the contour.

This may be verified as follows,

$$\frac{1}{2\pi i} \oint_C \frac{d \log [A(\zeta)/\zeta^p]}{d\zeta} d\zeta = \frac{1}{2\pi i} \oint_C \frac{d \log A(\zeta)}{d\zeta} d\zeta - \frac{1}{2\pi i} \oint_C \frac{d \log \zeta^p}{d\zeta} d\zeta = 0$$

Hence, the net increase of arg $A_0(\zeta)$ when ζ traverses the contour is zero. Furthermore, $A_0(\zeta)$ is Hölder continuous on C. These properties of the function $A_0(\zeta)$ imply that the auxiliary homogeneous Hilbert problem with boundary condition,

$$H^L(\zeta) = A_0(\zeta)H^R(\zeta)$$

can be reduced to a Plemelj boundary value problem with boundary condition,

$$\log H^L(\zeta) - \log H^R(\zeta) = \log A_0(\zeta)$$

The sectionally analytic function, which is the solution of this problem, takes the form,

$$H(\lambda) = \exp\left(\frac{1}{2\pi i}\oint_C \frac{\log A_0(\zeta)}{\zeta - \lambda}\, d\zeta\right)$$

We are now able, with the assistance of the auxiliary function $H(\lambda)$, to construct a solution of the homogeneous Hilbert problem with the boundary condition,

$$F^L(\zeta) = A(\zeta)F^R(\zeta) \tag{4.15}$$

For let us consider the function $G(\zeta)$ which is defined by the following relations,

$$G^L(\lambda) = H^L(\lambda) \qquad \text{when } \lambda \text{ is a point in } L$$

$$G^R(\lambda) = H^R(\lambda)/\lambda^p \qquad \text{when } \lambda \text{ is a point in } R$$

Substitution of the integral representation for the auxiliary solution $H(\lambda)$ yields the following representations for $G(\lambda)$,

$$G^L(\lambda) = \exp\left(\frac{1}{2\pi i}\oint_C \frac{\log\,[A(\zeta)/\zeta^p]}{\zeta - \lambda}\, d\zeta\right)$$

when λ is a point in the region L, and

$$G^R(\lambda) = \frac{1}{\lambda^p}\exp\left(\frac{1}{2\pi i}\oint_C \frac{\log\,[A(\zeta)/\zeta^p]}{\zeta - \lambda}\, d\zeta\right)$$

when λ is a point in the region R.

We can draw the following conclusions from these relations. The function $G(\lambda)$ is analytic inside and outside the contour C. Furthermore, $G(\lambda)$ is of algebraic growth at infinity because it satisfies the order property $G(\lambda) = O(1/\lambda^p)$ when λ tends to infinity. The boundary values of $G(\lambda)$ on the contour C are related to the boundary values of the function $H(\lambda)$,

$$G^L(\zeta) = H^L(\zeta) \quad \text{and} \quad G^R(\zeta) = H^R(\zeta)/\zeta^p$$

This implies that we may write

$$G^L(\zeta) = H^L(\zeta) = A_0(\zeta)H^R(\zeta) = \zeta^p A_0(\zeta)G^R(\zeta)$$

and thus

$$G^L(\zeta) = A(\zeta)G^R(\zeta)$$

Consequently, the sectionally analytic function $G(\lambda)$ constructed above satisfies all the conditions which we imposed on the solution of the homogeneous Hilbert problem and is, therefore, a solution of this problem.

The solution $G(\lambda)$, which is nonvanishing in all finite regions of the complex plane, is called the fundamental solution of the homogeneous Hilbert problem. $G(\lambda)$ is not the only solution. For let $P(\lambda)$ be a polynomial of degree m in the complex variable λ. Then the sectionally analytic function $P(\lambda)G(\lambda)$ is also a solution of the homogeneous Hilbert problem. This may be verified as follows. The boundary values $P^L(\zeta)G^L(\zeta)$ and $P^R(\zeta)G^R(\zeta)$ satisfy the boundary value condition,

$$P^L(\zeta)G^L(\zeta) = A(\zeta)P^R(\zeta)G^R(\zeta)$$

because $P^L(\zeta) = P^R(\zeta)$ on the boundary. Furthermore $P(\lambda)G(\lambda) = O(\lambda^{m-p})$ when λ tends to infinity. This implies that the sectionally analytic function $P(\lambda)G(\lambda)$ also satisfies the conditions imposed on a solution of the homogeneous Hilbert problem. We can show, however, that no other solution exists, and that all solutions $F(\lambda)$ can be written as the product of the fundamental solution and a polynomial $P(\lambda)$,

$$F(\lambda) = P(\lambda)G(\lambda)$$

For let $F(\lambda)$ be the solution of the homogeneous Hilbert problem. The function $F(\lambda)/G(\lambda)$ is analytic in the regions L and R and satisfies the boundary condition,

$$\frac{F^L(\zeta)}{G^L(\zeta)} = \frac{F^R(\zeta)}{G^R(\zeta)}$$

Consequently, the function $F(\lambda)/G(\lambda)$ is continuous and analytic in the whole complex plane. Furthermore, the function $F(\lambda)/G(\lambda)$ is of algebraic growth at infinity. According to Liouville's theorem, therefore, the function $F(\lambda)/G(\lambda)$ must be equal to a polynomial $P(\lambda)$ and thus

$$F(\lambda) = P(\lambda)G(\lambda)$$

This implies that the nontrivial solutions of the homogeneous Hilbert problem, which vanish at infinity, take the form,

$$F(\lambda) = P(\lambda)G(\lambda)$$

where $P(\lambda)$ is an arbitrary polynomial of degree $m \leqq p - 1$. Furthermore, there are no nontrivial solutions of the homogeneous problem which vanish at infinity when the index of the homogeneous problem is negative or vanishes.

B. The Inhomogeneous Hilbert Problem for a Contour

We now direct our attention to the solution of the inhomogeneous Hilbert problem. Let us again assume that the contour C encloses the origin, that the function $B(\zeta)$ is Hölder continuous on this contour, and that the function $A(\zeta)$ is Hölder continuous and nonvanishing on this contour.

To solve the inhomogeneous Hilbert problem, we need to construct a function $F(\lambda)$ which is sectionally analytic in the plane cut along the contour C, is of algebraic growth at infinity, and has boundary values $F^L(\zeta)$ and $F^R(\zeta)$ which satisfy the boundary condition,

$$F^L(\zeta) = A(\zeta)F^R(\zeta) + B(\zeta) \tag{4.17}$$

on the contour C.

Setting $B(\zeta) = 0$ we obtain the homogeneous Hilbert problem. Solving this problem, in the manner prescribed in the preceding section, we obtain the factorization,

$$A(\zeta) = G^L(\zeta)/G^R(\zeta)$$

of the coefficient $A(\zeta)$ where $G^L(\zeta)$ and $G^R(\zeta)$ are the boundary values of the fundamental solution of the homogeneous problem. Substitution of this expression for $A(\zeta)$ into equation (4.17) yields the boundary condition,

$$\frac{F^L(\zeta)}{G^L(\zeta)} - \frac{F^R(\zeta)}{G^R(\zeta)} = \frac{B(\zeta)}{G^L(\zeta)}$$

This reduces the inhomogeneous Hilbert problem to the boundary value problem of Plemelj which was solved in Section 4.7. Referring to this section, we can immediately write down the following integral representation for the solution of the inhomogeneous Hilbert problem,

$$F(\lambda) = \frac{G(\lambda)}{2\pi i} \oint_C \frac{B(\zeta)}{G^L(\zeta)} \frac{d\zeta}{\zeta - \lambda} + P(\lambda)G(\lambda)$$

The degree of the polynomial $P(\lambda)$ can be determined from the behavior of the sectionally analytic function $F(\lambda)$ at infinity. To investigate the behavior of this function at infinity let us consider the representation,

$$F^R(\lambda) = \frac{G^R(\lambda)}{2\pi i} \oint_C \frac{B(\zeta)}{G^L(\zeta)} \frac{d\zeta}{\zeta - \lambda} + P(\lambda)G^R(\lambda)$$

The Cauchy integral vanishes as $1/\lambda$ when λ tends to infinity and, since $G(\lambda)$ is the fundamental solution of the homogeneous Hilbert problem, $G(\lambda)$ vanishes as λ^{-p} when λ tends to infinity, where p is the index of the homogeneous problem. Hence, the first term on the right hand side of the representation for $F^R(\lambda)$ is $O(\lambda^{-p-1})$ when λ tends to infinity. Similarly, if m is the degree of the polynomial $P(\lambda)$, then the second term on the right hand side is $P(\lambda)G(\lambda) = O(\lambda^{m-p})$ when λ tends to infinity.

In most applications of the subject matter of this section to problems of mathematical physics and engineering, the sectionally analytic functions obtained as the solutions of Hilbert problems are the Fourier transforms of the solutions of integral equations or of partial differential equations. This implies that these functions must vanish at infinity. Imposing this condition on the solutions of the inhomogeneous Hilbert problem, we may distinguish between the following three possibilities depending on the index p of the homogeneous problem.

a. The index vanishes. Since

$$P(\lambda)G(\lambda) = O(\lambda^{m-p})$$

when λ tends to infinity, the only admissible polynomial is the trivial polynomial $P(\lambda) = 0$ and we obtain the unique solution,

$$F(\lambda) = \frac{G(\lambda)}{2\pi i} \oint_C \frac{B(\zeta)}{G^L(\zeta)} \frac{d\zeta}{\zeta - \lambda}$$

b. The index is positive. The admissible polynomial is of a degree $m \leqq p - 1$ and the solution,

$$F(\lambda) = \frac{G(\lambda)}{2\pi i} \oint_C \frac{B(\zeta)}{G^L(\zeta)} \frac{d\zeta}{\zeta - \lambda} + P_m(\lambda)G(\lambda)$$

may contain $m \leqq p - 1$ arbitrary constants, namely the coefficients of the polynomial.

c. The index is negative. We must again choose the trivial polynomial $P(\lambda) = 0$. Furthermore, expanding the integrand of the Cauchy integral in terms of λ

$$\begin{aligned} F(\lambda) &= \frac{G(\lambda)}{2\pi i} \oint_C \frac{B(\zeta)}{G^L(\zeta)} \frac{d\zeta}{\zeta - \lambda} \\ &= -\frac{G(\lambda)}{2\pi i\lambda}\left[\oint_C \frac{B(\zeta)}{G^L(\zeta)}\, d\zeta + \frac{1}{\lambda}\oint_C \frac{\zeta B(\zeta)}{G^L(\zeta)}\, d\zeta + \cdots \right. \\ &\qquad \left. + \cdots + \frac{1}{\lambda^m}\oint_C \frac{\zeta^m B(\zeta)}{G^L(\zeta)}\, d\zeta + \cdots \right] \end{aligned}$$

we must require, in order for $F(\lambda)$ to vanish at infinity, that the coefficients,

$$\oint_C \frac{\zeta^m B(\zeta)}{G^L(\zeta)}\, d\zeta = 0$$

in the expansion vanish for all $m = 0, 1, 2, \ldots, -(p+1)$. Hence, in this case, the unique solution of the inhomogeneous Hilbert problem, which vanishes at infinity, takes the form,

$$F(\lambda) = \frac{G(\lambda)}{2\pi i} \oint_C \frac{B(\zeta)}{G^L(\zeta)} \frac{d\zeta}{\zeta - \lambda}$$

subject to the auxiliary conditions,

$$\oint_C \frac{\zeta^m B(\zeta)}{G^L(\zeta)}\, d\zeta = 0$$

when $m = 0, 1, 2, \ldots, -(p+1)$.

4.11 SINGULAR INTEGRAL EQUATIONS OF THE CAUCHY TYPE

The analysis presented in the previous section may be utilized to obtain the solution of the following singular integral equation of the Cauchy type,

$$A(\zeta)f(\zeta) = B(\zeta) + \oint_C \frac{f(\alpha)}{\alpha - \zeta}\, d\alpha \tag{4.18}$$

The functions $A(\zeta)$ and $B(\zeta)$ are known functions which are defined and Hölder continuous on the contour C which is assumed to enclose the origin.

If we assume that the solution $f(\zeta)$ of the integral equation is Hölder continuous on the contour, we may define the sectionally analytic function,

$$F(\lambda) = \frac{1}{2\pi i} \oint_C \frac{f(\zeta)}{\zeta - \lambda}\, d\zeta$$

This function vanishes as $1/\lambda$ when λ tends to infinity.

According to the Plemelj formulas, the solution of the integral equation $f(\zeta)$ is related to the boundary values $F^L(\zeta)$ and $F^R(\zeta)$ of the sectionally analytic function $F(\lambda)$,

$$F^L(\zeta) - F^R(\zeta) = f(\zeta)$$

$$F^L(\zeta) + F^R(\zeta) = \frac{1}{\pi i} \oint_C \frac{f(\alpha)}{\alpha - \zeta}\, d\alpha$$

This implies that the solution $f(\zeta)$ of the integral equation can be obtained immediately from the first Plemelj formula, once the boundary values of $F(\lambda)$ are known. We shall first use the Plemelj formulas to reduce the integral equation (4.18) to an inhomogeneous Hilbert problem. Simple substitution from these formulas into the integral equation (4.18) yields the boundary value equation for the boundary values $F^L(\zeta)$ and $F^R(\zeta)$ of the sectionally analytic function $F(\lambda)$,

$$A(\zeta)[F^L(\zeta) - F^R(\zeta)] = B(\zeta) + \pi i[F^L(\zeta) + F^R(\zeta)]$$

which may also be written

$$F^L(\zeta) = \frac{A(\zeta) + \pi i}{A(\zeta) - \pi i} F^R(\zeta) + \frac{B(\zeta)}{A(\zeta) - \pi i} \tag{4.19}$$

The solution of the singular integral equation (4.18) has been reduced, therefore, to the search for a function $F(\lambda)$ which is sectionally analytic in the plane cut along the contour C, vanishes at infinity, and has boundary values $F^L(\zeta)$ and $F^R(\zeta)$ which satisfy the boundary condition (4.19) on the contour C. Since $A(\zeta)$ and $B(\zeta)$ are Hölder continuous on C, this means that we have reduced the problem of solving a singular integral equation to the problem of solving an inhomogeneous Hilbert problem. Referring to the analysis in the preceding section, we can immediately write down the sectionally analytic function which is the solution of this inhomogeneous Hilbert problem,

$$F(\lambda) = \frac{G(\lambda)}{2\pi i} \oint_C \frac{B(\zeta)}{G^L(\zeta)[A(\zeta) - \pi i]} \frac{d\zeta}{\zeta - \lambda} + P(\lambda)G(\lambda) \tag{4.20}$$

where $G(\lambda)$ is the fundamental solution of the homogeneous Hilbert problem with boundary condition,

$$G^L(\zeta) = \frac{A(\zeta) + \pi i}{A(\zeta) - \pi i} G^R(\zeta)$$

Let p be the index of the homogeneous Hilbert problem. The sectionally analytic function $G(\lambda) = O(1/\lambda^p)$ when λ tends to infinity. However, the function $F(\lambda)$ is required to vanish at infinity and we must distinguish therefore between the following cases.

a. The index vanishes. The only admissible polynomial is the trivial polynomial and we obtain the unique solution,

$$F(\lambda) = \frac{G(\lambda)}{2\pi i} \oint_C \frac{B(\zeta)}{G^L(\zeta)[A(\zeta) - \pi i]} \frac{d\zeta}{\zeta - \lambda}$$

b. The index is positive. The degree m of the polynomial $P(\lambda)$ must satisfy the condition $m \leqq p - 1$ and we obtain the solution,

$$F(\lambda) = \frac{G(\lambda)}{2\pi i} \oint_C \frac{B(\zeta)}{G^L(\zeta)[A(\zeta) - \pi i]} \frac{d\zeta}{\zeta - \lambda} + P(\lambda)G(\lambda)$$

which, in general, is determined up to $m \leqq p - 1$ arbitrary constants, namely the coefficients of the polynomial $P(\lambda)$.

c. The index is negative. In this case we must choose $P(\lambda)$ to be equal to zero. The unique solution takes the form,

$$F(\lambda) = \frac{G(\lambda)}{2\pi i} \oint_C \frac{B(\zeta)}{G^L(\zeta)[A(\zeta) - \pi i]} \frac{d\zeta}{\zeta - \lambda}$$

subject to the following auxiliary conditions,

$$\oint_C \frac{\zeta^m B(\zeta)}{G^L(\zeta)[A(\zeta) - \pi i]} d\zeta = 0$$

when $m = 0, 1, 2, \ldots, -(p+1)$.

The sectionally analytic function $F(\lambda)$ can now be used to determine the solution $f(\zeta)$ of the singular integral equation (4.18). For, according to Section 4.6, the boundary values $F^L(\zeta)$ and $F^R(\zeta)$ of the sectionally analytic function $F(\lambda)$ take the form,

$$F^L(\zeta) = \frac{1}{2} \frac{G^L(\zeta)B(\zeta)}{G^L(\zeta)[A(\zeta) - \pi i]} + \frac{G^L(\zeta)}{2\pi i} \oint_C \frac{B(\alpha)}{G^L(\alpha)[A(\alpha) - \pi i]} \frac{d\alpha}{\alpha - \zeta} + P(\zeta)G^L(\zeta)$$

and

$$F^R(\zeta) = -\frac{1}{2} \frac{G^R(\zeta)B(\zeta)}{G^L(\zeta)[A(\zeta) - \pi i]} + \frac{G^R(\zeta)}{2\pi i} \oint_C \frac{B(\alpha)}{G^L(\alpha)[A(\alpha) - \pi i]} \frac{d\alpha}{\alpha - \zeta} + P(\zeta)G^R(\zeta)$$

However, according to the first Plemelj formula,

$$f(\zeta) = F^L(\zeta) - F^R(\zeta)$$

and, by substitution of $F^L(\zeta)$ and $F^R(\zeta)$, we obtain therefore the following solution of the singular integral equation (4.18),

$$f(\zeta) = \frac{[G^L(\zeta) + G^R(\zeta)]B(\zeta)}{2G^L(\zeta)[A(\zeta) - \pi i]} + [G^L(\zeta) - G^R(\zeta)]P(\zeta) + \frac{G^L(\zeta) - G^R(\zeta)}{2\pi i} \oint_C \frac{B(\alpha)}{G^L(\alpha)[A(\alpha) - \pi i]} \frac{d\alpha}{\alpha - \zeta}$$

This equation expresses the solution of the integral equation in terms of the boundary values $G^L(\zeta)$ and $G^R(\zeta)$ of the fundamental solution of the homogeneous Hilbert problem.

The boundary values $G^L(\zeta)$ and $G^R(\zeta)$ satisfy the relation,

$$\frac{G^L(\zeta)}{G^R(\zeta)} = \frac{A(\zeta) + \pi i}{A(\zeta) - \pi i}$$

Hence, the solution of the singular integral equation may also be written

$$(4.21)\quad f(\zeta) = \frac{A(\zeta)B(\zeta)}{A^2(\zeta) + \pi^2} + \frac{2\pi i G^L(\zeta)}{A(\zeta) + \pi i} \left[P(\zeta) + \frac{1}{2\pi i} \oint_C \frac{B(\alpha)}{G^L(\alpha)[A(\alpha) - \pi i]} \frac{d\alpha}{\alpha - \zeta} \right]$$

EXAMPLE Consider the Hilbert equation,

$$g(\zeta) = \frac{1}{\pi} \oint_C \frac{f(\alpha)}{\alpha - \zeta} \, d\alpha$$

where $g(\zeta)$ is a known function which is defined and Hölder continuous on C. Comparing this equation with the standard form of the singular integral equation, we find

$$A(\zeta) = 0 \quad \text{and} \quad B(\zeta) = -\pi g(\zeta)$$

The corresponding homogeneous Hilbert problem is

$$G^L(\zeta) = -G^R(\zeta) \qquad \text{for } \zeta \text{ on } C$$

Hence, the index of the homogeneous problem is zero and we may set $G^L(\zeta) = -G^R(\zeta) = 1$. Furthermore the polynomial $P(\zeta)$ is zero. Substitution of these values into equation (4.21) yields the solution,

$$f(\zeta) = -\frac{1}{\pi} \oint_C \frac{g(\alpha)}{\alpha - \zeta} \, d\alpha$$

of the Hilbert equation.

4.12 BOUNDARY VALUE PROBLEMS FOR SECTIONALLY ANALYTIC FUNCTIONS IN A PLANE CUT ALONG A FINITE PATH

In section 4.10 we presented the solution of the homogeneous Hilbert problem for the case of a contour. Although the solution of the homogeneous Hilbert problem for the case of a finite path can be derived in a similar manner, the behavior of the solution at the end points of the path necessitates some additional analysis.

A. The Homogeneous Hilbert Problem for a Finite Path

The problem we pose is to construct a sectionally analytic function $F(\lambda)$ which has a boundary path Γ with end points a and b and is of finite degree at infinity. This function $F(\lambda)$ moreover should be bounded by $(a - \lambda)^\alpha$ when λ tends to a and by $(b - \lambda)^\beta$ when λ tends to b where $\alpha + 1$ and $\beta + 1$ are positive constants. On the boundary Γ the right and left boundary values $F^L(\zeta)$ and $F^R(\zeta)$ of $F(\lambda)$ should satisfy the boundary condition,

$$F^L(\zeta) = A(\zeta) F^R(\zeta) \tag{4.22}$$

where $A(\zeta)$ is Hölder continuous and nonvanishing on the path including its end points.

Choosing a branch of the multivalued function $\log A(\zeta)$ which is continuous on the path Γ, we consider the function,

$$\exp\left[\frac{1}{2\pi i}\int_\Gamma \frac{\log A(\zeta)}{\zeta - \lambda}\, d\zeta\right]$$

This function satisfies the boundary condition (4.22) but not necessarily the conditions which are imposed on the solution of the Hilbert problem at the end points of the path Γ. However, let us consider the function,

$$G(\lambda) = (a - \lambda)^{\alpha(a)}(b - \lambda)^{\beta(b)} \exp\left[\frac{1}{2\pi i}\int_\Gamma \frac{\log A(\zeta)}{\zeta - \lambda}\, d\zeta\right]$$

As we have shown in Section 4.5, the Cauchy integral,

$$\frac{1}{2\pi i}\int_\Gamma \frac{\log A(\alpha)}{\zeta - \lambda}\, d\zeta$$

may be written

$$\frac{1}{2\pi i}\int_\Gamma \frac{\log A(\zeta)}{\zeta - \lambda}\, d\zeta = -\frac{\log A(a)}{2\pi i}\log (a - \lambda) + H(\lambda, a)$$

in the neighborhood of the point a, where $H(\lambda, a)$ denotes a function which is bounded at the point a. In the neighborhood of the point a therefore $G(\lambda)$ can be approximated by the function,

$$(a - \lambda)^{\alpha(a) - (1/2\pi i)\log A(a)}$$

Hence, choosing an integer $\alpha(a)$ such that

$$\alpha(a) - R\left[\frac{1}{2\pi i}\log A(a)\right] + 1$$

is a positive number, the function $G(\lambda)$ has the required behavior in the neighborhood of the end point a of the path Γ. Similarly, we can show that the function $G(\lambda)$ will have the required behavior when λ tends to point b if we choose an integer $\beta(b)$ such that

$$\beta(b) + R\left[\frac{1}{2\pi i}\log A(b)\right] + 1$$

is a positive number. The function,

$$G(\lambda) = (a - \lambda)^{\alpha(a)}(b - \lambda)^{\beta(b)} \exp\left[\frac{1}{2\pi i}\int_\Gamma \frac{\log A(\zeta)}{\zeta - \lambda}\, d\zeta\right]$$

where the integers $\alpha(a)$ and $\beta(b)$ have been chosen in accordance with our specifications, is therefore a solution of the homogeneous Hilbert problem, namely the so-called fundamental solution. Since the Cauchy integral tends to zero as $1/\lambda$ when λ tends to infinity, the fundamental solution behaves as $1/\lambda^{p(\alpha,\beta)}$ when λ tends to infinity, where the integer $p(\alpha, \beta) = -[\alpha(a) + \beta(b)]$ is the index of the homogeneous Hilbert problem. The fundamental solution will have a zero of order $p(\alpha, \beta)$ at infinity when the index is positive and a pole of order $p(\alpha, \beta)$ at infinity when $p(\alpha, \beta)$ is negative. The fundamental solution is bounded at the end point a of the path Γ when the quantity $R[(1/2\pi i) \log A(a)]$ is an integer. For in this case we must choose the integer $\alpha(a)$ such that

$$\alpha(a) = R\left[\frac{1}{2\pi i} \log A(a)\right]$$

which implies that $G(\lambda) = O(1)$ when λ tends to a. Similarly, the fundamental solution is bounded at the end point b of the path Γ whenever the quantity $R[(1/2\pi i) \log A(b)]$ is an integer. The boundary values $G^L(\zeta)$ and $G^R(\zeta)$ of the fundamental solution take the form,

$$G^L(\zeta) = (a - \zeta)^{\alpha(a)}(b - \zeta)^{\beta(b)} \exp\left[\frac{1}{2} \log A(\zeta) + \frac{1}{2\pi i} \int_\Gamma \frac{\log A(v)}{v - \zeta}\, dv\right]$$

and

$$G^R(\zeta) = (a - \zeta)^{\alpha(a)}(b - \zeta)^{\beta(b)} \exp\left[-\frac{1}{2} \log A(\zeta) + \frac{1}{2\pi i} \int_\Gamma \frac{\log A(v)}{v - \zeta}\, dv\right]$$

These expressions can easily be obtained by means of the Plemelj formulas for the Cauchy integral,

$$\frac{1}{2\pi i} \int_\Gamma \frac{\log A(\zeta)}{\zeta - \lambda}\, d\zeta$$

To find the general solution $F(\lambda)$ of the homogeneous Hilbert problem, let us consider the boundary condition,

$$F^L(\zeta) = A(\zeta)F^R(\zeta)$$

which must be satisfied by the boundary values of this solution on the path Γ. Since the boundary values of the fundamental solution satisfy the condition,

$$G^L(\zeta) = A(\zeta)G^R(\zeta)$$

the ratios of the left and right boundary values of the functions $F(\lambda)$ and $G(\lambda)$ must satisfy the condition,

$$\frac{F^L(\zeta)}{G^L(\zeta)} - \frac{F^R(\zeta)}{G^R(\zeta)} = 0 \tag{4.23}$$

on the path Γ. If we construct therefore a sectionally analytic function $F(\lambda)/G(\lambda)$ with boundary path Γ on which its left and right boundary values satisfy the boundary condition (4.23), then the general solution of the homogeneous Hilbert problem is obtained as the product of this function and the fundamental solution. Such a function $F(\lambda)/G(\lambda)$ can easily be constructed. For the boundary condition implies that $F(\lambda)/G(\lambda)$ is continuous on the boundary. The function $F(\lambda)/G(\lambda)$ therefore is analytic in the whole complex plane including the boundary but with the possible exception of the end points. For our purposes it is sufficient if we assume, in addition, that the function $F(\lambda)/G(\lambda)$ is bounded at the endpoints a and b of the path Γ. In other words, we want the function $F(\lambda)/G(\lambda)$ to have at most a removable singularity at these points. This can be accomplished by assuming that the fundamental solution behaves as $F(\lambda)$ near the endpoints of the path Γ. Hence, we must choose our integers $\alpha(a)$ and $\beta(b)$ such that

$$-1 < \alpha(a) - R\left[\frac{1}{2\pi i}\log A(a)\right] \leqq 0$$

and

$$-1 < \beta(b) + R\left[\frac{1}{2\pi i}\log A(b)\right] \leqq 0$$

These conditions ensure that the function $F(\lambda)/G(\lambda)$ is analytic in the whole complex plane and since moreover $F(\lambda)/G(\lambda)$ is of finite degree at infinity, it must be a polynomial $P(\lambda)$. Thus we obtain the expression,

$$F(\lambda) = P(\lambda)G(\lambda)$$

for the general solution of the homogeneous Hilbert problem where $P(\lambda)$ denotes an arbitrary polynomial.

B. The Inhomogeneous Hilbert Problem for a Finite Path

Having obtained the solution of the homogeneous Hilbert problem for the case of a finite path Γ the solution of the corresponding inhomogeneous Hilbert problem satisfying a boundary condition,

$$F^L(\zeta) = A(\zeta)F^R(\zeta) + B(\zeta)$$

on this path can easily be found by means of the methods outlined in Section 4.10. According to the formulas derived in that section, the solution of the inhomogeneous problem takes the form,

$$F(\lambda) = \frac{G(\lambda)}{2\pi i}\int_\Gamma \frac{B(\zeta)}{G^L(\zeta)}\frac{d\zeta}{\zeta - \lambda} + P(\lambda)G(\lambda)$$

where $G(\lambda)$ is the fundamental solution of the homogeneous Hilbert problem and $P(\lambda)$ is an arbitrary polynomial. The choice of the values of the integers $\alpha(a)$ and $\beta(b)$ in the fundamental solution of the homogeneous Hilbert problem,

$$G(\lambda) = (a - \lambda)^{\alpha(a)}(b - \lambda)^{\beta(b)} \exp\left[\frac{1}{2\pi i}\int_\Gamma \frac{\log A(\zeta)}{\zeta - \lambda}\, d\zeta\right]$$

is in part determined by the required behavior of the solution of the inhomogeneous Hilbert problem in the neighborhood of the end points a and b of the path Γ. For example, if we require that $F(\lambda)$ is bounded by $(a - \lambda)^\nu$ when λ tends to a and by $(b - \lambda)^\nu$ when λ tends to b, where $-1 < \nu \leqq 0$, then we must choose the integers $\alpha(a)$ and $\beta(b)$ such that

$$-1 < \alpha(a) - R\left[\frac{1}{2\pi i} \log A(a)\right] \leqq 0$$

and

$$-1 < \beta(b) + R\left[\frac{1}{2\pi i} \log A(b)\right] \leqq 0$$

The behavior of the fundamental solution $G(\lambda)$ at infinity determines the choice of the polynomial $P(\lambda)$. Since the function $G(\lambda)$ behaves as $1/\lambda^{p(\alpha,\beta)}$ when λ tends to infinity, the choice of the polynomial $P(\lambda)$ depends on the values of the index $p(\alpha, \beta) = -[\alpha(a) + \beta(b)]$. For example, assuming that we want solutions $F(\lambda)$ of the inhomogeneous Hilbert problem which vanish when λ tends to infinity we must distinguish between the following cases.

1. The index $p(\alpha, \beta)$ is zero. Since in general the function $P(\lambda)G(\lambda)$ behaves as λ^{m-p} when λ tends to infinity where m is the degree of the polynomial $P(\lambda)$, we must require that $P(\lambda) = 0$ when $p(\alpha, \beta) = 0$. We obtain therefore the unique solution,

$$F(\lambda) = \frac{G(\lambda)}{2\pi i}\int_\Gamma \frac{B(\zeta)}{G^L(\zeta)} \frac{d\zeta}{\zeta - \lambda}$$

2. The index $p(\alpha, \beta)$ is positive. In this case any polynomial of degree $m \leqq p - 1$ is admissible and the solution,

$$F(\lambda) = \frac{G(\lambda)}{2\pi i}\int_\Gamma \frac{B(\zeta)}{G^L(\zeta)} \frac{d\zeta}{\zeta - \lambda} + P_m(\lambda)G(\lambda)$$

is determined up to at most $p - 1$ arbitrary constants.

3. The index $p(\alpha, \beta)$ is negative. We now must choose $P(\lambda) = 0$ and in addition impose the following auxiliary conditions,

$$\int_\Gamma \frac{B(\zeta)\zeta^m}{G^L(\zeta)}\, d\zeta = 0 \qquad m = 0, 1, \ldots, -(p + 1)$$

on the unique solution,

$$F(\lambda) = \frac{G(\lambda)}{2\pi i} \int_\Gamma \frac{B(\zeta)}{G^L(\zeta)} \frac{d\zeta}{\zeta - \lambda}$$

of the inhomogeneous Hilbert problem.

4.13 BOUNDARY VALUE PROBLEMS FOR SECTIONALLY ANALYTIC FUNCTIONS IN A PLANE CUT ALONG AN INFINITE STRAIGHT LINE

Boundary value problems of the Hilbert type, involving sectionally analytic functions which satisfy a homogeneous or inhomogeneous boundary condition on a straight line of infinite length, can be solved by a technique which is a straightforward generalization of the solution method of the Hilbert problem for a contour. The case in which the boundary path is an infinite line which is parallel to the real or imaginary axis is of special importance and arises frequently in the solution of the boundary value problems of mathematical physics by means of transform techniques.

In this section we shall generalize the results of Section 4.10 to the case in which the boundary is an infinite line which runs parallel to the real axis. First we shall consider the homogeneous Hilbert problem.

A. The Homogeneous Hilbert Problem for an Infinite Line

Assuming that the function $A(\zeta)$ is Hölder continuous and nonvanishing on any finite subinterval of the path $(-\infty + ic, \infty + ic)$ and satisfies the order relation $A(\zeta) = 1 + O(\zeta^\beta)$ when ζ tends to infinity on this path, where β is a negative number, the homogeneous Hilbert problem can be stated as follows: Construct a function $F(\lambda)$ which is sectionally analytic in the plane cut along the path $(-\infty + ic, \infty + ic)$, is of algebraic growth at infinity, and has boundary values $F^L(\zeta)$ and $F^R(\zeta)$ satisfying the condition,

$$F^L(\zeta) = A(\zeta)F^R(\zeta)$$

on the path.

First let us assume that

$$\lim_{R(\zeta)\to+\infty} \arg A(\zeta) - \lim_{R(\zeta)\to-\infty} \arg A(\zeta) = 0$$

when ζ traverses the path $(-\infty + ic, \infty + ic)$. In this case, the boundary condition of the homogeneous Hilbert problem can be transformed into the boundary condition,

$$\log F^L(\zeta) - \log F^R(\zeta) = \log A(\zeta)$$

of a Plemelj boundary value problem. The solution of this Plemelj problem can be written down immediately

$$\log F(\lambda) = \frac{1}{2\pi i} \int_{-\infty + ic}^{\infty + ic} \frac{\log A(\zeta)}{\zeta - \lambda} \, d\zeta$$

This implies that the solution of the homogeneous Hilbert problem takes the form,

$$F(\lambda) = \exp\left(\frac{1}{2\pi i} \int_{-\infty + ic}^{\infty + ic} \frac{\log A(\zeta)}{\zeta - \lambda} \, d\zeta\right)$$

The condition that the coefficient $A(\zeta)$ is Hölder continuous on any finite subinterval of the infinite path $(-\infty + ic, \infty + ic)$ and the condition that

$$\lim_{R(\zeta)\to+\infty} \log A(\zeta) - \lim_{R(\zeta)\to-\infty} \log A(\zeta) = 0$$

on this path are sufficient to ensure the existence of the integral in the expressions above. However, these integrals do not converge when the function $A(\zeta)$ changes phase at the end points of the infinite interval. In other words, when the index,

$$p = \frac{1}{2\pi i}\left[\lim_{R(\zeta)\to+\infty} \log A(\zeta) - \lim_{R(\zeta)\to-\infty} \log A(\zeta)\right]$$

is a positive or negative integer. In such a case we must introduce a convergence factor in order to obtain convergent integrals. We can easily construct such a convergence factor. For let us consider the function,

$$A_0(\zeta) = \left(\frac{\zeta - b}{\zeta - a}\right)^p A(\zeta)$$

where a is an arbitrary complex number in the upper half plane $I(\lambda) > c$ and b is an arbitrary complex number in the lower half plane $I(\lambda) < c$, as shown in Figure IV-7. The logarithm of the function $A_0(\zeta)$ above satisfies the condition,

$$\begin{aligned}
&\lim_{R(\zeta)\to+\infty} \log A_0(\zeta) - \lim_{R(\zeta)\to-\infty} \log A_0(\zeta) \\
&\quad = \lim_{R(\zeta)\to+\infty} i[\arg A(\zeta) + p \arg(\zeta - b) - p \arg(\zeta - a)] \\
&\qquad - \lim_{R(\zeta)\to-\infty} i[\arg A(\zeta) + p \arg(\zeta - b) - p \arg(\zeta - a)] = 0
\end{aligned}$$

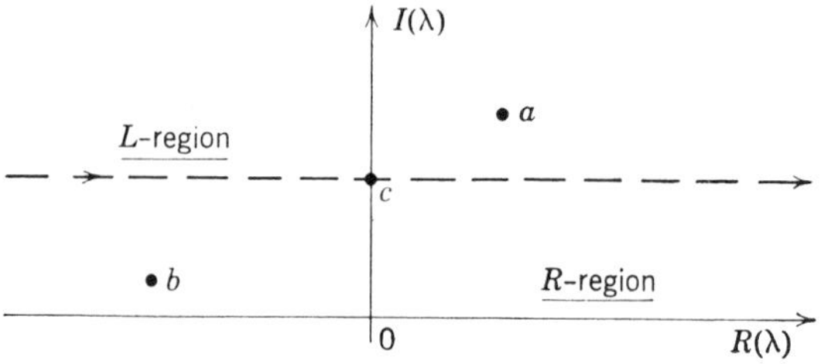

Figure IV-7

when ζ is located on the path $(-\infty + ic, \infty + ic)$. For, as can easily be verified from Figure IV-8,

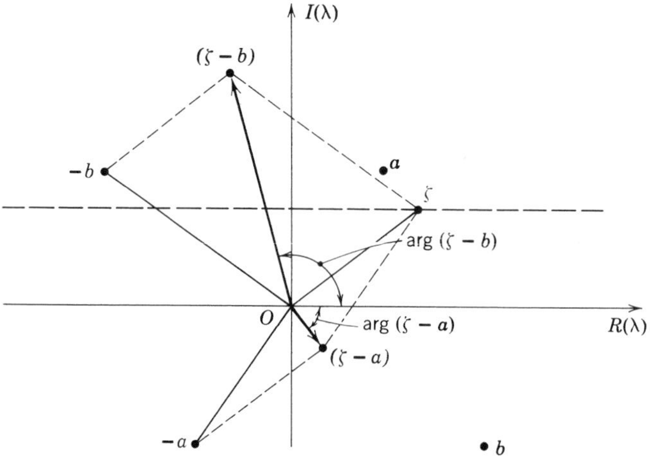

Figure IV-8

$$\lim_{R(\zeta)\to+\infty} p[\arg(\zeta - b) - \arg(\zeta - a)] = 0$$

and

$$\lim_{R(\zeta)\to-\infty} p[\arg(\zeta - b) - \arg(\zeta - a)] = 2\pi p$$

when ζ is located on the path $(-\infty + ic, \infty + ic)$.

This implies that the auxiliary homogeneous Hilbert problem for the sectionally analytic function $H(\lambda)$ which satisfies the boundary condition,

$$H^L(\zeta) = A_0(\zeta)H^R(\zeta)$$

can be solved by transformation to a boundary value problem of Plemelj with boundary condition,

$$\log H^L(\zeta) - \log H^R(\zeta) = \log A_0(\zeta)$$

The solution of this Plemelj problem is

$$H(\lambda) = \exp\left(\frac{1}{2\pi i}\int_{-\infty+ic}^{\infty+ic} \frac{\log A_0(\zeta)}{\zeta - \lambda}\, d\zeta\right)$$

$$= \exp\left(\frac{1}{2\pi i}\int_{-\infty+ic}^{\infty+ic} \frac{\log\left[A(\zeta)\left(\frac{\zeta - b}{\zeta - a}\right)^p\right]}{\zeta - \lambda}\, d\zeta\right)$$

It is now easy to show that the function $G(\lambda)$ which has the representations,

$$G^L(\lambda) = H^L(\lambda)/(\lambda - b)^p \qquad \text{when } \lambda \text{ is a point in the region } L$$

$$G^R(\lambda) = H^R(\lambda)/(\lambda - a)^p \qquad \text{when } \lambda \text{ is a point in the region } R$$

is a sectionally analytic function with the boundary line $(-\infty + ic, \infty + ic)$. On this boundary the boundary values, $G^L(\zeta)$ and $G^R(\zeta)$, of the function $G(\lambda)$ satisfy the condition,

$$G^L(\zeta) = H^L(\zeta)/(\zeta - b)^p = H^R(\zeta)A_0(\zeta)/(\zeta - b)^p$$
$$= G^R(\zeta)A_0(\zeta)(\zeta - a)^p/(\zeta - b)^p = A(\zeta)G^R(\zeta)$$

Consequently, the fundamental solution of the homogeneous Hilbert problem for the infinite straight line has the representation,

$$G^L(\lambda) = \frac{\exp\left(\frac{1}{2\pi i}\int_{-\infty+ic}^{\infty+ic} \frac{\log\left[A(\zeta)(\zeta - b)^p/(\zeta - a)^p\right]}{\zeta - \lambda}\, d\zeta\right)}{(\lambda - b)^p}$$

when λ is a point in the region L and the representation,

$$G^R(\lambda) = \frac{\exp\left(\frac{1}{2\pi i}\int_{-\infty+ic}^{\infty+ic} \frac{\log\left[A(\zeta)(\zeta - b)^p/(\zeta - a)^p\right]}{\zeta - \lambda}\, d\zeta\right)}{(\lambda - a)^p}$$

when λ is a point in the region R. The integer p is the index of the homogeneous Hilbert problem.

As in the case of the Hilbert problem for the contour, the general solution $F(\lambda)$ of the problem is obtained by multiplying the fundamental solution $G(\lambda)$ by a polynomial $P(\lambda)$,

$$F(\lambda) = P(\lambda)G(\lambda)$$

The degree of the polynomial is determined by the required algebraic behavior of the function $F(\lambda)$ at infinity.

In Section 3.4 we discussed the factor formulas of the Wiener-Hopf technique. In reference to these formulas it may be noted that the solution of the homogeneous Hilbert problem is equivalent to the factorization,

$$A(\zeta) = G^L(\zeta)/G^R(\zeta)$$

of the function $A(\zeta)$ into the two functions $G^L(\zeta)$ and $G^R(\zeta)$ which are the boundary values of a function $G(\lambda)$, which is sectionally analytic in the plane cut along the line $(-\infty + ic, \infty + ic)$.

B. The Inhomogeneous Hilbert Problem for an Infinite Line

Once we have found the fundamental solution of the homogeneous Hilbert problem, the solution of the inhomogeneous Hilbert problem poses no additional difficulties.

We now want to construct a function $F(\lambda)$ which is sectionally analytic in the plane cut along the path $(-\infty + ic, \infty + ic)$, is of algebraic growth at infinity, and has the boundary values $F^L(\zeta)$ and $F^R(\zeta)$ satisfying the boundary condition,

$$F^L(\zeta) = A(\zeta)F^R(\zeta) + B(\zeta) \tag{4.24}$$

on the path. We assume that $A(\zeta)$ and $B(\zeta)$ are Hölder continuous on any finite part of the boundary line and require moreover that $A(\zeta)$ and $B(\zeta)$ satisfy the conditions,

$$A(\zeta) = 1 + O(\zeta^{\alpha})$$

and

$$B(\zeta) = B(\infty) + O(\zeta^{\beta})$$

when ζ tends to infinity, where α and β are negative constants. Finally, we assume that $A(\zeta)$ is nonvanishing on the boundary.

The coefficient function $A(\zeta)$ can be factored as follows,

$$A(\zeta) = G^L(\zeta)/G^R(\zeta)$$

where $G^L(\zeta)$ and $G^R(\zeta)$ are the boundary values of the fundamental solution $G(\lambda)$ of the corresponding homogeneous Hilbert problem. Substitution of this expression for $A(\zeta)$ into equation (4.24) yields the boundary condition,

$$\frac{F^L(\zeta)}{G^L(\zeta)} - \frac{F^R(\zeta)}{G^R(\zeta)} = \frac{B(\zeta)}{G^L(\zeta)}$$

of a Plemelj boundary value problem. The solution of the inhomogeneous Hilbert problem can now be obtained immediately and takes the form,

$$F(\lambda) = \frac{G(\lambda)}{2\pi i} \int_{-\infty+ic}^{\infty+ic} \frac{B(\zeta)}{G^L(\zeta)} \frac{d\zeta}{\zeta - \lambda} + P(\lambda)G(\lambda)$$

where $P(\lambda)$ is an arbitrary polynomial. The degree of this polynomial and its relation to the index p of the homogeneous Hilbert problem depend on the algebraic behavior of $F(\lambda)$ at infinity. They can be determined in a manner similar to that outlined for the case of a contour in Section 4.10.

4.14 WIENER-HOPF INTEGRAL EQUATIONS AND HILBERT PROBLEMS

In the introduction to this chapter we noted that the Fourier transformation of a Wiener-Hopf type integral equation sometimes results in a functional equation which is defined on a line parallel to the real axis instead of in the usual strip in the space of the transform variable. In this section we shall be concerned with the solution of such integral equations by means of the techniques developed in the preceding sections of this chapter.

A. Homogeneous Wiener-Hopf Integral Equations of the Second Kind

First let us consider the homogeneous Wiener-Hopf integral equation of the second kind,

$$f(t) = \int_0^\infty k(t - t_0) f(t_0)\, dt_0$$

We assume that for some real number c the function $k(t) \exp(-ct)$ is absolutely integrable over the real axis. This implies that the Fourier transform,

$$K(\zeta) = \frac{1}{\sqrt{(2\pi)}} \int_{-\infty}^{\infty} k(t) e^{i\zeta t}\, dt$$

exists on the path $(-\infty + ic, \infty + ic)$ and, according to the Riemann-Lebesgue lemma, the function $K(\zeta)$ vanishes when ζ tends to infinity on this path. We assume, moreover, that $K(\zeta)$ is Hölder continuous and that the function $1 - \sqrt{(2\pi)} K(\zeta)$ is nonvanishing on any finite subinterval of the path $(-\infty + ic, \infty + ic)$.

We are interested in the solutions $f(t)$ of the integral equation which have the property that the function $f(t) \exp(-ct)$ is absolutely integrable on the real axis. To find these solutions we define two functions $f_+(t)$ and $f_-(t)$ such that

$$\begin{aligned} f_+(t) &= f(t) && \text{when } t \text{ is positive,} \\ &= 0 && \text{when } t \text{ is negative} \\ f_-(t) &= -f(t) && \text{when } t \text{ is negative,} \\ &= 0 && \text{when } t \text{ is positive.} \end{aligned}$$

The unilateral Fourier transforms of these functions,

$$F_+(\lambda) = \frac{1}{\sqrt{(2\pi)}} \int_0^{\infty} f_+(t) e^{i\lambda t}\, dt$$

and

$$F_-(\lambda) = \frac{1}{\sqrt{(2\pi)}} \int_{-\infty}^{0} f_-(t) e^{i\lambda t}\, dt$$

are analytic in the upper half plane $I(\lambda) > c$ and in the lower half plane $I(\lambda) < c$ respectively, and the integrals of both transforms converge on the path $(-\infty + ic, \infty + ic)$. Furthermore, it can be shown by the Riemann-Lebesgue lemma that $F_+(\lambda)$ vanishes when λ tends to infinity in the upper half plane $I(\lambda) > c$ and that $F_-(\lambda)$ vanishes when λ tends to infinity in the lower half plane $I(\lambda) < c$.

The three transforms $F_+(\zeta)$, $F_-(\zeta)$, and $K(\zeta)$ have the line of convergence $(-\infty + ic, \infty + ic)$ in common and Fourier transformation of the integral equation yields the functional equation,

$$F_+(\zeta)[1 - \sqrt{(2\pi)}K(\zeta)] - F_-(\zeta) = 0$$

In order to make our notation conform to the notations in the other sections of this chapter, we introduce the quantities, $F^L(\zeta) = F_+(\zeta)$, $F^R(\zeta) = F_-(\zeta)$, and $A(\zeta) = 1/[1 - \sqrt{(2\pi)}K(\zeta)]$, and we may write, therefore,

$$F^L(\zeta) = A(\zeta) F^R(\zeta)$$

The conclusions arrived at above imply that the solution of the integral equation can be obtained by the Fourier inversion of a function $F(\lambda)$ which is sectionally analytic in the plane cut along the boundary line $(-\infty + ic, \infty + ic)$. On this boundary line the left and right boundary values, $F^L(\zeta)$ and $F^R(\zeta)$, of this function $F(\lambda)$ satisfy the boundary condition,

$$F^L(\zeta) = A(\zeta) F^R(\zeta) \tag{4.25}$$

In other words, we have reduced the integral equation to a homogeneous Hilbert problem with boundary condition (4.25). Since $F(\lambda)$ is a Fourier transform, the solution of our Hilbert problem must vanish at infinity.

Let p be the index of the homogeneous Hilbert problem,

$$\begin{aligned} p &= \frac{1}{2\pi i}\left[\lim_{R(\zeta)\to+\infty} \log A(\zeta) - \lim_{R(\zeta)\to-\infty} \log A(\zeta)\right] \\ &= \frac{1}{2\pi i}\left[\lim_{R(\zeta)\to-\infty} \log[1 - \sqrt{(2\pi)}K(\zeta)] - \lim_{R(\zeta)\to+\infty} \log[1 - \sqrt{(2\pi)}K(\zeta)]\right] \end{aligned}$$

We introduce the convergence factor,

$$(\zeta - b)^p/(\zeta - a)^p$$

and define the function,

$$A_0(\zeta) = A(\zeta)(\zeta - b)^p/(\zeta - a)^p$$

where a and b are arbitrary complex numbers in the upper half plane $I(\lambda) > c$ and the lower half plane $I(\lambda) < c$ respectively.

According to the discussion presented in Section 4.13, we can now draw the following conclusions.

The solution $F(\lambda)$ of the homogeneous Hilbert problem with boundary condition (4.25) is the sectionally analytic function,

$$F(\lambda) = P(\lambda)G(\lambda)$$

with boundary line $(-\infty + ic, \infty + ic)$. The function $P(\lambda)$ is a polynomial and $G(\lambda)$, the fundamental solution of the homogeneous Hilbert problem, has the representation,

$$G^L(\lambda) = \frac{\exp\left(\dfrac{1}{2\pi i}\displaystyle\int_{-\infty+ic}^{\infty+ic} \frac{\log[(\zeta - b)^p/\{(\zeta - a)^p[1 - \sqrt{(2\pi)}K(\zeta)]\}]}{(\zeta - \lambda)}\, d\zeta\right)}{(\lambda - b)^p}$$

when λ is located in the upper half plane $I(\lambda) > c$, and the representation,

$$G^R(\lambda) = \frac{\exp\left(\dfrac{1}{2\pi i}\displaystyle\int_{-\infty+ic}^{\infty+ic} \frac{\log[(\zeta - b)^p/\{(\zeta - a)^p[1 - \sqrt{(2\pi)}K(\zeta)]\}]}{(\zeta - \lambda)}\, d\zeta\right)}{(\lambda - a)^p}$$

when λ is located in the lower half plane $I(\lambda) < c$.

The sectionally analytic function $F(\lambda)$ must vanish at infinity and the polynomial $P(\lambda)$ must be chosen accordingly. Hence, if the index p of the homogeneous Hilbert problem is negative or zero, there are no solutions $F(\lambda)$ which vanish at infinity with the exception of the trivial solution. Furthermore, if the index p is positive, we must choose a polynomial of degree m such that m is smaller than p.

Once we have found the function $F(\lambda)$, the solution of the integral equation can be obtained by Fourier inversion.

B. Inhomogeneous Wiener-Hopf Integral Equations of the Second Kind

Let us assume that the kernel and the solution of the inhomogeneous Wiener-Hopf integral equation of the second kind,

$$f(t) = h(t) + \int_0^\infty k(t - t_0)f(t_0)\, dt_0$$

satisfy the conditions imposed on the kernel and the solution of the homogeneous equation considered in the preceding section. Furthermore, we assume that the function $h(t)$ is defined and known for positive values of t but can be extended to the negative t axis by the definitions,

$$\begin{aligned} h_+(t) &= h(t) && \text{when } t \text{ is positive} \\ &= 0 && \text{when } t \text{ is negative} \\ h_-(t) &= h(t) && \text{when } t \text{ is negative} \\ &= 0 && \text{when } t \text{ is positive} \end{aligned}$$

where $h_-(t)$ is some unknown function which needs to be determined.

Assuming moreover that the function $h(t)e^{-ct}$ is absolutely integrable over the real axis, the Fourier transforms $H_+(\lambda)$ and $H_-(\lambda)$ share a half plane of analyticity with the functions $F_+(\lambda)$ and $F_-(\lambda)$ respectively and a line of convergence $(-\infty + ic, \infty + ic)$ with the transforms $F_+(\zeta)$, $F_-(\zeta)$, and $K(\zeta)$.

Fourier transforming the inhomogeneous integral equation, we obtain the functional equation,

$$F^L(\zeta) = A(\zeta)[F^R(\zeta) + H^R(\zeta)] + A(\zeta)H^L(\zeta) \tag{4.26}$$

where $H^L(\zeta) = H_+(\zeta)$, $H^R(\zeta) = H_-(\zeta)$. Consequently, we have reduced the inhomogeneous integral equation of the Wiener-Hopf type to an inhomogeneous Hilbert problem with boundary condition (4.26).

To obtain the sectionally analytic function $F(\lambda)$ with boundary values $F^L(\zeta)$ and $F^R(\zeta) + H^R(\zeta)$ on the line $(-\infty + ic, \infty + ic)$, we factor the function $A(\zeta)$ by means of the fundamental solution of the corresponding homogeneous problem,

$$A(\zeta) = 1/[1 - \sqrt{(2\pi)}K(\zeta)] = G^L(\zeta)/G^R(\zeta)$$

Substituting this expression for $A(\zeta)$ into the boundary condition (4.26), we find the Plemelj boundary condition,

$$\frac{F^L(\zeta)}{G^L(\zeta)} - \frac{F^R(\zeta) + H^R(\zeta)}{G^R(\zeta)} = \frac{H^L(\zeta)}{G^R(\zeta)}$$

The Plemelj boundary value problem can easily be solved by the methods outlined in Section 4.7 and yields in turn the following solution of the inhomogeneous Hilbert problem,

$$F(\lambda) = \frac{G(\lambda)}{2\pi i}\int_{-\infty+ic}^{\infty+ic} \frac{H^L(\zeta)}{G^R(\zeta)}\frac{d\zeta}{\zeta - \lambda} + P(\lambda)G(\lambda)$$

The nature of the polynomial $P(\lambda)$ is determined by the condition that the Fourier transform $F(\lambda)$ must vanish at infinity and we refer to Section 4.10 for a discussion of its relation to the index p of the homogeneous problem.

The solution of the inhomogeneous Wiener-Hopf equation can be found by Fourier inversion of the function $F(\lambda)$.

C. Wiener-Hopf Integral Equations of the First Kind

We now turn our attention to the solution of the Wiener-Hopf integral equation of the first kind,

$$h(t) = \int_0^\infty k(t - t_0)f(t_0)\,dt_0$$

where $h(t)$ is a known function which is defined for all positive values of t. This equation can be solved by defining a continuation of the integral equation on the negative t-axis by the relations,

$$\begin{aligned} h_+(t) &= h(t) &&\text{when } t \text{ is positive} \\ &= 0 &&\text{when } t \text{ is negative} \\ h_-(t) &= h(t) &&\text{when } t \text{ is negative} \\ &= 0 &&\text{when } t \text{ is positive} \end{aligned}$$

This introduces another unknown function $h_-(t)$ which we need to determine. Let us assume that the solution and kernel of the integral equation satisfy the conditions imposed on these functions in the preceding parts of this section. Furthermore, let $h(t)\exp(-ct)$ be absolutely integrable over the real axis. The Fourier transforms $H_+(\lambda)$ and $H_-(\lambda)$ are analytic in the upper half plane $I(\lambda) > c$ and the lower half plane $I(\lambda) < c$ respectively and share the line of convergence $(-\infty + ic, \infty + ic)$ with the functions $F_+(\lambda)$ and $K(\zeta)$. Consequently, Fourier transformation of the integral equation yields the following relation,

$$F^L(\zeta) = A(\zeta)F^R(\zeta) + A(\zeta)H^L(\zeta) \tag{4.27}$$

between the functions $F^L(\zeta) = F_+(\zeta)$, $F^R(\zeta) = H_-(\zeta)$, $H^L(\zeta) = H_+(\zeta)$, and $A(\zeta) = 1/[\sqrt{(2\pi)}K(\zeta)]$.

We have transformed therefore the integral equation into a homogeneous Hilbert problem with boundary condition (4.27). This problem, however, cannot be solved by a straightforward substitution of the relevant functions into the appropriate equations of Section 4.13. The function $K(\zeta)$ is the Fourier transform of the kernel $k(t)$ and vanishes when ζ tends to infinity. This implies that the integral,

$$\frac{1}{2\pi i}\int_{-\infty+ic}^{\infty+ic} \frac{\log A(\zeta)}{\zeta - \lambda}\,d\zeta$$

which is used to construct the fundamental solution, does not exist.

To eliminate this difficulty we introduce a new function $N(\zeta)$ such that the function $A(\zeta)N(\zeta)$ tends to one when ζ tends to infinity. We assume moreover that the function $N(\zeta)$ can be factored, $N(\zeta) = N^L(\zeta)/N^R(\zeta)$, so that $N^L(\zeta)$ and $N^R(\zeta)$ are nonvanishing on any finite section of the path $(-\infty + ic, \infty + ic)$ and are of algebraic growth at infinity. Subsequently we find the fundamental solution of the homogeneous Hilbert problem with the boundary condition,

$$M^L(\zeta) = A(\zeta)N(\zeta)M^R(\zeta)$$

The index of this problem is zero and we obtain the solution,

$$M(\lambda) = \exp\left(\frac{1}{2\pi i}\int_{-\infty+ic}^{\infty+ic} \frac{\log\,[A(\zeta)N(\zeta)]}{\zeta - \lambda}\,d\zeta\right)$$

Since we may write

$$G^L(\zeta) = \frac{M^L(\zeta)}{N^L(\zeta)} = A(\zeta)\frac{M^R(\zeta)}{N^R(\zeta)} = A(\zeta)G^R(\zeta)$$

this implies that $G(\lambda) = M(\lambda)/N(\lambda)$ is a solution of the homogeneous Hilbert problem with boundary condition, $G^L(\zeta) = A(\zeta)G^R(\zeta)$. The solution of the original inhomogeneous Hilbert problem with boundary condition (4.27) can now be obtained by substitution of the factorization $A(\zeta) = G^L(\zeta)/G^R(\zeta)$ into this boundary equation. This yields the Plemelj boundary value condition,

$$\frac{F^L(\zeta)}{G^L(\zeta)} - \frac{F^R(\zeta)}{G^R(\zeta)} = \frac{H^L(\zeta)}{G^R(\zeta)}$$

and the following solution of the inhomogeneous Hilbert problem,

$$F(\lambda) = \frac{G(\lambda)}{2\pi i}\int_{-\infty+ic}^{\infty+ic} \frac{H^L(\zeta)}{G^R(\zeta)}\frac{d\zeta}{\zeta - \lambda} + P(\lambda)G(\lambda)$$

This solution may also be written

$$F(\lambda) = \frac{M(\lambda)}{N(\lambda)}\frac{1}{2\pi i}\int_{-\infty+ic}^{\infty+ic} \frac{H^L(\zeta)N^R(\zeta)}{M^R(\zeta)}\frac{d\zeta}{\zeta - \lambda} + P(\lambda)M(\lambda)/N(\lambda)$$

Again we need to be careful that the definition of the appropriate functions above is commensurate with the condition that the Fourier transform $F(\lambda)$ must vanish at infinity. Such conditions have been specified for the polynomial $P(\lambda)$ in Section 4.10. However, the growth properties of the function $N(\lambda)$ should be taken into account in defining the appropriate $P(\lambda)$ in the representation for $F(\lambda)$ above.

Inversion of the Fourier transform $F(\lambda)$ yields the solution of the Wiener-Hopf equation of the first kind.

4.15 GREEN'S FUNCTIONS AND THE SOLUTION OF BOUNDARY VALUE PROBLEMS IN ELECTROSTATICS

In the final section of this chapter we shall illustrate the applicability of the theory discussed in the foregoing sections at the hand of a potential problem taken from the field of electrostatics. In that section we shall ask ourselves the following question: What is the potential inside a grounded, semi-infinite, hollow cylinder when we place a point charge of unit magnitude on the axis of this cylinder? In more mathematical terms: How can we construct a Green's function $G(\mathbf{r}\,|\,\mathbf{r}_0)$ which is the solution of the partial differential equation,

$$\nabla^2 G(\mathbf{r}\,|\,\mathbf{r}_0) = -\delta(\mathbf{r} - \mathbf{r}_0)/\varepsilon_0$$

subject to certain appropriate boundary conditions?

To familiarize ourselves with the kind of analysis that goes with the solution of such a problem, we shall first discuss, in more general terms, the solution by means of Green's functions of boundary value problems in electrostatics.

To determine the electrostatic field $\mathbf{E}(\mathbf{r})$, generated by a charge distribution with density $\rho(\mathbf{r})$ inside a region D with boundary surface S, we have to find a solution of the Maxwell equations,

$$\nabla \times \mathbf{E}(\mathbf{r}) = 0$$

and

$$\nabla \cdot \mathbf{E}(\mathbf{r}) = \rho(\mathbf{r})/\varepsilon_0$$

where ε_0 denotes the permittivity of empty space.

From the first equation we may infer that the electrostatic field vector is irrotational and can be written as the gradient of the electrostatic potential,

$$\mathbf{E}(\mathbf{r}) = -\nabla\phi(\mathbf{r})$$

If we now substitute this expression for the field vector into the second field equation we obtain the well-known equation of Poisson for the electrostatic potential,

$$\nabla^2\phi(\mathbf{r}) = -\rho(\mathbf{r})/\varepsilon_0$$

Furthermore, the electrostatic field is solenoidal,

$$\nabla \cdot \mathbf{E}(\mathbf{r}) = 0$$

in the regions of space which are devoid of charge. Hence, in those regions, the electrostatic potential can be found as the solution of Laplace's equation,

$$\nabla^2\phi(\mathbf{r}) = 0$$

The electrostatic potential therefore is the solution of the inhomogeneous Poisson equation in the regions of space containing charges and it is the solution of the homogeneous Laplace equation in the regions devoid of charges. The solutions of these equations can be determined uniquely, provided appropriate conditions are imposed on these solutions on the boundaries of the regions. Appropriate conditions are either Dirichlet type or Neumann type boundary conditions. This means that either the potential or its normal derivative is specified on the boundary of the region in which we want to solve the field equations. To describe a particular boundary value problem more specifically, one uses the following terminology.

A boundary value problem is called an interior Dirichlet problem if the region in which we want to solve the field equations is finite and bounded by surfaces on which the potential is specified. The boundary value problem is called an exterior Dirichlet problem if this region extends to infinity and is bounded internally by a closed surface on which the potential is specified.

In a similar manner we can now define an interior and an exterior Neumann problem by specifying on the boundary the normal derivative of the potential instead of the potential.

Boundary value problems of the type described above can be solved most easily by means of a Green's function technique. In this context a Green's function $G(\mathbf{r}\,|\,\mathbf{r}_0)$ is the electrostatic potential measured at an observation point $\mathbf{r}$ due to a point charge of unit magnitude at the source point $\mathbf{r}_0$. In other words, the Green's function is the solution of Poisson's equation,

$$\nabla^2 G(\mathbf{r}\,|\,\mathbf{r}_0) = -\delta(\mathbf{r} - \mathbf{r}_0)/\varepsilon_0$$

subject to certain appropriately chosen boundary conditions. The importance of the Green's function technique in the solution of the boundary value problems of mathematical physics is greatly enhanced by the fact that these boundary conditions can be chosen to facilitate the construction of the Green's function and thus the subsequent solution of the boundary value problem under consideration. The following boundary conditions are usually imposed on the solution of the Green's function equation.

1. The homogeneous Dirichlet condition,

$$G(\mathbf{r}^s\,|\,\mathbf{r}_0) = 0$$

where $\mathbf{r}^s$ denotes a point on the boundary. This type of boundary condition is most useful for the solution of exterior or interior Dirichlet problems.

2. The homogeneous Neumann condition,

$$\mathbf{n} \cdot \nabla G(\mathbf{r}^s\,|\,\mathbf{r}_0) = 0$$

where $\mathbf{n}$ denotes the outwardly directed unit normal to the boundary surface.

This boundary condition is imposed on a Green's function which is used in the solution of an exterior Neumann problem.

3. The inhomogeneous Neumann condition,

$$\mathbf{n} \cdot \nabla G(\mathbf{r}^s \,|\, \mathbf{r}_0) = -1/A\varepsilon_0$$

where A is the surface area of the boundary S. Physical consistency requires that we impose this condition on the Green's function for an interior Neumann problem. For integrating the equation,

$$\nabla^2 G(\mathbf{r} \,|\, \mathbf{r}_0) = -\delta(\mathbf{r} - \mathbf{r}_0)/\varepsilon_0$$

over the space enclosed by the surface S, we find

$$\int_V \nabla^2 G(\mathbf{r} \,|\, \mathbf{r}_0)\, d\mathbf{r} = -\frac{1}{\varepsilon_0} \int_V \delta(\mathbf{r} - \mathbf{r}_0)\, d\mathbf{r} = -1/\varepsilon_0 \tag{4.28}$$

Now let us apply the divergence theorem,

$$\int_V \nabla \cdot \mathbf{F}(\mathbf{r})\, d\mathbf{r} = \oint_S \mathbf{F}(\mathbf{r}^s) \cdot \mathbf{n}\, d\mathbf{r}^s$$

to the vector,

$$\mathbf{F}(\mathbf{r}) = \nabla G(\mathbf{r} \,|\, \mathbf{r}_0)$$

Substitution of the boundary condition imposed on the interior Neumann problem yields

$$\int_V \nabla \cdot \nabla G(\mathbf{r} \,|\, \mathbf{r}_0)\, d\mathbf{r} = \oint_S \nabla G(\mathbf{r}^s \,|\, \mathbf{r}_0) \cdot \mathbf{n}\, d\mathbf{r}^s = -1/\varepsilon_0$$

which agrees with the result (4.28) .

The solutions of the boundary value problems of electrostatics can be obtained in a formal manner with the assistance of the Green's functions defined above. For, multiplying the Poisson equation,

$$\nabla_0{}^2 \phi(\mathbf{r}_0) = -\rho(\mathbf{r}_0)/\varepsilon_0$$

by the Green's function $G(\mathbf{r} \,|\, \mathbf{r}_0)$ and multiplying the Green's function equation,

$$\nabla_0{}^2 G(\mathbf{r} \,|\, \mathbf{r}_0) = -\delta(\mathbf{r} - \mathbf{r}_0)/\varepsilon_0$$

by the potential function $\phi(\mathbf{r}_0)$ and subtracting the results, we obtain the equation,

$$G(\mathbf{r} \,|\, \mathbf{r}_0)\nabla_0{}^2\phi(\mathbf{r}_0) - \phi(\mathbf{r}_0)\nabla_0{}^2 G(\mathbf{r} \,|\, \mathbf{r}_0) = [\delta(\mathbf{r} - \mathbf{r}_0)\phi(\mathbf{r}_0) - G(\mathbf{r} \,|\, \mathbf{r}_0)\rho(\mathbf{r}_0)]/\varepsilon_0$$

Integrating both sides of this equation over the space enclosed by the boundary surface S, we find

$$\int_V [G(\mathbf{r}\,|\,\mathbf{r}_0)\nabla_0{}^2\phi(\mathbf{r}_0) - \phi(\mathbf{r}_0)\nabla_0{}^2 G(\mathbf{r}\,|\,\mathbf{r}_0)]\, d\mathbf{r}_0$$

$$= \phi(\mathbf{r})/\varepsilon_0 - \frac{1}{\varepsilon_0}\int_V G(\mathbf{r}\,|\,\mathbf{r}_0)\rho(\mathbf{r}_0)\, d\mathbf{r}_0$$

However, according to Green's theorem,

$$\int_V [G(\mathbf{r}\,|\,\mathbf{r}_0)\nabla_0{}^2\phi(\mathbf{r}_0) - \phi(\mathbf{r}_0)\nabla_0{}^2 G(\mathbf{r}\,|\,\mathbf{r}_0)]\, d\mathbf{r}_0$$

$$= \oint_S \left[G(\mathbf{r}\,|\,\mathbf{r}_0{}^s)\frac{\partial\phi(\mathbf{r}_0{}^s)}{\partial n_0} - \phi(\mathbf{r}_0{}^s)\frac{\partial G(\mathbf{r}\,|\,\mathbf{r}_0{}^s)}{\partial n_0}\right] d\mathbf{r}_0{}^s$$

Consequently, we obtain the following integral representation,

$$\phi(\mathbf{r}) = \int_V G(\mathbf{r}\,|\,\mathbf{r}_0)\rho(\mathbf{r}_0)\, d\mathbf{r}_0 + \varepsilon_0 \oint_S \left[G(\mathbf{r}\,|\,\mathbf{r}_0{}^s)\frac{\partial\phi(\mathbf{r}_0{}^s)}{\partial n_0} - \phi(\mathbf{r}_0{}^s)\frac{\partial G(\mathbf{r}\,|\,\mathbf{r}_0{}^s)}{\partial n_0}\right] d\mathbf{r}_0{}^s$$

for the potential at an interior point.

This representation enables us to compute the potential at an interior point $\mathbf{r}$ by integrating the product of the density of the charge distribution $\rho(\mathbf{r})$ and the Green's function $G(\mathbf{r}\,|\,\mathbf{r}_0)$ over the space enclosed by S and adding to this integral a surface integral which has in its integrand the boundary values of the potential and the Green's function.

We should observe that to evaluate the surface integral we have to know both the potential and its normal derivative on the boundary. However, to determine uniquely the solution of a boundary value problem, which involves either Poisson's equation or Laplace's equation, it is sufficient to know either the behavior of the potential or its normal derivative on the boundary. Hence, we are free to simplify the integrand of the surface integral by either eliminating the term containing the potential or the term containing the normal derivative of the potential on the boundary. In other words, for a Dirichlet problem, in which the value of the potential is given on the boundary, we want to get rid of the surface integral over the normal derivative of the potential, whereas for a Neumann problem we want to keep this integral and get rid of the surface integral over the potential. We can accomplish this by using an appropriate Green's function. For example, to solve a Dirichlet problem we construct a Green's function which satisfies a homogeneous Dirichlet condition,

$$G(\mathbf{r}\,|\,\mathbf{r}_0{}^s) = 0$$

In this case we obtain the integral representation,

$$\phi(\mathbf{r}) = \int_V G(\mathbf{r} \,|\, \mathbf{r}_0)\rho(\mathbf{r}_0)\, d\mathbf{r}_0 - \varepsilon_0 \oint_S \frac{\partial G(\mathbf{r} \,|\, \mathbf{r}_0{}^s)}{\partial n_0} \phi(\mathbf{r}_0{}^s)\, d\mathbf{r}_0^s$$

for the potential at an interior point. Hence, if the potential vanishes on the boundary, this representation yields the solution,

$$\phi(\mathbf{r}) = \int_V G(\mathbf{r} \,|\, \mathbf{r}_0)\rho(\mathbf{r}_0)\, d\mathbf{r}_0$$

of the Dirichlet problem.

On the other hand, if the density of the charge distribution vanishes, we obtain the integral representation,

$$\phi(\mathbf{r}) = -\varepsilon_0 \oint_S \frac{\partial G(\mathbf{r} \,|\, \mathbf{r}_0{}^s)}{\partial n_0} \phi(\mathbf{r}_0{}^s)\, d\mathbf{r}_0{}^s$$

for the solution of the Dirichlet problem.

From these considerations we may infer that the solution of a particular boundary value problem in electrostatics can be represented by a volume or a surface integral, once the appropriate Green's function has been found. Consequently, we have switched the emphasis from finding the solution of the boundary value problem to that of finding the appropriate Green's function for that particular boundary value problem.

For some problems the Green's function can easily be found. For example, the infinite free space Green's function takes the form,

$$G(\mathbf{r} \,|\, \mathbf{r}_0) = \frac{1}{4\pi\varepsilon_0} \frac{1}{|\mathbf{r} - \mathbf{r}_0|}$$

This function represents the potential measured at the observation point $\mathbf{r}$ due to a point charge of unit magnitude at the source point $\mathbf{r}_0$. This can be verified as follows. The Green's function vanishes as $1/\mathbf{r}$ when $|\mathbf{r}|$ tends to infinity and has therefore the correct behavior at large distances from the source. Furthermore, since $G(\mathbf{r} \,|\, \mathbf{r}_0)$ tends to infinity as $1/|\mathbf{r} - \mathbf{r}_0|$ when the observation point moves to the source point, the Green's function has the correct singular behavior close to the source point. Finally, the Green's function satisfies Poisson's equation,

$$\nabla^2 G(\mathbf{r} \,|\, \mathbf{r}_0) = -\delta(\mathbf{r} - \mathbf{r}_0)/\varepsilon_0$$

For, considering a region not containing the source point, we find

$$\nabla^2 G(\mathbf{r} \,|\, \mathbf{r}_0) = \nabla^2 \left[\frac{1}{4\pi\varepsilon_0} \frac{1}{|\mathbf{r} - \mathbf{r}_0|} \right] = \frac{1}{4\pi\varepsilon_0} \frac{1}{R^2} \frac{d}{dR} \left(R^2 \frac{d}{dR} \frac{1}{R} \right) = 0$$

which checks with the fact that in a source-free region the Green's function should satisfy Laplace's equation. At the source point, the function $G(\mathbf{r} \mid \mathbf{r}_0)$ is singular and in order to determine the strength of this singularity and verify the solution in a region which contains the source point we construct a sphere of radius a about this point. Integrating the Green's function equation,

$$\nabla^2 G(\mathbf{r} \mid \mathbf{r}_0) = -\delta(\mathbf{r} - \mathbf{r}_0)/\varepsilon_0$$

over the region bounded by the sphere, we find

$$\int_V \nabla^2 G(\mathbf{r} \mid \mathbf{r}_0)\, d\mathbf{r} = -\frac{1}{\varepsilon_0} \int_V \delta(\mathbf{r} - \mathbf{r}_0)\, d\mathbf{r} = -1/\varepsilon_0 \tag{4.29}$$

On the other hand, utilizing the explicit expression for the Green's function and applying the divergence theorem, we obtain

$$\int_V \nabla^2 G(\mathbf{r} \mid \mathbf{r}_0)\, d\mathbf{r} = \frac{1}{4\pi\varepsilon_0} \int_V \nabla \cdot \nabla\left(\frac{1}{|\mathbf{r} - \mathbf{r}_0|}\right) d\mathbf{r}$$

$$= \frac{1}{4\pi\varepsilon_0} \oint_S \mathbf{n} \cdot \nabla\left(\frac{1}{|\mathbf{r} - \mathbf{r}_0|}\right) d\mathbf{r}^s = \frac{1}{\varepsilon_0} \int_0^a R^2 \frac{\partial}{\partial R}\left(\frac{1}{R}\right) dR = -1/\varepsilon_0$$

and this result agrees with the result (4.29) obtained above.

The well-known integral representation for the electrostatic potential,

$$\phi(\mathbf{r}) = \frac{1}{4\pi\varepsilon_0} \int_V \frac{\rho(\mathbf{r}_0)}{|\mathbf{r} - \mathbf{r}_0|}\, d\mathbf{r}_0$$

$$+ \frac{1}{4\pi} \oint_S \left[\frac{1}{|\mathbf{r} - \mathbf{r}_0|} \frac{\partial \phi(\mathbf{r}_0{}^s)}{\partial n_0} - \phi(\mathbf{r}_0{}^s) \frac{\partial}{\partial n_0}\left(\frac{1}{|\mathbf{r} - \mathbf{r}_0{}^s|}\right)\right] d\mathbf{r}_0{}^s$$

can now be obtained immediately by substitution of the infinite free space Green's function into the expression,

$$\phi(\mathbf{r}) = \int_V G(\mathbf{r} \mid \mathbf{r}_0)\rho(\mathbf{r}_0)\, d\mathbf{r}_0 + \varepsilon_0 \oint_S \left[G(\mathbf{r} \mid \mathbf{r}_0{}^s) \frac{\partial \phi(\mathbf{r}_0{}^s)}{\partial n_0} - \phi(\mathbf{r}_0{}^s) \frac{\partial G(\mathbf{r} \mid \mathbf{r}_0{}^s)}{\partial n_0}\right] d\mathbf{r}_0{}^s$$

where V is the volume of an arbitrary region containing the source point $\mathbf{r}_0$ and S is the boundary surface of that region. This representation can be used to evaluate the potential at any point in space. The volume integral,

$$\frac{1}{4\pi\varepsilon_0} \int_V \frac{\rho(\mathbf{r}_0)}{|\mathbf{r} - \mathbf{r}_0|}\, d\mathbf{r}_0$$

represents the contribution to the potential of the free charge distribution inside the closed region. The contribution to the potential of the charge distribution outside this region is accounted for by the surface integral,

$$\frac{1}{4\pi}\oint_S \left[\frac{1}{|\mathbf{r}-\mathbf{r}_0{}^s|}\frac{\partial\phi(\mathbf{r}_0{}^s)}{\partial n_0} - \phi(\mathbf{r}_0{}^s)\frac{\partial}{\partial n_0}\left(\frac{1}{|\mathbf{r}-\mathbf{r}_0{}^s|}\right)\right] d\mathbf{r}_0{}^s$$

As is well known,

$$\omega(\mathbf{r}^s) = \varepsilon_0 \frac{\partial\phi(\mathbf{r}^s)}{\partial n}$$

represents the density of the surface charge distribution on the surface S, and the first term of the surface integral,

$$\frac{1}{4\pi}\oint_S \frac{1}{|\mathbf{r}-\mathbf{r}_0{}^s|}\frac{\partial\phi(\mathbf{r}_0{}^s)}{\partial n_0}\, d\mathbf{r}_0{}^s = \frac{1}{4\pi\varepsilon_0}\oint_S \frac{\omega(\mathbf{r}_0{}^s)}{|\mathbf{r}-\mathbf{r}_0{}^s|}\, d\mathbf{r}_0{}^s$$

can be interpreted therefore as the potential of a single layer. Similarly, the second term of the surface integral,

$$\frac{1}{4\pi}\oint_S \phi(\mathbf{r}_0{}^s)\frac{\partial}{\partial n_0}\left(\frac{1}{|\mathbf{r}-\mathbf{r}_0{}^s|}\right) d\mathbf{r}_0{}^s$$

can be interpreted as the potential of a double layer with density,

$$\tau(\mathbf{r}^s) = \varepsilon_0\,\phi(\mathbf{r}^s)$$

To construct the Green's function for a finite region, one makes use of the Green's function for the infinite region, $1/(4\pi\varepsilon_0|\mathbf{r}-\mathbf{r}_0|)$. This function has the correct singular behavior close to the source point. The Green's function for a finite region can now be obtained by adding to the infinite free space Green's function a solution $F(\mathbf{r}\,|\,\mathbf{r}_0)$ of the source-free equation,

$$\nabla^2 F(\mathbf{r}\,|\,\mathbf{r}_0) = 0$$

This solution of Laplace's equation is chosen such that the function,

$$F(\mathbf{r}\,|\,\mathbf{r}_0) + \frac{1}{4\pi\varepsilon_0}\frac{1}{|\mathbf{r}-\mathbf{r}_0|}$$

satisfies the boundary condition imposed on the Green's function for the finite region. It can now easily be verified that the function,

$$G(\mathbf{r}\,|\,\mathbf{r}_0) = F(\mathbf{r}\,|\,\mathbf{r}_0) + \frac{1}{4\pi\varepsilon_0}\frac{1}{|\mathbf{r}-\mathbf{r}_0|}$$

satisfies Poisson's equation,

$$\nabla^2 G(\mathbf{r}\,|\,\mathbf{r}_0) = -\delta(\mathbf{r}-\mathbf{r}_0)/\varepsilon_0$$

Hence, since it also satisfies the boundary conditions and has the correct singular behavior at the source point, it must be the Green's function we set out to construct.

In the next section we shall present a more complicated example of the construction of a Green's function.

4.16 GREEN'S FUNCTION FOR A POINT CHARGE ON THE AXIS OF AN INFINITE CYLINDER

The construction of a Green's function is not always an easy task and one must sometimes choose a somewhat roundabout method to obtain the required result. In this section we shall derive an expression for the Green's function for a boundary value problem that is closely related to the boundary value problem we referred to in the first few paragraphs of the preceding section.

Here we shall answer the question: "What is the potential at a point $\mathbf{r} = (r, \theta, z)$ inside a grounded, infinitely long, hollow cylinder of radius a when we place a point charge of unit magnitude on the axis of this cylinder?"

We shall choose the axis of symmetry of the cylinder to coincide with the z-axis of our coordinate system and we shall place the point charge at the origin of this system. The potential for this configuration is axially symmetric and the Green's function $G(r, z \mid 0, 0)$ is the solution of Poisson's equation in cylindrical coordinates,

$$\frac{1}{r}\frac{\partial}{\partial r}\left(r\frac{\partial G(r, z \mid 0, 0)}{\partial r}\right) + \frac{\partial^2 G(r, z \mid 0, 0)}{\partial z^2} = -\delta(r)\,\delta(z)/(2\pi\varepsilon_0\, r) \tag{4.30}$$

subject to the boundary condition,

$$G(a, z \mid 0, 0) = 0$$

and the condition that $G(r, z \mid 0, 0)$ is bounded when z tends to plus or minus infinity inside the cylinder.

Choosing a function $\phi(r, z)$ which is regular at all points inside the cylinder and satisfies the source-free equation,

$$\frac{1}{r}\frac{\partial}{\partial r}\left(r\frac{\partial \phi(r, z)}{\partial r}\right) + \frac{\partial^2 \phi(r, z)}{\partial z^2} = 0 \tag{4.31}$$

we obtain, by means of equations (4.30) and (4.31) and in the manner discussed in the preceding section, the following integral representation for the function $\phi(r, z)$ at the origin,

$$\phi(0, 0) = -2\pi\varepsilon_0\, a \int_{-\infty}^{\infty} \phi(a, z)\frac{\partial G(a, z)}{\partial r}\, dz$$

This representation leads, by simple substitution, to an integral equation,

$$\phi(0, 0) = -2\pi a \int_{-\infty}^{\infty} \phi(a, z)\omega(a, z)\, dz$$

for the density of the induced charge distribution on the surface of the cylinder,

$$\omega(a, z) = \varepsilon_0 \frac{\partial G(a, z)}{\partial r}$$

Within the wide limits outlined above, the function $\phi(r, z)$ can be chosen arbitrarily and we shall make the convenient choice,

$$\phi(r, z) = I_0(\zeta r)e^{i\zeta z}$$

where the parameter ζ can take values on the whole real axis. This choice yields the following integral equation with a Fourier kernel for the density of the induced charge distribution on the cylinder,

$$\int_{-\infty}^{\infty} \omega(a, z)e^{i\zeta z}\, dz = -\frac{1}{2\pi a I_0(\zeta a)}$$

Inverting the Fourier integral, we obtain immediately an expression for this quantity,

$$\omega(a, z) = -\frac{1}{4\pi^2 a}\int_{-\infty}^{\infty} \frac{e^{-i\zeta z}}{I_0(\zeta a)}\, d\zeta$$

Having found the density of the induced charge distribution, we can find the Green's function by adding to the potential,

$$\frac{1}{4\pi\varepsilon_0}\frac{1}{\sqrt{(z^2 + r^2)}}$$

which is due to the point charge at the origin, the potential,

$$\frac{1}{4\pi\varepsilon_0}\oint_S \frac{\omega(a, z_0)}{|\mathbf{r} - \mathbf{r}_0^{\,s}|}\, d\mathbf{r}_0^{\,s}$$

which is due to the induced charge distribution on the cylinder, where $\mathbf{r}_0^{\,s} = (a, \theta, z)$ denotes a point on the cylinder. In this manner we obtain the following integral representation for the Green's function,

$$\begin{aligned} G(r, z \,|\, 0, 0) &= \frac{1}{4\pi\varepsilon_0}\frac{1}{\sqrt{(z^2 + r^2)}} - \frac{1}{16\pi^3\varepsilon_0\, a}\oint_S \frac{d\mathbf{r}_0^{\,s}}{|\mathbf{r} - \mathbf{r}_0^{\,s}|}\int_{-\infty}^{\infty} \frac{e^{-i\zeta z_0}}{I_0(\zeta a)}\, d\zeta \\ &= G_0(r, z \,|\, 0, 0) + G_b(r, z \,|\, 0, 0) \end{aligned}$$

To evaluate the function $G_b(r, z \mid 0, 0)$ at an arbitrary point inside the cylinder we shall make use of a well-known technique of great utility in the investigation of axially symmetric boundary value problems. Following this technique, we first evaluate the function $G_b(r, z \mid 0, 0)$ for the special case when the observation point is located on the axis of the cylinder and subsequently find a general expression for this function by evaluating the integral,

$$G_b(r, z \mid 0, 0) = \frac{1}{2\pi} \int_0^{2\pi} G_b(0, z + ir\cos\theta \mid 0, 0)\, d\theta$$

Placing the observation point on the axis of the cylinder, we find

$$\begin{aligned} G_b(0, z \mid 0, 0) &= \frac{a}{2\varepsilon_0} \int_{-\infty}^{\infty} \frac{\omega(a, z_0)\, dz_0}{\sqrt{[(z_0 - z)^2 + a^2]}} \\ &= -\frac{1}{8\pi^2\varepsilon_0} \int_{-\infty}^{\infty} \frac{du}{\sqrt{(u^2 + a^2)}} \int_{-\infty}^{\infty} \frac{e^{-i\zeta(u+z)}}{I_0(\zeta a)}\, d\zeta \\ &= -\frac{1}{2\pi^2\varepsilon_0} \int_0^{\infty} \frac{\cos\zeta z}{I_0(\zeta a)}\, d\zeta \int_0^{\infty} \frac{\cos\zeta u}{\sqrt{(u^2 + a^2)}}\, du \end{aligned}$$

By substitution of the well-known integral representation,

$$K_0(\zeta a) = \int_0^{\infty} \frac{\cos\zeta u}{\sqrt{(u^2 + a^2)}}\, du$$

for the zeroth order modified Bessel function, this expression for the function $G_b(0, z \mid 0, 0)$ can be reduced to the simple relation,

$$G_b(0, z \mid 0, 0) = -\frac{1}{2\pi^2\varepsilon_0} \int_0^{\infty} \frac{K_0(\zeta a)}{I_0(\zeta a)} \cos\zeta z\, d\zeta$$

For an arbitrary point inside the cylinder, the function is now defined by the integral,

$$G_b(r, z \mid 0, 0) = \frac{1}{2\pi} \int_0^{2\pi} G_b(0, z + ir\cos\theta \mid 0, 0)\, d\theta$$

and evaluating this integral we obtain,

$$\begin{aligned} G_b(r, z \mid 0, 0) &= -\frac{1}{4\pi^3\varepsilon_0} \int_0^{2\pi} d\theta \int_0^{\infty} \frac{K_0(\zeta a)}{I_0(\zeta a)} \cos\zeta(z + ir\cos\theta)\, d\zeta \\ &= -\frac{1}{2\pi^3\varepsilon_0} \int_0^{\infty} \frac{K_0(\zeta a)}{I_0(\zeta a)} \cos\zeta z\, d\zeta \int_{-1}^{1} \frac{\cosh(\zeta r u)}{\sqrt{(1 - u^2)}}\, du \\ &= -\frac{1}{2\pi^2\varepsilon_0} \int_0^{\infty} \frac{K_0(\zeta a) I_0(\zeta r)}{I_0(\zeta a)} \cos\zeta z\, d\zeta \end{aligned}$$

where we made use of the integral representation,

$$\pi I_0(\zeta r) = \int_{-1}^{1} \frac{\cosh(\zeta r u)}{\sqrt{(1-u^2)}}\, du$$

Finally, we obtain therefore the following integral representation for the Green's function,

$$G(r, z \mid 0, 0) = \frac{1}{4\pi\varepsilon_0\sqrt{(z^2+r^2)}} - \frac{1}{2\pi^2\varepsilon_0}\int_0^\infty \frac{K_0(\zeta a)I_0(\zeta r)}{I_0(\zeta a)} \cos \zeta z \, d\zeta$$

By construction, this function satisfies the partial differential equation,

$$\nabla^2 G(r, z \mid 0, 0) = -\delta(r)\delta(z)/(2\pi\varepsilon_0 r)$$

in cylindrical coordinates. It has the correct singular behavior at the origin and it is bounded when z tends to plus or minus infinity inside the cylinder. Finally we must verify that it also satisfies the boundary condition,

$$G(a, z \mid 0, 0) = 0$$

This condition can be verified as follows. On the surface of the cylinder

$$G(a, z \mid 0, 0) = \frac{1}{4\pi\varepsilon_0\sqrt{(z^2+a^2)}} - \frac{1}{2\pi^2\varepsilon_0}\int_0^\infty K_0(\zeta a) \cos \zeta z \, d\zeta$$

However, evaluating the Fourier cosine transform for $K_0(a\zeta)$, we find

$$\int_0^\infty K_0(\zeta a) \cos \zeta z \, d\zeta = \frac{\pi}{2\sqrt{(z^2+a^2)}}$$

and we may conclude therefore that the Green's function vanishes on the boundary.

4.17 GREEN'S FUNCTION FOR A POINT CHARGE ON THE AXIS OF A SEMI-INFINITE CYLINDER

In 1956, Lauwerier presented in a prizewinning paper the answer to the following question: "What is the potential inside a grounded, semi-infinite, hollow cylinder when a point charge of unit magnitude is placed on the axis of the cylinder?" He obtained his answer by means of the function-theoretic techniques discussed in this chapter. In the preceding section we considered a closely related problem, namely the problem to determine the potential inside an infinite cylinder. The solution of that problem however is simple in comparison with that of the semi-infinite cylinder. For, due to the infinite z-interval, the density of the induced charge distribution on the infinite cylinder satisfies a Fourier integral equation. This density therefore can be obtained by inverting a Fourier transform and, once the density of the induced surface charge is known, the Green's function or potential of a unit charge can be found by integration. It is more difficult however to solve the same problem for a semi-infinite cylinder. For, in this case, the density of the induced surface charge distribution satisfies a Wiener-Hopf integral equation of the first kind instead of a Fourier integral equation. Moreover, the solution of the Wiener-Hopf integral equation cannot be obtained by the method discussed in Chapter III. The appropriate Fourier transforms do not have a strip of analyticity in common but share a line of convergence. A satisfactory solution can be obtained however by means of the techniques outlined in this chapter.

Let us assume that the generators of a semi-infinite cylinder of radius a are parallel to the positive z-axis and that a positive charge of unit magnitude is placed on the axis at the point $z = b$ as shown in Figure IV-9. Due

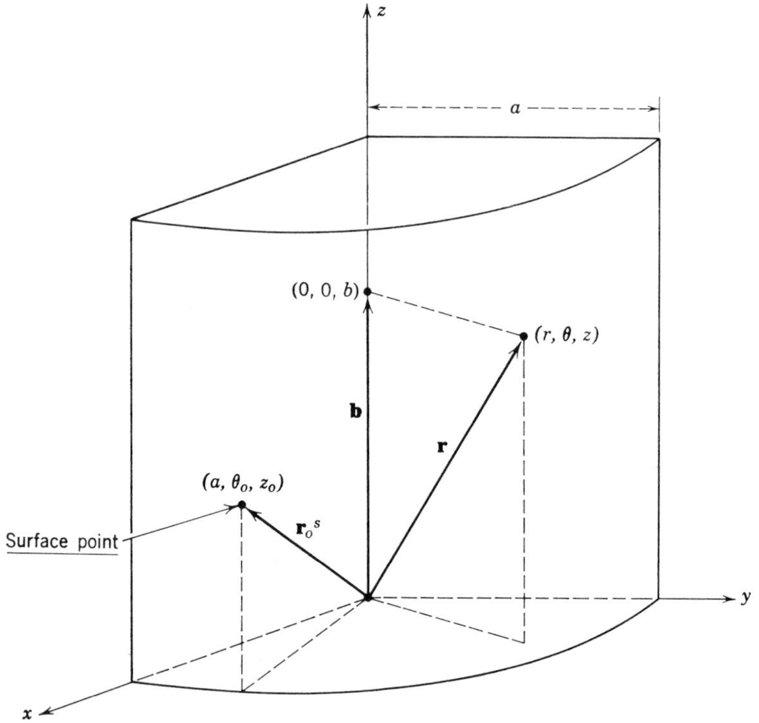

Figure IV-9

to this point charge, a surface charge of density $\omega(z, b)$ is induced on the surface of the cylinder, and, for the axially symmetric configuration considered, the surface charge density is a function of the coordinate z and the location $\mathbf{b} = (0, 0, b)$ of the point charge only. The potential or Green's function $G(r, z \mid 0, b)$ at a point $\mathbf{r} = (r, \theta, z)$ inside the cylinder is the sum of the potential,

$$\frac{1}{4\pi\varepsilon_0}\frac{1}{|\mathbf{r} - \mathbf{b}|} = \frac{1}{4\pi\varepsilon_0}\frac{1}{\sqrt{[(z-b)^2 + r^2]}}$$

due to the point charge at the point $\mathbf{b}$ and the potential,

$$\frac{1}{4\pi\varepsilon_0}\oint_S \frac{\omega(z_0, b)}{|\mathbf{r} - \mathbf{r}_0{}^s|}\,d\mathbf{r}_0{}^s = \frac{1}{4\pi\varepsilon_0}\int_0^\infty\int_0^{2\pi} \frac{a\omega(z_0, b)\,dz_0\,d\theta_0}{\sqrt{[(z-z_0)^2 + r^2 + a^2 + 2ar\cos\theta_0]}}$$

due to the induced charge distribution on the surface of the cylinder. Adding these two terms, we obtain the following integral representation for the Green's function,

$$G(r, z \mid 0, b) = \frac{1}{4\pi\varepsilon_0\sqrt{[(z-b)^2 + r^2]}} + \frac{1}{4\pi\varepsilon_0}\int_0^\infty\int_0^{2\pi} \frac{a\omega(z_0, b)\,dz_0\,d\theta_0}{\sqrt{[(z-z_0)^2 + r^2 + a^2 + 2ar\cos\theta_0]}}$$

The unknown quantity in this expression is the density of the induced charge distribution $\omega(z_0, b)$. To determine this quantity our next step is to reduce the representation of the Green's function to a Wiener-Hopf integral equation for the density $\omega(z_0, b)$. We can accomplish this by making use of the condition that the potential must vanish on the surface of the grounded conductor,

$$G(a, z \mid 0, b) = \frac{1}{4\pi\varepsilon_0\sqrt{[(z-b)^2 + a^2]}} + \frac{1}{4\pi\varepsilon_0}\int_0^\infty\int_0^{2\pi} \frac{a\omega(z_0, b)\,dz_0\,d\theta_0}{\sqrt{[(z-z_0)^2 + 2a^2 + 2a^2\cos\theta_0]}} = 0$$

The double integral can be reduced to a single integral by integrating over the angle θ_0,

$$n(a, z - z_0) = \int_0^{2\pi} \frac{a\,d\theta_0}{\sqrt{[(z-z_0)^2 + 2a^2 + 2a^2\cos\theta_0]}} = \frac{4a}{\sqrt{[(z-z_0)^2 + 4a^2]}}\,K\!\left(\frac{2a}{\sqrt{[(z-z_0)^2 + 4a^2]}}\right)$$

where $K(m)$ denotes the complete elliptic integral of the first kind,

$$K(m) = \int_0^{\pi/2} \frac{d\theta}{\sqrt{(1 - m^2\sin^2\theta)}}$$

Introducing moreover the function,

$$h(z) = -\frac{1}{\sqrt{[(z-b)^2 + a^2]}}$$

we obtain the following Wiener-Hopf integral equation of the first kind for the surface charge density $\omega(z, b)$,

$$\int_0^\infty n(a, z - z_0)\omega(z_0, b)\, dz_0 = h(z)$$

This equation holds for positive values of z only and to solve it by the methods outlined in Section 4.14 we must introduce another unknown function $f(z)$ which is defined by the relation,

$$\int_0^\infty n(a, z - z_0)\omega(z_0, b)\, dz_0 = f(z)$$

for all negative values of z.

The kernel of the Wiener-Hopf equation has a logarithmic singularity at the origin. This can be verified as follows. The complete elliptic integral $K(m)$ can be expressed in terms of the hypergeometric function $F(a, b|c|z)$,

$$K(m) = \frac{\pi}{2} F\left(\frac{1}{2}, \frac{1}{2} |1| \, m^2\right)$$

Furthermore,

$$\frac{\pi}{2} F\left(\frac{1}{2}, \frac{1}{2} |1| \, m^2\right) = -\frac{1}{2} F\left(\frac{1}{2}, \frac{1}{2} |1| \, 1 - m^2\right) \log(1 - m^2)$$
$$+ \sum_{p=0}^{\infty} \frac{(\frac{1}{2})_p (\frac{1}{2})_p}{p!\, p!} [\Psi(p+1) - \Psi(p + 1/2)](1 - m^2)^p$$

where Ψ denotes the logarithmic derivative of the gamma function. This implies that the kernel may be written

$$n(a, z) = \frac{4a}{\sqrt{(z^2 + 4a^2)}} \left[-\frac{1}{2} F\left(\frac{1}{2}, \frac{1}{2} |1| \, \frac{z^2}{z^2 + 4a^2}\right) \log\left(\frac{z^2}{z^2 + 4a^2}\right) \right.$$
$$\left. + \sum_{p=0}^{\infty} \frac{(\frac{1}{2})_p (\frac{1}{2})_p}{p!\, p!} [\Psi(p+1) - \Psi(p + 1/2)] \left(\frac{z^2}{z^2 + 4a^2}\right)^p \right]$$

which plainly shows the character of the singularity of the kernel at the origin. For the Fourier transform of the kernel we obtain

$$N(\zeta) = \frac{1}{\sqrt{(2\pi)}} \int_{-\infty}^{\infty} e^{i\zeta z} n(a, z)\, dz$$
$$= \frac{8a}{\sqrt{(2\pi)}} \int_0^\infty \frac{K[2a/\sqrt{(z^2 + 4a^2)}]}{\sqrt{(z^2 + 4a^2)}} \cos \zeta z\, dz = \frac{4\pi a}{\sqrt{(2\pi)}} I_0(a\zeta) K_0(a|\zeta|)$$

where I_0 and K_0 denote the modified Bessel functions of zeroth order.

Due to the behavior of $K_0(a|\zeta|)$ for small values of ζ,

$$K_0(a|\zeta|) \sim - \log a|\zeta|$$

the function $N(\zeta)$ has also a logarithmic singularity at the origin.

The unilateral Fourier transforms,

$$F_+(\lambda) = \frac{1}{\sqrt{(2\pi)}} \int_0^\infty \omega(z, b) e^{i\lambda z} \, dz$$

$$F_-(\lambda) = \frac{1}{\sqrt{(2\pi)}} \int_{-\infty}^0 f(z) e^{i\lambda z} \, dz$$

$$H_+(\lambda) = \frac{1}{\sqrt{(2\pi)}} \int_0^\infty h(z) e^{i\lambda z} \, dz$$

and the Fourier transform of the kernel are all defined and convergent on the real axis. In consequence of the properties of the functions $\omega(z, b)$, $f(z)$, and $h(z)$, the functions $F_+(\lambda)$ and $H_+(\lambda)$ are analytic in the upper half of the λ-plane and the function $F_-(\lambda)$ is analytic in the lower half of that plane. Hence, the transforms $F_+(\lambda)$, $F_-(\lambda)$, $H_+(\lambda)$, and $N(\lambda)$ have a line of convergence in common which cannot be extended to a strip in the complex plane. The techniques outlined in Chapter III cannot be used therefore but the solution of the Wiener-Hopf integral equations must be obtained by the methods of this chapter.

Introducing the functions $F^L(\zeta) = F_+(\zeta)$, $F^R(\zeta) = F_-(\zeta)$, and

$$A(\zeta) = \frac{1}{\sqrt{(2\pi)} N(\zeta)} = \frac{1}{4\pi a I_0(a\zeta) K_0(a\,|\zeta|)}$$

we obtain, by Fourier transformation of the integral equation, the following functional equation defined on the real axis,

$$F^L(\zeta) = A(\zeta) F^R(\zeta) + A(\zeta) H^L(\zeta) \tag{4.32}$$

Hence, the solution of the integral equation is reduced to an inhomogeneous Hilbert problem, namely, to construct a function $F(\lambda)$ which is sectionally analytic in the plane cut along the real axis and has boundary values $F^L(\zeta)$ and $F^R(\zeta)$ which satisfy the boundary condition (4.32) Furthermore, since $F^L(\zeta)$ and $F^R(\zeta)$ are Fourier transforms, $F(\lambda)$ must vanish at infinity.

Anticipating the solution of the corresponding homogeneous Hilbert problem with boundary condition,

$$G^L(\zeta) = A(\zeta) G^R(\zeta)$$

which will be verified at the end of this section, we write

$$A(\zeta) = G^L(\zeta)/G^R(\zeta)$$

By means of this expression for $A(\zeta)$ and the boundary condition for the inhomogeneous problem, we obtain a Plemelj boundary value problem with boundary condition,

$$\frac{F^L(\zeta)}{G^L(\zeta)} - \frac{F^R(\zeta)}{G^R(\zeta)} = \frac{H^L(\zeta)}{G^R(\zeta)}$$

The solution of this Plemelj problem leads to the following integral representation for the Fourier transform of the density of the induced charge distribution on the surface of the cylinder,

$$F^L(\lambda) = \frac{G^L(\lambda)}{2\pi i} \int_{-\infty}^{\infty} \frac{H^L(\zeta)}{G^R(\zeta)} \frac{d\zeta}{\zeta - \lambda}$$

Furthermore, since the function $H^R(\lambda)/G^R(\lambda)$ is analytic in the lower half plane and is continuous in this half plane including the real axis,

$$\frac{1}{2\pi i} \int_{-\infty}^{\infty} \frac{H^R(\zeta)}{G^R(\zeta)} \frac{d\zeta}{\zeta - \lambda} = 0$$

when λ is a point in the upper half plane. Hence, we may also write

$$F^L(\lambda) = \frac{G^L(\lambda)}{2\pi i} \int_{-\infty}^{\infty} \frac{H(\zeta)}{G^R(\zeta)} \frac{d\zeta}{\zeta - \lambda}$$

where $H(\zeta)$ is the Fourier transform,

$$\begin{aligned} H(\zeta) &= \frac{1}{\sqrt{(2\pi)}} \int_{-\infty}^{\infty} h(z) e^{i\zeta z}\, dz \\ &= -\frac{2}{\sqrt{(2\pi)}} \int_0^{\infty} \frac{\cos \zeta z}{\sqrt{[(z-b)^2 + a^2]}}\, dz = -\frac{2e^{ib\zeta}}{\sqrt{(2\pi)}} K_0(a\,|\zeta|) \end{aligned}$$

The density of the induced charge distribution can now be found by evaluating the inverse Fourier transform,

$$\begin{aligned} \omega(z, b) &= \frac{1}{\sqrt{(2\pi)}} \int_{-\infty + ic}^{\infty + ic} F^L(\alpha) e^{-i\alpha z}\, d\alpha \\ &= \frac{1}{\sqrt{(2\pi)}} \int_{-\infty + ic}^{\infty + ic} e^{-i\alpha z}\, d\alpha \frac{G^L(\alpha)}{2\pi i} \int_{-\infty}^{\infty} \frac{H(\zeta)}{G^R(\zeta)} \frac{d\zeta}{\zeta - \alpha} \end{aligned}$$

where c is an appropriately chosen positive constant. In view of the fact that

$$H(\zeta) = -\frac{2e^{i\zeta b}}{\sqrt{(2\pi)}} K_0(a\,|\zeta|)$$

and

$$A(\zeta) = \frac{G^L(\zeta)}{G^R(\zeta)} = \frac{1}{4\pi a I_0(a\zeta) K_0(a|\zeta|)}$$

we may also write

$$\omega(z, b) = -\frac{1}{8\pi^3 ai} \int_{-\infty+ic}^{\infty+ic} G^L(\alpha) e^{-i\alpha z}\, d\alpha \int_{-\infty}^{\infty} \frac{e^{i\zeta b}}{G^L(\zeta) I_0(a\zeta)} \frac{d\zeta}{\zeta - \alpha}$$

We now deform the Fourier inversion contour into the contour Γ shown in Figure IV-10. In terms of this contour we obtain

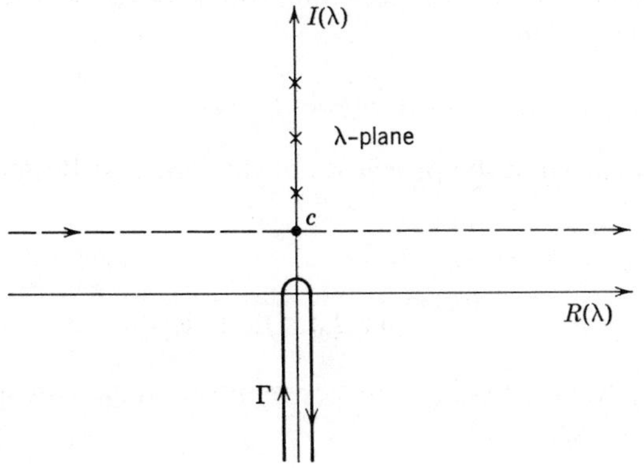

Figure IV-10

$$\omega(z, b) = -\frac{1}{4\pi^2 a} \int_{-\infty}^{\infty} \frac{e^{i\zeta(b-z)}}{I_0(a\zeta)} d\zeta$$
$$- \frac{1}{8\pi^3 ia} \int_{\Gamma} G^L(\alpha) e^{-i\alpha z}\, d\alpha \int_{-\infty}^{\infty} \frac{e^{i\zeta b}}{G^L(\zeta) I_0(a\zeta)} \frac{d\zeta}{\zeta - \alpha}$$
$$= \omega_\infty(a, z) - \frac{1}{8\pi^3 ia} \int_{\Gamma} G^L(\alpha) e^{-i\alpha z}\, d\alpha \int_{-\infty}^{\infty} \frac{e^{i\zeta b}}{G^L(\zeta) I_0(a\zeta)} \frac{d\zeta}{\zeta - \alpha}$$

where, according to the discussion in the preceding section, the quantity,

$$\omega_\infty(z, b) = -\frac{1}{4\pi^2 a} \int_{-\infty}^{\infty} \frac{e^{i\zeta(b-z)}}{I_0(a\zeta)} d\zeta$$

is the density of the surface charge induced on the surface of an infinite cylinder when a positive point charge of unit magnitude is placed at the point $z = b$ on the axis of this cylinder. This quantity appears in the expression for $\omega(z, b)$ because we cross a pole at $\lambda = \zeta$ when we deform the contour.

The Green's function or potential of a unit charge on the axis of a semi-infinite cylinder has therefore the integral representation,

$$G(r, z \mid 0, b) = \frac{1}{4\pi\varepsilon_0\sqrt{[(z-b)^2 + r^2]}} + \frac{1}{4\pi\varepsilon_0}\int_0^\infty n(r, z - z_0)\omega(z_0, b)\, dz_0$$

where the density $\omega(z, b)$ is presented above. Simplified expressions for the Green's function can be found at certain special locations of the observation and source points. However, this is not the place to go deeply into such asymptotic evaluations and we must refer the reader to the literature for a more detailed discussion.

We conclude this section by presenting the solution of the homogeneous Hilbert problem,

$$G^L(\zeta) = A(\zeta)G^R(\zeta) \tag{4.33}$$

Because of the asymptotic properties of the modified Bessel functions, the function

$$A(\zeta) = \frac{1}{4\pi a I_0(a\zeta)K_0(a\,|\zeta|)}$$

tends to infinity when ζ tends to plus or minus infinity. This implies that the integral,

$$\frac{1}{2\pi i}\int_{-\infty}^{\infty} \frac{\log A(\zeta)}{\zeta - \lambda}\, d\zeta$$

does not exist and that we cannot obtain the solution of the homogeneous Hilbert problem in the conventional manner. As explained in Section 4.14, to circumvent this difficulty we introduce a function $N(\zeta)$ such that $N(\zeta)A(\zeta)$ tends to one when $|\zeta|$ tends to infinity. The following function,

$$N(\zeta) = \frac{2\pi}{|\zeta|}$$

serves this purpose. We now consider the homogeneous Hilbert problem with the boundary condition,

$$M^L(\zeta) = B(\zeta)M^R(\zeta)$$

where $B(\zeta) = A(\zeta)N(\zeta)$. The function $B(\zeta)$ tends to one when $|\zeta|$ becomes large and we immediately find the following fundamental solution of the auxiliary Hilbert problem,

$$M(\lambda) = \exp\left(\frac{1}{2\pi i}\int_{-\infty}^{\infty}\frac{\log B(\zeta)}{\zeta - \lambda}\,d\zeta\right)$$

The boundary values of this sectionally analytic function can be obtained from the Plemelj formulas,

$$\lim_{\varepsilon\to 0}\frac{1}{2\pi i}\int_{-\infty}^{\infty}\frac{\log B(\alpha)}{\alpha - \zeta \mp \varepsilon}\,d\alpha = \pm\frac{1}{2}\log B(\zeta) + \frac{1}{2\pi i}\int_{-\infty}^{\infty}\frac{\log B(\alpha)}{\alpha - \zeta}\,d\alpha$$

With the help of these formulas we obtain the representations,

$$M^L(\zeta) = \frac{\exp\left(\pi i/4 + \dfrac{1}{2\pi i}\displaystyle\int_{-\infty}^{\infty}\frac{\log B(\alpha)}{\alpha - \zeta}\,d\alpha\right)}{\sqrt{[2a\,|\zeta|\,I_0(a\zeta)K_0(a\,|\zeta|)]}}$$

for the left boundary value, and

$$M^R(\zeta) = \sqrt{[2a\,|\zeta|\,I_0(a\zeta)K_0(a\,|\zeta|)]}\,\exp\left(\pi i/4 + \frac{1}{2\pi i}\int_{-\infty}^{\infty}\frac{\log B(\alpha)}{\alpha - \zeta}\,d\alpha\right)$$

for the right boundary value of $M(\lambda)$ on the real axis, where the constant factor $\exp(\pi i/4)$ has been introduced to obtain more symmetric expressions for $G^L(\zeta)$ and $G^R(\zeta)$ below.

We now factor the function $N(\zeta)$ in the following manner,

$$N(\zeta) = \frac{N^L(\zeta)}{N^R(\zeta)} = \frac{\sqrt{(2\pi/\zeta)}}{\sqrt{(\zeta/2\pi)}}$$

Consequently, since

$$\frac{M^L(\zeta)}{N^L(\zeta)} = G^L(\zeta) = A(\zeta)G^R(\zeta) = A(\zeta)\,\frac{M^R(\zeta)}{N^R(\zeta)}$$

we find the following integral representations for the solution of the homogeneous Hilbert problem,

$$G^L(\lambda) = \sqrt{\left(\frac{\lambda}{2\pi}\right)}\exp\left(\frac{\pi i}{4} + \frac{1}{2\pi i}\int_{-\infty}^{\infty}\frac{\log B(\zeta)}{\zeta - \lambda}\,d\zeta\right)$$

when λ is a point in the upper half plane, and

$$G^R(\lambda) = \sqrt{\left(\frac{2\pi}{\lambda}\right)}\exp\left(\frac{\pi i}{4} + \frac{1}{2\pi i}\int_{-\infty}^{\infty}\frac{\log B(\zeta)}{\zeta - \lambda}\,d\zeta\right)$$

when λ is a point in the lower half plane. The corresponding boundary values of these functions take the form,

$$G^L(\zeta) = \frac{\exp\left[\dfrac{\pi i}{4}\,\varepsilon(\zeta) + \dfrac{1}{2\pi i}\displaystyle\int_{-\infty}^{\infty} \dfrac{\log B(\alpha)}{\alpha - \zeta}\,d\alpha\right]}{\sqrt{[4\pi a I_0(a\zeta)K_0(a\,|\zeta|)]}}$$

and

$$G^R(\zeta) = \sqrt{[4\pi a I_0(a\zeta)K_0(a\,|\zeta|)]}\,\exp\left[\frac{\pi i}{4}\,\varepsilon(\zeta) + \frac{1}{2\pi i}\int_{-\infty}^{\infty} \frac{\log B(\alpha)}{\alpha - \zeta}\,d\alpha\right]$$

where $\varepsilon(\zeta)$ denotes the sign function introduced in Section 1.1.

CHAPTER V

DISTRIBUTIONS

5.0 INTRODUCTION

In the mathematical description of physical phenomena one frequently encounters operational quantities, such as the delta functions of Dirac and Heisenberg, which have meaning only when they, or products of these quantities with sufficiently smooth ordinary functions, occur under an integral sign. Devoid of meaning when interpreted as point functions defined on an interval, but having a well-defined meaning when interpreted as functionals on a space of sufficiently smooth ordinary functions, they sometimes appear to be the more natural mathematical entities for the description of physical phenomena. For example, in the physics of continua the parameters describing the fields on a macroscopic scale are appropriately taken space and time averages of the corresponding microscopic quantities. The charge density in an electric material, for instance, can be defined as an average,

$$\langle \rho(\mathbf{x}) \rangle = \frac{\displaystyle\int_R \rho_a(\mathbf{x}_0)\, d\mathbf{x}_0}{\displaystyle\int_R d\mathbf{x}_0}$$

where $\rho_a(\mathbf{x}_0)$ denotes the charge density on an atomic level at the space-time point $\mathbf{x}_0$ and $\int_R d\mathbf{x}_0$ is the extent of a space-time region surrounding the space-time point $\mathbf{x}$. Averaging procedures of this type result in smoothly varying field quantities such as the electric and magnetic field intensities of electromagnetic theory and the concentrations and particle currents of diffusion phenomena. The regions in space and the intervals in time over which the averages are taken are sufficiently large so that the fluctuations in space and time of the microscopic parameters can be ignored but are still sufficiently small so that these space-time regions can be treated as infinitesimally small on a microscopic scale. However, because they contain many particles and extend over many characteristic periods, they have a definite physical extension and are by no means points in the geometrical sense. Thus, the charge density $\langle \rho(\mathbf{x}) \rangle$ defined above is not the actual charge at the point $\mathbf{x}$ but is an average over all the microscopic charge concentrations in a small space-time region surrounding the point. It is therefore not a point function in the ordinary sense of the word but a quantity which can be derived from ordinary point functions by a suitable operation on these functions, in this case by an averaging procedure.

Other examples of mathematical entities of this type arise in quantum field theory. According to Bohr and Rosenfeld, the physically significant parameters, i.e., the physical quantities which can be observed, are appropriate space-time averages of the field and not the field itself. To circumvent the difficulties, such as infinite self-energy, inherent in an individual particle description, the physical model introduced in this case is that of a test body which is sufficiently heavy so that it contains many elementary particles but is still sufficiently light so that it is subject to the laws of quantum mechanics. The observable quantities T are now space-time averages of the form,

$$\langle T, f \rangle = \int_R T(x) f(x) \, dx$$

where $f(x)$ denotes a sufficiently smooth "weighting" or "testing" function which is of finite extent in space and time.

Mathematical entities of this type, i.e., continuous linear functionals on spaces of testing functions $f(x)$, have been the subject of intensive investigation during the last few decades. First recognized by Dirac as important new mathematical entities with widespread physical application, their theory was rigorously founded by Schwartz. In the next few sections we shall present the basic theory of these concepts according to the latter investigator avoiding where possible the abstract mathematical setting.

5.1 DEFINITION OF A SCHWARTZ DISTRIBUTION

The delta function of Dirac is probably the best-known and most useful example of an operational quantity that cannot be defined as a function in the ordinary sense but must be defined by its action on other functions. This quantity was introduced by Dirac to obtain a precise notation for dealing with certain kinds of infinities. Dirac defined the delta function as a function which vanishes for all nonzero values of its argument in such a way that the integral of this function over an arbitrary interval containing the origin is equal to unity.

$$\delta(x) = 0 \qquad \text{for all nonzero values of } x$$

and

$$\int_{-\infty}^{\infty} \delta(x)\,dx = 1$$

An approximation to the delta function is the step function which vanishes outside some small interval Δ about the origin and is equal to $1/\Delta$ on this interval. The delta function is obtained from this step function in the limit as Δ tends to zero.

Dirac observed that a pathological function such as the delta function cannot be defined as a point function in the usual sense of the definition of a function of a real variable but is a more general type of function. He states, "The delta function is not a quantity which can be generally used in mathematical analysis like an ordinary function but its use must be confined to certain simple types of expression for which it is obvious that no inconsistency can arise." Such use is exemplified by the well-known sifting property of the delta function,

$$\int_{-\infty}^{\infty} \delta(x)f(x)\,dx = f(0)$$

or the more general form,

$$\int_{-\infty}^{\infty} \delta(x-a)f(x)\,dx = f(a)$$

where $f(x)$ is a function which can be defined in the ordinary sense.

These expressions show that although no proper meaning can be attached to the quantity $\delta(x)$ as a point function of the real variable x it can be defined as an operational quantity through its action on other functions. Thus, an equation involving delta functions such as

$$\delta(ax) = \frac{1}{|a|}\,\delta(x)$$

has no meaning by itself but must be read as follows: The integral of the product of $\delta(ax)$ with a sufficiently smooth point function $f(x)$ over an interval containing the origin is equal to the integral of the product of $\delta(x)/|a|$ and the function $f(x)$ over a similar interval. For

$$\int_{-\infty}^{\infty} \delta(ax)f(x)\,dx = \frac{1}{|a|}\int_{-\infty}^{\infty} \delta(x)f(x/a)\,dx = \frac{1}{|a|}\,f(0) = \frac{1}{|a|}\int_{-\infty}^{\infty} \delta(x)f(x)\,dx$$

More generally, we can show that if $g(x)$ is a monotonic function of x which vanishes at the point $x = a$, then

$$\delta(g(x)) = \frac{\delta(x - a)}{|g'(a)|}$$

For let us make the substitutions $y = g(x)$ and $h(y) = f(x)/|g'(x)|$ in the integral,

$$\int_{-\infty}^{\infty} \delta(g(x))f(x)\, dx$$

Then

$$\int_{-\infty}^{\infty} \delta(g(x))f(x)\, dx = \int_{-\infty}^{\infty} \delta(y)h(y)\, dy = h(0) = \frac{f(a)}{|g'(a)|}$$

$$= \int_{-\infty}^{\infty} \frac{\delta(x - a)}{|g'(a)|} f(x)\, dx$$

which proves the identity above. In a similar manner we can show that if $g(x)$ is a monotonic function of x which vanishes at the points $x = a_0$, $a_1, \ldots, a_M$, then

$$\delta(g(x)) = \sum_{m=0}^{M} \frac{\delta(x - a_m)}{|g'(a_m)|}$$

Thus it is clear that the operational quantity $\delta(x)$ and the equations involving this quantity are meaningful only if they are first multiplied by some sufficiently smooth function and then integrated from minus infinity to plus infinity. In other words, only under an integral sign do these relations attain significance. These considerations now lead to a mathematically rigorous definition of a delta function as a continuous linear functional on a space of sufficiently smooth functions.

The concept of a continuous linear functional on a space of functions can most easily be introduced in analogy with the concept of an ordinary point function on an interval of the real axis. A real or complex valued function of a real variable assigns to each point of a given interval of the real axis a point on the real axis or in a region of the complex plane. In other words, a function is a mapping of a subset of the one-dimensional space of real numbers onto a subset of the space of all real or complex numbers. Analogously, we may define a functional as a mapping of a given space of functions into a subset of the space of all real or complex numbers. A functional, therefore, is a well-defined operation by which we assign a real or complex number to each and every function of a given space of functions. Thus, the space of functions on which a functional is defined is the counterpart of the interval of real numbers on which a function is defined, and the functional operation by which we assign to each function of a given space of functions a real or complex number is the counterpart of the function operation by which we assign to each number of a given interval a real or complex number. For example, if X denotes the space of all functions $f(x)$ which are integrable over the interval (a, b), then the integral,

$$\int_a^b f(x)\,dx$$

defines a functional on the space X. For the integral denotes a well-defined operation by which we assign to each and every function $f(x)$ of the space X a real or complex number, namely, the value of the definite integral of the function $f(x)$ over the interval (a, b). Similarly, if Y denotes the space of all functions $e^{i\lambda x}/\sqrt{(2\pi)}$ and $g(x)$ is absolutely integrable over the x axis, then the Fourier integral,

$$G(\lambda) = \frac{1}{\sqrt{(2\pi)}} \int_{-\infty}^{\infty} g(x) e^{i\lambda x}\,dx$$

defines a functional on the space Y. For this integral assigns to each function $e^{i\lambda x}/\sqrt{(2\pi)}$ of the space Y a real or complex number $G(\lambda)$.

The suitability of a particular function of a real variable for describing physical phenomena depends on its analytic properties such as continuity, differentiability, integrability, etc. These properties in turn depend on the structure or topology of the underlying real number system. For instance, to define the concept of continuity of a function of a real variable we must first investigate the convergence of sequences of real numbers. Analogously, the analytic properties of functionals must be defined with respect to the convergence properties of sequences of functions $f(x)$ of the underlying function space. In other words, they must be defined with respect to the structure or topology of that function space.

To construct a functional, therefore, we need the following mathematical entities. First, we need a space of functions, $f(x)$, defined on the real axis and having certain desirable analytical properties, such as continuity, differentiability, growth, decay, etc., in common. Of course many different spaces can be considered. For our purposes however we shall exclusively make use of so-called linear spaces. Such spaces have the property that a linear combination of the functions of a space is also a function of that space. Second, we need a definition of convergence for sequences of functions of the space. Third, we need an operation by which we can assign to each and every function of the space a real or complex number.

To be more specific, let $f(x)$ be a continuous real or complex valued function of the real variable x, which vanishes identically outside some finite interval of the x axis. If, in addition, $f(x)$ has continuous derivatives of all orders, then $f(x)$ will be called a testing function. For example, the function,

$$[\theta(x+a)-\theta(x-a)]\exp\left\{\frac{1}{x^2-a^2}\right\}$$

where $\theta(x)$ denotes the unit step function, is a testing function and many other examples of testing functions can be constructed. The space D of all functions $f(x)$ which have the properties delineated above is called the space of testing functions $f(x)$. D is a linear space, because any linear combination,

$$a_0 f_0(x) + a_1 f_1(x) + \cdots + a_m f_m(x)$$

of testing functions $f_0(x), f_1(x), \ldots, f_m(x)$, where $a_0, a_1, \ldots, a_m$ are arbitrary real or complex numbers, is also a testing function.

Having defined the testing functions $f(x)$ and the space D of all such functions, we must now introduce a definition of convergence of sequences of testing functions. The definition of convergence most suited for our purposes states that a sequence of testing functions $f_m(x)$ converges to zero if all the functions of the sequence vanish outside the same finite interval of the real axis and if the functions $f_m(x)$ and all their derivatives converge to zero uniformly as m tends to infinity. This implies that a sequence of testing functions $f_m(x)$ converges to a testing function $f(x)$ if the sequence of testing functions $f_m(x) - f(x)$ converges to zero in the sense of convergence defined above.

We now have a linear function space D of sufficient structure so that we can define functionals of far-reaching applicability on it. The functionals we shall consider are, first of all, so-called linear functionals. A linear functional T on the space D is an operation by which we assign to each and every testing function $f(x)$ of the space D a real or complex number, which we shall denote by (T, f), such that

$$(T, af_1 + bf_2) = a(T, f_1) + b(T, f_2)$$

and

$$(T, af) = a(T, f)$$

where f_1 and f_2 are arbitrary functions of the space D and a and b are arbitrary real or complex numbers. We shall require moreover that our linear functionals be continuous. This means that the sequence of numbers (T, f_m) converges to the number (T, f) if the sequence of testing functions f_m converges to the testing function f in the sense of convergence defined above,

$$\lim_{m\to\infty}(T, f_m) = \left(T, \lim_{m\to\infty} f_m\right)$$

A continuous linear functional on the space of testing function D is called a distribution. Distributions on the space D are the prototype of the continuous linear functionals with which we shall be concerned in the following pages.

We shall call a function $T(x)$ which is absolutely integrable on any finite interval of the real axis a locally integrable function. A regular distribution T is a continuous linear functional that can be represented by the integral,

$$(T, f) = \int_{-\infty}^{\infty} T(x)f(x)\,dx$$

Distributions that cannot be represented by an integral are called singular distributions, However, as a matter of convenience we shall sometimes use the notation,

$$(T, f) = \int_{-\infty}^{\infty} T(x)f(x)\,dx$$

even when the distribution T is singular and the integral can have a symbolic meaning only. Similarly we shall sometimes use the notation $T(x)$ for the singular distribution T, in which case we must avoid attaching to this symbolism the usual connotation that T is a function of x or that T is the regular distribution generated by the function $T(x)$. For example, Dirac's delta function is a singular distribution that assigns to every testing function of the space D its value at the origin. The proper notation for this distribution is δ and its value when operating on the testing function $f(x)$ is properly written as

$$(\delta, f) = f(0)$$

However, the historically developed notations,

$$\delta = \delta(x)$$

and

$$(\delta, f) = \int_{-\infty}^{\infty} \delta(x)f(x)\,dx = f(0)$$

will also be used.

We shall now consider some well-known distributions on the space D. As we have remarked before, any locally integrable function $T(x)$ can be used to define a regular distribution T on the space D of testing functions $f(x)$. Such a regular distribution has the integral representation,

$$(T, f) = \int_{-\infty}^{\infty} T(x)f(x)\,dx$$

Since an arbitrary constant a is locally integrable it can be used to define a regular distribution a on the space D and the values of this constant can be represented by the integral,

$$(a, f) = \int_{-\infty}^{\infty} af(x)\,dx = a \int_{-\infty}^{\infty} f(x)\,dx$$

This leads to the definition of the unit distribution 1 on the space D of testing functions $f(x)$ as the distribution which is defined by the operation,

$$(1, f) = \int_{-\infty}^{\infty} f(x)\,dx$$

In the preceding discussion we frequently made use of Dirac's delta function for illustrative purposes. This important singular distribution δ on the space D of testing functions $f(x)$ can be defined as the operational quantity which assigns to a testing function of the space D its value at the origin,

$$(\delta, f) = f(0)$$

Many identities involving this distribution are known. Proofs of some of the identities in the following list will be provided in subsequent discussions.

1. $$\delta(x) = \delta(-x)$$
2. $$x\delta(x) = 0$$
3. $$\delta(ax) = \delta(x)/|a|$$
4. $$\delta(ax - b) = \delta(x - b/a)/|a|$$
5. $$\delta(x^2 - a^2) = [\delta(x - a) + \delta(x + a)]/2|a|$$
6. $$f(x)\delta(x - a) = f(a)\delta(x - a)$$
7. $$\delta(a - b) = \int_{-\infty}^{\infty} \delta(x - a)\,\delta(x - b)\,dx$$
8. $$\delta\left(\frac{1}{x} - \frac{1}{y}\right) = xy\,\delta(x - y) = x^2\,\delta(x - y) = y^2\,\delta(x - y)$$

Another important singular distribution on the space D of testing functions $f(x)$ is the so-called principal value distribution $P(1/x)$. This distribution is defined by the Cauchy principal value integral of the function $1/x$,

$$\left(P\frac{1}{x}, f\right) = \lim_{\varepsilon \to 0} \int_{|x| \geqq \varepsilon} \frac{f(x)}{x}\,dx$$

The singularity of this distribution follows from the fact that the function $1/x$ is not integrable at the origin. Another representation of the same distribution may be written

$$\left(P\frac{1}{x}, f\right) = \lim_{\varepsilon\to 0}\frac{1}{2}\int_{-\infty}^{\infty}\left[\frac{1}{x+i\varepsilon}+\frac{1}{x-i\varepsilon}\right]f(x)\,dx$$

By means of the principal value distribution and the identity,

$$(x-\nu)\delta(x-\nu) = 0$$

we can obtain the solution, in the distributional sense, of the following simple functional equation,

$$(x-\nu)\psi(x) = g(x)$$

defined on some interval $a \leqq x \leqq b$ of the real axis. If the point ν is located in the complex plane or on the real axis but not on the interval (a, b), then the solution of this equation is simply

$$\psi(x) = \frac{g(x)}{x-\nu}$$

and is a function which exists in the ordinary sense. However, if ν is a point on the interval (a, b), then the solution of this equation must be interpreted as a distribution. For, from the identity $(x-\nu)\delta(x-\nu)=0$ we may infer that if $(x-\nu)\psi(x)=0$, then $\psi(x)$ must be a multiple of the delta distribution $\delta(x-\nu)$. The distributional solution of the equation may be written therefore as

$$\psi(x\,|\,\nu) = \lambda(\nu)\,\delta(x-\nu) + g(x)P\frac{1}{x-\nu}$$

where the strength $\lambda(\nu)$ of the concentration of the delta distribution at the point $x=\nu$ must be determined from auxiliary conditions which are imposed on the distribution $\psi(x\,|\,\nu)$. The solution of this equation, which was first obtained by Dirac, has far-reaching consequences in transport theory.

The Heisenberg delta functions,

$$\delta^{\pm}(x) = \frac{1}{2}\,\delta(x) \mp \frac{1}{2\pi i}\,P\frac{1}{x}$$

are also singular distributions on the space D of testing functions $f(x)$. Symbolically these distributions can be represented by Cauchy integrals. For example,

$$(\delta^{+}, f) = -\lim_{\varepsilon\to 0}\frac{1}{2\pi i}\int_{-\infty}^{\infty}\frac{f(x)}{x+i\varepsilon}\,dx$$

For, according to the Plemelj formulas which were derived in Chapter IV, we may write

$$\lim_{\varepsilon \to 0} \frac{1}{2\pi i} \int_{-\infty}^{\infty} \frac{f(x)}{x + i\varepsilon}\, dx = -\frac{1}{2} f(0) + \frac{1}{2\pi i} \int_{-\infty}^{\infty} \frac{f(x)}{x}\, dx$$

$$= -\frac{1}{2}(\delta, f) + \frac{1}{2\pi i}\left(P\frac{1}{x}, f\right) = (-\delta^{+}, f)$$

In a similar manner we can show that

$$(\delta^{-}, f) = \lim_{\varepsilon \to 0} \frac{1}{2\pi i} \int_{-\infty}^{\infty} \frac{f(x)}{x - i\varepsilon}\, dx$$

We obtain therefore the following limit representations for the Heisenberg delta functions,

$$\delta^{\pm}(x) = \mp \lim_{\varepsilon \to 0} \frac{1}{2\pi i} \frac{1}{x \pm i\varepsilon}$$

Some interesting identities can be derived connecting the Heisenberg delta functions, the Dirac delta function, and the principal value distribution. For example, since

$$\delta^{\pm}(x) = \frac{1}{2}\delta(x) \mp \frac{1}{2\pi i} P\frac{1}{x}$$

we obtain, by addition and subtraction, the following identities,

$$\delta(x) = \delta^{+}(x) + \delta^{-}(x)$$

and

$$\frac{1}{\pi i} P\frac{1}{x} = \delta^{-}(x) - \delta^{+}(x)$$

Replacing the terms on the right hand side of these identities by the appropriate limit representations,

$$\delta^{\pm}(x) = \mp \lim_{\varepsilon \to 0} \frac{1}{2\pi i} \frac{1}{x \pm i\varepsilon}$$

of Heisenberg's delta functions, we obtain the following well-known limit representation for the delta function of Dirac,

$$\delta(x) = \lim_{\varepsilon \to 0} \frac{1}{\pi} \frac{\varepsilon}{x^2 + \varepsilon^2}$$

and the limit representation,

$$P\frac{1}{x} = \lim_{\varepsilon \to 0} \frac{x}{x^2 + \varepsilon^2}$$

for the principal value distribution.

5.2 ALGEBRAIC AND ANALYTIC OPERATIONS ON DISTRIBUTIONS

Before presenting the basic rules for the algebraic and analytic manipulation of distributions, let us first introduce briefly some useful concepts and definitions.

Since a distribution T on the space D of testing functions $f(x)$ is a continuous linear functional and not a point function in the ordinary sense, the statement that this distribution vanishes at the point x on the real axis needs some elaboration. We shall say that a distribution T vanishes at the point x on the real axis if there exists an open interval, containing the point x, such that $(T, f) = 0$ for all testing functions $f(x)$ which vanish outside this interval. For example, $(\delta, f) = 0$ for all functions of the space D on any open interval not containing the origin. The delta function therefore vanishes at all points on the real axis with the exception of the origin. The set of all the points of the real axis which are located outside the open intervals on which a distribution vanishes is called the support of that distribution. For example, if the distribution T vanishes on the open interval $a < x < b$, and nowhere else, then the support of the distribution T consists of the closed intervals $-\infty < x \leqq a$ and $b \leqq x < \infty$. Conversely, if the distribution vanishes on the open intervals $-\infty < x < a$ and $b < x < \infty$, where a is smaller than b, then the support of the distribution is the closed interval $a \leqq x \leqq b$. In other words, the support of a distribution is the smallest closed set of points on the real axis outside which the distribution vanishes. The support of the delta function for example is the single point $x = 0$.

If a distribution vanishes outside some finite interval on the real axis, then the distribution is said to have bounded support and is called a distribution of bounded support. The delta function is obviously an example of a distribution of bounded support.

An interesting proposition, which will prove to be useful in this chapter, may be formulated as follows. Let $a(x)$ be a continuous function of the real variable x. If $a(x)$ has continuous derivatives of all orders and $a(x) = 1$ for all values of x on an interval containing the support of a distribution T, then, as can easily be shown, the distribution T is invariant under the operation by which all the testing functions $f(x)$ of the space D are multiplied by $a(x)$,

$$(T, f) = (T, af)$$

For the functions

$$f(x) = a(x)f(x) + (1 - a(x))f(x), \quad a(x)f(x), \quad \text{and} \quad (1 - a(x))f(x)$$

are testing functions of the space D. Moreover, the function $(1 - a(x))f(x)$ vanishes on the support of the distribution T, so that $(T, (1 - a)f) = 0$. Hence,

$$(T, f) = (T, af + (1 - a)f) = (T, af) + (T, (1 - a)f) = (T, af)$$

We shall now discuss briefly the basic definitions pertaining to some algebraic and analytic operations on distributions. It will be observed that these definitions closely resemble, and in many cases are identical to, the definitions for the corresponding operations on ordinary functions. This is no accident. For, in general, the definitions for operations on distributions have been chosen such that they reduce to their counterparts for operations on ordinary functions whenever these operations are performed on distributions which are also functions in the ordinary sense.

We shall say that two distributions S and T on the space D are equal if

$$(S, f) = (T, f)$$

for all testing functions $f(x)$ of the space D. For instance, if S and T are regular distributions, then S is equal to T if

$$\int_{-\infty}^{\infty} S(x)f(x)\,dx = \int_{-\infty}^{\infty} T(x)f(x)\,dx$$

for all functions $f(x)$ of the space D.

The algebraic operations of taking the sum of two distributions and multiplying a distribution by a constant can be defined as follows. If S and T are arbitrary distributions on the space D, then the sum $S + T$ of these two distributions is defined by the relation,

$$(S + T, f) = (S, f) + (T, f)$$

for all testing functions $f(x)$ of the space D. This definition implies that the sum of two distributions is again a continuous linear functional on the space D and thus, again, a distribution. If S and T are regular distributions generated by the locally integrable functions $S(x)$ and $T(x)$, then the definition of addition of two distributions reduces to the definition of the sum $S(x) + T(x)$ of two ordinary functions,

$$\begin{aligned}(S + T, f) &= \int_{-\infty}^{\infty} [S(x) + T(x)]f(x)\,dx \\ &= \int_{-\infty}^{\infty} S(x)f(x)\,dx + \int_{-\infty}^{\infty} T(x)f(x)\,dx \\ &= (S, f) + (T, f)\end{aligned}$$

The product aT of an arbitrary real or complex constant a and a distribution T is defined by the relation,

$$(aT, f) = (T, af) = a(T, f)$$

for all functions f of the space D. This product aT is again a distribution on the space D. If T is a regular distribution generated by the locally integrable function $T(x)$, then the definition of the product of a distribution by a constant corresponds to the rule,

$$(aT, f) = \int_{-\infty}^{\infty} aT(x)f(x)\,dx = a\int_{-\infty}^{\infty} T(x)f(x)\,dx = a(T, f)$$

of the integral of the product of a function and a constant.

Defining an operational rule for the multiplication of two distributions which corresponds to the operational rule for the multiplication of two ordinary functions is possible in certain special cases only. One such case is the following. Let $A(x)$ denote a continuous function which possesses continuous derivatives of all orders. Then the function $A(x)$ generates a regular distribution A,

$$(A, f) = \int_{-\infty}^{\infty} A(x)f(x)\,dx$$

Furthermore, the product $A(x)f(x)$ of the function $A(x)$ and an arbitrary testing function $f(x)$ of the space D is also a testing function of the space D. We may now define the product AT of the distribution A and an arbitrary distribution T on the space D by the rule,

$$(AT, f) = (T, Af)$$

Clearly this product AT is again a distribution on the space D. If moreover the distribution T is generated by the locally integrable function $T(x)$, then

$$(AT, f) = \int_{-\infty}^{\infty} A(x)T(x)f(x)\,dx = \int_{-\infty}^{\infty} T(x)A(x)f(x)\,dx = (T, Af)$$

and the product AT of the two distributions A and T is the distribution generated by the product of the two functions $A(x)$ and $T(x)$.

For example, the function x is continuous and has continuous derivatives of all orders. We may write, therefore,

$$(x\delta(x), f) = (\delta(x), xf) = 0 \cdot f(0)$$

and we obtain the identity,

$$x\delta(x) = 0$$

Similarly, if $g(x)$ is a continuous function which has continuous derivatives of all orders, then

$$(g(x)\delta(x-a), f) = (\delta(x-a), g(x)f(x)) = g(a)f(a) = g(a)(\delta(x-a), f)$$

which yields the identity,

$$g(x)\delta(x-a) = g(a)\delta(x-a)$$

The limit of a sequence of distributions T_m on the space D can be defined as follows. A sequence of distributions T_m on the space D converges to another distribution T on the space D if the sequence of ordinary numbers (T_m, f) converges to the number (T, f) for all testing functions $f(x)$ of the space D. As an example let us consider the ordinary function

$$T(x \mid a) = \frac{1}{2\pi} \int_{-a}^{a} e^{i\omega x}\, d\omega = \frac{\sin ax}{\pi x}$$

This function is locally integrable and defines the regular distribution, $T(a)$,

$$(T(a), f) = \int_{-\infty}^{\infty} T(x \mid a) f(x)\, dx = \frac{1}{\pi} \int_{-\infty}^{\infty} \frac{\sin ax}{x} f(x)\, dx$$

on the space D of testing functions $f(x)$. The sequence of distributions $T(a)$ converges to the delta function $\delta(x)$ in the limit as a tends to infinity. For

$$\lim_{a\to\infty} (T(a), f) = \lim_{a\to\infty} \frac{1}{\pi} \int_{-\infty}^{\infty} \frac{\sin ax}{x} f(x)\, dx = f(0) = (\delta, f)$$

for all testing functions $f(x)$ of the space D. In the sense of convergence of distributions, we obtain therefore the following integral representation of the delta function,

$$\delta(x) = \frac{1}{2\pi} \int_{-\infty}^{\infty} e^{i\omega x}\, d\omega$$

The delta function can also be represented as the limit of a sequence of ordinary functions. For example, in the preceding section we obtained the limit representation,

$$\delta(x) = \lim_{\varepsilon\to 0} \frac{1}{\pi} \frac{\varepsilon}{x^2 + \varepsilon^2}$$

Many so-called delta convergent sequences are known. For example, if a denotes a real number, then

$$\delta(x) = \lim_{a\to\infty} \frac{a}{\sqrt{\pi}} e^{-a^2x^2}$$

Similarly,

$$\delta(x) = \lim_{a \to \infty} \frac{1}{\pi} \frac{\sin ax}{x}$$

We shall now define some operations on distributions pertaining to transformations of the underlying space of the real variable x.

The translation over a distance a of a distribution T on the space D is defined by the relation,

$$(T(x-a), f) = (T, f(x+a))$$

For example, the relation,

$$(\delta(x-a), f) = (\delta, f(x+a))$$

defines a translation of the delta function over a distance a. If T is a regular distribution generated by the locally integrable function $T(x)$, then the translation of the distribution T over a distance a corresponds to a translation of the function $T(x)$ over this distance,

$$(T(x-a), f) = \int_{-\infty}^{\infty} T(x-a)f(x)\,dx$$

$$= \int_{-\infty}^{\infty} T(x)f(x+a)\,dx = (T, f(x+a))$$

A distribution T is said to be invariant with respect to translations over a distance a or to be periodic with period a, if

$$(T(x-a), f) = (T, f(x+a)) = (T, f)$$

An example of such a distribution is the regular distribution,

$$(e^{i\omega x}, f) = \int_{-\infty}^{\infty} e^{i\omega x} f(x)\,dx$$

which is generated by the locally integrable function $e^{i\omega x}$. Since

$$(e^{i\omega(x \pm 2n\pi)}, f) = (e^{i\omega x}, f)$$

this distribution is invariant with respect to translations over distances $2n\pi$ where n is an arbitrary positive integer.

The reflection of a distribution T in the origin is defined by the relation,

$$(T(-x), f) = (T, f(-x))$$

Again, the consistency of this definition with the corresponding definition of the reflection of an ordinary function in the origin can easily be verified at the hand of a regular distribution T which is generated by a locally integrable function $T(x)$. For in this case we find, by means of the rule of transformation of an integral,

$$(T(-x), f) = \int_{-\infty}^{\infty} T(-x)f(x)\,dx = \int_{-\infty}^{\infty} T(x)f(-x)\,dx = (T, f(-x))$$

The reflection of the delta function in the origin is defined by the relation,

$$(\delta(-x), f) = (\delta, f(-x)) = (\delta, f)$$

Hence, $\delta(x) = \delta(-x)$. A distribution which is invariant under reflections in the origin is called a centrally symmetric or even distribution. The delta function therefore is a centrally symmetric distribution. Similarly, a distribution which behaves under the reflection transformation as

$$(T(-x), f) = (T, f(-x)) = -(T, f)$$

is called a skew symmetric or odd distribution.

A similarity transformation of the distribution T on the space D is defined as the operation,

$$(T(x/a), f) = |a|(T, f(ax))$$

For example,

$$(\delta(x/a), f) = |a|(\delta, f(ax))$$

Since $f(ax)$ is again a testing function of the space D, we may also write

$$(\delta(x/a), f) = |a|(\delta, f)$$

Hence

$$\delta(x/a) = |a|\delta(x)$$

or

$$\delta(x) = |a|\delta(ax)$$

As another example let us consider the distribution $\delta(ax - b)$. Subjecting this distribution to a similarity transformation, we find

$$(\delta(ax - b), f) = \frac{1}{|a|}(\delta(x - b), f(x/a)) = \frac{1}{|a|}(\delta(x - b/a), f(x))$$

Hence, we obtain the identity,

$$\delta(ax - b) = \frac{1}{|a|}\delta(x - b/a)$$

In analogy with the definition of homogeneous functions, a distribution T on the space D is said to be homogeneous of degree v if $T(ax) = a^v T(x)$ where a is a positive constant. For example, if a is a positive constant, then

$$\delta(ax) = \frac{1}{a}\,\delta(x)$$

The delta function therefore is homogeneous of degree -1. If the distribution T is homogeneous of degree v, then

$$(T(ax), f) = a^v(T(x), f)$$

However, according to the definition of a similarity transformation, we may also write

$$(T(ax), f) = \frac{1}{a}\,(T, f(x/a))$$

and we obtain the relation,

$$(T, f(x/a)) = a^{v+1}(T, f)$$

Finally let us consider a testing function $f(x, \lambda)$ of the space D which is also a function of the real or complex variable λ. If T is a regular distribution on the space D, then T has the representation,

$$(T, f(x, \lambda)) = \int_{-\infty}^{\infty} T(x) f(x, \lambda)\, dx$$

As explained in Section 2.2, under certain circumstances the integral represents a function of the variable λ and can be differentiated under the integral sign

$$\frac{\partial}{\partial \lambda}(T, f(x, \lambda)) = \int_{-\infty}^{\infty} T(x) \frac{\partial f}{\partial \lambda}\, dx$$

and we may write therefore

$$\frac{\partial}{\partial \lambda}(T, f(x, \lambda)) = \left(T, \frac{\partial f}{\partial \lambda}\right)$$

This rule for the interchange of functional operation and differentiation with respect to a parameter, made plausible at the hand of a regular distribution, can be shown to be true for all distributions on the space D, provided that the testing function $f(x, \lambda)$ and its derivatives satisfy certain conditions. For instance, it is sufficient to require that the functions $f(x, \lambda)$ vanish outside the same finite interval of the x-axis for all values of λ in a given region R and that the partial derivatives $f^{(m)}(x, \lambda)$ and $\partial f^{(m)}(x, \lambda)/\partial \lambda$ exist and are continuous functions of x and λ for all values of x on this interval and for all values of λ in the region R.

Similarly, under certain circumstances we can formulate a rule for the interchange of functional operation and integration with respect to a parameter,

$$\int_\Gamma (T(x), f(x, \zeta))\, d\zeta = \left(T, \int_\Gamma f(x, \zeta)\, d\zeta\right)$$

where Γ is a given path or contour in the complex plane. For the formulation and proof of these important operations we must however refer the reader to the literature.

5.3 THE DERIVATIVE OF A DISTRIBUTION

In the preceding section we presented the definitions of the more important algebraic and analytic operations on distributions with the exception of the very important operation of taking the derivative of a distribution.

A workable definition of the derivative of a distribution, i.e., a definition which yields consistent results when we differentiate a distribution that is also a function in the ordinary sense, can most easily be obtained by first considering the case of a regular distribution T generated by a continuously differentiable function $T(x)$. Such a distribution can be represented by the integral,

$$(T, f) = \int_{-\infty}^{\infty} T(x) f(x)\, dx$$

and we note that for a regular distribution the integral representation has a real and not merely a symbolic meaning. Now let us consider the integral,

$$\int_{-\infty}^{\infty} T'(x) f(x)\, dx$$

For the particular functions $T(x)$ and $f(x)$ considered, this integral can be evaluated by means of the classical rule of integration by parts,

$$\int_{-\infty}^{\infty} T'(x) f(x)\, dx = [T(x) f(x)]_{-\infty}^{\infty} - \int_{-\infty}^{\infty} T(x) f'(x)\, dx$$

However, a testing function $f(x)$ of the space D vanishes outside some finite interval on the real axis and we obtain therefore

$$\int_{-\infty}^{\infty} T'(x) f(x)\, dx = -\int_{-\infty}^{\infty} T(x) f'(x)\, dx$$

or, in the distributional notation,

$$(T', f) = -(T, f')$$

In the theory of distributions this rule for the derivative of a regular distribution, which is generated by a continuously differentiable function $T(x)$, is used to define the derivative of a distribution on the space D including the singular distributions. The derivative of a distribution on the space D of testing functions $f(x)$ is defined therefore by the relation,

$$(T', f) = -(T, f')$$

Thus, the operation of the distributional derivative T' of the distribution T on a testing function $f(x)$ of the space D yields a real or complex number which is equal to the negative of the real or complex number obtained when the distribution operates on the derivative $f'(x)$ of the testing function $f(x)$. Since the derivative of a testing function of the space D is also a testing function of the space D, it is clear that the derivative of a distribution on D is again a distribution on D.

Repeated application of the rule of integration by parts on the integral representation of an appropriately defined regular distribution leads to the following rule for taking the m-th derivative $T^{(m)}$ of a distribution T on the space D,

$$(T^{(m)}, f) = (-1)^m (T, f^{(m)})$$

Again, the m-th derivative of a testing function of the space D is a testing function of the space D and the m-th derivative of a distribution on the space D is a distribution on the space D. Now it is clear why we insisted on testing functions which have continuous derivatives of all orders, because without this provision it would have been impossible to define the derivatives of a distribution in the manner above. It is moreover an immediate consequence of this definition that a distribution will have distributional derivatives of all orders.

In view of the definition of a distributional derivative, the following rules can easily be verified.

1. The derivative of the sum of two distributions S and T is equal to the sum of the derivatives of the distributions S and T,

$$((S+T)', f) = -(S+T, f') = -(S, f') - (T, f') = (S', f) + (T', f)$$

2. The derivative of the product of a distribution and a constant is equal to the product of the constant and the derivative of the distribution,

$$((aT)', f) = a(T', f)$$

3. The derivative of the product of a distribution T and a continuous function $A(x)$ which has continuous derivatives of all orders is equal to the sum of the distributions $A'T$ and TA',

$$((AT)', f) = (AT', f) + (A'T, f)$$

For,

$$\begin{aligned}((AT)', f) &= -(AT, f') = -(T, Af') \\ &= -(T, (Af)') + (T, A'f) \\ &= (T', Af) + (T, A'f) \\ &= (T'A, f) + (TA', f)\end{aligned}$$

In the remainder of this section we shall present some examples of the derivatives of the distributions most frequently encountered in theoretical physics and engineering. By means of these examples we shall show how some of the singular distributions, such as Dirac's delta function and the principal value distribution, can be obtained by repeated differentiation of a regular distribution.

To obtain the singular delta distribution we start by evaluating the derivatives of the regular distribution $|x|$ which is generated by the ordinary function $|x|$,

$$(|x|, f) \quad \int_{-\infty}^{\infty} |x| f(x)\, dx.$$

According to the definitions above we may write

$$(|x|', f) = -(|x|, f') = -\int_{-\infty}^{\infty} |x| f'(x)\, dx = \int_{-\infty}^{0} xf'(x)\, dx - \int_{0}^{\infty} xf'(x)\, dx$$

Integration by parts yields the expression,

$$(|x|', f) = \int_{0}^{\infty} f(x)\, dx - \int_{-\infty}^{0} f(x)\, dx = (\theta(x) - \theta(-x), f) = (\varepsilon, f)$$

where $\theta(x)$ is the unit step function and $\varepsilon(x)$ denotes the sign function.

The singular delta distribution can now be obtained as the derivative of the regular θ distribution which is generated by the unit step function $\theta(x)$,

$$(\theta, f) = \int_{0}^{\infty} f(x)\, dx$$

For, according to the definitions above,

$$(\theta', f) = -(\theta, f') = -\int_{0}^{\infty} f'(x)\, dx = f(0) = (\delta, f)$$

We have obtained therefore the relation,

$$\delta(x) = \theta'(x)$$

which, since $\theta(x) = \frac{1}{2}(1 + \varepsilon(x))$, where $\varepsilon(x)$ denotes the sign function, may also be written as

$$\delta(x) = \tfrac{1}{2}\varepsilon'(x)$$

The derivatives of the delta function are defined by the relations,

$$(\delta^{(m)}, f) = (-1)^m(\delta, f^{(m)}) = (-1)^m f^{(m)}(0)$$

For example, subjecting the distribution $\delta^{(m)}(ax - b)$ to a similarity transformation, we find

$$(\delta^{(m)}(ax - b), f) = \frac{1}{|a|}(\delta^{(m)}(x - b), f(x/a))$$

and, by the rules of differentiation,

$$(\delta^{(m)}(ax - b), f) = \frac{(-1)^m}{|a|}(\delta(x - b), f^{(m)}(x/a))$$

$$= \frac{(-1)^m}{|a|\, a^m}(\delta(x - b/a), f^{(m)}(x)) = \frac{1}{|a|\, a^m}(\delta^{(m)}(x - b/a), f)$$

Consequently, we have obtained the identity,

$$\delta^{(m)}(ax - b) = \frac{1}{|a|\, a^m}\delta^{(m)}(x - b/a)$$

The following identities involving the Dirac delta function and its derivatives are immediate consequences of the definition of a distributional derivative and the rules pertaining to the operation with delta functions and their derivatives:

1. $$\delta'(-x) = -\delta'(x)$$
2. $$x\delta'(x) = -\delta(x)$$
3. $$x^2\,\delta'(x) = 0$$
4. $$f(x)\delta'(x) = f(0)\delta'(x) - f'(x)\delta(x)$$
5. $$\delta'(b - a) = \int \delta'(b - x)\delta(x - a)\, dx$$

Integral and limit representations of the derivative of the delta function can be obtained by formal differentiation of the corresponding representations of the delta function itself. For example, we can obtain in this manner the following representations,

$$\delta'(x) = \frac{1}{2\pi}\int_{-\infty}^{\infty} i\omega e^{i\omega x}\, d\omega$$

and

$$\delta'(x) = -\lim_{\varepsilon \to 0} \frac{1}{\pi} \frac{2\varepsilon x}{(\varepsilon^2 + x^2)^2}$$

Of course, such formal manipulations do not constitute rigorous proofs of these expressions.

With the help of the results obtained above we can derive a rule for evaluating the derivative of a piecewise smooth function $T(x)$ which has a jump discontinuity of magnitude b at the point $x = a$. For such a function has the representation,

$$T(x) = S(x) + b\theta(x - a)$$

where the function $S(x)$ is continuous at all points including the point $x = a$ and $\theta(x)$ denotes the unit step function. This representation generates a regular distribution,

$$(T, f) = (S, f) + b(\theta(x - a), f)$$

with a distributional derivative,

$$(T', f) = (S', f) + b(\theta'(x - a), f) = (S', f) + b(\delta(x - a), f)$$

We obtain therefore the following representation for the derivative of the piecewise smooth function $T(x)$,

$$T'(x) = S'(x) + b\,\delta(x - a)$$

For example, the sign function $\varepsilon(x)$ has a jump discontinuity of magnitude 2 at the point $x = 0$ and can be represented as,

$$\varepsilon(x) = -1 + 2\theta(x)$$

Its derivative therefore takes the form,

$$\varepsilon'(x) = 2\,\delta(x)$$

a result which we have obtained before by other means.

In general, if $T(x)$ is a piecewise smooth function which has jump discontinuities of magnitude $b_0, b_1, \ldots, b_M$ at the points $a_0, a_1, \ldots, a_M$, then it has the representation,

$$T(x) = S(x) + \sum_{m=0}^{M} b_m \theta(x - a_m)$$

where $S(x)$ is a continuous function which has a piecewise continuous derivative. The derivative of the function $T(x)$ has the representation,

$$T'(x) = S'(x) + \sum_{m=0}^{M} b_m \delta(x - a_m)$$

This result can easily be generalized to expressions for the higher derivatives, but we shall not write out the ensuing rather complicated formulas.

The singular principal value distribution $P(1/x)$ which has the symbolic representation,

$$\left(P\frac{1}{x}, f\right) = \lim_{\varepsilon \to 0} \int_{|x| \geqq \varepsilon} \frac{f(x)}{x} \, dx$$

can be obtained by differentiating the regular distribution $\log |x|$ which is generated by the ordinary function $\log |x|$,

$$(\log |x|, f) = \int_{-\infty}^{\infty} \log |x| \, f(x) \, dx$$

For, according to the definition of the derivative of a distribution,

$$\left(\frac{d}{dx} \log |x|, f\right) = -(\log |x|, f') = -\int_{-\infty}^{\infty} \log |x| \, f'(x) \, dx$$

$$= \lim_{\varepsilon \to 0} \int_{|x| \geqq \varepsilon} \frac{f(x)}{x} \, dx$$

where the integral on the left hand side was evaluated by integration by parts. We may write therefore

$$\left(P\frac{1}{x}, f\right) = \left(\frac{d}{dx} \log |x|, f\right)$$

or

$$P\frac{1}{x} = \frac{d}{dx} \log |x|$$

The derivative of the principal value distribution can be evaluated in a manner which closely resembles the subtraction technique for dispersion relations. For we may write

$$\left(P'\frac{1}{x}, f\right) = -\left(P\frac{1}{x}, f'\right) = -\lim_{\varepsilon \to 0} \int_{|x| \geqq \varepsilon} \frac{f'(x)}{x} \, dx$$

However, the testing function $f(x)$ has the representation,

$$f(x) = f(0) + xg(x)$$

where $g(x)$ is continuous over the real axis including the origin and vanishes as $1/x$ when x tends to plus or minus infinity. Thus, since

$$\frac{f'(x)}{x} = \frac{f(x) - f(0)}{x^2} + g'(x)$$

we may write

$$\left(P'\frac{1}{x}, f\right) = -\int_{-\infty}^{\infty} g'(x)\,dx - \lim_{\varepsilon\to 0}\int_{|x|\geqq\varepsilon} \frac{f(x)-f(0)}{x^2}\,dx$$

$$= -\lim_{\varepsilon\to 0}\int_{|x|\geqq\varepsilon} \frac{f(x)-f(0)}{x^2}\,dx$$

The principal value integral on the right hand side, which we shall write as

$$\left(P\frac{1}{x^2}, f\right) = \lim_{\varepsilon\to 0}\int_{|x|\geqq\varepsilon} \frac{f(x)-f(0)}{x^2}\,dx$$

defines a new singular distribution which we shall denote by $P(1/x^2)$. We have obtained therefore the relation,

$$\left(P'\frac{1}{x}, f\right) = -\left(P\frac{1}{x^2}, f\right)$$

or

$$P'\frac{1}{x} = -P\frac{1}{x^2}$$

In a similar manner we obtain the following expression for the m-th derivative of the principal value distribution,

$$P^{(m)}\frac{1}{x} = (-1)^m m!\, P\frac{1}{x^{m+1}}$$

where the singular distribution $P(1/x^{m+1})$ is defined by the Cauchy integral,

$$\left(P\frac{1}{x^{m+1}}, f\right) = \lim_{\varepsilon\to 0}\int_{|x|\geqq\varepsilon} \frac{f(x)-f(0)-\cdots-x^{m-1}f^{(m-1)}(0)/(m-1)!}{x^{m+1}}\,dx$$

The singular distribution,

$$\delta^+(x) = \frac{1}{2}\,\delta(x) - \frac{1}{2\pi i}\,P\frac{1}{x}$$

which is known as Heisenberg's delta function can be obtained by differentiating the regular distribution $\log(x+i0)$ which is generated by the locally integrable function,

$$\log(x+i0) = \lim_{\varepsilon\to 0}\log(x+i\varepsilon)$$

For we may write

$$\log(x+i\varepsilon) = \log|x+i\varepsilon| + i\arg(x+i\varepsilon)$$

and

$$i \lim_{\varepsilon\to 0} \arg(x + i\varepsilon) = i \lim_{\varepsilon\to 0} \arctan \frac{\varepsilon}{x} = i\pi\theta(-x)$$

where $\theta(x)$ denotes the unit step function.

Hence

$$\lim_{\varepsilon\to 0} \log(x + i\varepsilon) = \log|x| + i\pi\theta(-x)$$

and we obtain therefore the expression,

$$\left(\frac{d}{dx}\log(x + i0), f\right) = \lim_{\varepsilon\to 0}\left(\frac{1}{x + i\varepsilon}, f\right) = \left(P\frac{1}{x} - i\pi\delta(x), f\right)$$

This may also be written,

$$\lim_{\varepsilon\to 0} \frac{1}{x + i\varepsilon} = P\frac{1}{x} - i\pi\delta(x)$$

This implies that Heisenberg's delta function can be defined as

$$\delta^{+}(x) = \frac{1}{2}\delta(x) - \frac{1}{2\pi i} P\frac{1}{x} = -\lim_{\varepsilon\to 0} \frac{1}{2\pi i} \frac{1}{x + i\varepsilon}$$

In a similar manner we obtain the representation,

$$\delta^{-}(x) = \frac{1}{2}\delta(x) + \frac{1}{2\pi i} P\frac{1}{x} = \lim_{\varepsilon\to 0} \frac{1}{2\pi i} \frac{1}{x - i\varepsilon}$$

Combining the results obtained for the derivatives of the delta function and the principal value distribution, we can immediately write down the following expressions,

$$\delta^{+(m)}(x) = \frac{1}{2}\delta^{(m)}(x) - \frac{1}{2\pi i} P^{(m)}\frac{1}{x} = \frac{1}{2}\delta^{(m)}(x) - \frac{(-1)^m m!}{2\pi i} P\frac{1}{x^{m+1}}$$

and

$$\delta^{-(m)}(x) = \frac{1}{2}\delta^{(m)}(x) + \frac{1}{2\pi i} P^{(m)}\frac{1}{x} = \frac{1}{2}\delta^{(m)}(x) + \frac{(-1)^m m!}{2\pi i} P\frac{1}{x^{m+1}}$$

for the derivatives of the Heisenberg delta functions.

5.4 TEMPERED DISTRIBUTIONS AND THEIR FOURIER TRANSFORMS

The main topic of discussion of Chapter II was the Fourier transformation of an ordinary function of a real or complex variable and its applications.

In that chapter we derived, in a rather inexact but expedient manner, the Fourier transformations of such distributions as the Dirac and Heisenberg delta functions and the principal value distribution. Now, being better acquainted with these important mathematical entities and knowing them to be singular distributions on the space of testing functions D, we may well ask for a derivation of their Fourier transforms within the framework of the theory of distributions. Such a derivation requires the introduction of a new space of testing functions, namely, the space S of the so-called good functions $g(x)$, and of the continuous linear functionals on this space, namely, the so-called tempered distributions or the distributions of slow growth.

A continuous function $g(x)$ is called a good function or a rapidly descending function if it has continuous derivatives of all orders and if it and its derivatives vanish more rapidly than $1/|x|^n$, as $|x|$ tends to infinity, for all values of n. In other words, if $g(x)$ is a good function, then the functions $|x|^n g^{(m)}(x)$ tend to zero when $|x|$ tends to infinity for all non-negative values of m and n. A sequence of good functions $g(x)$ converges to zero if the sequence of functions $|x|^n g_\nu{}^{(m)}(x)$ converges to zero uniformly on the real axis for all non-negative values of m and n. This definition of convergence implies that a sequence of good functions $g_\nu(x)$ converges to another good function $g(x)$ if the sequence $|x|^n[g_\nu{}^{(m)}(x) - g^{(m)}(x)]$ converges to zero uniformly on the real axis for all non-negative values of m and n.

The space of all good functions $g(x)$ which have the properties delineated above is called the space S of good functions $g(x)$. As an immediate consequence of the definition of a good function, we may draw the conclusion that all the testing functions $f(x)$ of the space D are also good functions that belong to the space S. However, it is also clear that the space S is larger than the space D. For the space S contains the functions of exponential decay such as e^{-x^2} which, since they do not vanish outside some finite interval on the real axis, are certainly not functions of the space D.

An outstanding property of a good function is that its Fourier transform is also a good function. For, if $g(x)$ is a good function and $G(\omega)$ is its Fourier transform,

$$G(\omega) = \frac{1}{\sqrt{(2\pi)}} \int_{-\infty}^{\infty} g(x) e^{i\omega x}\, dx$$

then it follows immediately from the Riemann-Lebesgue lemma that $G(\omega)$ vanishes as $|\omega|$ tends to infinity. Furthermore, integrating the Fourier integral m times by parts, we find

$$|\omega|^n G(\omega) = \frac{|\omega|^n(-1)^n}{(i\omega)^n \sqrt{(2\pi)}} \int_{-\infty}^{\infty} g^{(n)}(x) e^{i\omega x}\, dx$$

and the expression on the right vanishes when $|\omega|$ tends to infinity according to the same lemma. Finally, differentiating the Fourier integral m times with respect to ω, we find

$$G^{(m)}(\omega) = \frac{1}{\sqrt{(2\pi)}} \int_{-\infty}^{\infty} (ix)^m g(x) e^{i\omega x} \, dx$$

Since $g(x)$ is a good function we may infer that $(ix)^m g(x)$ is also a good function. Repeating therefore the first part of the argument, but now for the good function $(ix)^m g(x)$, we obtain the result that $|\omega|^n G^{(m)}(\omega)$ also vanishes when $|\omega|$ tends to infinity.

Thus, we may draw the conclusion that good functions are mapped by Fourier transformation into other good functions and that the space S of all good functions is mapped by Fourier transformation into itself. Since a testing function $f(x)$ of the space D is also a good function of the space S, this implies that the Fourier transform $F(\omega)$ of a testing function $f(x)$ of the space D is also a good function of the space S. The Fourier transformation,

$$F(\omega) = \frac{1}{\sqrt{(2\pi)}} \int_{-\infty}^{\infty} f(x) e^{i\omega x} \, dx$$

of a testing function $f(x)$ of the space D is moreover the restriction to the real axis of a function,

$$F(\lambda) = \frac{1}{\sqrt{(2\pi)}} \int_{-\infty}^{\infty} f(x) e^{i\lambda x} \, dx$$

which is analytic in the whole complex λ-plane, including the real axis, and is therefore an entire function. This statement can easily be verified by means of the discussion in Section 2.3. For, since $f(x)$ is a testing function of the space D, there exists a finite interval $(-a, a)$ on the real axis outside which the function $f(x)$ vanishes. The function $F(x)$ therefore has the integral representation,

$$F(\lambda) = \frac{1}{\sqrt{(2\pi)}} \int_{-a}^{a} f(x) e^{i\lambda x} \, dx$$

The integrand of this integral is an entire function of the complex variable λ and a continuous function of the real variable x on the interval $(-a, a)$. According to Section 2.3, this implies that the integral is the representation of a function $F(\lambda)$ which is analytic in the whole complex plane and is therefore an entire function.

The functionals on the space S appropriate for our purposes are the so-called tempered distributions or the distributions of slow growth. A tempered distribution is a linear functional on the space S which is continuous in the sense of convergence for sequences of good functions. In other words, if T is a tempered distribution and g_m is a sequence of good functions which converges to zero, then the sequence of real or complex numbers (T, g_m) converges to zero. We note without proof that a tempered distribution on the space S is also a distribution on the space D. For instance, the delta function and its derivatives are examples of distributions on the space D which are also tempered distributions. However, there are distributions on the space D that are not tempered distributions.

Since the tempered distributions are distributions on the space D, all the rules for the algebraic and analytic operations on distributions on the space D are also valid for the corresponding operations on tempered distributions. It should be realized that such an operation or sequence of operations on tempered distributions, although always yielding a distribution on the space D, does not necessarily result in another tempered distribution. However, among the more important operations on tempered distribtions that result in other tempered distributions are the addition of two tempered distributions, the multiplication of a tempered distribution by a constant, and the operation of taking a derivative of a tempered distribution.

As in the case of regular distributions on the space D of testing functions $f(x)$, we can define regular tempered distributions on the space S of good functions $g(x)$ by the integral operation,

$$(T, g) = \int_{-\infty}^{\infty} T(x)g(x)\, dx$$

In this case it is sufficient to require that the function $T(x)$ be absolutely integrable over any finite subinterval on the real axis and that it tend to infinity more slowly than some power of x. In other words, the function $T(x)$ is at most of the order of x^m, where m is some positive number, and its growth is dominated by any power of x larger than m. In the following, such functions will be called functions of slow growth. Good functions of course are functions of slow growth and any good function therefore can be used to define a tempered distribution. A polynomial is also a function of slow growth, because any polynomial of degree m dominates the growth of the polynomials of degree smaller than m.

We shall now turn our attention to the definition of the Fourier transform of a tempered distribution. If the locally integrable function $T(x)$ is absolutely integrable over the real axis, then $T(x)$ is a function of slow growth which defines a regular tempered distribution,

$$(T, g) = \int_{-\infty}^{\infty} T(x)g(x)\, dx$$

on the space S of good functions $g(x)$. The Fourier transform,

$$F(T, \omega) = \frac{1}{\sqrt{(2\pi)}} \int_{-\infty}^{\infty} T(x)e^{i\omega x}\, dx$$

of the function $T(x)$ is also a function of slow growth as may easily be inferred from the continuity and boundedness of the function $F(T, \omega)$ on the real axis. Thus, the Fourier transform $F(T, \omega)$ of the function $T(x)$ can also be used to generate a regular tempered distribution F on the space S.

An interesting relationship exists between the regular tempered distribution T and its Fourier transform $F(T)$. For, if $G^*(\omega)$ denotes the complex conjugate of the Fourier transform $G(\omega)$ of the good function $g(x)$, then, according to Parseval's equality introduced in Section 2.5, we may write

$$\int_{-\infty}^{\infty} F(T, \omega)G^*(\omega)d\omega = \int_{-\infty}^{\infty} T(x)g^*(x)\, dx$$

From this equality we may infer that the regular tempered distribution $F(T)$, in its action on the good functions of the space S, assigns to the complex conjugate of the Fourier transform $G(\omega)$ of the good function $g(x)$ the same value as is assigned to the complex conjugate $g^*(x)$ of the good function $g(x)$ by the regular tempered distribution $T(x)$,

$$(F(T), G^*) = (T, g^*)$$

The regular tempered distribution $F(T)$, on the space S, which satisfies this relationship is called the Fourier transform of the regular tempered distribution T. This definition can now be extended to all tempered distributions on the space S. Thus, the Fourier transform $F(T)$ of the tempered distribution T on the space S is the functional on the space S which satisfies the relationship,

$$(F(T), G^*) = (T, g^*)$$

where $G^*(\omega)$ denotes the complex conjugate of the Fourier transform of the good function $g(x)$. Since the Fourier transform of a good function is also a good function, it can easily be verified that the Fourier transform of a tempered distribution on the space S is also a tempered distribution.

The concept of the Fourier transform of a tempered distribution will now be illustrated at the hand of several examples. The Fourier transform $F(\delta)$ of the delta function $\delta(x)$ can be defined as follows,

$$(F(\delta), G^*) = (\delta, g^*)$$

However,

$$(\delta, g^*) = g^*(0) = \frac{1}{\sqrt{(2\pi)}} \int_{-\infty}^{\infty} G^*(\omega)\, d\omega$$

Hence

$$(F(\delta), G^*) = \frac{1}{\sqrt{(2\pi)}} \int_{-\infty}^{\infty} G^*(\omega)\, d\omega$$

and we obtain therefore the expression,

$$F(\delta) = \frac{1}{\sqrt{(2\pi)}}$$

for the Fourier transform of the delta function. This transform has been obtained by other means in Section 2.5.

In a similar manner, we can find the Fourier transform of the m-th derivative of the delta function. This transform is defined by the relation,

$$(F(\delta^{(m)}), G^*) = (\delta^{(m)}, g^*)$$

and since

$$(\delta^{(m)}, g^*) = (-1)^m g^{*(m)}(0) = \frac{1}{\sqrt{(2\pi)}} \int_{-\infty}^{\infty} (-i\omega)^m G^*(\omega)\, d\omega$$

the Fourier transform of the m-th derivative of the delta function is

$$F(\delta^{(m)}) = \frac{(-i\omega)^m}{\sqrt{(2\pi)}}$$

The Fourier transform of a constant A is equal to

$$F(A) = A\sqrt{(2\pi)}\delta(\omega)$$

For, by definition,

$$(F(A), G^*) = (A, g^*)$$

However,

$$(A, g^*) = A \int_{-\infty}^{\infty} g^*(x)\, dx = A\sqrt{(2\pi)}G^*(0)$$

Hence

$$(F(A), G^*) = A\sqrt{(2\pi)}G^*(0)$$

and we obtain, therefore,

$$F(A) = A\sqrt{(2\pi)}\delta(\omega)$$

The Fourier transform, $F(x^m)$, of the m-th power of x is defined by the relation,

$$(F(x^m), G^*) = (x^m, g^*)$$

Now

$$(x^m, g^*) = \int_{-\infty}^{\infty} x^m g^*(x)\, dx = \sqrt{(2\pi)} i^m G^{*(m)}(0)$$

and we find therefore that

$$(F(x^m), G^*) = \sqrt{(2\pi)} i^m G^{*(m)}(0)$$

or

$$F(x^m) = \sqrt{(2\pi)}(-i)^m \, \delta^{(m)}(\omega)$$

This implies that the Fourier transform of the polynomial,

$$P_m(x) = A_0 x^m + A_1 x^{m-1} + \cdots + A_m$$

takes the form,

$$F(P_m) = \sqrt{(2\pi)}[A_0(-i)^m \delta^{(m)}(\omega) + A_1(-i)^{m-1} \delta^{\,m-1}(\omega) + \cdots + A_m \delta(\omega)]$$

or, in an obvious notation,

$$F(P_m) = \sqrt{(2\pi)} P_m\left(-i \frac{d}{d\omega}\right)\delta(\omega)$$

Conversely, we can show that

$$\sqrt{(2\pi)} F\left[P_m\left(\frac{d}{dx}\right)\delta(x)\right] = P_m(-i\omega)$$

For, the Fourier transform of the m-th derivative of the delta function is

$$F(\delta^{(m)}) = \frac{(-i\omega)^m}{\sqrt{(2\pi)}}$$

and thus

$$F[A_0 \delta^{(m)}(x) + A_1 \delta^{(m-1)}(x) + \cdots + A_m \delta(x)]$$

$$= \frac{1}{\sqrt{(2\pi)}} [A_0(-i\omega)^m + A_1(-i\omega)^{m-1} + \cdots + A_m]$$

Another important Fourier transform is the transform of the sign function $\varepsilon(x)$. This transform, $F(\varepsilon)$, is defined by the relation,

$$(F(\varepsilon), G^*) = (\varepsilon, g^*)$$

Introducing the integral representation,

$$\varepsilon(x) = \frac{i}{\pi} \int_{-\infty}^{\infty} \frac{e^{-i\omega x}}{\omega} \, d\omega$$

of Section 1.1, we find

$$(\varepsilon, g^*) = \frac{2i}{\sqrt{(2\pi)}} \int_{-\infty}^{\infty} \frac{G^*(\omega)}{\omega} \, d\omega = (F(\varepsilon), G^*)$$

This implies that the Fourier transform of the sign function may be written as

$$F(\varepsilon) = \frac{2i}{\sqrt{(2\pi)}} P \frac{1}{\omega} = \frac{2}{\sqrt{(2\pi)}} P \frac{1}{(-i\omega)}$$

The Fourier transform, $F(P(1/x))$, of the principal value distribution can also be obtained by means of the integral representation of the sign function. For, writing

$$\left(F\left(P\frac{1}{x}\right), G^*\right) = \left(P\frac{1}{x}, g^*\right) = \lim_{\varepsilon\to 0} \int_{|x|\geqq\varepsilon} \frac{g^*(x)}{x}\, dx$$

we find, upon substitution of this representation into the Cauchy integral,

$$\left(F\left(P\frac{1}{x}\right), G^*\right) = \frac{\pi i}{\sqrt{(2\pi)}} \int_{-\infty}^{\infty} \varepsilon(\omega) G^*(\omega)\, d\omega$$

From this expression we may conclude that

$$F\left(P\frac{1}{x}\right) = \frac{\pi i}{\sqrt{(2\pi)}} \varepsilon(\omega)$$

Combining the results obtained above, we can immediately find the Fourier transform of the unit step function,

$$\theta(x) = \tfrac{1}{2} + \tfrac{1}{2}\varepsilon(x)$$

For we may write

$$F(\theta) = F\left(\frac{1}{2}\right) + F\left(\frac{1}{2}\varepsilon\right) = \frac{1}{2}\sqrt{(2\pi)}\delta(\omega) + \frac{1}{\sqrt{(2\pi)}} P \frac{1}{(-i\omega)} = \sqrt{(2\pi)}\delta^+(\omega)$$

where

$$\delta^+(\omega) = \frac{1}{2}\delta(\omega) - \frac{1}{2\pi i} P \frac{1}{\omega}$$

is Heisenberg's delta function. Similarly, since

$$\theta(-x) = \tfrac{1}{2} - \tfrac{1}{2}\varepsilon(x)$$

we find

$$F(\theta(-x)) = \sqrt{(2\pi)}\delta^-(\omega)$$

where

$$\delta^-(\omega) = \frac{1}{2}\delta(\omega) + \frac{1}{2\pi i} P \frac{1}{\omega}$$

is the complex conjugate of Heisenberg's delta function.

The Fourier transforms of Heisenberg's delta functions can also be obtained by combination of the Fourier transforms of other distributions. For

$$\delta^+(x) = \frac{1}{2}\,\delta(x) - \frac{1}{2\pi i}\,P\,\frac{1}{x}$$

and thus

$$F(\delta^+) = \frac{1}{2}\,F(\delta) - \frac{1}{2\pi i}\,F\!\left(P\,\frac{1}{x}\right) = \frac{1}{\sqrt{(2\pi)}}\left[\frac{1}{2} - \frac{1}{2}\,\varepsilon(\omega)\right] = \frac{\theta(-\omega)}{\sqrt{(2\pi)}}$$

In a similar manner we find

$$F(\delta^-) = \frac{\theta(\omega)}{\sqrt{(2\pi)}}$$

Denoting by $F(T)$ the tempered distribution which is the Fourier transform of the distribution T on the space S we may state the following general rules.

1. The Fourier transform of the m-th derivative of the distribution T is equal to the distribution $(-i\omega)^m F(T)$,

$$F(T^{(m)}) = (-i\omega)^m F(T)$$

For example,

$$F(\delta^{(m)}) = \frac{(-i\omega)^m}{\sqrt{(2\pi)}}$$

2. The Fourier transform of the distribution $(ix)^m T$ is equal to the m-th derivative of the distribution $F(T)$,

$$F((ix)^m T) = F^{(m)}(T)$$

For example,

$$F((ix)^m) = \sqrt{(2\pi)}\,\delta^{(m)}(\omega)$$

3. The Fourier transform of the translation $T(x-a)$ of the distribution T over a distance a is equal to the distribution $e^{i\omega a}F(T)$,

$$F(T(x-a)) = e^{i\omega a}F(T)$$

For example,

$$F(\delta(x-a)) = \frac{e^{i\omega a}}{\sqrt{(2\pi)}}$$

$$F(\delta^{(m)}(x-a)) = \frac{(-i\omega)^m e^{i\omega a}}{\sqrt{(2\pi)}}$$

4. The Fourier transform of the distribution $e^{-iax}T$ is equal to the translation of the distribution F over a distance a,

$$F(Te^{-iax}) = F(T(\omega - a))$$

For example,

$$F(e^{-iax}) = \sqrt{(2\pi)}\delta(\omega - a)$$
$$F((ix)^m e^{-iax}) = \sqrt{(2\pi)}\delta^{(m)}(\omega - a)$$

5. The Fourier transform of the distribution $T(ax)$ is equal to the distribution $(1/|a|)F(T(\omega/a))$,

$$F(T(ax)) = \frac{1}{|a|} F(T(\omega/a))$$

For example,

$$F(\delta(ax)) = \frac{1}{|a|\sqrt{(2\pi)}}$$

The rules above closely resemble the corresponding rules derived in Section 2.5 for the Fourier transforms of ordinary functions.

5.5 THE CAUCHY REPRESENTATION OF DISTRIBUTIONS

There are several areas of interest common to the theory of distributions and to the theory of analytic functions which forms the main topic of discussion of this book. One such area can be established by considering a continuous linear functional T acting on a particular testing function $1/(x - \lambda)$ of a new space of testing functions E. This functional generates a function $T_C(\lambda)$ of the complex variable λ. The properties of this function can be studied within the framework of the theory developed in the foregoing chapters. A second area of interest common to the theory of distributions and to the theory of analytic functions can be established by considering, for example, a regular distribution $T(\lambda)$ which is generated by a locally integrable function $T(x, \lambda)$ depending on a complex variable λ. Such a distribution can be interpreted as a generalized analytic function. The concept of a generalized analytic function, introduced at the hand of regular distributions, can be extended to that of a generalized analytic function defined by an arbitrary distribution on the space D. Generalized analytic functions, although more general mathematical structures than ordinary analytic functions, have many properties in common with the latter. For example, the concept of analytic continuation can be introduced for these functions yielding a powerful tool for the investigation of the properties of singular distributions.

Starting with the introduction of a new space E of testing functions $\phi(x)$, we shall present in this section a discussion of the first mentioned area of interest common to the theory of distributions and that of analytic functions.

A. Cauchy Representations of Distributions on the Space E

In this section we shall consider a new space E of testing functions $\phi(x)$. Similarly as for the testing functions $f(x)$ of the space D, we shall require that the functions $\phi(x)$ of the space E are continuous and have continuous derivatives of all orders. In contrast to the testing functions $f(x)$ of the space D, however, the testing functions $\phi(x)$ of the space E are not required to vanish outside some finite interval on the real axis. In addition, we shall introduce the following distinct definition of convergence for functions $\phi(x)$ of the space E: A sequence of functions $\phi_m(x)$ of the space E converges to zero if the functions $\phi_m(x)$ and all their derivatives converge to zero uniformly on every finite subinterval of the real axis. Thus, a sequence of functions $\phi_m(x)$ of the space E converges to another function $\phi(x)$ of the space E if the sequence of functions $\phi_m(x) - \phi(x)$ converges to zero in the sense of convergence delineated above. We note, that the testing functions $f(x)$ of the space D are also functions of the space E but that not all the functions of the space E are functions of the space D. For the functions of the space D vanish outside some finite interval on the real axis and a limitation of this type has not been imposed on the functions $\phi(x)$ of the space E.

A linear functional T on the space E of testing functions $\phi(x)$ is a distribution on the space E if it is continuous with respect to the definition of convergence for sequences of functions $\phi_m(x)$ of the space E introduced above. In other words, if T is a distribution on the space E, then the sequence of real or complex numbers (T, ϕ_m) converges to zero whenever the sequence of functions $\phi_m(x)$ converges to zero in the sense of convergence of sequences of functions of the space E.

Distributions on the space E have the useful property that they vanish outside some finite interval on the real axis and for this reason they are called distributions of bounded support. All distributions of bounded support on the space D are also distributions on the space E.

Now let us consider the function,

$$\frac{1}{2\pi i(x - \lambda)}$$

If λ denotes a point located in the upper or lower half plane but not on the real axis, then this function is continuous and has continuous derivatives of all orders for all values of x and is therefore a function of the space E. Thus, if T is a continuous linear functional on the space E, then the operation,

$$T_C(\lambda) = \frac{1}{2\pi i}\left(T(x), \frac{1}{x - \lambda}\right)$$

generates a function $T_C(\lambda)$ of the complex variable λ for all values of λ outside the real axis. Now let us consider the restriction of this function $T_C(\lambda)$ to the real axis. In other words, we want to know if it is possible to assign a meaning to the limit,

$$T_C(\omega) = \lim_{\varepsilon \to 0} T_C(\omega \pm i\varepsilon)$$

We can show that this limit is well defined for all values of ω which are located outside the support of the distribution T. For, let $a(x)$ be a continuous function of the real variable x which has continuous derivatives of all orders. Let us assume moreover that this function $a(x)$ vanishes for all values of x outside some finite interval (a, b) containing the support of the distribution T and is equal to one on the support of this distribution. Since $a(x)$ vanishes identically for all values of x outside the interval (a, b), the function $a(x)/(x - \omega)$ is continuous and has continuous derivatives of all orders for all values of ω outside the interval (a, b) and is therefore a function of the space E. In Section 5.2, we have shown moreover that the distribution T is invariant with respect to the transformation by which the functions of the space E are multiplied by the function $a(x)$. Thus the operation,

$$T_C(\omega) = \frac{1}{2\pi i}\left(T(x), \frac{a(x)}{x - \omega}\right) = \frac{1}{2\pi i}\left(T(x), \frac{1}{x - \omega}\right)$$

is well defined for all values of ω outside the interval $(a\ b,)$ or, more precisely, outside the support of the distribution T, because we have assumed that the interval (a, b) contains the support of this distribution.

We may conclude therefore that the function,

$$T_C(\lambda) = \frac{1}{2\pi i}\left(T(x), \frac{1}{x - \lambda}\right)$$

is a well-defined function of the complex variable λ for all values of λ outside the support of the distribution T. In a similar manner, it can be shown that the derivatives of the function $T_C(\lambda)$ with respect to λ exist for all values of λ outside the support of the distribution T. We shall refer to this fact by saying that the function,

$$T_C(\lambda) = \frac{1}{2\pi i}\left(T(x), \frac{1}{x - \lambda}\right)$$

is a sectionally analytic function in the complex λ-plane with a boundary on the real axis consisting of the support of the distribution T. In other words, the support of the distribution T does not belong to the region of analyticity of the function $T_C(\lambda)$.

The sectionally analytic function $T_C(\lambda)$ defined above will be called the Cauchy representation of the distribution T. Thus, the Cauchy representation of a distribution T on the space E is the function $T_C(\lambda)$ of the complex variable λ,

$$T_C(\lambda) = \frac{1}{2\pi i}\left(T(x), \frac{1}{x-\lambda}\right)$$

which is generated by performing the operation characteristic for the distribution T on the special testing function $1/[2\pi i(x-\lambda)]$ of the space E.

For example, if $T(x)$ is a locally integrable function which vanishes outside some finite interval on the real axis and is the restriction to this interval of an analytic function $T(\lambda)$ which vanishes for large values of λ, then the regular distribution T,

$$(T, \phi) = \int_{-\infty}^{\infty} T(x)\phi(x)\,dx$$

is a distribution of bounded support. The Cauchy representation of this distribution takes the form of the ordinary Cauchy integral,

$$T_C(\lambda) = \frac{1}{2\pi i}\int_{-\infty}^{\infty} \frac{T(x)}{x-\lambda}\,dx$$

which, as we have shown in Chapter I, may be written as

$$\begin{aligned} T_C(\lambda) &= T(\lambda) \qquad &&\text{when } I(\lambda) > 0 \\ &= 0 &&\text{when } I(\lambda) < 0 \end{aligned}$$

The Dirac delta function is also a distribution of bounded support. In this case we find

$$\delta_C(\lambda) = \frac{1}{2\pi i}\left(\delta(x), \frac{1}{x-\lambda}\right) = -\frac{1}{2\pi i\lambda}$$

We shall now proceed to present a short discussion of some of the properties of the Cauchy representation of a distribution T on the space E. The discussion will be formal and the reader is referred to the literature for the rigorous proofs of some of the statements and propositions.

The Cauchy representation $T_C(\lambda)$ of a distribution T on the space E has an important property in common with the Cauchy representations of ordinary analytic functions, namely, it vanishes at least as $1/\lambda$ when λ tends to infinity. This property is an immediate consequence of the continuity of the linear functional T on the space E of testing functions $\phi(x)$. For, since the function $1/(x-\lambda)$ and its derivatives are testing functions of the space E and the sequences of these functions vanish as λ tends to infinity, the sequence of real or complex numbers

$$\frac{1}{2\pi i}\left(T(x), \frac{1}{x-\lambda}\right)$$

must vanish also when λ tends to infinity. This implies in turn that the function $T_C(\lambda)$ vanishes for large values of λ. Furthermore, expanding the sectionally analytic function in a Laurent series about the point at infinity,

$$T_C(\lambda) = A_0 + A_1/\lambda + A_2/\lambda^2 + \cdots$$

we may infer from the vanishing of $T_C(\lambda)$ that A_0 must be equal to zero. The function $T_C(\lambda)$ therefore behaves as $1/\lambda$ when λ tends to infinity.

The derivative with respect to λ of the Cauchy representation $T_C(\lambda)$ of a distribution T on the space E is equal to the Cauchy representation of the distributional derivative T' of that distribution,

$$\frac{1}{2\pi i}\frac{\partial}{\partial\lambda}\left(T(x), \frac{1}{x-\lambda}\right) = \frac{1}{2\pi i}\left(T'(x), \frac{1}{x-\lambda}\right)$$

For the distributional derivative of T is defined by the relation,

$$\frac{1}{2\pi i}\left(T'(x), \frac{1}{x-\lambda}\right) = -\frac{1}{2\pi i}\left(T(x), \frac{\partial}{\partial x}\frac{1}{x-\lambda}\right)$$

and, since

$$\frac{\partial}{\partial x}\frac{1}{x-\lambda} = -\frac{\partial}{\partial\lambda}\frac{1}{x-\lambda}$$

we find

$$\frac{1}{2\pi i}\left(T'(x), \frac{1}{x-\lambda}\right) = \frac{1}{2\pi i}\left(T(x), \frac{\partial}{\partial\lambda}\frac{1}{x-\lambda}\right) = \frac{1}{2\pi i}\frac{\partial}{\partial\lambda}\left(T(x), \frac{1}{x-\lambda}\right)$$

Denoting the Cauchy representation of the distributional derivative of a distribution T by $T_C'(\lambda)$,

$$T_C'(\lambda) = \frac{1}{2\pi i}\left(T'(x), \frac{1}{x-\lambda}\right)$$

we may write therefore

$$\frac{\partial}{\partial\lambda} T_C(\lambda) = T_C'(\lambda)$$

In a similar manner we find

$$\frac{\partial^m}{\partial\lambda^m} T_C(\lambda) = T_C^{(m)}(\lambda)$$

where $T_C^{(m)}(\lambda)$ denotes the Cauchy representation,

$$T_C^{(m)}(\lambda) = \frac{1}{2\pi i}\left(T^{(m)}(x), \frac{1}{x-\lambda}\right)$$

of the m-th distributional derivative of the distribution T on the space E.

For example, the Cauchy representation,

$$\delta_C^{(m)}(\lambda) = \frac{1}{2\pi i}\left(\delta^{(m)}(x), \frac{1}{x-\lambda}\right)$$

of the m-th derivative of Dirac's delta function is equal to the m-th derivative with respect to λ of the Cauchy representation of this function. Thus we find

$$\delta_C^{(m)}(\lambda) = \frac{\partial^m}{\partial \lambda^m}\delta_C(\lambda) = \frac{(-1)^{m+1}m!}{2\pi i \lambda^{m+1}}$$

As we have observed before, the support of a distribution T on the space E is contained in a finite interval on the real axis. In other words, a distribution on the space E is a distribution of bounded support.

Let C be a contour enclosing the support of the distribution T on the space E which has the Cauchy representation $T_C(\lambda)$. Integrating the function $T_C(\lambda)$ over the contour C, we find

$$\oint_C T_C(\zeta)\, d\zeta = \frac{1}{2\pi i}\oint_C \left(T(x), \frac{1}{x-\zeta}\right) d\zeta$$

Assuming that we may interchange the order of integration and functional operation, we find

$$\oint_C T_C(\zeta)\, d\zeta = \left(T(x), \frac{1}{2\pi i}\oint_C \frac{d\zeta}{x-\zeta}\right) = (T(x), -1)$$

Thus, the contour integral of the Cauchy representation of a distribution T on the space E over a contour enclosing the support of that distribution is equal to the real or complex number assigned by the distribution T to the testing function $\phi(x) = -1$. This property of the Cauchy representation of a distribution T closely resembles Cauchy's integral theorem, according to which the integral,

$$\frac{1}{2\pi i}\oint_C \frac{d\zeta}{\lambda - \zeta}$$

over a contour C enclosing the point λ is equal to -1.

EXAMPLES The Cauchy representation $\delta_C(\lambda)$ of Dirac's delta function is

$$\delta_C(\lambda) = \frac{1}{2\pi i}\left(\delta(x), \frac{1}{x-\lambda}\right) = -\frac{1}{2\pi i \lambda}$$

and if C is a contour enclosing the origin, then

$$\oint_C \delta_C(\zeta)\, d\zeta = -\frac{1}{2\pi i}\oint_C \frac{d\zeta}{\zeta} = -1 = (\delta, -1) = -\delta(x)$$

We obtain therefore the following contour integral representation,

$$\delta(x) = \frac{1}{2\pi i} \oint_C \frac{d\zeta}{\zeta}$$

of Dirac's delta function.

Similarly, the Cauchy integral representation of the distribution,

$$T(x) = \sum_{m=0}^{M} A_m \, \delta^{(m)}(x)$$

is

$$T_C(\lambda) = \sum_{m=0}^{M} \frac{(-1)^{m+1} A_m \, m!}{2\pi i \lambda^{m+1}}$$

Integrating the function $T_C(\lambda)$ over an arbitrary contour enclosing the origin, we find

$$\oint_C T_C(\zeta)\, d\zeta = \sum_{m=0}^{M} \frac{(-1)^{m+1} A_m \, m!}{2\pi i} \oint_C \frac{d\zeta}{\zeta^{m+1}} = \sum_{m=0}^{M} A_m (\delta^{(m)}, -1) = -A_0$$

and thus

$$(T, -1) = -A_0$$

In the more general case, we consider a function $F(\lambda)$ which is analytic in a strip $-a \leqq I(\lambda) \leqq a$ where a is some positive number. If C is an arbitrary contour enclosing the support of the distribution T on the space E and lying wholly inside the strip $-a \leqq I(\lambda) \leqq a$, then we may write

$$\oint_C T_C(\zeta) F(\zeta)\, d\zeta = \frac{1}{2\pi i} \oint_C \left(T(x), \frac{1}{x - \zeta} \right) F(\zeta)\, d\zeta$$

Supposing again that we may interchange the order of integration and functional operation, we find

$$\oint_C T_C(\zeta) F(\zeta)\, d\zeta = \left(T(x), \frac{1}{2\pi i} \oint_C \frac{F(\zeta)}{x - \zeta}\, d\zeta \right) = (T, -F(x))$$

In words, the contour integral of the product of an analytic function $F(\lambda)$ and the Cauchy representation $T_C(\lambda)$ of a distribution T on the space E over a contour lying wholly inside the region of analyticity of the function $F(\lambda)$ and enclosing the support of the distribution T is equal to the real or complex number assigned by the distribution T to the function $-F(x)$. It should be noted that the analytic function $F(\lambda)$ and its restriction to the real axis satisfy all the conditions imposed on a testing function of the space E so that the operation (T, F) is well defined. The statement above closely resembles the

Cauchy integral theorem for ordinary analytic functions,

$$\frac{1}{2\pi i}\oint_C \frac{F(\zeta)}{\lambda - \zeta} = -F(\lambda)$$

where C is a contour enclosing the point λ.

EXAMPLES The support of Dirac's delta function is concentrated at the origin. Any contour therefore which encloses the origin also encloses the support of the delta distribution. Now let $F(\lambda)$ denote an arbitrary function which is analytic in the strip $-a \leqq I(\lambda) \leqq a$ where a is an arbitrary positive number and let C be a contour enclosing the origin and lying wholly inside this strip. Then

$$\oint_C \delta_C(\zeta)F(\zeta)\,d\zeta = -\frac{1}{2\pi i}\oint_C \frac{F(\zeta)}{\zeta}\,d\zeta = -F(0) = (\delta, -F(x))$$

where $\delta_C(\lambda)$ is the Cauchy representation of the delta function,

$$\delta_C(\lambda) = -\frac{1}{2\pi i\lambda}$$

In a similar manner we find

$$\oint_C \delta_C{}^{(m)}(\zeta)F(\zeta)\,d\zeta = \frac{(-1)^{m+1}m!}{2\pi i}\oint_C \frac{F(\zeta)}{\zeta^{m+1}}\,d\zeta$$

$$= (-1)^{m+1}F^{(m)}(0) = (\delta^{(m)}, -F(x))$$

where $\delta_C{}^{(m)}(\lambda)$ denotes the Cauchy representation,

$$\delta_C{}^{(m)}(\lambda) = \frac{(-1)^{m+1}m!}{2\pi i\lambda^{m+1}}$$

of the m-th derivative of Dirac's delta function.

B. Cauchy Representations of Distributions on the Space *B*.

Up to this point in the discussion we have been concerned with the Cauchy representation of distributions on the space E of testing functions $\phi(x)$. As we have remarked before, the distributions on the space E are distributions with bounded support and such well-known distributions as the Heisenberg delta functions,

$$\delta^{\pm}(x) = \mp\frac{1}{2\pi i}\lim_{\varepsilon\to 0}\frac{1}{x \pm i\varepsilon} = \frac{1}{2}\delta(x) \mp \frac{1}{2\pi i}P\frac{1}{x}$$

and the principal value distributions,

$$P\frac{1}{x^m}$$

do not fall into this category. It has been shown by Bremermann and Durand however that Cauchy representations can also be defined for distributions which do not have bounded support but which are distributions on a new space of testing functions. This new space B contains those testing functions of the space E which, together with all their derivatives, vanish at least as fast as $1/|x|$ when $|x|$ tends to infinity. All other properties of the functions of the space B, including the convergence properties, are the same as those of the functions of the space E. A distribution on the space B can now be defined as a linear functional on the space B that is continuous with respect to the definition of convergence for the functions of the space B. For example, a locally integrable function $T(x)$ which behaves as $1/|x|^p$ when $|x|$ tends to infinity, where p is a positive constant, generates a regular distribution on the space B. For, if $\phi(x)$ is a function of the space B, then ϕ vanishes at least as fast as $1/|x|$ when $|x|$ tends to infinity. The product $T(x)\phi(x)$ therefore vanishes at least as fast as $1/|x|^{p+1}$ for large values of $|x|$, implying that the integral,

$$(T, \phi) = \int_{-\infty}^{\infty} T(x)\phi(x)\,dx$$

exists. In complete analogy with the corresponding definition of a Cauchy representation of a distribution on the space E, we can now define the Cauchy representation of a distribution T on the space B as the function,

$$T_C(\lambda) = \frac{1}{2\pi i}\left(T(x), \frac{1}{x-\lambda}\right)$$

This function is sectionally analytic with a boundary on the real axis consisting of the support of the distribution T. It vanishes moreover as least as fast as $1/\lambda$ when λ tends to infinity.

EXAMPLES The Cauchy representation of Heisenberg's delta function,

$$\delta^+(x) = -\frac{1}{2\pi i}\lim_{\varepsilon\to 0}\frac{1}{x+i\varepsilon}$$

is defined by the relation,

$$\delta_C{}^+(\lambda) = \frac{1}{2\pi i}\left(\delta^+(x), \frac{1}{x-\lambda}\right) = -\frac{1}{2\pi i}\lim_{\varepsilon\to 0}\frac{1}{2\pi i}\int_{-\infty}^{\infty}\frac{1}{x+i\varepsilon}\frac{dx}{x-\lambda}$$

Evaluating the Cauchy integral according to the rules laid down in Chapter I we find

$$\delta_C{}^{+}(\lambda) = -\lim_{\varepsilon\to 0}\frac{1}{2\pi i}\frac{1}{\lambda + i\varepsilon} \qquad \text{when } I(\lambda) > 0$$

$$= 0 \qquad \text{when } I(\lambda) < 0$$

The Cauchy representation of Heisenberg's delta function $\delta^{+}(x)$ may be written therefore as

$$\delta_C{}^{+}(\lambda) = -\frac{1}{2\pi i\lambda} \qquad \text{when } I(\lambda) > 0$$

$$= 0 \qquad \text{when } I(\lambda) < 0$$

The Cauchy representation of Heisenberg's delta function,

$$\delta^{-}(x) = \lim_{\varepsilon\to 0}\frac{1}{2\pi i}\frac{1}{x - i\varepsilon}$$

can be obtained in a similar manner. In this case we must evaluate the Cauchy integral,

$$\delta_C{}^{-}(\lambda) = \frac{1}{2\pi i}\lim_{\varepsilon\to 0}\frac{1}{2\pi i}\int_{-\infty}^{\infty}\frac{1}{x - i\varepsilon}\frac{1}{x - \lambda}\,dx$$

and we find

$$\delta_C{}^{-}(\lambda) = 0 \qquad \text{when } I(\lambda) > 0$$

$$= -\frac{1}{2\pi i\lambda} \qquad \text{when } I(\lambda) < 0$$

The Cauchy integral representation $P_C{}^{m}(\lambda)$ of the principal value distribution $P(1/x^m)$ can also be obtained by means of Cauchy's integral theorem of Section 1.1,

$$P_C{}^{m}(\lambda) = \frac{1}{2\pi i}\left(\frac{1}{x^m}, \frac{1}{x - \lambda}\right) = \frac{1}{2\pi i}\int_{-\infty}^{\infty}\frac{1}{x^m}\frac{dx}{x - \lambda} = \frac{1}{\lambda^m} \qquad \text{when } I(\lambda) > 0$$

$$= -\frac{1}{2\lambda^m} \qquad \text{when } I(\lambda) < 0$$

Combining the results of the last two examples with the Cauchy representation of Dirac's delta function, we may also write

$$\delta_C{}^{+}(\lambda) = \frac{1}{2}\,\delta_C(\lambda) - \frac{1}{2\pi i}\,P_C(\lambda)$$

and

$$\delta_C^{-}(\lambda) = \frac{1}{2}\,\delta_C(\lambda) + \frac{1}{2\pi i}\,P_C(\lambda)$$

for the Cauchy representations of the Heisenberg delta functions $\delta^{\pm}(x)$.

It can again be shown that the m-th derivative with respect to λ of a Cauchy representation of a distribution T on the space B is equal to the Cauchy representation of the m-th distributional derivative $T^{(m)}$ of the distribution T,

$$\frac{\partial^m}{\partial\lambda^m}\,T_C(\lambda) = T_C^{(m)}(\lambda)$$

For example, in Section 5.3 we have shown that the m-th derivative of the Heisenberg delta function $\delta^{+}(x)$ may be written as

$$\delta^{+(m)}(x) = \frac{1}{2}\,\delta^{(m)}(x) - \frac{(-1)^m m!}{2\pi i}\,P\,\frac{1}{x^{m+1}}$$

In view of the results obtained above, the Cauchy representation of the m-th derivative of the Heisenberg delta function takes the form,

$$\begin{aligned}
\delta_C^{+(m)}(\lambda) &= \frac{(-1)^{m+1} m!}{2\pi i}\,\frac{1}{2\lambda^{m+1}} - \frac{(-1)^m m!}{2\pi i}\,\frac{1}{2\lambda^{m+1}} && \text{when } I(\lambda) > 0 \\
&= \frac{(-1)^{m+1} m!}{2\pi i}\,\frac{1}{2\lambda^{m+1}} + \frac{(-1)^m m!}{2\pi i}\,\frac{1}{2\lambda^{m+1}} && \text{when } I(\lambda) < 0
\end{aligned}$$

or

$$\begin{aligned}
\delta_C^{+(m)}(\lambda) &= -\frac{(-1)^m m!}{2\pi i}\,\frac{1}{\lambda^{m+1}} && \text{when } I(\lambda) > 0 \\
&= 0 && \text{when } I(\lambda) < 0
\end{aligned}$$

However, we have found before that the Cauchy representation of Heisenberg's delta function $\delta^{+}(x)$ is

$$\begin{aligned}
\delta_C^{+}(\lambda) &= -\frac{1}{2\pi i}\,\frac{1}{\lambda} && \text{when } I(\lambda) > 0 \\
&= 0 && \text{when } I(\lambda) < 0
\end{aligned}$$

Taking the m-th derivative of this quantity, we find

$$\begin{aligned}
\frac{\partial^m}{\partial\lambda^m}\,\delta^{+}(\lambda) &= -\frac{(-1)^m m!}{2\pi i}\,\frac{1}{\lambda^{m+1}} && \text{when } I(\lambda) > 0 \\
&= 0 && \text{when } I(\lambda) < 0
\end{aligned}$$

Comparing this expression with that for the Cauchy representation of the m-th distributional derivative of the Heisenberg delta function, we obtain the equality

$$\frac{\partial^m}{\partial \lambda^m} \delta_C{}^+(\lambda) = \delta_C{}^{+(m)}(\lambda)$$

as was to be expected.

As in the case of the Cauchy representation of a distribution on the space E, we can also obtain a generalized Cauchy integral theorem for the Cauchy representation of a distribution on the space B. For, if T is a distribution on the space B and $F(\lambda)$ is an analytic function of the complex variable λ in the strip $-b \leqq I(\lambda) \leqq b$ which vanishes at least as fast as $1/\lambda$ when λ tends to infinity in this strip, then

$$(T, -F(x)) = \int_{-\infty - ia}^{\infty - ia} T_C(\zeta)F(\zeta)\, d\zeta - \int_{-\infty + ia}^{\infty + ia} T_C(\zeta)F(\zeta)\, d\zeta$$

where $T_C(\lambda)$ denotes the Cauchy representation of the distribution T and a is a real number such that $0 < a < b$. This may be shown as follows. Writing

$$\int_{-\infty - ia}^{\infty - ia} T_C(\zeta)F(\zeta)\, d\zeta - \int_{-\infty + ia}^{\infty + ia} T_C(\zeta)F(\zeta)\, d\zeta$$
$$= \frac{1}{2\pi i}\int_{-\infty - ia}^{\infty - ia} \left(T(x), \frac{1}{x-\zeta}\right)F(\zeta)\, d\zeta - \frac{1}{2\pi i}\int_{-\infty + ia}^{\infty + ia} \left(T(x), \frac{1}{x-\zeta}\right)F(\zeta)\, d\zeta$$

and assuming that we may interchange the order of integration and functional operation, we find

$$\int_{-\infty - ia}^{\infty - ia} T_C(\zeta)F(\zeta)\, d\zeta - \int_{-\infty + ia}^{\infty + ia} T_C(\zeta)F(\zeta)\, d\zeta$$
$$= \left(T(x), \frac{1}{2\pi i}\int_{-\infty - ia}^{\infty - ia} \frac{F(\zeta)}{x-\zeta}\, d\zeta - \frac{1}{2\pi i}\int_{-\infty + ia}^{\infty + ia} \frac{F(\zeta)}{x-\zeta}\, d\zeta\right)$$

However, $F(\lambda)$ is analytic in the strip $-b \leqq I(\lambda) \leqq b$, which contains the strip $-a \leqq I(\lambda) \leqq a$, and vanishes at least as fast as $1/\lambda$ when λ tends to infinity in this strip. Thus we may write, according to Cauchy's integral theorem,

$$\frac{1}{2\pi i}\int_{-\infty - ia}^{\infty - ia} \frac{F(\zeta)}{x-\zeta}\, d\zeta - \frac{1}{2\pi i}\int_{-\infty + ia}^{\infty + ia} \frac{F(\zeta)}{x-\zeta}\, d\zeta = -F(x)$$

and we obtain therefore the stated result,

$$(T, -F(x)) = \int_{-\infty - ia}^{\infty - ia} T_C(\zeta)F(\zeta)\, d\zeta - \int_{-\infty + ia}^{\infty + ia} T_C(\zeta)F(\zeta)\, d\zeta$$

Since the restriction on the real axis of the function $F(\lambda)$ is a function of the space B, the operation on the left hand side of this expression is well defined.

EXAMPLE The Cauchy representation $\delta_C{}^+(\lambda)$ of Heisenberg's delta function is

$$\delta_C{}^+(\lambda) = -\frac{1}{2\pi i}\frac{1}{\lambda} \qquad \text{when } I(\lambda) > 0$$

$$= 0 \qquad \text{when } I(\lambda) < 0$$

and we find, therefore,

$$(\delta^+, -F(x)) = \frac{1}{2\pi i}\int_{-\infty+ia}^{\infty+ia} \frac{F(\zeta)}{\zeta}\, d\zeta$$

This expression may also be written as

$$(\delta^+, F(x)) = \frac{1}{2\pi i}\int_{\Gamma} \frac{F(\zeta)}{\zeta}\, d\zeta$$

where Γ is the path shown in Figure V-1.

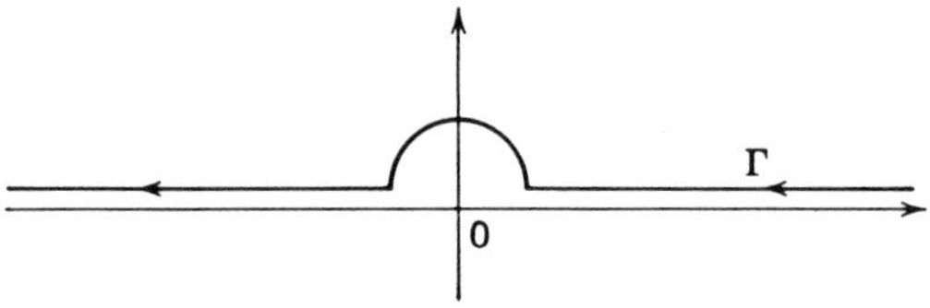

Figure V-1

We obtain therefore the following contour integral representation of Heisenberg's delta function,

$$\delta^+(x) = \frac{1}{2\pi i}\int_{\Gamma} \frac{d\zeta}{\zeta}$$

In a similar manner we can obtain the integral representation of Heisenberg's δ^- function,

$$\delta^-(x) = \frac{1}{2\pi i}\int_{\Omega} \frac{d\zeta}{\zeta}$$

where Ω is the path of Figure V-2.

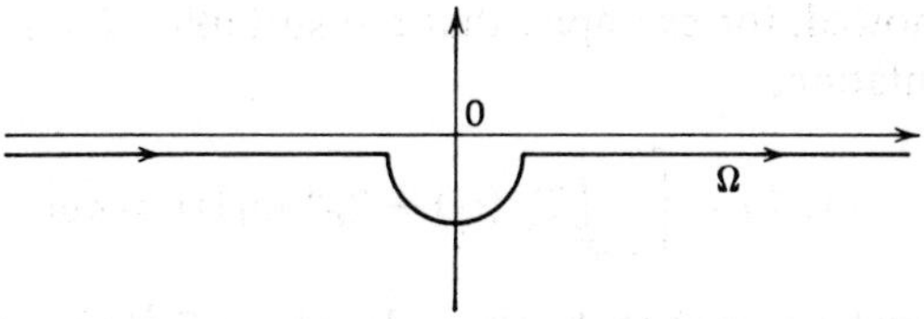

Figure V-2

C. CAUCHY REPRESENTATIONS AND PLEMELJ FORMULAS

In Chapter IV we presented a discussion of the properties of sectionally analytic functions which can be represented by a Cauchy integral,

$$F(\lambda) = \frac{1}{2\pi i} \int_{-\infty}^{\infty} \frac{f(\omega)}{\omega - \lambda} \, d\omega$$

where $f(\omega)$ is Hölder continuous or integrable on the real axis. Among the more important results obtained in that chapter is the first Plemelj formula,

$$f(\omega) = F^L(\omega) - F^R(\omega)$$

by which the function $f(\omega)$ can be represented in terms of the boundary values $F^L(\omega)$ and $F^R(\omega)$ of the sectionally analytic function $F(\lambda)$ on the real axis. Representations of this type, as we have shown in Section 4.11, can be used to obtain the solution of certain singular integral equations of the Cauchy type and serve many other important purposes. Since the Cauchy integral,

$$F(\lambda) = \frac{1}{2\pi i} \int_{-\infty}^{\infty} \frac{f(\omega)}{\omega - \lambda} \, d\omega$$

representing the sectionally analytic function $F(\lambda)$, and the Cauchy representation,

$$T_C(\lambda) = \frac{1}{2\pi i} \left(T(x), \frac{1}{x - \lambda} \right)$$

of a distribution T on the space E or B closely resemble each other, we may well ask: "Does the Plemelj representation of the function $f(\omega)$ has a distributional counterpart by which the distribution T can be represented in terms of the boundary values of the sectionally analytic function $T_C(\lambda)$ on the real axis?" This question has been answered in the affirmative by Bremermann and Durand who showed, for example, that a distribution T on the space E or B has the representation,

$$(T, f) = \int_{-\infty}^{\infty} [T_C{}^L(\omega) - T_C{}^R(\omega)] f(\omega)\, d\omega$$

for all testing functions $f(x)$ of the space D, where $T_C{}^L(\omega)$ and $T_C{}^R(\omega)$ are the boundary values on the real axis of the Cauchy representation,

$$T_C(\lambda) = \frac{1}{2\pi i}\left(T(x), \frac{1}{x - \lambda}\right)$$

of the distribution T. For a rigorous proof of this statement we must refer the reader to the literature but, in order to gain some insight in the functional operations involved, we shall try to make the validity of this formula plausible. To this purpose let us consider the expression,

$$\lim_{\varepsilon \to 0} \int_{-\infty}^{\infty} [T_C(\omega + i\varepsilon) - T_C(\omega - i\varepsilon)] f(\omega)\, d\omega$$

$$= \lim_{\varepsilon \to 0} \frac{1}{2\pi i} \int_{-\infty}^{\infty} \left(T(x), \frac{1}{x - (\omega + i\varepsilon)} - \frac{1}{x - (\omega - i\varepsilon)}\right) f(\omega)\, d\omega$$

Assuming that we may interchange the order of integration and functional operation, we find

$$\lim_{\varepsilon \to 0} \int_{-\infty}^{\infty} [T_C(\omega + i\varepsilon) - T_C(\omega - i\varepsilon)] f(\omega)\, d\omega$$

$$= \left(T(x), \lim_{\varepsilon \to 0}\left[\frac{1}{2\pi i} \int_{-\infty}^{\infty} \frac{f(\omega)}{\omega - (x + i\varepsilon)}\, d\omega - \frac{1}{2\pi i} \int_{-\infty}^{\infty} \frac{f(\omega)}{\omega - (x - i\varepsilon)}\, d\omega\right]\right)$$

However, according to the Plemelj formulas, which certainly hold for the testing functions $f(x)$ of the space E, we may write

$$\lim_{\varepsilon \to 0} \frac{1}{2\pi i} \int_{-\infty}^{\infty} \frac{f(\omega)}{\omega - (x + i\varepsilon)}\, d\omega - \lim_{\varepsilon \to 0} \frac{1}{2\pi i} \int_{-\infty}^{\infty} \frac{f(\omega)}{\omega - (x - i\varepsilon)}\, d\omega = f(x)$$

and we obtain therefore the representation,

$$(T, f) = \lim_{\varepsilon \to 0} \int_{-\infty}^{\infty} [T_C(\omega + i\varepsilon) - T_C(\omega - i\varepsilon)] f(\omega)\, d\omega$$

$$= \int_{-\infty}^{\infty} [T_C{}^L(\omega) - T_C{}^R(\omega)] f(\omega)\, d\omega$$

EXAMPLES The Cauchy representation of Dirac's delta function is

$$\delta_C(\lambda) = -\frac{1}{2\pi i}\frac{1}{\lambda}$$

and we may write

$$\delta_C{}^L(\omega) = -\frac{1}{2\pi i}\lim_{\varepsilon\to 0}\frac{1}{\omega + i\varepsilon}$$

and

$$\delta_C{}^R(\omega) = -\frac{1}{2\pi i}\lim_{\varepsilon\to 0}\frac{1}{\omega - i\varepsilon}$$

Substitution of these expressions for the boundary values of the function $\delta_C(\lambda)$ into the representation formula above yields the following integral representation of Dirac's delta function,

$$(\delta, f) = \lim_{\varepsilon\to 0}\frac{1}{2\pi i}\int_{-\infty}^{\infty}\left[\frac{1}{\omega - i\varepsilon} - \frac{1}{\omega + i\varepsilon}\right] f(\omega)\, d\omega$$

This formula implies the limit representation,

$$\delta(x) = \lim_{\varepsilon\to 0}\frac{1}{\pi}\frac{\varepsilon}{x^2 + \varepsilon^2}$$

or conversely, by means of the limit representation, the integral representation above can be verified.

In a similar manner the formula,

$$(T, f) = \int_{-\infty}^{\infty}[T_C{}^L(\omega) - T_C{}^R(\omega)] f(\omega)\, d\omega$$

can be used to obtain, by means of the Cauchy representation of Heisenberg's delta function, an integral representation and a limit representation of this distribution. For, the Cauchy representation of this distribution may be written as

$$\delta_C{}^+(\lambda) = -\frac{1}{2\pi i}\frac{1}{\lambda} \qquad \text{when } I(\lambda) > 0$$

$$= 0 \qquad \text{when } I(\lambda) < 0$$

and we find, therefore,

$$\delta_C{}^{+L}(\omega) = -\lim_{\varepsilon\to 0}\frac{1}{2\pi i}\frac{1}{\omega + i\varepsilon}$$

and

$$\delta_C{}^{+R}(\omega) = 0$$

Substitution yields the integral representation,

$$(\delta^+, f) = -\lim_{\varepsilon \to 0} \frac{1}{2\pi i} \int_{-\infty}^{\infty} \frac{f(\omega)}{\omega + i\varepsilon} \, d\omega$$

from which we can obtain the limit representation,

$$\delta^+(x) = -\lim_{\varepsilon \to 0} \frac{1}{2\pi i} \frac{1}{x + i\varepsilon}$$

The integral representation,

$$(\delta^-, f) = \lim_{\varepsilon \to 0} \frac{1}{2\pi i} \int_{-\infty}^{\infty} \frac{f(\omega)}{\omega - i\varepsilon} \, d\omega$$

and the corresponding limit representation,

$$\delta^-(x) = \lim_{\varepsilon \to 0} \frac{1}{2\pi i} \frac{1}{x - i\varepsilon}$$

for Heisenberg's δ^- function can be obtained from the Cauchy representation of this distribution by a similar argument.

Finally, since the Cauchy representation $P_C(\lambda)$ of the principal value distribution $P(1/x)$ is given by

$$P_C(\lambda) = \frac{1}{2\lambda} \qquad \text{when } I(\lambda) > 0$$

$$= -\frac{1}{2\lambda} \qquad \text{when } I(\lambda) < 0$$

we find the boundary values

$$P_C{}^L(\omega) = \lim_{\varepsilon \to 0} \frac{1}{2} \frac{1}{\omega + i\varepsilon}$$

and

$$P_C{}^R(\omega) = -\lim_{\varepsilon \to 0} \frac{1}{2} \frac{1}{\omega - i\varepsilon}$$

and we obtain therefore the following integral representation,

$$\left(P\frac{1}{x}, f\right) = \lim_{\varepsilon \to 0} \frac{1}{2} \int_{-\infty}^{\infty} \left[\frac{1}{\omega + i\varepsilon} + \frac{1}{\omega - i\varepsilon}\right] f(\omega) \, d\omega$$

for the principal value distribution.

5.6 GENERALIZED ANALYTIC FUNCTIONS

If $f(x)$ is an arbitrary testing function of the space D and $T(x, \lambda)$ is a locally integrable function of the variable x which is also an analytic function of the complex variable λ in some given region R of the complex plane, then, as we have seen in Section 2.3, the integral,

$$\int_{-\infty}^{\infty} T(x, \lambda) f(x)\, dx$$

is a representation of an analytic function of λ in the region R. Considered as a continuous linear functional on the space D of testing functions $f(x)$, this integral defines therefore a whole family of functions of the complex variable λ which are all analytic in the same region R of the complex plane. In this case, the regular distribution $T(\lambda)$ defined on the space D of testing functions $f(x)$ by the operation,

$$(T(\lambda), f) = \int_{-\infty}^{\infty} T(x, \lambda) f(x)\, dx$$

is called a regular generalized analytic function of the complex variable λ in the region R. The regular generalized analytic function $T(\lambda)$ should not be confused with the Cauchy representation $T_C(\lambda)$ of a distribution T introduced in the preceding section. The Cauchy representation $T_C(\lambda)$ is defined by the operation,

$$T_C(\lambda) = \frac{1}{2\pi i}\left(T(x), \frac{1}{x - \lambda}\right)$$

of a distribution T on a very special testing function of the space E or B, to wit, the function $1/[2\pi i(x - \lambda)]$. On the other hand, a regular generalized analytic function $T(\lambda)$ is defined by the operation,

$$(T(\lambda), f) = \int_{-\infty}^{\infty} T(x, \lambda) f(x)\, dx$$

of a regular distribution T, depending on a complex variable λ, on all the testing functions of the space D. For each individual testing function $f(x)$ of the space D the operation,

$$(T(\lambda), f) = \int_{-\infty}^{\infty} T(x, \lambda) f(x)\, dx$$

defines an ordinary analytic function and a class of such analytic functions is generated by this operation when the testing function $f(x)$ traverses the space D.

Referring again to Section 2.3, we found that the integral,

$$\int_{-\infty}^{\infty} T(x, \lambda) f(x)\, dx$$

can be differentiated under the integral sign,

$$\int_{-\infty}^{\infty} \frac{\partial T}{\partial \lambda} f(x)\, dx$$

at a point of analyticity of the function $T(x, \lambda)$ and, since the derivative of an analytic function is also an analytic function, the last integral is the representation of an analytic function in the region R. The continuous linear functional $\partial T/\partial \lambda$ defined on the space D by the operation,

$$\left(\frac{\partial T}{\partial \lambda}, f\right) = \int_{-\infty}^{\infty} \frac{\partial T(x, \lambda)}{\partial \lambda} f(x)\, dx$$

is a regular distribution on the space D and a regular generalized analytic function in the region R. It will be called the derivative of the regular generalized analytic function $T(\lambda)$ with respect to λ,

$$\frac{\partial}{\partial \lambda}(T(\lambda), f) = \left(\frac{\partial T}{\partial \lambda}, f\right)$$

Continuing in this manner, we can obtain a Taylor series representation of the regular generalized analytic function $T(\lambda)$ in a point of analyticity $\lambda = a$,

$$T(\lambda) = T(a) + (\lambda - a)\frac{\partial T(a)}{\partial \lambda} + \frac{1}{2}(\lambda - a)^2 \frac{\partial^2 T(a)}{\partial \lambda^2} + \cdots$$

This representation of the regular generalized analytic function $T(\lambda)$ is defined by the operations,

$$\begin{aligned}(T(\lambda), f) &= \left(T(a) + (\lambda - a)\frac{\partial T(a)}{\partial \lambda} + \ldots, f\right) \\ &= (T(a), f) + (\lambda - a)\left(\frac{\partial T(a)}{\partial \lambda}, f\right) + \cdots\end{aligned}$$

on the space D of testing functions $f(x)$, and the expansion coefficients $\partial^m T(a)/\partial \lambda^m$ are again regular distributions on the space D.

Similarly we can find a Laurent series representation of the regular generalized analytic function $T(\lambda)$ in the neighborhood of an isolated singularity $\lambda = a$ of the generating function $T(x, \lambda)$. For, expanding the function $T(x, \lambda)$ in a Laurent series about the point $\lambda = a$, we find

$$T(x, \lambda) = \sum_{m=-\infty}^{\infty} A_m(x)(\lambda - a)^m$$

where the expansion coefficients $A_m(x)$ have been defined in Section 1.2,

$$A_m(x) = \frac{1}{2\pi i} \oint_C \frac{T(x, \zeta)}{(\zeta - a)^{m+1}}\, d\zeta$$

and C is a contour enclosing the singularity at the point $\lambda = a$ but no other singularities of the function $T(x, \lambda)$. Substituting this representation for the function $T(x, \lambda)$ into the integral

$$(T(\lambda), f) = \int_{-\infty}^{\infty} T(x, \lambda) f(x)\, dx$$

we find

$$(T(\lambda), f) = \sum_{m=-\infty}^{\infty} (A_m(x), f)(\lambda - a)^m$$

This operation defines the Laurent series representation of the regular generalized analytic function $T(\lambda)$,

$$T(\lambda) = \sum_{m=-\infty}^{\infty} (\lambda - a)^m A_m$$

where the coefficients A_m are defined by the operation,

$$(A_m, f) = \frac{1}{2\pi i} \oint_C \frac{(T(x, \zeta), f)}{(\zeta - a)^{m+1}}\, d\zeta$$

as regular distributions on the space D.

These notions, introduced at the hand of regular distributions, can be extended immediately to generalized analytic functions defined by singular distributions on the space D of testing functions $f(x)$. In general, therefore, a distribution $T(\lambda)$ on the space of testing functions D is said to be a generalized analytic function of the complex variable λ in a region R of the complex plane, if the operation $(T(\lambda), f)$ defines an ordinary analytic function of λ in the region R for all testing functions $f(x)$ of the space D. Thus, for a particular testing function $f(x)$ of the space D the operation $(T(\lambda), f)$ defines an ordinary function of the complex variable λ and a whole class of such functions is generated by this operation as the function $f(x)$ traverses the space D. The derivative with respect to λ of such a generalized analytic function and the Taylor and Laurent series representations of such functions can be defined in complete analogy with the corresponding concepts for regular generalized analytic functions.

The concept of the analytic continuation of an ordinary function of a complex variable which plays such an important role in the application of function-theoretic techniques in mathematical physics and engineering can also be formulated for generalized analytic functions. For, let $T(\lambda)$ denote a distribution on the space D of testing functions $f(x)$ and a generalized analytic function of the complex variable λ in a region $R(T)$ of the complex plane. Furthermore, let $(S(\lambda), f)$ denote the analytic continuation of the ordinary analytic function $(T(\lambda), f)$ from its region of analyticity $R(T)$ into the region $R(S)$. If the ordinary analytic function $(S(\lambda), f)$ is the analytic continuation of the ordinary analytic function $(T(\lambda), f)$ into the region $R(S)$ for all testing functions $f(x)$ of the space D, then the functional $S(\lambda)$ is a generalized analytic function and the analytic continuation of the generalized analytic function $T(\lambda)$ into the region $R(S)$. For, as we have remarked in Section 1.6, the analytic continuation $(S(\lambda), f)$ of the ordinary function $(T(\lambda), f)$ can be obtained by means of a Taylor series expansion technique. However, the radius of convergence of such a Taylor series is determined by the singularities of the function $(T(\lambda), f)$ as a function of λ and does not depend on the particular testing function considered. Thus, the radius of convergence is the same for all testing functions of the space D, and the Taylor series,

$$(T(\lambda), f) = \left(T(a) + (\lambda - a)\frac{\partial T(a)}{\partial \lambda} + \ldots, f \right)$$

defines a continuous linear functional on the space D for all values of λ inside the radius of convergence. This distribution therefore is a generalized analytic function on the region enclosed by the radius of convergence. From this we may infer that the ordinary analytic functions $(S(\lambda), f)$ on the region $R(S)$, obtained by successive Taylor series expansions from the ordinary analytic functions $(T(\lambda), f)$ on the region $R(T)$, are the values of a continuous linear functional $S(\lambda)$ which is a generalized analytic function on the region $R(S)$ and may be considered to be the analytic continuation of the generalized analytic function $T(\lambda)$ into the region $R(S)$.

To illustrate the applicability of the technique of analytic continuation of generalized analytic functions, we shall present a few examples of the regularization of a function with an algebraic singularity.

In the foregoing sections we frequently encountered the principal value distribution $P(1/x)$ which is defined, on the space D, by the operation,

$$\left(P\frac{1}{x}, f \right) = \lim_{\varepsilon \to 0} \int_{|x| \geqq \varepsilon} \frac{f(x)}{x}\, dx$$

where $f(x)$ is a testing function of the space D. By means of the Cauchy principal value definition the, in general, divergent integral,

$$\int_{-\infty}^{\infty} \frac{f(x)}{x}\, dx$$

is assigned a definite value by deleting from the interval of integration an infinitesimal small interval $|x| < \varepsilon$. However, considered as a functional on the space D of testing functions $f(x)$, the integral can also be made definite by choosing from among the testing functions of the space D only those functions $f(x)$ which vanish in a neighborhood of the origin. For, the integral is well defined for all testing functions $f(x)$ which vanish in such a neighborhood. In general, if the function $T(x)$ has a nonintegrable singularity at the point $x = a$, then the integral,

$$\int_{-\infty}^{\infty} T(x)f(x)\,dx$$

is well defined in the ordinary sense for all testing functions $f(x)$ which vanish at the point a. Thus, although we cannot define a continuous linear functional T by the integral,

$$\int_{-\infty}^{\infty} T(x)f(x)\,dx$$

for all functions $f(x)$ of the space D, we can define a so-called regularization of the function $T(x)$ or of the integral,

$$\int_{-\infty}^{\infty} T(x)f(x)\,dx$$

as the distribution which is defined by this integral for all testing functions $f(x)$ which vanish in a neighborhood of the point a.

A regularization of the function $1/x$ is a distribution $1/x$ which is defined by the integral,

$$\left(\frac{1}{x}, f\right) = \int_{-\infty}^{\infty} \frac{f(x)}{x}\,dx$$

for all testing functions $f(x)$ which vanish in a neighborhood of the origin. An example of such a regularization of the function $1/x$ is the distribution $1/x$ defined by the integral,

$$\left(\frac{1}{x}, f\right) = \int_{-\infty}^{\infty} \frac{f(x) - f(0)[\theta(x+1) - \theta(x-1)]}{x}\,dx$$

where $\theta(x)$ is the unit step function. Similarly, a regularization of the function $1/x^m$ is the distribution $1/x^m$ which is defined by the operation,

$$\left(\frac{1}{x^m}, f\right) = \int_{-\infty}^{\infty} \frac{f(x) - \sum_{n=0}^{m-1} \dfrac{f^{(n)}(0)x^n}{n!}[\theta(x+1) - \theta(x-1)]}{x^m}\,dx$$

In general, if $T(x)$ is a function with a nonintegrable singularity at the origin and the function $x^m T(x)$ is locally integrable, then a regularization of the function $T(x)$ is the distribution T which is defined by the operation,

$$(T, f) = \int_{-\infty}^{\infty} T(x)\Big[f(x) - \Big\{f(0) + f'(0)x + \cdots + \frac{1}{(m-1)!} f^{(m-1)}(0)x^{m-1}\Big\}\{\theta(x+1) - \theta(x-1)\}\Big]\, dx$$

Let us return to our example of the regularization of the function $1/x$ defined by the operation,

$$\left(\frac{1}{x}, f\right) = \int_{-\infty}^{\infty} \frac{f(x)}{x}\, dx$$

where $f(x)$ is a testing function of the space D which vanishes in a neighborhood of the origin. We note that the delta distribution $\delta(x)$ vanishes everywhere except at the origin. In other words, the support of the delta distribution consists of the single point $x = 0$, a fact that can also be referred to by saying that the delta distribution $\delta(x)$ is concentrated at the origin. This implies that we can add a delta distribution $\delta(x)$ to the regularization $1/x$ of the function $1/x$ without changing the result. For

$$\left(\frac{1}{x} + \delta(x), f\right) = \left(\frac{1}{x}, f\right) + (\delta, f) = \left(\frac{1}{x}, f\right) + f(0)$$

However, the testing function $f(x)$ vanishes in a neighborhood of the origin and thus

$$\left(\frac{1}{x} + \delta(x), f\right) = \left(\frac{1}{x}, f\right)$$

In general, if the function $T(x)$ has a nonintegrable singularity at the point a, then a regularization T of this function is determined up to an arbitrary linear combination of the delta distribution $\delta(x - a)$ and its derivatives. For, the delta function $\delta(x - a)$ and its derivatives $\delta^{(m)}(x - a)$ are all concentrated at the point $x = a$. Hence

$$\begin{aligned}\Big(T + \sum_m A_m \delta^{(m)}(x-a), f\Big) &= (T, f) + \sum_m A_m(\delta^{(m)}(x-a), f)\\ &= (T, f) + \sum_m A_m(-1)^m f^{(m)}(a) = (T, f)\end{aligned}$$

since the testing functions $f(x)$ of the regularization T of the function $T(x)$ at the point a vanish in a neighborhood of this point.

As an example, let us consider the function $x^{\lambda}\theta(x)$ where λ is a complex parameter and $\theta(x)$ denotes the unit step function. This function is locally integrable for all values of λ in the right half plane $R(\lambda) > -1$ and generates a regular distribution $x^{\lambda}\theta(x)$ defined by the operation,

$$(x^{\lambda}\theta, f) = \int_0^{\infty} x^{\lambda} f(x)\, dx$$

on the space D of testing functions $f(x)$ for all values of λ in this half plane. Now let $f(x)$ be a testing function of the space D. Then the integral,

$$\int_0^{\infty} x^{\lambda} f(x)\, dx$$

is the representation of an ordinary function $(x^{\lambda}\theta, f)$ of the complex variable λ which is analytic in the right half plane $R(\lambda) > -1$. However, the following evaluation of this integral,

$$\int_0^{\infty} x^{\lambda} f(x)\, dx = \int_0^1 x^{\lambda}[f(x) - f(0)]\, dx + \int_1^{\infty} x^{\lambda} f(x)\, dx + \frac{f(0)}{\lambda + 1}$$

is the representation of a function of the complex variable λ which is analytic in all points of the right half plane $R(\lambda) > -2$ with the exception of the point $\lambda = -1$. At this point the function has a simple pole with residue $f(0)$. Thus the function,

$$(x^{\lambda}\theta, f) = \int_0^{\infty} x^{\lambda} f(x)\, dx$$

which is analytic for all values of λ in the right half plane $R(\lambda) > -1$, can be analytically continued by the evaluation,

$$(x^{\lambda}\theta, f) = \int_0^1 x^{\lambda}[f(x) - f(0)]\, dx + \int_1^{\infty} x^{\lambda} f(x)\, dx + \frac{f(0)}{\lambda + 1}$$

into the strip $-2 < R(\lambda) \leqq -1$. The function $(x^{\lambda}\theta, f)$ defined by this evaluation is therefore analytic in the right half plane $R(\lambda) > -2$ with the exception of the point $\lambda = -1$ at which it has a simple pole with residue $f(0)$. Since

$$\frac{f(0)}{\lambda + 1} = -\, f(0) \int_1^{\infty} x^{\lambda}\, dx$$

when $-2 < R(\lambda) < -1$, the function $(x^{\lambda}\theta, f)$ has the simple representation,

$$(x^{\lambda}\theta, f) = \int_0^{\infty} x^{\lambda}[f(x) - f(0)]\, dx$$

inside the strip $-2 < R(\lambda) < -1$.

These conclusions derived for the ordinary function $(x^\lambda \theta, f)$ imply that the generalized analytic function $x^\lambda \theta(x)$ defined by the operation,

$$(x^\lambda \theta, f) = \int_0^\infty x^\lambda f(x)\, dx$$

on the space D of testing functions $f(x)$ for all values of λ in the right half plane $R(\lambda) > -1$, can be analytically continued into the strip $-2 < R(\lambda) \leqq -1$ by means of the generalized analytic function $x^\lambda \theta(x)$ which is defined by the functional,

$$(x^\lambda \theta, f) = \int_0^1 x^\lambda [f(x) - f(0)]\, dx + \int_1^\infty x^\lambda f(x)\, dx + \frac{(\delta, f)}{\lambda + 1}$$

This generalized analytic function is analytic in the half plane $R(\lambda) > -2$ with the exception of the point $\lambda = -1$ at which it has a simple pole with residue $\delta(x)$. Inside the strip $-2 < R(\lambda) < -1$ the defining functional takes the simple form,

$$(x^\lambda \theta, f) = \int_0^\infty x^\lambda [f(x) - f(0)]\, dx$$

Thus, by means of the principle of analytic continuation, we can define a regularization of the function $x^\lambda \theta(x)$ in the half plane $R(\lambda) > -2$ as a distribution $x^\lambda \theta(x)$ which is defined by the functional,

$$(x^\lambda \theta, f) = \int_0^1 x^\lambda [f(x) - f(0)]\, dx + \int_1^\infty x^\lambda f(x)\, dx + \frac{(\delta, f)}{\lambda + 1}$$

on the space D of testing functions $f(x)$. This distribution is analytic in the half plane $R(\lambda) > -2$ with the exception of the point $\lambda = -1$ at which it has a simple pole with residue $\delta(x)$.

More generally, we can consider the analytic continuation,

$$\int_0^1 x^\lambda \left[f(x) - \sum_{m=0}^{M-1} \frac{f^{(m)}(0) x^m}{m!} \right] dx + \int_1^\infty x^\lambda f(x)\, dx + \sum_{m=0}^{M-1} \frac{f^{(m)}(0)}{m!(\lambda + m + 1)}$$

into the strip $-(M + 1) < R(\lambda) < -1$ of the function $(x^\lambda \theta, f)$ which is defined and analytic in the half plane $R(\lambda) > -1$ and can be represented in this half plane by the integral,

$$(x^\lambda \theta, f) = \int_0^\infty x^\lambda f(x)\, dx$$

The continuation of this function is analytic in the half plane $R(\lambda) > -(M + 1)$ with the exception of the points $\lambda = -M, -(M - 1), \ldots, -1$ at which it has simple poles with residues $f^{(m)}(0)/m!$. Since in the strip $-(M+1) < R(\lambda) < -M$,

$$\sum_{m=0}^{M-1} \frac{f^{(m)}(0)}{m!} \frac{1}{\lambda+m+1} = -\sum_{m=0}^{M-1} \frac{f^{(m)}(0)}{m!} \int_1^\infty x^{\lambda+m+1}\,dx$$

the analytic continuation of the function $(x^\lambda\theta, f)$ takes the simple form,

$$\int_0^\infty x^\lambda \left[f(x) - f(0) - f'(0)x - \cdots - \frac{f^{(M-1)}(0)}{(M-1)!} x^{M-1} \right] dx$$

inside this strip. These facts can again be exploited to define a generalized analytic function on the space D of testing functions $f(x)$ by the operation,

$$(x^\lambda\theta, f) = \int_0^1 x^\lambda \left[f(x) - \sum_{m=0}^{M-1} \frac{f^{(m)}(0)x^m}{m!} \right] dx + \int_1^\infty x^\lambda f(x)\,dx + \sum_{m=0}^{M-1} \frac{(-1)^m(\delta^{(m)}, f)}{m!(\lambda+m+1)}$$

This generalized analytic function is the analytic continuation into the strip $-(M+1) < R(\lambda) < -1$ of the generalized analytic function $x^\lambda\theta(x)$ which is defined in the half space $R(\lambda) > -1$ as a regular distribution by the operation,

$$(x^\lambda\theta, f) = \int_0^\infty x^\lambda f(x)\,dx$$

The continuation of this generalized analytic function is analytic in the half plane $R(\lambda) > -(M+1)$ with the exception of the points $\lambda = -M$, $-(M-1), \ldots, -1$ at which it has simple poles with residues $(-1)^m\delta^{(m)}(x)/m!$ Inside the strip $-(M+1) < R(\lambda) < -M$ the functional defining the analytic continuation of the generalized analytic function $x^\lambda\theta(x)$ takes the simple form,

$$(x^\lambda\theta, f) = \int_0^\infty x^\lambda \left[f(x) - \sum_{m=0}^{M-1} \frac{f^{(m)}(0)x^m}{m!} \right] dx$$

Finally, we may infer from the considerations above that the distribution $x^\lambda\theta(x)$ which is defined by the operation,

$$(x^\lambda\theta, f) = \int_0^1 x^\lambda \left[f(x) - \sum_{m=0}^{M-1} \frac{f^{(m)}(0)}{m!} x^m \right] dx + \int_1^\infty x^\lambda f(x)\,dx + \sum_{m=0}^{M-1} \frac{(-1)^m(\delta^{(m)}, f)}{m!(\lambda+m+1)}$$

on the space D of testing functions $f(x)$ is a regularization of the function $x^\lambda\theta(x)$ in the half plane $R(\lambda) > -(M+1)$. The distribution is analytic in this half plane with the exception of the points $\lambda = -M$, $-(M-1), \ldots, -1$ at which it has simple poles with residues $(-1)^m \delta^{(m)}(x)/m!$ Furthermore, inside the strip $-(M+1) < R(\lambda) < -M$ the distribution is defined by the simple functional,

$$(x^\lambda\theta, f) = \int_0^\infty x^\lambda\left[f(x) - \sum_{m=0}^{M-1} \frac{f^{(m)}(0)x^m}{m!}\right] dx$$

The derivative of the function $x^\lambda\theta(x)$ can also be defined by means of the analytic continuation technique. Knowing that the function $x^{\lambda-1}\theta(x)$ is well defined and analytic for all values of λ in the half plane $R(\lambda) > 0$, we first consider the derivative of the function $x^\lambda\theta(x)$ for these values of λ. This derivative exists in the ordinary sense and is given by the expression,

$$(x^\lambda\theta)' = \lambda x^{\lambda-1}\theta(x)$$

or considering it as a distributional derivative, we may write

$$((x^\lambda\theta)', f) = \lambda(x^{\lambda-1}\theta, f) = -(x^\lambda\theta, f')$$

However, as we have shown above, the generalized analytic functions $\lambda x^{\lambda-1}\theta(x)$ and $x^\lambda\theta(x)$ can be analytically continued into the left half plane and the continuation of these functions are analytic in this half plane with the exception of simple poles at the points $-1, -2, \ldots$. Thus, as an immediate consequence of the principle of analytic continuation, we may decide that the relation,

$$(x^\lambda\theta)' = \lambda x^{\lambda-1}\theta(x)$$

is valid for all values of λ with the exception of the points $\lambda = -1, -2, \ldots$.

Now let us consider the function $|x|^\lambda\theta(-x)$. This function is well defined and analytic for all values of λ in the half plane $R(\lambda) > -1$. Furthermore, for these values of λ we may write

$$\int_{-\infty}^0 (-x)^\lambda f(x)\, dx = \int_0^\infty x^\lambda f(-x)\, dx$$

or, in distributional notation,

$$(|x|^\lambda\theta(-x), f) = (x^\lambda\theta(x), f(-x))$$

By the principle of analytic continuation, this relation can now be extended into the left half plane and the regularization of the function $|x|^\lambda\theta(-x)$ can be defined as the distribution $|x|^\lambda\theta(-x)$ on the space D of testing functions $f(x)$ such that

$$(|x|^\lambda\theta(-x), f) = (x^\lambda\theta(x), f(-x)) = \int_0^1 x^\lambda\left[f(-x) - \sum_{m=0}^{M-1} \frac{f^{(m)}(0)(-x)^m}{m!}\right] dx$$
$$+ \int_1^\infty x^\lambda f(-x)\, dx + \sum_{m=0}^{M-1} \frac{(\delta^{(m)}, f)}{m!(\lambda+m+1)}$$

This distribution is analytic in the half plane $R(\lambda) > -(M+1)$ with the exception of the points $\lambda = -M, -(M-1), \ldots, -1$, at which it has simple poles with residues $\delta^{(m)}(x)/m!$. The functional, defining this distribution, takes the simple form,

$$(|x|^{\lambda}\theta(-x), f) = \int_0^{\infty} x^{\lambda}\left[f(-x) - \sum_{m=0}^{M-1} \frac{f^{(m)}(0)(-x)^m}{m!}\right] dx$$

inside the strip $-(M+1) < R(\lambda) < -M$.

Regularizations of many other functions with algebraic singularities can be obtained by means of the analytic continuation technique. We must, however, refer the reader to the literature for these highly interesting developments.

5.7 DISTRIBUTIONS AND BOUNDARY VALUES OF ANALYTIC FUNCTIONS

In Chapter II we presented a discussion on the theory of Fourier transforms in the complex plane and the implications of this theory for certain subjects of theoretical physics. Avoiding technical detail, we shall present in this section a short review of the generalization to distributions of some of these developments. It should be noted however that no attempt has been made to make this review general and exhaustive.

First let us consider the Fourier transform of a tempered distribution with bounded support. The Fourier transform of such a distribution takes a particularly simple form, namely, we can show that if T is a tempered distribution with bounded support then its Fourier transform $F(T)$ is given by

$$F(T, \omega) = \frac{1}{\sqrt{(2\pi)}}(T, e^{i\omega x})$$

For, let us assume that the function $a(x)$ is continuous and has continuous derivatives of all orders. If, moreover, $a(x)$ is equal to one on some interval (a, b) which contains the support of the distribution T and vanishes outside the interval $(a - \varepsilon, b + \varepsilon)$ where ε is an arbitrarily small positive constant, then the function $a(x)e^{i\omega x}$ is a testing function of the space S. We may write, therefore,

$$(F(T, \omega), G^*) = \frac{1}{\sqrt{(2\pi)}}\left(T, \int_{-\infty}^{\infty} G^*(\omega)e^{i\omega x}\, d\omega\right)$$

$$= \frac{1}{\sqrt{(2\pi)}}\left(T, a(x)\int_{-\infty}^{\infty} G^* e^{i\omega x}\, d\omega\right)$$

Assuming now that we may interchange the order of integration and functional operation, we find

$$(F(T, \omega), G^*) = \frac{1}{\sqrt{(2\pi)}} \int_{-\infty}^{\infty} (T, a(x)e^{i\omega x}) G^*(\omega)\, d\omega$$

and we obtain therefore

$$F(T, \omega) = \frac{1}{\sqrt{(2\pi)}} (T, a(x)e^{i\omega x})$$

or, by means of the proposition of Section 5.2,

$$F(T, \omega) = \frac{1}{\sqrt{(2\pi)}} (T, e^{i\omega x})$$

For example, the delta function of Dirac is a tempered distribution with bounded support and thus

$$F(\delta, \omega) = \frac{1}{\sqrt{(2\pi)}} (\delta, e^{i\omega x}) = \frac{1}{\sqrt{(2\pi)}}$$

To obtain the representation,

$$F(T, \omega) = \frac{1}{\sqrt{(2\pi)}} (T, e^{i\omega x})$$

we have assumed that T is a distribution with bounded support. This condition can be relaxed if we move from the real axis into the complex plane and consider testing functions $e^{i\lambda x}$ where λ is a complex variable. For example, if T is a tempered distribution which vanishes for negative values of x, in other words, if $T(x)$ is zero in some neighborhood of every point on the negative real axis, then the Fourier transform $F(T, \lambda)$ of this distribution may be written as

$$F(T, \lambda) = \frac{1}{\sqrt{(2\pi)}} (T, e^{i\lambda x})$$

for all values of λ in the upper half of the complex plane. For let us introduce the continuous function $a(x)$ which has continuous derivatives of all orders. Moreover, let $a(x)$ be equal to one for all non-negative values of x and equal to zero for all values of x smaller than some arbitrarily small negative number $-\varepsilon$. Then, since $a(x) \exp(i\omega x - \gamma x)$ vanishes exponentially when x tends to plus or minus infinity, the function $a(x) \exp(i\lambda x)$ is a testing function of the space S and we find, by means of a similar argument as before, that

$$F(T, \lambda) = \frac{1}{\sqrt{(2\pi)}} (T, e^{i\lambda x})$$

Considered as a function of λ, the tempered distribution $F(T, \lambda)$ is analytic in the upper half of the complex plane. Similarly, if the tempered distribution T vanishes for positive values of x, then we can show that the Fourier transform,

$$F(T, \lambda) = \frac{1}{\sqrt{(2\pi)}}(T, e^{i\lambda x})$$

exists for all values of λ in the lower half plane $I(\lambda) < 0$ and defines in that half plane an analytic function of the complex variable λ. These considerations may be utilized, as has been done by Bremermann and Durand, to define unilateral Fourier transforms of tempered distributions.

In Section 2.12 we found that the cause and effect relationship between the response $X(x)$ and the driving force $F(x)$ of a translational-invariant linear physical system can be expressed by means of the convolution,

$$X(x) = \int_{-\infty}^{\infty} G(x - x_0)F(x_0)\, dx_0$$

of the driving force and the Green's function of the system. The Green's function, which is defined as the response of the system to an impulse force of unit magnitude, completely determines the nature of the response to a more general driving force. A distributional formulation of the cause and effect relationship of linear physical systems can be drawn along similar lines. To outline this development we first need to generalize the concept of the convolution of two functions to that of two distributions.

The convolution $T * f$ of a distribution T and a testing function $f(x)$ can be defined, in analogy with the convolution of two ordinary functions, as the functional,

$$C(x) = T * f = (T(x_0), f(x - x_0))$$

where we should remember that the notation $T(x_0)$ implies that the distribution T operates on the function $f(x - x_0)$ in its capacity as a function of the variable x_0. We use moreover the symbol $C(x)$ to denote the function of x generated by this operation. If T is a distribution on the space E and $f(x)$ is a testing function of the space D, then $C(x)$ is also a testing function of the space D. To illustrate the type of argument that is involved to prove such a statement, let us consider the following somewhat detailed proof.

We have to show that, under the conditions stated, $C(x)$ is continuous, has continuous derivatives of all orders, and vanishes identically outside some finite interval on the real axis. The continuity of $C(x)$ is an immediate consequence of the fact that $f(x - x_0)$ is a testing function of the space D for all fixed values of x_0. Thus, if x tends to a then $f(x - x_0)$ tends to $f(a - x_0)$ in the sense of convergence defined for testing functions of the space D.

From this consideration we may infer that $C(x)$ tends to $C(a)$ as x tends to a and is continuous in x. In like fashion we can show that

$$\lim_{\varepsilon \to 0} \frac{f(x - x_0 + \varepsilon) - f(x - x_0)}{\varepsilon} = f'(x - x_0)$$

exists in the sense of convergence defined for testing functions of the space D, where the prime denotes differentiation with respect to the argument. This implies that

$$C'(x) = \lim_{\varepsilon \to 0} \frac{C(x + \varepsilon) - C(x)}{\varepsilon} = \left(T(x_0), \lim_{\varepsilon \to 0} \frac{f(x - x_0 + \varepsilon) - f(x - x_0)}{\varepsilon} \right)$$

$$= (T(x_0), f'(x - x_0))$$

exists. By a similar argument as for the function $C(x)$ we can now show that $C'(x)$ is continuous and, repeating the analysis above (replacing $C(x)$ by $C'(x)$) we can prove the existence and continuity of all higher derivatives. Furthermore, since

$$f'(x - x_0) = -\frac{df(x - x_0)}{dx_0}$$

we find

$$\frac{d^m C(x)}{dx^m} = (T(x_0), f^{(m)}(x - x_0)) = (T^{(m)}(x_0), f(x - x_0))$$

Finally we must show that the function $C(x) = T * f$ vanishes identically outside some finite interval on the real axis. To this purpose we define a function $a(x)$ which is continuous and has continuous derivatives of all orders. In addition, we assume that $a(x)$ is equal to one on the support of T and vanishes outside some finite interval (a, b) that contains this support. Since $T(x)$ as a distribution on the space E is of bounded support, such an interval exists. The function $a(x)f(x - x_0)$ therefore can only be different from zero on a finite interval consisting of the intersection of the interval (a, b) and an interval $(-d + x_0, d + x_0)$ outside which the function $f(x - x_0)$ vanishes, where $(-d, d)$ denotes the interval outside which $f(x)$ vanishes. The function $a(x)f(x - x_0)$ is identically equal to zero for all values of x outside this intersection. Thus we may infer that the function,

$$C(x) = (T(x_0), a(x)f(x - x_0)) = (T(x_0), f(x - x_0))$$

vanishes outside some finite interval on the real axis and is a testing function of the space D.

In contrast to the statement just substantiated, it can be shown that if T is a distribution on the space D and $f(x)$ is a testing function of this space, then the function $C(x)$ defined by the convolution of T and $f(x)$,

$$C(x) = T * f = (T(x_0), f(x - x_0))$$

is a function of the space E. However, if T is a tempered distribution and $g(x)$ is a good function, then the function $C(x)$ defined by the convolution of T and $g(x)$,

$$C(x) = T * g = (T(x_0), g(x - x_0))$$

is also a good function. Finally, if T is a distribution on the space D and $\phi(x)$ is a function of the space E, then the convolution

$$C(x) = (T(x_0), \phi(x - x_0))$$

is a function of the space E. This function vanishes for all negative values of x, provided the distribution T vanishes for all negative values of x.

Now let us turn our attention to the definition of the convolution of two distributions. In particular, let us consider the case in which T is a regular distribution on the space D and S denotes a regular distribution on the space E. The convolution of the distribution with bounded support S and a testing function $f(x)$ of the space D yields, as we have seen, another testing function of the space D. If $S(x)$ is the locally integrable function that generates the regular distribution S, then the convolution of the distribution S and the testing function $f(x)$ may be written as

$$C(x) = S * f = \int_{-\infty}^{\infty} S(x_0) f(x - x_0)\, dx_0$$

Furthermore, since $C(x)$ is a testing function of the space D, the convolution of this function and the regular distribution T may be written as

$$T * C = \int_{-\infty}^{\infty} T(y_0) C(y - y_0)\, dy_0$$

This convolution represents a testing function of the space E. If we now insert the integral,

$$C(y - y_0) = \int_{-\infty}^{\infty} S(x_0) f(y - y_0 - x_0)\, dx_0$$

introduce the new variable $u_0 = x_0 + y_0$, and interchange the order of integration, we find

$$T * C = T * (S * f) = \int_{-\infty}^{\infty} \left[\int_{-\infty}^{\infty} T(y_0) S(u_0 - y_0)\, dy_0 \right] f(y - u_0)\, du_0$$

This result may also be written as

$$T * (S * f) = \int_{-\infty}^{\infty} X(u_0) f(y - u_0)\, du_0 = X * f$$

where we have introduced the convolution,

$$X(x) = \int_{-\infty}^{\infty} T(x_0) S(x - x_0)\, dx_0$$

of the functions $T(x)$ and $S(x)$. This function $X(x)$, which is the convolution of the regular distributions T and S, generates a regular distribution on the space D. The relation,

$$T * (S * f) = X * f$$

can now be used to define the distribution X which is the convolution of an arbitrary distribution T on the space D and an arbitrary distribution S on the space E.

X is a distribution on the space D, and the following relations can readily be derived,

$$T * S = S * T$$

$$(X, f) = (T * S, f) = (T(x), (S(x_0), f(x + x_0)))$$

It can be shown moreover that if G is a tempered distribution and F is a distribution on the space E, then the convolution of these distributions,

$$X = G * F$$

is a tempered distribution. Denoting the Fourier transform of these distributions by $X(\omega)$, $G(\omega)$, and $F(\omega)$, respectively, we have shown in Chapter II, that if G is a regular tempered distribution and F is a regular distribution on the space E, then their distributional convolution,

$$X = G * F$$

which, as we have seen, is a regular distribution corresponding to the locally integrable function,

$$\int_{-\infty}^{\infty} G(x - x_0) F(x_0)\, dx_0$$

can be reduced by Fourier transformation to the simple relationship,

$$X(\omega) = G(\omega) F(\omega)$$

between their Fourier transforms in frequency space. This relationship can also be obtained when G is an arbitrary tempered distribution and F is an arbitrary distribution on the space E.

Turning our attention now to a case of great physical interest, we consider the situation in which both G and F are distributions on the space D that vanish on the negative real axis. In other words, the support of the distributions G and F is located on the positive real axis. In subsequent discussions we shall call such distributions causal distributions. In a similar manner as before, we may define the convolution X of the causal distributions G and F by the relation,

$$G * (F * f) = X * f$$

where $f(x)$ is a testing function of the space D. This relation is well defined. For, although the convolution $F * f$ is a testing function of the space E, the convolution $G * (F * f)$ is a testing function of the space D. The convolution,

$$X = G * F$$

of the two causal distributions G and F on the space D is also a causal distribution on the space D. In other words, it can be shown that the support of the distribution X is located on the positive real axis.

These considerations can be utilized, as has been done by Taylor, to obtain distributional counterparts of the causality conditions for linear physical processes. The distributional translation of the dictum that no effect precedes its cause reads as follows: The response X of a causal system to a driving force F which is a causal distribution is also a causal distribution. As a logical consequence of this statement and the foregoing discussion, we find that if the response X of a linear system to a driving force F, which is a causal distribution on the space D, is a causal distribution on the space D, then there exists a distribution G such that

$$X = G * F$$

where G is also a causal distribution on the space D. The distribution G is called the Green's distribution.

Titchmarsh's theorem, which is of fundamental importance in the analysis of causal physical phenomena, has been generalized to similar theorems covering the situation in which the causal processes are described by distributions.

Fundamental in this development is a theorem by Schwartz stating that a necessary and sufficient condition for a tempered distribution to be a causal tempered distribution is for its Fourier transform to be a tempered causal transform.

In the statement of this theorem we have introduced the following terminology. As before, we agree to call a tempered distribution a causal tempered distribution if the support of this distribution is located on the positive real axis. In a less exact but more descriptive wording, a causal tempered distribution vanishes for all negative values of x. Furthermore, a distribution on a particular function space is said to be a causal transform if it is is the boundary value, in the sense of convergence of distributions on that space, of a function that is analytic in the upper half of the complex plane and is bounded by a polynomial uniformly in this half plane. For example, if $G(\lambda)$ is analytic in the half plane $I(\lambda) > 0$ and is bounded by a polynomial uniformly in this half plane, then

$$G(\omega) = \lim_{\gamma \to 0} G(\omega + i\gamma)$$

in the sense of convergence of distributions on the space S, is a causal tempered distribution.

The theorem of Schwartz generalizes to distributions the first part of Titchmarsh's theorem for causal functions introduced in Section 2.11. This first part of Titchmarsh's theorem concerns the equivalence of causality and the existence of a causal transform.

The second part of Titchmarsh's theorem for causal functions, namely, the part in which the equivalence of causality and the existence of dispersion relations is stated, was first generalized to distributions by Taylor. Taylor has shown that a necessary and sufficient condition for a tempered distribution T to be causal is for the distribution,

$$G(\omega) = F(T, \omega)/(\omega^2 + 1)^n$$

where $F(T, \omega)$ denotes the Fourier transform of the distribution T, to be a distribution on the space DL for some integer n and for $G(\omega)$ to satisfy the subtracted dispersion relation,

$$G(\omega) = \sum_{m=0}^{2n+1} A_m(\omega)\omega^m + \frac{i}{\pi} G(\omega) * P\frac{1}{\omega}$$

where $(\omega^2 + 1)^{2n+1} A_m(\omega)$ is constant.

In the formulation of this theorem we have introduced a new space of testing functions DL, namely, the space of all continuous functions $f(x)$ which are absolutely integrable over the real axis and have continuous derivatives of all orders that are also absolutely integrable over the real axis. The topology on this space is established by defining a sequence of functions $f_m(x)$ to converge to zero if

$$\lim_{m \to \infty} \int_{-\infty}^{\infty} \left| \frac{d^p f_m(x)}{dx^p} \right| dx = 0$$

for all positive integers p. The distributions on this space are the so-called bounded distributions.

In a similar manner, we can define the space of testing functions DL^2 as the space of all continuous functions $f(x)$ which are absolutely square integrable over the real axis and have continuous derivatives of all orders that are also absolutely square integrable over the real axis.

With respect to distributions on the space DL^2, Beltrami and Wohlers obtained a theorem that closely resembles Titchmarsh's theorem for ordinary functions. They were able to show that the following two conditions are equivalent necessary and sufficient conditions for a distribution $G(\omega)$ on the space DL^2 to be a tempered causal transform.

a. $G(\omega)$ is the Fourier transform of the product of a polynomial and a square integrable causal function.
b. The real and imaginary parts of the distribution $G(\omega) = D(\omega) + iA(\omega)$ form a pair of Hilbert transforms,

$$D(\omega) = -\frac{1}{\pi} A(\omega) * P\frac{1}{\omega}$$

and

$$A(\omega) = \frac{1}{\pi} D(\omega) * P\frac{1}{\omega}$$

They have shown moreover that if $G(\omega)$ is a tempered causal transform on the space DL^2, then the Fourier transform of this distribution and its Cauchy representation,

$$G_C(\lambda) = \frac{1}{2\pi i}\left(G(\omega), \frac{1}{\omega - \lambda}\right)$$

in the upper half of the complex plane are one and the same. By means of Titchmarsh's theorem and this representation they obtained, furthermore, a generalization to distributions of the highly useful decomposition of a square integrable function $F(\omega)$ into a positive and a negative frequency part,

$$F(\omega) = F_+(\omega) - F_-(\omega)$$

introduced in Section 2.11. The distributional counterpart of this proposition reads as follows:

If $G(\omega)$ is a distribution on the space DL^2 and the Fourier transform of the product of a polynomial and a function that is square integrable over the real axis, then

$$G(\omega) = G_+(\omega) - G_-(\omega)$$

where $G_+(\omega)$ is the boundary value, in the sense of convergence of distributions on the space S, of a function that is analytic in the upper half of the complex plane, whereas $G_-(\omega)$ is the boundary value, in the same sense of convergence, of a function that is analytic in the lower half of the complex plane.

For, if $g(x)$ denotes the function of which $G(\omega)$ is the Fourier transform, then $g(x)$ can be written as the difference,

$$g(x) = g_+(x) - g_-(x)$$

of the functions $g_+(x) = \theta(x)g(x)$ and $g_-(x) = [\theta(x) - 1]g(x)$, where $\theta(x)$ is the unit step function. The function $g_+(x)$ is the product of a polynomial and a square integrable causal function. According to Titchmarsh's theorem therefore, the Fourier transform $G_+(\omega)$ of this function is a causal tempered distribution, i.e., it is the boundary value, in the sense of convergence of distributions on the space S, of a function that is analytic in the upper half of the complex plane. In a similar manner we can show that the Fourier transform $G_-(\omega)$ of the function $g_-(x)$ is the boundary value, in the sense of convergence of distributions on the space S, of a function that is analytic in the lower half of the complex plane. In this fashion we obtain the decomposition,

$$G(\omega) = F(g) = G_+(\omega) - G_-(\omega)$$

This is a distributional counterpart of the first Plemelj formula. To formally obtain a distributional counterpart of the second Plemelj formula we note, as stated above, that the Fourier transform $G_+(\lambda)$ has the Cauchy representation,

$$G_+(\lambda) = \frac{1}{2\pi i}\left(G_+(\omega), \frac{1}{\omega - \lambda}\right)$$

in the upper half of the complex plane. Thus,

$$G_+(\omega) = \lim_{\varepsilon \to 0} G_+(\omega + i\varepsilon) = \frac{1}{\pi i}\left(G_+(\zeta), \frac{1}{\zeta - \omega}\right)$$

Similarly we may write

$$G_-(\omega) = \lim_{\varepsilon \to 0} G_-(\omega - i\varepsilon) = -\frac{1}{\pi i}\left(G_-(\zeta), \frac{1}{\zeta - \omega}\right)$$

Addition now yields the result,

$$G_+(\omega) + G_-(\omega) = \frac{1}{\pi i}\left(G(\zeta), \frac{1}{\zeta - \omega}\right) = -\frac{1}{\pi i}\, G(\omega) * P\frac{1}{\omega}$$

which is a distributional counterpart of the second Plemelj formula for ordinary functions.

These relations can be shown to have wider validity. Some indication in this direction is given by the following example. One can formally define Plemelj formulas for the Dirac delta function,

$$\delta_+(\omega) - \delta_-(\omega) = \delta(\omega)$$

$$\delta_+(\omega) + \delta_-(\omega) = -\frac{1}{\pi i}\,\delta(\omega) * P\frac{1}{\omega}$$

However, we have found before,

$$\delta(\omega) = \delta^+(\omega) + \delta^-(\omega)$$

and

$$-\frac{1}{\pi i}\,P\frac{1}{\omega} = \delta^+(\omega) - \delta^-(\omega)$$

where

$$\delta^{\pm}(\omega) = \pm\delta_{\pm}(\omega) = \frac{1}{2}\,\delta(\omega) \mp \frac{1}{2\pi i}\,P\frac{1}{\omega}$$

are the Heisenberg delta functions.
From the relation above, we infer that

$$\frac{1}{2\pi}\,P\frac{1}{\omega} = \frac{1}{2i}\,[\delta^+(\omega) - \delta^-(\omega)] = \frac{1}{2i}\,[\delta_+(\omega) + \delta_-(\omega)] = \frac{1}{2\pi}\,\delta(\omega) * P\frac{1}{\omega}$$

In a similar fashion we can define the Plemelj formulas for the principal value distribution,

$$P_+(\omega) - P_-(\omega) = P\frac{1}{\omega}$$

and

$$P_+(\omega) + P_-(\omega) = -\frac{1}{\pi i}\,P\frac{1}{\omega} * P\frac{1}{\omega}$$

and derive the relation,

$$\frac{1}{2}\,\delta(\omega) = \frac{1}{2}\,[\delta^+(\omega) + \delta^-(\omega)] = -\frac{1}{2\pi i}\,[P_+(\omega) + P_-(\omega)] = -\frac{1}{2\pi^2}\,P\frac{1}{\omega} * P\frac{1}{\omega}$$

Summarizing, we have obtained the relations,

$$\frac{1}{2}\,\delta(\omega) = -\frac{1}{2\pi^2}\,P\frac{1}{\omega} * P\frac{1}{\omega}$$

and

$$\frac{1}{2\pi} P \frac{1}{\omega} = \frac{1}{2\pi} \delta(\omega) * P \frac{1}{\omega}$$

Thus, since,

$$\delta^{+}(\omega) = \frac{1}{2} \delta(\omega) - \frac{1}{2\pi i} P \frac{1}{\omega}$$

we may draw the conclusion that the real and imaginary parts of Heisenberg's delta function form a pair of Hilbert transforms.

CHAPTER VI

APPLICATIONS IN NEUTRON TRANSPORT THEORY

6.0 INTRODUCTION

Distributions have been used with great success by Case, van Kampen, Wigner and many others in the solution, by means of normal mode expansion techniques, of initial and boundary value problems arising in the mathematical description of linear transport phenomena.

In 1955, in a paper on the theory of plasma oscillations, van Kampen investigated the solution of the linearized Boltzmann equation,

$$\frac{\partial f}{\partial t} + ikvf(v, t) = -ikh(v)\int_{-\infty}^{\infty} f(v, t)\, dv$$

for the longitudinal velocity distribution function $f(v, t)$ by writing this function as a superposition of normal modes,

$$f(v \mid \omega)e^{-i\omega t}$$

Normalizing the velocity-dependent part such that

$$\int_{-\infty}^{\infty} f(v \mid \nu)\, dv = 1 \qquad \nu = \omega/k$$

he obtained, by substituting the normal mode $f(v \mid \nu)\exp(-i\nu kt)$ into the

Boltzmann equation, the following equation for the eigenfunctions $f(v \mid \nu)$.

$$(\nu - v) f(v \mid \nu) = h(v)$$

Observing that this equation must be solved in the spirit of the theory of distributions, he obtained the following general solution,

$$f(v \mid \nu) = b(\nu)\,\delta(v - \nu) + h(v) P \frac{1}{\nu - v}$$

where $P(1/(\nu - v))$ denotes the principal value distribution, $\delta(v - \nu)$ is Dirac's delta distribution, and the function $b(\nu)$ can be determined from the normalization condition imposed on the eigenfunctions $f(v \mid \nu)$.

Van Kampen then proceeded to show that the system of eigenfunctions $f(v \mid \nu)$ is complete for all functions of the real variable v that are square integrable in the sense of Lebesgue over the real axis. In his proof he made use of the theory of singular integral equations in conjunction with the decomposition of Fourier transforms in positive and negative frequency parts as described in Section 2.11.

The theory of these eigendistributions was extended by Case in a paper published in 1959. In that paper, Case showed that the Landau and van Kampen treatments of the initial value problem arising in the theory of plasma oscillations are equivalent. Introducing an adjoint equation,

$$\frac{\partial \chi}{\partial t} + ikv\chi(v, t) = -ik \int_{-\infty}^{\infty} h(v)\chi(v, t)\, dv$$

he showed moreover that the functions $f(v \mid \nu)$ and $\chi(v \mid \nu)$ are orthogonal and he obtained a modification of van Kampen's proof for the completeness of the eigenfunctions $f(v \mid \nu)$. Also in 1959, Case, van Kampen, and Wigner independently proposed to use distributions in solving, by means of normal mode expansion techniques, some boundary and initial value problems of neutron transport theory. In Case's paper powerful orthogonality and completeness theorems are presented for the eigenfunctions $\phi(\mu \mid \nu)$ which are the counterparts in neutron transport theory of the eigenfunctions $f(v \mid \nu)$ of plasma physics. In subsequent years the results of Case's paper have been extended by him and many others. These investigations have lead to the solution in closed form of many boundary and initial value problems for which previously no analytical solution techniques were available.

In this chapter we shall present an outline of Case's technique. In the discussion of these ideas we shall limit ourselves to an investigation of the stationary transport of monoenergetic neutrons in a uniform medium that scatters neutrons isotropically and elastically. Assuming moreover that the transport media of interest are of finite extent in the x-direction only, we want to find the angular neutron density $\Phi(x, \mu)$, that is, the number of neutrons per unit volume at the point x that move in a direction making an angle $\theta = \arccos \mu$ with the positive x-axis. This quantity is a solution of the, in general, inhomogeneous transport equation,

$$\mu \frac{\partial \Phi(x, \mu)}{\partial x} + \Phi(x, \mu) = \frac{c}{2} \int_{-1}^{1} \Phi(x, \mu)\, d\mu + S(x, \mu)$$

subject to certain prescribed boundary conditions on the free surfaces of the medium. In this equation the coefficient c denotes the number of secondaries produced per collision. To be definite, we shall assume in general that c is smaller than one and that the transport medium therefore is composed of an absorbing but not a fissionable material. No loss of generality is incurred by this assumption and the extension of our arguments to other values of c is either straightforward or immediate. In the formulation of the transport equation it has been assumed moreover that length is measured in units of the neutron mean free path in the particular medium considered.

The transport equation is a balance equation which expresses the fact that in the stationary state the net number of neutrons,

$$\mu \frac{\partial \Phi}{\partial x}$$

that leaves the direction μ due to streaming plus the number of neutrons

$$\Phi(x, \mu)$$

that leaves the direction μ due to scattering must be equal to the number of neutrons,

$$\frac{c}{2} \int_{-1}^{1} \Phi(x, \mu)\, d\mu$$

that is scattered into the direction μ plus the number of neutrons,

$$S(x, \mu)$$

produced by external sources into the direction μ.

In the normal mode approach to the solution of the inhomogeneous transport equation we expand the function $\Phi(x, \mu)$,

$$\Phi(x, \mu) = \sum a(\nu) \psi(x, \mu \mid \nu)$$

in terms of the elementary solutions $\psi(x, \mu \mid \nu)$ of the homogeneous, or source-free, transport equation,

$$\mu \frac{\partial \psi(x, \mu)}{\partial x} + \psi(x, \mu) = \frac{c}{2} \int_{-1}^{1} \psi(x, \mu)\, d\mu$$

The summation sign in the expansion formula above denotes in general an integration over the continuum states and a summation over those eigenfunctions representing modes with eigenvalues in the discrete part of the spectrum.

Such expansions are familiar from the theory of ordinary differential equations in which we consider expansions in terms of the eigenfunctions of the singular Sturm-Liouville operator or other differential operators of mathematical physics. The spectral theory of such operators can also be treated by means of powerful techniques from the theory of analytic functions and distributions. These techniques will not be discussed in this book, however, and the reader is referred to the literature for their exposition.

Imposition of symmetry and boundary conditions on the normal mode expansion for the solution of the inhomogeneous transport equation results, as we shall see, in a singular integral equation for the expansion coefficients. The solution of this integral equation can be obtained by means of the methods outlined in Section 4.11.

To obtain explicit analytical expressions for the normal modes, we note that the variable x does not appear explicitly in the homogeneous transport equation. This implies, as we have explained in Section 2.6, that this equation is invariant under translations of the x-axis and suggests that we look for solutions of the form,

$$\psi(x, \mu \mid v) = \phi(\mu \mid v) f(x \mid v)$$

Substitution of this expression into the homogeneous transport equation yields the following relation between the functions $\phi(\mu \mid v)$ and $f(x|v)$,

$$\frac{1}{f(x)} \frac{df(x)}{dx} = -\frac{\phi(\mu) - \dfrac{c}{2} \displaystyle\int_{-1}^{1} \phi(\mu)\, d\mu}{\mu \phi(\mu)}$$

The left hand side of this equation depends only on x whereas the right hand side depends only on μ. A change in x therefore does not affect the right hand side and a change in μ has no influence on the left hand side. This implies that the left hand side and the right hand side of this equation are equal to the same constant which we shall denote by $-1/v$. We obtain therefore the following separated equations,

$$\frac{df(x \mid v)}{dx} + \frac{1}{v} f(x \mid v) = 0$$

and

$$(v - \mu)\phi(\mu \mid v) = \frac{cv}{2} \int_{-1}^{1} \phi(\mu \mid v)\, d\mu$$

The solution of the first equation is simply

$$f(x \mid \nu) = e^{-x/\nu}$$

and the normal modes take the form,

$$\psi(x, \mu \mid \nu) = \phi(\mu \mid \nu) e^{-x/\nu}$$

The solutions $\phi(\mu \mid \nu)$ of the second equation and their properties will be the topic of discussion of the next section.

6.1 PROPERTIES OF ANGULAR EIGENFUNCTIONS: ORTHOGONALITY

The angular eigenfunctions $\phi(\mu \mid \nu)$ are the solutions of the integral equation,

$$(\nu - \mu)\phi(\mu \mid \nu) = \frac{c\nu}{2} \int_{-1}^{1} \phi(\mu \mid \nu)\, d\mu$$

The integral on the right hand side of this equation cannot vanish and since the equation is homogeneous we can, without loss of generality, normalize the function $\phi(\mu \mid \nu)$ so that

$$\int_{-1}^{1} \phi(\mu \mid \nu)\, d\mu = 1 \tag{6.1}$$

The equation for the angular eigenfunctions assumes therefore the following simple form,

$$(\nu - \mu)\phi(\mu \mid \nu) = \frac{c}{2}\,\nu \tag{6.2}$$

We note that the variable μ takes its values on the interval $-1 \leqq \mu \leqq 1$, and that for values of ν which are located on this interval the eigenvalue equation is singular. It has been observed by Case, van Kampen, and Wigner that in this case the eigenfunctions must be defined in terms of the singular distributions introduced in Chapter V. In Section 5.1 we remarked that if the values of the parameter ν are located on the interval of definition of the variable μ, then, according to Dirac, the solutions of a singular equation of the type (6.2) can be written as the sum of a delta distribution and a principal value distribution,

$$\phi(\mu \mid \nu) = \lambda(\nu)\, \delta(\nu - \mu) + \frac{c\nu}{2} P \frac{1}{\nu - \mu}$$

The coefficient $\lambda(\nu)$ is in general a completely arbitrary function of the parameter ν. In our case, however, we have introduced the normalization (6.1) and substitution yields therefore a relation,

$$\lambda(\nu) = 1 + \frac{c\nu}{2} \int_{-1}^{1} \frac{d\mu}{\mu - \nu}$$

for the function $\lambda(\nu)$. Since ν is a point on the interval $-1 \leqq \mu \leqq 1$, the integral must be evaluated as a Cauchy principal value integral,

$$\int_{-1}^{1} \frac{d\mu}{\mu - \nu} = \lim_{\varepsilon \to 0} \left\{ \int_{-1}^{\nu - \varepsilon} \frac{d\mu}{\mu - \nu} + \int_{\nu + \varepsilon}^{1} \frac{d\mu}{\mu - \nu} \right\} = \log \frac{1 - \nu}{1 + \nu} = -2 \operatorname{arctanh} \nu$$

Thus, for all values of ν on the interval $-1 \leqq \mu \leqq 1$, we can obtain a value of $\lambda(\nu)$,

$$\lambda(\nu) = 1 - c\nu \operatorname{arctanh} \nu$$

so that the corresponding singular eigenfunctions,

$$\phi(\mu \mid \nu) = \lambda(\nu)\, \delta(\nu - \mu) + \frac{c\nu}{2} P \frac{1}{\nu - \mu}$$

satisfy the normalization condition (6.1). We may therefore conclude that the interval $(-1, 1)$ constitutes the continuous part of the spectrum of the eigenvalue equation (6.2) and that the continuum eigenfunctions are singular eigendistributions of the form,

$$\phi(\mu \mid \nu) = (1 - c\nu \operatorname{arctanh} \nu)\, \delta(\nu - \mu) + \frac{c\nu}{2} P \frac{1}{\nu - \mu}$$

For all values of ν outside the closed interval $(-1, 1)$ the solution of the eigenvalue equation is of course simply the function,

$$\phi(\mu \mid \nu) = \frac{c}{2} \frac{\nu}{\nu - \mu}$$

In this case the normalization condition imposed on the eigenfunctions $\phi(\mu \mid \nu)$ requires that,

$$\frac{c\nu}{2} \int_{-1}^{1} \frac{d\mu}{\nu - \mu} = 1$$

In other words, the admissible values of ν are the roots of the following dispersion equation,

$$\frac{c\nu}{2} \log \frac{\nu + 1}{\nu - 1} = c\nu \operatorname{arctanh} 1/\nu = 1$$

This equation has only two roots, namely, there are two real roots $\pm\nu_0$ for all values of c that are smaller than one, two purely imaginary roots $\pm\nu_0$ for all values of c that are larger than one, and two roots which coalesce at infinity when c is equal to one. The discrete part of the spectrum of the eigenvalue equation (6.2) contains therefore only two points $\pm\nu_0$ and the corresponding discrete eigenfunctions are of the form,

$$\phi(\mu \mid \pm\nu_0) = \frac{c\nu_0}{2}\frac{1}{\nu_0 \mp \mu}$$

Having obtained explicit expressions for the continuum and discrete angular eigenfunctions, we can use these expressions to investigate the orthogonality and completeness properties of this system of functions.

It has been shown by Case that the system of functions $\phi(\mu \mid \nu)$, $\phi(\mu \mid \pm\nu_0)$ is orthogonal with weighting factor μ over the interval $-1 \leqq \mu \leqq 1$. This statement can readily be verified by multiplying the eigenvalue equation,

$$(\nu - \mu)\phi(\mu \mid \nu) = c\,\nu/2$$

by the eigenfunction $\phi(\mu \mid \alpha)$ and the eigenvalue equation,

$$(\alpha - \mu)\phi(\mu \mid \alpha) = c\alpha/2$$

by the eigenfunction $\phi(\mu \mid \nu)$. Subtracting the results and integrating the result of this subtraction over the interval $-1 \leqq \mu \leqq 1$, we obtain the equation,

$$\left(\frac{1}{\alpha} - \frac{1}{\nu}\right)\int_{-1}^{1} \phi(\mu \mid \nu)\phi(\mu \mid \alpha)\mu \, d\mu = 0$$

from which we may infer that

$$\int_{-1}^{1} \phi(\mu \mid \nu)\phi(\mu \mid \alpha)\mu \, d\mu = 0$$

for all values of α that are different from ν. We can show moreover that

$$\int_{-1}^{1} \phi(\mu \mid \nu)\phi(\mu \mid \alpha)\mu \, d\mu = M(\nu)\,\delta(\nu - \alpha)$$

and that

$$\int_{-1}^{1} \phi^2(\mu \mid \pm\nu_0)\mu \, d\mu = M(\pm\nu_0)$$

where the normalization factors $M(\nu)$ and $M(\pm\nu_0)$ may be written as

$$M(\nu) = \nu[\lambda^2(\nu) + \pi^2 c^2 \nu^2/4]$$

and

$$M(\pm\nu_0) = \pm\frac{c\nu_0}{2}\left[\frac{1 - {\nu_0}^2(1 - c)}{{\nu_0}^2 - 1}\right]$$

The first result can be derived as follows. We write

$$M(\nu, \alpha) = \int_{-1}^{1} \mu\phi(\mu \mid \nu)\phi(\mu \mid \alpha)\, d\mu$$

and introducing a function $\Phi(\mu)$ that is Hölder continuous on the interval $-1 \leqq \mu \leqq 1$, we consider the integral,

$$\int_{-1}^{1} \Phi(\alpha)M(\nu, \alpha)\, d\alpha = \int_{-1}^{1} \mu\phi(\mu \mid \nu)\, d\mu \int_{-1}^{1} \Phi(\alpha)\phi(\mu \mid \alpha)\, d\alpha$$

Substitution of the explicit expressions for the continuum angular eigenfunctions yields

$$\int_{-1}^{1} \Phi(\alpha)M(\nu, \alpha)\, d\alpha = \nu\lambda^2(\nu)\Phi(\nu) + \frac{c\lambda(\nu)}{2}\int_{-1}^{1} \alpha\Phi(\alpha)\, d\alpha \int_{-1}^{1} \frac{\mu\, \delta(\nu - \mu)}{\alpha - \mu}\, d\mu$$
$$+ \frac{c\nu}{2}\int_{-1}^{1} \lambda(\alpha)\Phi(\alpha)\, d\alpha \int_{-1}^{1} \frac{\mu\, \delta(\alpha - \mu)}{\nu - \mu}\, d\mu + \frac{c^2\nu}{4}\int_{-1}^{1} \frac{\mu}{\nu - \mu}\, d\mu \int_{-1}^{1} \frac{\alpha\Phi(\alpha)}{\alpha - \mu}\, d\alpha$$

Interchanging the order of integration of the last integral on the right hand side of this equation by means of the Poincaré-Bertrand transformation formula of Section 4.9, we may write

$$\int_{-1}^{1} \Phi(\alpha)M(\nu, \alpha)\, d\alpha = \nu[\lambda^2(\nu) + \pi^2c^2\nu^2/4]\Phi(\nu) + \int_{-1}^{1} \Phi(\alpha)G(\nu, \alpha)\, d\alpha$$

where

$$G(\nu, \alpha) = \frac{c\alpha\lambda(\nu)}{2}\int_{-1}^{1} \frac{\mu\, \delta(\nu - \mu)}{\alpha - \mu}\, d\mu + \frac{c\nu\lambda(\alpha)}{2}\int_{-1}^{1} \frac{\mu\, \delta(\alpha - \mu)}{\nu - \mu}\, d\mu$$
$$+ \frac{c^2\nu\alpha}{4}\int_{-1}^{1} \frac{\mu}{(\nu - \mu)(\alpha - \mu)}\, d\mu$$
$$= \frac{c\nu\alpha}{2(\alpha - \nu)}[\lambda(\nu) - \lambda(\alpha) + c\nu \operatorname{arctanh} \nu - c\nu \operatorname{arctanh} \alpha] = 0$$

We have, therefore,

$$\int_{-1}^{1} \Phi(\alpha)M(\nu, \alpha)\, d\alpha = \nu[\lambda^2(\nu) + \pi^2c^2\nu^2/4]\Phi(\nu)$$

and it follows from this equation that

$$M(\nu, \alpha) = \nu[\lambda^2(\nu) + \pi^2c^2\nu^2/4]\delta(\nu - \alpha)$$

Similarly, if we integrate the product $\mu\phi^2(\mu \mid \pm\nu_0)$ over the fundamental interval, we find

$$M(\pm\nu_0) = \int_{-1}^{1} \phi^2(\mu \mid \pm\nu_0)\mu\, d\mu = \pm\frac{c\nu_0}{2}\left[\frac{1 - \nu_0{}^2(1 - c)}{\nu_0{}^2 - 1}\right]$$

As we shall show in subsequent sections of this chapter, the system of angular eigenfunctions is complete for functions belonging to certain physically significant function spaces. This implies, for example, that if the function $\Phi(\mu)$ satisfies certain given conditions on the interval $-1 \leqq \mu \leqq 1$, then it can be represented by the expansion,

$$\Phi(\mu) = a(\nu_0)\phi(\mu \mid \nu_0) + a(-\nu_0)\phi(\mu \mid -\nu_0) + \int_{-1}^{1} a(\nu)\phi(\mu \mid \nu)\, d\nu$$

In view of the orthogonality relations for the functions $\phi(\mu \mid \nu)$ and $\phi(\mu \mid \pm\nu_0)$ this means that the expansion coefficients $a(\pm\nu_0)$ can be written as

$$a(\pm\nu_0) = \frac{1}{M(\pm\nu_0)} \int_{-1}^{1} \Phi(\alpha)\phi(\alpha \mid \pm\nu_0)\alpha\, d\alpha$$

whereas the continuum coefficients $a(\nu)$ take the form,

$$a(\nu) = \frac{1}{M(\nu)} \int_{-1}^{1} \Phi(\alpha)\phi(\alpha \mid \nu)\alpha\, d\alpha$$

Substitution now yields the following representation of the function $\Phi(\mu)$ in terms of the angular eigenfunctions

$$\Phi(\mu) = \int_{-1}^{1} \Phi(\nu)\nu\, d\nu \left[\frac{\phi(\mu \mid \nu_0)\phi(\nu \mid \nu_0)}{M(\nu_0)} + \frac{\phi(\mu \mid -\nu_0)\phi(\nu \mid -\nu_0)}{M(-\nu_0)} + \int_{-1}^{1} \frac{\phi(\mu \mid \alpha)\phi(\nu \mid \alpha)}{M(\alpha)}\, d\alpha\right]$$

where, in conformity with traditional usage in neutron transport theory, the product of the two continuum eigenfunctions $\phi(\mu \mid \alpha)$ and $\phi(\nu \mid \alpha)$ should be interpreted as

$$\phi(\mu \mid \alpha)\phi(\nu \mid \alpha) = [\lambda^2(\alpha) + \pi^2 c^2 \alpha^2/4]\, \delta(\alpha - \mu)\, \delta(\alpha - \nu) + \frac{c\alpha}{2(\nu - \mu)}\, [\phi(\nu \mid \alpha) - \phi(\mu \mid \alpha)]$$

As an immediate consequence of the expansion formula above, we obtain the following completeness relation,

$$\delta(\nu - \mu) = \frac{\nu\phi(\mu \mid \nu_0)\phi(\nu \mid \nu_0)}{M(\nu_0)} + \frac{\nu\phi(\mu \mid -\nu_0)\phi(\nu \mid -\nu_0)}{M(-\nu_0)} + \int_{-1}^{1} \frac{\nu\phi(\mu \mid \alpha)\phi(\nu \mid \alpha)}{M(\alpha)}\, d\alpha$$

for the system of angular eigenfunctions over the interval $-1 \leqq \mu \leqq 1$.

We note that the convention for the product of two continuum eigenfunctions delineated above is consistent with the following interpretation of the product of two principal value distributions,

$$P\frac{1}{\mu-\nu}\,P\frac{1}{\mu-\alpha}=\frac{1}{\nu-\alpha}\left[P\frac{1}{\mu-\nu}-P\frac{1}{\mu-\alpha}\right]+\pi^2\,\delta(\nu-\mu)\,\delta(\alpha-\mu)$$

This interpretation requires that the order of integration of a double Cauchy integral should be interchanged according to the rule,

$$\begin{aligned}\int d\mu\int d\alpha F(\alpha,\mu)P\frac{1}{\mu-\nu}\,P\frac{1}{\mu-\alpha}\\
&=\int d\alpha\int d\mu F(\alpha,\mu)P\frac{1}{\mu-\nu}\,P\frac{1}{\mu-\alpha}\\
&=\int d\alpha\int d\mu F(\alpha,\mu)\left[\pi^2\,\delta(\nu-\mu)\,\delta(\alpha-\mu)+\frac{1}{\nu-\alpha}\left\{P\frac{1}{\mu-\nu}-P\frac{1}{\mu-\alpha}\right\}\right]\\
&=\pi^2F(\nu,\nu)+\int\frac{d\alpha}{\nu-\alpha}\int d\mu F(\alpha,\mu)\left[P\frac{1}{\mu-\nu}-P\frac{1}{\mu-\alpha}\right]\end{aligned}$$

The results obtained in this fashion are completely consistent with those obtained by means of the conventional Poincaré-Bertrand transformation formula of Section 4.9,

$$\begin{aligned}\int d\mu\int d\alpha F(\alpha,\mu)P\frac{1}{\mu-\nu}\,P\frac{1}{\mu-\alpha}\\
&=\pi^2F(\nu,\nu)+\int d\alpha\int d\mu F(\alpha,\mu)P\frac{1}{\mu-\nu}\,P\frac{1}{\mu-\alpha}\end{aligned}$$

when the product of the principal value distributions in the integrand of the double integral on the right hand side of the equation is interpreted as

$$P\frac{1}{\mu-\nu}\,P\frac{1}{\mu-\alpha}=\frac{1}{\nu-\alpha}\left[P\frac{1}{\mu-\nu}-P\frac{1}{\mu-\alpha}\right]$$

Introducing more complicated weighting factors, we can show that the eigenfunctions are orthogonal with respect to these weighting factors on arbitrary subintervals of the fundamental interval $-1\leqq\mu\leqq 1$. However, the reader is referred to the literature for these interesting and highly useful developments.

Having discussed the orthogonality properties of the angular eigenfunctions, we now turn our attention to their completeness properties.

6.2 PROPERTIES OF ANGULAR EIGENFUNCTIONS: COMPLETENESS

In a beautiful analysis applying the theory of singular integral equations of the Cauchy type, Case has shown that the system of continuum functions

$\phi(\mu \mid \nu)$ is complete for functions which are Hölder continuous in the extended sense on a proper subinterval of the fundamental interval $-1 \leqq \mu \leqq 1$. He has shown, moreover, that in the case of the important half range intervals $-1 \leqq \mu \leqq 0$ and $0 \leqq \mu \leqq 1$ the system of continuum functions must be augmented by the discrete eigenfunctions $\phi(\mu \mid -\nu_0)$ and $\phi(\mu \mid \nu_0)$ respectively, whereas on the full range, $-1 \leqq \mu \leqq 1$, the system of continuum functions must be enlarged by both functions, $\phi(\mu \mid \nu_0)$ and $\phi(\mu \mid -\nu_0)$.

Following Case's analysis, we consider the expansion in terms of the continuous functions $\phi(\mu \mid \nu)$ of a function $f(\mu)$ which is Hölder continuous in the extended sense on a subinterval (a, b) of the fundamental interval. This means that the function $f(\mu)$ is Hölder continuous on any closed subinterval of the interval (a, b) and is bounded by the functions $g(\mu)/(\mu - a)^\alpha$ and $h(\mu)/(\mu - b)^\beta$ near the end points a and b of the interval (a, b) respectively, where the functions $g(\mu)$ and $h(\mu)$ are Hölder continuous on (a, b), including the end points, and α and β are constants such that $0 \leqq \alpha < 1$ and $0 \leqq \beta < 1$.

The completeness of the continuum functions $\phi(\mu \mid \nu)$ for such functions $f(\mu)$ can be established by means of the theory of singular integral equations of the type introduced in Chapter IV. For, let us assume that the function $f(\mu)$ has the integral representation,

$$f(\mu) = \int_a^b a(\nu)\phi(\mu \mid \nu)\, d\nu \tag{6.3}$$

Substitution of the eigendistribution,

$$\phi(\mu \mid \nu) = \lambda(\nu)\, \delta(\nu - \mu) + \frac{c\nu}{2} P \frac{1}{\nu - \mu}$$

yields a singular integral equation of the Cauchy type,

$$f(\mu) = \lambda(\mu)a(\mu) + \int_a^b \frac{c}{2} \frac{\nu a(\nu)}{\nu - \mu}\, d\nu \tag{6.4}$$

for the function $a(\nu)$. If we can show therefore that this integral equation has a solution $a(\nu)$ for functions $f(\mu)$ which are Hölder continuous in the extended sense on the interval (a, b), we have established at the same time the integral representation (6.3). The proof of the existence of the function $a(\nu)$ is by construction. We first assume that $a(\nu)$ is Hölder continuous in the extended sense on the interval (a, b). On the basis of this assumption and the Hölder continuity of the function $f(\mu)$, we are able to construct a solution of the singular integral equation by means of the methods outlined in Chapter IV.

Let us assume therefore that the function $a(\nu)$ is Hölder continuous in the extended sense on the interval (a, b). As explained in Section 4.11, the singular integral equation (6.4) can be reduced to a boundary equation for the boundary values of a sectionally analytic function $F(z)$ that has the Cauchy integral representation,

$$F(z) = \frac{1}{2\pi i} \int_a^b \frac{c}{2} \frac{\nu a(\nu)}{\nu - z} \, d\nu$$

For, making appropriate substitutions from the Plemelj formulas,

$$F^L(\nu) - F^R(\nu) = a(\nu)c\nu/2 \tag{6.5}$$

and

$$F^L(\nu) + F^R(\nu) = \frac{1}{\pi i} \int_a^b \frac{c}{2} \frac{\mu a(\mu)}{\mu - \nu} \, d\mu$$

into the singular integral equation, we obtain the relation,

$$F^L(\nu) = \frac{\lambda(\nu) - \pi i c\nu/2}{\lambda(\nu) + \pi i c\nu/2} F^R(\nu) + \frac{f(\nu)c\nu/2}{\lambda(\nu) + \pi i c\nu/2}$$

between the boundary values $F^L(\nu)$ and $F^R(\nu)$ of the function $F(z)$ on the path (a, b). Thus, introducing the functions,

$$A(\nu) = \frac{\lambda(\nu) - \pi i c\nu/2}{\lambda(\nu) + \pi i c\nu/2} = \frac{1 - c\nu \operatorname{arctanh} \nu - \pi i c\nu/2}{1 - c\nu \operatorname{arctanh} \nu + \pi i c\nu/2}$$

and

$$B(\nu) = \frac{f(\nu)c\nu/2}{\lambda(\nu) + \pi i c\nu/2} = \frac{f(\nu)c\nu/2}{1 - c\nu \operatorname{arctanh} \nu + \pi i c\nu/2}$$

we want to construct a sectionally analytic function $F(z)$ with boundary path (a, b) such that the boundary values $F^L(\nu)$ and $F^R(\nu)$ of this function satisfy the boundary condition,

$$F^L(\nu) = A(\nu)F^R(\nu) + B(\nu)$$

on the path (a, b). The function $F(z)$ moreover should behave as $1/z$ when z tends to infinity and should be bounded by $(a - z)^\alpha$ and $(b - z)^\beta$ when z tends to the end point a or b, respectively, where $\alpha + 1$ and $\beta + 1$ are positive constants. Once the solution of this Hilbert problem has been found, the function $a(\nu)$ in the expansion formula,

$$f(\mu) = \int_a^b a(\nu)\phi(\mu \,|\, \nu) \, d\nu$$

can be obtained immediately from the first Plemelj formula (6.5) for the jump in the sectionally analytic function $F(z)$ when it crosses the path (a, b) upon moving from the upper into the lower half plane. Assisted by the technique developed in Section 4.12, we first obtain the solution of the corresponding homogeneous Hilbert problem with boundary condition,

$$F^L(\nu) = A(\nu)F^R(\nu)$$

on the path (a, b). The fundamental solution $G(z)$ of this problem can be written down immediately

$$G(z) = (a - z)^{\alpha(a)}(b - z)^{\beta(b)} \exp\left\{-\frac{1}{\pi}\int_a^b \frac{\theta(\nu)}{\nu - z}\,d\nu\right\}$$

where the real valued function $\theta(\nu)$ is defined by the relations,

$$\theta(\nu) = \frac{i}{2}\log A(\nu) = \arg\,[\lambda(\nu) + \pi i c\nu/2] = \arctan\frac{\pi c\nu/2}{1 - c\nu\,\text{arctanh}\,\nu}$$

The function $\theta(\nu)$ increases from $-\pi$ to π, when ν traverses the interval from -1 to $+1$, and vanishes at the origin. The conditions imposed on the solution of the inhomogeneous Hilbert problem at the end points a and b of the interval require that we choose the integers $\alpha(a)$ and $\beta(b)$ in the fundamental solution such that

$$-1 < \alpha(a) + \frac{1}{\pi}\,\theta(a) \leqq 0$$

and

$$-1 < \beta(b) - \frac{1}{\pi}\,\theta(b) \leqq 0$$

In view of the behavior of $\theta(\nu)$ over the interval $-1 \leqq \nu \leqq 1$, we can now easily construct the following table of admissible values of the integers $\alpha(a)$ and $\beta(b)$, and of the index $p(\alpha, \beta) = -[\alpha(a) + \beta(b)]$ of the homogeneous Hilbert problem.

Table VI-1

a	$\alpha(a)$	b	$\beta(b)$	$p(\alpha, \beta)$
$a = -1$	1	$b = 1$	1	-2
$a = -1$	1	$0 \leqq b < 1$	0	-1
$a = -1$	1	$-1 < b < 0$	-1	0
$-1 < a \leqq 0$	0	$b = 1$	1	-1
$-1 < a \leqq 0$	0	$0 \leqq b < 1$	0	0
$-1 < a \leqq 0$	0	$a \leqq b < 0$	-1	1
$0 < a < 1$	-1	$b = 1$	1	0
$0 < a < 1$	-1	$a < b < 1$	0	1

The solution $F(z)$ of the inhomogeneous Hilbert problem with boundary condition,

$$F^L(\nu) = A(\nu)F^R(\nu) + B(\nu)$$

on the path (a, b) takes the form,

$$F(z) = \frac{G(z)}{2\pi i}\int_a^b \frac{B(\nu)}{G^L(\nu)}\frac{d\nu}{\nu - z} + P(z)G(z)$$

where

$$B(\nu) = \frac{f(\nu)c\nu/2}{\lambda(\nu) + \pi i c\nu/2}$$

As we have observed in Section 4.12, the character of the solution $F(z)$ and the choice of the polynomial $P(z)$ depend on the behavior at infinity of the fundamental solution $G(z)$. This behavior in turn is determined by the values of the index $p(\alpha, \beta) = -[\alpha(a) + \beta(b)]$. In our case $F(z)$ must vanish as $1/z$ when z tends to infinity and we find, therefore, that the admissible solutions of the inhomogeneous Hilbert problem and the corresponding expressions for the expansion function $a(\nu)$ are related to the particular interval of definition (a, b) of the function $f(\nu)$ in the following manner.

1. The index $p(\alpha, \beta)$ vanishes. According to Table VI-1, this case arises, for example, when the function $f(\mu)$ is Hölder continuous in the extended sense on a proper subinterval $(-1 < a \leqq 0 \leqq b < 1)$ of the interval $(-1 \leqq \mu \leqq 1)$. In Section 4.12, we found that in this case the inhomogeneous Hilbert problem has the unique solution,

$$F(z) = \frac{G(z)}{2\pi i}\int_a^b \frac{c}{2}\frac{\nu f(\nu)}{[\lambda(\nu) + \pi i c\nu/2]G^L(\nu)}\frac{d\nu}{\nu - z}$$

The solution of the integral equation,

$$f(\nu) = \lambda(\nu)a(\nu) + \int_a^b \frac{c}{2}\frac{\mu a(\mu)}{\mu - \nu}\,d\mu$$

can now be obtained by means of the first Plemelj formula,

$$F^L(\nu) - F^R(\nu) = a(\nu)c\nu/2$$

for the Cauchy integral,

$$F(z) = \frac{1}{2\pi i}\int_a^b \frac{c}{2}\frac{\nu a(\nu)}{\nu - z}\,d\nu$$

The boundary values of the sectionally analytic function $F(z)$ can be written down immediately

$$F^L(\nu) = \frac{G^L(\nu)}{2} \frac{f(\nu)c\nu/2}{[\lambda(\nu) + \pi i c\nu/2]G^L(\nu)} + \frac{G^L(\nu)}{2\pi i} \int_a^b \frac{c}{2} \frac{\mu f(\mu)}{[\lambda(\mu) + \pi i c\mu/2]G^L(\mu)} \frac{d\mu}{\mu - \nu}$$

and

$$F^R(\nu) = -\frac{G^R(\nu)}{2} \frac{f(\nu)c\nu/2}{[\lambda(\nu) + \pi i c\nu/2]G^L(\nu)} + \frac{G^R(\nu)}{2\pi i} \int_a^b \frac{c}{2} \frac{\mu f(\mu)}{[\lambda(\mu) + \pi i c\mu/2]G^L(\mu)} \frac{d\mu}{\mu - \nu}$$

Substitution of these expressions for the boundary values $F^L(\nu)$ and $F^R(\nu)$ into the first Plemelj formula yields the following relation for the expansion function $a(\nu)$,

$$a(\nu) = \frac{\lambda(\nu) f(\nu)}{[\lambda^2(\nu) + \pi^2 c^2 \nu^2/4]} - \frac{G^L(\nu)}{[\lambda(\nu) - \pi i c\nu/2]} \int_a^b \frac{c}{2} \frac{\mu f(\mu)}{[\lambda(\mu) + \pi i c\mu/2]G^L(\mu)} \frac{d\mu}{\mu - \nu}$$

2. The index $p(\alpha, \beta)$ is positive. As may be observed from Table VI-1, this can happen only when the end points a and b of the interval (a, b) are located on the same side of the origin. For instance, the partial range intervals $-1 < \mu < 0$ and $0 < \mu < 1$ fall into this category. The solution of the inhomogeneous Hilbert problem, obtained for this case in Section 4.12, takes the form,

$$F(z) = \frac{G(z)}{2\pi i} \int_a^b \frac{c}{2} \frac{\nu f(\nu)}{[\lambda(\nu) + \pi i c\nu/2]G^L(\nu)} \frac{d\nu}{\nu - z} + P_m(z)G(z)$$

where the admissible polynomial is of a degree $m \leqq p(\alpha, \beta) - 1$. The expansion coefficient,

$$a(\nu) = \frac{\lambda(\nu) f(\nu)}{[\lambda^2(\nu) + \pi^2 c^2 \nu^2/4]} - \frac{2\pi i P_m(\nu) G^L(\nu)}{[\lambda(\nu) - \pi i c\nu/2]} - \frac{G^L(\nu)}{[\lambda(\nu) - \pi i c\nu/2]} \int_a^b \frac{c}{2} \frac{\mu f(\mu)}{[\lambda(\mu) + \pi i c\mu/2]G^L(\mu)} \frac{d\mu}{\mu - \nu}$$

can again be found from the first Plemelj formula. Since the polynomial $P_m(\nu)$ is determined up to $m \leqq p(\alpha, \beta) - 1$ arbitrary constants, the function $a(\nu)$ cannot be determined in a unique fashion when the index of the auxiliary homogeneous Hilbert problem is positive.

3. The index $p(\alpha, \beta)$ is negative. This very important category includes the so-called full range and half range expansions over the interval, $-1 \leqq \mu \leqq 1$, and the intervals, $-1 \leqq \mu \leqq 0$ and $0 \leqq \mu \leqq 1$, respectively. In Section 4.12 we found that the inhomogeneous Hilbert problem has the unique solution,

$$F(z) = \frac{G(z)}{2\pi i} \int_a^b \frac{c}{2} \frac{\nu f(\nu)}{[\lambda(\nu) + \pi i c\nu/2]G^L(\nu)} \frac{d\nu}{\nu - z}$$

provided that the following auxiliary conditions are satisfied,

$$\int_a^b \frac{c}{2} \frac{\nu f(\nu)}{[\lambda(\nu) + \pi i c\nu/2]} \frac{\nu^m}{G^L(\nu)} \, d\nu = 0$$

for all values of m $= 0, \ldots, -[p(\alpha, \beta) + 1]$. It is clear, however, that these conditions cannot be satisfied for any arbitrary function $f(\nu)$ which is Hölder continuous in the extended sense on the interval (a, b). A way out of this dilemma is to consider expansions of the function $f(\mu)$ in terms of the continuum *and* the discrete eigenfunctions $\phi(\mu \mid \nu)$, $\phi(\mu \mid \pm\nu_0)$, instead of expansions involving the continuum functions only. In other words, the space of continuum functions $\phi(\mu \mid \nu)$ is not complete for functions $f(\mu)$ which are Hölder continuous in the extended sense on the intervals $-1 \leqq \mu \leqq 1$, $0 \leqq \mu \leqq 1$, and $-1 \leqq \mu \leqq 0$, but must be augmented by either one or both of the discrete eigenfunctions $\phi(\mu \mid \pm\nu_0)$. Expansion of the function $f(\mu)$ in terms of this augmented system puts at our disposal enough undetermined coefficients to satisfy the auxiliary conditions.

For example, let us consider a function $f(\mu)$ which is Hölder continuous in the extended sense on the interval $-1 \leqq \mu \leqq 1$. From Table VI-1, we find that the homogeneous Hilbert problem has an index $p(\alpha, \beta) = -2$, and therefore two auxiliary conditions are imposed on the solution of the homogeneous Hilbert problem. Expanding the function $f(\mu)$,

$$f(\mu) = a(\nu_0)\phi(\mu \mid \nu_0) + a(-\nu_0)\phi(\mu \mid -\nu_0) + \int_{-1}^{1} a(\nu)\phi(\mu \mid \nu) \, d\nu$$

in terms of the continuum and discrete eigenfunctions, we define a new function $g(\mu)$,

$$g(\mu) = f(\mu) - a(\nu_0)\phi(\mu \mid \nu_0) - a(-\nu_0)\phi(\mu \mid -\nu_0) = \int_{-1}^{1} a(\nu)\phi(\mu \mid \nu) \, d\nu$$

By repeating the analysis leading to the solution of the inhomogeneous Hilbert problem, we find that the following auxiliary conditions must be satisfied,

$$\int_{-1}^{1} \frac{c}{2} \frac{\nu g(\nu)}{[\lambda(\nu) + \pi i c\nu/2]} \frac{\nu^m}{G^L(\nu)} \, d\nu = 0$$

where $m = 0$ and $m = 1$. Inserting the function,

$$g(\nu) = f(\nu) - a(\nu_0)\phi(\nu \mid \nu_0) - a(-\nu_0)\phi(\nu \mid -\nu_0)$$

we obtain two linear algebraic equations for the expansion coefficients $a(\nu_0)$ and $a(-\nu_0)$ which enable us to express these coefficients in terms of the function $f(\nu)$ and, simultaneously, to satisfy the auxiliary conditions. The expressions obtained for the expansion coefficients $a(\nu_0)$ and $a(-\nu_0)$ should of course agree with those obtained by means of the orthogonality relations satisfied by the functions $\phi(\mu \mid \nu)$ and $\phi(\mu \mid \pm\nu_0)$ on the interval $-1 \leqq \mu \leqq 1$.

In the case of the interval $0 \leqq \mu \leqq 1$, we find that $p(\alpha, \beta) = -1$ and we can expect one auxiliary condition on the solution of the inhomogeneous Hilbert problem. We now consider the half range expansion,

$$f(\mu) = a(\nu_0)\phi(\mu \mid \nu_0) + \int_0^1 a(\nu)\phi(\mu \mid \nu)\, d\nu$$

and define a new function,

$$g(\mu) = f(\mu) - a(\nu_0)\phi(\mu \mid \nu_0) = \int_0^1 a(\nu)\phi(\mu \mid \nu)\, d\nu$$

By means of the auxiliary condition,

$$\int_0^1 \frac{c}{2} \frac{\nu g(\nu)}{[\lambda(\nu) + \pi i c\nu/2]} \frac{\nu^m}{G^L(\nu)}\, d\nu = 0$$

where $m = 0$, we are able to express the coefficient $a(\nu_0)$ in terms of the known function $f(\nu)$.

We shall now apply these ideas to obtain some explicit analytical expressions for the coefficients $a(\nu)$, $a(\nu_0)$, and $a(-\nu_0)$ for the full and half range expansions of a function $f(\mu)$.

6.3 FULL RANGE EXPANSION COEFFICIENTS

We consider the expansion in terms of the angular eigenfunctions $\phi(\mu \mid \nu)$ and $\phi(\mu \mid \pm\nu_0)$ of a function $f(\mu)$ which is defined and Hölder continuous in the extended sense on the interval $-1 \leqq \mu \leqq 1$. Since $\alpha(-1) = 1$ and $\beta(1) = 1$, the fundamental solution of the auxiliary homogeneous Hilbert problem takes the form,

$$G(z) = (1 - z^2) \exp\left\{\frac{1}{2\pi i} \int_{-1}^1 \frac{\log A(\nu)}{\nu - z}\, d\nu\right\}$$

where

$$A(\nu) = \frac{\lambda(\nu) - i\pi c\nu/2}{\lambda(\nu) + i\pi c\nu/2} = \frac{1 - c\nu \operatorname{arctanh} \nu - i\pi c\nu/2}{1 - c\nu \operatorname{arctanh} \nu + i\pi c\nu/2}$$

The function $G(z)$ can be brought into a more convenient form as follows. The integral,

$$H(z) = \frac{1}{2\pi i} \int_{-1}^1 \frac{d\nu}{\nu - z} = -\frac{1}{\pi i} \operatorname{arctanh} 1/z$$

is the representation of a sectionally analytic function $H(z)$ with boundary path $(-1, 1)$ and, according to the Plemelj formulas, the boundary values of this function are given by the expressions,

$$H^L(v) = \frac{1}{2} + \frac{1}{2\pi i}\int_{-1}^{1} \frac{d\mu}{\mu - v} = \frac{1}{2} - \frac{1}{\pi i}\text{arctanh } v$$

and

$$H^R(v) = -\frac{1}{2} + \frac{1}{2\pi i}\int_{-1}^{1} \frac{d\mu}{\mu - v} = -\frac{1}{2} - \frac{1}{\pi i}\text{ arctanh } v$$

The boundary values of the sectionally analytic function,

$$K(z) = 1 - cz \text{ arctanh } 1/z = 1 + \pi iczH(z)$$

may be written therefore as

$$K^L(v) = 1 - cv \text{ arctanh } v + \pi icv/2$$

and

$$K^R(v) = 1 - c\, v \text{ arctanh } v - \pi icv/2$$

This implies that

$$A(v) = \frac{1 - cv \text{ arctanh } v - i\pi cv/2}{1 - cv \text{ arctanh } v + i\pi cv/2} = \frac{[1 - cz \text{ arctanh } 1/z]^R}{[1 - cz \text{ arctanh } 1/z]^L}$$

Thus, we may replace the line integral,

$$\frac{1}{2\pi i}\int_{-1}^{1} \frac{\log A(v)}{v - z}\, dv$$

by the contour integral,

$$\frac{1}{2\pi i}\oint_C \frac{\log [1 - c\zeta \text{ arctanh } 1/\zeta]}{\zeta - z}\, d\zeta$$

where C denotes an arbitrary contour encircling the path $(-1, 1)$, as shown in Figure VI-1. This statement can easily be verified by letting the contour C

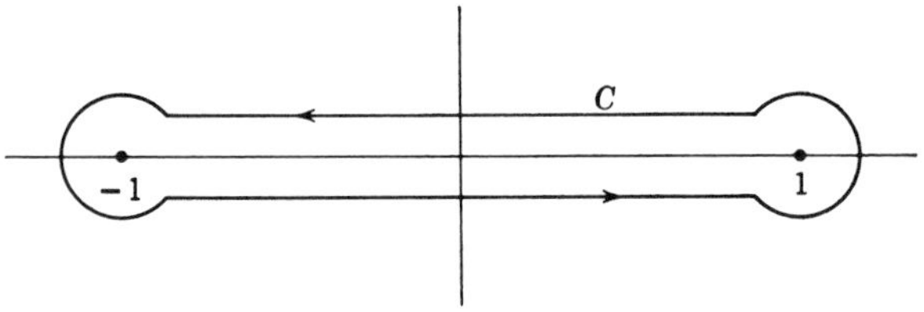

Figure VI-1

shrink to the path $(-1, 1)$. For, if $\zeta = \nu + i\varepsilon$ is a point on the contour located in the upper half plane, then

$$\lim_{\varepsilon \to 0} (1 - c\zeta \operatorname{arctanh} 1/\zeta) = 1 - c\nu \operatorname{arctanh} \nu + i\pi c\nu/2$$

Similarly, if $\zeta = \nu - i\varepsilon$ denotes a point on the contour located in the lower half plane, then

$$\lim_{\varepsilon \to 0} (1 - c\zeta \operatorname{arctanh} 1/\zeta) = 1 - c\nu \operatorname{arctanh} \nu - i\pi c\nu/2$$

Thus, in the limit as the contour C tends to the path $(-1, 1)$,

$$\begin{aligned}\lim_{\varepsilon \to 0} \frac{1}{2\pi i} \oint_C \frac{\log(1 - c\zeta \operatorname{arctanh} 1/\zeta)}{\zeta - z}\, d\zeta &= \frac{1}{2\pi i} \int_{-1}^{1} \frac{\log(1 - c\nu \operatorname{arctanh} \nu - i\pi c\nu/2)}{\nu - z}\, d\nu \\ &\quad + \frac{1}{2\pi i} \int_{1}^{-1} \frac{\log(1 - c\nu \operatorname{arctanh} \nu + i\pi c\nu/2)}{\nu - z}\, d\nu \\ &= \frac{1}{2\pi i} \int_{-1}^{1} \frac{\log A(\nu)}{\nu - z}\, d\nu\end{aligned}$$

To evaluate the contour integral,

$$\frac{1}{2\pi i} \oint_C \frac{\log(1 - c\zeta \operatorname{arctanh} 1/\zeta)}{\zeta - z}\, d\zeta$$

it should be noted that the integrand has a simple pole at the point z and branch points at the zeros $\pm\, \nu_0$ of the function $1 - c\zeta \operatorname{arctanh} 1/\zeta$. To avoid cumbersome integrations along branch cuts in the complex plane, we use a trick suggested by Case and construct a function $M(z)$ which is analytic in the plane outside the contour C, vanishes at infinity, and has the property that

$$\frac{1}{2\pi i} \oint_C \frac{\log M(\zeta)}{\zeta - z}\, d\zeta = \frac{1}{2\pi i} \int_{-1}^{1} \frac{\log A(\nu)}{\nu - z}\, d\nu$$

The function,

$$M(z) = \frac{(1 - z^2)(1 - cz \operatorname{arctanh} 1/z)}{({\nu_0}^2 - z^2)(1 - c)}$$

has the required properties. For, the function $1 - cz \operatorname{arctanh} 1/z$ tends to $1 - c$ as z tends to infinity and the function $M(z)$ therefore tends to one for large values of z. $M(z)$ moreover is analytic and nonvanishing in the whole complex plane with the exception of the boundary $-1 \leqq \nu \leqq 1$. On the boundary

$$\frac{M^R(\nu)}{M^L(\nu)} = \frac{(1 - cz \operatorname{arctanh} 1/z)^R}{(1 - cz \operatorname{arctanh} 1/z)^L} = A(\nu)$$

The integrand of the contour integral,

$$\frac{1}{2\pi i} \oint_C \frac{\log M(\zeta)}{\zeta - z} \, d\zeta$$

has a simple pole at the point z and we obtain therefore by the residue theorem,

$$\frac{1}{2\pi i} \oint_C \frac{\log M(\zeta)}{\zeta - z} \, d\zeta = \frac{1}{2\pi i} \int_{-1}^{1} \frac{\log A(\nu)}{\nu - z} \, d\nu$$

$$= -\log \frac{(1 - z^2)(1 - cz \operatorname{arctanh} 1/z)}{({\nu_0}^2 - z^2)(1 - c)}$$

where the minus sign is incurred because the contour C is traversed in the positive direction and the pole at the point z is located outside the contour.

In view of the relations obtained above, the fundamental solution of the homogeneous Hilbert problem may now be written as

$$G(z) = (1 - z^2) \exp\left\{\frac{1}{2\pi i} \int_{-1}^{1} \frac{\log A(\nu)}{\nu - z} \, d\nu\right\} = \frac{({\nu_0}^2 - z^2)(1 - c)}{1 - cz \operatorname{arctanh} 1/z}$$

The solution of the inhomogeneous Hilbert problem takes the form,

$$F(z) = \frac{G(z)}{2\pi i} \int_{-1}^{1} \frac{c}{2} \frac{\nu g(\nu)}{G^L(\nu)[\lambda(\nu) + \pi i c \nu/2]} \frac{d\nu}{\nu - z}$$

and substitution of the left boundary values of $G(z)$,

$$G^L(\nu) = \frac{({\nu_0}^2 - \nu^2)(1 - c)}{1 - c\nu \operatorname{arctanh} \nu + i\pi c \nu/2}$$

yields the simpler expression,

$$F(z) = \frac{1}{2\pi i} \frac{{\nu_0}^2 - z^2}{1 - cz \operatorname{arctanh} 1/z} \int_{-1}^{1} \frac{c}{2} \frac{\nu g(\nu)}{{\nu_0}^2 - \nu^2} \frac{d\nu}{\nu - z} \tag{6.6}$$

for the solution of the inhomogeneous Hilbert problem. In a similar manner we obtain for the auxiliary conditions, which must be imposed on this solution, the expression,

$$\int_{-1}^{1} \frac{\nu g(\nu)}{{\nu_0}^2 - \nu^2} \nu^m \, d\nu = 0$$

where $m = 0$ or $m = 1$. However, since

$$\frac{1}{\nu_0^2 - \nu^2} = \frac{1}{2\nu_0}\left[\frac{1}{\nu_0 - \nu} + \frac{1}{\nu_0 + \nu}\right] = \frac{1}{2\nu}\left[\frac{1}{\nu_0 - \nu} - \frac{1}{\nu_0 + \nu}\right]$$

the auxiliary conditions may also be written as

$$\int_{-1}^{1} \frac{\nu g(\nu)}{\nu_0 \pm \nu}\, d\nu = 0 \tag{6.7}$$

We make use of this fact to simplify the expression for the solution of the inhomogeneous Hilbert problem still further. For we note that

$$\frac{1}{(\nu_0^2 - \nu^2)(\nu - z)} = \frac{1}{2\nu_0}\left[\frac{1}{(\nu_0 - z)(\nu_0 - \nu)} + \frac{1}{(\nu_0 - z)(\nu - z)} + \frac{1}{(\nu_0 + z)(\nu - z)} - \frac{1}{(\nu_0 + z)(\nu_0 + \nu)}\right]$$

Substitution into equation (6.6) yields therefore the Cauchy integral representation,

$$F(z) = \frac{1}{2\pi i}\frac{1}{1 - cz \operatorname{arctanh} 1/z}\int_{-1}^{1} \frac{c}{2}\frac{\nu g(\nu)}{\nu - z}\, d\nu$$

for the solution of the inhomogeneous Hilbert problem.

By means of the Plemelj formula,

$$F^L(\nu) - F^R(\nu) = a(\nu)c\nu/2$$

the expansion function $a(\nu)$ can immediately be expressed in terms of the boundary values $F^L(\nu)$ and $F^R(\nu)$ of the function $F(z)$. We obtain in this manner

$$a(\nu) = \frac{1}{[\lambda^2(\nu) + \pi^2 c^2 \nu^2/4]}\left\{\lambda(\nu)g(\nu) - \int_{-1}^{1} \frac{c}{2}\frac{\mu g(\mu)}{\mu - \nu}\, d\mu\right\} \tag{6.8}$$

Furthermore, substitution of the function,

$$g(\nu) = f(\nu) - a(\nu_0)\phi(\nu \mid \nu_0) - a(-\nu_0)\phi(\nu \mid -\nu_0)$$

where

$$\phi(\nu \mid \pm\nu_0) = \frac{c}{2}\frac{\nu_0}{\nu_0 \mp \nu}$$

into equation (6.7) immediately yields the following expressions for the coefficients $a(\nu_0)$ and $a(-\nu_0)$,

$$a(\pm\nu_0) = \frac{1}{M(\pm\nu_0)}\int_{-1}^{1} \nu f(\nu)\phi(\nu \mid \pm\nu_0)\, d\nu$$

where

$$M(\pm\nu_0) = \pm\frac{c\nu_0}{2}\left[\frac{1-(1-c)\nu_0^2}{\nu_0^2-1}\right]$$

These expressions could have been obtained in a more straightforward manner by means of the orthogonality relations for the functions $\phi(\mu \mid \nu)$ and $\phi(\mu \mid \pm\nu_0)$ on the interval $(-1, 1)$. The derivation above however verifies the consistency of the integral equation approach.

6.4 HALF RANGE EXPANSION COEFFICIENTS

Now let us consider the expansion of a function $f(\mu)$, which is defined and Hölder continuous in the extended sense on the interval $0 \leqq \mu \leqq 1$, in terms of the angular eigenfunctions $\phi(\mu \mid \nu)$. In this case, the exponents $\alpha(a)$ and $\beta(b)$ in the fundamental solution $G(z)$ of the homogeneous Hilbert problem take the values $\alpha(0) = 0$ and $\beta(1) = 1$. The fundamental solution may be written therefore as

$$G(z) = (1-z)\exp\left\{\frac{1}{2\pi i}\int_0^1 \frac{\log A(\nu)}{\nu - z}\,d\nu\right\}$$

where

$$A(\nu) = \frac{\lambda(\nu) - \pi i c\nu/2}{\lambda(\nu) + \pi i c\nu/2} = \frac{1 - c\nu \operatorname{arctanh} \nu - i\pi c\nu/2}{1 - c\nu \operatorname{arctanh} \nu + i\pi c\nu/2}$$

Some highly useful identities, related to this function $G(z)$, can be derived. For example, the function,

$$\frac{1}{G(z)} = \frac{\exp\left\{-\dfrac{1}{2\pi i}\displaystyle\int_0^1 \frac{\log A(\nu)}{\nu - z}\,d\nu\right\}}{1-z}$$

is sectionally analytic with boundary path $(0, 1)$ and vanishes as $1/z$ when z tends to infinity. This implies that the function $1/G(z)$ can be represented by the Cauchy integral,

$$\frac{1}{G(z)} = \frac{1}{2\pi i}\oint_C \frac{1/G(\zeta)}{\zeta - z}\,d\zeta$$

where C is an arbitrary contour which encloses the origin and is traversed in the negative direction, as shown in Figure VI-2.

In view of the fact that

$$\frac{G^L(\nu)}{G^R(\nu)} = \frac{\lambda(\nu) - \pi i c\nu/2}{\lambda(\nu) + \pi i c\nu/2}$$

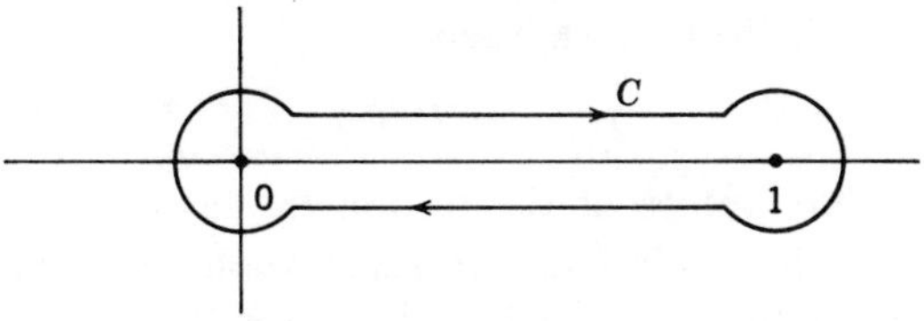

Figure VI-2

we obtain, by letting the contour C shrink to the path (0, 1), the first identity,

$$\frac{1}{G(z)} = \frac{1}{2\pi i}\int_0^1 \left[\frac{1}{G^L(v)} - \frac{1}{G^R(v)}\right]\frac{dv}{v-z} = \int_0^1 \frac{c}{2}\,\frac{v}{[\lambda(v) + \pi icv/2]G^L(v)}\,\frac{dv}{v-z}$$

(6.9)

If z tends to a point v on the interval (0, 1), the second Plemelj formula yields

$$\frac{1}{2}\left[\frac{1}{G^L(v)} + \frac{1}{G^R(v)}\right] = \int_0^1 \frac{c}{2}\,\frac{\mu}{[\lambda(\mu) + \pi ic\mu/2]G^L(\mu)}\,\frac{d\mu}{\mu - v}$$

or, again using the expression for the ratio of the functions $G^L(v)$ and $G^R(v)$,

$$\int_0^1 \frac{c}{2}\,\frac{\mu}{[\lambda(\mu) + \pi ic\mu/2]G^L(\mu)}\,\frac{d\mu}{\mu - v} = \frac{\lambda(v)}{[\lambda(v) + \pi icv/2]G^L(v)}$$

To obtain the second identity, let us consider the function,

$$H(z) = \frac{({v_0}^2 - z^2)(1-c)}{G(z)G(-z)(1 - cz \operatorname{arctanh} 1/z)}$$

We can verify immediately that this function is sectionally analytic with boundary path (0, 1) and tends to one when z tends to infinity. The boundary values of $H(z)$ on the path (0, 1) may be written as

$$H^L(v) = \frac{({v_0}^2 - v^2)(1-c)}{G^L(v)G^L(-v)[1 - cv \operatorname{arctanh} v + \pi icv/2]}$$

and

$$H^R(v) = \frac{({v_0}^2 - v^2)(1-c)}{G^R(v)G^R(-v)[1 - cv \operatorname{arctanh} v - \pi icv/2]}$$

However,

$$G^L(v) = \frac{1 - cv \operatorname{arctanh} v - \pi icv/2}{1 - cv \operatorname{arctanh} v + \pi icv/2}\,G^R(v)$$

and substitution yields the following relation,

$$H^L(\nu) = H^R(\nu)$$

between the boundary values of the sectionally analytic function $H(z)$ on the boundary (0, 1). This implies that $H(z)$ is also continuous on the boundary and must be therefore an entire function. However, an entire function which is equal to one at infinity must be equal to one everywhere else in the complex plane and we may conclude therefore that

$$\frac{(\nu_0^2 - z^2)(1 - c)}{G(z)G(-z)(1 - cz \operatorname{arctanh} 1/z)} = 1$$

The second identity now follows at once,

$$G(z)G(-z) = \frac{(1 - c)(\nu_0^2 - z^2)}{1 - cz \operatorname{arctanh} 1/z} \tag{6.10}$$

We could have established this result by means of the fundamental solution of the homogeneous Hilbert problem for the interval $(-1, 1)$. For,

$$G(z) = (1 - z) \exp\left\{\frac{1}{2\pi i}\int_0^1 \frac{\log A(\nu)}{\nu - z}\, d\nu\right\}$$

and

$$G(-z) = (1 + z) \exp\left\{\frac{1}{2\pi i}\int_{-1}^0 \frac{\log A(\nu)}{\nu - z}\, d\nu\right\}$$

Multiplying these functions, we find

$$G(z)G(-z) = (1 - z^2) \exp\left\{\frac{1}{2\pi i}\int_{-1}^1 \frac{\log A(\nu)}{\nu - z}\, d\nu\right\}$$

However, in the preceding section we found that the Cauchy integral on the right hand side of this expression is equal to

$$\log \frac{(1 - c)(\nu_0^2 - z^2)}{(1 - z^2)(1 - cz \operatorname{arctanh} 1/z)}$$

and subsitution yields again the second identity. For later use we shall need the limit as z tends to ν_0 of the product $G(z)\, G(-z)$,

$$\lim_{z \to \nu_0} G(z)G(-z) = (1 - c)\frac{2\nu_0^2(1 - \nu_0^2)}{1 - \nu_0^2(1 - c)} \tag{6.11}$$

Another useful limit may be written as

$$\lim_{z \to 0} G(z)G(-z) = G^2(0) = (1 - c)\nu_0^2 \tag{6.12}$$

With the help of the fundamental solution $G(z)$ of the homogeneous Hilbert problem we are now able to obtain the solution,

$$F(z) = \frac{G(z)}{2\pi i} \int_0^1 \frac{c}{2} \frac{\nu g(\nu)}{[\lambda(\nu) + \pi i c\nu/2] G^L(\nu)} \frac{d\nu}{\nu - z}$$

of the inhomogeneous Hilbert problem where

$$g(\nu) = f(\nu) - a(\nu_0)\phi(\nu \mid \nu_0)$$

The index of the homogeneous problem is $p(\alpha, \beta) = -1$ and we must therefore impose the following auxiliary condition,

$$\int_0^1 \frac{c}{2} \frac{\nu g(\nu)}{[\lambda(\nu) + \pi i c\nu/2]} \frac{d\nu}{G^L(\nu)} = 0$$

Substitution of the function $g(\nu)$ defined above immediately yields the following expression for the expansion coefficient $a(\nu_0)$,

$$a(\nu_0) = -\frac{2G(\nu_0)}{c\nu_0} \int_0^1 \frac{c}{2} \frac{\nu f(\nu)}{[\lambda(\nu) + \pi i c\nu/2]} \frac{d\nu}{G^L(\nu)}$$

where we made use of the first identity (6.9). The continuum function $a(\nu)$ can be found by means of the first Plemelj formula for the function $F(z)$,

$$a(\nu) = \frac{2}{c\nu} [F^L(\nu) - F^R(\nu)]$$

$$= \frac{\lambda(\nu) g(\nu)}{[\lambda^2(\nu) + \pi^2 c^2 \nu^2/4]} - \frac{G^L(\nu)}{[\lambda(\nu) - \pi i c\nu/2]} \int_0^1 \frac{c}{2} \frac{\mu g(\mu)}{[\lambda(\mu) + \pi i c\mu/2] G^L(\mu)} \frac{d\mu}{\mu - \nu}$$

To simplify this expression we make use of the second identity (6.10) and we write

$$a(\nu) = \frac{1}{[\lambda^2(\nu) + \pi^2 c^2 \nu^2/4]} \left\{ \lambda(\nu) g(\nu) - \frac{(1-c)(\nu_0{}^2 - \nu^2)}{G(-\nu)} \int_0^1 \frac{c}{2} \frac{\mu g(\mu)}{[\lambda(\mu) + \pi i c\mu/2] G^L(\mu)} \frac{d\mu}{\mu - \nu} \right\}$$

Now let us consider the auxiliary condition,

$$\int_0^1 \frac{c}{2} \frac{\nu g(\nu)}{[\lambda(\nu) + \pi i c\nu/2]} \frac{d\nu}{G^L(\nu)} = 0$$

By means of the identity,

$$G^L(\nu)[\lambda(\nu) + \pi i c\nu/2] = \frac{(1-c)(\nu_0{}^2 - \nu^2)}{G(-\nu)}$$

and the partial fraction expansion,

$$\frac{1}{{\nu_0}^2 - \nu^2} = \frac{1}{2\nu_0}\left[\frac{1}{\nu + \nu_0} - \frac{1}{\nu - \nu_0}\right]$$

we readily obtain the following relation,

$$\int_0^1 \frac{c}{2}\frac{\nu g(\nu)G(-\nu)}{\nu - \nu_0}\,d\nu = \int_0^1 \frac{c}{2}\frac{\nu g(\nu)G(-\nu)}{\nu + \nu_0}\,d\nu$$

from the auxiliary condition. Making use of this relation and the partial fraction expansion,

$$\frac{1}{(\mu - \nu)({\nu_0}^2 - \mu^2)} = \frac{1}{2\nu_0}\left[\frac{1}{(\nu_0 - \nu)(\nu_0 - \mu)} + \frac{1}{(\nu_0 - \nu)(\mu - \nu)} + \frac{1}{(\nu_0 + \nu)(\mu - \nu)} - \frac{1}{(\nu_0 + \nu)(\nu_0 + \mu)}\right]$$

we see that the continuum expansion coefficient may also be written as

$$a(\nu) = \frac{1}{[\lambda^2(\nu) + \pi^2 c^2 \nu^2/4]}\left\{\lambda(\nu)g(\nu) + \frac{1}{G(-\nu)}\int_0^1 \frac{c}{2}\frac{\mu g(\mu)G(-\mu)}{\mu - \nu_0}\,d\mu - \frac{1}{G(-\nu)}\int_0^1 \frac{c}{2}\frac{\mu g(\mu)G(-\mu)}{\mu - \nu}\,d\mu\right\}$$

6.5 SUMMARY

Summarizing the results obtained in the preceeding sections on the properties of the angular eigenfunctions $\phi(\mu \mid \nu)$ and $\phi(\mu \mid \pm\nu_0)$, we consider a function $f(\mu)$ which is defined and Hölder continuous in the extended sense on a subinterval (a, b) of the interval $-1 \leqq \mu \leqq 1$.

This function can be expanded in terms of the solutions of the eigenvalue equation,

$$(\nu - \mu)\phi(\mu \mid \nu) = \frac{c}{2}\nu \tag{6.2}$$

which are normalized such that

$$\int_{-1}^{1} \phi(\mu \mid \nu)\,d\mu = 1$$

If the point ν is located outside the interval $-1 \leqq \mu \leqq 1$, then equation (6.2) has two solutions,

$$\phi(\mu \mid \pm\nu_0) = \frac{c\nu_0}{2}\frac{1}{\nu_0 \mp \mu}$$

corresponding to the two discrete eigenvalues $\pm \nu_0$ which are the roots of the transcendental equation,

$$1 - c\nu \operatorname{arctanh} 1/\nu = 0$$

These roots are purely imaginary when c is larger than one, they coalesce at infinity when c is equal to one, and they are real for all values of c which are smaller than one.

If the point ν is located on the interval $-1 \leqq \mu \leqq 1$, then the solutions of equation (6.2) are the singular eigendistributions,

$$\phi(\mu \mid \nu) = \lambda(\nu)\, \delta(\nu - \mu) + \frac{c\nu}{2} P \frac{1}{\nu - \mu}$$

The normalization condition now serves to determine the strength $\lambda(\nu)$ of the concentration of delta functions at the point ν,

$$\lambda(\nu) = 1 - c\nu \operatorname{arctanh} \nu$$

The system of eigenfunctions and eigendistributions, $\phi(\mu \mid \pm\nu_0)$, $\phi(\mu \mid \nu)$ is orthogonal with respect to the weighting factor μ over the interval $-1 \leqq \mu \leqq 1$ and, with respect to more complicated weighting factors, over an arbitrary subinterval of the fundamental interval $-1 \leqq \mu \leqq 1$. The full range orthogonality relations are,

$$\int_{-1}^{1} \phi(\mu \mid \nu)\phi(\mu \mid \alpha)\mu \, d\mu = M(\nu)\, \delta(\nu - \alpha)$$

$$\int_{-1}^{1} \phi^2(\mu \mid \pm\nu_0)\mu \, d\mu = M(\pm\nu_0)$$

$$\int_{-1}^{1} \phi(\mu \mid \nu)\phi(\mu \mid \pm\nu_0)\mu \, d\mu = 0$$

$$\int_{-1}^{1} \phi(\mu \mid \nu_0)\phi(\mu \mid -\nu_0)\mu \, d\mu = 0$$

where the normalization factors may be written as

$$M(\nu) = \nu[\lambda^2(\nu) + \pi^2 c^2 \nu^2/4]$$

and

$$M(\pm\nu_0) = \pm \frac{c\nu_0}{2}\left[\frac{1 - \nu_0{}^2(1 - c)}{\nu_0{}^2 - 1}\right]$$

Restricting ourselves to the important cases of the full and half range expansions, we find that the system of functions $\phi(\mu \mid \nu)$, $\phi(\mu \mid \pm\nu_0)$ is complete for functions $f(\mu)$ which are defined and Hölder continuous in the extended sense on the interval $-1 \leqq \mu \leqq 1$, and we may write

$$f(\mu) = a(v_0)\phi(\mu \mid v_0) + a(-v_0)\phi(\mu \mid -v_0) + \int_{-1}^{1} a(v)\phi(\mu \mid v)\, dv$$

The system $\phi(\mu \mid v)$, $\phi(\mu \mid v_0)$ is complete for functions $f(\mu)$ which are defined and Hölder continuous in the extended sense on the interval (0, 1) and in this case we obtain the half range expansion,

$$f(\mu) = a(v_0)\phi(\mu \mid v_0) + \int_{0}^{1} a(v)\phi(\mu \mid v)\, dv$$

Finally, the system of angular eigenfunctions $\phi(\mu \mid v)$, $\phi(\mu \mid -v_0)$ is complete for functions $f(\mu)$ which are defined and Hölder continuous in the extended sense on the interval $(-1, 0)$, and the half range expansion over this interval takes the form,

$$f(\mu) = a(-v_0)\phi(\mu \mid -v_0) + \int_{-1}^{0} a(v)\phi(\mu \mid v)\, dv$$

The expansion coefficients $a(v_0)$, $a(-v_0)$, and $a(v)$ can be obtained either by the full or half range orthogonality relations or by substitution of the distribution,

$$\phi(\mu \mid v) = \lambda(v)\, \delta(v - \mu) + \frac{cv}{2} P \frac{1}{v - \mu}$$

into the integral representation,

$$g(\mu) = f(\mu) - a(v_0)\phi(\mu \mid v_0) - a(-v_0)\phi(\mu \mid -v_0) = \int_{a}^{b} a(v)\phi(\mu \mid v)\, dv$$

The latter technique leads to a singular integral equation,

$$g(\mu) = \lambda(\mu)a(\mu) + \int_{a}^{b} \frac{c}{2} \frac{va(v)}{v - \mu}\, dv$$

the solution of which yields the expansion coefficients. A proof for the existence of the function $a(v)$, and thus a proof of the completeness of the system of angular eigenfunctions, can also be constructed by means of this integral equation. For let $G(z)$ be the solution of the homogeneous Hilbert problem involving the boundary condition,

$$G^L(v) = \frac{\lambda(v) - \pi icv/2}{\lambda(v) + \pi icv/2}\, G^R(v)$$

on the path (a, b). The solution $F(z)$ of the corresponding inhomogeneous Hilbert problem with boundary condition,

$$F^L(v) = \frac{\lambda(v) - \pi i c v/2}{\lambda(v) + \pi i c v/2} F^R(v) + \frac{g(v) c v/2}{\lambda(v) + \pi i c v/2}$$

may be expressed in terms of the function $G(z)$ and a polynomial,

$$F(z) = \frac{G(z)}{2\pi i} \int_a^b \frac{c}{2} \frac{v g(v)}{[\lambda(v) + \pi i c v/2] G^L(v)} \frac{dv}{v - z} + P(z) G(z)$$

Choosing the functions $G(z)$ and $P(z)$ so that $F(z)$ is sectionally analytic with boundary path (a, b), vanishes at infinity as $1/z$, and is bounded by $(a - z)^\alpha$ and $(b - z)^\beta$ when z tends to a and b, respectively, where $\alpha + 1$ and $\beta + 1$ are positive constants, we find that the function,

$$a(v) = \frac{2}{cv} [F^L(v) - F^R(v)]$$

is Hölder continuous in the extended sense on the interval (a, b) and is the solution of the singular integral equation.

6.6 SOME ONE-DIMENSIONAL BOUNDARY VALUE PROBLEMS OF TIME-INDEPENDENT NEUTRON TRANSPORT THEORY

Having developed the mathematical apparatus of the normal mode expansion technique for solving the one-dimensional steady state transport equation,

$$\mu \frac{\partial \Phi(x, \mu)}{\partial x} + \Phi(x, \mu) = \frac{c}{2} \int_{-1}^{1} \Phi(x, \mu) \, d\mu + S(x, \mu)$$

we shall now apply this technique to the solution of some simple boundary value problems of neutron transport theory involving this equation. As we have remarked before, the normal mode technique centers about the expansion of the solution of the transport equation,

$$\Phi(x, \mu) = a(v_0)\psi(x, \mu \mid v_0) + a(-v_0)\psi(x, \mu \mid -v_0) + \int a(v)\psi(x, \mu \mid v) \, dv$$

in terms of the normal modes or elementary solutions,

$$\psi(x, \mu \mid v) = e^{-x/v} \phi(\mu \mid v)$$

and

$$\psi(x, \mu \mid \pm v_0) = e^{\mp x/v_0} \phi(\mu \mid \pm v_0)$$

of the homogeneous transport equation,

$$\mu \frac{\partial \psi(x, \mu \mid \nu)}{\partial x} + \psi(x, \mu \mid \nu) = \frac{c}{2} \int_{-1}^{1} \psi(x, \mu \mid \nu) \, d\mu$$

The properties of the angular eigenfunctions $\phi(\mu \mid \nu)$, $\phi(\mu \mid \pm\nu_0)$ have been discussed in detail in previous sections. The expansion coefficients $a(\nu)$ and $a(\pm\nu_0)$ can be determined by means of boundary and symmetry conditions.

A. The Infinite Medium Green's Function

As a first example of the applicability of the normal mode expansion technique, we shall obtain a representation for the Green's function

$$G(x, \mu | x_0, \mu_0)$$

describing the spatial and angular distribution of neutrons in a non-multiplying medium of infinite extent due to a delta source,

$$S(x, \mu) = \frac{\delta(x - x_0) \, \delta(\mu - \mu_0)}{4\pi}$$

This source, of unit strength, generates monoenergetic neutrons at the point x_0 which move in a direction making an angle $\theta_0 = \arccos \mu_0$ with the positive x-axis. Mathematically, we want to find therefore the solution of the inhomogeneous transport equation,

$$\mu \frac{\partial G(x, \mu \mid x_0, \mu_0)}{\partial x} + G(x, \mu \mid x_0, \mu_0)$$
$$= \frac{c}{2} \int_{-1}^{1} G(x, \mu \mid x_0, \mu_0) \, d\mu + \frac{\delta(x - x_0) \, \delta(\mu - \mu_0)}{4\pi}$$

which vanishes at infinity. This solution can be found by expansion in terms of the elementary solutions $\psi(x, \mid \nu)$, $\mu \psi(x, \mu \mid \pm\nu_0)$ of the homogeneous transport equation which satisfy the same boundary conditions. Since the infinite medium Green's function vanishes when x tends to infinity in the positive or negative direction, we must use the modes

$$\psi(x, \mu \mid \nu) = \phi(\mu \mid \nu) e^{-x/\nu} \qquad \nu < 0$$
$$\psi(x, \mu \mid -\nu_0) = \phi(\mu \mid -\nu_0) e^{x/\nu_0}$$

for the representation of the Green's function for values of x which are smaller than x_0, and we must choose the modes

$$\psi(x, \mu \mid \nu) = \phi(\mu \mid \nu) e^{-x/\nu} \qquad \nu > 0$$
$$\psi(x, \mu \mid \nu_0) = \phi(\mu \mid \nu_0) e^{-x/\nu_0}$$

for the expansion of the Green's function for values of x which are larger than x_0. We consider therefore the expansion,

$$G(x, \mu \mid x_0, \mu_0) = -a(-\nu_0)\psi(x, \mu \mid -\nu_0) - \int_{-1}^{0} a(\nu)\psi(x, \mu \mid \nu)\, d\nu \qquad x < x_0$$

$$G(x, \mu \mid x_0, \mu_0) = a(\nu_0)\psi(x, \mu \mid \nu_0) + \int_{0}^{1} a(\nu)\psi(x, \mu \mid \nu)\, d\nu \qquad x > x_0$$

where the minus sign in front of the terms for $x < x_0$ has been chosen for later convenience. To obtain the expansion coefficients, we first integrate the transport equation over the interval $(x_0 - \varepsilon, x_0 + \varepsilon)$ and let ε tend to zero. In this manner we find that the Green's function suffers a jump discontinuity of magnitude $\delta(\mu - \mu_0)/4\pi\mu$ at the point x_0,

$$\lim_{\varepsilon \to 0} [G(x_0 + \varepsilon, \mu \mid x_0, \mu_0) - G(x_0 - \varepsilon, \mu \mid x_0, \mu_0)] = \frac{\delta(\mu - \mu_0)}{4\pi\mu}$$

Substituting the expansion formula for the Green's function into this expression, we obtain the following integral equation for the expansion coefficients,

$$a(\nu_0)e^{-x_0/\nu_0}\phi(\mu \mid \nu_0) + a(-\nu_0)e^{x_0/\nu_0}\phi(\mu \mid -\nu_0) + \int_{-1}^{1} a(\nu)e^{-x_0/\nu}\phi(\mu \mid \nu)\, d\nu = \frac{\delta(\mu - \mu_0)}{4\pi\mu}$$

The expansion coefficients can most easily be obtained from this equation by means of the orthogonality relations for the eigenfunctions $\phi(\mu \mid \nu)$, $\phi(\mu \mid \pm\nu_0)$ on the fundamental interval $-1 \leqq \mu \leqq 1$. Multiplying the equation by $\mu\, \phi(\mu \mid \pm\nu_0)$ and integrating the result over the interval $-1 \leqq \mu \leqq 1$, we find the following expressions for the expansion coefficients $a(\pm\nu_0)$,

$$a(\pm\nu_0) = \frac{\phi(\mu_0 \mid \pm\nu_0)e^{\pm x_0/\nu_0}}{4\pi M(\pm\nu_0)}$$

where $M(\pm\nu_0)$ denote the normalization factors,

$$M(\pm\nu_0) = \pm\frac{c\nu_0}{2}\left[\frac{1 - \nu_0^2(1 - c)}{\nu_0^2 - 1}\right]$$

of the preceding section.
Multiplying the equation by $\mu\phi(\mu \mid \nu)$ and integrating the result over the interval $-1 \leqq \mu \leqq 1$, the expansion coefficient,

$$a(\nu) = \frac{\phi(\mu_0 \mid \nu)e^{x_0/\nu}}{4\pi M(\nu)}$$

is obtained, where

$$M(v) = v[\lambda^2(v) + \pi^2 c^2 v^2/4]$$

These results can also be found of course by means of the expressions for the expansion coefficients derived in the preceding section. For example, substitution of the function,

$$g(v) = \frac{\delta(v - v_0)}{4\pi v} - a(v_0)e^{-x_0/v_0}\phi(v \mid v_0) - a(-v_0)e^{x_0/v_0}\phi(v \mid -v_0)$$

into the equation,

$$a(v) = \frac{e^{x_0/v}}{[\lambda^2(v) + \pi^2 c^2 v^2/4]}\left[\lambda(v)g(v) - \int_{-1}^{1} \frac{c}{2}\frac{\mu g(\mu)}{\mu - v}\, d\mu\right]$$

which corresponds to equation (6.8), yields the same expression for the coefficient $a(v)$ as the one obtained by means of the orthogonality relations.

With the help of the expressions for the expansion coefficients $a(\pm v_0)$, $a(v)$ we can immediately obtain the following representation of the infinite medium Green's function in terms of the eigenfunctions $\phi(\mu \mid v)$, $\phi(\mu \mid \pm v_0)$,

$$G(x,\mu \mid x_0,\mu_0) = -\frac{\phi(\mu_0 \mid - v_0)\phi(\mu \mid - v_0)}{4\pi\, M(-v_0)} e^{(x-x_0)/v_0} - \int_{-1}^{0} \frac{\phi(\mu_0 \mid v)\phi(\mu \mid v)}{4\pi M(v)} e^{-(x-x_0)/v}\, dv \qquad x < x_0$$

$$G(x, \mu \mid x_0, \mu_0) = \frac{\phi(\mu_0 \mid v_0)\phi(\mu \mid v_0)}{4\pi M(v_0)} e^{-(x-x_0)/v_0} + \int_{0}^{1} \frac{\phi(\mu_0 \mid v)\phi(\mu \mid v)}{4\pi M(v)} e^{-(x-x_0)/v}\, dv \qquad x > x_0$$

These formulas can be written more compactly as,

$$G(x, \mu \mid x_0, \mu_0) = \frac{\phi(\mu_0 \mid \pm v_0)\phi(\mu \mid \pm v_0)}{4\pi M(v_0)} e^{-|x-x_0|/v_0} + \int_{0}^{1} \frac{\phi(\mu_0 \mid \pm v)\phi(\mu \mid \pm v)}{4\pi M(v)} e^{-|x-x_0|/v}\, dv$$

where the positive sign must be taken when $x > x_0$ and the negative sign when $x < x_0$.

The quantities of intrinsic physical interest which can be derived from the infinite medium Green's function are the neutron density,

$$\rho(x) = \int_{-1}^{1} G(x, \mu \mid x_0, \mu_0)\, d\mu$$

and the neutron current,

$$j(x) = \int_{-1}^{1} \mu G(x, \mu \mid x_0, \mu_0)\, d\mu$$

These quantities can easily be computed by means of the explicit expression for the infinite medium Green's function above and the observation that the angular eigenfunctions $\phi(\mu \mid \nu)$, $\phi(\mu \mid \pm\nu_0)$ are normalized so that

$$\int_{-1}^{1} \phi(\mu \mid \nu)\, d\mu = 1$$

and thus

$$\int_{-1}^{1} \mu\phi(\mu \mid \nu)\, d\mu = \nu(1 - c)$$

We obtain therefore, by means of simple integration, the following expressions,

$$\rho(x \mid x_0, \mu_0) = \frac{\phi(\mu_0 \mid \pm\nu_0) e^{-|x - x_0|/\nu_0}}{4\pi M(\nu_0)} + \int_0^1 \frac{\phi(\mu_0 \mid \pm\nu) e^{-|x - x_0|/\nu}}{4\pi M(\nu)}\, d\nu$$

and

$$j(x \mid x_0, \mu_0) = \pm(1 - c)\left[\frac{\nu_0\, \phi(\mu_0 \mid \pm\nu_0) e^{-|x - x_0|/\nu_0}}{4\pi M(\nu_0)} + \int_0^1 \frac{\nu\phi(\mu_0 \mid \pm\nu) e^{-|x - x_0|/\nu}}{4\pi M(\nu)}\, d\nu\right]$$

for the neutron density and the neutron current respectively.

In the case of a plane isotropic source,

$$S(x) = \frac{\delta(x - x_0)}{4\pi}$$

the jump discontinuity suffered by the Green's function at the point $x = x_0$ takes the form,

$$G(x_0 + 0, \mu \mid x_0) - G(x_0 - 0, \mu \mid x_0) = \frac{1}{4\pi\mu}$$

This implies that we may write the following integral equation for the expansion coefficients,

$$a(\nu_0) e^{-x_0/\nu_0} \phi(\mu \mid \nu_0) + a(-\nu_0) e^{x_0/\nu_0} \phi(\mu \mid -\nu_0) + \int_{-1}^{1} a(\nu) e^{-x_0/\nu} \phi(\mu \mid \nu)\, d\nu = \frac{1}{4\pi\mu}$$

By means of the orthogonality relations for the eigenfunctions $\phi(\mu \mid \nu)$, $\phi(\mu \mid \pm\nu_0)$ over the full range $-1 \leqq \mu \leqq 1$, we immediately obtain the following expressions for the expansion coefficients,

$$a(\pm\nu_0) = \frac{e^{\pm x_0/\nu_0}}{4\pi M(\pm\nu_0)}$$

and

$$a(\nu) = \frac{e^{x_0/\nu}}{4\pi M(\nu)}$$

From these relations we may infer that the infinite medium Green's function, due to a plane isotropic source $(1/4\pi)\,\delta(x - x_0)$, may be written as

$$G(x, \mu \mid x_0) = \frac{\phi(\mu \mid \pm\nu_0)e^{-|x-x_0|/\nu_0}}{4\pi M(\nu_0)} + \int_0^1 \frac{\phi(\mu \mid \pm\nu)e^{-|x-x_0|/\nu}}{4\pi M(\nu)}\,d\nu$$

where the positive sign must be chosen when $x > x_0$ and the negative sign when $x < x_0$. Of course, this expression can be obtained more easily by integrating the infinite medium Green's function $G(x, \mu \mid x_0, \mu_0)$ over the interval $-1 \leqq \mu \leqq 1$,

$$G(x, \mu \mid x_0) = \int_{-1}^{1} G(x, \mu \mid x_0, \mu_0)\,d\mu_0$$

It is readily verified that the neutron density and the neutron current take the form,

$$\rho(x) = \frac{e^{-|x-x_0|/\nu_0}}{4\pi M(\nu_0)} + \int_0^1 \frac{e^{-|x-x_0|/\nu}}{4\pi M(\nu)}\,d\nu$$

and

$$j(x) = \pm(1-c)\left[\frac{\nu_0\, e^{-|x-x_0|/\nu_0}}{4\pi M(\nu_0)} + \int_0^1 \frac{\nu e^{-|x-x_0|/\nu}}{4\pi M(\nu)}\,d\nu\right]$$

B. The Half Space Green's Function

The half space Green's function can easily be obtained with the help of the infinite medium Green's function described in the preceding section. We want to find the spatial and angular distribution of neutrons in a half space $x \geqq 0$, which is occupied by a nonmultiplying medium, due to a delta source,

$$S(x, \mu) = \frac{\delta(x - x_0)\,\delta(\mu - \mu_0)}{4\pi}$$

when no neutrons are incident upon the vacuum-material interface at $x = 0$. This implies that we have to find the solution of the inhomogeneous transport equation,

$$\mu \frac{\partial G(x, \mu \mid x_0, \mu_0)}{\partial x} + G(x, \mu \mid x_0, \mu_0) = \frac{c}{2} \int_{-1}^{1} G(x, \mu \mid x_0, \mu_0)\, d\mu + \frac{\delta(x - x_0)\, \delta(\mu - \mu_0)}{4\pi}$$

in the half space $x \geqq 0$, subject to the homogeneous boundary conditions,

$$G(0, \mu \mid x_0, \mu_0) = 0$$

and

$$\lim_{x \to \infty} G(x, \mu \mid x_0, \mu_0) = 0$$

The solution of this boundary value problem can be written as

$$G(x, \mu \mid x_0, \mu_0) = G_\infty(x, \mu \mid x_0, \mu_0) + \Phi(x, \mu)$$

where $G_\infty(x, \mu \mid x_0, \mu_0)$ denotes the infinite medium Green's function. Substituting this expression for $G(x, \mu \mid x_0, \mu_0)$ into the inhomogeneous transport equation, we find that the function $\Phi(x, \mu)$ is the solution of the homogeneous transport equation,

$$\mu \frac{\partial \Phi(x, \mu)}{\partial x} + \Phi(x, \mu) = \frac{c}{2} \int_{-1}^{1} \Phi(x, \mu)\, d\mu$$

which vanishes at infinity and satisfies the inhomogeneous boundary condition,

$$\Phi(0, \mu) = -G_\infty(0, \mu \mid x_0, \mu_0)$$

at the vacuum-material interface. The solution of this boundary value problem can be obtained by expanding $\Phi(x, \mu)$ in terms of the normal modes, $\psi(x, \mu \mid \nu)$, $\psi(x, \mu \mid \pm \nu_0)$. Actually, since $\Phi(x, \mu)$ must vanish at infinity, a half range expansion,

$$\Phi(x, \mu) = a(\nu_0)\psi(x, \mu \mid \nu_0) + \int_0^1 a(\nu)\psi(x, \mu \mid \nu)\, d\nu$$

is appropriate. From this expansion we obtain, by means of the boundary condition at $x = 0$, the following integral equation for the expansion coefficients,

$$a(\nu_0)\phi(\mu \mid \nu_0) + \int_0^1 a(\nu)\phi(\mu \mid \nu)\, d\nu = -G_\infty(0, \mu \mid x_0, \mu_0)$$

This equation was solved in Section 6.4. In that section we found that

$$a(\nu_0) = \frac{2G(\nu_0)}{c\nu_0} \int_0^1 \frac{c}{2} \frac{\nu G_\infty(0, \nu \mid x_0, \mu_0)}{[\lambda(\nu) + \pi i c\nu/2]G^L(\nu)} \, d\nu$$

where $G(\nu_0)$ denotes the value of the fundamental solution of the auxiliary homogeneous Hilbert problem at the point ν_0. We also found that the coefficient $a(\nu)$ may be written as

$$a(\nu) = -\frac{\lambda(\nu)[G_\infty(0, \nu \mid x_0, \mu_0) + a(\nu_0)\phi(\nu \mid \nu_0)]}{[\lambda^2(\nu) + \pi^2 c^2 \nu^2/4]}$$

$$+ \frac{(1-c)(\nu_0^2 - \nu^2)}{[\lambda^2(\nu) + \pi^2 c^2 \nu^2/4]G(-\nu)} \int_0^1 \frac{c}{2} \frac{\mu[G_\infty(0, \mu \mid x_0, \mu_0) + a(\nu_0)\phi(\mu \mid \nu_0)]}{[\lambda(\mu) + \pi i c\mu/2]G^L(\mu)} \frac{d\mu}{\mu - \nu}$$

In the foregoing subsection we derived the following expression for the value of the infinite medium Green's function at the origin,

$$G_\infty(0, \nu \mid x_0, \mu_0) = -\frac{\phi(\mu_0 \mid -\nu_0)\phi(\nu \mid -\nu_0)}{4\pi M(-\nu_0)} e^{-x_0/\nu_0}$$

$$- \int_{-1}^0 \frac{\phi(\mu_0 \mid \mu)\phi(\nu \mid \mu)}{4\pi M(\mu)} e^{x_0/\mu} \, d\mu$$

Substitution of this expression into the integral representations for the expansion coefficients obtained above yields

$$a(\nu_0) = -\frac{G(\nu_0)}{G(-\nu_0)} \frac{\phi(\mu_0 \mid -\nu_0)}{4\pi M(-\nu_0)} e^{-x_0/\nu_0} + \frac{G(\nu_0)}{\nu_0} \int_{-1}^0 \frac{\mu}{G(\mu)} \frac{\phi(\mu_0 \mid \mu)}{4\pi M(\mu)} e^{x_0/\mu} \, d\mu$$

and

$$a(\nu) = \frac{c\nu_0^2(1-c)}{[\lambda^2(\nu) + \pi^2 c^2 \nu^2/4]G(-\nu)G(-\nu_0)} \frac{\phi(\mu_0 \mid -\nu_0)}{4\pi M(-\nu_0)} e^{-x_0/\nu_0}$$

$$+ \frac{(1-c)(\nu_0 + \nu)}{[\lambda^2(\nu) + \pi^2 c^2 \nu^2/4]G(-\nu)} \int_{-1}^0 \frac{(\nu_0 - \mu)}{G(\mu)} \frac{\phi(\mu_0 \mid \mu)\phi(\nu \mid \mu)}{4\pi M(\mu)} e^{x_0/\mu} \, d\mu$$

Thus, the normal mode representation of the half space Green's function takes the form,

$$G(x, \mu \mid x_0, \mu_0) = G_\infty(x, \mu \mid x_0, \mu_0) + a(\nu_0)\psi(x, \mu \mid \nu_0) + \int_0^1 a(\nu)\psi(x, \mu \mid \nu) \, d\nu$$

where $G_\infty(x, \mu \mid x_0, \mu_0)$ denotes the infinite medium Green's function and the expansion coefficients are presented above. Integrating this representation over μ, we obtain the following expressions for the neutron density and the neutron current,

$$\rho(x \mid x_0, \mu_0) = \rho_\infty(x \mid x_0, \mu_0) + a(\nu_0)e^{-x/\nu_0} + \int_0^1 a(\nu)e^{-x/\nu}\, d\nu$$

and

$$j(x \mid x_0, \mu_0) = j_\infty(x \mid x_0, \mu_0) + (1-c)\left[\nu_0\, a(\nu_0)e^{-x/\nu_0} + \int_0^1 \nu a(\nu)e^{-x/\nu}\, d\nu\right]$$

where $\rho_\infty(x \mid x_0, \mu_0)$ and $j_\infty(x \mid x_0, \mu_0)$ denote the density and current in the infinite medium configuration.

The half space Green's function $G(x, \mu \mid x_0)$ for a plane isotropic source can again be obtained by integrating the function $G(x, \mu \mid x_0, \mu_0)$ over the interval $-1 \leqq \mu_0 \leqq 1$,

$$G(x, \mu \mid x_0) = \int_{-1}^1 G(x, \mu \mid x_0, \mu_0)\, d\mu_0$$

$$= G_\infty(x, \mu \mid x_0) + b(\nu_0)\psi(x, \mu \mid \nu_0) + \int_0^1 b(\nu)\psi(x, \mu \mid \nu)\, d\nu$$

where the expansion coefficients $b(\nu_0)$ and $b(\nu)$ may be written as

$$b(\nu_0) = -\frac{G(\nu_0)}{G(-\nu_0)}\frac{e^{-x_0/\nu_0}}{4\pi M(-\nu_0)} + \frac{G(\nu_0)}{\nu_0}\int_{-1}^0 \frac{\mu}{G(\mu)}\frac{e^{x_0/\mu}}{4\pi M(\mu)}\, d\mu$$

and

$$b(\nu) = \frac{c\nu_0^{\,2}(1-c)}{[\lambda^2(\nu) + \pi^2 c^2 \nu^2/4]G(-\nu)G(-\nu_0)}\frac{e^{-x_0/\nu_0}}{4\pi M(-\nu_0)}$$

$$+ \frac{(1-c)(\nu_0+\nu)}{[\lambda^2(\nu) + \pi^2 c^2 \nu^2/4]G(-\nu)}\int_{-1}^0 \frac{(\nu_0 - \mu)}{G(\mu)}\frac{\phi(\nu \mid \mu)}{4\pi M(\mu)} e^{x_0/\mu}\, d\mu$$

For the neutron density and the net current we find

$$\rho(x \mid x_0) = \rho_\infty(x \mid x_0) + b(\nu_0)e^{-x_0/\nu_0} + \int_0^1 b(\nu)e^{-x/\nu}\, d\nu$$

and

$$j(x \mid x_0) = j_\infty(x \mid x_0) + (1-c)\left[\nu_0\, b(\nu_0)e^{-x/\nu_0} + \int_0^1 \nu b(\nu)e^{-x/\nu}\, d\nu\right]$$

where the expansion coefficients $b(\nu_0)$ and $b(\nu)$ are given above and $\rho_\infty(x \mid x_0)$ and $j_\infty(x \mid x_0)$ denote the corresponding infinite medium neutron density and current.

C. The Half Space Albedo Problem

In the following example of the half space albedo problem we are concerned with the distribution of neutrons in a half space, occupied by a homogeneous source-free medium which scatters neutrons isotropically and elastically, when a monodirectional neutron beam is incident on the vacuum-material interface. In this case, the neutron angular density $\Phi(x, \mu)$ is the solution of the transport equation,

$$\mu \frac{\partial \Phi(x, \mu)}{\partial x} + \Phi(x, \mu) = \frac{c}{2} \int_{-1}^{1} \Phi(x, \mu)\, d\mu$$

in the half space $x \geqq 0$ which vanishes when x tends to infinity and satisfies the boundary condition,

$$\Phi(0, \mu) = \delta(\mu - \mu_0) \qquad \mu_0 > 0, 0 < \mu \leqq 1$$

on the vacuum-material interface.

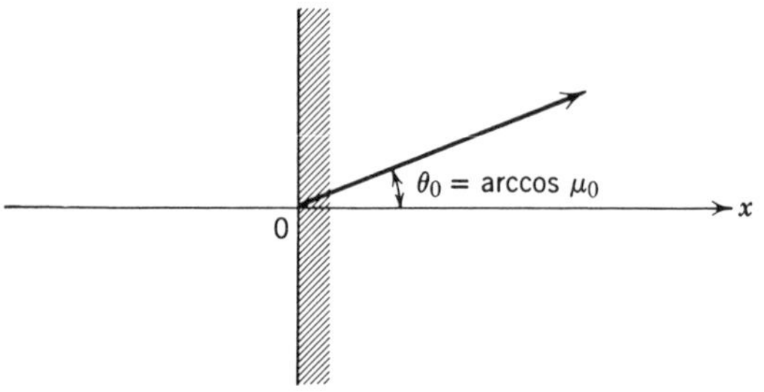

Figure VI-3

The neutron angular density $\Phi(x, \mu)$ should vanish at infinity, and the half range expansion of this function in terms of the normal modes $\psi(x, \mu \mid \nu)$ and $\psi(x, \mu \mid \nu_0)$,

$$\Phi(x, \mu) = a(\nu_0)\psi(x, \mu \mid \nu_0) + \int_0^1 a(\nu)\psi(x, \mu \mid \nu)\, d\nu$$

is therefore appropriate. By imposing on this solution the boundary condition at $x = 0$, we obtain the following integral equation for the expansion coefficients,

$$a(\nu_0)\phi(\mu \mid \nu_0) + \int_0^1 a(\nu)\phi(\mu \mid \nu)\, d\nu = \delta(\mu - \mu_0) \qquad 0 \leqq \mu \leqq 1.$$

The solution of this equation can easily be obtained by means of the formulas derived in Section 6.4. For the expansion coefficient $a(\nu_0)$ we find

$$a(\nu_0) = -\frac{2G(\nu_0)}{c\nu_0}\int_0^1 \frac{c}{2}\frac{\nu\,\delta(\nu-\mu_0)}{[\lambda(\nu)+\pi i c\nu/2]G^L(\nu)}\,d\nu$$

$$= -\frac{\mu_0}{\nu_0}\frac{G(\nu_0)}{[\lambda(\mu_0)+\pi i c\mu_0/2]G^L(\mu_0)} = -\frac{\mu_0}{\nu_0}\frac{G(-\mu_0)G(\nu_0)}{(1-c)(\nu_0{}^2-\mu_0{}^2)}$$

The coefficient $a(\nu)$ is given by

$$a(\nu) = \frac{\lambda(\nu)}{[\lambda^2(\nu)+\pi^2c^2\nu^2/4]}\{\delta(\nu-\mu_0) - a(\nu_0)\phi(\nu\,|\,\nu_0)\}$$

$$+\frac{(1-c)(\nu^2-\nu_0{}^2)}{[\lambda^2(\nu)+\pi^2c^2\nu^2/4]G(-\nu)}\int_0^1 \frac{c}{2}\frac{\mu[\delta(\mu-\mu_0)-a(\nu_0)\phi(\mu\,|\,\nu_0)]}{[\lambda(\mu)+\pi i c\mu/2]G^L(\mu)}\frac{d\mu}{\mu-\nu}$$

The first part of the integral yields the value,

$$\frac{1}{[\lambda^2(\nu)+\pi^2c^2\nu^2/4]}\frac{G^L(\nu)[\lambda(\nu)+\pi i c\nu/2]}{G^L(\mu_0)[\lambda(\mu_0)+\pi i c\mu_0/2]}\frac{c}{2}\frac{\mu_0}{\nu-\mu_0}$$

and the second part may be written as

$$\frac{\lambda(\nu)a(\nu_0)\phi(\nu\,|\,\nu_0)}{[\lambda^2(\nu)+\pi^2c^2\nu^2/4]} + \frac{1}{[\lambda^2(\nu)+\pi^2c^2\nu^2/4]}\frac{G^L(\nu)[\lambda(\nu)+\pi i c\nu/2]}{G^L(\mu_0)[\lambda(\mu_0)+\pi i c\mu_0/4]}\frac{c}{2}\frac{\mu_0}{\nu_0-\nu}$$

where we have made use of the first and second identities (6.9) and (6.10). Combining these results and remembering that

$$\left[1-\frac{f(x)}{f(x_0)}\right]\delta(x-x_0) = 0$$

we obtain the following expression,

$$a(\nu) = \frac{G^L(\nu)[\lambda(\nu)+\pi i c\nu/2]\mu_0(\nu_0-\mu_0)}{G^L(\mu_0)[\lambda(\mu_0)+\pi i c\mu_0/2]\nu(\nu_0-\nu)}\frac{\phi(\mu_0\,|\,\nu)}{[\lambda^2(\nu)+\pi^2c^2\nu^2/4]}$$

for the expansion coefficient $a(\nu)$.

Thus, we find that the expansion of the solution $\Phi(x, \mu)$ of the albedo problem in terms of the normal modes may be written

$$\Phi(x, \mu) = a(\nu_0)\psi(x, \mu\,|\,\nu_0) + \int_0^1 a(\nu)\psi(x, \mu\,|\,\nu)\,d\nu$$

where the expansion coefficients are given above. For the neutron density we obtain in this case

$$\rho(x) = a(\nu_0)e^{-x/\nu_0} + \int_0^1 a(\nu)e^{-x/\nu}\,d\nu$$

which reduces at the vacuum-material interface to

$$\rho(0) = a(\nu_0) + \int_0^1 a(\nu)\, d\nu$$

This expression can readily be evaluated by noting that

$$a(\nu_0)\phi(\mu \mid \nu_0) + \int_0^1 a(\nu)\phi(\mu \mid \nu)\, d\nu = \delta(\mu - \mu_0)$$

Multiplying both sides of this equation by

$$\frac{c}{2} \frac{(\nu_0 - \mu)}{[\lambda(\mu) + \pi i c\mu/2]G^L(\mu)}$$

and integrating over the interval (0, 1), we find

$$a(\nu_0) + \int_0^1 a(\nu)\, d\nu = \frac{(\nu_0 - \mu_0)G(0)}{\nu_0[\lambda(\mu_0) + \pi i c\mu_0/2]G^L(\mu_0)}$$

since

$$\int_0^1 \frac{c}{2} \frac{(\nu_0 - \mu)\phi(\mu \mid s)}{[\lambda(\mu) + \pi i c\mu/2]G^L(\mu)}\, d\mu = \frac{c}{2} \frac{\nu_0}{G(0)}$$

With the help of this result and the second identity (6.10), we obtain therefore the neat expression,

$$\rho(0) = \frac{\nu_0}{\nu_0 + \mu_0} \frac{G(-\mu_0)}{G(0)}$$

for the neutron density on the vacuum-material interface.

The net current in the half space takes the form,

$$j(x) = \int_{-1}^1 \mu\Phi(x, \mu)\, d\mu = (1 - c)\left[\nu_0\, a(\nu_0)e^{-x/\nu_0} + \int_0^1 \nu a(\nu)e^{-x/\nu}\, d\nu\right]$$

and the net current on the vacuum-material interface may be written

$$j(0) = (1 - c)\left[\nu_0\, a(\nu_0) + \int_0^1 \nu a(\nu)\, d\nu\right]$$

Multiplying the equation,

$$a(\nu_0)\,\phi(\mu \mid \nu_0) + \int_0^1 a(\nu)\phi(\mu \mid \nu)\, d\nu = \delta(\mu - \mu_0)$$

throughout by

$$\frac{c\mu}{2} \frac{(\nu_0 - \mu)}{[\lambda(\mu) + \pi i c\mu/2]G^L(\mu)}$$

and integrating the result over the interval (0, 1), we find

$$j(0) = (1-c)\left[\nu_0 a(\nu_0) + \int_0^1 \nu a(\nu)\, d\nu\right] = \frac{\mu_0}{\nu_0 + \mu_0} G(-\mu_0)$$

where we have made use of the relation,

$$\int_0^1 \frac{c\mu}{2} \frac{(\nu_0 - \mu)\phi(\mu \mid s)}{[\lambda(\mu) + \pi i c\mu/2]G^L(\mu)}\, d\mu = c\nu_0/2 \qquad \text{when } s = \nu_0$$

$$= c\nu/2 \qquad \text{when } s = \nu$$

and the second identity (6.10).

D. The Milne Problem

As in the case of the half space albedo problem, we are concerned with the spatial and angular distribution of neutrons in a half space $x \geqq 0$ which is occupied by a nonmultiplying medium without sources. In contrast to the albedo problem, however, we now require that no neutrons are incident on the vacuum-material interface but that neutrons are entering the half space at infinity and are leaving the half space at $x = 0$. Assuming, as usual, that the medium scatters neutrons isotropically and without loss of speed, we are interested in the solution of the homogeneous transport equation,

$$\mu \frac{\partial \Phi(x, \mu)}{\partial x} + \Phi(x, \mu) = \frac{c}{2} \int_{-1}^{1} \Phi(x, \mu)\, d\mu$$

subject to the boundary conditions:

a. No neutrons are incident on the vacuum-material interface,

$$\Phi(0, \mu) = 0 \qquad 0 \leqq \mu \leqq 1$$

b. A net flux $\psi(x, \mu \mid -\nu_0)$ of the neutrons enters the half space at infinity,

$$\lim_{x \to \infty} \Phi(x, \mu) = \psi(x, \mu \mid -\nu_0)$$

In other words, the behavior of the angular neutron density $\Phi(x, \mu)$ for large values of x is characterized by the slowest growing mode,

$$\phi(\mu \mid -\nu_0) \exp(x/\nu_0).$$

Proceeding in the customary fashion, we expand the angular neutron density $\Phi(x, \mu)$ in terms of the normal modes, $\psi(x, \mu \mid \nu)$, $\psi(x, \mu \mid \pm\nu_0)$,

$$\Phi(x, \mu) = a(\nu_0)\psi(x, \mu \mid \nu_0) + a(-\nu_0)\psi(x, \mu \mid -\nu_0) + \int_{-1}^{1} a(\nu)\psi(x, \mu \mid \nu)\, d\nu$$

The second boundary condition can immediately be satisfied by setting

$$a(-\nu_0) = 1 \quad \text{and} \quad a(\nu) = 0$$

for all negative values of ν, and we write therefore

$$\Phi(x, \mu) = \psi(x, \mu \mid -\nu_0) + a(\nu_0)\psi(x, \mu \mid \nu_0) + \int_0^1 a(\nu)\psi(x, \mu \mid \nu)\, d\nu$$

Invoking the boundary condition at $x = 0$, we obtain the following integral equation for the expansion coefficients,

$$-\phi(\mu \mid -\nu_0) = a(\nu_0)\phi(\mu \mid \nu_0) + \int_0^1 a(\nu)\phi(\mu \mid \nu)\, d\nu$$

Of course, this equation can also be interpreted as the half range expansion of the function $-\phi(\mu \mid -\nu_0)$ in terms of the functions $\phi(\mu \mid \nu)$ and $\phi(\mu \mid \nu_0)$. According to Section 6.4, the expansion coefficient $a(\nu_0)$ may be written as

$$a(\nu_0) = \frac{2G(\nu_0)}{c\nu_0} \int_0^1 \frac{c}{2} \frac{\nu\phi(\nu \mid -\nu_0)}{[\lambda(\nu) + \pi i c\nu/2]G^L(\nu)}\, d\nu = \frac{G(\nu_0)}{G(-\nu_0)}$$

whereas the coefficient $a(\nu)$ takes the form,

$$\begin{aligned} a(\nu) &= -\frac{\lambda(\nu)[\phi(\nu \mid -\nu_0) + a(\nu_0)\phi(\nu \mid \nu_0)]}{[\lambda^2(\nu) + \pi^2 c^2 \nu^2/4]} \\ &\quad + \frac{(1-c)(\nu_0^2 - \nu^2)}{[\lambda^2(\nu) + \pi^2 c^2 \nu^2/4]G(-\nu)} \int_0^1 \frac{c}{2} \frac{\mu[\phi(\mu \mid -\nu_0) + a(\nu_0)\phi(\mu \mid \nu_0)]}{[\lambda(\mu) + \pi i c\mu/2]G^L(\mu)} \frac{d\mu}{\mu - \nu} \\ &= -\frac{c\nu_0^2(1-c)}{[\lambda^2(\nu) + \pi^2 c^2 \nu^2/4]G(-\nu)G(-\nu_0)} \end{aligned}$$

For the representation of the solution of the Milne problem in terms of the normal modes $\psi(x, \mu \mid \nu)$, $\psi(x, \mu \mid \pm\nu_0)$ we obtain therefore the expression,

$$\Phi(x, \mu) = \psi(x, \mu \mid -\nu_0) + a(\nu_0)\psi(x, \mu \mid \nu_0) + \int_0^1 a(\nu)\psi(x, \mu \mid \nu)\, d\nu$$

where the expansion coefficients $a(\nu_0)$ and $a(\nu)$ are given above. This representation immediately leads to the expressions,

$$\rho(x) = e^{x/\nu_0} + a(\nu_0)e^{-x/\nu_0} + \int_0^1 a(\nu)e^{-x/\nu}\, d\nu$$

and

$$j(x) = (1-c)\left[-\nu_0\, e^{x/\nu_0} + \nu_0\, a(\nu_0)e^{-x/\nu_0} + \int_0^1 \nu a(\nu)e^{-x/\nu}\, d\nu\right]$$

for the neutron density and net neutron current respectively. The vacuum-material interface values of these quantities can be obtained by a procedure similar to that by which we obtained the corresponding quantities for the albedo problem in the foregoing section. Thus we find

$$\rho(0) = 1 + a(\nu_0) + \int_0^1 a(\nu)\, d\nu$$

$$= 1 - \frac{2G(0)}{c\nu_0} \int_0^1 \frac{c}{2} \frac{\phi(\mu\,|-\nu_0)(\nu_0 - \mu)}{[\lambda(\mu) + \pi i c\mu/2]G^L(\mu)}\, d\mu = \frac{2G(0)}{G(-\nu_0)}$$

and

$$j(0) = (1 - c)\left[-\nu_0 + \nu_0\, a(\nu_0) + \int_0^1 \nu a(\nu) d\nu\right]$$

$$= (1 - c)\left[-\nu_0 - \frac{2}{c} \int_0^1 \frac{c\mu}{2} \frac{(\nu_0 - \mu)\phi(\mu\,|-\nu_0)}{[\lambda(\mu) + \pi i c\mu/2]G^L(\mu)}\, d\mu\right] = -\frac{2\nu_0{}^2(1 - c)}{G(-\nu_0)}$$

Another quantity of physical interest is the so-called Milne extrapolation length L. This is the distance beyond the vacuum-material interface at which the asymptotic neutron density,

$$\rho(x) = e^{x/\nu_0} + a(\nu_0)e^{-x/\nu_0}$$

vanishes. The point z_0 at which the asymptotic neutron density vanishes is called the extrapolated end point. At the extrapolated end point therefore

$$\rho(z_0) = e^{z_0/\nu_0} + a(\nu_0)e^{-z_0/\nu_0} = 0$$

Substitution of the value $G(\nu_0)/G(-\nu_0)$ for the expansion coefficient $a(\nu_0)$ leads to the expression,

$$L = -z_0 = \frac{\nu_0}{2} \log\left[-\frac{G(-\nu_0)}{G(\nu_0)}\right]$$

A closely related quantity is the so-called linear extrapolation distance. The straight line,

$$\rho_s(x) = \frac{1}{\nu_0}[1 - a(\nu_0)]x + [1 + a(\nu_0)]$$

agrees in value and slope with the corresponding values of the asymptotic neutron density at the vacuum-material interface. The distance beyond this interface at which the function $\rho_s(x)$ vanishes is called the linear extrapolation distance d,

$$d = \frac{\nu_0[a(\nu_0) + 1]}{a(\nu_0) - 1}$$

Case has solved a more general Milne problem that can be formulated as follows: Find the solution of the homogeneous transport equation,

$$\mu \frac{\partial \Phi(x, \mu)}{\partial x} + \Phi(x, \mu) = \frac{c}{2} \int_{-1}^{1} \Phi(x, \mu)\, d\mu$$

in the half space $x \geqq 0$, which is subject to the boundary conditions,

$$\Phi(0, \mu) = 0 \qquad \mu \geqq 0$$

$$\lim_{x \to \infty} \Phi(x, \mu) = \psi(x, \mu \mid -s) \qquad 0 \leqq s \leqq 1$$

In a similar way as before, we find that the solution $\Phi(x, \mu)$ of this problem may be written as

$$\Phi(x, \mu) = \psi(x, \mu \mid -s) + a(v_0 \mid s)\psi(x, \mu \mid v_0) + \int_0^1 a(v \mid s)\psi(x, \mu \mid v)\, dv$$

where $0 \leqq s \leqq 1$ and the expansion coefficients are given by the equations,

$$a(v_0 \mid s) = \frac{sG(v_0)}{v_0 G(-s)}$$

and

$$a(v \mid s) = -\frac{(1 - c)(v_0 + v)(v_0 + s)}{[\lambda^2(v) + \pi^2 c^2 v^2/4]G(-v)G(-s)}\, \phi(v \mid -s)$$

where $0 \leqq s \leqq 1$.

In terms of the solution $\Phi(x, \mu \mid -v_0)$ and $\Phi(x, \mu \mid -s)$ of the two Milne problems above, the Green's function for a half space can be represented by the expression,

$$\begin{aligned} G(x, \mu \mid x_0, \mu_0) &= G_\infty(x, \mu \mid x_0, \mu_0) \\ &\quad - \frac{\phi(\mu \mid -v_0)}{4\pi M(-v_0)} [\Phi(x, \mu \mid -v_0) - \psi(x, \mu \mid -v_0)] e^{-x_0/v_0} \\ &\quad - \int_0^1 \frac{\phi(\mu_0 \mid -s)}{4\pi M(s)} [\Phi(x, \mu \mid -s) - \psi(x, \mu \mid -s)] e^{-x_0/s}\, ds \end{aligned}$$

where $G_\infty(x, \mu \mid x_0, \mu_0)$ denotes the infinite medium Green's function. As can easily be verified, this representation of the Green's function reduces to that of the preceding section if we substitute the explicit expressions for the solutions of the Milne problems.

E. Half Space with Constant Isotropic Source

As a final example of a half space boundary value problem, we shall determine the distribution of neutrons in a half space $x \geqq 0$, occupied by a nonmultiplying absorbing medium, when there is a constant isotropic source S. Assuming again that the medium scatters neutrons isotropically and elastically and supposing in addition that no neutrons are incident on the vacuum-material interface, we solve the inhomogeneous transport equation,

$$\mu \frac{\partial \Phi(x, \mu)}{\partial x} + \Phi(x, \mu) = \frac{c}{2} \int_{-1}^{1} \Phi(x, \mu)\, d\mu + S$$

subject to the conditions,

$$\Phi(0, \mu) = 0 \qquad \mu > 0$$

and

$$\lim_{x \to \infty} \Phi(x, \mu) = \text{bounded}$$

We write the solution of this equation as a sum,

$$\Phi(x, \mu) = \Phi_h(x, \mu) + S/(1 - c)$$

of the solution $\Phi_h(x, \mu)$ of the source-independent equation and a particular solution $S/(1 - c)$ of the source-dependent equation and we shall assume in addition that the function $\Phi_h(x, \mu)$ satisfies the boundary conditions,

$$\Phi_h(0, \mu) = -S/(1 - c)$$

and

$$\lim_{x \to \infty} \Phi_h(0, \mu) = 0$$

We now expand the solution of the source-independent equation in terms of the normal modes choosing the half range expansion,

$$\Phi_h(x, \mu) = a(\nu_0)\psi(x, \mu \mid \nu_0) + \int_0^1 a(\nu)\psi(x, \mu \mid \nu)\, d\nu$$

that vanishes at infinity. Imposing on this solution the boundary conditions at the origin, we obtain the following equation for the expansion coefficients,

$$a(\nu_0)\phi(\mu \mid \nu_0) + \int_0^1 a(\nu)\phi(\mu \mid \nu)\, d\nu = -\frac{S}{1 - c}$$

Proceeding as in the case of the Milne and other half space problems, we find

$$a(\nu_0) = \frac{2G(\nu_0)S}{c\nu_0(1 - c)} \int_0^1 \frac{c}{2} \frac{\nu}{[\lambda(\nu) + \pi i c\nu/2]G^L(\nu)}\, d\nu = \frac{2G(\nu_0)S}{c\nu_0(1 - c)}$$

and

$$a(\nu) = -\frac{\lambda(\nu)[S/(1-c) + a(\nu_0)\phi(\nu \mid \nu_0)]}{[\lambda^2(\nu) + \pi^2 c^2 \nu^2/4]}$$

$$+ \frac{(1-c)(\nu_0{}^2 - \nu^2)}{[\lambda^2(\nu) + \pi^2 c^2 \nu^2/4]G(-\nu)} \int_0^1 \frac{c\mu}{2} \frac{[S/(1-c) + a(\nu_0)\phi(\mu \mid \nu_0)]}{[\lambda(\mu) + \pi i c\mu/2]G^L(\mu)} \frac{d\mu}{\mu - \nu}$$

$$= -\frac{(\nu + \nu_0)S}{[\lambda^2(\nu) + \pi^2 c^2 \nu^2/4]G(-\nu)}$$

Thus, the half space angular density for the constant isotropic source may be written as

$$\Phi(x, \mu) = S/(1-c) + a(\nu_0)\psi(x, \mu \mid \nu_0) + \int_0^1 a(\nu)\psi(x, \mu \mid \nu)\, d\nu$$

where the expansion coefficients $a(\nu_0)$ and $a(\nu)$ are presented above. The neutron density and net neutron current are readily seen to be

$$\rho(x) = 2S/(1-c) + a(\nu_0)e^{-x/\nu_0} + \int_0^1 a(\nu)e^{-x/\nu}\, d\nu$$

and

$$j(x) = (1-c)\left[\nu_0\, a(\nu_0)e^{-x/\nu_0} + \int_0^1 \nu a(\nu)e^{-x/\nu}\, d\nu\right]$$

The following expressions for these quantities at the origin,

$$\rho(0) = 2S/(1-c) - \frac{2G(0)}{c\nu_0} \int_0^1 \frac{c}{2} \frac{(\nu_0 - \mu)S/(1-c)}{[\lambda(\mu) + \pi i c\mu/2]G^L(\mu)}\, d\mu$$

$$= \frac{2G(0)}{c\nu_0} \frac{S}{1-c}\left[1 - \frac{G(0)}{\nu_0}\right]$$

and

$$j(0) = -\frac{2S}{c} \int_0^1 \frac{c\mu}{2} \frac{(\nu_0 - \mu)}{[\lambda(\mu) + \pi i c\mu/2]G^L(\mu)}\, d\mu$$

can be obtained by the procedure with which we became familiar in the preceding two sections.

F. Bare Slab Criticality Problem

As a final example of a boundary value problem in neutron transport theory that can be solved by means of Case's expansion technique, we shall consider the distribution of neutrons in a bare slab of fissionable material.

In contrast to the infinite medium and half space problems, boundary value problems in neutron transport theory involving slab configurations usually cannot be solved in closed form but must be solved partly by closed form analytical techniques and partly by analytical or numerical approximation methods.

We shall consider the distribution of neutrons in a bare slab of a fissionable material assuming that in all other respects the material properties of the medium are the same as in the case of the albedo and Milne half space problems. Our twofold aim is to derive an expansion of the angular neutron density in terms of the elementary solutions of the homogeneous transport equation and to obtain a criticality condition, i.e., a relation between the parameters describing the nuclear properties of the slab material and the thickness of the slab. Our problem statement requires us to solve the homogeneous transport equation,

$$\mu \frac{\partial \Phi(x, \mu)}{\partial x} + \Phi(x, \mu) = \frac{c}{2} \int_{-1}^{1} \Phi(x, \mu)\, d\mu$$

subject to the homogeneous boundary value conditions,

$$\Phi(-a, \mu) = 0 \qquad \mu \geqq 0$$

and

$$\Phi(a, \mu) = 0 \qquad \mu \leqq 0$$

on the boundaries of the slab.

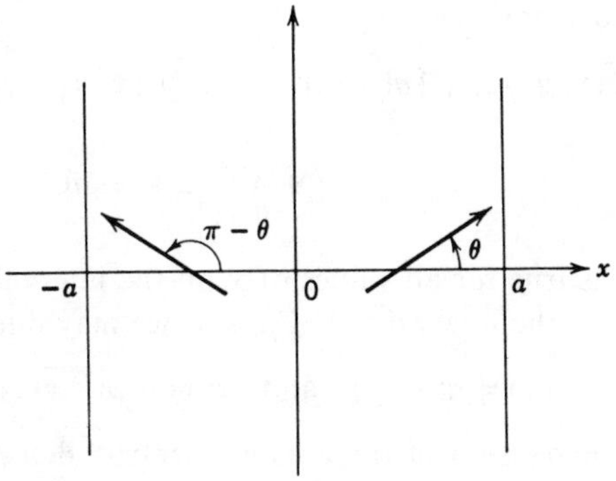

Figure VI-4

Starting out by expanding the angular density $\Phi(x, \mu)$ in terms of the full range elementary system,

$$\Phi(x, \mu) = a(\nu_0)\psi(x, \mu \,|\, \nu_0) + a(-\nu_0)\psi(x, \mu \,|\, -\nu_0) + \int_{-1}^{1} a(\nu)\psi(x, \mu \,|\, \nu)\, d\nu$$

the expansion coefficients are obtained by means of symmetry arguments and the boundary conditions. From the symmetry of the slab configuration we may infer that the number of neutrons at the point x moving in a direction which makes an angle θ with the positive x-axis must be equal to the number of neutrons at the point $-x$ moving in a direction which makes an angle $\pi - \theta$ with the positive x-axis. Thus

$$\Phi(x, \mu) = \Phi(-x, -\mu)$$

and we may write therefore

$$a(\nu_0)\psi(x, \mu \mid \nu_0) + a(-\nu_0)\psi(x, \mu \mid -\nu_0) + \int_{-1}^{1} a(\nu)\psi(x, \mu \mid \nu)\, d\nu$$
$$= a(\nu_0)\psi(-x, -\mu \mid \nu_0) + a(-\nu_0)\psi(-x, -\mu \mid -\nu_0)$$
$$+ \int_{-1}^{1} a(\nu)\psi(-x, -\mu \mid \nu)\, d\nu$$

however, as can easily be verified from the explicit analytical expressions for the elementary solutions,

$$\psi(-x, -\mu \mid \pm\nu_0) = \psi(x, \mu \mid \mp\nu_0)$$

and

$$\psi(-x, -\mu \mid \nu) = \psi(x, \mu \mid -\nu)$$

Hence we may also write

$$[a(\nu_0) - a(-\nu_0)]\psi(x, \mu \mid \nu_0) + [a(-\nu_0) - a(\nu_0)]\psi(x, \mu \mid -\nu_0)$$
$$+ \int_{-1}^{1} [a(\nu) - a(-\nu)]\psi(x, \mu \mid \nu)\, d\nu = 0$$

Since this relation is true for all values of x on the interval $-a \leqq x \leqq a$ and for all values of μ on the interval $-1 \leqq \mu \leqq 1$, we may infer that

$$a(\nu_0) = a(-\nu_0) \quad \text{and} \quad a(\nu) = a(-\nu)$$

The normal mode expansion of the angular neutron density takes therefore the form

$$\Phi(x, \mu) = \psi(x, \mu \mid \nu_0) + \psi(x, \mu \mid -\nu_0) + \int_{-1}^{1} a(\nu)\psi(x, \mu \mid \nu)\, d\nu$$

where we have made use of the homogeneity of the transport equation and the boundary conditions to normalize the expansion coefficients so that $a(\nu_0)$ is equal to one. By means of the boundary conditions imposed on the angular density at the free surfaces of the slab we now obtain a singular integral equation for the expansion coefficients $a(\nu)$. Because of the symmetry, one of these conditions is sufficient and choosing the boundary condition at $x = -a$ we find the equation,

$$\psi(-a, \mu \mid \nu_0) + \psi(-a, \mu \mid -\nu_0) = -\int_{-1}^{1} a(\nu)\psi(-a, \mu \mid \nu)\, d\nu$$

which may also be written as

$$\psi(-a, \mu \mid \nu_0) + \psi(-a, \mu \mid -\nu_0) = -\int_0^1 a(\nu)[\psi(-a, \mu \mid \nu) + \psi(-a, \mu \mid -\nu)]\, d\nu$$

This equation must be satisfied for all positive values of μ. Substitution of the explicit analytical expressions for the functions

$$\psi(-a, \mu \mid \nu) \quad \text{and} \quad \psi(-a, \mu \mid \pm \nu_0)$$

into this equation yields the singular integral equation,

$$\lambda(\mu)b(\mu) + \int_0^1 \frac{c}{2}\frac{\nu b(\nu)}{\nu - \mu}\, d\nu = -\phi(\mu \mid \nu_0)e^{a/\nu_0} - \phi(\mu \mid -\nu_0)e^{-a/\nu_0}$$
$$- \int_0^1 \frac{c}{2}\frac{\nu b(\nu)e^{-2a/\nu}}{\nu + \mu}\, d\nu$$

where we have introduced the function,

$$b(\nu) = a(\nu)e^{a/\nu}$$

The solution of this integral equation is obtained in two steps. Introducing the function,

$$f(\mu) = -\int_0^1 \frac{c}{2}\frac{\nu b(\nu)e^{-2a/\nu}}{\nu + \mu}\, d\nu - e^{a/\nu_0}\phi(\mu \mid \nu_0) - e^{-a/\nu_0}\phi(\mu \mid -\nu_0)$$

and assuming for the moment that the function $f(\mu)$ is known, we can obtain the solution of the singular equation,

$$f(\mu) = \lambda(\mu)b(\mu) + \int_0^1 \frac{c}{2}\frac{\nu b(\nu)}{\nu - \mu}\, d\nu$$

by means of the methods outlined in Section 4.12. This solution takes the form,

$$b(\nu) = \frac{1}{[\lambda^2(\nu) + \pi^2 c^2 \nu^2/4]}\left\{\lambda(\nu)f(\nu) - \frac{(1 - c)(\nu_0^2 - \nu^2)}{G(-\nu)}\int_0^1 \frac{c}{2}\frac{\mu f(\mu)}{[\lambda(\mu) + \pi i c\mu/2]G^L(\mu)}\frac{d\mu}{\mu - \nu}\right\}$$

where the following auxiliary condition must be satisfied,

$$\int_0^1 \frac{c}{2} \frac{\nu f(\nu)}{[\lambda(\nu) + \pi i c\nu/2] G^L(\nu)} d\nu = 0$$

Substitution of the function $f(\nu)$ into the penultimate equation yields a Fredholm integral equation for the function $b(\nu)$ which can be solved by analytical or numerical approximation techniques. For the particulars of such approximate solutions we have to refer the reader to the literature. Let us however consider the auxiliary condition more closely. Substitution of the function $f(\nu)$ and application of the identities,

$$\frac{1}{G(z)} = \int_0^1 \frac{c}{2} \frac{\nu}{[\lambda(\nu) + \pi i c\nu/2] G^L(\nu)} \frac{d\nu}{\nu - z}$$

and

$$G(\nu_0)G(-\nu_0) = \frac{2(1-c)\nu_0^2(1-\nu_0^2)}{1-\nu_0^2(1-c)}$$

leads to the expression,

$$G(-\nu_0)e^{a/\nu_0} - G(\nu_0)e^{-a/\nu_0} = \frac{2(1-c)\nu_0(1-\nu_0^2)}{1-\nu_0^2(1-c)} \int_0^1 \frac{\nu b(\nu)e^{-2a/\nu}}{G(-\nu)} d\nu$$

This implies that for given $b(\nu)$ and known material composition of the medium we can deduce the critical thickness of the slab from this relation. Conversely for given $b(\nu)$ and known thickness of the slab, the material composition of the medium can be found. A relation of this type is known physically as a criticality condition. Mathematically it is the characteristic or dispersion equation from which we can determine the eigenvalues of the homogeneous transport equation.

CHAPTER VII

APPLICATIONS IN PLASMA PHYSICS

7.0 INTRODUCTION

In this chapter we shall present some applications of the analytic function and distribution techniques, introduced in the previous chapters, to the field of plasma physics.

A plasma is a highly ionized gas consisting mainly of a large number of negatively charged electrons and positively charged ions. In contrast to a gas of neutral particles, however, the aggregate of all the charged particles constituting a plasma exhibits the coherent static and dynamic behavior that is characteristic of an ordered medium. This behavior is a result of the long range electromagnetic interaction between the charged particles and of the screening of the electromagnetic fields, which are generated by external charge and current distributions and/or incomplete internal charge neutralization, by the highly mobile free charges. This screening process results in an electrically nearly neutral and field-free region of space in which the cloud of charged particles is suspended. A slight perturbation in the equilibrium configuration of such a nearly neutral and field-free plasma, for example a perturbation due to local charge separation, results in the generation of restoring forces and consequent oscillations of the plasma about the equilibrium configuration.

An elementary theory of such electron density oscillations can be based on the following model. We consider the situation in which an equal number of electrons and ions are uniformly distributed so that the resultant space charge is zero. A small disturbance in the neutral charge distribution causes the electrons to oscillate about a position of equilibrium. Of course, the ions will also oscillate. However, the electrons are much lighter than the ions and, because of the high frequency of the electron oscillations with respect to the frequency of the ion oscillations, we may, in first approximation, consider the ions to be immovable. If $N(\mathbf{r}, t)$ denotes the average electron density and $\mathbf{v}(r, t)$ is the average electron velocity at a particular space point $\mathbf{r}$ at time t, the equations describing the time rate of change of these quantities are the continuity equation,

$$\frac{\partial N(\mathbf{r}, t)}{\partial t} + \nabla \cdot (N\mathbf{v}) = 0$$

and the equation of motion,

$$m \frac{\partial \mathbf{v}(\mathbf{r}, t)}{\partial t} = e\mathbf{E}(\mathbf{r}, t)$$

where the electric field can be determined from the field equation,

$$\nabla \cdot \mathbf{E}(\mathbf{r}, t) = e[N(\mathbf{r}, t) - n_0]/\varepsilon_0$$

and n_0 denotes the uniform equilibrium electron density.

Assuming that the electron density and the electron velocity are slightly perturbed from their equilibrium values,

$$N(\mathbf{r}, t) = n_0 + n(\mathbf{r}, t)$$

and

$$\mathbf{v}(\mathbf{r}, t) = 0 + \mathbf{v}(\mathbf{r}, t)$$

the equations of state may be linearized and we find, in first approximation, the system,

$$\frac{\partial n(\mathbf{r}, t)}{\partial t} + n_0 \nabla \cdot \mathbf{v}(\mathbf{r}, t) = 0$$

$$m \frac{\partial \mathbf{v}(\mathbf{r}, t)}{\partial t} = e\mathbf{E}(\mathbf{r}, t)$$

$$\nabla \cdot \mathbf{E}(\mathbf{r}, t) = en(\mathbf{r}, t)/\varepsilon_0$$

Eliminating the velocity and the intensity of the electric field, we obtain the following equation for the perturbation in the electron density,

$$\frac{\partial^2 n(\mathbf{r}, t)}{\partial t^2} + \frac{n_0 e^2}{m\varepsilon_0} n(\mathbf{r}, t) = 0$$

This equation may also be written

$$\frac{\partial^2 n(\mathbf{r}, t)}{\partial t^2} + \omega_p{}^2 n(\mathbf{r}, t) = 0$$

where

$$\omega_p = \left[\frac{n_0 e^2}{m\varepsilon_0}\right]^{1/2}$$

is the electron plasma frequency in MKS units.

According to Section 2.7, this equation is the equation of motion of a physical system oscillating about a position of stable equilibrium. Thus, we find that the electron density oscillates about the equilibrium density with the plasma frequency ω_p. Furthermore, in this approximation the density oscillations are localized. This is the so-called case of a zero temperature plasma. In such a "cold" plasma the frequency of the electron density oscillations is independent of the wave length λ. As a result, the group velocity, which is defined as the derivative of the frequency of oscillation with respect to the wave number $k = 2\pi/\lambda$, vanishes and an initially localized perturbation in the electron density does not propagate through the plasma but causes local density fluctuations only. Temperature effects, however, may result in density oscillations in which the frequency is a function of the wave number. Now the group velocity will not be zero and the density fluctuations will not be localized but may propagate in space as well as change in time.

In the following sections of this chapter we shall be concerned with such collective motions of the aggregate of all particles rather than with the motions of the individual particles. In particular we shall be interested in the small amplitude longitudinal oscillations of a plasma about an equilibrium configuration. We shall study therefore the medium-like behavior of a plasma and we shall make use of smooth particle and field averages. This implies that we shall assume that the plasma oscillations of interest have wave lengths which are appreciably larger than the interparticle spacing and periods that are very much smaller than the mean time between collisions of electrons with the surrounding ions and gas molecules.

The natural mathematical vehicle for the description of the physical processes we have in mind is the Boltzmann transport equation. The derivation of this equation, accompanied by a discussion of the physical conditions under which such an equation is applicable, will be the subject of the next section.

7.1 THE COLLISIONLESS BOLTZMANN EQUATION

As we have remarked before, the transport of neutrons in a uniform medium can accurately be described by a linear Boltzmann or Boltzmann transport equation. To derive such an equation, one assumes that the frequency of neutron-neutron collisions is low compared to the frequency of the collisions of neutrons with the atoms or molecules of the transport medium. This approximation, which results in a linear transport equation, is justified because the neutron number density is usually very much lower than the number density of the atomic nuclei of the surrounding medium.

The behavior of a gas of neutral particles, such as atoms or molecules, can also be described by a Boltzmann equation for the particle distribution function $\Psi(\mathbf{r}, \mathbf{v}, t)$,

$$\frac{D\Psi}{Dt} = \left[\frac{\partial\Psi}{\partial t}\right]_{\text{col.}}$$

where D/Dt denotes the displacement derivative.

The left hand side of this balance equation is a measure of the time rate of change of the number of molecules in a unit volume of phase space due to streaming and the influence of external forces, whereas the right hand side accounts for the time rate of change of the number of molecules in the same volume element of phase space due to interparticle collisions.

The molecules of a neutral gas are freely moving and only intermolecular collisions are important. Furthermore, since the intermolecular forces are of short range, only binary collisions have to be taken into account in a dilute neutral gas. This has the result that the collision term on the right hand side of the Boltzmann equation is quadratically nonlinear in the distribution function. Assuming that the duration of intermolecular collisions is short with respect to the time between consecutive collisions and that the frequency of intermolecular collisions is high it can be shown that the particle distribution function deviates only slightly from a Maxwellian equilibrium distribution.

Now let us consider the case of a high temperature strongly ionized gas or plasma. Because of the long range nature of electromagnetic forces, each constituent of such a plasma interacts continuously with all the other particles but the effects of the interaction, such as momentum transfer, are in general small. Thus we may picture an almost freely moving particle which traverses with low speed the field produced by all the other particles and a particle configuration which does not change effectively over appreciable periods of time.

This picture of a nearly quiescent particle configuration is rudely destroyed however when a charged particle makes a close collision with a neutral atom or molecule of the gas or a close coulomb collision with one of the other charged particles. For the short range forces acting in such close interactions usually result in appreciable momentum transfer and a consequent violent disruption of the particle configuration. However, in the case of the low density high temperature plasmas we shall be concerned with, it can be shown that the time rate of change of the particle configuration due to such short range collisions is small compared to the time rate of change of this configuration due to particle streaming and to oscillations produced by the long range averaged electromagnetic fields. In first approximation therefore we may neglect the effects of the close collisions and consider the so-called collisionless Boltzmann or Vlasov equation,

$$\frac{D\Psi(\mathbf{r}, \mathbf{v}, t)}{Dt} = 0$$

It is moreover entirely sufficient to investigate the electron motions independent of the motions of the ions. The ion mass is very much larger than the electron mass and the intrinsic ion plasma frequency, which is inversely proportional to the square root of the ion mass, is low enough that its overall effect on the electron motion can be ignored. We may assume therefore, for wave lengths larger than the interionic spacings, that a uniform distribution of immovable, infinitely heavy ions provides a positively charged background for the electron motion.

We can now derive a more explicit expression for the collisionless Boltzmann equation for the electron distribution function $\Psi(\mathbf{r}, \mathbf{v}, t)$. Let us consider a volume element $d\mathbf{r}\, d\mathbf{v}$ in six-dimensional position and velocity space. Then $\Psi(\mathbf{r}, \mathbf{v}, t)\, d\mathbf{r}\, d\mathbf{v}$ is the number of electrons in the range $\mathbf{r}$ to $\mathbf{r} + d\mathbf{r}$ and $\mathbf{v}$ to $\mathbf{v} + d\mathbf{v}$. Under influence of external and/or self-consistent electromagnetic fields, but in absence of interparticle collisions, the electrons move in such a manner that at time $t + dt$ the position vectors of the electrons are $\mathbf{r} + \mathbf{v}\, dt$ and their velocity vectors are $\mathbf{v} + \mathbf{a}\, dt$ where $\mathbf{a}$ is the instantaneous electron acceleration imparted to the electrons by the electromagnetic force fields. Conservation of electrons requires that

$$\Psi(\mathbf{r}, \mathbf{v}, t)\, d\mathbf{r}\, d\mathbf{v} = \Psi(\mathbf{r} + \mathbf{v}\, dt, \mathbf{v} + \mathbf{a}\, dt, t + dt)\, d\mathbf{r}\, d\mathbf{v}$$

or, expanding the function $\Psi(r + \mathbf{v}\, dt, \mathbf{v} + \mathbf{a}\, dt, t + dt)$ in a Taylor series about the point $\mathbf{r}, \mathbf{v}, t$, we find, in first approximation and in absence of collisions, the transport equation,

$$\frac{\partial\Psi(\mathbf{r}, \mathbf{v}, t)}{\partial t} + \mathbf{v} \cdot \nabla_{\mathbf{r}} \Psi(\mathbf{r}, \mathbf{v}, t) + \mathbf{a} \cdot \nabla_{\mathbf{v}} \Psi(\mathbf{r}, \mathbf{v}, t) = 0 \tag{7.1}$$

Here $\nabla_{\mathbf{r}}$ denotes the gradient operator in real space whereas $\nabla_{\mathbf{v}}$ is the gradient operator in velocity space. We shall now assume that the plasma forms an isolated system shielded from the influence of electro-magnetic fields which are generated by external charge and current distributions. The local electron acceleration $\mathbf{a}$ therefore is due to the self-consistent electromagnetic fields, i.e., the average electromagnetic fields which arise by induction from internal macroscopic space charges and currents. If $\mathbf{E}$ and $\mathbf{B}$ denote the intensity vectors of this field, then, as we have seen in Section 2.8, the electron acceleration can be found by means of the following equation for the Lorentz force,

$$m\mathbf{a} = e[\mathbf{E} + \mathbf{v} \times \mathbf{B}] \tag{7.2}$$

To completely describe the electron motion, therefore, the collisionless Boltzmann equation must be complemented by the Maxwell equations for the electromagnetic field,

$$\nabla \times \mathbf{E} + \frac{\partial \mathbf{B}}{\partial t} = 0 \tag{7.3}$$

$$c^2 \nabla \times \mathbf{B} - \frac{\partial \mathbf{E}}{\partial t} = \mathbf{J}/\varepsilon_0 \tag{7.4}$$

$$\nabla \cdot \mathbf{E} = \rho/\varepsilon_0 \tag{7.5}$$

$$\nabla \cdot \mathbf{B} = 0 \tag{7.6}$$

where c is the speed of light, ε_0 is the permittivity of empty space, and the units chosen are those of the rationalized MKS system.

The charge and current densities are given by integrals of the distribution function over velocity space. The charge density may be written

$$\rho(\mathbf{r}, t) = e \int \Psi(\mathbf{r}, \mathbf{v}, t)\, d\mathbf{v} - en_0$$

and the current density takes the form,

$$\mathbf{J}(\mathbf{r}, t) = e \int \mathbf{v}\, \Psi(\mathbf{r}, \mathbf{v}, t)\, d\mathbf{v}$$

where n_0 is the fixed ion number density and e is the electron charge.

The formidable system of nonlinear differential equations and integro-differential equations comprising the Vlasov and Maxwell equations can be simplified considerably by the following limitations on our objectives. First, we shall limit our interests to the study of plasma oscillations which are set up by small local perturbations in a spatially uniform and time-independent neutral electron distribution $n_0 \psi_0(\mathbf{v})$, which is normalized such that the electron number density is equal to the number density of the fixed ion background. Since the number density of the ion background is n_0, we must have

$$n_0 \int \psi_0(\mathbf{v})\, d\mathbf{v} = n_0$$

from which we may infer that the equilibrium distribution $\psi_0(\mathbf{v})$ is normalized to one,

$$\int \psi_0(\mathbf{v})\, d\mathbf{v} = 1$$

Supposing that the unperturbed plasma configuration is field-free, an assumption which is consistent with our previous supposition of vanishing external fields, we find moreover that

$$\int \mathbf{v}\psi_0(\mathbf{v})\, d\mathbf{v} = 0$$

The electron distribution function $\Psi(\mathbf{r}, \mathbf{v}, t)$ may be written therefore as the sum of a steady, homogeneous, neutral equilibrium distribution $n_0\,\psi_0(\mathbf{v})$ and a distribution function $\psi(\mathbf{r}, \mathbf{v}, t)$ which is a measure of the small departure from equilibrium of the electron distribution at a particular point in phase space,

$$\Psi(\mathbf{r}, \mathbf{v}, t) = n_0\,\psi_0(\mathbf{v}) + \psi(\mathbf{r}, \mathbf{v}, t)$$

Substituting this expression for the distribution function into the collisionless Boltzmann equation and the Maxwell equations and neglecting terms of second order of smallness, we obtain the following system of linear equations,

$$\frac{\partial \psi}{\partial t} + \mathbf{v} \cdot \nabla_{\mathbf{r}} \psi + \frac{en_0}{m} [\mathbf{E} + \mathbf{v} \times \mathbf{B}] \cdot \nabla_{\mathbf{v}} \psi_0(\mathbf{v}) = 0 \tag{7.7}$$

$$\nabla \times \mathbf{E} + \frac{\partial \mathbf{B}}{\partial t} = 0 \tag{7.8}$$

$$c^2 \nabla \times \mathbf{B} - \frac{\partial \mathbf{E}}{\partial t} = \mathbf{J}/\varepsilon_0 \tag{7.9}$$

$$\nabla \cdot \mathbf{E} = \rho/\varepsilon_0 \tag{7.10}$$

$$\nabla \cdot \mathbf{B} = 0 \tag{7.11}$$

where the charge and current densities are given by the integrals,

$$\rho(\mathbf{r}, t) = e \int \psi(\mathbf{r}, \mathbf{v}, t)\, d\mathbf{v} \tag{7.12}$$

and

$$\mathbf{J}(\mathbf{r}, t) = e \int \mathbf{v}\psi(\mathbf{r}, \mathbf{v}, t)\, d\mathbf{v} \tag{7.13}$$

This system of equations can be simplified still further by restricting ourselves to the investigation of the collective motions of the electrons in a direction parallel to the electric field vector **E**. In the case of such longitudinal modes of oscillation the system of equations can be reduced to the two coupled equations,

$$\frac{\partial \psi}{\partial t} + \mathbf{v} \cdot \nabla_{\mathbf{r}} \psi + \frac{en_0}{m} \mathbf{E}(\mathbf{r}, t) \cdot \nabla_{\mathbf{v}} \psi_0(\mathbf{v}) = 0 \tag{7.14}$$

and

$$\nabla \cdot \mathbf{E} = \rho/\varepsilon_0 \tag{7.15}$$

where $\rho(\mathbf{r}, t)$ is defined by equation (7.12).

In many situations it is more convenient to work with the scalar potential $\phi(\mathbf{r}, t)$ than with the electric field vector $\mathbf{E}(\mathbf{r}, t)$. The scalar potential is defined by the relation,

$$\mathbf{E}(\mathbf{r}, t) = -\nabla\phi(\mathbf{r}, t) \tag{7.16}$$

In terms of the scalar potential the linearized collisionless Boltzmann equation may be written as

$$\frac{\partial \psi}{\partial t} + \mathbf{v} \cdot \nabla_{\mathbf{r}} \psi(\mathbf{r}, \mathbf{v}, t) = \frac{en_0}{m} \nabla\phi(\mathbf{r}, t) \cdot \nabla_{\mathbf{v}} \psi_0(\mathbf{v}) \tag{7.17}$$

where $\phi(\mathbf{r}, t)$ is a solution of Poisson's equation,

$$\nabla^2\phi(\mathbf{r}, t) = -\rho(\mathbf{r}, t)/\varepsilon_0 \tag{7.18}$$

7.2 LONGITUDINAL OSCILLATIONS IN AN UNBOUNDED PLASMA; PROBLEM STATEMENT

In this and subsequent sections, we shall be concerned with a plasma of infinite extent. This enables us to Fourier transform the collisionless Boltzmann equation for the perturbation $\psi(\mathbf{r}, \mathbf{v}, t)$ in the electron distribution function $\Psi(\mathbf{r}, \mathbf{v}, t)$,

$$\frac{\partial \psi(\mathbf{r}, \mathbf{v}, t)}{\partial t} + \mathbf{v} \cdot \nabla_{\mathbf{r}} \psi(\mathbf{r}, \mathbf{v}, t) = \frac{en_0}{m} \nabla\phi(\mathbf{r}, t) \cdot \nabla_{\mathbf{v}} \psi_0(\mathbf{v})$$

and the Poisson equation,

$$\nabla^2\phi(\mathbf{r}, t) = -\frac{e}{\varepsilon_0} \int \psi(\mathbf{r}, \mathbf{v}, t)\, d\mathbf{v}$$

from real space into the space of the Fourier transform variable by introducing the Fourier transforms,

$$\psi(\mathbf{k}, \mathbf{v}, t) = \frac{1}{(2\pi)^{3/2}} \int_{-\infty}^{\infty} \psi(\mathbf{r}, \mathbf{v}, t) e^{-i\mathbf{k}\cdot\mathbf{r}}\, d\mathbf{r}$$

and

$$\phi(\mathbf{k}, \mathbf{v}, t) = \frac{1}{(2\pi)^{3/2}} \int_{-\infty}^{\infty} \phi(\mathbf{r}, t) e^{-i\mathbf{k}\cdot\mathbf{r}}\, d\mathbf{r}$$

where we distinguish between the functions $\psi(\mathbf{r}, \mathbf{v}, t)$, $\phi(\mathbf{r}, t)$ and their Fourier transforms $\psi(\mathbf{k}, \mathbf{v}, t)$, $\phi(\mathbf{k}, t)$ by means of the variable index $\mathbf{k}$. In $\mathbf{k}$-space, the collisionless Boltzmann equation takes the form,

$$\frac{\partial \psi(\mathbf{k}, \mathbf{v}, t)}{\partial t} + i\mathbf{k} \cdot \mathbf{v}\psi(\mathbf{k}, \mathbf{v}, t) = \frac{n_0 e}{m} \phi(\mathbf{k}, t) i\mathbf{k} \cdot \nabla_{\mathbf{v}} \psi_0(\mathbf{v}) \tag{7.19}$$

where the Fourier amplitude $\phi(\mathbf{k}, t)$ of the scalar potential $\phi(\mathbf{r}, t)$ of the self-consistent field is related to the Fourier amplitude of the distribution function by the equation,

$$\phi(\mathbf{k}, t) = \frac{e}{\varepsilon_0 k^2} \int \psi(\mathbf{k}, \mathbf{v}, t)\, d\mathbf{v} \tag{7.20}$$

In this and subsequent sections we shall mainly work in $\mathbf{k}$-space. The Fourier transform from $\mathbf{k}$-space to physical space can be done routinely and does not lead to additional complications or particularly revealing discoveries from the standpoint of the physics of the problem.

It is furthermore convenient to choose the axes in velocity space in a direction parallel and perpendicular to the vector $\mathbf{k}$. Denoting the longitudinal component of the velocity vector by v,

$$v = \mathbf{k} \cdot \mathbf{v}/k$$

and combining the transversal velocity components in a vector $\mathbf{u}$, we may write

$$\mathbf{v} = \mathbf{u} + \frac{\mathbf{k}}{k} v$$

where $\mathbf{k} \cdot \mathbf{u} = 0$ and $k = |\mathbf{k}|$.

Since we are interested exclusively in longitudinal modes of oscillation, we define a new distribution function $f(\mathbf{k}, v, t)$ in $\mathbf{k}$-space, by integrating the Fourier amplitude $\psi(\mathbf{k}, \mathbf{v}, t)$ of the perturbation $\psi(\mathbf{r}, \mathbf{v}, t)$ in the electron distribution function over $\mathbf{u}$-space. Thus

$$f(\mathbf{k}, v, t) = \int \psi(\mathbf{k}, \mathbf{v}, t)\, d\mathbf{u} \tag{7.21}$$

Integrating the collisionless Boltzmann equation in $\mathbf{k}$-space over the transversal velocity components, we find

$$\frac{\partial f(\mathbf{k}, v, t)}{\partial t} + ikvf(\mathbf{k}, v, t) = -ikh(k, v) \int_{-\infty}^{\infty} f(\mathbf{k}, v, t)\, dv \tag{7.22}$$

where we have introduced the functions,

$$h(k, v) = -\frac{\omega_p^{\,2}}{k^2}\frac{df_0(v)}{dv} \tag{7.23}$$

and

$$f_0(v) = \int \psi_0(\mathbf{v})\, d\mathbf{u} \tag{7.24}$$

and where ω_p denotes the plasma frequency. We note, moreover, that the amplitude of the scalar potential of the electric field may now be written as

$$\phi(\mathbf{k}, t) = \frac{e}{\varepsilon_0 k^2}\int_{-\infty}^{\infty} f(\mathbf{k}, v, t)\, dv \tag{7.25}$$

In the next several sections of this chapter we shall discuss some techniques for the solution of the following initial value problem: Find the solutions of the collisionless Boltzmann equation in **k**-space,

$$\frac{\partial f(\mathbf{k}, v, t)}{\partial t} + ikvf(\mathbf{k}, v, t) = -ikh(k, v)\int_{-\infty}^{\infty} f(\mathbf{k}, v, t)\, dv$$

subject to the initial value condition,

$$f(\mathbf{k}, v, 0) = g(\mathbf{k}, v)$$

and determine, by means of these solutions, the temporal behavior of the Fourier amplitude,

$$\phi(\mathbf{k}, t) = \frac{e}{\varepsilon_0 k^2}\int_{-\infty}^{\infty} f(\mathbf{k}, v, t)\, dv$$

of the scalar potential of the electric field.

We note that the function $g(\mathbf{k}, v)$ is the Fourier transform with respect to the space coordinates of the initial perturbation in the equilibrium velocity distribution integrated over the transversal velocity components.

Solutions of this initial value problem have been obtained and investigated by many people by means of widely diverse mathematical techniques. Vlasov seems to have been the first to obtain the transport formulation of the present problem but his solution is of limited validity. In a basic paper published in 1946, Landau formulated the initial value problem in its present form and obtained the first consistent solution by means of a unilateral Fourier or Laplace transform technique. In that same paper he discussed his discovery of the phenomenon of Landau damping, i.e., the collisionless damping of longitudinal plasma oscillations. Since Landau's fundamental work, several other solution techniques have been developed with highly interesting mathematical and physical implications, such as the normal mode technique of Case and van Kampen.

In the next section we shall start our review of these techniques with a discussion of the Landau solution of the initial value problem posed above.

7.3 LANDAU'S TRANSFORM SOLUTION OF THE INITIAL VALUE PROBLEM

Let us repeat the problem statement: Find the solution of the collisionless Boltzmann equation in **k**-space,

$$\frac{\partial f(\mathbf{k}, v, t)}{\partial t} + ikvf(\mathbf{k}, v, t) = -ikh(k, v)\int_{-\infty}^{\infty} f(\mathbf{k}, v, t)\, dv$$

subject to the initial condition,

$$f(\mathbf{k}, v, 0) = g(\mathbf{k}, v)$$

and determine, by means of this solution, the temporal behavior of the amplitude,

$$\phi(\mathbf{k}, t) = \frac{e}{\varepsilon_0 k^2}\int_{-\infty}^{\infty} f(\mathbf{k}, v, t)\, dv$$

of the scalar potential of the self-consistent field. Landau obtained the solution of this problem by introducing the unilateral Fourier transforms,

$$F(\mathbf{k}, v, \lambda) = \frac{1}{\sqrt{(2\pi)}}\int_{0}^{\infty} f(\mathbf{k}, v, t)e^{i\lambda t}\, dt$$

and

$$\Phi(\mathbf{k}, \lambda) = \frac{1}{\sqrt{(2\pi)}}\int_{0}^{\infty} \phi(\mathbf{k}, t)e^{i\lambda t}\, dt$$

By means of these transforms the collisionless Boltzmann equation in **k**-space takes the form,

$$F(\mathbf{k}, v, \lambda) = \frac{g(\mathbf{k}, v)}{ik(v - \lambda/k)} - \frac{h(k, v)}{v - \lambda/k}\int_{-\infty}^{\infty} F(\mathbf{k}, v, \lambda)\, dv$$

while the potential function in k-space may be written as,

$$\Phi(\mathbf{k}, \lambda) = \frac{e}{\varepsilon_0 k^2}\int_{-\infty}^{\infty} F(\mathbf{k}, v, \lambda)\, dv$$

Integrating the collisionless Boltzmann equation over v, we find

$$\int_{-\infty}^{\infty} F(\mathbf{k}, v, \lambda)\, dv = \frac{1}{ik} \int_{-\infty}^{\infty} \frac{g(\mathbf{k}, v)}{v - \lambda/k}\, dv + \frac{\omega_p{}^2}{k^2} \int_{-\infty}^{\infty} F(\mathbf{k}, v, \lambda)\, dv \int_{-\infty}^{\infty} \frac{df_0(v)}{dv} \frac{dv}{v - \lambda/k}$$

and from this equation and the equation for $\Phi(\mathbf{k}, \lambda)$ we may infer that

$$\Phi(\mathbf{k}, \lambda) = \frac{N(\mathbf{k}, \lambda)}{D(k, \lambda)}$$

The numerator $N(\mathbf{k}, \lambda)$ in this expression takes the form,

$$N(\mathbf{k}, \lambda) = \frac{2\pi e}{\varepsilon_0 k^3} G(\mathbf{k}, \lambda)$$

where the function $G(\mathbf{k}, \lambda)$ is represented by the Cauchy integral,

$$G(\mathbf{k}, \lambda) = \frac{1}{2\pi i} \int_{-\infty}^{\infty} \frac{g(\mathbf{k}, v)}{v - \lambda/k}\, dv$$

The expression for the denominator $D(k, \lambda)$ also contains a Cauchy integral,

$$D(k, \lambda) = 1 - \frac{\omega_p{}^2}{k^2} \int_{-\infty}^{\infty} \frac{df_0(v)}{dv} \frac{dv}{v - \lambda/k}$$

It is interesting to note that the numerator $N(\mathbf{k}, \lambda)$ depends on the initial value of the perturbation in the equilibrium distribution, whereas the denominator $D(k, \lambda)$ depends on the equilibrium distribution itself.

In terms of the functions $G(\mathbf{k}, \lambda)$ and $D(k, \lambda)$, the Fourier transform $F(\mathbf{k}, v, \lambda)$ may now be written

$$F(\mathbf{k}, v, \lambda) = \frac{1}{ik} \frac{1}{v - \lambda/k} \left[g(\mathbf{k}, v) + 2\pi i \frac{G(\mathbf{k}, \lambda)}{D(k, \lambda)} \frac{\omega_p{}^2}{k^2} \frac{df_0(v)}{dv} \right]$$

7.4 THE TIME-DEPENDENT BEHAVIOR OF THE POTENTIAL OF THE SELF-CONSISTENT FIELD

In this section we shall investigate the time-dependent behavior of the Fourier amplitude $\phi(\mathbf{k}, t)$ of the potential of the self-consistent field.

Let us assume that the function $\phi(\mathbf{k}, t)$ is at most of exponential growth for large values of t. In particular, let us assume that $\Phi(\mathbf{k}, t)$ is at most of the order of exp (at) when t tends to infinity and is absolutely integrable over any finite time interval. According to Section 2.2, the Fourier integral

$$\Phi(\mathbf{k}, \lambda) = \frac{1}{\sqrt{(2\pi)}} \int_0^{\infty} \phi(\mathbf{k}, t) e^{i\lambda t}\, dt$$

is absolutely and uniformly convergent in the upper half plane $I(\lambda) \geqq a$, and is the representation of a function $\Phi(k, \lambda)$ which is analytic in the upper half plane $I(\lambda) > a$. This function, moreover, is continuous and bounded for all finite values of λ in the upper half plane $I(\lambda) \geqq a$ and vanishes when λ tends to infinity in this half plane. The Fourier amplitude of the scalar potential can be found therefore by evaluating the inversion integral,

$$\phi(\mathbf{k}, t) = \frac{1}{\sqrt{(2\pi)}} \int_{-\infty+ib}^{\infty+ib} \Phi(\mathbf{k}, \zeta) e^{-i\zeta t} \, d\zeta$$

where b is an arbitrary number larger than a.

As we have found in the preceding section,

$$\Phi(\mathbf{k}, \lambda) = \frac{N(\mathbf{k}, \lambda)}{D(k, \lambda)} = \frac{2\pi e}{\varepsilon_0 k^3} \frac{G(\mathbf{k}, \lambda)}{D(k, \lambda)}$$

where the function $G(\mathbf{k}, \lambda)$ can be represented by a Cauchy integral,

$$G(\mathbf{k}, \lambda) = \frac{1}{2\pi i} \int_{-\infty}^{\infty} \frac{g(\mathbf{k}, v)}{v - \lambda/k} \, dv$$

and the function in the denominator may be written as,

$$D(k, \lambda) = 1 - \frac{\omega_p^{\,2}}{k^2} \int_{-\infty}^{\infty} \frac{df_0(v)}{dv} \frac{dv}{v - \lambda/k}$$

From these expressions, it follows immediately that the behavior of $\Phi(\mathbf{k}, \lambda)$ as a function of λ is closely related to the behavior of the functions $g(\mathbf{k}, v)$ and $f_0(v)$ as functions of v. In other words, the behavior of the function $\Phi(\mathbf{k}, \lambda)$ in the complex λ-plane is determined by the amplitude of the initial perturbation in the equilibrium distribution (appearing in the numerator) and by the equilibrium distribution (appearing in the denominator).

Now let us assume, with Landau, that the amplitude $g(\mathbf{k}, v)$ of the initial perturbation and the equilibrium distribution $f_0(v)$ are the restrictions to the real axis of functions that are analytic in the whole complex velocity plane. In other words, the functions $g(\mathbf{k}, z)$ and $f_0(z)$ are entire functions of the complex variable $z = \lambda/k$, where z is the complex phase velocity. As we have remarked in Section 2.13, this condition is necessary and sufficient for the function,

$$G^R(\mathbf{k}, \lambda) = \frac{1}{2\pi i} \int_{-\infty}^{\infty} \frac{g(\mathbf{k}, v)}{v - \lambda/k} \, dv + g(\mathbf{k}, \lambda/k)$$

to be the analytic continuation of the function,

$$G^L(\mathbf{k}, \lambda) = \frac{1}{2\pi i} \int_{-\infty}^{\infty} \frac{g(\mathbf{k}, v)}{v - \lambda/k} \, dv$$

into the lower half of the complex λ-plane. Furthermore, the function $G(\mathbf{k}, \lambda)$ defined by the relations,

$$G(\mathbf{k}, \lambda) = G^L(\mathbf{k}, \lambda) \qquad \text{when } I(\lambda) > 0$$
$$= G^R(\mathbf{k}, \lambda) \qquad \text{when } I(\lambda) < 0$$

is an entire function which can be represented by the Cauchy integral,

$$G(\mathbf{k}, \lambda) = \frac{1}{2\pi i} \int_\Gamma \frac{g(\mathbf{k}, v)}{v - \lambda/k}\, dv$$

where Γ denotes the Landau contour shown in Figure VII-1.

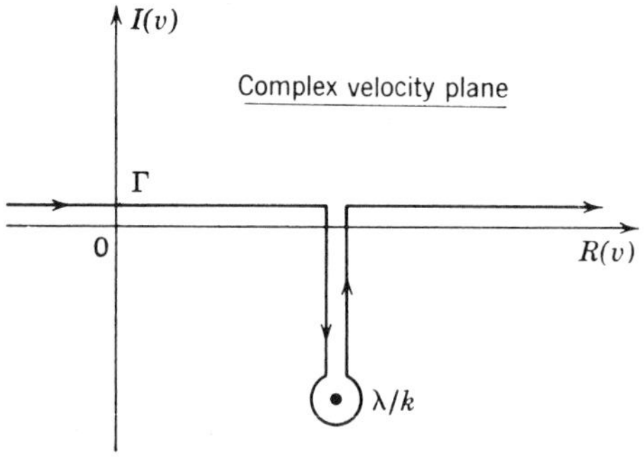

Figure VII-1

Similar conclusions can be drawn with respect to the function $D(k, \lambda)$, defined by the relations,

$$D(k, \lambda) = D^L(k, \lambda) \qquad \text{when } I(\lambda) > 0$$
$$= D^R(k, \lambda) \qquad \text{when } I(\lambda) < 0$$

where $D^L(k, \lambda)$ has the integral representation,

$$D^L(k, \lambda) = 1 - \frac{\omega_p^2}{k^2} \int_{-\infty}^{\infty} \frac{df_0(v)}{dv} \frac{dv}{v - \lambda/k}$$

and $D^R(k, \lambda)$, the analytic continuation of the function $D^L(k, \lambda)$ into the lower half plane, is defined by the expression,

$$D^R(k, \lambda) = 1 - \frac{\omega_p^2}{k^2} \int_{-\infty}^{\infty} \frac{df_0(v)}{dv} \frac{dv}{v - \lambda/k} - 2\pi i \frac{\omega_p^2}{k^2} \frac{df_0(\lambda/k)}{dv}$$

Of course, the entire function $D(k, \lambda)$ can also be represented by the integral relation,

$$D(k, \lambda) = 1 - \frac{\omega_p^2}{k^2} \int_\Gamma \frac{df_0(v)}{dv} \frac{dv}{v - \lambda/k}$$

The function $D(k, \lambda)$, together with its analytic continuation into the lower half plane, is often called the dielectric function.

From these considerations we may conclude that the function $\Phi(\mathbf{k}, \lambda)$ can be written as the ratio of two entire functions,

$$\Phi(\mathbf{k}, \lambda) = \frac{N(\mathbf{k}, \lambda)}{D(k, \lambda)}$$

This function therefore is analytic in the whole complex λ-plane with the exception of possible singularities at the zeros of the dielectric function $D(k, \lambda)$. These singularities, moreover, must all be located below the line $I(\lambda) = a + \varepsilon$ where ε is some arbitrarily small positive number. For reasons to be explained later, the equation

$$D(k, \lambda) = 0$$

is called the dispersion equation.

Thus, assuming that the Fourier amplitude of the initial perturbation and of the equilibrium distribution are the restrictions to the real axis of entire functions, we may conclude that the singularities of the function $\Phi(\mathbf{k}, \lambda) = N(\mathbf{k}, \lambda)/D(k, \lambda)$ as a function of the complex variable λ are determined solely by the zeros of the dielectric function $D(k, \lambda)$ which depends on the equilibrium distribution only.

To obtain information about the behavior in time of the Fourier amplitude of the scalar potential from its integral representation,

$$\phi(\mathbf{k}, t) = \frac{1}{\sqrt{(2\pi)}} \int_{-\infty+ib}^{\infty+ib} \frac{N(\mathbf{k}, \zeta)}{D(k, \zeta)} e^{-i\zeta t}\, d\zeta$$

we may now proceed along two similar but different routes. We may be satisfied, as Landau was, to obtain information about the long time behavior of the function $\phi(\mathbf{k}, t)$, or we may impose additional restrictions on the function $\Phi(\mathbf{k}, \lambda) = N(\mathbf{k}, \lambda)/D(k, \lambda)$ to obtain a series representation of the function $\phi(\mathbf{k}, t)$.

The asymptotic behavior of the function $\phi(\mathbf{k}, t)$ for large values of t can be obtained by means of the techniques outlined in Section 2.14.

Assuming that the singularities of the function,

$$\Phi(\mathbf{k}, \lambda) = N(\mathbf{k}, \lambda)/D(k, \lambda)$$

are poles of the first order and that the residues of the function

$$\Phi(\mathbf{k}, \lambda) \exp(-i\lambda t)$$

at these poles do not vanish, we may move the path of integration into the lower half plane taking care that no poles are crossed in this procedure. In this manner we obtain the new path of integration Ω of Figure

VII-2. As we have found in Section 2.14, in the limit of large values of t, the function,

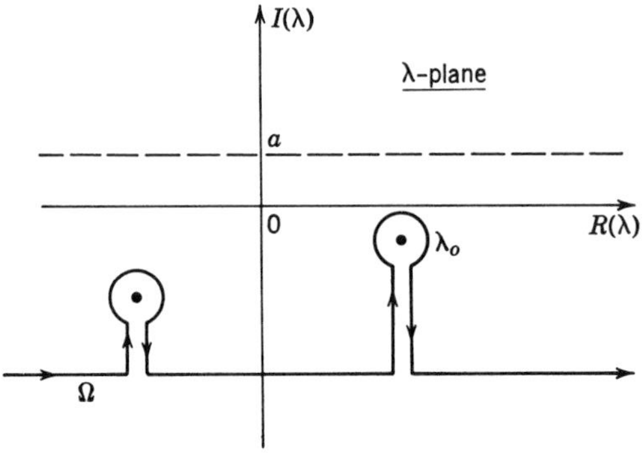

Figure VII-2

$$\phi(\mathbf{k}, t) = \frac{1}{\sqrt{(2\pi)}} \int_{\Omega} \frac{N(\mathbf{k}, \zeta)}{D(k, \zeta)} e^{-i\zeta t} \, d\zeta$$

has the asymptotic behavior

$$\phi(\mathbf{k}, t) \sim e^{-i\lambda_0(k)t}$$

where $\lambda_0(k)$ is the root of the dispersion equation,

$$D(k, \lambda) = 0$$

located closest to the line $I(\lambda) = a$.

Thus, after a sufficiently long time, the field performs harmonic oscillations of exponentially decreasing, steady, or exponentially growing amplitude. The frequency of the oscillations is $\omega_0(k)$ and the rate of decrease or increase of the amplitude is given by the exponent $\gamma_0(k)$. For, as $\gamma_0(k)$ becomes larger in absolute magnitude, the rate of decay or growth of the oscillations becomes greater. We shall call $\gamma_0(k)$ the amplification exponent.

If the amplification exponent $\gamma_0(k)$ is a positive number, the oscillations in the field are exponentially growing and we shall say that the equilibrium velocity distribution is unstable against self-excitation by plasma oscillations.

If the root $\gamma_0(k)$is located on the real axis and the amplification exponent vanishes, steady sinusoidal oscillations of frequency $\omega_0(k)$ will be observed after a sufficiently long time.

Finally, if $\gamma_0(k)$ is a negative number and all the zeros of the dielectric function are located in the lower half of the complex plane, then, after sufficiently long times, the field is exponentially damped. In this latter case, and when $\gamma_0(k)$ vanishes, the equilibrium velocity distribution is said to be stable against self-excitation by plasma oscillations. In both of these situations, the equilibrium velocity distribution cannot support exponentially growing plasma oscillations.

The exponential damping of the field, observed when all the roots of the dispersion equation are located in the lower half of the complex λ-plane, is called Landau damping, after Landau who was the first to call attention to this phenomenon.

The reason why the equation $D(k, \lambda) = 0$ is called the dispersion equation is now also clear. For, a root of this equation, the "complex frequency" $\lambda(k) = \omega(k) + i\gamma(k)$, is in general a function of the wave number k, and if the real part of λ, the physical frequency $\omega(k)$, depends on k, the group velocity does not vanish and we observe a dispersive type of wave propagation.

It should be emphasized that the conclusions drawn above are vitally linked to the assumption that the initial distribution is the restriction to the real axis of a function that is analytic in the whole complex velocity plane. We shall call this assumption the Landau assumption or Landau condition. If the initial perturbation satisfies the Landau condition, then the singularities of the function

$$\Phi(\mathbf{k}, \lambda) = \frac{N(\mathbf{k}, \lambda)}{D(k, \lambda)}$$

are determined by the zeros of the dielectric function only.

To obtain a series representation of the amplitude of the scalar potential,

$$\phi(\mathbf{k}, t) = \frac{1}{\sqrt{(2\pi)}} \int_{-\infty+ib}^{\infty+ib} \Phi(\mathbf{k}, \zeta) e^{-i\zeta t}\, d\zeta$$

which is valid for all times, and not only asymptotically, we consider the function,

$$\phi(\mathbf{k}, t \,|\, R) = \frac{1}{\sqrt{(2\pi)}} \int_{-R+ib}^{R+ib} \Phi(\mathbf{k}, \zeta) e^{-i\zeta t}\, d\zeta$$

Closing the path of integration $(-R + ib, R + ib)$ in the lower half plane by a semicircle CR of radius R and center at the point $(0, b)$, we find

$$\frac{1}{\sqrt{(2\pi)}} \oint_C \Phi(\mathbf{k}, \zeta) e^{-i\zeta t}\, d\zeta = 2\pi i \sum_m \operatorname{Res}\left[\frac{N(\mathbf{k}, \lambda)}{D(k, \lambda)} \frac{e^{-i\lambda t}}{\sqrt{(2\pi)}}, \lambda = \lambda_m\right]$$

where λ_m denotes a pole of the function $\Phi(\mathbf{k}, \lambda) = N(\mathbf{k}, \lambda)/D(k, \lambda)$ enclosed by the contour C, which consists of the path $(-R + ib, R + ib)$ and the semicircle CR, shown in Figure VII-3. Supposing that the contribution of this semicircle

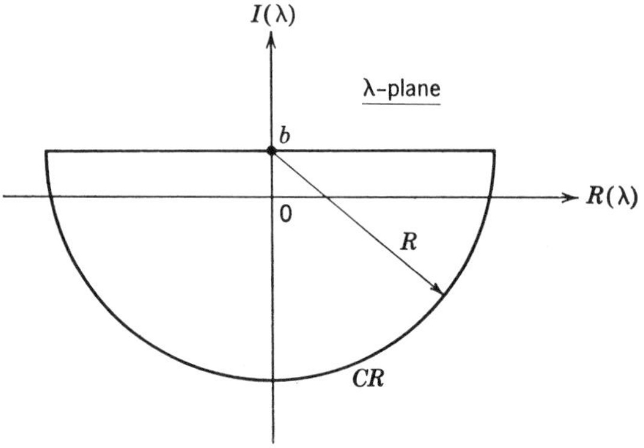

Figure VII-3

to the contour integral vanishes in the limit as R tends to infinity, we obtain a series representation of the amplitude of the potential,

$$\phi(\mathbf{k}, t) = \lim_{R \to \infty} \phi(\mathbf{k}, t \mid R) = -2\pi i \sum_m \operatorname{Res}\left[\frac{N(\mathbf{k}, \lambda)}{D(k, \lambda)} \frac{e^{-i\lambda t}}{\sqrt{(2\pi)}}, \lambda = \lambda_m\right]$$

If the roots of the dispersion equation are reasonably widely spaced, and if there is one root of greatest imaginary part, then we find that after sufficiently long times one of the modes will overpower all other modes in the expansion and we may draw the same conclusions, about steady state, damped, or growing plasma oscillations, as before.

We note therefore that, under the Landau assumptions about the analyticity of the initial perturbation in the equilibrium velocity distribution, the natural frequencies of the field can be found as the roots of a dispersion equation,

$$D(k, \lambda) = 0$$

and a prediction as to whether the plasma will exhibit damped, steady state, or growing oscillations can be based on the location of these roots in the complex plane. It is interesting to note that each wave number can give rise to many roots of the dispersion equation and that there can be many different frequencies corresponding to the same wave number.

Several papers have been written in which the authors have tried, although generally adhering to the same mathematical techniques as the ones used by Landau, to obtain the solution of the initial value problem under mathematically less stringent conditions on the functions involved and to place Landau's conclusions on a mathematically more rigorous foundation.

Outstanding among these is the paper written by Backus in which a rigorous justification of Landau's transform technique has been presented. Tracing the Landau solution in detail, Backus obtained rigorous proofs of the following statements.

1. In an equilibrium velocity distribution, which has an integrable derivative, there are no perturbations $f(\mathbf{k}, v, t)$ which have a growth rate larger than the plasma frequency. In other words, no disturbance in the electron distribution can grow faster than exp $(\omega_p t)$. This implies that all the solutions of the initial value problem grow sufficiently slow to have unilateral Fourier transforms with respect to time and that the transform technique is applicable.

2. Assuming that the initial perturbation $g(\mathbf{k}, v)$ in an equilibrium velocity distribution with an integrable derivative is integrable, Landau's expression for the solution $f(\mathbf{k}, v, t)$ of the initial value problem is correct and $f(\mathbf{k}, v, 0) = g(\mathbf{k}, v)$.

3. Landau's assumptions about the analyticity of the continuations of the equilibrium distribution and the initial perturbation off the real axis are sufficient but not necessary conditions.

According to Backus, a differentiable equilibrium velocity distribution is stable against self-excitation by plasma oscillations if the integral of the absolute value of the amplitude $f(\mathbf{k}, v, t)$ of the perturbation in the equilibrium distribution,

$$\int_{-\infty}^{\infty} |f(\mathbf{k}, v, t)| \, dv$$

is bounded for all times. This criterion for stability should be contrasted with Landau's criterion in which the requirement for stability is that the amplitude of the potential,

$$\phi(\mathbf{k}, t) = \frac{e}{\varepsilon_0 k^2} \int_{-\infty}^{\infty} f(\mathbf{k}, v, t) \, dv$$

is bounded for all times. Thus, the condition that the amplitude of the perturbation should be integrable is replaced by the condition that the amplitude of the perturbation should be absolutely integrable.

The criterion for stability of Backus seems to be preferable to Landau's criterion for the following reasons.

First, if the integral of the absolute value of the function $f(\mathbf{k}, v, t)$ vanishes, then the perturbation $f(\mathbf{k}, v, t)$ must be zero. This is not true in Landau's criterion, for the amplitude of the potential $\phi(\mathbf{k}, t)$ can be zero even when the amplitude of the perturbation $f(\mathbf{k}, v, t)$ is large with respect to the equilibrium distribution.

Second, the criterion of Backus has the mathematical significance that if the integral of the absolute value of the amplitude of the initial perturbation is bounded, then the initial value equation for $f(\mathbf{k}, v, t)$ has a unique solution and the integral of $|f(\mathbf{k}, v, t)|$ is bounded for all times. Based on this definition of stability, Backus was able to obtain a rigorous proof of the following assertion of Landau:

If the dispersion equation,

$$D(\lambda, k) = 1 - \frac{\omega_p{}^2}{k^2} \int_{-\infty}^{\infty} \frac{df_0(v)}{dv} \frac{dv}{v - \lambda/k} \tag{7.26}$$

has simple zeros in the upper half of the complex λ-plane or multiple zeros on the real axis, and if the initial perturbation is the restriction to the real axis of a function that is analytic in a strip about the real axis in the complex velocity plane, then the equilibrium distribution $f_0(v)$, having an integrable derivative, is unstable against self-excitation by plasma oscillations.

Backus proved moreover that if the initial perturbation $g(\mathbf{k}, v)$ and the derivative $df_0(v)/dv$ of the equilibrium distribution are integrable and integrable square and the dispersion equation (7.26) has no roots in the upper half of the complex λ-plane and has zeros on the real axis that are at most of first order, then the equilibrium velocity distribution $f_0(v)$ is stable. However, if the initial perturbation $g(\mathbf{k}, v)$ is integrable but not integrable square, then under the same conditions the distribution $f_0(v)$ can be unstable.

The physical interpretation of these statements is that the equilibrium velocity distribution can support growing plasma oscillations when the dispersion equation has roots in the upper half of the complex plane. However, if the dispersion equation has no roots in the upper half of the complex plane, then a differentiable equilibrium velocity distribution with a sufficiently smooth derivative is stable against excitation by sufficiently smooth initial disturbances. Moreover, if we smooth the initial disturbance, equilibrium velocity distributions with rough derivatives may move into the stable group and vice versa.

Landau's analytical observation of exponentially damped or growing plasma oscillations depends strongly on his supposition that the equilibrium velocity distribution and the initial perturbation are the restriction to the real axis of functions that are analytic in the whole complex velocity plane. In the recent literature on the subject the following two objections have been voiced against this assumption:

1. The assumption is unphysical. For, so one argues, how can one explain the unphysical notion that the behavior of the electric field is influenced by the behavior of electron distribution functions off the real axis.

2. The assumption is unnecessarily restrictive. In other words, one can show the existence of Landau damping, or for that matter the existence of damping much slower or much faster than the exponentially fast Landau damping, under much weaker conditions on the distribution functions.

We are inclined to disregard the first objection. For, since there are distribution functions that are the restriction to the real axis of entire functions, there is no reason why we should not make use of this fact to prove mathematically, at least for this type of distribution, the existence of Landau damping. It is true, as has been stated by Weitzner, that analyticity is usually found to be an "accessory after the fact" and to support this statement Weitzner calls attention to two examples, one from the field of potential theory and the other from the field of scattering theory. However it is also true, as has been stated recently by Källén, that analyticity may have definite physical connotations. In a paper on analyticity in quantum electrodynamics, Källén shows that an, on first sight mathematically merely expedient, analytic continuation of a physical quantity off the real axis into the complex plane can have a definite physical interpretation. At the hand of an example, he shows that the particular continuation is equivalent to an average over space and time of the quantity involved. He shows, moreover, that in this particular case the points off the real axis are physically more significant than the points on the real axis. In the context of his example, this is a paradoxical statement that runs contrary to the conventional nomenclature of that field in which points on the real axis are called "physical" and points off the real axis are called "unphysical."

Weitzner has shown that the second objection against Landau's assumption of analyticity, namely, the objection that this assumption is too restrictive, is certainly valid and he arrived at some highly interesting conclusions in the process. He has shown, for the case of a Maxwellian equilibrium velocity distribution, that the amplitude of the potential of the self-consistent field will vanish much slower than an exponential if we abandon the assumption that the initial perturbation is the restriction to the real axis of an entire function in favor of the imposition of some milder conditions on this function.

For example, let us assume that the equilibrium velocity distribution $f_0(v)$ is nonvanishing on the whole real v-axis and has derivatives that vanish at a finite number of points only.

Now let us consider the functions $F(k, \lambda)$ and $G(\mathbf{k}, \lambda)$ defined as analytic functions in the upper half plane, $I(\lambda) \geqq 0$, by the integrals,

$$F(k, \lambda) = \int_{-\infty}^{\infty} \frac{df_0(v)}{dv} \frac{dv}{v - \lambda/k}$$

and

$$G(\mathbf{k}, \lambda) = \frac{1}{2\pi i}\int_{-\infty}^{\infty} \frac{g(\mathbf{k}, v)}{v - \lambda/k}\, dv$$

We now assume that the equilibrium velocity distribution $f_0(v)$ and the amplitude of the initial perturbation $g(\mathbf{k}, v)$ are sufficiently smooth and vanish sufficiently fast when v tends to plus or minus infinity so that $F(k, \lambda) = O(1/\lambda^2)$ and $G(\mathbf{k}, \lambda) = O(1/\lambda)$ when λ tends to infinity in the upper half plane $I(\lambda) \geqq 0$, and the derivatives $\partial F/\partial\lambda$ and $\partial G/\partial\lambda$ are absolutely integrable. Imposition of simple differentiability and Hölder continuity conditions on the functions $df_0(v)/dv$ and $g(\mathbf{k}, v)$ and some limitations on their growth is sufficient for our purpose. We assume, moreover, that the function

$$D(k, \lambda) = 1 - (\omega_p{}^2/k^2)F(k, \lambda)$$

has no zeros in the upper half plane including the real axis. We consider the inversion integral,

$$\phi(\mathbf{k}, t) = \frac{1}{\sqrt{(2\pi)}}\int_{-\infty}^{\infty} \frac{N(\mathbf{k}, \omega)}{D(k, \omega)}\, e^{-i\omega t}\, d\omega$$

where we have moved the path of integration to the real axis. Integration by parts yields the expression,

$$\phi(\mathbf{k}, t) = \frac{1}{it\sqrt{(2\pi)}}\int_{-\infty}^{\infty} \frac{\partial}{\partial\omega}\left[\frac{N(\mathbf{k}, \omega)}{D(k, \omega)}\right] e^{-i\omega t}\, d\omega$$

The integrand is absolutely integrable and therefore, by the Riemann-Lebesgue lemma of Section 2.5 the integral is smaller than some small positive number for sufficiently large values of t. This implies that the potential is at most of the order of $1/t$ when t tends to infinity and that the damping is only as fast as $1/t$ instead of exponentially fast. Thus, we find that imposition of milder conditions on the initial perturbation leads to damping that is much slower than the exponentially fast damping found by Landau under the condition that the initial perturbation is the restriction to the real axis of an entire function.

As an example, let us consider the effect on the potential of the self-consistent field when we superimpose an initial perturbation of the form,

$$\begin{aligned} g(k, v) &= (v - v_0)^2 e^{-(v-v_0)^2} \qquad && v > v_0 \\ &= 0 && v \leqq v_0 \end{aligned}$$

where v_0 is an arbitrary real number, on a Maxwellian equilibrium velocity distribution. In this case, the integral,

$$G(k, \lambda) = \frac{1}{2\pi i}\int_{v_0}^{\infty} \frac{(v - v_0)^2 e^{-(v-v_0)^2}}{v - \lambda/k}\, dv$$

is the representation of a sectionally analytic function with a boundary path (v_0, ∞). On the boundary, the left and right boundary values of this function are related by the Plemelj formula,

$$G^L(\omega) - G^R(\omega) = \frac{1}{k^2}(\omega - \omega_0)^2 e^{-(\omega-\omega_0)^2/k^2}$$

where $\omega = vk$ and $\omega_0 = v_0 k$. We now consider the contour integral,

$$\frac{1}{\sqrt{(2\pi)}} \oint_C \frac{N(\mathbf{k}, \zeta)}{D(k, \zeta)} e^{-i\zeta t} \, d\zeta$$

where C denotes the rectangular contour shown in Figure VII-4 and the

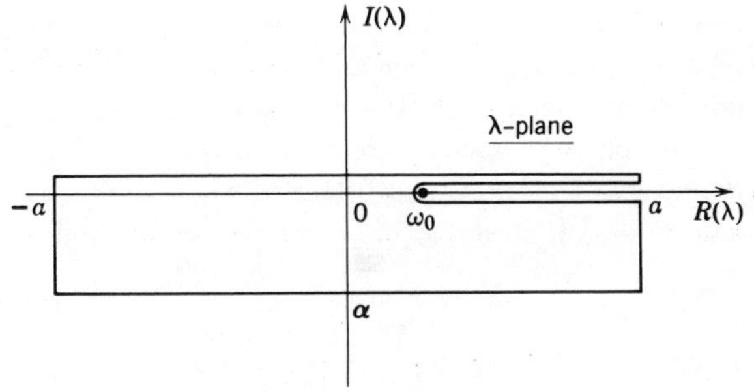

Figure VII-4

small negative number α has been chosen so that no zeros of the dielectric function are located inside or on C. As we shall find in Section 7.7, this is always possible provided the equilibrium velocity distribution is Maxwellian. For in that case we can show that the roots of the dispersion equation are all located in the lower half of the complex λ-plane and that for each value of k there is a root with a greatest imaginary part. In the limit as a tends to infinity we find,

$$\frac{1}{\sqrt{(2\pi)}} \oint_C \frac{N(\mathbf{k}, \zeta)}{D(k, \zeta)} e^{-i\zeta t} \, d\zeta$$

$$= \frac{1}{\sqrt{(2\pi)}} \int_{-\infty + i\alpha}^{\infty + i\alpha} \frac{N(\mathbf{k}, \zeta)}{D(k, \zeta)} e^{-i\zeta t} \, d\zeta + \frac{1}{\sqrt{(2\pi)}} \int_{\infty}^{-\infty} \frac{N(\mathbf{k}, \omega)}{D(k, \omega)} e^{-i\omega t} \, d\omega$$

$$+ \frac{1}{\sqrt{(2\pi)}} \int_{\infty}^{\omega_0} \frac{N^R(\mathbf{k}, \omega)}{D(k, \omega)} e^{-i\omega t} \, d\omega + \frac{1}{\sqrt{(2\pi)}} \int_{\omega_0}^{\infty} \frac{N^L(\mathbf{k}, \omega)}{D(k, \omega)} e^{-i\omega t} \, d\omega = 0$$

Consequently, we may write, for large values of t,

$$\phi(\mathbf{k}, t) = \frac{1}{\sqrt{(2\pi)}} \int_{-\infty}^{\infty} \frac{N(\mathbf{k}, \omega)}{D(k, \omega)} e^{-i\omega t} \, d\omega$$

$$= \sqrt{(2\pi)} \frac{e}{\varepsilon_0 k^5} \int_{\omega_0}^{\infty} \frac{(\omega - \omega_0)^2 e^{-(\omega-\omega_0)^2/k^2}}{D(k, \omega)} e^{-i\omega t} \, d\omega + O(e^{-\alpha t})$$

Three successive integrations by parts now yield the relation,

$$\phi(\mathbf{k}, t) = \sqrt{(2\pi)} \frac{2ie}{\varepsilon_0 k^5} \frac{e^{-i\omega_0 t}}{D(k, \omega_0)} \frac{1}{t^3} + O(1/t^4) + O(e^{-\alpha t})$$

Thus, perturbing a Maxwellian velocity distribution with the initial disturbance $g(k, v)$ defined above, we observe, after a sufficiently long time, damped sinusoidal oscillations with frequency ω_0 in the field. The oscillations moreover are not exponentially damped but are damped with a damping factor which goes like $1/t^3$.

Other interesting results have been obtained by Weitzner for the case in which the equilibrium velocity distribution and the initial perturbation vanish identically for all particle speeds greater than some given cutoff speed $v = v_0 = \omega_0/k$ and smaller than the cutoff speed $v = -v_0 = -\omega_0/k$. Assuming that the functions $df_0(v)/dv$ and $g(\mathbf{k}, v)$ are continuously differentiable the integrals,

$$F(k, \lambda) = \int_{-v_0}^{v_0} \frac{df_0(v)}{dv} \frac{dv}{v - \lambda/k}$$

and

$$G(\mathbf{k}, \lambda) = \frac{1}{2\pi i} \int_{-v_0}^{v_0} \frac{g(\mathbf{k}, v)}{v - \lambda/k} \, dv$$

are the representations of functions $F(k, \lambda)$ and $G(\mathbf{k}, \lambda)$ which are sectionally analytic and have the boundary $(-\omega_0, \omega_0)$ in the complex λ-plane. The function $G(\mathbf{k}, \lambda)$ is at most of the order of $1/\lambda$ when λ tends to infinity in the upper half plane, whereas an integration by parts shows that the function,

$$F(k, \lambda) = \int_{-v_0}^{v_0} \frac{f_0(v)}{(v - \lambda/k)^2} \, dv$$

vanishes as $1/\lambda^2$ when λ tends to infinity in this half plane. Now let us assume that $f_0(v)$ is an even equilibrium velocity distribution. The dispersion equation,

$$D(k, \lambda) = 1 - \frac{\omega_p^2}{k^2} F(k, \lambda)$$

will have roots in the upper half of the complex λ-plane, including the real axis, if the value of the function $F(k, \lambda)$ at the point $\lambda = \omega_0$ is greater than the positive number $k^2/\omega_p{}^2$. For the function $F(k, \lambda)$ is real and positive for all values of λ on the intervals $-\infty < \omega < -\omega_0$ and $\omega_0 < \omega < \infty$. Furthermore, $F(k, \lambda)$ is continuous and increases monotonically from zero to $F(k, -\omega_0)$ on the interval $-\infty < \omega \leq -\omega_0$ and decreases monotonically from $F(k, \omega_0)$ to zero on the interval $\omega_0 \leqq \omega < \infty$, as has been sketched in Figure VII-5.

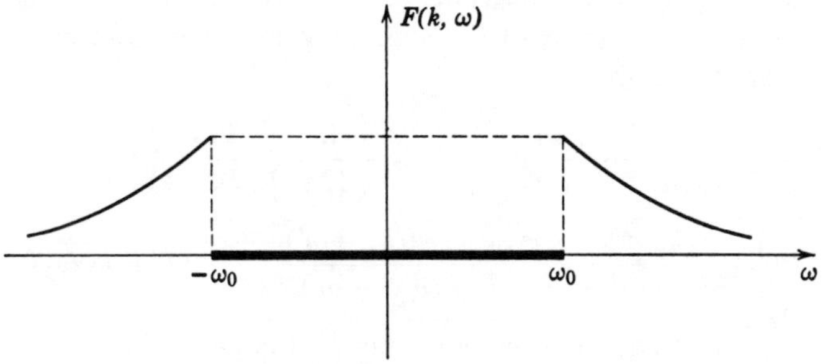

Figure VII-5

If $\lambda = \omega'$ is a root of the dispersion equation located on the interval $\omega_0 < \omega < \infty$, then

$$F(k, \omega') = k^2/\omega_p{}^2 = F(k, -\omega')$$

However, we have just shown that $F(k, \omega')$ must be smaller than $F(k, \omega_0)$ and thus $F(k, \omega_0)$ must be larger than $k^2/\omega_p{}^2$. Now let us consider the contour integral,

$$\frac{1}{\sqrt{(2\pi)}} \oint_C \frac{N(\mathbf{k}, \zeta)}{D(k, \zeta)} e^{-i\zeta t} \, d\zeta$$

where C denotes the contour of Figure VII-6. According to the residue

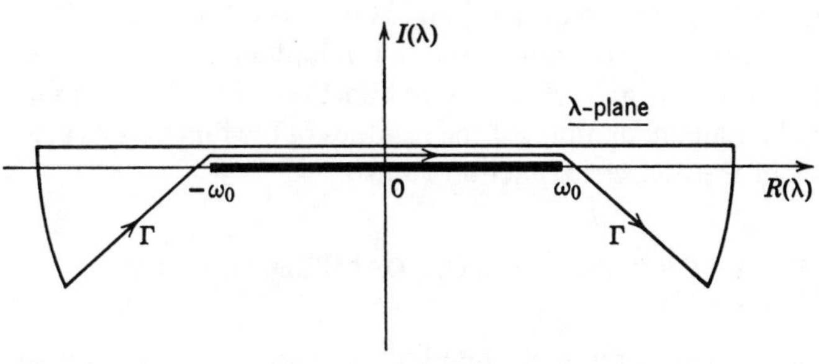

Figure VII-6

theorem of Section 1.3, we may write

$$\frac{1}{\sqrt{(2\pi)}}\oint_C \frac{N(\mathbf{k},\zeta)}{D(k,\zeta)}e^{-i\zeta t}\,d\zeta = 2\pi i\sum \text{Res}\left[\frac{N(\mathbf{k},\lambda)}{D(k,\lambda)}\frac{e^{-i\lambda t}}{\sqrt{(2\pi)}},\ \text{zeros of } D(k,\lambda)\right]$$

$$= 2\pi i\left[\frac{N(\mathbf{k},\omega')}{\partial D(k,\omega')/\partial\lambda}\frac{e^{-i\omega' t}}{\sqrt{(2\pi)}} + \frac{N(\mathbf{k},-\omega')}{\partial D(k,-\omega')/\partial\lambda}\frac{e^{+i\omega' t}}{\sqrt{(2\pi)}}\right]\theta[F(k,\omega_0) - k^2/\omega_p{}^2]$$

where θ denotes the unit step function. The contributions to the contour integral of the circular parts of the contour vanish when R tends to infinity and we obtain therefore

$$\phi(\mathbf{k},t) = \frac{1}{\sqrt{(2\pi)}}\int_{-\infty}^{\infty}\frac{N(\mathbf{k},\omega)}{D(k,\omega)}e^{-i\omega t}\,d\omega = \frac{1}{\sqrt{(2\pi)}}\int_\Gamma \frac{N(\mathbf{k},\zeta)}{D(k,\zeta)}e^{-i\zeta t}\,d\zeta$$

$$- i\sqrt{(2\pi)}\left[\frac{N(k,\omega')}{\partial D(k,\omega')/\partial\lambda}e^{-i\omega' t} + \frac{N(\mathbf{k},-\omega')}{\partial D(k,-\omega')/\partial\lambda}e^{i\omega' t}\right]\theta[F(k,\omega_0) - k^2/\omega_p{}^2]$$

If the dispersion equation has no roots on the interval $\omega_0 < \omega < \infty$, and $F(k, \omega_0)$ is smaller then $k^2/\omega_p{}^2$, then the θ function vanishes and the amplitude of the potential of the self-consistent field has the integral representation,

$$\phi(\mathbf{k},t) = \frac{1}{\sqrt{(2\pi)}}\int_\Gamma \frac{N(\mathbf{k},\zeta)}{D(k,\zeta)}e^{-i\zeta t}\,d\zeta$$

Supposing the equilibrium velocity distribution and the amplitude of the initial perturbation are sufficiently smooth, we can show, in a similar manner as before, that the potential is at most of the order of $1/t^m$ when t tends to infinity, where m is some positive integer depending on the smoothness properties of the functions $f_0(v)$ and $g(\mathbf{k}, v)$. However, if $F(k, \omega_0)$ is larger than $k^2/\omega_p{}^2$, and the dispersion equation has a root on the interval $\omega_0 < \omega < \infty$, then, after a sufficiently long time, we find steady state plasma oscillations with the frequency ω'.

Finally we should note that we can also have damping that is faster than the exponentially fast Landau damping. Hayes has shown, for a Maxwellian equilibrium velocity distribution and an initial disturbance which is the restriction to the real axis of an entire function, that the damping can be faster than the Landau damping if the residues of the function $N(\mathbf{k}, \lambda)/D(k, \lambda)$ at the zeros of the dielectric function vanish.

7.5 CRITERIA FOR GROWING OR DAMPED PLASMA OSCILLATIONS

As we have noted in the preceding section, from the Landau assumptions about the analyticity of the equilibrium velocity distribution and the amplitude of the initial disturbance, we may infer that the singular behavior of the unilateral transform of the amplitude of the potential function,

$$\Phi(\mathbf{k}, \lambda) = \frac{N(\mathbf{k}, \lambda)}{D(k, \lambda)}$$

is determined exclusively by the roots of the dispersion equation,

$$D(k, \lambda) = 1 - \frac{\omega_p{}^2}{k^2} \int_\Gamma \frac{df_0(v)}{dv} \frac{dv}{v - \lambda/k} = 0$$

Physically this means that the answer to the question whether or not the equilibrium distribution can support exponentially growing, steady state, or exponentially damped plasma oscillations depends on the sign of the imaginary part of the complex phase velocity λ/k; in other words, on the location of the roots of the dispersion equation in the complex plane.

It is interesting to note that some criteria exist which enable us to determine, on the basis of a rather superficial knowledge of the analytic behavior of the equilibrium velocity distribution, whether or not the dispersion equation has roots in the upper half of the complex plane. In other words, we can determine whether or not a given equilibrium distribution can support growing plasma oscillations without actually solving the dispersion equation.

In this section we shall present an outline of some of the better known criteria.

A. Jackson's Criterion for Bell-Shaped Equilibrium Velocity Distributions

Let us assume that the unperturbed velocity distribution $f_0(v)$ is bell-shaped with a single maximum at the point $v = v_m$, as shown in Figure VII-7. The derivative of this function is positive for all values of v smaller than the speed v_m, at which it crosses the v-axis, and negative for all values of v larger than the speed v_m. If λ_0 is a root of the dispersion equation, we may write

$$\int_\Gamma \frac{df_0(v)}{dv} \frac{dv}{v - \lambda_0/k} = \frac{k^2}{\omega_p{}^2}$$

where Γ denotes the Landau contour.

Now let us assume that the root $\lambda_0 = \omega_0 + i\gamma_0$ has a positive imaginary part. In this case the Landau contour may be taken to coincide with the real axis and we find

$$\int_{-\infty}^{\infty} \frac{df_0(v)}{dv} \frac{dv}{v - \lambda_0/k} = \frac{k^2}{\omega_p{}^2}$$

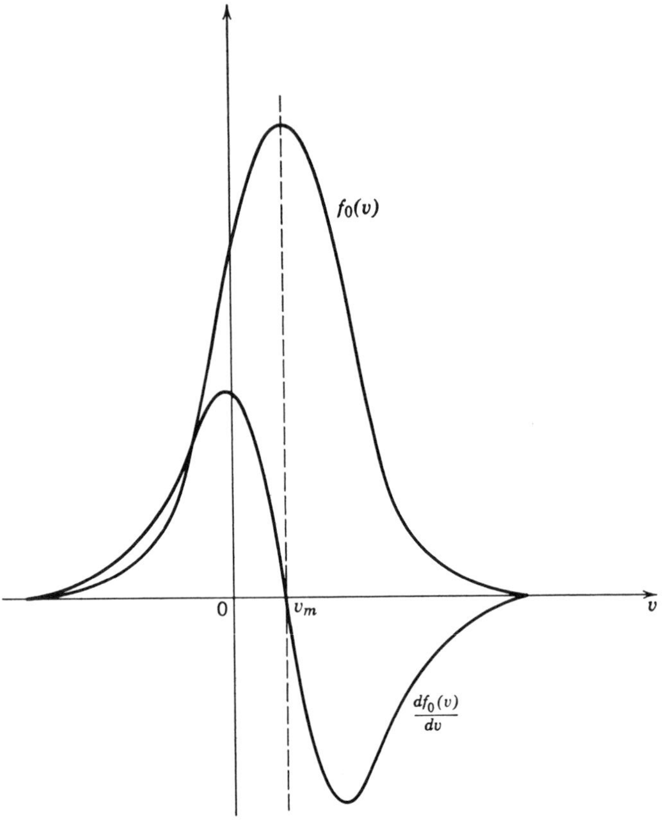

Figure VII-7

Decomposing this equation into its real and imaginary parts, we may also write

$$\int_{-\infty}^{\infty} \frac{df_0(v)}{dv} \frac{v - \omega_0/k}{(v - \omega_0/k)^2 + \gamma_0{}^2/k^2}\, dv = \frac{k^2}{\omega_p{}^2}$$

and

$$\int_{-\infty}^{\infty} \frac{df_0(v)}{dv} \frac{1}{(v - \omega_0/k)^2 + \gamma_0{}^2/k^2}\, dv = 0$$

If we multiply the second of the last two equations by the factor $(v_m - \omega_0/k)$ and subtract the result from the first equation, we find

$$\int_{-\infty}^{\infty} \frac{df_0(v)}{dv} \frac{v - v_m}{(v - \omega_0/k)^2 + \gamma_0{}^2/k^2}\, dv = \frac{k^2}{\omega_p{}^2}$$

Because of the behavior of the functions $df_0(v)/dv$ and $(v - v_m)$, the integrand is negative definite over the whole integration interval and the integral must have a negative value therefore. This conclusion contradicts the fact that the right hand side of the equation is a positive quantity, and our assumption about the sign of the imaginary part of the root λ_0 must be in error. Hence, if $f_0(v)$ is a bell-shaped equilibrium velocity distribution, then the dispersion equation,

$$D(k, \lambda) = 1 - \frac{\omega_p{}^2}{k^2} \int_\Gamma \frac{df_0(v)}{dv} \frac{dv}{v - \lambda/k} = 0$$

will have no roots in the upper half of the complex λ-plane.

There is no danger that we shall also obtain a contradiction when we start our argument with the assumption that the root λ_0 is located in the lower half plane. For in this case, the Landau contour cannot be taken to coincide with the real axis and the dispersion equation takes the form,

$$\int_\Gamma \frac{df_0(v)}{dv} \frac{dv}{v - \lambda/k} = \int_{-\infty}^{\infty} \frac{df_0(v)}{dv} \frac{dv}{v - \omega/k} + 2\pi i \frac{df_0(\lambda/k)}{dv} = \frac{k^2}{\omega_p{}^2}$$

The additional term, $2\pi i[df_0(\lambda/k)/dv]$, invalidates our proof by contradiction.

Thus, we have derived the following criterion valid for bell-shaped equilibrium velocity distributions.

Criterion of Jackson: A bell-shaped equilibrium velocity distribution cannot support growing plasma oscillations and is stable for disturbances satisfying the Landau condition.

The most useful example of such a bell-shaped distribution is a Maxwellian. Hence, a small perturbation, which is the restriction to the real axis of an entire function, in a Maxwellian equilibrium distribution does not lead to oscillations that grow exponentially with time. In other words, if the initial disturbance satisfies the Landau condition, then the uniform state described by a Maxwellian velocity distribution is stable against self-excitation by plasma oscillations.

B. Penrose's Criterion for Non-Maxwellian Equilibrium Velocity Distributions

In the preceding section, we have shown by means of Jackson's criterion that bell-shaped zero-order velocity distributions cannot support exponentially growing plasma oscillations and that the oscillations set up in such a distribution by a small perturbation, which is the restriction to the real axis of an entire function, are either steady state or exponentially damped oscillations.

In this section we shall consider Penrose's criterion. This criterion can be used to determine whether or not a more arbitrary equilibrium velocity distribution will lead to roots of the dispersion equation which are located in the upper half plane and thus to perturbations in the equilibrium distribution that can grow exponentially with time.

Penrose's criterion is based on the following observation. If the dispersion equation,

$$D(k, \lambda) = 1 - \frac{\omega_p^{\,2}}{k^2} \int_\Gamma \frac{df_0(v)}{dv} \frac{dv}{v - \lambda/k} = 0$$

has a root λ_0 in the upper half of the complex λ-plane, then the function,

$$F(k, \lambda) = \int_{-\infty}^{\infty} \frac{df_0(v)}{dv} \frac{dv}{v - \lambda/k}$$

takes on a positive value,

$$F(k, \lambda_0) = k^2/\omega_p^{\,2}$$

for that particular value λ_0. Conversely therefore, if the function $F(k, \lambda)$ is positive for values of λ in the upper half plane, then there exists a wave number k,

$$k = \omega_p \sqrt{F(k, \lambda_0)}$$

leading to exponentially growing plasma oscillations and the particular equilibrium velocity distribution considered is unstable for small perturbations satisfying the Landau condition.

To find whether or not the function $F(k, \lambda)$ is positively valued at some points in the upper half of the complex λ-plane we map the upper half of this plane into the complex w-plane by means of the transformation,

$$w = F(k, \lambda) = \int_{-\infty}^{\infty} \frac{df_0(v)}{dv} \frac{dv}{v - \lambda/k}$$

Supposing that the derivative of the equilibrium distribution function $f_0(v)$ is Hölder continuous on the finite real axis and at infinity, the left boundary value of the function $F(k, \lambda)$ may be written, according to the formula of Plemelj of Section 4.6,

$$F^L(k, \omega) = \lim_{\varepsilon \to 0} F^L(\omega + i\varepsilon) = \int_{-\infty}^{\infty} \frac{df_0(v)}{dv} \frac{dv}{v - \omega/k} + \pi i \frac{df_0(\omega/k)}{dv}$$

The sectionally analytic function $F(k, \lambda)$ is analytic in the upper half of the complex λ-plane and its left boundary value $F^L(k, \omega)$ is bounded and continuous on the real axis. Consequently, according to Section 1.3, the transformation $w = F(k, \lambda)$ maps the upper half of the complex λ-plane into the interior of a positively directed curve C which is the image in the w-plane of the real axis in the λ-plane under the transformation $w = F(k, \lambda)$. The function $F(k, \lambda)$ vanishes when λ tends to infinity in the upper half of the complex λ-plane including the real axis. Consequently, a semicircle in the upper half of the complex λ-plane of infinite radius and center at the origin is mapped into the origin of the complex w-plane. Similarly, the points at infinity on the real axis in the λ-plane are mapped into the point $w = 0$, and the curve C starts and terminates at the origin in the complex w-plane.

For example, if $f_0(v)$ is a Maxwellian the transformation,

$$w = F(k, \lambda) = \int_{-\infty}^{\infty} \frac{df_0(v)}{dv} \frac{dv}{v - \lambda/k}$$

maps the upper half of the complex λ-plane into the interior of a heart-shaped curve in the w-plane as shown in Figure VII-8. The curve C itself is the

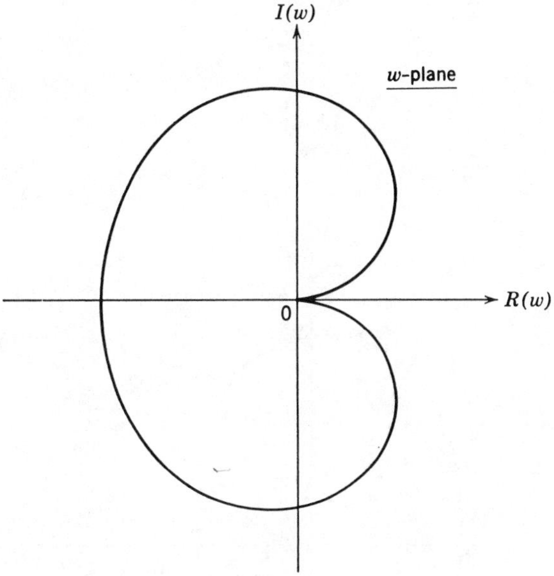

Figure VII-8

image in the w-plane of the real axis of the λ-plane.

Now let us assume that the function $F(k, \lambda)$ is positive for some value of λ in the upper half plane. The transformation $w = F(k, \lambda)$ maps this point λ onto the positive real axis in the w-plane. In this case therefore the curve C must enclose part of the positive real axis. Furthermore, remembering that the curve C is positively directed, there must be a point A, shown in Figures VII-9 and VII-10, at which the curve C crosses the real axis in the direction

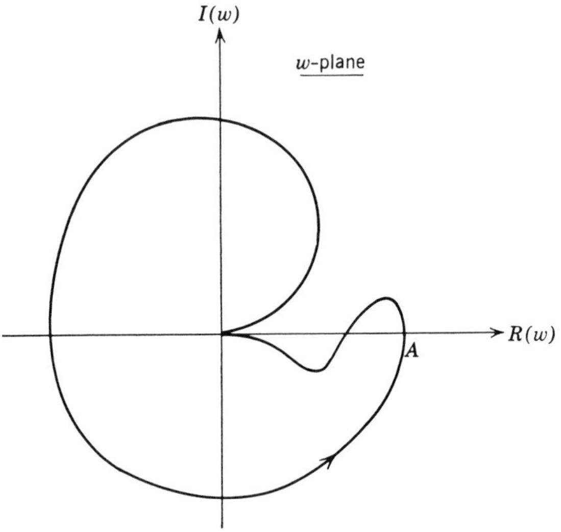

Figure VII-9

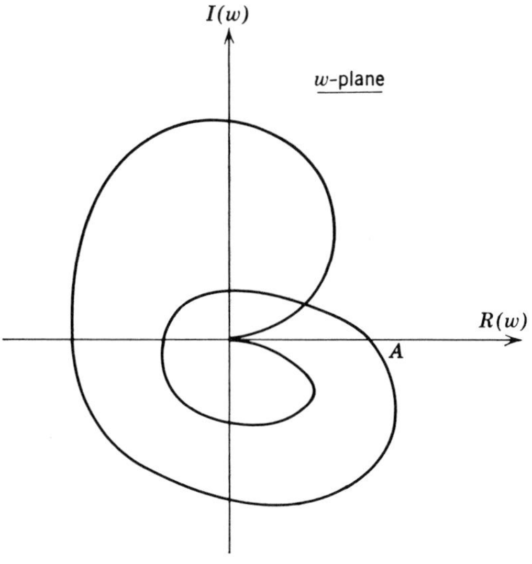

Figure VII-10

from the lower half of the complex w-plane into the upper half of the complex w-plane. However, on the curve C we have

$$w = F^L(k, \omega) = \int_{-\infty}^{\infty} \frac{df_0(v)}{dv} \frac{dv}{v - \omega/k} + \pi i \frac{df_0(\omega/k)}{dv}$$

Consequently, at a point A, the integral

$$\int_{-\infty}^{\infty} \frac{df_0(v)}{dv} \frac{dv}{v - \omega/k}$$

has a positive value, whereas the derivative $df_0(\omega/k)/dv$ vanishes and changes its sign from negative to positive. This implies that the equilibrium velocity distribution $f_0(v)$ has a minimum at the point A. Moreover, the principal value integral above may also be written

$$\begin{aligned}\int_{-\infty}^{\infty} & \frac{df_0(v)}{dv} \frac{dv}{v - \omega/k} \\ &= \lim_{\varepsilon \to 0} \left[\int_{-\infty}^{\omega/k - \varepsilon} \frac{d[f_0(v) - f_0(\omega/k)]}{v - \omega/k} + \int_{\omega/k + \varepsilon}^{\infty} \frac{d[f_0(v) - f_0(\omega/k)]}{v - \omega/k} \right] \\ &= \int_{-\infty}^{\infty} \frac{f_0(v) - f_0(\omega/k)}{(v - \omega/k)^2} \, dv\end{aligned}$$

and we may state therefore the following criterion.

Criterion of Penrose: An equilibrium velocity distribution $f_0(v)$ can support growing plasma oscillations if and only if the function $f_0(v)$ has a minimum at the point $v = \omega/k$ at which the integral,

$$\int_{-\infty}^{\infty} \frac{f_0(v) - f_0(\omega/k)}{(v - \omega/k)^2} \, dv$$

is positive.

In the case of a Maxwellian equilibrium velocity distribution, the map of the upper half of the complex λ-plane under the transformation $w = F(k, \lambda)$ is shown in Figure VII-8. Since the curve C does not enclose part of the positive real axis, we may conclude that a Maxwellian equilibrium velocity distribution cannot support growing plasma oscillations if the initial perturbation satisfies the Landau condition. We arrived at the same conclusion by means of the criterion of Jackson of the preceding section.

If the dispersion equation,

$$F(k, \lambda) = k^2/\omega_p{}^2$$

has no roots in the upper half of the complex plane, a modification of Penrose's criterion enables us to determine whether or not roots of the dispersion equation are located on the upper bank of the real axis. For in that case the curve C touches the real axis but does not cross it. We may state therefore: The dispersion equation,

$$F^L(k, \omega) = \lim_{\varepsilon \to 0} F(\omega + i\varepsilon) = k^2/\omega_p{}^2$$

has a root on the real axis but not in the upper half of the complex plane if and only if the derivatives $df_0(\omega/k)/dv$ and $d^2 f_0(\omega/k)/dv^2$ vanish at a point $v = \omega/k$ at which the integral,

$$\int_{-\infty}^{\infty} \frac{f_0(v) - f_0(\omega/k)}{(v - \omega/k)^2}\, dv$$

is positive.

C. The Criterion of Nyquist

The criterion of Nyquist is closely related to, but not identical with, the criterion of Penrose. It is based on the following properties of the function,

$$D(k, \lambda) = 1 - \frac{\omega_p{}^2}{k^2} \int_{-\infty}^{\infty} \frac{df_0(v)}{dv} \frac{dv}{v - \lambda/k}$$

when the derivative of the zero order velocity distribution function is Hölder continuous on the real axis and at infinity.

1. The function $D(k, \lambda)$ is analytic for all values of λ in the upper half of the complex plane.
2. The left boundary value of the function $D(k, \lambda)$,

$$D^L(k, \omega) = 1 - \frac{\omega_p{}^2}{k^2} \int_{-\infty}^{\infty} \frac{df_0(v)}{dv} \frac{dv}{v - \omega/k} - \pi i \frac{\omega_p{}^2}{k^2} \frac{df_0(\omega/k)}{dv}$$

   is bounded and continuous for all values of ω.
3. If λ traverses the boundary of the whole upper half of the complex λ-plane in the positive direction, then the function $D(k, \lambda)$ maps this boundary into a positively directed curve C in the complex $w = D(k, \lambda)$-plane. This curve starts and terminates at the point $w = 1$, as shown in Figure VII-12.
4. The polar angle of the vector **p**, drawn from the origin to a point on the curve C, increases by 2π when the curve C encircles the origin and does not change when C does not encircle the origin.

5. If N is the number of revolutions of the vector **p**, then, by the principle of the argument of Section 1.3, the number of zeros of the function

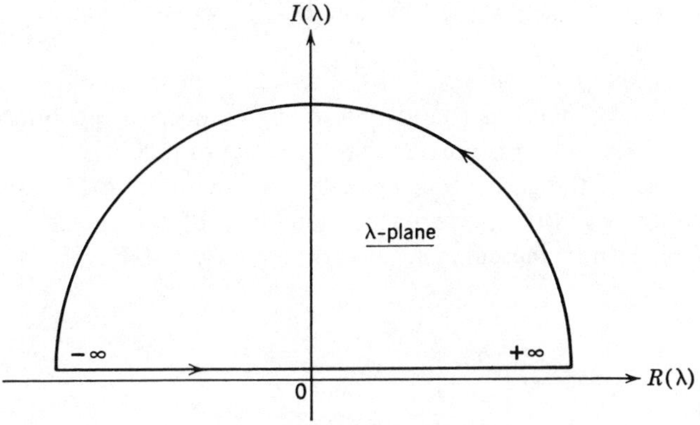

Figure VII-11

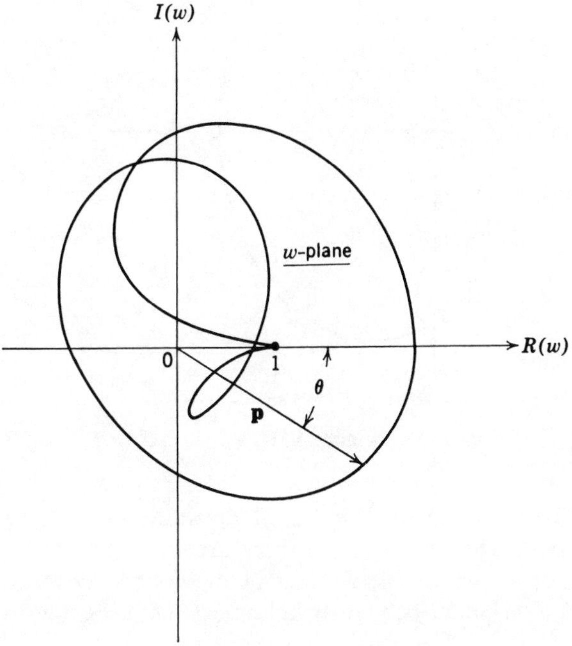

Figure VII-12

$D(k, \lambda)$ in the upper half of the complex λ-plane is equal to N. In other words, for every zero of the function $D(k, \lambda)$ in the upper half of the complex λ-plane, the vector **p** will experience one revolution about the origin in the complex w-plane.

From these properties of the function $D(k, \lambda)$ we may infer the following criterion.

Nyquist's Criterion: An equilibrium velocity distribution can support growing plasma oscillations if and only if the number of revolutions of the vector **p** about the origin is greater than or equal to one.

For example, if the zero order velocity distribution is a Maxwellian, the transformation $w = D(k, \lambda)$ maps the boundary of the upper half of the complex λ-plane into the curve C shown in Figure VII-13. This curve does

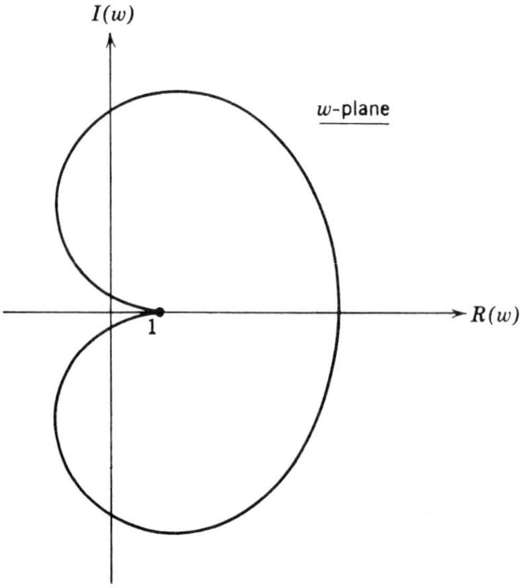

Figure VII-13

not encircle the origin and the number of revolutions of the vector **p** about the origin is zero. This implies that there are no roots of the dispersion equation $D(k, \lambda) = 0$ in the upper half of the complex λ-plane and that a Maxwellian equilibrium velocity distribution cannot support growing plasma oscillations.

Interesting numerical results have been obtained by Jackson, at the hand of the Nyquist diagram procedure, for a so-called "bump-in-tail" or two-peaked equilibrium velocity distribution, such as the one shown in Figure VII-14. Increasing the separation of the two peaks of an at first stable velocity

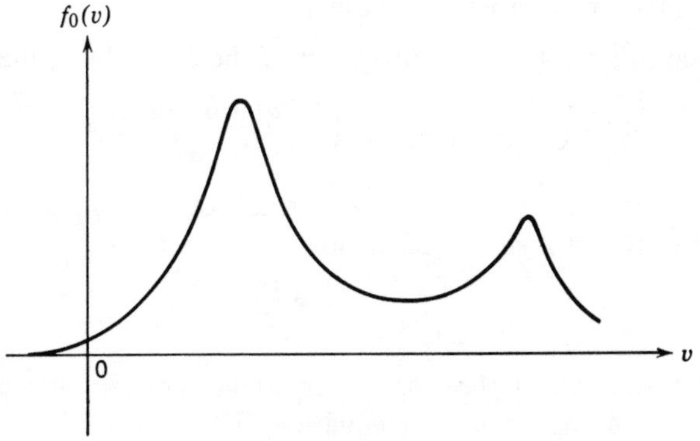

Figure VII-14

distribution, he obtained an unstable velocity distribution. This fact is demonstrated very nicely at the hand of the series of Nyquist diagrams, shown in Figure VII-15, which have been taken from Jackson's paper.

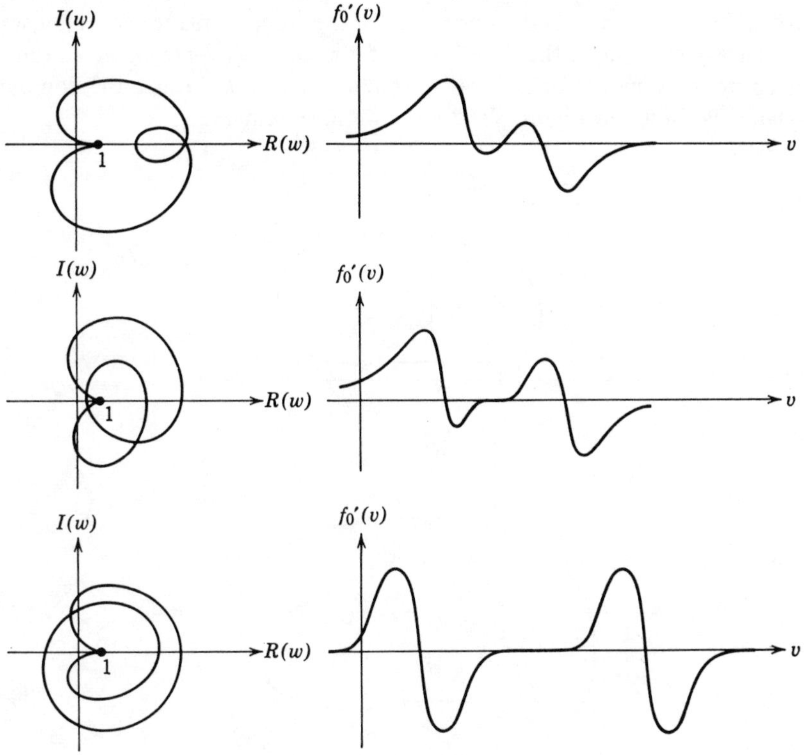

Figure VII-15

D. McGune's Exact Inversion Procedure

McGune considered the exact inversion of the dispersion equation,

$$D(k, \lambda) = 1 - \frac{\omega_p{}^2}{k^2} \int_{-\infty}^{\infty} \frac{df_0(v)}{dv} \frac{dv}{v - \lambda/k}$$

for the case when λ is a point in the upper half of the complex plane.

He observed that if λ_0 is a root of this equation, then

$$\lambda_0 = \frac{1}{2\pi i} \oint_C \zeta \frac{\partial \log D(k, \zeta)}{\partial \zeta} d\zeta$$

where the contour C, in the upper half plane, encloses the point λ_0 and no other roots of the dispersion equation. For, according to the residue theorem of Section 1.3,

$$\frac{1}{2\pi i} \oint_C \zeta \frac{\partial \log D(k, \zeta)}{\partial \zeta} d\zeta = \text{Res}\left[\zeta \frac{\partial \log D(k, \zeta)}{\partial \zeta}, \zeta = \lambda_0\right] = \lambda_0$$

This formula may be used in conjunction with the Nyquist criterion of the preceding section in a procedure to locate and actually compute the roots of the dispersion equation in the upper half of the complex plane. For, choosing an arbitrary contour in the upper half of the complex λ-plane, we can map this contour by means of the transformation $w = D(k, \lambda)$ into the complex w-plane, as shown in Figure VII-16. As we have remarked

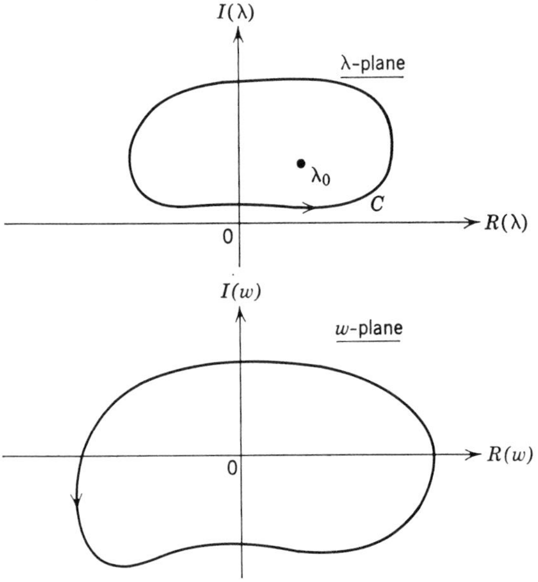

Figure VII-16

in the preceding section, the contour C encloses a root of the dispersion equation if and only if the image of this contour encloses the origin in the complex w-plane. The root itself can then be computed from McGune's formula by means of a contour integration. If it appears, from a Nyquist diagram, that the contour C encloses more than one root of the dispersion equation, i.e., if the image of the contour C encircles the origin in the w-plane more than once, we can deform the contour C until the image of the new contour encircles the origin in the w-plane only once.

7.6 LONG AND SHORT WAVE LENGTH PLASMA OSCILLATIONS

If the disturbance $g(\mathbf{k}, v)$ is the restriction to the real axis of an entire function, then, as we have observed in the preceding sections, the natural frequencies of the field are the roots of the dispersion equation,

$$D(k, \lambda) = 1 - \frac{\omega_p{}^2}{k^2} \int_\Gamma \frac{df_0(v)}{dv} \frac{dv}{v - \lambda/k} = 0$$

In the limit of small and large wave numbers, simple analytical expressions can be obtained for the frequency and amplification exponent of the oscillations.

A. Long Wave Length Plasma Oscillations

We shall now follow a procedure introduced by Jackson to obtain approximate expressions, in terms of the wave number, for the frequency and the amplification exponent of long wave length longitudinal plasma oscillations.

It is convenient to assume that the equilibrium velocity distribution is the restriction to the real axis of an entire function. It should be noted however that this condition on the function $f_0(v)$, although sufficient, is not at all necessary for the following discussions. This assumption implies that the Cauchy integral,

$$F(k, \lambda) = \int_{-\infty}^{\infty} \frac{df_0(v)}{dv} \frac{dv}{v - \lambda/k}$$

is the representation of a function $F(k, \lambda)$ which is analytic in the upper half of the complex λ-plane. Consequently, if λ_0 is a point in this half plane, the function $F(k, \lambda)$ can be expanded in a Taylor series about this point and we may write

$$F(k, \lambda) = \sum_{m=0}^{\infty} \frac{(\lambda - \lambda_0)^m}{m!} \frac{\partial^m F(k, \lambda_0)}{\partial \lambda^m}$$

This series is a valid representation of the function $F(k, \lambda)$ for all values of λ in the upper half plane. According to Section 1.1, the derivatives of this function take the form,

$$\frac{\partial^m F(k, \lambda_0)}{\partial \lambda^m} = \frac{m!}{k^m} \int_{-\infty}^{\infty} \frac{df_0(v)}{dv} \frac{dv}{(v - \lambda_0/k)^{m+1}} = \frac{1}{k^m} \int_{-\infty}^{\infty} \frac{f_0^{(m+1)}(v)}{v - \lambda_0/k}\, dv$$

and we obtain therefore the following series representation for the function $F(k, \lambda)$,

$$F(k, \lambda) = \sum_{m=0}^{\infty} \frac{(\lambda - \lambda_0)^m}{m!\, k^m} \int_{-\infty}^{\infty} \frac{f_0^{(m+1)}(v)}{v - \lambda_0/k}\, dv$$

Now let us assume that $\lambda_0 = \omega + i\varepsilon$ where ε is a small positive number. Then

$$F(k, \lambda) = \sum_{m=0}^{\infty} \frac{i^m(\gamma - \varepsilon)^m}{m!\, k^m} \int_{-\infty}^{\infty} \frac{f_0^{(m+1)}(v)}{(v - \omega/k) - i\varepsilon/k}\, dv$$

and, in the limit as ε tends to zero, we obtain, by means of the Plemelj boundary value formula of Section 4.6,

$$F(k, \lambda) = \sum_{m=0}^{\infty} \frac{i^m}{m!} \left(\frac{\gamma}{k}\right)^m \left[\int_{-\infty}^{\infty} \frac{f_0^{(m+1)}(v)}{v - \omega/k}\, dv + \pi i f_0^{(m+1)}(\omega/k)\right]$$

Choosing a zero order velocity distribution such that the uppermost root of the dispersion equation,

$$D(k, \lambda) = 1 - \frac{\omega_p^2}{k^2} F(k, \lambda) = 0$$

is located close to and just above the real axis, we may write

$$D(k,\lambda) = 1 - \frac{\omega_p^2}{k^2} \sum_{m=0}^{\infty} \frac{i^m}{m!} \left(\frac{\gamma}{k}\right)^m \left[\int_{-\infty}^{\infty} \frac{f_0^{(m+1)}(v)}{v - \omega/k}\, dv + \pi i f_0^{(m+1)}(\omega/k)\right] = 0$$

Consequently, if the imaginary part of the complex phase velocity λ/k is small, we obtain, to zeroth order in γ/k, the relation,

$$\int_{-\infty}^{\infty} \frac{df_0(v)}{dv} \frac{dv}{v - \omega/k} = \frac{k^2}{\omega_p^2}$$

For small values of the quantity kv/ω, in particular in the case of long wave length oscillations, the denominator of the integrand can be expanded in powers of the wave number and we find

$$\int_{-\infty}^{\infty} \frac{df_0(v)}{dv} \left(1 + \frac{kv}{\omega} + \frac{k^2 v^2}{\omega^2} + \cdots\right) dv = -\frac{k\omega}{\omega_p^2}$$

Assuming that the function $f_0(v)$ vanishes at plus and minus infinity faster than an arbitrary power of v the contribution to the integral of the first and third terms in the integrand vanish. The second term yields the contribution,

$$\frac{k}{\omega}\int_{-\infty}^{\infty} v\frac{df_0(v)}{dv}\,dv = -\frac{k}{\omega}$$

whereas the contribution to the integral of the fourth term in the integrand may be written as

$$\frac{k^3}{\omega^3}\int_{-\infty}^{\infty} v^3\frac{df_0(v)}{dv}\,dv = -3\frac{k^3}{\omega^3}\langle v^2\rangle$$

where

$$\langle v^2\rangle = \int_{-\infty}^{\infty} v^2 f_0(v)\,dv$$

is the mean square velocity of the distribution function $f_0(v)$.

Hence, taking into account the first nonvanishing term in the expansion, we obtain the Langmuir-Tonks dispersion relation,

$$\omega^2 = \omega_p{}^2$$

whereas, if we include terms to fourth order, we obtain the Landau-Vlasov dispersion equation,

$$\omega^2 = \omega_p{}^2 + 3k^2\langle v^2\rangle$$

The Landau-Vlasov equation is a dispersion equation in the true sense of the word. It relates the frequency of the oscillations to the wave number. The group velocity does not vanish, implying that the effect of an initially localized disturbance propagates through the system.

Now let us turn our attention to the amplification exponent or imaginary part of the complex frequency $\lambda = \omega + i\gamma$. To first order in the quantity γ/k, the series representation of the dielectric function $D(k, \lambda)$ yields the relation,

$$\frac{\gamma}{k}\int_{-\infty}^{\infty}\frac{d^2f_0(v)}{dv^2}\frac{dv}{v-\omega/k} = -\pi\frac{df_0(\omega/k)}{dv} \tag{7.27}$$

A more convenient expression for the integral on the left hand side of this equation can be obtained by differentiating the zeroth order expression,

$$\int_{-\infty}^{\infty}\frac{df_0(v)}{dv}\frac{dv}{v-\omega/k} = \frac{k^2}{\omega_p{}^2}$$

with respect to k. In this manner we find

$$\int_{-\infty}^{\infty} \frac{df_0(v)}{dv} \frac{dv}{(v - \omega/k)^2} = 2k \bigg/ \left[\omega_p{}^2 \frac{d}{dk} \left(\frac{\omega}{k} \right) \right]$$

and, integrating by parts, we may write

$$\int_{-\infty}^{\infty} \frac{d^2 f_0(v)}{dv^2} \frac{dv}{v - \omega/k} = 2k \bigg/ \left[\omega_p{}^2 \frac{d}{dk} \left(\frac{\omega}{k} \right) \right]$$

Substitution of this integral into equation (7.27) now yields the following equation of Jackson for the amplification exponent,

$$\gamma = \frac{\pi}{2} \omega \left(1 - \frac{k}{\omega} \frac{d\omega}{dk} \right) \frac{\omega_p{}^2}{k^2} \frac{df_0(\omega/k)}{dv}$$

To summarize, if the equilibrium velocity distribution function and the initial disturbance are the restrictions to the real axis of entire functions, and the equilibrium distribution satisfies the additional conditions delineated above, then the asymptotic time behavior of the field will show damped sinusoidal oscillations with a frequency,

$$\omega = \pm \sqrt{(\omega_p{}^2 + 3k^2 \langle v^2 \rangle)}$$

and an amplification exponent,

$$\gamma = \frac{\pi}{2} \omega \left(1 - \frac{k}{\omega} \frac{d\omega}{dk} \right) \frac{\omega_p{}^2}{k^2} \frac{df_0(\omega/k)}{dv}$$

It should be noted that the analysis above is based on the supposition that the dielectric function $D(k, \lambda)$ has an isolated zero of greatest imaginary part located close to the real axis. In that case, after a sufficiently long time, the mode characterized by this zero will grow faster, or is damped slower, than any other mode in the expansion of the field. Thus, the long time behavior of the field depends largely on this single isolated zero, a fact which allows us to refer to the equation,

$$\omega^2 = \omega_p{}^2 + 3k^2 \langle v^2 \rangle$$

as the dispersion equation. In general, however, the dielectric function $D(k, \lambda)$ has more than one zero corresponding to a particular wave number and a large number of possible frequencies can be associated with a single wave number. If these zeros are closely spaced, the long time behavior of the potential is influenced by more than one zero of the dielectric function and a dispersion equation of the type above loses its significance.

B. Short Wave Length Plasma Oscillations

We shall now turn our attention to the case of the other extreme, i.e., to the case of longitudinal plasma oscillations of very short wave length. We assume, and the suppositions of this section are all justified when the particular equilibrium velocity distribution is Maxwellian, that the uppermost root of the dispersion equation,

$$D(k, \lambda) = 1 - \frac{\omega_p^{\,2}}{k^2} \int_\Gamma \frac{df_0(v)}{dv} \frac{dv}{v - \lambda/k} = 0$$

is located in the lower half plane and that, when k increases, ω tends to plus or minus infinity, γ and γ/k tend to minus infinity, and ω/k is vanishingly small.

In other words, for very large values of k, the uppermost root of the dispersion equation is assumed to be located close to the negative imaginary axis and far down in the lower half of the complex plane, as shown in Figure VII-17. Assuming moreover that the function $df_0(v)/dv$ vanishes exponentially

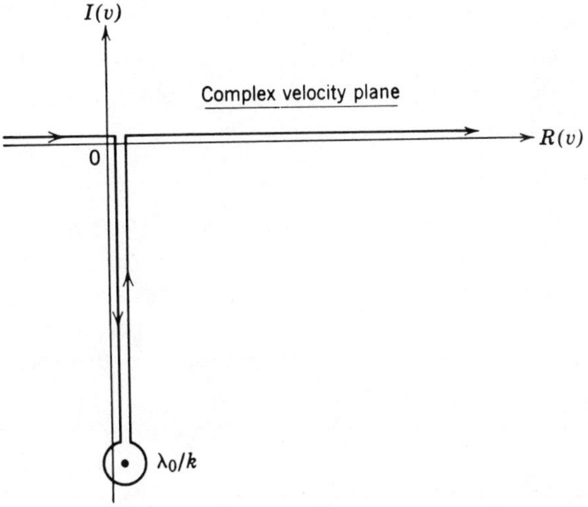

Figure VII-17

fast for large positive and negative values of v, so that the contribution to the integral,

$$\int_\Gamma \frac{df_0(v)}{dv} \frac{dv}{v - \lambda/k}$$

of the part of the Landau contour coinciding with the real axis is vanishingly small, the integral above is reduced to a contour integral around the pole

$\lambda_0/k = (\omega_0 + i\gamma_0)/k$ where ω_0/k is very small. Consequently,

$$\int_\Gamma \frac{df_0(v)}{dv}\frac{dv}{v-\lambda/k} = 2\pi i \operatorname{Res}\left[\frac{df_0(v)}{dv}\frac{1}{v-\lambda/k}, v = (\omega_0 + i\gamma_0)/k\right]$$

$$= 2\pi i \frac{df_0(\lambda_0/k)}{dv} = \frac{k^2}{{\omega_p}^2}$$

from which we may infer that the amplification exponent γ_0 of the short wave length longitudinal plasma oscillations can be determined as the root of the transcendental equation,

$$\frac{df_0(\lambda_0/k)}{dv} = \frac{1}{2\pi i}\frac{k^2}{{\omega_p}^2}$$

7.7 SOME SPECIAL EQUILIBRIUM VELOCITY DISTRIBUTIONS

Up to this point, the discussion has been kept quite general in the sense that no explicit analytical expressions for the equilibrium velocity distribution have been introduced. In this section we shall become more specific and consider the consequences of the theoretical constructs of the preceding sections when the equilibrium velocity distribution is a singular delta function, a Lorentzian, or a Maxwellian.

A. A Zero Temperature Plasma

First we shall consider the case in which the plasma is initially at zero temperature and all the electrons are at rest. In other words, we want to determine the long time behavior of the potential of the self-consistent field when a zero temperature electron distribution is perturbed by a small disturbance satisfying the Landau condition. In this case, the equilibrium velocity distribution is a Dirac delta function,

$$f_0(v) = \delta(v)$$

and the dielectric function takes the form,

$$D(k, \lambda) = 1 - \frac{{\omega_p}^2}{k^2}\int_{-\infty}^{\infty} \frac{d\delta(v)}{dv}\frac{dv}{v-\lambda/k}$$

Consequently, by the rules of Section 5.3, we obtain the dispersion equation,

$$1 - \frac{\omega_p^2}{k^2}\int_{-\infty}^{\infty} \frac{\delta(v)}{(v-\lambda/k)^2}\,dv = 1 - \frac{{\omega_p}^2}{\lambda^2} = 0$$

The roots $\lambda = \omega = \pm\omega_p$ of the dispersion equation are located on the real axis and the amplitude of the electric potential is represented therefore by the integral,

$$\phi(\mathbf{k}, t) = \frac{1}{\sqrt{(2\pi)}} \int_{-\infty+ib}^{\infty+ib} \Phi(\mathbf{k}, \zeta) e^{-i\zeta t} \, d\zeta$$

where b is a small positive number. Closing the path of integration in the lower half plane by a semicircle CR of radius R and center at the point $(0, b)$ we consider the contour integral,

$$\oint_C \Phi(\mathbf{k}, \zeta) e^{-i\zeta t} \, d\zeta$$

where C is the contour shown in Figure VII-18. By the residue theorem of

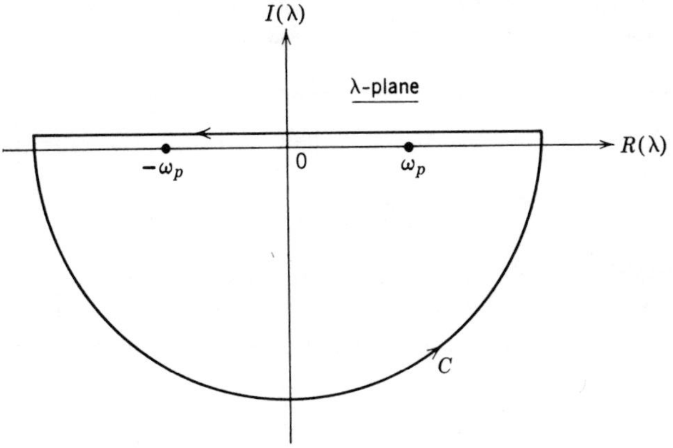

Figure VII-18

Section 1.3, we find

$$\oint_C \Phi(\mathbf{k}, \zeta) e^{-i\zeta t} \, d\zeta = 2\pi i \sum \text{Res} \, [\Phi(\mathbf{k}, \lambda) e^{-i\lambda t}, \lambda = \pm\omega_p]$$

The function $\Phi(\mathbf{k}, \lambda)$ takes the form,

$$\Phi(\mathbf{k}, \lambda) = \frac{N(\mathbf{k}, \lambda)}{D(k, \lambda)} = \frac{\lambda^2 N(\mathbf{k}, \lambda)}{(\lambda + \omega_p)(\lambda - \omega_p)}$$

and, assuming that the zeros of the function $N(\mathbf{k}, \lambda)$ do not coincide with the points $\lambda = \pm\omega_p$, we may write

$$\oint_C \Phi(\mathbf{k}, \zeta) e^{-i\zeta t} \, d\zeta = \int_{CR} \Phi(\mathbf{k}, \zeta) e^{-i\zeta t} \, d\zeta + \int_{R+ib}^{-R+ib} \Phi(\mathbf{k}, \zeta) e^{-i\zeta t} \, d\zeta$$

$$= \pi i \omega_p [N(\mathbf{k}, \omega_p) e^{-i\omega_p t} - N(\mathbf{k}, -\omega_p) e^{i\omega_p t}]$$

Hence, if the contribution of the path CR to the contour integral vanishes in the limit as R tends to infinity, we obtain the following expression for the amplitude of the potential,

$$\phi(\mathbf{k}, t) = \frac{1}{\sqrt{(2\pi)}} \int_{-\infty + ib}^{\infty + ib} \Phi(\mathbf{k}, \zeta) e^{-i\zeta t} \, d\zeta$$

$$= \frac{1}{2} \sqrt{(2\pi)} i\omega_p [N(\mathbf{k}, -\omega_p) e^{i\omega_p t} - N(\mathbf{k}, \omega_p) e^{-i\omega_p t}]$$

Thus, we may conclude that a small disturbance, satisfying the Landau condition, in a zero temperature plasma generates steady sinusoidal oscillations in the field. The frequency of these oscillations is equal to the plasma frequency. Since the frequency is independent of the wave number, the group velocity vanishes and the disturbance remains localized.

B. The Two-Stream Velocity Distribution

We shall now show that the so-called two-stream equilibrium velocity distribution,

$$f_0(v) = \tfrac{1}{2}[\delta(v - v_0) + \delta(v + v_0)]$$

can be unstable to self-excitation by plasma oscillations.

Substitution of this expression for $f_0(v)$ into the dielectric function yields, in a similar manner as for the zero temperature plasma, the dispersion equation,

$$1 - \frac{1}{2} \frac{\omega_p^2}{k^2} \left[\frac{1}{(v_0 - \lambda/k)^2} + \frac{1}{(v_0 + \lambda/k)^2} \right] = 0$$

and the roots of this equation can be determined from the relation,

$$\lambda^2 = k^2 v_0^2 + \frac{1}{2} \omega_p^2 \pm \frac{1}{2} \omega_p^2 \left(1 + \frac{8k^2 v_0^2}{\omega_p^2} \right)^{1/2}$$

For values of kv_0 very much smaller than the plasma frequency ω_p, we may expand the square root expression in terms of the quantity kv_0/ω_p, and, retaining only terms of first order in kv_0/ω_p, we obtain the following four roots of the dispersion equation,

$$\lambda = \pm ikv_0; \qquad \lambda = \pm \tfrac{1}{2}\omega_p$$

Since one of the roots of the dispersion equation is located in the upper half of the complex λ-plane, it follows, by an analysis similar to that of the preceding section, that the amplitude of the electric potential will have one growing mode, the time rate of growth of which is determined by the amplification factor $\gamma = kv_0$. This is the so-called two-stream instability.

C. THE LORENTZIAN EQUILIBRIUM VELOCITY DISTRIBUTION

In this section we consider the case in which the equilibrium velocity distribution is a Lorentzian,

$$f_0(v) = \frac{1}{\pi} \frac{a}{(v - v_m)^2 + a^2}$$

where v_m is the maximum speed and $2a$ is the half-width of the distribution, as shown in Figure VII-19. Now the dispersion equation takes the form,

$$1 + \frac{2a}{\pi} \frac{\omega_p{}^2}{k^2} \int_\Gamma \frac{v - v_m}{[(v - v_m)^2 + a^2]^2} \frac{dv}{v - \lambda/k} = 0$$

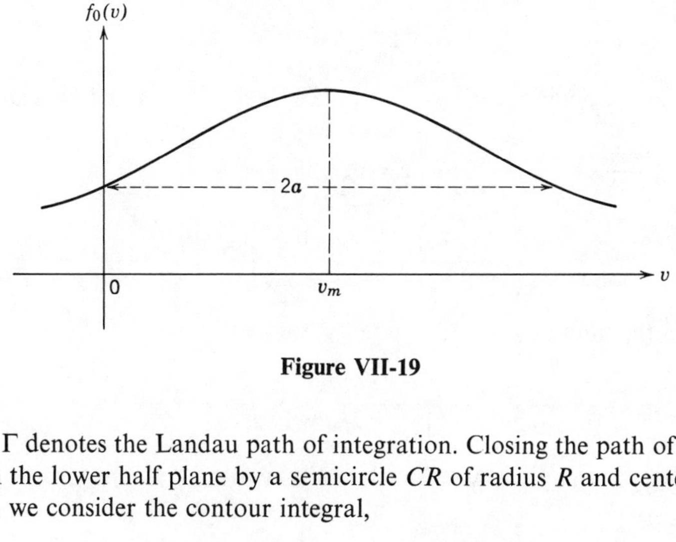

Figure VII-19

where Γ denotes the Landau path of integration. Closing the path of integration in the lower half plane by a semicircle CR of radius R and center at the origin, we consider the contour integral,

$$\oint_C \frac{\zeta - v_m}{[(\zeta - v_m)^2 + a^2]^2} \frac{d\zeta}{\zeta - \lambda/k}$$

where C is the contour shown in Figure VII-20. Since $z = v_m - ia$ is the only pole of the integrand enclosed by the contour C, we obtain, by means of the residue theorem of Section 1.3,

$$\oint_C \frac{\zeta - v_m}{[(\zeta - v_m)^2 + a^2]^2} \frac{d\zeta}{\zeta - \lambda/k}$$

$$= 2\pi i \operatorname{Res}\left[\frac{z - v_m}{[(z - v_m)^2 + a^2]^2} \frac{1}{z - \lambda/k}, z = v_m - ia\right]$$

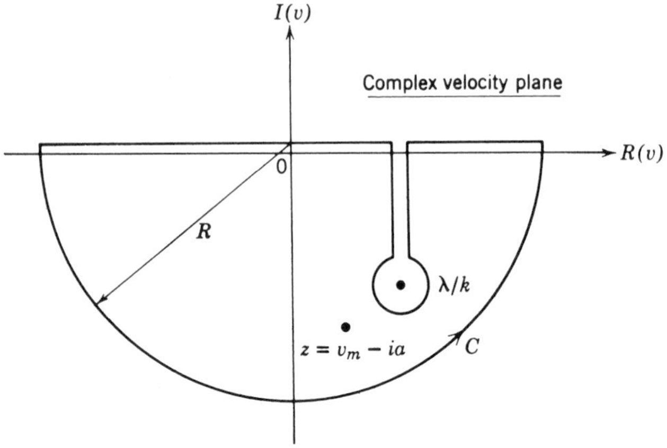

Figure VII-20

The pole at the point $z = v_m - ia$ is a pole of second order and consequently,

$$\operatorname{Res}\left[\frac{z - v_m}{[(z - v_m)^2 + a^2]^2}\frac{1}{z - \lambda/k}, z = v_m - ia\right]$$

$$= \frac{\partial}{\partial z}\left[\frac{z - v_m}{(z - v_m - ia)^2}\frac{1}{z - \lambda/k}\right]_{z = v_m - ia} = \frac{1}{4ai(v_m - ia - \lambda/k)^2}$$

Hence, in the limit as R tends to infinity, we find

$$\int_\Gamma \frac{\zeta - v_m}{[(\zeta - v_m)^2 + a^2]^2}\frac{d\zeta}{\zeta - \lambda/k} = -\frac{\pi}{2a(v_m - ia - \lambda/k)^2}$$

The dispersion equation takes therefore the simple form,

$$1 - \frac{{\omega_p}^2}{k^2}\frac{1}{(v_m - ia - \lambda/k)^2} = 0$$

Consequently, we may conclude that a small disturbance, satisfying the Landau condition, in a Lorentzian equilibrium velocity distribution leads to damped sinusoidal oscillations in the field. The frequency of the oscillations can be determined from the equation,

$$\omega = kv_m \pm \omega_p$$

whereas the damping decrement $\gamma = -ka$.

D. The Maxwellian Equilibrium Velocity Distribution

The physically most significant equilibrium velocity distribution is the normalized Maxwellian,

$$f_0(v) = \sqrt{\left(\frac{m}{2\pi KT}\right)} e^{-mv^2/2KT}$$

where K denotes the Boltzmann constant and T is the temperature in degrees Kelvin. The mean square thermal velocity of this distribution can easily be calculated

$$\langle v^2 \rangle = \int_{-\infty}^{\infty} v^2 f_0(v)\, dv = KT/m$$

and the root mean square thermal velocity a is therefore,

$$a = \sqrt{\langle v^2 \rangle} = \sqrt{(KT/m)}$$

In terms of the root mean square thermal velocity the distribution function $f_0(v)$ takes the form,

$$f_0(v) = \frac{1}{a\sqrt{(2\pi)}} e^{-v^2/2a^2}$$

and substitution of this function into the dielectric function yields the expression,

$$D(k, \lambda) = 1 + \frac{1}{a^3\sqrt{(2\pi)}} \frac{\omega_p^{\ 2}}{k^2} \int_\Gamma \frac{ve^{-v^2/2a^2}}{v - \lambda/k}\, dv$$

where Γ denotes the Landau path of integration. To simplify this expression we introduce the new variables, $u = v/(a\sqrt{2})$ and $z = \lambda/(ak\sqrt{2})$, and obtain

$$D(k, z) = 1 + \frac{1}{k^2 d^2} \frac{1}{\sqrt{\pi}} \int_\Omega \frac{ue^{-u^2}}{u - z}\, du$$

where d denotes the Debye length,

$$d = \sqrt{\left(\frac{\varepsilon_0 KT}{n_0 e^2}\right)} = a/\omega_p$$

and Ω is a Landau path of integration.

The dispersion equation can also be written in terms of the familiar error integral. For, since $f_0(v)$ is a Maxwellian, the roots of the dispersion equation must be located in the lower half plane. Consequently,

$$\frac{1}{\sqrt{\pi}} \int_\Omega \frac{ue^{-u^2}}{u - z}\, du = \frac{1}{\sqrt{\pi}} \int_{-\infty}^{\infty} \frac{ue^{-u^2}}{u - z}\, du + 2i\sqrt{\pi} z e^{-z^2}$$

Now let us consider the integral,

$$M(z) = \frac{1}{\sqrt{\pi}} \int_{-\infty}^{\infty} \frac{ue^{-u^2}}{u - z}\, du$$

With the help of the known integral,

$$\frac{1}{\sqrt{\pi}} \int_{-\infty}^{\infty} e^{-u^2}\, du = 1$$

it can easily be verified that

$$\frac{e^{z^2}}{z}[M(z) - 1] = \frac{1}{\sqrt{\pi}} \int_{-\infty}^{\infty} \frac{e^{z^2-u^2}}{u - z}\, du$$

Furthermore,

$$\frac{\partial}{\partial u}\frac{e^{z^2-u^2}}{u - z} + \frac{\partial}{\partial z}\frac{e^{z^2-u^2}}{u - z} = -2e^{z^2-u^2}$$

Integrating this expression over u from minus to plus infinity we find

$$\frac{\partial}{\partial z} \int_{-\infty}^{\infty} \frac{e^{z^2-u^2}}{u - z}\, du = -2\sqrt{\pi}e^{z^2}$$

and integrating this result over z from $-i\infty$ to z, we obtain

$$\frac{1}{\sqrt{\pi}} \int_{-\infty}^{\infty} \frac{e^{z^2-u^2}}{u - z}\, du = -2\int_{-i\infty}^{z} e^{s^2}\, ds$$

Substitution now yields the expression,

$$\frac{e^{z^2}}{z}[M(z) - 1] = -2\int_{-i\infty}^{z} e^{s^2}\, ds$$

which may also be written as

$$\frac{e^{z^2}}{z}[M(z) - 1] = -2\int_{0}^{z} e^{s^2}\, ds - i\sqrt{\pi}$$

This implies that the dispersion equation takes the form,

$$k^2d^2 + \frac{1}{\sqrt{\pi}} \int_{\Omega} \frac{ue^{-u^2}}{u - z}\, du = 1 + k^2d^2 + iz\sqrt{\pi}e^{-z^2} - 2ze^{-z^2}\int_{0}^{z} e^{s^2}\, ds = 0$$

This equation can be written even more compactly in terms of the Hilbert transform of the Gaussian,

$$Z(z) = \frac{1}{\sqrt{\pi}} \int_{-\infty}^{\infty} \frac{e^{-t^2}}{t - z}\, dt \qquad I(z) > 0 \tag{7.28}$$

The $Z(z)$-function, represented by this integral, is called the plasma dispersion function. It is of considerable importance for theoretical work in plasma physics and in the analysis of neutron cross section data. Several efficient computer subroutines exist for its evaluation and it has been extensively tabulated. The integral representation (7.28) defines the plasma dispersion function as an analytic function of the complex variable z in the upper half plane only. However, according to Section 2.13, the analytic continuation of this function into the lower half plane takes the form,

$$Z(z) = \frac{1}{\sqrt{\pi}} \int_{-\infty}^{\infty} \frac{e^{-u^2}}{u - z}\, du + 2i\sqrt{\pi} e^{-z^2}$$

Consequently, we may write

$$\begin{aligned} Z(z) &= \frac{1}{\sqrt{\pi}} \int_{-\infty}^{\infty} \frac{e^{-u^2}}{u - z}\, du && \text{when } I(z) > 0 \\ &= \frac{1}{\sqrt{\pi}} \int_{-\infty}^{\infty} \frac{e^{-u^2}}{u - z}\, du + 2i\sqrt{\pi} e^{-z^2} && \text{when } I(z) < 0 \end{aligned}$$

or, introducing the Landau path Ω, we obtain the following integral representation of the plasma dispersion function valid in the whole complex plane,

$$Z(z) = \frac{1}{\sqrt{\pi}} \int_{\Omega} \frac{e^{-u^2}}{u - z}\, du$$

If z is a point in the upper half plane, then

$$Z(z) = \frac{i}{\sqrt{\pi}} \int_{-\infty}^{\infty} e^{-u^2}\, du \int_{0}^{\infty} e^{i(z-u)p}\, dp = \frac{i}{\sqrt{\pi}} \int_{0}^{\infty} e^{izp - p^2/4}\, dp \int_{-\infty + ip/2}^{\infty + ip/2} e^{-\zeta^2}\, d\zeta$$

However, according to Cauchy's theorem, and referring to Figure VII-21,

$$\int_{-\infty + ip/2}^{\infty + ip/2} e^{-\zeta^2}\, d\zeta = \int_{-\infty}^{\infty} e^{-u^2}\, du = \sqrt{\pi}$$

and we may write therefore,

$$Z(z) = i \int_{0}^{\infty} e^{izp - p^2/4}\, dp = 2e^{-z^2} \int_{z}^{i\infty} e^{s^2}\, ds = e^{-z^2}\left[i\sqrt{\pi} - 2 \int_{0}^{z} e^{s^2}\, ds \right]$$

This formula, shown to be true for values of z in the upper half plane, can be shown to be valid for all values of z by the principle of analytic continuation.

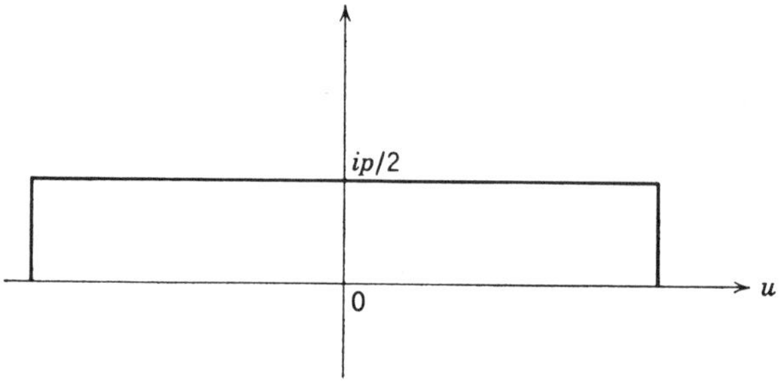

Figure VII-21

The plasma dispersion function satisfies some interesting and useful symmetry relations. We list, without proof,

$$
\begin{aligned}
Z^*(z) &= Z(z^*) - 2i\sqrt{\pi}\exp[-(z^*)^2] \\
Z(-z) &= -Z(z) + 2i\sqrt{\pi}\exp(-z^2) \\
Z(z^*) &= -Z^*(-z) \\
Z'(z) &= -2[1 + zZ(z)]
\end{aligned}
$$

With the help of the plasma dispersion function, the dispersion equation for a Maxwellian equilibrium velocity distribution may be written

$$1 + k^2d^2 + zZ(z) = 0$$

Highly interesting results on the number, order, and location of the roots of this dispersion equation have been obtained by Hayes and by Saenz. For instance, there exists a theorem by Picard which states that an entire functio n, that is not a polynomial, takes every value, with but one possible exception, an infinite number of times. Thus, the function exp z takes all values an infinite number of times except the value zero which it never attains. Similarly, the function sin z takes all values an infinite number of times with no exceptions. For the complicated proof of Picard's theorem we must refer the reader to the literature.

The implications of Picard's theorem for the dispersion equation of a Maxwellian equilibrium velocity distribution are immediate. For the left hand side of the equation,

$$zZ(z) = -(1 + k^2d^2)$$

is an entire function, and it takes all values, with but one possible exception, an infinite number of times. Consequently, for a given value of k, the dispersion equation has an infinite number of roots unless, for that particular value of k, the quantity $1 + k^2d^2$ takes the special value, which the function

$zZ(z)$ attains, only a finite number of times. Hayes has shown that the exceptional value occurs at $k = 0$ and that the dispersion equation has only two real roots for that particular value of the wave number.

If z is a root of the dispersion equation, then $-z^*$ is also a root of this equation. For, taking complex conjugates, we find

$$1 + k^2d^2 + z^*Z^*(z) = 0$$

However,

$$Z^*(z) = -Z(-z^*)$$

and consequently,

$$1 + k^2d^2 + (-z^*)Z(-z^*) = 0$$

The roots of the dispersion equation are simple. For let z_0 be a zero of the function,

$$E(z) = 1 + k^2d^2 + zZ(z)$$

Then, as we have shown in Section 7.5, z_0 must lie in the lower half plane, $I(z_0) < 0$. Taking the derivative of the function $E(z)$ with respect to z, we find

$$E'(z) = (1 - 2z^2)Z(z) - 2z$$

where we have made use of the derivative relation,

$$Z'(z) = -2[1 + zZ(z)]$$

If z_0 is a zero of the function $E(z)$, then

$$z_0 Z(z_0) = -(1 + k^2d^2) \tag{7.29}$$

and, in order for z_0 to be a zero of second or higher order, we must also have

$$E'(z_0) = (1 - 2z_0{}^2)Z(z_0) - 2z_0 = 0 \tag{7.30}$$

From equations (7.29) and (7.30), we may infer that

$$z_0 = \pm \frac{\sqrt{[2(1 + k^2d^2)]}}{2kd}$$

and that z_0 must be real in order to satisfy equations (7.29) and (7.30) simultaneously. This is in contradiction with our assumption that z_0 has a nonzero negative imaginary part and the roots of the dispersion equation must be simple therefore.

Furthermore, it has been shown by Hayes and by Saenz that for non-vanishing wave numbers the dispersion equation has a root of greatest imaginary part located in the lower half plane. Saenz moreover was able to compute that root and to verify Landau's results. Very little is known however about the location of the other roots of the dispersion equation for a Maxwellian equilibrium velocity distribution.

In Section 7.6 we found, for a rather general velocity distribution, that the frequency of the long wave length, damped, sinusoidal oscillations, set up in the field by a disturbance which satisfies the Landau condition, is related to the plasma frequency and the mean square thermal velocity,

$$\omega^2 = \omega_p{}^2 + 3k^2\langle v^2 \rangle$$

We found, moreover, that the amplification exponent of such oscillations can be computed by means of Jackson's formula,

$$\gamma = \frac{\pi}{2}\,\omega\left(1 - \frac{k}{\omega}\frac{d\omega}{dk}\right)\frac{\omega_p{}^2}{k^2}\frac{df_0(\omega/k)}{dv}$$

For a Maxwellian equilibrium velocity distribution this implies that the long wave length, small amplitude oscillations in the field have the frequency,

$$\omega = \pm\sqrt{\left(\omega_p{}^2 + \frac{3KT}{m}k^2\right)}$$

and an amplification exponent,

$$\gamma = -\sqrt{\left(\frac{\pi}{8}\right)}\left(\frac{\omega_p{}^2}{a^3k}\right)\frac{\omega_p{}^2}{k^2}\,e^{-\omega^2/2a^2k^2}$$

In the approximation of Section 7.6, the amplification exponent and the frequency of the short wave length oscillations can be found by means of the expression,

$$2\pi i\,\frac{\omega_p{}^2}{k^2}\frac{df_0(\lambda_0/k)}{dv} = 1$$

In the case of a Maxwellian equilibrium velocity distribution this equation takes the form,

$$-2\pi i\,\frac{\omega_p{}^2}{k^2}\frac{\lambda_0}{a^3k\sqrt{(2\pi)}}\,e^{-\lambda_0{}^2/2a^2k^2} = 1$$

Hence, to lowest order in ω_0/k, we find

$$\sqrt{(2\pi)}\,\frac{\omega_p{}^2}{a^3k^2}\frac{\gamma_0}{k}\,e^{-(2i\gamma_0\omega_0 - \gamma_0{}^2)/2a^2k^2} = 1$$

Imposing the condition,

$$\frac{\gamma_0\,\omega_0}{a^2k^2} = -\pi$$

the left hand side of the equation is positive and we can obtain the amplification exponent from the equation,

$$\sqrt{(2\pi)}\,\frac{\omega_p{}^2}{a^3k^2}\,\frac{\gamma_0}{k}\,e^{\gamma_0{}^2/2a^2k^2} = -1$$

7.8 VAN KAMPEN'S NORMAL MODE SOLUTION OF THE INITIAL VALUE PROBLEM FOR A MAXWELLIAN EQUILIBRIUM VELOCITY DISTRIBUTION

In the preceding sections we have been concerned with the Landau technique for the solution of the initial value problem representing the mathematical description of the evolution of an initially small disturbance in a uniform electron plasma in the absence of magnetic fields. We shall now turn our attention to the normal mode technique of Case and van Kampen for the solution of the same initial value problem. This technique is similar to the normal mode technique by which we solved boundary value problems in neutron transport theory in Chapter VI.

In this section we shall consider van Kampen's solution, by means of a normal mode expansion technique, of the initial value problem of Section 7.2 when the equilibrium velocity distribution is a Maxwellian.

To obtain the solution of the linear transport equation in **k**-space,

$$\frac{\partial f(\mathbf{k}, v, t)}{\partial t} + ikvf(\mathbf{k}, v, t) = -ikh(k, v)\int_{-\infty}^{\infty} f(\mathbf{k}, v, t)\,dv$$

subject to the initial value condition,

$$f(\mathbf{k}, v, 0) = g(\mathbf{k}, v)$$

we observe that this equation is translational-invariant and we introduce elementary solutions or normal modes of the form,

$$f(\mathbf{k}, v, t) = f(\mathbf{k}, v\,|\,\omega)e^{-i\omega t}$$

Substitution of such a mode into the transport equation above leads to the following eigenvalue equation for the eigenfunctions $f(\mathbf{k}, v\,|\,\omega)$,

$$(v - \omega/k)f(\mathbf{k}, v\,|\,\omega) = -h(k, v)\int_{-\infty}^{\infty} f(\mathbf{k}, v\,|\,\omega)\,dv$$

Introducing the phase velocity $\alpha = \omega/k$ and normalizing the eigenfunctions so that

$$\int_{-\infty}^{\infty} f(\mathbf{k}, v\,|\,\alpha)\,dv = 1$$

we obtain, without loss of generality, the simpler eigenvalue equation,

$$(v - \alpha)f(\mathbf{k}, v \mid \alpha) = -h(k, v)$$

where we want to recall the definition,

$$h(k, v) = -\frac{\omega_p{}^2}{k^2}\frac{df_0(v)}{dv}$$

and note that, in this section, the equilibrium velocity distribution $f_0(v)$ is assumed to be Maxwellian.

As we have remarked in Section 5.1, if α is a point on the real axis, then the solutions of this eigenvalue equation take the form,

$$f(\mathbf{k}, v \mid \alpha) = b(k, \alpha)\,\delta(\alpha - v) + h(k, v)P\frac{1}{\alpha - v}$$

where $\delta(\alpha - v)$ is the Dirac delta function and $P[1/(\alpha - v)]$ denotes the principal value distribution.

The strength $b(k, \alpha)$ of the concentration of delta functions at the point $v = \alpha$ on the real axis can be determined by means of the normalization condition imposed on the eigenfunctions. This condition yields the relation,

$$b(k, \alpha) = 1 + \int_{-\infty}^{\infty} \frac{h(k, v)}{v - \alpha}\,dv$$

where, since α is a point on the real axis, the integral must be interpreted as a Cauchy principal value integral.

Hence, to each real value of α there corresponds a strength $b(k, \alpha)$, implying that the real eigenvalues α are in the continuous spectrum. The singular eigenfunctions $f(\mathbf{k}, v \mid \alpha)$ corresponding to these real eigenvalues are the continuum eigenfunctions,

$$f(\mathbf{k}, v \mid \alpha) = \left[1 + \int_{-\infty}^{\infty} \frac{h(k, v)}{v - \alpha}\,dv\right]\delta(\alpha - v) + h(k, v)P\frac{1}{\alpha - v}$$

In the case of a Maxwellian equilibrium velocity distribution these are the only eigenfunctions. For let us assume that α is a point off the real axis. For complex phase velocities $\alpha = z$ the eigenvalue equation,

$$(v - z)f(\mathbf{k}, v \mid z) = -h(k, v)$$

is no longer singular and its regular solutions may be written

$$f(\mathbf{k}, v \mid z) = \frac{h(k, v)}{z - v}$$

The normalization condition imposed on the eigenfunctions implies that the function,

$$B(k, z) = 1 + \int_{-\infty}^{\infty} \frac{h(k, v)}{v - z}\, dv$$

must vanish.

Note that this function is not the dielectric function defined in Section 7.4. The function $B(k, z)$ is sectionally analytic in the plane cut along the real axis and is defined by the relations,

$$B(k, z) = B^L(k, z) = 1 + \int_{-\infty}^{\infty} \frac{h(k, v)}{v - z}\, dv \qquad I(z) > 0$$

$$B(k, z) = B^R(k, z) = 1 + \int_{-\infty}^{\infty} \frac{h(k, v)}{v - z}\, dv \qquad I(z) < 0$$

Hence, according to Section 2.13, the function $B^R(k, z)$ is not the analytic continuation of the function $B^L(k, z)$ into the lower half plane.

We can show, by means of the method of Section 7.5, that the function $B(k, z)$ does not vanish off the real axis when $f_0(v)$ is a Maxwellian equilibrium velocity distribution, and we may conclude that in the case of such a distribution all the eigenvalues are real and in the continuous spectrum.

It is interesting to note the following consequences of the definitions above. According to the Plemelj formulas of Section 4.6, the left and right boundary values of the sectionally analytic function $B(k, z)$ may be written

$$B^L(k, \alpha) = 1 + \int_{-\infty}^{\infty} \frac{h(k, v)}{v - \alpha}\, dv + \pi i h(k, \alpha)$$

$$B^R(k, \alpha) = 1 + \int_{-\infty}^{\infty} \frac{h(k, v)}{v - \alpha}\, dv - \pi i h(k, \alpha)$$

This implies that the strength of the concentration of delta functions,

$$b(k, \alpha) = 1 + \int_{-\infty}^{\infty} \frac{h(k, v)}{v - \alpha}\, dv$$

is related to the boundary values of the function $B(k, z)$, namely,

$$2b(k, \alpha) = B^L(k, \alpha) + B^R(k, \alpha)$$

The solution $f(\mathbf{k}, v, t)$ of the initial value problem can be expanded in terms of the elementary solutions or normal modes,

$$f(\mathbf{k}, v \mid \alpha) e^{-ik\alpha t}$$

and the following integral representation can be obtained,

$$f(\mathbf{k}, v, t) = \int_{-\infty}^{\infty} a(k, \alpha) f(\mathbf{k}, v \mid \alpha) e^{-ik\alpha t} \, d\alpha$$

where $a(k, \alpha)$ denotes the expansion coefficient. In the customary way, this function can be determined by the initial value condition $f(\mathbf{k}, v, 0) = g(\mathbf{k}, v)$ which is imposed on the solutions of the initial value problem. Thus we may write

$$g(\mathbf{k},v) = \int_{-\infty}^{\infty} a(k,\alpha) f(\mathbf{k},v \mid \alpha) \, d\alpha$$

and substitution of the explicit expression,

$$f(\mathbf{k}, v \mid \alpha) = b(k, \alpha) \, \delta(\alpha - v) + h(k, v) P \frac{1}{\alpha - v}$$

for the continuum eigenfunctions leads to the following singular integral equation of the Cauchy type,

$$g(\mathbf{k}, v) = b(k, v) a(k, v) + h(k, v) \int_{-\infty}^{\infty} \frac{a(k, \alpha)}{\alpha - v} \, d\alpha$$

for the expansion coefficient $a(k, \alpha)$.

To obtain the solution of this equation, van Kampen assumed that the initial disturbance in the equilibrium velocity distribution and the derivative of the equilibrium velocity distribution are square integrable over the whole real velocity axis. He subsequently made use of the positive and negative frequency decomposition of a square integrable function of Section 2.11 to obtain the solution of the singular integral equation and to show, by construction, that the space of eigenfunctions $f(\mathbf{k}, v \mid \alpha)$ is complete for functions that are square integrable over the real axis. For initial disturbances that have the same measure of smoothness as the Maxwellian equilibrium velocity distribution but are concentrated about much higher velocities (the bump-in-tail disturbances), he was moreover able to show the existence of collective motions corresponding to plasma oscillations that are damped with the Landau damping decrement. For more details on his solution technique we refer the reader to the literature.

The solution of the integral equation for the expansion coefficient $a(k, \alpha)$ can also be obtained when the derivative of the equilibrium velocity distribution and the initial disturbance in this distribution satisfy less strong conditions. For let us assume that the functions $h(v)$ and $g(\mathbf{k}, v)$ are Hölder continuous on all finite subintervals of the real velocity axis and at infinity. Supposing for the moment that the solution $a(k, \alpha)$ of the singular integral equation,

$$g(\mathbf{k}, v) = b(k, v)a(k, v) + h(k, v) \int_{-\infty}^{\infty} \frac{a(k, \alpha)}{\alpha - v} \, d\alpha$$

satisfies the same condition, we introduce the integral representations,

$$G(\mathbf{k}, z) = \frac{1}{2\pi i} \int_{-\infty}^{\infty} \frac{g(\mathbf{k}, v)}{v - z} \, dv$$

$$H(k, z) = \frac{1}{2\pi i} \int_{-\infty}^{\infty} \frac{h(k, v)}{v - z} \, dv$$

$$A(k, z) = \frac{1}{2\pi i} \int_{-\infty}^{\infty} \frac{a(k, v)}{v - z} \, dv$$

The functions $G(\mathbf{k}, z)$, $H(k, z)$, and $A(k, z)$ are sectionally analytic in the plane bounded by the real axis and vanish as $1/z$ when z tends to infinity. On the real axis the left and right boundary values of these functions are related by the Plemelj formulas,

$$G^L(\mathbf{k}, v) - G^R(\mathbf{k}, v) = g(\mathbf{k}, v)$$

$$G^L(\mathbf{k}, v) + G^R(\mathbf{k}, v) = \frac{1}{\pi i} \int_{-\infty}^{\infty} \frac{g(\mathbf{k}, \alpha)}{\alpha - v} \, d\alpha$$

$$H^L(k, v) - H^R(k, v) = h(k, v)$$

$$H^L(k, v) + H^R(k, v) = \frac{1}{\pi i} \int_{-\infty}^{\infty} \frac{h(k, \alpha)}{\alpha - v} \, d\alpha$$

$$A^L(k, v) - A^R(k, v) = a(k, v)$$

$$A^L(k, v) + A^R(k, v) = \frac{1}{\pi i} \int_{-\infty}^{\infty} \frac{a(k, \alpha)}{\alpha - v} \, d\alpha$$

With the help of these relations we can now reduce the singular integral equation for the expansion coefficient $a(k, \alpha)$ to the following functional equation on the real line,

$$\begin{aligned} G^L(\mathbf{k}, v) - G^R(\mathbf{k}, v) &= b(k, v)[A^L(k, v) - A^R(k, v)] \\ &\quad + \pi i[H^L(k, v) - H^R(k, v)][A^L(k, v) + A^R(k, v)] \end{aligned}$$

However,

$$b(k, v) = 1 + \int_{-\infty}^{\infty} \frac{h(k, \alpha)}{\alpha - v} \, d\alpha = 1 + \pi i[H^L(k, v) + H^R(k, v)]$$

and consequently,

$$G^L(\mathbf{k}, v) - A^L(k, v)[1 + 2\pi i H^L(k, v)] = G^R(\mathbf{k}, v) - A^R(k, v)[1 + 2\pi i H^R(k, v)]$$

Now let us define the function,

$$M(z) = G(\mathbf{k}, z) - A(k, z)[1 + 2\pi i H(k, z)]$$

This function is sectionally analytic in the complex z-plane cut along the real axis. On this axis the left and right boundary values of this function satisfy the boundary condition,

$$M^L(v) = M^R(v)$$

Hence, since the boundary values of the sectionally analytic function $M(z)$ are continuous over the boundary, the function $M(z)$ is analytic in the whole complex z-plane and is therefore an entire function. Moreover, since $M(z)$ vanishes as $1/z$ when z tends to infinity, we may conclude, by means of Liouville's theorem, that $M(z)$ must vanish in the whole complex plane.

We may write, therefore,

$$A(k, z) = \frac{G(\mathbf{k}, z)}{1 + 2\pi i H(k, z)}$$

The expansion coefficient $a(k, \alpha)$ can now be found by means of the first Plemelj formula,

$$a(k, \alpha) = A^L(k, \alpha) - A^R(k, \alpha) = \frac{G^L(\mathbf{k}, \alpha)}{1 + 2\pi i H^L(k, \alpha)} - \frac{G^R(\mathbf{k}, \alpha)}{1 + 2\pi i H^R(k, \alpha)}$$

Since the equilibrium velocity distribution is Maxwellian, we can show, by means of the criteria of Section 7.5, that the functions $1 + 2\pi i H^L(k, z)$ and $1 + 2\pi i H^R(k, z)$ do not vanish in the upper and lower half plane respectively, including the real axis. The expressions for $A(k, z)$ and $a(k, \alpha)$ are well defined therefore.

Thus we have shown, under the conditions imposed on the functions involved, that the singular integral equation,

$$g(\mathbf{k}, v) = \int_{-\infty}^{\infty} a(k, \alpha) f(\mathbf{k}, v \mid \alpha)\, d\alpha$$

where $f(\mathbf{k}, v \mid \alpha)$ denotes the singular continuum eigenfunction,

$$f(\mathbf{k}, v \mid \alpha) = b(k, \alpha)\, \delta(\alpha - v) + h(k, v) P \frac{1}{\alpha - v}$$

has a solution $a(k, \alpha)$ and, by construction, we have obtained a proof that the space of eigenfunctions $f(\mathbf{k}, v \mid \alpha)$ is complete for functions that are Hölder continuous on the real axis and at infinity.

The solution of the initial value problem may now be written

$$f(\mathbf{k}, v, t) = \int_{-\infty}^{\infty} a(k, \alpha) f(\mathbf{k}, v \,|\, \alpha) e^{-ik\alpha t} \, d\alpha$$

where the expansion coefficient $a(k, \alpha)$ and the singular continuum eigenfunctions $f(\mathbf{k}, v \,|\, \alpha)$ are presented above.

We can formally compare the Landau formula for the amplitude of the potential of the electric field with van Kampen's formula for the same quantity. In view of the equations derived above, the amplitude of the potential takes the form,

$$\begin{aligned} \phi(\mathbf{k}, t) &= \frac{e}{\varepsilon_0 k^2} \int_{-\infty}^{\infty} f(\mathbf{k}, v, t) \, dv \\ &= \frac{e}{\varepsilon_0 k^2} \int_{-\infty}^{\infty} \left[\frac{G^L(\mathbf{k}, \alpha)}{1 + 2\pi i H^L(k, \alpha)} - \frac{G^R(\mathbf{k}, \alpha)}{1 + 2\pi i H^R(k, \alpha)} \right] e^{-ik\alpha t} \, d\alpha \end{aligned}$$

where we have made use of the normalization condition imposed on the eigenfunctions $f(\mathbf{k}, v|\alpha)$. Consider the second integral on the right hand side of this equation. Since the denominator of the integrand has no zeros in the lower half plane including the real axis, and the functions $G^L(\mathbf{k}, z)$ and $H^R(k, z)$ are analytic in this region, we may conclude that the integrand as a function of the complex variable z has no singularities below and on the real axis. Furthermore, the integrand vanishes as $1/z$ when z tends to infinity in the lower half plane. From these properties of the integrand we may infer, according to Section 1.5, that the integral,

$$\int_{-\infty}^{\infty} \frac{G^R(\mathbf{k}, \alpha)}{1 + 2\pi i H^R(k, \alpha)} e^{-ik\alpha t} \, d\alpha$$

vanishes identically for all positive values of t. Consequently, van Kampen's formula for the function $\phi(\mathbf{k}, t)$ may be written

$$\phi(\mathbf{k}, t) = \frac{e}{\varepsilon_0 k^2} \int_{-\infty}^{\infty} \frac{G^L(\mathbf{k}, \alpha)}{1 + 2\pi i H^L(k, \alpha)} e^{-ik\alpha t} \, d\alpha$$

However,

$$G^L(\mathbf{k}, \alpha) = \lim_{\varepsilon \to 0} \frac{1}{2\pi i} \int_{-\infty}^{\infty} \frac{g(\mathbf{k}, v)}{v - (\alpha + i\varepsilon)} \, dv$$

and

$$H^L(k, \alpha) = \lim_{\varepsilon \to 0} \frac{1}{2\pi i} \int_{-\infty}^{\infty} \frac{h(k, v)}{v - (\alpha + i\varepsilon)} \, dv$$

where ε is a small positive number. We may write therefore

$$\phi(\mathbf{k}, t) = \frac{e}{\varepsilon_0 k^2} \frac{1}{2\pi i} \int_{-\infty}^{\infty} e^{-ik\alpha t} \left[\frac{\displaystyle\int_{-\infty}^{\infty} \frac{g(\mathbf{k}, v)}{v - (\alpha + i\varepsilon)} dv}{1 + \displaystyle\int_{-\infty}^{\infty} \frac{h(k, v)}{v - (\alpha + i\varepsilon)} dv} \right] d\alpha$$

and this expression is formally equivalent to Landau's formula for the amplitude of the potential of the self-consistent field.

7.9 CASE'S NORMAL MODE SOLUTION OF THE INITIAL VALUE PROBLEM FOR GENERAL EQUILIBRIUM VELOCITY DISTRIBUTIONS

The van Kampen technique for the solution of the initial value problem of the preceding section has been extended in a decisive manner by Case. Case considered equilibrium velocity distributions which are more general than the isotropic distribution functions considered by van Kampen and, by introducing an adjoint transport equation, he was able to put the spectral theory of the transport equation for the distribution function $f(\mathbf{k}, v, t)$ on a firmer basis.

Let us again consider the eigenvalue equation,

$$(v - \alpha) f(\mathbf{k}, v \,|\, \alpha) = -h(k, v)$$

where

$$h(k, v) = -\frac{\omega_p^{\,2}}{k^2} \frac{df_0(v)}{dv}$$

In the preceding section we concluded that in the case of a Maxwellian equilibrium distribution all the eigenvalues of this equation are in the continuous spectrum. However, if the equilibrium velocity distribution is not a Maxwellian the discrete spectrum does not have to be empty and the continuum eigenfunctions do not have to be the only eigenfunctions of this equation. In the case of more general equilibrium velocity distributions the spectrum of the eigenvalue equation above can be subdivided into a continuous and a discrete part.

In the continuous part of the spectrum we find:

1. The real eigenvalues α that are not zeros of the function $h(k, v)$. To this class of eigenvalues correspond the singular eigenfunctions,

$$f(\mathbf{k}, v \,|\, \alpha) = b(k, \alpha)\, \delta(\alpha - v) + h(k, v) P \frac{1}{\alpha - v}$$

of the preceding section. As we have shown in that section, the condition

$$\int_{-\infty}^{\infty} f(\mathbf{k}, v \mid \alpha)\, dv = 1$$

imposed on the eigenfunctions leads to the following expression for the strength $b(k, \alpha)$ of the concentration of delta functions at the point $v = \alpha$,

$$b(k, \alpha) = 1 + \int_{-\infty}^{\infty} \frac{h(k, v)}{v - \alpha}\, dv \tag{7.31}$$

where the integral is a Cauchy principal value integral.

2. The real eigenvalues α that are zeros of the function $h(k, v)$ but not of the function $b(k, v)$. In this case, the continuum eigenfunctions may be written

$$f(\mathbf{k}, v \mid \alpha) = b(k, \alpha)\, \delta(\alpha - v) + \frac{h(k, v)}{\alpha - v}$$

where, since the function $h(k, v)$ vanishes at the point $v = \alpha$, the second term on the right hand side denotes a regular distribution, supposing of course that the function $h(k, v)/(\alpha - v)$ is locally integrable. The strength of the concentration of delta functions at the point $v = \alpha$ can again be computed by means of equation (7.31) above.

In the discrete part of the spectrum we find:

3. The real eigenvalues α that are zeros of both $h(k, v)$ and $b(k, v)$. In this case the discrete eigenfunctions take the form,

$$f(\mathbf{k}, v \mid \alpha_m) = \frac{h(k, v)}{\alpha_m - v} \qquad m = 1, 2, \ldots, M$$

This implies, according to the normalization condition imposed on the eigenfunctions, that the eigenvalues in this part of the spectrum are the zeros of the dispersion equation,

$$\int_{-\infty}^{\infty} \frac{h(k, v)}{v - \alpha}\, dv = -1 \tag{7.32}$$

where the integral can be evaluated in the ordinary sense. We shall assume, for simplicity, that these zeros are simple.

4. The eigenvalues α that are located in the complex plane off the real axis. The discrete eigenfunctions corresponding to these complex eigenvalues are regular and may be written

$$f(\mathbf{k}, v \mid \alpha_m) = \frac{h(k, v)}{\alpha_m - v}$$

The normalization condition imposed on the eigenfunctions leads again to the dispersion equation (7.32) and the complex eigenvalues are the zeros of this equation which for simplicity we shall again assume to be simple.

Up to this point, the spectral theory of the linear transport equation describing the temporal behavior of longitudinal plasma oscillations has been developed along the same lines as the spectral theory of the neutron transport equation. However, in contrast to the eigenfunctions obtained in the case of the neutron transport equation, the eigenfunctions $f(\mathbf{k}, v \mid \alpha)$ do not form an orthogonal system.

Orthogonality of course is of decisive importance for a successful expansion technique and it is fortunate that we are able to construct a function space, the functions of which are orthogonal to the eigenfunctions $f(\mathbf{k}, v \mid \alpha)$. The functions of this adjoint space are the eigenfunctions of the adjoint equation,

$$\frac{\partial \chi(\mathbf{k}, v, t)}{\partial t} + ikv\chi(\mathbf{k}, v, t) = -ik \int_{-\infty}^{\infty} h(k, v)\chi(\mathbf{k}, v, t)\, dv$$

The substitution $\chi(\mathbf{k}, v, t) = \chi(\mathbf{k}, v \mid \alpha)e^{-i\omega t}$ reduces this equation to an eigenvalue equation,

$$(v - \alpha)\chi(\mathbf{k}, v \mid \alpha) = -\int_{-\infty}^{\infty} h(k, v)\chi(\mathbf{k}, v \mid \alpha)\, dv$$

for the adjoint eigenfunctions $\chi(\mathbf{k}, v \mid \alpha)$.

Imposing the normalization condition,

$$\int_{-\infty}^{\infty} h(k, v)\chi(\mathbf{k}, v \mid \alpha)\, dv = 1$$

on the adjoint eigenfunctions, we can easily show that the functions $f(\mathbf{k}, v \mid \alpha)$ and $\chi(\mathbf{k}, v \mid \alpha)$ are orthogonal. For multiplying the eigenvalue equation,

$$(v - \alpha)f(\mathbf{k}, v \mid \alpha) = -h(k, v)$$

by the adjoint function $\chi(\mathbf{k}, v \mid \beta)$, multiplying the adjoint equation,

$$(v - \beta)\chi(\mathbf{k}, v \mid \beta) = -1$$

by the function $f(\mathbf{k}, v \mid \alpha)$, and subtracting the results, we find

$$(\beta - \alpha)f(\mathbf{k}, v \mid \alpha)\chi(\mathbf{k}, v \mid \beta) = f(\mathbf{k}, v \mid \alpha) - h(k, v)\chi(\mathbf{k}, v \mid \beta)$$

If we now integrate this equation over the real v-axis and make use of the normalization conditions imposed on the functions $f(\mathbf{k}, v \mid \alpha)$ and $\chi(\mathbf{k}, v \mid \beta)$, we obtain the result,

$$(\beta - \alpha) \int_{-\infty}^{\infty} f(\mathbf{k}, v \mid \alpha)\chi(\mathbf{k}, v \mid \beta)\, dv = 0$$

Thus, supposing that α and β are different eigenvalues, we find

$$\int_{-\infty}^{\infty} f(\mathbf{k}, v \mid \alpha)\chi(\mathbf{k}, v \mid \beta)\, dv = 0$$

The spectral properties of the adjoint equation are closely related to those of the eigenvalue equation. The spectrum of the adjoint equation can also be divided into a continuous and a discrete part.

The continuous part of the spectrum consists of:

1. The real eigenvalues α that are not zeros of the function $h(k, v)$. The eigenfunctions corresponding to these eigenvalues are the continuum functions,

$$\chi(\mathbf{k}, v \mid \alpha) = \beta(k, \alpha)\,\delta(\alpha - v) + P\,\frac{1}{\alpha - v}$$

The strength of the concentration of delta functions at the point $v = \alpha$ can be ascertained by multiplying the function $\chi(\mathbf{k}, v \mid \alpha)$ by $h(k, v)$ and integrating the result over the real axis. Using the normalization condition imposed on the adjoint functions, we find

$$h(k, \alpha)\beta(k, \alpha) = 1 + \int_{-\infty}^{\infty} \frac{h(k, v)}{v - \alpha}\, dv$$

The function $\beta(k, \alpha)$ can be related immediately to the strength $b(k, \alpha)$ of the concentration of delta functions in the continuum eigenfunctions $f(\mathbf{k}, v \mid \alpha)$. For

$$b(k, \alpha) = 1 + \int_{-\infty}^{\infty} \frac{h(k, v)}{v - \alpha}\, dv$$

and we obtain therefore the relation,

$$b(k, \alpha) = h(k, \alpha)\beta(k, \alpha)$$

between the strengths of the concentration of delta functions in the ordinary and the adjoint continuum eigenfunctions.

2. The real eigenvalues α that are zeros of the function $h(k, v)$ but not of the function $b(k, v)$. This is a special case. For we shall not impose the adjoint normalization condition on the eigenfunctions corresponding to these eigenvalues. The eigenfunctions satisfying the eigenvalue equation,

$$(v - \alpha)\chi(\mathbf{k}, v \mid \alpha) = -\int_{-\infty}^{\infty} h(k, v)\chi(\mathbf{k}, v \mid \alpha)\, dv$$

are the Dirac delta functions,

$$\chi(\mathbf{k}, v \mid \alpha) = \delta(\alpha - v)$$

For substituting this function into the eigenvalue equation, we obtain the relation,

$$(v - \alpha)\,\delta(v - \alpha) = -h(k, \alpha) = 0$$

and, as we have shown in Section 5.1, this is a well-known identity satisfied by the Dirac delta function.

The discrete part of the spectrum consists of:

3. The real eigenvalues α that are zeros of both $h(k, v)$ and $\beta(k, v)$. The eigenfunctions corresponding to these eigenvalues take the form,

$$\chi(\mathbf{k}, v \mid \alpha_m) = \frac{1}{\alpha_m - v} \qquad m = 1, 2, \ldots, M.$$

The normalization condition imposed on the adjoint eigenfunctions yields the dispersion equation,

$$\int_{-\infty}^{\infty} \frac{h(k, v)}{v - \alpha}\, dv = -1 \tag{7.32}$$

where, since $h(k, v)$ vanishes at the point $v = \alpha$, the integral is an infinite integral defined in the ordinary sense.

4. The complex eigenvalues. The eigenfunctions corresponding to these eigenvalues may be written,

$$\chi(\mathbf{k}, v \mid \alpha_m) = \frac{1}{\alpha_m - v}$$

and the normalization condition imposed on these eigenvalues leads to the dispersion equation (7.32). Thus, the complex eigenvalues in the discrete spectrum can be found as the roots of this dispersion equation.

As we have shown, the eigenfunctions $f(\mathbf{k}, v \mid \alpha)$ and $\chi(\mathbf{k}, v \mid \beta)$ are orthogonal for all values of α and β that are not equal to each other. Now let us compute, by means of the explicit expression for the eigenfunctions found above, integrals of the form,

$$\int_{-\infty}^{\infty} f(\mathbf{k}, v \mid \alpha)\chi(\mathbf{k}, v \mid \beta)\, dv$$

where α can be equal to β. If $f(\mathbf{k}, v \mid \alpha)$ and $\chi(\mathbf{k}, v \mid \beta)$ are continuum eigenfunctions of the first group, we find, by means of the method of Section 6.1, the normalization constant,

$$N(k, \alpha) = \int_{-\infty}^{\infty} f(\mathbf{k}, v \mid \alpha)\chi(\mathbf{k}, v \mid \beta)\, dv = \frac{b^2(k, \alpha) + \pi^2 h^2(k, \alpha)}{h(k, \alpha)}\,\delta(\alpha - \beta)$$

For the continuum eigenfunctions of the second group we obtain the result,

$$\int_{-\infty}^{\infty} f(\mathbf{k}, v \mid \alpha)\chi(\mathbf{k}, v \mid \beta)\, dv = N(k, \alpha) = b(k, \alpha)\, \delta(\alpha - \beta)$$

Hence, in this case, the normalization constant is equal to the strength of the concentration of delta functions at the point $v = \alpha$.

For the discrete eigenfunctions in the third and fourth groups the following integral relation is obtained,

$$\int_{-\infty}^{\infty} f(\mathbf{k}, v \mid \alpha_m)\chi(\mathbf{k}, v \mid \alpha_n)\, dv = N(\alpha_m) = \delta_{mn} \int_{-\infty}^{\infty} \frac{h(k, v)}{(v - \alpha_m)^2}\, dv$$

Let us assume that the space of eigenfunctions $f(\mathbf{k}, v \mid \alpha)$ is complete for functions that are Hölder continuous on the real axis. We are now prepared to obtain the solution, by means of a normal mode expansion technique, of the initial value problem describing the temporal behavior of the amplitude of the disturbance in the equilibrium velocity distribution, namely the solution of the linear transport equation,

$$\frac{\partial f(\mathbf{k}, v, t)}{\partial t} + ikvf(\mathbf{k}, v, t) = -ikh(k, v) \int_{-\infty}^{\infty} f(\mathbf{k}, v, t)\, dv$$

subject to the initial value condition,

$$f(\mathbf{k}, v, t = 0) = g(\mathbf{k}, v)$$

For, let us consider the following representation of the solution $f(\mathbf{k}, v, t)$ in terms of the eigenfunctions $f(\mathbf{k}, v \mid \alpha)$,

$$f(\mathbf{k}, v, t) = \sum_m a(k, m)f(\mathbf{k}, v \mid \alpha_m)e^{-ik\alpha_m t} + \int_{-\infty}^{\infty} a(k, \alpha)f(\mathbf{k}, v \mid \alpha)e^{-ik\alpha t}\, d\alpha$$

At time $t = 0$ we find

$$g(\mathbf{k}, v) = \sum_m a(k, m)f(\mathbf{k}, v \mid \alpha_m) + \int_{-\infty}^{\infty} a(k, \alpha)f(\mathbf{k}, v \mid \alpha)\, d\alpha$$

or, defining a new function,

$$w(\mathbf{k}, v) = g(\mathbf{k}, v) - \sum_m a(k, m)f(\mathbf{k}, v \mid \alpha_m)$$

we obtain the singular integral equation,

$$w(\mathbf{k}, v) = \int_{-\infty}^{\infty} a(k, \alpha)f(\mathbf{k}, v \mid \alpha)\, d\alpha = b(k, v)a(k, v) + h(k, v) \int_{-\infty}^{\infty} \frac{a(k, \alpha)}{\alpha - v}\, d\alpha$$

for the expansion coefficient $a(k, \alpha)$.

Now we can show, in the manner of the preceding section, that this integral equation has a solution $a(k, \alpha)$ for functions $w(\mathbf{k}, v)$ that are Hölder continuous on the real axis and this solution takes the form,

$$a(k, \alpha) = A^L(k, \alpha) - A^R(k, \alpha) = \frac{W^L(\mathbf{k}, \alpha)}{1 + 2\pi i H^L(k, \alpha)} - \frac{W^R(\mathbf{k}, \alpha)}{1 + 2\pi i H^R(k, \alpha)}$$

The functions $A^L(k, \alpha)$ and $A^R(k, \alpha)$ are the boundary values of the function,

$$A(k, z) = \frac{W(\mathbf{k}, z)}{1 + 2\pi i H(k, z)}$$

which is sectionally analytic in the plane cut along the real axis, where the function $W(\mathbf{k}, z)$ can be represented by a Cauchy integral,

$$W(\mathbf{k}, z) = \frac{1}{2\pi i} \int_{-\infty}^{\infty} \frac{w(\mathbf{k}, v)}{v - z}\, dv$$

Arriving at this point, we must be careful. For we did not require the equilibrium function to be a Maxwellian. Hence, the denominator $1 + 2\pi i H(k, z)$ may have zeros in the complex plane. However, the zeros of the denominator,

$$1 + 2\pi i H(k, z) = 1 + \int_{-\infty}^{\infty} \frac{h(k, v)}{v - z}\, dv$$

are just the complex eigenvalues in the discrete part of the spectrum, and the function $W(\mathbf{k}, z)$ also vanishes at such a zero. For,

$$W(\mathbf{k}, \alpha_m) = \frac{1}{2\pi i} \int_{-\infty}^{\infty} \frac{w(\mathbf{k}, v)}{v - \alpha_m}\, dv = -\frac{1}{2\pi i} \int_{-\infty}^{\infty} w(\mathbf{k}, v)\chi(\mathbf{k}, v \mid \alpha_m)\, dv = 0$$

because the discrete adjoint eigenfunctions are orthogonal to the function,

$$w(\mathbf{k}, v) = g(\mathbf{k}, v) - \sum_m a(k, m) f(\mathbf{k}, v \mid \alpha_m) = \int_{-\infty}^{\infty} a(k, \alpha) f(\mathbf{k}, v \mid \alpha)\, d\alpha \tag{7.33}$$

The expansion coefficients $a(k, m)$ can be found by multiplying the expansion (7.33) by the discrete adjoint eigenfunctions $\chi(\mathbf{k}, v \mid \alpha_m)$ and integrating over the fundamental interval. In this manner we find

$$a(k, m) = \frac{1}{N(k, \alpha_m)} \int_{-\infty}^{\infty} \chi(\mathbf{k}, v \mid \alpha_m) g(\mathbf{k}, v)\, dv$$

where

$$N(k, \alpha_m) = \int_{-\infty}^{\infty} \frac{h(k, v)}{(v - \alpha_m)^2}\, dv$$

is the normalization constant for the discrete eigenfunctions.

Furthermore, making use of the orthogonality of the eigenfunctions and the adjoint eigenfunctions, we find that the expansion coefficient of the continuum modes takes the form,

$$a(k, \alpha) = \frac{1}{b^2(k, \alpha) + \pi^2 h^2(k, \alpha)} \left[b(k, \alpha) g(\mathbf{k}, \alpha) - h(k, \alpha) \int_{-\infty}^{\infty} \frac{g(\mathbf{k}, v)}{v - \alpha} \, dv \right]$$

We have obtained therefore the representation,

$$f(\mathbf{k}, v, t) = \sum_m a(k, m) f(\mathbf{k}, v \mid \alpha_m) e^{-ik\alpha_m t} + \int_{-\infty}^{\infty} a(k, \alpha) f(\mathbf{k}, v \mid \alpha) e^{-ik\alpha t} \, d\alpha$$

for the solution of the Fourier transform of the linearized Vlasov equation where the expansion coefficients $a(k, m)$ and $a(k, \alpha)$ and the eigenfunctions $f(\mathbf{k}, v \mid \alpha_m)$ and $f(\mathbf{k}, v \mid \alpha)$ have been presented above. Moreover, by construction, we have shown that the space of eigenfunctions $f(\mathbf{k}, v \mid \alpha)$ is complete for functions which are Hölder continuous on the real axis.

APPENDIX **A**

PATHS, CONTOURS AND REGIONS IN THE COMPLEX PLANE

In this book on the applications of analytic functions and distributions in mathematical physics and engineering we are concerned with functions of a complex variable, in other words, with functions which are defined in the complex plane. Consequently, certain geometrical entities such as paths, contours, simply and multiply connected regions, etc., are basic to all our considerations. In this appendix we explain some of the nomenclature which we use regarding such entities.

For instance, we frequently refer to paths and contours in the complex plane. The basic constituent of such a path or contour is a simple and smooth arc. A simple and smooth arc is a curve in the complex plane which does not intersect itself and which has a continuously turning tangent at each of its points. Such an arc can be represented by a continuous and continuously differentiable function $\lambda(t) = \omega(t) + i\gamma(t)$ of some parameter t. We say that the arc is rectifiable if we can assign a definite length,

$$s(t) = \int_a^t \sqrt{\left[\left(\frac{d\omega}{dt}\right)^2 + \left(\frac{d\gamma}{dt}\right)^2\right]}\, dt$$

to any portion of the arc. Rectifiable arcs can be represented by a continuous and continuously differentiable function $\lambda(s) = \omega(s) + i\gamma(s)$ where the parameter s denotes the length of the arc between the point $\lambda(s)$ and some fixed reference point $\lambda(0)$. The parameter s is usually called the arc length. A regular path or curve Γ can now be constructed from such arcs by joining a finite number of them end to end in such a manner that the path does not intersect itself. This means that a path is a simple curve which has a continuously turning tangent in all but a finite number of points. In other words, a path has no double points and is piecewise differentiable. An arc or path which is closed is called a contour. We therefore use the word contour exclusively to denote a closed arc or path, and refrain from using the redundant word closed in connection with the name contour.

In two dimensions we are concerned with simply and multiply connected regions. A simply connected region is a domain in the complex plane which has the following two properties. First, any two points, which are located in the region, can be connected by a continuous path which lies wholly in the region. Second, any contour in the region can be contracted continuously to a point in the region, without ever leaving the region. Examples of such simply connected regions are the open region $|\lambda - a| < r$ and the closed region $|\lambda - a| \leqq r$. The regions $\rho < |\lambda - a| < r$ and $\rho \leqq |\lambda - a| \leqq r$ are examples of an open and a closed doubly connected region respectively. A doubly connected region can be reduced to a simple connected region by the insertion of a barrier, as shown in Figure A-1. Similarly an m-fold multiply

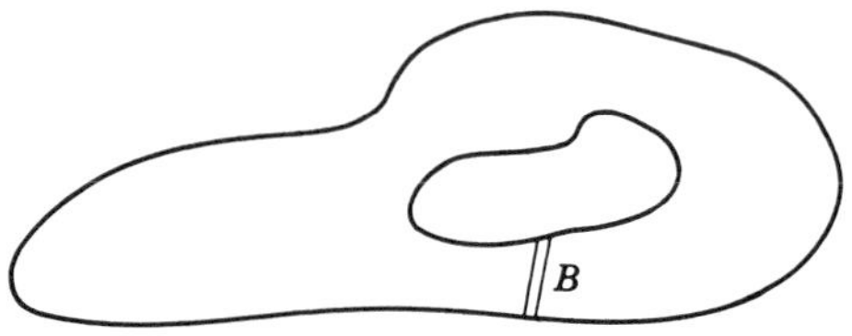

Figure A-1

connected region can be rendered simply connected by the insertion of $m - 1$ barriers.

It is intuitively obvious, but very hard to prove rigorously, that a contour divides the complex plane into two separate regions, a region interior to the contour and a region exterior to the contour. For a finite contour one of these regions is bounded and the other region is unbounded. If, upon traversing the contour, we leave the bounded region on our left, we say that the contour is traversed in the positive direction. The region on the left of the contour we denote by L and the region on the right of the contour by R. The contour is said to be traversed in the negative direction if the direction of motion leaves the bounded region on the right as shown in Figure A-2 and Figure A-3. The concept of a left neighborhood and a right neighborhood of a contour can be extended to the concept of a left and a right neighborhood of a path by

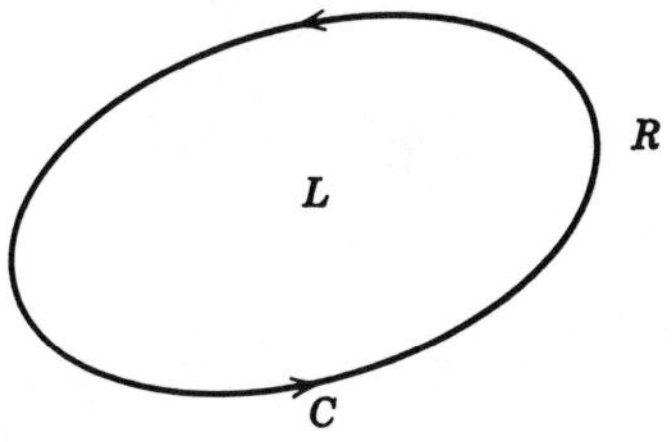

Figure A-2

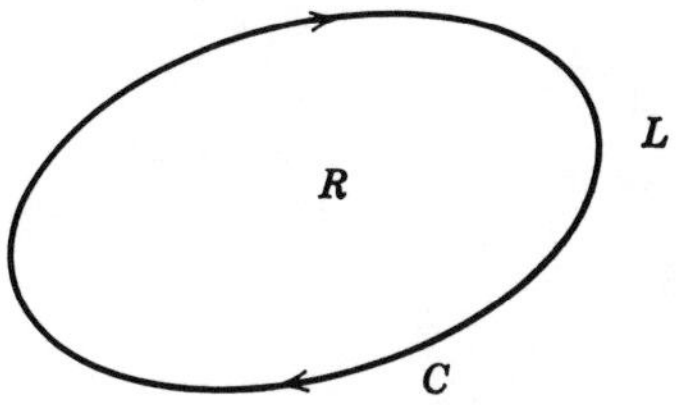

Figure A-3

first closing the path by another path to form a contour. On this contour we can choose a direction and in this manner we can assign a direction and a left and right neighborhood to the original path.

APPENDIX B

ORDER RELATIONS

To describe the properties of growth and decay of a function of a real or complex variable relative to the same properties of some given function we use the so-called big O, small o, and equivalence relations.

We use the notation $F(\lambda) = O[G(\lambda)]$, when λ tends to some given limit, if the absolute value of the ratio $F(\lambda)/G(\lambda)$ is bounded by some given positive constant A when λ tends to its limit. In this case we say that $F(\lambda)$ is at most of the order of $G(\lambda)$ or that $F(\lambda)$ is big O of $G(\lambda)$. For instance, if $F(\omega)$ is bounded when ω tends to infinity, we write $F(\omega) = O(1)$ when ω tends to infinity. Examples of the big O notation are $\sin \omega = O(1)$ when $-\infty < \omega < \infty$, $\sin \omega = O(\omega)$ when $-\infty < \omega < \infty$, $\omega^2 = O(\omega)$ when ω tends to zero, $\exp(-\omega) = O(1)$ when ω tends to infinity, and $\exp(-\lambda) = O(\lambda^p)$ when λ tends to infinity in the right half plane $R(\lambda) \geqq 0$, where $R(p) \geqq 0$.

The notation $F(\lambda) = o[G(\lambda)]$, when λ tends to some given limit, implies that the ratio $F(\lambda)/G(\lambda)$ tends to zero when λ tends to its limit. In this case we say that $F(\lambda)$ is of a smaller order than $G(\lambda)$ or that $F(\lambda)$ is small o of $G(\lambda)$. Of course, if the ratio $F(\lambda)/G(\lambda)$ tends to zero when λ tends to its limit it also stays bounded when λ tends to this limit. Consequently, the order relation $F(\lambda) = o[G(\lambda)]$ implies the order relation $F(\lambda) = O[G(\lambda)]$. In other words, the small o relation is stronger than the big O relation. Examples of the small o notation are $\omega^p = o(e^{\omega})$ when ω tends to infinity, $(\log \omega)^p = o(e^{\omega})$ when ω tends to infinity, $(\log \omega)^p = o(\omega^2)$ when ω tends to infinity, $\cos \omega = 1 + o(\omega)$ when ω tends to zero, etc.

If the ratio of the two functions $F(\lambda)$ and $G(\lambda)$ tends to unity when λ tends to some given limit we write $F(\lambda) \sim G(\lambda)$ when λ tends to its limit. In this case we say that the function $F(\lambda)$ is asymptotically equivalent to the function $G(\lambda)$ in the neighborhood of the limit point. Examples of the equivalence notation are $\omega + 1 \sim \omega$ when ω tends to infinity and $\cosh \omega \sim e^{\omega}/2$ when ω tends to infinity.

BIBLIOGRAPHY

The following books and articles will provide the reader with useful references, supplementary reading material, and discussions of more advanced topics related to the material presented in this book. It should be realized, however, that this bibliography is by no means exhaustive and that the author may have failed to include a more relevant article or book.

CHAPTER I. ANALYTIC FUNCTIONS

For a very clear introduction to the theory of analytic functions and many examples of the application of this theory to problems of mathematical physics, see:

1. P. M. Morse and H. Feshbach, *Methods of Theoretical Physics*, Vol. I and II, McGraw-Hill, New York, 1953.

Other introductions to the theory of analytic functions of an applied nature are:

2. R. V. Churchill, *Complex Variables and Applications*, McGraw-Hill, New York, 1960.
3. Z. Nehari, *Introduction to Complex Analysis*, Allyn and Bacon, New York, 1961.
4. B. A. Fuchs and B. V. Shabat, *Functions of a Complex Variable and some of their Applications*, Addison-Wesley, Reading, Mass., 1964.
5. J. W. Dettman, *Applied Complex Variables*, Macmillan, New York, 1965.
6. G. F. Carrier, M. Krook, and C. E. Pearson, *Functions of a Complex Variable*, McGraw-Hill, New York, 1966.

More advanced discussions of a more theoretical nature can be found in:

7. E. T. Copson, *An Introduction to the Theory of Functions of a Complex Variable*, Oxford Univ. Press, Oxford, 1950.
8. E. C. Titchmarsh, *The Theory of Functions*, Oxford Univ. Press, Oxford, 1952.
9. E. T. Whittaker and G. N. Watson, *A Course of Modern Analysis*, Cambridge Univ. Press, London, 1952.

10. E. Hille, *Analytic Function Theory*, Vol. I and II, Ginn and Co., Boston, 1959.
11. A. I. Markushevich, *Theory of Functions of a Complex Variable*, Vol. I, II, III, Prentice-Hall, Englewood Cliffs, N.J., 1965.
12. L. V. Ahlfors, *Complex Analysis*, McGraw-Hill, New York, 1966.

CHAPTER II. FOURIER TRANSFORMS, CAUSALITY, AND DISPERSION RELATIONS

Highly enjoyable and easily readable introductions to the basic mathematics of this chapter can be found in:

1. C. Lanczos, *Discourse on Fourier Series*, Hafner Publishing, New York, 1966.
2. G. P. Tolstov, *Fourier Series*, Prentice-Hall, Englewood Cliffs, N.J., 1962.

For lucid introductions to the theory of Fourier transforms and to the applications of this theory to problems in mathematical physics and engineering, see:

3. I. N. Sneddon, *Fourier Transforms*, McGraw-Hill, New York, 1951.
4. P. M. Morse and H. Feshbach, *Methods of Theoretical Physics*, Vol. I and II, McGraw-Hill, New York, 1953.
5. A. Papoulis, *The Fourier Integral and Its Applications*, McGraw-Hill, New York, 1962.

Publications of a more advanced and theoretical nature are:

6. R. E. A. C. Paley and N. Wiener, *Fourier Transforms in the Complex Domain, Am. Math. Soc. Coll. Pub. No. 19*, Am. Math. Soc., Providence, 1931.
7. E. C. Titchmarsh, *Introduction to the Theory of Fourier Integrals*, Oxford Univ. Press, Oxford, 1937.
8. N. Wiener, *The Fourier Integral and Certain of its Applications*, Dover Publications, New York, 1950.

A wide literature exists on causality and dispersion relations. The historical papers on this subject are:

9. R. Kronig, "Theory of Dispersion of X-Rays," *J. Am. Opt. Soc.*, **12**, 547 (1926).
10. H. A. Kramers, "La Diffusion de la Lumiere par les Atomes." *Collected Scientific Papers*, North-Holland Publishing Co., Amsterdam, 1956.
11. R. Kronig. "A Supplementary Condition in Heisenberg's Theory of Elementary Particles," *Physica* **12**, 543 (1946).

An enjoyable dialogue on causality and dispersion relations can be found in:

12. R. Hagedorn, "Causality and Dispersion Relations," in *Preludes in Theoretical Physics in Honor of V. F. Weisskopf*, edited by A. Shalit, North-Holland Publishing Co., Amsterdam, 1966.

Discussions on causality and dispersion relations within the framework of classical electrodynamics and nonrelativistic quantum mechanics can be found in:

13. W. Schützer and J. Tiomno, "On the Connection of the Scattering and Derivative Matrices with Causality," *Phys. Rev.* **83**, 249 (1951).

14. J. S. Toll, *The Dispersion Relation for Light and its Application to Problems Involving Electron Pairs*, Ph.D. Thesis, Princeton University, 1952.
15. F. Rohrlich and R. L. Gluckstern, "Forward Scattering of Light by a Coulomb Field," *Phys. Rev.* **86**, 1 (1952).
16. H. A. Bethe and F. Rohrlich, "Small Angle Scattering of Light by a Coulomb Field," *Phys. Rev.* **86**, 10 (1952).
17. N. G. van Kampen, "S-Matrix and Causality Condition I, Maxwell Field," *Phys. Rev.* **89**, 1072 (1953).
18. N. G. van Kampen, "S-Matrix and Causality Condition II, Non-Relativistic Particles," *Phys. Rev.* **91**, 1267 (1953).
19. E. P. Wigner, "On the Development of the Compound Nucleus Model," *Am. J. Phys.* **23**, 371 (1955).
20. J. S. Toll, "Causality and Dispersion Relation: Logical Foundations," *Phys. Rev.* **104**, 1760 (1956).

Excellent discussions of the concepts of causality and dispersion relations in quantum field theory and the physics of elementary particles can be found in:

21. J. Hamilton, "Dispersion Relations for Elementary Particles," *Progress in Nuclear Physics*, **8**, 145, Edited by O. R. Frisch, Pergamon Press, New York, 1960.
22. N. N. Bogoliubov, B. V. Medvedev, and M. K. Polivanov, "Probleme der Theorie der Dispersions Beziehungen," *Fortschritte der Physik*, **6**, 169 (1958).
23. E. Corinaldesi, "An Introduction to Dispersion Relations," *Il Nuovo Cimento*, **14**, Supplemento, 370 (1959).
24. N. N. Bogoliubov and D. V. Shirkov, *Introduction to the Theory of Quantized Fields*, Interscience, New York, 1959.
25. J. Hilgevoord, *Dispersion Relations and Causal Description*, Ph. D. Thesis, University of Amsterdam, 1960.
26. J. D. Jackson, "Introduction to Dispersion Relation Techniques," in *Dispersion Relations*, edited by J. R. Screaton, Wiley, New York, 1961.
27. M. L. Goldberger, *Dispersion Relations and Elementary Particles*, Wiley, New York, 1961.
28. M. L. Goldberger and K. M. Watson, *Collision Theory*, Wiley, New York, 1964.

For a rigorous discussion of Titchmarsh's theorem, see:

29. E. C. Titchmarsh, *Introduction to the Theory of Fourier Integrals*, Oxford Univ. Press, Oxford, 1937.

A mathematically concise statement of theorems relevant to the subject matter of Section 2.13 can be found in:

30. D. S. Greenstein, "On the Analytic Continuation of Functions which Map the Upper Half Plane into Itself," *J. Math. An. and Appl.* **1**, 355 (1960).

For related material, see also:

31. C. L. Dolph, J. B. McLeod, D. Thoe, "The Analytic Continuation of the Resolvent Kernel and Scattering Operator Associated with the Schroedinger Operator," *J. Math. An. and Appl.* **16**, 311 (1966).

and the excellent review article

32. C. L. Dolph, "Recent Developments in some Non-Self-Adjoint Problems of Mathematical Physics," *Bull. Am. Math. Soc.* **67**, 1 (1961).

Excellent presentations of the material on asymptotic expansions discussed in Section 2.14 can be found in:

33. G. Doetsch, *Guide to the Applications of Laplace Transforms*, Van Nostrand, New York, 1961.
34. A. Erdelyi, *Asymptotic Expansions*, Dover Publications, New York, 1956.
35. N. G. de Bruyn, *Asymptotic Methods in Analysis*, North-Holland Publishing Co., Amsterdam, 1960.
36. H. Jeffreys, *Asymptotic Approximations*, Oxford Univ. Press, Oxford, 1962.
37. E. T. Copson, *Asymptotic Expansions*, Cambridge Univ. Press, Cambridge, 1965.
38. H. A. Lauwerier, *Asymptotic Expansions*, Mathematical Centre Tracts, Mathematisch Centrum, Amsterdam, 1966.

See also the monumental work, awaiting a translator:

39. G. Doetsch, *Handbuch der Laplace Transformation*, Vol. I, II, and III, Birkhauser Verlag, Basel und Stuttgart, 1956.

For the application to neutron transport theory of the contents of Section 2.15, see:

40. K. M. Case, F. de Hoffmann, and G. Placzek, *Introduction to the Theory of Neutron Diffusion*, U. S. Government Printing Office, Washington, 1953.

CHAPTER III. THE WIENER-HOPF TECHNIQUE

The outstanding reference on the subject and a book of great practical utility is:

1. B. Noble, *The Wiener-Hopf Technique and its Application in the Solution of Partial Differential Equations*, Pergamon, New York, 1956.

Several interesting applications of the Wiener-Hopf technique to the solution of integral equations arising in mathematical physics can be found in:

2. P. M. Morse and H. Feshbach, *Methods of Theoretical Physics*, Vol. I and II, McGraw-Hill, New York, 1953.

Other discussions of the subject of a more theoretical nature can be found in:

3. E. Hopf, *Mathematical Problems of Radiative Equilibrium*, Cambridge Tracts, No. 31, Cambridge Univ. Press, London, 1931.
4. R. E. A. C. Paley and N. Wiener, *Fourier Transforms in the Complex Domain, Am. Math. Soc. Coll. Publ., No. 19*, Am. Math. Soc., Providence, 1931.
5. E. C. Titchmarsh, *Introduction to the Theory of Fourier Integrals*, Oxford Univ. Press, Oxford, 1937.

Fundamental papers on the theory and application of the Wiener-Hopf technique are:

6. N. Wiener and E. Hopf, "Über eine Klasse Singulärer Integral Gleichungen," *Sitz. Ber. Preuss. Ak. Wiss.* **30**, 696 (1931).
7. E. Reissner, "On a Class of Singular Integral Equations," *J. Math. Phys.* **20**, 219 (1941).

8. V. A. Fock, "On Certain Integral Equations of Mathematical Physics," *Dokl. Ak. Nauk. SSSR.* **37**, 147 (1942).
9. V. A. Fock, "On Certain Integral Equations of Mathematical Physics," *Math. Sb.* (NS), **14**, 3 (1944).
10. E. T. Copson, "On an Integral Equation Arising in the Theory of Diffraction," *Quart. J. Math., Oxford*, **17**, 19 (1946).
11. G. Placzek and W. Seidel, "Milne's Problem in Transport Theory," *Phys. Rev.* **72**, 550 (1947).
12. H. Levine and J. Schwinger, "On the Radiation of Sound from an Unflanged Circular Pipe," *Phys. Rev.* **73**, 383 (1948).
13. A. E. Heins, "Water Waves over a Channel of Finite Depth with a Dock," *Am. J. Math.* **70**, 730 (1948).
14. A. E. Heins, "The Scope and Limitations of the Method of Wiener and Hopf," *Comm. Pure. Applied Math.* **9**, 447 (1956).
15. L. A. Vainstein, *Propagation in Semi-Infinite Wave Guides*, New York University, Institute of Mathematical Sciences, Division of Electromagnetic Research, Report EM-63, 1954.

More recent developments in the Wiener-Hopf technique have been reported by:

16. H. C. Kranzer and J. Radlow, "Asymptotic Factorization for Perturbed Wiener-Hopf Problems," *J. Math. An. and Appl.* **4**, 240 (1962).
17. H. C. Kranzer and J. Radlow, "An Asymptotic Method for Solving Perturbed Wiener-Hopf Problems," *J. Math. and Mech.* **14**, 41 (1965).
18. J. Kane, "The Superposition Principle and Diffraction in Sectors," *J. Math. and Mech.* **15**, 207 (1966).

CHAPTER IV. BOUNDARY VALUE PROBLEMS FOR SECTIONALLY ANALYTIC FUNCTIONS

The following three books on the subject matter of this chapter are highly recommended:

1. N. I. Mushkhelishvili, *Singular Integral Equations*, P. Noordhof, N. V., Groningen, 1953.
2. N. I. Mushkhelishvili, *Some Basic Problems of the Mathematical Theory of Elasticity*, P. Noordhof, N. V., Groningen, 1953.
3. F. D. Gakhov, *Boundary Value Problems*, Addison-Wesley, Reading, Mass., 1966.

For a very interesting discussion of some of the topics of this chapter, see also:

4. N. Levinson, "Simplified Treatment of Integrals of the Cauchy Type, the Hilbert Problem, and Singular Integral Equations, with an Appendix on the Poincaré-Bertrand Transformation Formula," *Rev. Soc. Ind. Appl. Math.* **7**, 474 (1965).

The solution of Wiener-Hopf type integral equations by techniques from the theory of sectionally analytic functions was first attempted by:

5. I. M. Rapoport, "On a Class of Singular Integral Equations," *Dokl. Ak. Nauk. SSSR*, **59**, 1403 (1948).

6. J. Sparenberg, "Applications of the Theory of Sectionally Holomorphic Functions to Wiener-Hopf Type Integral Equations," *Proc. Koninkl. Ak. Wet. Amsterdam*, **A59**, 29 (1956).

For interesting recent developments in the theory of singular integral equations of the Cauchy type, see:

7. A. S. Peters, "The Solution of Certain Integral Equations with Cauchy Kernels," *Comm. Pure and Appl. Math.* **18**, 129 (1965).
8. K. M. Case, "Singular Integral Equations," *J. Math. Physics* **7**, 2121 (1966).
9. K. M. Case, "Singular Solutions of Certain Integral Equations," *J. Math. Physics*, 2125 (1966).

The boundary value problems of Sections 4.15, 4.16, and 4.17 have been discussed in much more detail in:

10. J. D. Jackson, *Classical Electrodynamics*, Wiley, New York, 1962.
11. C. J. Bouwkamp and N. G. de Bruyn, "The Electrostatic Field of a Point Charge Inside a Cylinder," *J. Appl. Phys.* **18**, 562 (1947).
12. H. A. Lauwerier, "The Surface Charge of a Semi-Infinite Cylinder due to an Axial Point Charge," *Appl. Sci. Res.* **B8**, 277 (1960).

For applications of the theory of sectionally analytic functions for the solution of integral equations arising in the physics of elementary particles, see:

13. J. D. Jackson, "Introduction to Dispersion Relation Techniques," in *Dispersion Relations*, edited by J. R. Screaton, Wiley, New York, 1961.
14. M. L. Goldberger and K. M. Watson, *Collision Theory*, Wiley, New York, 1964.

For applications of the theory of sectionally analytic functions in diffraction theory, see:

15. H. Honl, A. W. Maue, K. Westphal, "Theorie der Beugungs," *Handbook of Physics*, Vol. 25, Springer-Verlag, New York, 1961.

For applications of singular integral equations in waveguide theory, see:

16. L. Lewin, "The Use of Singular Integral Equations in the Solution of Waveguide Problems," in *Advances in Microwaves*, Vol. I, Leo Young, ed., Academic Press, New York, 1966.

CHAPTER V. DISTRIBUTIONS

Several excellent monographs and textbooks on the theory of distributions and their applications in mathematics, physics, and engineering have been published. Among the more prominent are:

1. L. Schwartz, *Theorie des Distributions*, Vol. I and II, Hermann, Paris, 1951.
2. I. M. Gelfand and G. E. Shilov, *Generalized Functions*, Vol. I: *Properties and Operations*, Academic Press, New York, 1964.
3. H. Bremermann, *Distributions, Complex Variables and Fourier Transforms*, Addison-Wesley, Reading, Mass., 1965.
4. A. H. Zemanian, *Distribution Theory and Transform Analysis*, McGraw-Hill, New York, 1965.

5. E. J. Beltrami and M. R. Wohlers, *Distributions and the Boundary Values of Analytic Functions*, Academic Press, New York, 1966.
6. J. Arsac, *Fourier Transforms and the Theory of Distributions*, Prentice-Hall, Englewood Cliffs, N.J., 1966.
7. E. M. de Jager, *Applications of Distributions in Mathematical Physics*, Mathematisch Centrum, Amsterdam, 1964.
8. A. Erdelyi, *Operational Calculus and Generalized Functions*, Holt, Rinehart, and Winston, New York, 1967.
9. A. Friedman, *Generalized Functions and Partial Differential Equations*, Prentice-Hall, Englewood Cliffs, N.J., 1963.
10. B. Friedman, *Principles and Techniques of Applied Mathematics*, Wiley, New York, 1956.
11. I. Halpern, *Introduction to the Theory of Distributions*, Univ. of Toronto Press, Toronto, 1952.
12. M. J. Lighthill, *An Introduction to Fourier Analysis and Generalized Functions*, Cambridge Univ. Press, London, 1958.
13. J. P. Marchand, *Distributions*, Interscience, New York, 1962.
14. J. Mikusinski, *Operational Calculus*, Pergamon, London, 1959.

References for the introduction to this chapter are:

15. N. Bohr and L. Rosenfeld, "Zur Frage der Messbarkeit der Elektromagnetischen Fieldgrosse," *Kgl. Danske Vid. Sels. Mat-fys. Medd.* **12** (1933).
16. N. Bohr and L. Rosenfeld, "Field and Charge Measurements in Quantum Electrodynamics," *Phys. Rev.* **78**, 794 (1950).
17. L. Rosenfeld, *Theory of Electrons*, North-Holland Publishing Co., Amsterdam, 1951.
18. P. A. M. Dirac, *Quantum Mechanics*, Oxford Univ. Press, Oxford, 1947.
19. A. Messiah, *Quantum Mechanics*, Wiley, New York, 1965.
20. G. Källén, "Intuitive Analyticity," in *Preludes in Theoretical Physics in Honor of V. F. Weisskopf*, edited by A. Shalit, North-Holland Publishing Co., Amsterdam, 1966.

Key references on the subject matter of Sections 5.5 and 5.7 are:

21. J. G. Taylor, "Dispersion Relations and Schwartz's Distributions," *Annals of Physics* **5**, 391 (1958).
22. H. J. Bremermann and L. Durand, III, "On Analytic Continuation, Multiplication and Fourier Transformation of Schwartz Distributions," *J. Math. Phys.* **2**, 240 (1961).
23. E. J. Beltrami and M. R. Wohlers, "Distributional Boundary Values of Functions Holomorphic in a Half Plane," *J. Math. and Mech.* **15**, 137 (1966).
24. E. J. Beltrami and M. R. Wohlers, "Distributional Boundary Value Theorems and Hilbert Transforms," *Arch. Rat. Mech. Anal.* **18**, 304 (1965).
25. H. A. Lauwerier, "The Hilbert Problem for Generalized Functions," *Arch. Rat. Mech. Anal.* **13**, 157 (1963).
26. R. W. B. Best, *Fourier and Hilbert Transforms of Generalized Functions of One Real Variable*, FOM-Report 66-30, Associatie EURATOM-FOM, FOM-Instituut voor Plasma-fysica, Rynhuizen, The Netherlands, 1966.

CHAPTER VI. APPLICATIONS IN NEUTRON TRANSPORT THEORY

Several excellent text and reference books on linear transport theory have appeared:

1. B. Davison, *Neutron Transport Theory*, Oxford Univ. Press, Oxford, 1957.
2. A. M. Weinberg and E. P. Wigner, *The Physical Theory of Neutron Chain Reactors*, Univ. Chicago Press, Chicago, 1958.
3. G. M. Wing, *An Introduction to Transport Theory*, Wiley, New York, 1962.
4. K. M. Case and P. F. Zweifel, *Linear Transport Theory*, Addison-Wesley, Reading, Mass., 1967.

Many papers have already appeared on the Case–van Kampen–Wigner technique. The basic papers on this subject are:

5. N. G. van Kampen, "On the Theory of Stationary Waves in Plasmas," *Physica*, **21**, 949 (1955).
6. K. M. Case, "Plasma Oscillations," *Annals of Physics*, **8**, 349 (1959).
7. K. M. Case, "Elementary Solutions of the Transport Equation and their Applications," *Annals of Physics*, **9**, 1 (1960).
8. E. P. Wigner, "Problems of Nuclear Reactor Theory," *Proc. Symp. Appl. Math. Am. Math. Soc.* **11**, 89 (1961).
9. K. M. Case, *Recent Developments in Neutron Transport Theory*, University of Michigan Memorial Phoenix Report, Univ. of Michigan, 1962.
10. R. E. Aamodt and K. M. Case, "Useful Identities for Half Space Problems in Linear Transport Theory," *Annals of Physics*, **21**, 284 (1963).
11. I. Kuscer, N. J. McCormick, and G. C. Summerfield, "Orthogonality of Case's Eigenfunctions in One-Speed Transport Theory," *Annals of Physics*, **30**, 411 (1964).

Applications of the Case–van Kampen–Wigner technique in time-independent, mono-energetic, isotropic problems of neutron transport theory have been reported by:

12. G. L. Mitsis, *Transport Solutions to the One-Dimensional Critical Problem*, ANL-6459, 1961. *See also: Nuclear Science and Engineering*, **17**, 55 (1963).
13. R. Zelazny, "Exact Solution of a Critical Problem for a Slab," *J. Math. Physics*, **2**, 538 (1961).
14. R. Zelazny and A. Kuszell, "Albedo Problem for a Slab," *Physica*, **27**, 797 (1961).
15. W. Kofink, *New Solutions of the Boltzmann Equation for Monoenergetic Neutron Transport in Spherical Geometry*, ORNL Report 3216, 1961.
16. M. R. Mendelson and G. C. Summerfield, "One-Speed Neutron Transport in Two Adjacent Half-Spaces," *J. Math Physics*, **5**, 668 (1964).
17. N. J. McCormick and M. R. Mendelson, "Transport Solution of the One-Speed Slab Albedo Problem," *Nuclear Science and Engineering*, **20**, 462 (1964).
18. A. M. Jacobs and J. J. McInerney, "On the Green's Function of Monoenergetic Neutron Transport Theory," *Nuclear Science and Engineering*, **22**, 119 (1965).
19. I. Kuscer and N. J. McCormick, "On the Use of the Poincaré-Bertrand Transformation Formula in Neutron Transport Theory," *Nuclear Science and Engineering*, **23**, 404 (1965).

Solutions of time-independent, monoenergetic, anisotropic problems of neutron transport theory by means of the Case–van Kampen–Wigner technique have been reported by:

20. R. Zelazny, A. Kuszell, and J. Mika, "Solution of the One-Velocity Boltzmann Equation with First-Order Anisotropic Scattering in Plane Geometry," *Annals of Physics*, **16**, 69 (1961).
21. J. Mika, "Neutron Transport with Anisotropic Scattering," *Nuclear Science and Engineering*, **11**, 415 (1961).
22. J. J. McInerney, "Green's Function for a Bare Slab with Anisotropic Scattering," *Nuclear Science and Engineering*, **16**, 460 (1963).
23. F. Shure and M. Natelson, "Anisotropic Scattering in Half-Space Transport Problems," *Annals of Physics*, **26**, 274 (1964).
24. N. J. McCormick and I. Kuscer, "Half-Space Neutron Transport with Linearly Anisotropic Scattering," *J. Math. Physics*, **6**, 1939 (1965).
25. D. H. Sattinger, "A Singular Eigenfunction Expansion in Anisotropic Transport Theory," *J. Math. An. and Appl.* **15**, 497 (1966).
26. S. Pahor, "A New Approach to Half-Space Transport Problems," *Nuclear Science and Engineering*, **26**, 192 (1966).

Time-independent multigroup and slowing down problems have been solved by:

27. R. Zelazny and A. Kuszell, "Two-Group Approach in Neutron Transport Theory in Plane Geometry," *Annals of Physics*, **16**, 81 (1961).
28. R. Zelazny and A. Kuszell, "Multigroup Neutron Transport Theory," in *Physics of Fast and Intermediate Reactors*, **II**, 51, IAEA, Vienna (1962).
29. R. J. Bednarz and J. R. Mika, "Energy Dependent Boltzmann Equation in Plane Geometry," *J. Math. Physics*, **9**, 1285 (1963).
30. J. J. McInerney, "A Solution of the Space-Angle-Dependent Neutron Slowing Down Problem," *Nuclear Science and Engineering*, **22**, 215 (1965).

Time-dependent problems have been solved by means of the Case–van Kampen–Wigner technique by:

31. J. U. Koppel, "A Method of Solving the Time Dependent Neutron Thermalization Problem," *Nuclear Science and Engineering*, **16**, 101 (1963).
32. A. Claesson, *The Solution of a Velocity Dependent Slowing-Down Problem Using Case's Eigenfunction Expansion*, Report AE-164, Stockholm, 1964.
33. R. L. Bowden and C. D. Williams, "A Solution of the Initial-Value Transport Problem for Monoenergetic Neutrons in Slab Geometry," *J. Math. Physics*, **5**, 1527 (1964).
34. I. Kuscer and P. Zweifel, "Time-Dependent One-Speed Albedo Problem for a Semi-Infinite Medium," *J. Math. Physics*, **6**, 1125 (1965).

For the function theoretic analysis of the spectral properties of singular Sturm–Liouville and Schroedinger operators referred to in the introduction to this chapter, see:

35. H. Weyl, "Über Gewöhnliche Lineare Differentialgleichungen mit Singulären Stellen und Ihre Eigenfunktionen," *Göttinger Nachrichten*, 37-64, 442-467, 1909, *Math. Annalen*, **68**, 220 (1910).
36. E. C. Titchmarsh, *Eigenfunction Expansions I*, Oxford Univ. Press, Oxford, 1962.

For generalizations of this analysis to Dirac's radial relativistic wave equation, see:

37. B. W. Roos and W. Sangren, "Spectral Theory of Dirac's Radial Relativistic Wave Equation," *J. Math. Physics*, **3**, 882 (1962).
38. B. W. Roos and W. Sangren, "Expansions Associated with a Pair of Singular First Order Differential Equations," *J. Math. Physics*, **4**, 999 (1963).

For a treatment of these problems in the framework of the theory of generalized functions or distributions, see:

39. Yu. M. Berezanskii, *Eigenfunction Expansions for Self-Adjoint Operators*, Naukova Dumka, Kiev, 1965.
40. I. M. Gelfand and G. E. Shilov, *Generalized Functions*, Vol. III: *Theory of Differential Equations*, Academic Press, New York, 1967.

CHAPTER VII. APPLICATIONS IN PLASMA PHYSICS

Excellent discussions of the subject matter of this chapter can be found in:

1. J. D. Jackson, *Classical Electrodynamics*, Wiley, New York, 1962.
2. T. H. Stix, *The Theory of Plasma Waves*, McGraw-Hill, New York, 1962.
3. D. Montgomory and D. Tidman, *Plasma Kinetic Theory*, McGraw-Hill, New York, 1964.
4. N. G. van Kampen and B. U. Felderhoff, *Theoretical Methods in Plasma Physics*, North-Holland Publishing Co., Amsterdam, 1967.
5. K. M. Case and P. F. Zweifel, *Linear Transport Theory*, Addison-Wesley, Reading, Mass., 1967.
6. H. Grad, ed., "Magneto-Fluid and Plasma Dynamics," *Proceedings of Symposia in Appl. Math.* **18**, Am. Math. Soc., Providence, 1967.

Basic papers on plasma oscillations are:

7. L. Tonks and I. Langmuir, "Oscillations in Ionized Gases," *Phys. Rev.* **33**, 196 (1929).
8. A. A. Vlasov, "The Oscillation Properties of an Electron Gas," *J. Exptl. Theoret. Phys.* (*USSR*), **8**, 291 (1938).
9. L. Landau, "On the Vibrations of the Electron Plasma," *J. of Phys. USSR*, **10**, 25 (1946).
10. D. Bohm and E. P. Gross, "Theory of Plasma Oscillations, A. Origin of Mediumlike Behavior," *Phys. Rev.* **75**, 1851 (1949).
11. D. Bohm and E. P. Gross, "Theory of Plasma Oscillations, B. Excitation and Damping of Oscillations," *Phys. Rev.* **75**, 1864 (1949).
12. N. G. van Kampen, "On the Theory of Stationary Waves in Plasmas," *Physica*, **21**, 949 (1955).
13. N. G. van Kampen, "The Dispersion Equation for Plasma Waves," *Physica*, **23**, 647 (1957).
14. K. M. Case, "Plasma Oscillations," *Ann. Phys.* **7**, 349 (1959).

Landau's solution of the initial value problem by means of unilateral Fourier transforms and analytic continuation in the plane of the transform variable has been investigated in many papers. Key references are:

15. L. Landau, "On the Vibrations of the Electron Plasma," *J. of Phys., USSR*, **10**, 25 (1946).
16. J. D. Jackson, "Longitudinal Plasma Oscillations," *J. Nucl. Eng. Part C, Plasma Physics*, **1**, 171 (1960).
17. G. Backus, "Linearized Plasma Oscillations in Arbitrary Electron Velocity Distributions," *J. Math Physics*, **1**, 178 (1960).
18. O. Penrose, "Electrostatic Instabilities of a Uniform Non-Maxwellian Plasma," *Phys. Fluids*, **3**, 258 (1960).
19. H. Weitzner, "Plasma Oscillations and Landau Damping," *Phys. Fluids*, **6**, 1123 (1963).
20. H. Weitzner, "Long Wave Length Plasma Oscillations," *Phys. Fluids*, **7**, 476 (1964).
21. H. Weitzner, "Exponential Damping of Collisionless Plasma Oscillations," *Comm. Pure Appl. Math.* **18**, 307 (1965).
22. J. Hayes, "Damping of Plasma Oscillations in the Linear Theory," *Phys. Fluids*, **4**, 1387 (1961).
23. J. Hayes, "On Non-Landau Damped Solutions to the Linearized Vlasov Equation," *Il Nuovo Cimento*, **30**, 1048 (1963).
24. A. W. Saenz, "Longtime Behavior of the Electric Potential and Stability in the Linearized Vlasov Theory," *J. Math. Physics*, **6**, 859 (1965).
25. A. W. Saenz, *Rigorous Treatment of the Propagation and Damping of Small Amplitude Plasma Waves in an Initially Maxwellian Plasma*, U. S. Naval Research Laboratory Report NRL-6125, 1964.
26. A. J. Turski, "Transient and Oscillating Solution of the Boltzmann-Vlasov Equation in Linearized Plasmas," *Ann. Phys.* **35**, 240 (1965).
27. E. C. Taylor, "Landau Solution of the Plasma Oscillation Problem," *Phys. Fluids*, **8**, 2250 (1965).
28. J. E. McGune, "Exact Inversion of Dispersion Relations," *Phys. Fluids*, **9**, 2082 (1966).
29. J. Denavit, "First and Second Order Landau Damping in Maxwellian Plasmas," *Phys. Fluids*, **8**, 471 (1965).
30. J. Denavit, "Landau Damping and the Velocity Fourier Transform of the Initial Perturbation," *Phys. Fluids*, **9**, 134 (1966).

The analytic continuation of the dispersion equation into the lower half of the complex plane is discussed by:

31. D. S. Greenstein, "On the Analytic Continuation of Functions which Map the Upper Half Plane into Itself," *J. Math. An. and Appl.* **1**, 355 (1960).
32. B. D. Fried and S. D. Conte, *The Plasma Dispersion Function*, Academic Press, New York, 1961.

For the comment on "physical" and "un-physical" parts of the complex plane and Källén's work, see:

33. G. Källén, "Intuitive Analyticity," in *Preludes in Theoretical Physics in Honor of V. F. Weisskopf*, edited by A. Shalit, North-Holland Publishing Co., Amsterdam, 1966.

The normal mode technique for the solution of the initial value problem has been utilized in:

34. N. G. van Kampen, "On the Theory of Stationary Waves in Plasmas," *Physica*, **21**, 949 (1955).
35. K. M. Case, "Plasma Oscillations," *Am. Phys.* **7**, 349 (1959).
36. R. S. Zelazny, "The General Solution of the Initial Value Problem for Longitudinal Plasma Oscillations," *Ann. Phys.* **19**, 177 (1962).
37. B. U. Felderhoff, "A Theory of Fluctuations in Plasmas," *Physica*, **30**, 1771 (1964).
38. J. E. McGune, "Three Dimensional Normal Modes of a Vlasov Plasma with and without Magnetic Field," *Phys. Fluids*, **9**, 1788 (1966).

Boundary value problems have been considered by:

39. F. C. Shure, *Boundary Value Problems in Plasma Oscillations*, Ph.D. Thesis, Univ. of Michigan, Ann Arbor, 1962.
40. R. E. Aamodt and K. M. Case, "Useful Identities for Half Space Problems in Linear Transport Theory," *Ann. Phys.* **21**, 284 (1963).

For studies on the influence of a magnetic field, the reader is referred to:

41. I. B. Bernstein, "Waves in a Plasma in a Magnetic Field," *Phys. Rev.* **109**, 10 (1956).
42. D. E. Baldwin and G. Rowlands, "Plasma Oscillations Perpendicular to a Weak Magnetic Field," *Phys. Fluids*, **9**, 2444 (1966).

For nonlinear effects, see:

43. I. B. Bernstein, J. M. Greene, and M. D. Kruskal, "Exact Non-Linear Plasma Oscillations," *Phys. Rev.* **108**, 546 (1957).
44. W. E. Drummond and D. Pines, *Nuclear Fusion Supplement*, Part 2, 1049 (1962).
45. A. A. Vedenov, E. P. Velikov, and R. Z. Sagdeev, *Soviet Physics, Uspehi*, **4**, 332 (1961).

INDEX

The subject index includes names associated with a subject, like Case-van Kampen-Wigner technique. Names mentioned with publications or in personal references will be found in the Bibliography.